ROUTLEDGE HANDBOOK OF PUBLIC CRIMINOLOGIES

Featuring contributions from scholars from across the globe, *Routledge Handbook of Public Criminologies* is a comprehensive resource that addresses the challenges related to public conversations around crime and policy. In an era of fake news, misguided rhetoric about immigrants and refugees, and efforts to toughen criminal laws, criminologists seeking to engage publicly around crime and policy arguably face an uphill battle. This handbook outlines the foundations of and developments in public criminology, underscoring the need not only to understand earlier ideas and debates, but also how scholars pursue public-facing work through various approaches. The first of its kind, this collection captures diverse and critical perspectives on the practices and challenges of actually doing public criminology.

The book presents real-world examples that help readers better understand the nature of public criminological work, as well as the structural and institutional barriers and enablers of engaging wider audiences. Contributors address policies around crime and crime control, media landscapes, and changing political dynamics. In examining attempts to bridge the gaps between scholarship, activism, and outreach, the essays featured here capture important tensions related to inequality and social difference, including the ways in which criminology can be complicit in perpetuating inequitable practices and structures, and how public criminology aims—but sometimes fails—to address them.

The depth and breadth of material in the book will appeal to a wide range of academics, students, and practitioners. It is an important resource for early career researchers, more established scholars, and professionals, with accessible content that can also be used in upper-level undergraduate classes.

Kathryn Henne is Professor of Regulation and Governance at the Australian National University. Her work focuses on the interface between deviance, technologies of policing, and inequality. She is the author of *Testing for Athlete Citizenship: Regulating Doping and Sex in Sport* (2015) and co-editor (with Blayne Haggart and Natasha Tusikov) of *Information, Technology and Control in a Changing World* (2019).

Rita Shah is an Assistant Professor of Criminology at Eastern Michigan University. Her research examines the ways in which correctional systems are socially and legally constructed and critically analyses criminological methods and pedagogy. She is the author of *The Meaning of Rehabilitation and its Impact on Parole: There and Back Again in California* (Routledge, 2017), which queries the concept of rehabilitation to determine how, on a legislative and policy level, the term is defined as a goal of correctional systems.

ROUTLEDGE HANDBOOK OF PUBLIC CRIMINOLOGIES

Edited by Kathryn Henne and Rita Shah

NEW YORK AND LONDON

First published 2020
by Routledge
52 Vanderbilt Avenue, New York, NY 10017

and by Routledge
2 Park Square, Milton Park, Abingdon, Oxon, OX14 4RN

Routledge is an imprint of the Taylor & Francis Group, an informa business

© 2020 selection and editorial matter, Kathryn Henne and Rita Shah; individual chapters, the contributors

The right of Kathryn Henne and Rita Shah to be identified as the authors of the editorial material, and of the authors for their individual chapters, has been asserted in accordance with sections 77 and 78 of the Copyright, Designs and Patents Act 1988.

All rights reserved. No part of this book may be reprinted or reproduced or utilized in any form or by any electronic, mechanical, or other means, now known or hereafter invented, including photocopying and recording, or in any information storage or retrieval system, without permission in writing from the publishers.

Trademark notice: Product or corporate names may be trademarks or registered trademarks, and are used only for identification and explanation without intent to infringe.

Library of Congress Cataloging-in-Publication Data
Names: Henne, Kathryn E., 1982- editor. | Shah, Rita, editor.
Title: Routledge handbook of public criminologies / Kathryn Henne & Rita Shah.
Description: New York, NY : Routledge, 2020. | Includes bibliographical references and index.
Identifiers: LCCN 2019041535 (print) | LCCN 2019041536 (ebook) | ISBN 9781138479296 (hardback) | ISBN 9781351066105 (ebook)
Subjects: LCSH: Criminology. | Criminal law–Public opinion. | Criminology–Social aspects.
Classification: LCC HV6025 .R68 2020 (print) | LCC HV6025 (ebook) | DDC 364–dc23
LC record available at https://lccn.loc.gov/2019041535
LC ebook record available at https://lccn.loc.gov/2019041536

ISBN: 978-1-138-47929-6 (hbk)
ISBN: 978-1-351-06610-5 (ebk)

Typeset in Bembo
by Swales & Willis, Exeter, Devon, UK

CONTENTS

List of Illustrations — viii
Notes on Contributors — ix
Foreword: The State of Public Criminology—Progress and Challenges — xiv
Elliott Currie

Introduction: Public Criminology Reconsidered—An Invitation — 1
Rita Shah and Kathryn Henne

PART I
The Emergence of Public Criminologies — 9

1 Everything Still to Play for: Revisiting "Public Criminologies: Diverse Perspectives on Academia and Policy" — 11
   Lynn Chancer and Eugene McLaughlin

2 Re-thinking Public Criminology: Politics, Paradoxes, and Challenges — 21
   Eamonn Carrabine, Maggy Lee, and Nigel South

3 Where Is the Public in Public Criminology? Towards a Participatory Public Criminology — 34
   Stuart Henry

4 The Challenge of Transformative Justice: Insurgent Knowledge and Public Criminology — 49
   Michelle Brown

5 Articulation of Liberation Criminologies and Public Criminologies: Advancing a Countersystem Approach and Decolonization Paradigm 59
Biko Agozino and Kimberley Ducey

PART II
Engaging Publics 73

6 A Revolution in Prosecution: The Campaign to End Mass Incarceration in Philadelphia 75
Jill McCorkel

7 Reflections from an Accidental Public Scholar 87
Peter B. Kraska

8 Engaging the Public: Access to Justice for Those Most Vulnerable 95
Emily I. Troshynski

9 Public Feminist Criminologies: Reflections on the Activist-Scholar in Violence against Women Policy 107
Anastasia Powell and Ruth Liston

10 Liberating Abortion Pills in Legally Restricted Settings: Activism as Public Criminology 120
Mariana Prandini Assis

PART III
Barriers and Challenges 131

11 Strangers Within: Carving Out a Role for Engaged Scholarship in the University Space 133
Monique Marks

12 The Push and Pull of Going "Public": Barriers and Risks to Mobilizing Criminological Knowledge 141
Krystle Shore

13 Public Criminology in China: Neither Public nor Criminology 152
Jianhua Xu and Weidi Liu

14 A Case for a Public Pacific Criminology? 163
Miranda Forsyth, Sinclair Dinnen, and Fiona Hukula

15 The Challenges of Academics Engaging in Environmental Justice Activism 179
Joshua Ozymy and Melissa Jarrell

PART IV
Critiques and Critical Reflections — 191

16 You're a Criminologist? What Can You Offer Us? Interrogating Criminological Expertise in the Context of White Collar Crime — 193
Fiona Haines

17 Our North Is the South: Lessons from Researching Police-Community Encounters in São Paulo and Los Angeles — 203
Sebastian Sclofsky

18 Confronting Politics of Death in Papua — 213
Budi Hernawan

19 Rethinking How "the Public" Counts in Public Criminology — 228
David A. Maldonado

20 Does the Public Need Criminology? — 238
Vincenzo Ruggiero

PART V
Future Trajectories — 247

21 Starting the Conversation in the Classroom: Pedagogy as Public Criminology — 249
Lori Sexton

22 You Are on Indigenous Land: Acknowledgment and Action in Criminology — 259
Lisa Monchalin

23 Time to Think about Patriarchy? Public Criminology in an Era of Misogyny — 271
Meda Chesney-Lind

24 Value-Responsible Design and Sexual Violence Interventions: Engaging Value-Hypotheses in Making the Criminological Imagination — 286
Renee Shelby

25 Abolitionism as a Philosophy of Hope: "Inside-Outsiders" and the Reclaiming of Democracy — 299
David Scott

Index — *311*

ILLUSTRATIONS

Tables

5.1	A Comparison of Liberation Criminology and Liberation Sociology	63
18.1	The Indonesian Human Development Index	215
24.1	Potential Value-Hypotheses and "Questions of Action" in Sexual Violence	291

Figures

13.1	Mentions of "Criminologist" and "Sociologist" in China's Newspapers	155
13.2	Screenshot of Baidu Search about Criminal Psychologists	156
13.3	Mentions of "Criminologist" and "Criminal Psychologist" in China's Newspapers	158
14.1	The Sub-Division of the Pacific Islands into Three Broad Cultural Areas or Sub-Regions of the Pacific	165

NOTES ON CONTRIBUTORS

Biko Agozino is Professor of Sociology and Africana Studies at Virginia Tech and editor of the *African Journal of Criminology and Justice Studies*. He most recently authored *Critical, Creative and Centered Scholar-Activism: The Fourth Dimensionalism of Agwuncha Arthur Nwankw* (FDP, 2016), which joins a collection of other work exploring the relationships between colonization, race, ethnicity, and treatment by the criminal justice system.

Mariana Prandini Assis holds a Ph.D. in Politics from The New School for Social Research and is a postdoctoral fellow at The Schulich School of Law at Dalhousie University. She is a feminist Human Rights lawyer in Brazil. Her research interests include feminist legal and political theory, women's and human rights, and legal mobilization.

Michelle Brown is a Professor of Sociology at the University of Tennessee. She is author of *The Culture of Punishment* (NYU Press, 2009) and co-editor of the journal *Crime Media Culture* and the *Routledge International Handbook of Visual Criminology*; and senior editor for *The Oxford Encyclopedia of Crime, Media, and Popular Culture*. Her current work focuses on visuality, transformative justice, and the role of abolition in dismantling the carceral state.

Eamonn Carrabine is a Professor of Sociology at the University of Essex. His recent books include the *Routledge International Handbook of Visual Criminology* (with Michelle Brown) and *Crime and Social Theory*.

Lynn Chancer is Professor of Sociology at Hunter College and Executive Officer of the Sociology Ph.D. program at the Graduate Center of the City University of New York. She is the author of five books and two edited volumes including *High Profile Crimes: When Legal Cases Become Social Causes* and *After the Rise and Stall of American Feminism: Taking Back a Revolution*. Along with Eugene McLaughlin, she is a former editor of the journal *Theoretical Criminology* and presently a contributing editor of the *Journal of Psychosocial Studies*.

Meda Chesney-Lind is a Professor of Women's Studies at the University of Hawaii at Manoa. Her area of focus is on women in the criminal justice system, whether that be as victims, offenders, or workers. Her interest in girls and the juvenile justice system led her to co-author the book *Fighting for Girls: New Perspectives on Gender and Violence* (SUNY Press, 2010).

Notes on Contributors

Elliott Currie is a Professor of Criminology, Law and Society at the University of California, Irvine, and Adjunct Professor in the Faculty of Law, School of Justice, Queensland University, and Adjunct Professor in the Faculty of Law, School of Justice, Queensland University of Technology. He is the author of *Confronting Crime* (1985), *Crime and Punishment in America* (2013), and *Progressive Justice in the Age of Repression: Strategies for Challenging the Rise of the Right* (co-edited with Walter S. Dekeseredy; Routledge, 2019). His most recent book, *A Peculiar Indifference: Race, Violence, and Social Justice*, will be published in 2020.

Sinclair Dinnen is an Associate Professor of Pacific Affairs at the Australian National University. He has published in multiple leading journals, wrote many book chapters, and has co-edited seven books, most recently *Hybridity on the Ground in Peacebuilding and Development* (2018). His research interests include comparative criminology, justice and policing, conflict and peacebuilding, and regulatory pluralism.

Kimberley Ducey is an Associate Professor of Sociology at the University of Winnipeg. For her work in promoting liberation sociology, she was awarded the Québec's Forces AVENIR Award. She is the author of multiple books, including *Racist America: Roots, Current Realities and Future Reparations* (Routledge, 2018), and is currently working on *George Yancy: A Critical Reader*.

Miranda Forsyth is an Associate Professor at RegNet, the School of Regulation and Global Governance at the Australian National University. Her research interests include the interoperation of state and non-state justice systems. She is a lead investigator in a four-year project that is investigating ways to best overcome accusations of sorcery and the related violence in Papua New Guinea, and the author of *Weaving Intellectual Property Policy in Small Island Developing States* (2014).

Fiona Haines is Professor of Criminology at the University of Melbourne and Adjunct Professor at RegNet, the School of Regulation and Global Governance at Australian National University. An internationally renowned expert in regulation and compliance, she studies industrial disasters, globalization, and white collar and corporate crime. Her most recent book is *Regulatory Transformations: Rethinking Economy Society Interactions* (2015).

Stuart Henry is an Emeritus Professor of Criminal Justice and former Director of the School of Public Affairs at San Diego State University. His areas of expertise are criminological theory, corporate/white-collar crime, school violence, and sociology of crime. He is the author/editor of 35 books and over 100 articles and book chapters. Currently, he is working on a book manuscript entitled *The Social Construction of Crime*.

Budi Hernawan is a political anthropologist based at *Driyarkara* School of Philosophy in Jakarta, Indonesia. His research interests focus on political violence and peacebuilding in the context of Indigenous communities in Asia and the Pacific. He has extensive experience in conflict and post-conflict areas and in engaging the UN Human Rights Council and the UN Security Council.

Fiona Hukula is a Senior Research Fellow and Building Safer Communities Program Leader at the Papua New Guinea National Research Institute, and sits on multiple national committees and organization boards. She is the author/co-author of multiple publications on the topics of crimes, urban issues, and gender violence in Papua New Guinea. Her research interests are urban studies, gender, and socio-legal studies.

Notes on Contributors

Melissa Jarrell is an Associate Professor of Criminal Justice at Texas A&M University-Corpus Christi. Her areas of interest include environment crime, justice, and victimization. She has published in journals such as *Environmental Justice* and *Environmental Politics*, and is the author of *Environmental Crime and the Media: News Coverage of Petroleum Refining Industry Violations* (2007).

Peter B. Kraska is a Professor in the School of Justice Studies at Eastern Kentucky University. He is an internationally recognized researcher on topics of police/criminal justice militarization and has presented his findings to the U.S. Senate as well as on media outlets such as *60 Minutes*, *BBC*, and the *Wallstreet Journal*. He has published in numerous academic journals and is the author of seven books.

Maggy Lee is a Professor of Sociology at the University of Hong Kong. Her research focuses on migration and human trafficking and she is the author of *Trafficking and Global Crime Control* (2011) and *The Borders of Punishment: Migration, Citizenship, and Social Exclusion* (2013). She has also worked with governmental and non-governmental organizations as an expert on this area of research.

Ruth Liston is Lecturer in Criminology and Justice Studies at RMIT University (Melbourne, Australia). Ruth's research is focused on teaching criminology, youth justice, and preventing gender-based violence. Her research career has extended beyond the academy through her previous role in government policy and research, as well as undertaking commissioned research for the violence against women sector.

Weidi Liu is a doctoral student in the School of Criminology and Justice Studies at the University of Massachusetts Lowell. His research interests include criminological theory testing, organized crime, and quantitative methods.

David A. Maldonado is a doctoral student in the Graduate School of Education at University of California, Berkeley. He is a formerly incarcerated student and one of the founding members of the Underground Scholars Initiative. He grew up in Berkeley and Oakland, is a proud student parent, and is proud to be clean and sober in active recovery.

Monique Marks is a Professor at Durban University of Technology. She is the author of over 45 articles and reports as well as four books, including *Police Reform from the Bottom Up: Officers and their Unions as Agents of Change* (Routledge, 2011). Her areas of interest include youth social movements, police relations, police organizational change, and security governance. She is also a member of the Board of Trustees of the Safer South Africa Foundation.

Jill McCorkel is an Associate Professor of Sociology and Criminology at Villanova University. Her research examines the social and political consequences of mass incarceration and how race, class, and gender inequalities are perpetuated by laws and systems. Her work has been published in multiple academic journals, and she is the author of *Breaking Women: Gender, Race, and the New Politics of Imprisonment* (2013).

Eugene McLaughlin is Professor of Criminology at City University, London. His current research and writing clusters around the nature, dynamics, and impact of scandals, the significance of "trial by media," the mediatization of criminal justice, and celebrity sex offenders. He also has a long-standing interest in theorizing that seeks to extend the scope of criminology's research agenda. Along with Lynn Chancer, he is a former editor of the journal *Theoretical Criminology*.

Notes on Contributors

Lisa Monchalin is Algonquin, Métis, Huron, and Scottish and teaches in the Department of Criminology at Kwantlen Polytechnic University in British Columbia. She is the first Indigenous woman in Canada to hold a Ph.D. in Criminology. Her work focuses on finding justice for Indigenous peoples; her work has been published in many journals and she is the author of *The Colonial Problem: An Indigenous Perspective on Crime and Injustice in Canada* (2016).

Joshua Ozymy is a Professor of Political Science at Texas A&M University-Corpus Christi. His research agenda focuses on topics of environmental policies, how they fail to protect the public from harm, and the consequences of these policies. His work has been published in *Environmental Politics*, *Review of Policy Research*, and *Global Environmental Politics*.

Anastasia Powell is Associate Professor in Criminology and Justice Studies at RMIT University (Melbourne, Australia). Anastasia's research lies at the intersections of gender, violence, justice, technology, and digital culture. Recent books include *Digital Criminology* (Routledge, 2018 with Gregory Stratton and Robin Cameron) and *Sexual Violence in a Digital Age* (2017, with Nicola Henry).

Vincenzo Ruggiero is a Professor of Sociology and the director of the Centre for Social and Criminological Research at Middlesex University. He is the author of countless books, articles, and book chapters. His most recent book is entitled *Visions of Political Violence* (Routledge, 2019). His research interests include organized crime, corporate crime, penal systems, political violence, and social movements.

Sebastian Sclofsky is an Assistant Professor of Criminal Justice at California State University, Stanislaus. His research agenda focuses on the effects of policing, police violence, and development of policing in Latin America. His work has been published in the *Journal of Social Justice*, *International Studies Perspectives*, and *International Studies Review*, along with opinion pieces in media outlets.

David Scott is a Senior Lecturer of Criminology at The Open University. His current research interests revolve around penal abolition: historical relationships, ethical foundations, and anti-carceral approaches to punishment. His most recent book is entitled *Against Imprisonment* (2018) and he is currently co-editing the *International Handbook of Penal Abolition* (Routledge, 2020) and *Contesting Carceral Logic* (Routledge, 2021).

Lori Sexton is an Associate Professor of Criminal Justice and Criminology at the University of Missouri, Kansas City. Her research focuses on prisons, punishment, and the lived experience of penal sanctions among transgender prisoners. She is the author (with Kristi Holsinger) of *Toward Justice: Broadening the Study of Criminal Justice* (Routledge, 2017). Her work has been funded by the National Science Foundation, the National Institute of Justice, and the Fletcher Jones Foundation.

Renee Shelby is a Ph.D. candidate in the School of History and Sociology at the Georgia Institute of Technology. Her research is situated at the intersection of feminist science studies and critical legal studies and investigates how ideas about gender and race inform knowledge about sexual violence through technology, culture, and the law. This research was assisted by a Mellon/ACLS Dissertation Completion Fellowship from the American Council of Learned Societies.

Krystle Shore is a Ph.D. candidate in Sociology at the University of Waterloo. Her primary research focus is policing, and she is particularly interested in surveillance, police responses to marginalized groups, and police culture and militarization. She is also interested in how institutional forces in academe, such as the push for knowledge mobilization, can shape and censor critical or activist scholarship.

Nigel South is a Professor of Sociology and is the Director for the Centre of Criminology at the University of Essex. He recently co-authored *Water, Crime and Security in the Twenty-First Century: Too Dirty, Too Little, Too Much* (2018) and co-edited *Women and the Criminal Justice System* (2018). He is the European Editor of *Critical Criminology* and an Associate Editor of *Deviant Behavior*.

Emily I. Troshynski is an Associate Professor of Criminal Justice at the University of Nevada, Las Vegas. Her research agenda involves understanding the social causes of deviance, violence, victimization, and uncovering how law and society inform justice system policies and practices. She has published several book chapters and her work has appeared in *Trends in Organized Crime* and the *International Journal of Crime*, among many others.

Jianhua Xu is an Associate Professor of Sociology at the University of Macau. His research interests include policing and migrant workers in China, social problems in China, urban sociology, and victimology. His work has been published many journals, including *The British Journal of Criminology*, *Journal of Research in Crime and Delinquency*, and *Qualitative Sociology Review*.

FOREWORD

THE STATE OF PUBLIC CRIMINOLOGY—PROGRESS AND CHALLENGES

Elliott Currie

The central message of this exciting volume is that public criminology has come a long way in the last several years. Those of us who have been working to promote the idea of a more inclusive, engaged, and morally thoughtful criminology have much to be proud of, and the varied articles presented here illustrate why.

Twelve years ago, I wrote an article setting out some arguments in support of public criminology, at a time when there was much less of it than there is today (Currie, 2007). I was by no means the first to make that case, but I think it may be useful to step back and look at where we are today through the lens of where I thought we were then. Seen from this vantage point, there is a lot of good news.

To begin with, as this collection makes clear, there is simply more of what could reasonably be called public criminology under way, and in more areas and more places, than was true a decade or so ago. This volume gives a sense of that growth—encompassing a much more wide-ranging theoretical and critical discussion of what public criminology is and should be, and also showcasing a much wider range of campaigns, sometimes successful ones, in which criminologists have engaged with critical issues in the real world in a variety of contexts. From mass incarceration, to reproductive rights, police violence, harm reduction, domestic violence and sexual violence, we're seeing the principles of public criminology being put into practice in communities in many countries, and with significant collaboration between academic criminologists and constituencies that have all too often been ignored.

Likewise, a central theme in the vision of public criminology—the imperative to move beyond narrow definitions of the discipline, narrow conceptions of what the field of criminology is, to include a broader range of critical issues as legitimate and vital subjects of study and action—has been richly realized in the last few years. In 2007, I wrote that the largely self-inflicted isolation of the conventional discipline had kept us from studying a number of issues of "growing global concern." I specifically mentioned crimes against humanity, trafficking in human beings, and terrorism, but I also had in mind others: environmental harms, international corporate corruption, the intensifying global traffic in firearms, and more. On this score, there has been a real transformation since then, with the growth of green criminology, queer criminology, and, most recently, the rise of Southern criminology. I'm not suggesting that we've altogether thrown off the shackles of traditional definitions of the field. But the change is very real. Seen from the perspective of only a few years ago, this seems to me like a true flowering of the broader and less insular criminology that I felt, back then, was being held back by a disciplinary inertia that promoted business as usual by default. It's safe to say that, around the world, criminology will never be the same again. And that's a very good thing.

Other good news involves developments in the world beyond the discipline—some of which have been influenced by the work of public criminology. One of the most important, at least in the United States, is the emergence of unanticipated cracks in the monolith of the relentless growth of mass incarceration. My 2007 piece on public criminology began with the assertion, shared by many others, that the United States embodied the worst of all possible worlds when it came to crime and punishment: we had both the worst levels of serious violent crime in the advanced industrial world and the world's highest incarceration rate. The fact that the country had produced a default response to crime that went squarely against the grain of nearly everything that serious criminologists had to say about the factors that truly made for a secure society was, I thought, an illuminating indicator of just how marginal the discipline of criminology had become in the world outside of academia. But shortly after that piece was published, the American prison boom slowed for the first time in decades and even began the slight reversal that has continued ever since. Even more strikingly, during this political season we have witnessed a phenomenon we have not seen for many, many years—the emergence of a critique of mass incarceration among serious candidates for political office. Today, in fact, potential presidential candidates in the Democratic Party have been scrambling to distance themselves from the mainstream party's "tough on crime" rhetoric of the 1980s, 1990s, and early 2000s and, in some cases, to hastily concoct excuses for their own participation in pushing the legislation and policies that underpinned the prison boom. Most remarkably, we've seen presidential candidates fielding detailed plans for criminal justice reform that aim to further reduce prison populations and to provide a better chance for people coming out of confinement. Surprisingly, this has been an oddly bipartisan effort, which includes an unusual alliance between far-right donors and long-established liberal reform organizations. I don't think many of us really saw this coming 12 years ago: I certainly didn't. How much the efforts of public criminology, or any criminology, helped to fuel this unexpected shift is hard to say. But it is also hard to believe that the relentless work to get information out and into the public realm about the failures and injustices of America's prison system had no part in it.

Something similar could be said about the sudden emergence of gun control as an acceptable, even mandatory, issue for mainstream politicians in the United States. Those living in other countries may find the recent stirrings of political support for more gun regulation in the United States to be fairly paltry: but this is the United States, a country where the power and money of the organized firearms industry had kept any discussion whatever of gun regulation out of the political mainstream for as long as anyone can remember. But now we have Democratic presidential candidates openly proposing detailed strategies for the prevention of gun violence that include significant measures to regulate the sale and ownership of guns. Again, how much the efforts of public criminology helped to bring about this change is hard to quantify. It is clear that the main force behind what has become a powerful grassroots movement for gun control came not from academic experts, but from militant young people, especially survivors of mass shooting incidents at their schools, who took to the streets and to social media to mount the most visible and consequential anti-gun violence protests in our history. But again, it is a movement that makes regular use of the data and analysis that has been steadily provided by an intrepid band of academic criminologists who continued in the face of sharply restricted funding for their work.

These developments are very significant and very welcome. But they're not the whole story. The good news co-exists with the perpetuation of long-standing barriers to the development of an effective public criminology, as well as new—or intensified—challenges on a global level that will test our commitment and our resources in different ways.

One of the most stubborn obstacles is the continuing institutional inertia and outright resistance of much of academic social science and its infrastructure of funding sources and professional associations. This was the main focus of my 2007 critique: the conventions of the discipline and the structure and culture of the major research universities operated, in mutually reinforcing ways, to undercut the capacity of criminology to affect real-world policy in a progressive direction. I'd have to say that on the whole this seems still true in much of the world today.

Most of the scholars who have been engaged in doing this work, for example, are reasonably well employed at educational institutions that give them a modicum of job security, resources, and institutional authority. But it remains true that many of them are clustered in a relatively few institutions, and visibly absent from others. A fair number of universities around the world have distinguished themselves by having provided supportive environments for this work, and for having strong and visionary leadership willing to stick their necks out to support socially engaged scholarship in criminology. But many others have continued to be inhospitable—sometimes explicitly, more often subtly. The result is that scholars who want to do this kind of engaged criminology often feel like "strangers within," as Monique Marks puts it in her contribution to this volume. Students in many places are still discouraged from a career focus that fuses scholarship with social action: they are warned that it can have an adverse impact on getting hired and getting promoted, and the warning may be right. This kind of scholarship rarely finds its way into the so-called flagship journals in the field, and it often—though by no means always—gets ignored in government and foundation funding decisions. We continue to lack resources, training programs, or publication venues on the scale that would be transformative. This reinforces a long-standing situation in which an insular field mostly still talks only to itself, and in language that no one but other academics understand. And that in turn distances even potentially useful scholarship from any possible engagement with other constituencies, and particularly from the communities most burdened by systemic legal injustices and endemic harms. The single most important thing that would facilitate the flourishing of public criminology is to ensure that the people who do this work can make a decent living at it. On this score we have some way to go.

These continuing impediments to the flourishing of public criminology are especially troubling at a time when we face new or intensified challenges on many different levels—political, social, cultural, environmental—that urgently call for our attention and which will require public criminologists to up their game.

One is the continued dominance in many countries around the world of a profoundly punitive model of crime control deeply rooted in the acceptance of mass incarceration as its unquestioned core. In the widespread euphoria over the unexpected easing of the prison boom in the United States, we have often ignored the much more consequential continuity in our reliance on the prison. The United States remains by far the world's largest incarcerator, and there is at present no political movement of consequence within the dominant political parties that envisions moving beyond the decarceration of minor offenders to mount a full-on challenge to the reliance on incarceration and harsh sentencing more generally. Something like the American model, moreover, continues to be exported to other countries around the world, some of which have seen an explosion of prison populations in recent years. That's especially true in some of the more stricken countries of the global South where extremely high levels of violence have been met mainly by ramping up the institutions of repressive force. Forcing a real public discussion of alternatives to this more stubborn reality of incarceration will be an urgent task for public criminology in the future.

Relatedly, against the often exaggerated talk of a global "crime drop" lies the reality of what I have sometimes called the "violence divide": the stark and often growing disparity between those parts of the world where serious violence is relatively rare and those where it remains endemic and woven deeply into the fabric of community life. Those international differences, particularly between parts of Latin America and the Caribbean and the industrialized countries of North America, Asia, and Europe, are often attributed simplistically to the usual suspects: organized gangs and the drug trade. But the reality is deeper, more varied, and more pervasive. A major aspect of the divide, for example, is the global stratification of gender-based violence, which has reached astonishing levels in some of the countries of the global South. Historically, violence against women has been one of the most important arenas for work that fits the model of public criminology, and one where engaged criminology has been most frequently successful in catalyzing social change. But what we are up against now in some parts of the world is a high, and in some places rising level, of misogynistic violence that will challenge our best thinking and our best efforts at social and political mobilization. More generally, the violence divide, with its outsized impact on women, children, and youth, provides a window into the ways in which a toxic constellation of forces—economic deprivation, political corruption and state failure, stunning social neglect, traumatic histories of military intervention and colonial exploitation, and a massive and largely unregulated flow of firearms into the regions most affected—all work together to create situations of great peril and human suffering, which in turn helps to fuel a desperate mass migration in search of safety. Creating effective global strategies to address this very real crisis will be another tough, but necessary, challenge for public criminology in the coming years.

That is also true for our efforts to deal with the criminological aspects of the massive movements of population across borders more generally—a development that has brought danger and great harm to uprooted populations and that has led to conditions of confinement in many countries that are both socially disastrous and morally abhorrent. Criminologists have recently done important work on immigration, perhaps especially in dismantling myths about the criminality of migrants. But the scale and human impact of the current movement of populations is unprecedented, and it calls for a level of critical analysis and mobilization that we haven't yet been able to muster. And in the absence of the presentation of compelling alternatives, an exclusive and punitive right-wing response has prevailed in many places across the globe.

It has also helped to power another critical development: the rise of punitive and corrupt right-wing regimes, committed to brutal austerity measures that promise to increase deprivation and desperation at the bottom while unleashing State violence to contain the resulting disorder. Back in 2007, I wrote that the forces arrayed against honest and humane practices with respect to crime and justice were very strong, and in many places around the world were "increasingly in the saddle." Again, this was before nationalist, anti-immigrant regimes endorsing particularly harsh and heedless conceptions of "law and order" mounted the saddle in Brazil, Poland, Hungary, Honduras, and, of course, the United States.

Closely aligned with the rise of these punitive and exclusive regimes has been an intensified attack on science and on reasoned discourse and honest exploration of social issues. In 2007, I worried about the possibility of social scientific truths being "overwhelmed" in the current political climate by what I called "calculated untruth." I argued that one of the reasons why supporting public criminology, and public social science in general, had become especially urgent was that "the values of honest science are under siege as they have never before been in my lifetime" (Currie, 2007, p. 188). That was written a decade before Donald Trump took office. And the problem has clearly gotten worse since then. My sense is that the effort to obfuscate and erase reality in the service of political agendas has entered a new phase, made more dangerous because of the advance of digital and communications technologies that make distorting reality easier than ever before. Countering this with forceful, articulate, and well-disseminated analysis will be a crucial task for public criminology.

Finally, the most important—and most troubling—development of all has been the impact of environmental crime and heedless resource exploitation on the health of the planet itself. As Rob White (2019, p. 153) has written, "No one and nothing can escape the impact of the transgressions presently impinging upon the biosphere." A strong public criminology will play a critical role in exposing, explaining, and combatting those transgressions. Again, good work is already being done in this vein. But much more needs to be done, and we don't have that much time to do it.

There are many more of these challenges, but even that abbreviated list gives some sense of the depth and urgency of the issues a vital public criminology should step up to deal with in the coming years. I don't think we should be daunted by those challenges, but we will need to build a vibrant international infrastructure of support for the work ahead. This book, happily, is a big step in that direction. Hats off to the editors, the contributors, and all those who have had the courage and persistence to have moved the project of public criminology this far.

References

Currie, E. (2007). Against marginality: Arguments for a public criminology. *Theoretical Criminology*, *11*(2), 175–190.

White, R. (2019). Resisting ecocide: Engaging in the politics of the future. In W. DeKeseredy and E. Currie (Eds.). *Progressive justice in an age of repression: Strategies for challenging the rise of the right* (pp. 153–167). New York: Routledge.

INTRODUCTION

Public Criminology Reconsidered—An Invitation

Rita Shah and Kathryn Henne

Introduction

Amid rising populist and authoritarian sentiments across the globe, the current political moment—which could be understood as a "hot climate" (Loader & Sparks, 2011)—has sparked renewed interest in and discussion about criminologists participating in public fora. Reflecting on the United States, for example, Stuart (2017) observes how calls for research to have a so-called "real world" impact seem all the more pressing. Despite efforts to reform the U.S. criminal justice system, the 2016 election empowered a president who has promoted tough-on-crime rhetoric, appointed officials who have enforced oppressive policies, and endorsed practices that criminalize people who already experience various forms of marginalization.

In response to shifting governmental priorities and wider political change, many criminologists have framed public criminology as a necessary call to action. Traditionally thought of as efforts to "narrow the yawning gap between public perceptions and the best available scientific evidence on issues of public concern" (Uggen & Inderbitzin, 2010, p. 726), public criminology often works in concert with governmental actors to achieve their goals. For example, in the United States, Petersilia (2008) worked as an embedded criminologist with the aim of implementing evidence-based practices in the California prison system. While such efforts attempt to bridge the gap between research objectives and policy goals, they often focus on changes that uphold the status quo.

Although important, this view of public criminology has been the subject of critique. In particular, as Piché explains (2015, p. 71), this approach to public criminology can reify "dominant constructions of 'crime' and justice," fail "to work with the individuals and groups most harmed by interpersonal and state violence," and prioritizes "the participation of extra-academic publics to audiences of scholarly work." The acknowledgment of such shortcomings, alongside these calls for renewal, presents an opportunity to query what lessons we can learn from debates about public criminology.

This handbook showcases 25 chapters that provide a range of critical reflections on public engagement, attending to past and present practices as well as possible futures. This collection also raises questions about our obligations as scholars who are committed to generating and sharing criminological knowledge. What are our ethical obligations and responsibilities to wider publics, particularly those most likely to be affected—or targeted—by criminal justice policy? What are the risks and potential unintended consequences, particularly in the contemporary moment? And, what does this assumption of criminologists "going public" miss?

In considering these questions, we, as editors of this handbook, caution against the tendency to think of public criminology as a relationship premised on experts reaching out to publics (see also Nelund, 2014). In keeping with Loader and Sparks (2011, p. 2), we recognize there are many "ways in which criminologists, and those who produce knowledge about crime and its control under allied banners, have sought, and might in future seek, to engage with and influence public responses to crime." Like Hughes (2017, p. 369), we hope to highlight public criminological engagement as "a form of reflexive criminological labor," one that "aims to create a dialogic relation between the criminologist and various publics in which the agenda of each is brought to the table and in which each adjusts to the other." In doing so, we want to draw attention to public-facing work that does "not privilege the conversation with the state and its crime-control agencies, but ... instead also seek[s] to support work beyond the state, for example, with movements for social justice and human rights" (p. 369). Accordingly, the chapters featured in this collection showcase a plurality of public criminologies and the many activities they entail, which include—but are certainly not limited to—media and community outreach, policy advising, activism, expert testimony, civic-oriented education, and knowledge co-production (see Chancer & McLaughlin, 2007).

We also caution against viewing public criminology as limited to a distinct set of practices that appeal primarily to the state. As Rock (2014) argues, public criminology has tended to focus on research that is publicly funded, distributed through public channels, or done in concert with government organizations. Neither the "public" nor "criminology" is a uniform or homogeneous domain. Scholars have critically considered and critiqued the idea of a single public (e.g., Fraser, 1990). Indeed, in his foundational writings on public sociology, Burawoy (2005, p. 8) is clear "there is no shortage of publics if we but care to seek them out." Academics have also questioned what constitutes criminology (Bosworth & Hoyle, 2011), recognizing that it is perhaps best understood as an "interdiscipline" (Binder, 1987). Perhaps more importantly, scholars have warned that much criminological research lacks contemporary relevance, because it fails to grasp the complex and changing social, economic, and regulatory conditions in which crime, deviance, and forms of social control take shape (see Braithwaite, 2000).

As an acknowledgement of these debates, this handbook does not provide a definitive account of what *a* public criminology can or should do. Instead, it offers reflections and critiques that unveil and complicate common understandings of public criminology. In doing so, this collection captures the myriad ways in which criminologists approach "their responsibilities as citizens to participate in the broader public conversation" (Chancer & McLaughlin, 2007, p. 158). As such, it appreciates the need not only to understand earlier ideas and debates about public criminology, but also how they have materialized in ways that limit the scope and impact of public criminologies to date. Furthermore, this handbook discusses how scholars grapple with the shortcomings of more traditional forms of public criminology, attempts to extend critical thinking about "the public" and the field of criminology, and puts forth avenues for future engagement.

Public Criminologies for the Contemporary Moment

Despite the recognition of globalization's influence on the proliferation of crime and criminalized activities (Rotman, 2000), criminology is still coming to grips with how these dynamics manifest in different parts of the world (see Carrington, Hogg, & Sozzo, 2016). Although the devastating impacts of wars on drugs, tough-on-crime policies, and state violence are well documented, punitive responses are seemingly on the rise globally. They extend to areas such as environmental advocacy; immigration and statelessness; minority, queer, and transgender rights; and reproductive politics. Even though we see similar trends across different contexts, criminology, as Carrington, Hogg, and Sozzo (2016, p. 2) suggest, nonetheless tends to "make universal knowledge claims" and "fails to reflect their geo-political specificity." Heeding their advice, this handbook features "new and diverse perspectives [within] criminological research agendas" in order "to make them more inclusive and befitting of the world in which we live" (p. 2). We admit, though, it is not as comprehensive as we would like, and we acknowledge the need for broader and deeper analysis beyond North America and Western Europe.

Importantly, this handbook attends to questions of power and inequality not only as they pertain to specific situations and locations, but also as they implicate the field of criminology. Scholars have stressed that criminology has supported inequitable forms of social control, many of which cross-cut concerns of class, disability, gender, sexuality, and race (e.g., Belknap, 2015; Lynch, 2000; Nelund, 2014; Henne & Troshynski, 2019). This tendency is in part linked to what some scholars refer to as the discipline's overlooked history as a science of oppression, which has aided in legitimating state-sanctioned forms of subjugation (Lynch, 2000). As Haggerty (2004, p. 215) reminds us, "The motivation to 'do something' about crime [has] brought state functionaries into contact with criminological knowledge," positioning criminology as a desirable partner in "state efforts to govern crime." Criminology, even when striving for independence or objectivity, is thus vulnerable to state capture and co-optation. These risks are both inherent to and exacerbated by governmental collaboration (Piché, 2015). In response to these concerns, many of the chapters in this handbook offer nuanced readings of different formations of power, including gendered, globalized, racialized, and socio-economic inequalities, while accounting for expressed concerns about common practices of public criminology.

Among these critiques is public criminology's sometimes "troubling lack of attention to power and power relations" (Nelund, 2014, p. 68). According to Nelund (2014), public criminology can contribute to the privileging of certain kinds of knowledges over others. She states (Nelund, 2014, p. 72),

> Naming it public criminology is a discursive move... If public criminology is engaged, political, pragmatic, and accessible, then other criminologies are detached, objective, and aloof. Not only does this set up a binary, it creates a hierarchy based on traditional markers of scientific thought that excludes alternative ways of producing knowledge.

Fraser's (1990) observations that traditional notions of the public sphere often exclude marginalized persons are also applicable here. As Nelund (2014) explains, public criminological engagement, by not questioning who constitutes its audience, can perpetuate narrow constructions of "the public" and its needs, often to the detriment of those persons who occupy its peripheries. By doing so, public criminology can also perpetuate tacit notions of what knowledge is and who it serves, making it all the more difficult for alternative and grassroots knowledges to gain traction in criminological debates.

These power relations inevitably inform who emerges as experts and how they are perceived and understood. As Uggen and Inderbitzin (2010, p. 734) acknowledge, a "pathology" of public criminology is its "lack of diversity among the voices represented as experts on crime." Accordingly, feminist and queer scholars, scholars of color, and other underrepresented academics, such as those in disability studies, are often excluded from public discourse about crime. This exclusion replicates larger inequalities and forms of marginalization within academia and society at large (Belknap, 2015; Greene, Gabbidon, & Wilson, 2017; Woods, 2014). We therefore cannot ignore the resulting tensions underpinning who becomes recognized as an expert. Indeed, Ruggiero (2012, p. 157) argues that public criminologists recognized as experts are actually "esoteric and elitist," as they tend to "seek the help of experts working in adjacent areas," and treat the communities they advocate for in paternalistic, rather than collaborative, ways. Currie (2007, p. 178), too, frames the tendency to "sometimes think that the way to affect the world of social policy is to get 'access' to legislators and then persuade them to do the right thing" as a decidedly narrow approach to public criminology. We concur and seek to trouble some of these assumptions through this collection.

This handbook captures a wider range of public criminologies and makes a concerted effort not to limit its scope to attempts at effecting change through policy-oriented engagement. It aligns with Belknap's (2015, p. 5) notion of an activist criminology, in which criminologists participate "in social and/or legal justice at individual, organizational, and/or policy levels, which goes beyond typical research, teaching, and service." A key implication of her call "is broadening the diversity of criminologists to provide a lens that more accurately reflects what we study (crime and the responses to it)" (p. 5). Accordingly, the authors featured here draw on a variety of knowledges, many of which are not found in canonical criminological texts. As such, this collection embraces a wider range of what we see as praxis-oriented criminologies informed by different theoretical traditions and normative stances.

This task comes with challenges: in our attempts to include more perspectives in the handbook, we came to further appreciate that frontline commitments mean many scholars often cannot publish about their public engagement. Many of the scholars and activists doing the work called for by Belknap (2015) and others are overburdened by demands for their time. This aligns with observations that work informed by critical race and feminist perspectives illustrates how interlocking racialized and gendered hierarchies shape academic labor in practice (e.g., Gutiérrez Y Muhs, Niemann, González, & Harris, 2012; Nash, 2019). We see this in everyday life: scholars of color, queer academics, scholar-activists, and critical allies manage heavy workloads that embody forms of labor—be it mentorship, service, and community outreach, among other commitments—that academic incentive structures rarely acknowledge or take into account. Moreover, such work is often criticized or devalued as being "too political" (i.e., not objective or even biased) or "*me*search" (i.e., limited to one's own experience). In many cases, these contributions constitute different kinds of public criminology, even though they may diverge from traditional notions of a public criminology that relies on "objective" and "apolitical" experts (see Nelund, 2014; Ruggiero, 2012; Wacquant, 2011). Academics have refuted the idea "that we can have scholarship that has no political allegiance and comes from no particular position" (Nelund, 2014, p. 73). As Belknap (2015, p. 7) suggests, the "inclusivity of scholars with diverse demographic characteristics and life experiences is vital for a broad criminological lens," as it enhances scholarly inquiry. In part because of these realities, this handbook is merely a snapshot of the wide range of activities that could fall under the umbrella of public criminology.

We should also note that the inequalities underpinning what comes to count as public criminology surpass problems of academic labor. As Carrington, Hogg and Sozzo (2016, pp. 2–3) argue, we need to think reflexively about how knowledge production "privileges theories, assumptions, and methods based largely on empirical specificities of the global North,"[1] the effects of which have "stunted the intellectual development and vitality of criminology, both in the South and globally." In other words, geopolitics informs how we come to know and explain our worlds—an issue missing from public criminological debates. Braithwaite (2005) makes a similar point in his discussion of public social science: Not only do scholars and institutions in the North Atlantic strongly influence global knowledge production, they also hegemonically stifle the necessary "[c]ross-cutting cultural, economic, and political diversity that can engender transformative theory" (p. 347). While we do not tackle bigger questions of disciplinary silos and their wide-ranging effects, this handbook does confront related challenges by highlighting criminological pluralism rather than pursuing a narrow criminological agenda or dwelling on concerns as to whether criminology is a fractured field (see Bosworth & Hoyle, 2011). We do so with the hope that this approach better equips academics to make relevant and meaningful public contributions when addressing contemporary social problems within a globalized context.

Aims and Organization of this Handbook

Concerns of justice underpin the motivation for this handbook. It takes seriously the need for criminology—and by extension, public criminologies—to critically (re)consider its place and purpose in responding to the major issues of our time. The goal of this handbook is to invite readers to critically reflect on questions of public criminology, some of which surpass core concerns of criminological inquiry. In particular, we ask readers to reflect on the ways in which both the field of criminology and various state and nonstate actors can perpetuate violence, both intentionally and not (see Cunneen & Tauri, 2019; Muhammad, 2011; Piché, 2015; Wacquant, 2011) and to consider potential avenues for transformative change.

But we do not want to simply raise critiques. Rather, we emphasize a reflexive approach to criminology and public criminologies to support the pursuit of social justice. As editors, we hope this project supports others seeking to cultivate and instill hope collectively and institutionally—that is, as Braithwaite (2004, p. 9) suggests, by contributing to the creation of "rules, norms, and practices that ensure that we have some room not only to dream of the extraordinary, but also to do the extraordinary."[2] To do so, this collection brings together a diverse group of scholars with a variety of insights informed by their backgrounds, geographic and social location, and academic experiences.

Given our ambition to problematize "public criminology" (and, in doing so, arguably criminology), this project is inherently incomplete; it is an ongoing project, one that can be thought of as an "an open future" (Grosz, 2000, p. 1017). Similar to Grosz's (2000, p. 1020) reflection on feminist histories and futures, we see the history of public criminology as "a volatile one," one that can be written and re-written in the "production of conceivable futures." We therefore do not aim to offer a prescriptive notion of what this project should look like in the future. Instead, we offer this book as an invitation to reimagining what is—and has been—possible as public criminology. That said, we do want to recognize that many scholars navigate tenuous and complicated dynamics in the present. Attempts at meaningful engagement are difficult: They entail ongoing negotiations that require not only managing power relations, but also time, energy, and emotion that can exceed traditional academic expectations—and often without institutional support.

This handbook's contributors are keenly attuned to the difficulties of public criminological engagement as they discuss their work on crime and crime control, media landscapes, and the changing political climates in different parts of the world. In short, this collection captures how they "do" public criminologies, including the domains in which they work, the tactics they use, and the challenges they face. These grounded examples distinguish the handbook from other contributions in the area: By illustrating strategies for bridging the gap between scholarship, activism, and engagement, they offer a strong anchor for broader discussions of the status and possibilities of public criminologies. Taken together, many of the chapters center concerns of inequality and social difference, including the ways in which criminology can be complicit in perpetuating inequitable practices and structures, and how public criminology aims—and sometimes fails—to address them.

The handbook opens with Currie's reflection on growth within public criminology, including the breath of public outlets and continued resilience of scholars in the face of resistance to such activism. He also reminds us that as public criminology grows, we must be cognizant of and prepared to address the challenges we face on a global scale, the barriers placed on such work by academia itself, and the need to pay close attention to what Currie calls the "violence divide." His concerns are further discussed in the book's five parts.

Part I covers foundational ideas and debates about public criminology, including reflections on initial calls to take public criminology seriously. The authors present critical perspectives on the wider dissemination of criminological knowledge, how public criminology can mean different things to different people, and debates that shaped public criminological agendas. Instead of narrating the history of public criminology, they collectively problematize its origins, scope, and methods, highlighting the need for more reflexive consideration and transnational sensibilities.

Part II showcases accounts by scholars who have untaken different modes of taking criminology public, considering the ways in which they do so and their practices of translating research for different contexts. Specifically, they reflect on their engagement with government officials, policy development, activism, community outreach, and academic institutions. The authors also address relationships with different partners and audiences, the challenges and rewards of such engagement, and various vantage points and theories that inform their praxis. Finally, the authors are attentive to the distinct concerns when working with marginalized and ethnically diverse populations.

Part III examines barriers, both formal and discursive, to pursuing public criminologies. Authors from Australia, Asia and the Pacific, North America, South Africa, and the United Kingdom weigh in on the structural, institutional, and hegemonic forces that shape public criminological practices, which can censor critical voices or undermine meaningful or long-term engagement with different communities. The chapters introduce new empirical research on how the "impact agenda" implicates public criminologies, reflections on the public reception of expert views, feminist and community strategies, and dilemmas in navigating state-level censorship.

Part IV of the handbook is dedicated to explicit critiques of public criminological methods and approaches, some of which posit alternatives informed by different critical and radical traditions. Importantly, the authors also capture critical race and feminist theoretical perspectives. These chapters address critiques regarding criminology's privileging of particular kinds of expertise and the global North, as well as the burden of doing public work given assumptions of whose voices are valued.

Part V looks at possible futures of public criminologies, addressing a variety of concerns linked to power dynamics that cross-cut questions of knowledge production, changing political landscapes, and distinct formations of inequality. Specifically, it reflects on whether and how public modes of engagement can avoid being co-opted by impact agendas, which publics are ignored or overlooked, questions about more democratic forms of knowledge creation, and the broadening scope of criminological inquiry in light of wider societal change.

Notes

1 We use "Global North" and "Global South" as they have become conventional terms in the field through the recognition of Southern Criminology and its reliance on Southern Theory. We do, however, acknowledge that many scholars in other fields often use "Two-Thirds World" or "Three-Fourths World" so that they do not evoke narrow, binary assumptions of global difference.
2 While readers likely know John Braithwaite's criminological work, they may not be as familiar with Valerie Braithwaite's research, which spans social psychology and regulation. We encourage criminologists interested in collective hope to engage with her work.

References

Belknap, J. (2015). Activist criminology: Criminologists' responsibility to advocate for social and legal justice. *Criminology*, *53*(1), 1–22.
Binder, A. (1987). Criminology: Discipline or interdiscipline?. *Issues in Integrative Studies*, *5*, 41–67.
Bosworth, M., & Hoyle, C. (Eds.). (2011). *What is criminology?*. Oxford: Oxford University Press.

Braithwaite, J. (2000). The new regulatory state and the transformation of criminology. *The British Journal of Criminology*, *40*(2), 222–238.
Braithwaite, J. (2005). For public social science. *The British Journal of Sociology*, *56*(3), 345–353.
Braithwaite, V. (2004). Collective hope. *The ANNALS of the American Academy of Political and Social Science*, *592*, 6–15.
Burawoy, M. (2005). For public sociology. *American Sociological Review*, *70*(1), 4–28.
Carrington, K., Hogg, R., & Sozzo, M. (2016). Southern criminology. *The British Journal of Criminology*, *56*(1), 1–20.
Chancer, L., & McLaughlin, E. (2007). Public criminologies: Diverse perspectives on academia and policy. *Theoretical Criminology*, *11*(2), 155–173.
Cunneen, C., & Tauri, J. M. (2019). Indigenous peoples, criminology, and criminal justice. *Annual Review of Criminology*, *2*, 359–381.
Currie, E. (2007). Against marginality: Arguments for a public criminology. *Theoretical Criminology*, *11*(2), 175–190.
Fraser, N. (1990). Rethinking the public sphere: A contribution to the critique of actually existing democracy. *Social Text*, *25/26*, 56–80.
Greene, H. T., Gabbidon, S. L., & Wilson, S. K. (2017). Included? The status of African American scholars in the discipline of criminology and criminal justice since 2004. *Journal of Criminal Justice Education*, *29*(1), 96–115.
Grosz, E. (2000). Histories of a feminist future. *Signs: Journal of Women in Culture & Society*, *25*(4), 1017–1020.
Gutiérrez Y Muhs, G., Niemann, Y. F., González, C. G., & Harris, A. P. (Eds.). (2012). *Presumed incompetent: The intersections of race and class for women in academia*. Boulder: University Press of Colorado.
Haggerty, K. (2004). Displaced expertise: Three constraints on the policy-Relevance of criminological thought. *Theoretical Criminology*, *8*(2), 211–231.
Henne, K., & Troshynski, E. I. (2019). Intersectional criminologies for the contemporary moment: Crucial questions of power, praxis, and technologies of control. *Critical Criminology: An International Journal*, *27*(1), 55–71.
Hughes, G. (2017). Public criminology. In A. Brisman, E. Carrabine, & N. South (Eds.), *The Routledge companion to criminological theory and concepts* (pp. 367–371). London: Routledge.
Loader, I., & Sparks, R. (2011). *Public criminology?*. London: Routledge.
Lynch, M. J. (2000). The power of oppression: Understanding the history of criminology as a science of oppression. *Critical Criminology*, *9*(1/2), 144–152.
Muhammad, K. G. (2011). *The condemnation of blackness: Race, crime, and the making of modern urban America*. Cambridge, MA: Harvard University Press.
Nash, J. C. (2019). *Black feminism reimagined: After intersectionality*. Durham, NC: Duke University Press.
Nelund, A. (2014). Troubling publics: A feminist analysis of public criminology. *Radical Criminology*, *4*, 67–84.
Petersilia, J. (2008). Influencing public policy: An embedded criminologist reflects on California prison reform. *Journal of Experimental Criminology*, *4*(4), 335–356.
Piché, J. (2015). Assessing the boundaries of public criminology: On what does (not) count. *Social Justice*, *42*(2), 70–90.
Rock, P. (2014). The public faces of public criminology. *Criminology and Criminal Justice*, *14*(4), 412–433.
Rotman, E. (2000). The globalization of criminal violence. *Cornell Journal of Law and Public Policy*, *10*(1), 1–43.
Ruggiero, V. (2012). How public is public criminology?. *Crime, Media, Culture*, *8*(2), 151–160.
Stuart, F. (2017). Public criminology for whom? Bringing "organic" public scholarship out of the shadows. *The Criminologist*, *42*(2), 1, 3–6.
Uggen, C., & Inderbitzin, M. (2010). Public criminologies. *Criminology & Public Policy*, *9*(4), 725–749.
Wacquant, L. (2011). From "public criminology" to the reflexive sociology of criminological production and consumption: A review of *Public Criminology?* by Ian Loader and Richard Sparks. (London: Routledge, 2010). *The British Journal of Criminology*, *51*(2), 438–448.
Woods, J. B. (2014). Queer contestations and the future of critical "queer" criminology. *Critical Criminology*, *22*(1), 5–19.

PART I

The Emergence of Public Criminologies

1

EVERYTHING STILL TO PLAY FOR

Revisiting "Public Criminologies: Diverse Perspectives on Academia and Policy"

Lynn Chancer and Eugene McLaughlin

In May 2007, we wrote an introduction to a special issue of *Theoretical Criminology* entitled "Public Criminologies: Diverse Perspectives on Academia and Policy" (Chancer & McLaughlin, 2007a). It was an important moment to be deliberating the idea, both in and outside university walls. Fields beyond criminology were also having this conversation. For instance, in 2003 Robert Putnam used his address to the American Political Science Association conference to foreground the public role of political science. In the field of sociology, Michael Burawoy (2005) had defined "public sociology" at his 2004 American Sociological Association address to include four kinds of interventions: professional, critical, policy, and public.

We argued that Anglo-American criminology was popular in terms of courses given and student interest, having established itself as a distinctive academic discipline in many universities. Academic posts and specialist research centers had increased in number and kind. The membership of professional associations and a rapidly expanding number of specialist groups and sub-disciplines had grown, national and international conferences were well attended, and new journals specializing in rapidly evolving and diversifying subfields of criminology kept appearing. Yet, as we also noted, considerable anxiety and unease were palpable about the broader social purpose, policy relevance, and political recognition and public standing of criminology. Criminologists were having to come to terms with the relentless politicization of crime, law and order, the determination to govern through state violence and criminalization, and a punitive turn that saw mass incarceration grow to become an institutionalized Leviathan involving, at its height, the imprisonment of 2.2 million people. In the same instance, Bratton and Giuliani were advertising the "New York miracle" as a criminal justice strategy worth exporting. And, of course, 9/11 had unleashed a "war on terror" that legitimized the introduction of ever more expansive and intrusive surveillance and securitization practices. We summed up this contradictory experience as follows (Chancer & McLaughlin, 2007a, p. 157):

> Criminologists have had to confront the embarrassing fact that in a society saturated with "crime talk", they have utmost difficulty in communicating with politicians, policy makers, professionals and the public. Criminological reasoning is now mediated and

contested by a range of vociferous interest groups, activists and a multitude of institutional actors and public opinions.

Assessing the situation over ten years later, though, where is public criminology now, and to what extent have critical and other criminologists succeeded in publicizing academic knowledge while shaping awareness of national and international problems? It is gratifying to be contributing to this volume, itself reflective of increased interest in and value accorded public criminology. At the same time, overall, what has been accomplished (and not), and what can be surmised from the time of our special issue (Chancer & McLaughlin, 2007b) through pressing concerns at present and going forward?

Looking back on the positive side, sociologists and criminologists—albeit secondarily to social movement activists and well-known writers, such as Michelle Alexander (Alexander, 2010)—deserve credit for helping make mass incarceration and prison in the United States matters of (now) widespread concern. It seems clear that the issue of poor and minority young men receiving lengthy and punitive terms as a result of harsher prison sentencing is arguably the major "cause célèbre" of progressive idealistic students across college and university campuses in the United States. Mass incarceration has grown into a pressing public criminological issue indeed, with students often joining organizations like Petey Greene to do in-prison tutoring; interdisciplinary conferences abounding in and outside sociology and criminology departments; and progressive professors continuing to engage in editorial writing and visits to state and local policy makers. In all this, criminologists from Todd Clear (Clear & Frost, 2013) and Christian Parenti (2008) through Michael Jacobson (2005) and Loïc Wacquant (2011) have contributed to widely circulating critiques and cries for reform of harsh punitive mandatory sentencing laws and the torturous uses of violence and solitary confinement within prison walls. Feminist criminologists have contributed greatly to related critiques, including Kimberly Cook and Saundra Westervelt's (2018; see also Westervelt & Cook, 2013) work on death penalty exonerees and Elizabeth Bernstein's (2010, 2018) stellar work on carceral feminism. Kristin Bumiller's (2008) intersectional concerns about feminists making strange bedfellows with conservatives over the issues of violence against women illustrated the paradox of contributing to mass incarceration while promulgating what can be an excessively punitive approach to sexual assault and domestic violence sentencing. Partly due to the collective persuasiveness of criminologists' work, conservative Republicans entered the public fray fairly early in the game, with "prison reform" currently a pet concern of Republicans from the Koch Brothers to Donald Trump.

Analogously, criminological critiques of immigration policy in the United States and in Europe have been influential. In the former case, critical criminologists David Brotherton and Philip Kretsedemas (2018) recently published a collection of essays centering on the criminalization of immigration in the United States and the sprouting of detention centers concurrent with the prison boom. In Europe, too, criminologists have actively campaigned against crimmigration policies and practices. The Border Criminologies initiative,[1] founded and coordinated by Mary Bosworth at the Centre for Criminology, Oxford, is a remarkable international project dedicated to exposing and challenging the multiple injustices of border control regimes. The long tradition in the United Kingdom of critical criminologists being active in miscarriage-of-justice campaigns is exemplified in the role played by Phil Scraton (2016) in uncovering the truth about the institutional cover-up associated with the Hillsborough disaster, where 96 football fans were crushed to death and hundreds more were injured. In 2016, new inquests into the disaster concluded that the fans were unlawfully killed.

Since the publication of the special issue (Chancer & McLaughlin, 2007b), there have also been diverse and eclectic attempts to map the future possibilities and challenges confronting public criminology. This includes the grounded considerations of the troubling relationship between knowledge, action, and commitment by criminologists who have operated inside policy making. Joan Petersilia (2008), reflecting on working on Californian prison reform under Governor Schwarzenegger, foregrounded the idea of the "embedded criminologist" who works with criminal justice agencies and policy makers to "loosen up the policy environment," hopefully creating space for evidence-led interventions. Concrete lessons to be learned include communicating without pretense or jargon; publishing understandable research findings in accessible outlets; knowing exactly who you are working with; understanding the political realities of policy making, including the importance of timing; attentiveness to implementation issues; demonstrating the value of methodological rigor; and being realistic. She also reminds us that a criminologist is but one of many players in the game (Petersilia, 2008, p. 353):

> The science of criminology and our role in public policy is necessary but ultimately insufficient to alter fundamentally our nation's justice system ... scientific knowledge does not drive crime policy and probably never will. There are other powerful, legitimate, players at the table—for example, staff, legislators, the public, and offenders themselves—and scientific knowledge is just one important consideration. Criminologists have a role to play in this mosaic, but we should not delude ourselves of our centrality.

The final sobering point made by Petersilia (2008, p. 353) is that embedding oneself in policy research and development is not for the faint-hearted:

> my recent experiences convince me that our university reward structures are not the main culprit, but, rather, the hard and overwhelming nature of the work, the inflexibility of unrealistic time frames, and the public scrutiny and sometimes mean-spirited attacks that presumed power and visibility bring. In thinking about my experiences, if I had known all the rules at the start, and how daunting and consuming it was, I might not have done it. I came to wonder how many of us, including myself, have what it takes to engage truly in public criminology over the long haul. It is not that academics do not work hard, but rather that our culture is one of autonomy, academic freedom, and professional civility that did not characterize this bureaucracy.

In other words, being an embedded criminologist requires hard work.

Joanne Belknap (2015), among others, is pushing for another form of hard work—a fully transformative "activist criminology" where struggling against intersecting injustices "disproportionately drives those of us historically kept out of the academy due to our race, gender, class sexual identity and/or other marginalizations" (2015, p. 1; see also Arrigo, 2016). Activist criminological perspectives developed by African American, LGBTQ+, radical feminist, ex-convict scholars, and insurgent criminologists are expanding the scope and depth of the discipline, challenging the intersectional inequities entrenched in the discipline, and radicalizing teaching and research (Burgess-Proctor, 2006; Henne & Shah, 2015; Potter, 2015). And there are intriguing possibilities in re-constructing public criminology through subaltern studies, postcolonial studies, and decoloniality, which will force an intellectually energizing expansion of what, how, and where we research. In the sphere of criminal justice, "activist criminology" allies itself with social movements and subjugated communities campaigning against issues such as mass incarceration, racial profiling, and gendered violence. Natural alignments have grown with the "anger + activism + action" dynamics driving some of the most high-profile and influential contemporary justice movements including #BlackLivesMatter, #OccupyWallStreet, #MeToo, and #TimesUp campaigns.

But perhaps the most vigorously debated position in public criminology is that of Loader and Sparks (2010, 2011, 2014). Despite the title of their book (2010), they present both a sociological critique of criminology and the case for a civic rather than public criminology. They conceptualize the public work undertaken by criminologists as that of hard working "democratic underlabourers" whose primary responsibility is to champion a better, wiser politics of crime and its regulation (2010, p. 177). They insist that retaining distinctions between academic criminology (as a professional activity) and criminal justice activism, policy making, and politics is strategically and ethically important as is encouraging a plurality of voices. Intervening in matters of public concern and heated dispute necessitates the mobilization of expert criminological knowledge and the exercise of professional judgment and skepticism toward "common sense" thinking. But criminologists need to also "cultivate the will and necessary tools to make sense of the place and functions of crime and punishment in contemporary political culture" (p. 112). Interventions must be able to generate controversy in the opening up and extension of public debate, as well as contesting and provoking received public "opinion" and highly politicized standpoints.

For Loader and Sparks, it is the civic responsibility of criminologists to table alternative institutional arrangements and practices for thinking about and responding to crime and forge connections with groups in civil society who are seeking to advance progressive policies. In doing so, it is possible that criminologists can contribute to the creation of a more multi-dimensional deliberative politics of crime, criminal justice, law, and order. Furthermore, public criminology (Loader & Sparks, 2010, p. 132):

> is committed both to participating within, and to facilitating and extending, institutional spaces that supplement representative politics with inclusive public deliberation about crime and justice matters, whether locally, nationally, or in emergent transnational spaces. In this regard, the public value of democratic under-labouring lies not in "cooling" down controversies about crime and social responses to it, but in playing its part in figuring out ways to bring the "heat" within practices of democratic governance

In other words, criminologists must let go of the notion that engagement can be de-politicized. Criminologists also have to let go of expectations that their knowledge will have privileged status in the public realm (Loader & Sparks, 2011, p. 736):

> criminological knowledge cannot—and should not—determine outcomes, silence the claims of others or override normative conflicts. Entering the democratic fray as a criminologist means bringing what one knows to bear on matters of concern in ways that inform, provoke and unsettle conventional wisdoms—not in ways that claim to end the contest by playing the trump card of expertise.

Thus, criminologists must negotiate their roles as team players in a democratic process, which is distinct from being the "leader" in a hierarchical decision-making system.

A survey of the immediate responses to Loader and Sparks evidenced a discipline that continues to remain split between those who hold fatalistic (or, what they would call, realistic) views and those who hold positive views on the value of pursuing public criminology (see Christie et al., 2011; Clear, 2010). And it is perfectly possible, as we noted above, to mobilize historical and contemporary examples to support or refute criminology's public value. As Tonry (2010, p. 793) concludes, "research driven evidence influences policy and practice in some places, at sometimes and on some subjects." Wacquant (2011, p. 442) provides the most trenchant critique of Loader and Sparks, noting that they have nothing to say about the working realities of the neo-liberal university:

the managerial makeover of the university and the generalized degradation of the conditions of employment, research and teaching on justice; increased dependency on external funding aimed at short-term technical issues; the growing weight of policy institutes on campus and the rise of "think tanks" off campus; the proliferation of para-governmental outfits that foster and fabricate a bogus science plugged directly into the policy-making machine; the overt and covert intrusion of the concerns of politicians, themselves anxious to demonstrate their manly resolve to tame crime in synch with the demands and cycles of a media microcosm driven by the restless quest for audience ratings.

Wacquant could also have flagged institutional pressures to avoid non-fundable research topics and adopt quantitative methodologies.

What is remarkable is the speed with which criminologists discussing public criminology leaned inwards, deliberating professional interests rather than a proper consideration of the multiple publics who might be interested in what criminologists have to say (Rock, 2010). This echoes Gan's (2016) concerns about how professional sociologists, in effect, hijacked the public sociology debate to discuss themselves in primarily academic mediums. One outcome of this professional politicking is the perpetuation of aggressive "business as usual" disputes in a different guise. Building on these points, we would argue that the trajectory and dynamics of public criminology may be gleaned from "outside in" rather than "inside out"—establishing how others see us rather than obsessing on who we are. We need to know much more about before whom we stand.

On the other hand, and fully acknowledging these inputs, a critically significant intellectual question remains: public criminology is obviously alive, influential, and debated, but can it make the kind of "real world" difference that is necessary in a (nearly) 2020s context within which a variety of authoritarian regimes have risen to new strength and visibility globally? In the interests of thinking through what more can be done in the following decade, perhaps further efforts might be helpful as follows. For one thing sociologists and criminologists have only begun to understand ways that the "crime issue" has been used emotionally—or what can be called "psychosocially"—to further anti-immigrant sentiments that have played key roles in political outcomes from London to Jerusalem, Washington, DC to Budapest. Yet psychosocial criminology, capable of returning to Frankfurt School themes concerning the rise of authoritarianism and populism, has not become nearly as well-known in criminology as theories that—whether acknowledged or not—often assume "rational actors" increasingly out of line with contemporary historical trends.

Moreover, as Katherine Beckett (1997) referred to these psychosocial politics of "making crime pay," old and new forms of social media—and the ability of new and old moral panics to "go viral"—are developments that criminologists need, more than ever, to get to grips with in the interests of public criminology. In the aforementioned special issue (Chancer & McLaughlin, 2007a, p. 169), we argued that mass-media and popular culture

> have become increasingly complex. Are there opportunities to be engaged with film and performance as well as radio, with blogging as well as with the circulation of television and print news? Evident, at a minimum, is that "doing" public criminology is closely related to how sophisticated we can become in understanding and participating in a dynamically evolving range of 24/7 mass-media forums. This will not be easy because attempts to establish a public presence will take place against a backdrop of the thinning out of intellectual debate in the media and deepening public skepticism regarding "expert knowledge."

And at this point we have to acknowledge that the treacherous digital media landscape that has unfolded since the publication of the special issue (Chancer & McLaughlin, 2007b) has certainly complicated matters. We have witnessed a revolution in the 24/7 production, dissemination, and consumption of crime and criminal justice news that includes the reconfiguration of crime news as sensational infotainment, new genres of crime journalism, and the advent of citizen crime journalism. Technologically savvy progressive social movements have been able to leverage the power of the internet in a remarkable manner, enabling them to radicalize the whole notion of social protest, launching local, national, and global campaigns with astonishing speed that can disrupt civic life and the political status quo. Numerous opportunities now exist, at least in theory, for "news-making" or "talking-head" criminologists to communicate through on-line news sites and to use their own social media platforms to overcome the communication constraints associated with the legacy news media.

The rise of public journalism may overcome the issue raised by Rock (2014, p. 429):

> Why … do they nevertheless often take us to be little more than second or third rank experts whose forms of knowing are inferior to those of people who can convey more immediate impressions of an event—the victims, witnesses, practitioners and journalists? Crime news and crime programmes are still doggedly dominated by tales of the personal and the emotional, by the human interest story where there is a preference for the authenticity of vivid feeling conveyed very soon after the event rather than dispassionate analysis wrought by experts in later tranquility. Experiential knowledge about egregious crime over and again trumps the disinterested and the scholarly in the public forum.

However, there remain practical issues relating to the time and resources needed to tailor relevant communications to different audiences with limited attention spans.

Perhaps more significantly, anyone venturing into the digital life-world runs the serious risk of being sucked into the post-factual free-for-all of disinformation loops, "fake news," bogus research findings, alternative facts, hyped headlines, rumor bombs, false accusations, conspiracy fictions, trolling, gaslighting, hacking, scandal hunting, click-bait, toxic rhetoric, manipulation of public opinion and sentiments, and molding political sentiments and preferences. And, of course, there is the outrage and feeding frenzy generated by regurgitated moral panics, scandals, and "trials by media" that invert the rules and principles of due process. Claims to scientific expertise are likely to be ignored, willfully misinterpreted, or challenged and rebuked with resort to invective. Arendt's (2000, p. 568) analysis of propaganda and the function of organized lying in the political realm takes on renewed significance at this juncture:

> It has frequently been noted that the surest long-term result of brainwashing in the long run is a peculiar type of cynicism—an absolute refusal to believe in the truth of anything, no matter how well this truth may be established. In other words, the result of a consistent and total substitution of lies for factual truth is not that the lies will now be accepted as truth, and truth be defamed as lies, but that the sense by which we take our bearings in the real world—and the category of truth vs falsehood is among the mental means to this end—is being destroyed. And for this trouble there is no remedy.

Criminologists have been slow to analyze the game-changing ramifications of this post-factual world for their work, and particularly the challenges that this poses in different ways when emanating both from the left and the right.

Esping Andersen (2000, p. 63) describes our predicament in the following manner:

> We are like drivers in a dense fog. We can remember but no longer see our city of departure, and before us we can, at best, eye some blurry outline of our destination. In dense fog, we can easily get lost and end up in a fatal crash.

Here is just one example of what is at stake in a remarkable interview between CNN reporter Alisyn Camerota and Newt Gingrich in July 2016 (McIntyre, 2018, pp. 3–4):

Camerota: Violent crime is down. The economy is ticking up.
Gingrich: It is not down in the biggest cities.
Camerota: Violent crime, murder rate is down. It is down.
Gingrich: Then how come it is up in Chicago and up in Baltimore and up in Washington?
Camerota: There are pockets where certainly we are not tackling murder.
Gingrich: Your national capital, your third biggest city.
Camerota: But violent crime across the country is down.
Gingrich: The average American, I will bet you this morning, does not think crime is down, does not think we are safer.
Camerota: But it is. We are safer and it is down.
Gingrich: No, that's just your view
Camerota: It's a fact. These are national FBI facts.
Gingrich: But what I said is also a fact … The current view is that liberals have a whole set of statistics that theoretically may be right, but it's not where human beings are.
Camerota: But what you are saying is, but hold on Mr. Speaker because you're saying liberals use these numbers, they use this sort of magic math. These are the FBI statistics. They're not a liberal organization. They're a crime fighting organization.
Gingrich: No, but what I said is equally true. People feel more threatened.
Camerota: Feel it yes. They feel it, but the facts don't support it.
Gingrich: As a political candidate, I'll go with how people feel and let you go with the theoreticians.

Thus, an additional struggle is how to navigate the emotional dimensions of narratives around crime, which often cannot be separated from the presentation of data and facts.

All criminologists can agree that the unremitting 24/7 inter-mediatization of two of the most politically tricky of topics—crime and criminal justice—further complicates ambitions to engage in public work. Nicole Rafter (2007) has contended that whether we like it or not, the public's seemingly insatiable desire for crime and criminal justice fiction also has an important defining role within any consideration of "public" criminology. A crimino-centric mediascape of unprecedented choice and access is saturated with crime fiction; crime dramas; true crime docu-series; docudramas; and immersive podcast series investigating unsolved crimes, hidden crimes, high profile crime, mistakenly solved crimes, and notorious crimes. In 2014, NPR's *Serial* became the fastest podcast ever to reach five million iTunes downloads (Opam, 2014) and over 19 million people watched the Netflix's *Making a Murderer* in its first 35 days (Nededog, 2016). Driven by the advent of on-demand broadcasting options and social media, the academic International Crime Fiction Association conferences has now been joined by CrimeCon, a conference for fans of true crime and citizen detectives.

Academic criminologists would seem to have little to no participatory role to play in the latest binge-watching phenomenon despite the fact that the podcasts are "increasingly sophisticated and nuanced in recent years, beginning to ask ever more complex questions" (Yardley, Kelly, & Robinson-Edwards, 2018, p. 15). As yet, though, no celebrity criminologist has materialized to lay claim to the subject matter. David Wilson, branded by sections of the media as the U.K.'s "leading criminologist," has attempted to cross the divide between academic and populist/popular criminology but has had to work within the sensationalist serial killer logics of the production companies. This stands in sharp contrast to the agenda-setting media engagement activities of other academic disciplines. For example, in the U.K., Brian Cox, a professor of particle physics and Royal Society professor of public understanding of science, has been at the forefront of challenging those who cast doubt on the status and the value of scientific expertise and knowledge. His television series average millions of viewers and his sold-out science events for schools, "Brian Cox Live," draws capacity crowds at venues normally used for rock concerts. Michael Sandel, the Harvard University public philosopher "with the global profile of a rock star" undertakes high profile media work to "find in the political and legal controversies of our day an occasion for philosophy" and "to bring moral and political philosophy to bear on contemporary public discourse" (Sandel, 2006, p. 5). And Sandel's "Justice" course, one of the most popular taught at Harvard, is also the basis of a television series that is freely available online. The irony is that criminology has always been a central part of popular culture because crime and justice are written into the script of everyday life. And yet, as we discussed above, criminologists are not normally turned to, neither where criminology is extremely popular inside the academy, nor for expert advice in the intermediated public world outside.

As in the special issue (Chancer & McLaughlin, 2007b), we conclude by noting that *Theoretical Criminology*, with its use of interdisciplinary sources, the free flow of ideas, self-reflexivity, the probing of philosophical presumptions, and foresight capacity has to be the basis for a resurgence of public criminology. Criminology's endeavors cannot be judged solely by whether or not they are instantaneously "practical," "relevant," and "applicable." Without the hard work of theoretical recrafting and invigorating of the criminological imagination, we will end up simply reacting to political events, governmental shifts, client–customer negotiations, and/or changes in public opinion. Equally importantly, we will not have the intellectual tools to build knowledge and understanding of the future "crime shocks" resultant from the acceleration and expansion of militarized neoliberalism, rising authoritarian populism and fundamentalism, escalating incarceration, mass surveillance and securitization practices, corporate pillage, intensifying inequalities and social divisions, calamitous climate change, and relentless digital disruptions actively driving and shaping a chaotic inter-mediatized future. And, as Hirschman (1981, p. 305) reminds us, "morality belongs at the center of our work and it can only get there if social scientists are morally alive and make themselves vulnerable to moral concerns—then they will produce morally significant works, consciously or otherwise."

Note

1 For more information, see the Border Criminologies website: www.law.ox.ac.uk/research-subject-groups/centre-criminology/centreborder-criminologies

References

Alexander, M. (2010). *The new Jim Crow*. New York: New Press.
Arendt, H. (2000). Truth and politics. In P. Baehr (Ed.), *The portable Hannah Arendt* (pp. 545–575). New York: Penguin Books.
Arrigo, B. A. (Ed.). (2016). Critical criminology as academic activism: On praxis and pedagogy, resistance and revolution [Special issue]. *Critical Criminology, 24*, 4.
Beckett, K. (1997). *Making crime pay: Law and order in contemporary American politics*. New York: Oxford University Press.

Belknap, J. (2015). Activist criminology: Criminologists' responsibility to advocate for social and legal justice. *Criminology, 53*(1), 1–22.

Bernstein, E. (2010). Militarized humanitarianism meets carceral feminism: The politics of sex, rights, and freedom in contemporary anti-trafficking campaigns. *Signs: Journal of Women in Culture and Society, 36*(1), 45–71.

Bernstein, E. (2018). *Brokered subjects: Sex, trafficking, and the politics of freedom*. Chicago, IL: University of Chicago Press.

Brotherton, D. C., & Kretsedemas, P. (Eds.). (2018). *Immigration policy in the age of punishment: Detention, deportation, and border control*. New York: Columbia University Press.

Bumiller, K. (2008). *In an abusive state: How neoliberalism appropriated the feminist movement against sexual violence*. Durham, NC: Duke University Press.

Burawoy, M. (2005). For public sociology. *American Sociological Review, 70*(1), 4–28.

Burgess-Proctor, A. (2006). Intersections of race, class, gender, and crime: Future directions for feminist criminology. *Feminist Criminology, 1*(1), 27–47.

Chancer, L., & McLaughlin, E. (2007a). Public criminologies: Diverse perspectives on academia and policy. *Theoretical Criminology, 11*(2), 155–173.

Chancer, L., & McLaughlin, E. (Eds.). (2007b). Public criminologies [Special issue]. *Theoretical Criminology, 11*(2).

Christie, N., Currie, E., Kennedy, H., Laycock, G., Morgan, R., Sim, J., … Walters, R. (2011). A symposium of reviews of *public criminology?* By Ian Loader and Richard Sparks (Oxford: Key ideas in criminology, Routledge, 2010, 196pp.). *British Journal of Criminology, 51*(4), 707–738.

Clear, T. R. (Ed.). (2010). Public criminologies [Special section]. *Criminology & Public Policy, 9*(4), 721–805.

Clear, T. R., & Frost, N. (2013). *The punishment imperative: The rise and failure of mass incarceration in America*. New York: New York University Press.

Cook, K., & Westervelt, D. D. (2018). Power and accountability: Life after death row in the United States. In W. S. DeKeseredy & M. Dragiewicz (Eds.), *The Routledge handbook of critical criminology* (2nd ed., pp. 269–279). Abingdon: Routledge.

Esping Andersen, G. (2000). Two societies, one sociology and no theory. *British Journal of Sociology, 51*(1), 59–78.

Gans, H. J. (2016). Public sociology and its publics. *The American Sociologist, 47*(1), 3–11.

Henne, K., & Shah, R. (2015). Unveiling white logic in criminological research: An intertextual analysis. *Contemporary Justice Review, 18*(2), 105–120.

Hirschman, A. (1981). *Essays in trespassing*. Cambridge: Cambridge University Press.

Jacobson, M. (2005). *Downsizing prisons: How to reduce crime and end mass incarceration*. New York: New York University Press.

Loader, I., & Sparks, R. (2010). *Public criminology?* London: Routledge.

Loader, I., & Sparks, R. (2011). Criminology and democratic politics: Reply to critics. *British Journal of Criminology, 51*(4), 734–738.

Loader, I., & Sparks, R. (2014). The question of public criminology: Seeking resources of hope for a better politics of crime. *International Annals of Criminology, 52*(1–2), 155–177.

McIntyre, L. (2018). *Post-truth*. Cambridge, MA: MIT Press.

Nededog, J. (2016, February 12). Here's how popular Netflix's "Making a Murder" really was according to a research company. *Business Insider*. Retrieved from www.businessinsider.com/netflix-making-a-murderer-ratings-2016-2

Opam, K. (2014, November 18). "Serial" breaks iTunes record for fastest podcast to reach 5 million downloads and streams. *The Verge*. Retrieved from www.theverge.com/2014/11/18/7241715/serial-breaks-itunes-record-for-fastest-podcast-to-reach-5-million

Parenti, C. (2008). *Lockdown America: Police and prisons in the age of crisis* (New ed.). New York: Verso.

Petersilia, J. (2008). Influencing public policy: An embedded criminologist reflects on California prison reform. *Journal of Experimental Criminology, 4*(4), 335–356.

Potter, H. (2015). *Intersectionality and criminology: Disrupting and revolutionizing studies of crime*. New York: Routledge.

Rafter, N. (2007). Crime, film and criminology: Recent sex movies. *Theoretical Criminology, 11*(3), 407–420.

Rock, P. (2010). Comment on "Public Criminologies". *Criminology & Public Policy, 9*(4), 751–767.

Rock, P. (2014). The public faces of public criminology. *Criminology & Criminal Justice, 14*(4), 412–433.

Sandel, M. (2006). *Public philosophy: Essays in morality in politics*. Cambridge, MA: Harvard University Press.

Scraton, P. (2016). *Hillsborough: The Truth*. London: Transworld Publishers.

Tonry, M. (2010). "Public criminology" and evidence-based policy. *Criminology & Public Policy, 9*(4), 783–797.

Wacquant, L. (2011). From "Public Criminology" To the reflexive sociology of criminological production and consumption: A review of Public Criminology? by Ian Loader and Richard Sparks. *British Journal of Criminology, 51*(2), 438–448.

Westervelt, S. D., & Cook, K. J. (2013). *Life after death row: Exonerees' search for community and identity.* New Brunswick, NY: Rutgers University Press.

Yardley, E., Kelly, E., & Robinson-Edwards, S. (2018). Forever trapped in the imaginary of late capitalism? The serialized true crime podcast as a wake-up call in times of criminological slumber. *Crime, Media, Culture*. Advanced online publication. doi:10.1177/1741659018799375.

2
RE-THINKING PUBLIC CRIMINOLOGY

Politics, Paradoxes, and Challenges

Eamonn Carrabine, Maggy Lee, and Nigel South

Introduction

Our starting point is a co-authored paper published in 2000 as a contribution to a special issue of *Social Justice* addressing the theme of "Criminal Justice and Globalization at the New Millennium." The title and focus of that paper was "Social wrongs and human rights in late modern Britain," which reflected our interest in contributing to a "sociological criminology" (Carrabine, Iganski, Lee, Plummer, & South, 2004) and a belief, nicely captured by Ruggiero (2012, p. 15), that sociology—or a sociological criminology—may "survive" (and thrive) "best when it is engaged with public issues, and when it develops into social criticism." Following Turner (2004), Ruggiero suggests that without such "political and public commitments," there is a risk of appearing to reflect only "esoteric, elitist and eccentric intellectual interest[s]." Here, we return to the original paper to build on the proposal for a public criminology that we outlined there. The aim is to further develop the argument that such an approach can help us to think more effectively about social wrongs and their impacts on people and the environment in a global context. We argue, in fact, that the criminological compass has for too long pointed to the global North and a re-thinking of what "public criminology" might mean offers an opportunity for some re-orientation.

Public Criminology, Social Wrongs, and Human Rights at and beyond the New Millennium

In the run up to 2000, it seemed to us that there was an oddly Victorian echo to some of the dominant narratives of anxiety in Britain at the time: fear of crime, divisions between "haves" and "have nots," concerns about young people and associations with violence, and much talk about the erosion of so-called traditional values. Both the right and the left were outbidding each other to demonstrate they took crime seriously. If one looked at prisons as a barometer of the condition of democracy, then the outlook was bleak.

In response we outlined our propositions for a public criminology that would:

- engage with moral indifference and intolerance (e.g., the criminalization of poverty; discourses of ambivalence and condemnation; incapacitation/containment as strategies to treat society's "waste products");
- engage with both public issues and private troubles;

- take information, power and action "back to the people";
- explicitly break boundaries and make positive connections with other arenas of social action (e.g. improving services; providing a space for ordinary publics to make claims for social justice and their human rights);
- be transparent;
- be evidence-based;
- be applied in orientation; and
- show commitment to empowerment and practical (not idealistic) change, as well as to social justice and human rights.

Regrettably, at the turn of the millennium and apparently still today, aspirations to promote social justice and human rights have faced obstacles set in place by contemporary forces that bias arguments, inflame xenophobia, and promote individualism at the expense of common interests. Arguably, the prospects for widespread support for a social justice perspective have been eroded. To a moderate extent, this development may be due to a form of campaign and compassion fatigue (Cohen, 2001). It is more devastating because of varied disappointing associations with other articulations and exploitative impositions of the language of justice. Hence, we note again Harvey's (1996, p. 342) argument that:

> too many colonial peoples have suffered at the hands of western imperialism's particular justice, too many African-Americans have suffered at the hands of white man's justice, too many women from the justice imposed by a patriarchal order and too many workers from the justice imposed by capitalists, to make the concept [of social justice] anything other than problematic.

Harvey's list of the "too many" who have suffered injustice remains a reflection of the world we know. We have made little progress. Depressingly, if we have moved forward at all it is in recognizing that the list is even longer. Almost two decades on from our earlier essay, globalization has created neither an open world, nor a protected planet. Internal nationalism, international conflicts, and heightened levels of fears of "outsiders" in an age of mass mobility have made non-citizens and so-called "illegals," as well as borders and walls, the subjects of emotive politics and of breaches of rights.

These politics of divisions and divisiveness detract from a plethora of social harms and their uneven consequences, and "compartmentalize or decontextualize the sources of suffering" (Burawoy, 2006, p. 4). They encourage a view that authoritarian, populist solutions can be found for all social ills, and that calls for action in response to global warming or environmental degradation, or regarding damages done to the lives and lands of Indigenous peoples, need not be taken seriously. Human rights have often been compounded or confused with "the rights of states and markets" and misused by "colonizing powers and their satrapies" as "the ideological advance guard of occupation and recolonization, whether for geopolitical or economic ends" (pp. 4–6).

In the next sections, we consider these continuing challenges before revisiting the idea of a public criminology beyond parochialism (Burawoy, 2005b). In particular, we highlight migration control as a site of conflict and struggle over the human rights and human security of those who do not have citizenship privileges.

Migration Control in an Age of Mass Mobility

One of the most significant markers of the globally divided world today is migration control. People problematized as "immigrants," including asylum seekers, trafficked and smuggled migrants, sex workers, and labor migrants taking up "dirty, dangerous and demeaning" jobs, are the latest in a long line of "suitable enemies" (Christie, 1986): both a symbol of, and a target for, all social anxieties and thus legitimating a drift towards the criminalization and de-humanization of non-citizens—or what Dauvergne (2008) has termed the processes of "making people illegal." Migrants have consistently been portrayed in populist discourse as a source of insecurity, as so-called fake refugees, welfare scroungers or potential criminals, rather than people who are exposed to considerable dangers on their migratory journeys. Toughened up border control (e.g., fortified fences, land, air and sea rapid patrol teams armed with high-tech detection equipment) has meant people are diverted to ever more dangerous routes and toward taking greater risks in border crossing, resulting in numerous deaths from dehydration in the desert, drowning at sea, and direct (e.g., shootings) or indirect (e.g., landmines) violence.

Since 2014, the International Organization for Migration (IOM) has documented nearly 25,000 migrant deaths around the world though the quality and coverage of data on "missing migrants" clearly varies from region to region (IOM, 2017). In 2015 the discovery of mass graves and suspected human trafficking camps in the jungles of southern Thailand and northern Malaysia prompted a migration crisis in the region and an inquiry into alleged obstruction of justice. In the United States, the Trump Administration's pledge to build a 2,000-mile "great wall" along the southern U.S.-Mexico border, the identification of undocumented immigrants as "a significant threat to national security and public safety" (*The Economist*, 2018), and the threatened withdrawal of federal funding from sanctuary cities all exemplify the deeply entrenched social inequality and difference in migration control and the persistently restrictive and punitive approaches of drawing sharp boundaries between those who have citizenship privileges and those who do not.

Significantly, migrants around the world have been subjected to arrests and crackdowns, detention, deportation, and prisoner transfers under a convergence between the criminal law and administrative powers, or "crimmigration" (Stumpf, 2006). The "usual suspects"—poor men and women of color, reflecting familiar inequalities of gender, race, and socioeconomic status—tend to bear the brunt of the "harms of crimmigration control … inflicted through coercion, incarceration, exclusion, and deportation" (Bowling, 2013, p. 298). Critical scholars have argued that the securitization and militarization of migration control have gathered pace at a time when the processes of inclusion and exclusion at the borders of, and within, states have become much more diffuse (Bosworth, Parmar, & Vazquez, 2018; Franko Aas & Bosworth, 2013). Non-citizens have been caught up in a proliferation of expansive border zones where the "border" function has extended both inward and outward in time and space. Pre-emptive practices are aimed at blocking unwanted migrants from travelling in the first place—for example, through biometric surveillance, large-scale data matching, and carrier sanctions. There has been a dispersal of control functions beyond the physical border to internal spaces such as the workplace (through raids), the streets (through street stops and what have been known as "collateral arrests") (Chou, 2018), through extra-territorial strategies of off-shore interdiction and detention in neighboring countries (e.g., the U.S. network of off-shore processing camps that extended from Guantanamo to the Bahamas and Panama; the notorious detention facilities on Nauru and Manus Island as part of Australia's controversial "Pacific Solution"), and through overseas development and humanitarian aid initiatives in migration "management" (Frelick, Kysel, & Podkul, 2016; Lee, 2013). In the process, migration control has been dispersed from main destination countries in the global North to so-called sending countries in the South and from specialist immigration enforcement authorities to an ever-expanding array of international agencies, public and private bodies, including medical authorities and welfare agencies, that exclude migrants from essential services under what Weber (2013, p. 114) has described as a ubiquitous, "structurally embedded border."

While countries have long responded to "strangers" in times of war and those deemed "threatening" through practices of quarantine and containment, the use of detention of non-citizens has increased dramatically worldwide as a state response to unwanted migration

(Bosworth & Turnbull, 2014; Flynn, 2014). According to the Global Detention Project (2016), for example, the size of American immigration detention and removal operations has spiraled since the 1990s. The number of people placed in immigration detention in the United States increased from some 85,000 people in 1995 to 204,459 in 2001, peaking at 477,523 during fiscal year 2012, before declining to around 353,000 in 2016. Immigration detention centers are very painful places for detainees. There is no pretense that the purpose of immigration detention can provide rehabilitation or reform, merely incapacitation or deportation. Critics have highlighted a number of human rights violations associated with the increase in use of detention as an immigration enforcement mechanism, including the right not to be arbitrarily detained. There are also pervasive problems with the conditions of detention (e.g., inappropriate and excessive use of restraints, inadequate access to healthcare), and the lack of due process safeguards (Amnesty International USA, 2008; Human Rights Watch, 2017). Researchers in the United States and other jurisdictions have also found that immigration detention has a profound impact on those who are detained, particularly on mental and physical health, compounded by factors such as the absence of a statutory time limit on detention, and hence the uncertainty and anxiety over the duration of detention (Bosworth & Turnbull, 2014).

Following on from the experiences and practices of oppression and human rights violations described above, we turn to a consideration of the victimization and continuing exploitation of Indigenous peoples and their environments, particularly in the global South.

Indigenous Peoples and Environments Affected by Exploitation and Injustice

Indigenous communities today still live with the legacies and injustices of the past, which, in turn, have left challenges for the future. This is especially the case in relation to external forces of exploitation and resulting degradation of the lands and waters upon which they depend, and which may have not only material but also spiritual significance. Highlighting these threats and conditions throws into sharp relief some of the limitations and parochialism of previous explorations of a public criminology, which have reflected a Northern orientation—that is, a rather passive view of the circumstances of those troubled by public and private power, and importantly, a view that has often been neglectful of gender in relation to visibility within any public sphere. We address these points in turn.

As Mowforth (2014, para. 1) has noted, "Indigenous groups are now represented globally by a range of international organizations," including the United Nations Permanent Forum on Indigenous Issues, Assembly of First Nations, Survival International, the World Council of Indigenous Peoples, Indigenous Environmental Network, among others. These entities have provided the platforms for a number of supportive Declarations (Mowforth, 2014) and encouraged—as, for example, in several Latin American nations—the incorporation of ideas of multicultural citizenship and of rights for indigenous groups into laws and constitutions. As Mowforth (para. 2) argues, however, there have also been restraints and limits on such rights and "in most cases the recognition is only on paper." To elaborate:

> It is clear that indigenous peoples have been recognized, but it is also clear that legal recognition does not mean that the rights, territories, resources and cultures of Indigenous peoples are respected. Governments, corporations, loggers, campesino farmers, cattle-ranching companies, and many others still covet their land and resources, and continue to find ways to acquire them.
>
> *(Mowforth, 2014, para. 3)*

A public criminology might then ask, "*How widely* is all this known?", "*Where* is it known?", and, to put it bluntly, "*Who* cares?" It should also prompt us to think about *why* these questions matter. One answer, reflecting our re-orientation of a public criminology in this essay, is that addressing these questions can tell us something about the distribution of knowledge and power in the global North. Public criminology has so far simply reflected and replicated what Franko Aas (2012, p. 6) has described as the apparently "context-free nature of western social theory and its assumptions about the universality of its knowledge production." Hence, such a public criminology has encouraged an unreflective gaze at the conventional "academic wall map," which, based on "the immense production of books, journal articles and conferences dedicated to U.S. realities" tends to situate "the centre of gravity" as "situated in the core western, particularly Anglophone countries." Elsewhere, Rodríguez Goyes and South (2017a, p. 167) have examined the resulting processes of "epistemicide, absences and amnesia" in relation to numerous cases of, and struggles against, the "theft of nature and the poisoning of the land" (Rodríguez Goyes et al., 2017b, pp. 1–9)[1] throughout Latin America, while Carrington and colleagues (2015, p. 15) have called for acknowledgment of spatial particularities and for the democratization of epistemologies "by levelling the power imbalances that privilege knowledges produced in the metropolitan centers of the North." Without recognizing—indeed emphasizing—the global divisions within the notion of a "public," then a "public criminology" simply reflects the complacency of "Northern knowledge."

Colonialism, imperialism, and earlier forms of transnational commercial enterprise were built on assertions of the benefits of external financial investment and the superiority of western/White scientific knowledge. This latter claim is particularly important to remember when trying to think about an evidence base for a public criminology working in support of advocacy for the rights of Indigenous peoples. Our current moment is not a post-colonial age. The power and legacy of "the colonial" and the colonizers have not gone away, and the redefining of rights and displacement of traditional owners and indigenous people have been facilitated by both epistemic force—the suppression of knowledge—and physical force—the use of police and army forces (Rodríguez Goyes & South, 2017a, 2017b).

While evidence (i.e., science, empirical research findings) can be *biased*, it can also be *contested*. As Smith writes:

> From the vantage point of the colonized, … the term "research" is inextricably linked to European imperialism and colonialism. The word itself … is probably one of the dirtiest words in the indigenous world's vocabulary. … The ways in which scientific research is implicated in the worst excesses of colonialism remains a powerful remembered history for many of the world's colonized peoples.
>
> *(Smith, 1999, p. 1)*

In practical actions of resistance, Indigenous protestors have mobilized to protect lands and waters. They have combined traditional knowledge with new science regarding the damage, violence, and harm that exploitative developments may cause. Their efforts are active public criminology. For example, in 2016, hundreds of indigenous protestors and their allies gathered near the crossing of the Missouri and Cannon Ball rivers in the ancestral territories of the Standing Rock Sioux tribe to pursue non-violent action with the aim of preventing the building of the Dakota Access Oil Pipeline. The protestors rightly feared that oil leaks from the pipeline would pollute water used by the tribal community. As Whyte (2016) argues, however, this protest was about more; it was also about the legacy of colonization, the attempt to preserve and protect heritage, and—both now and into the future—about climate justice, recognizing the damage caused by oil economies. Their protests draw attention to a particular set of injustices. It is among Indigenous communities displaced by rising sea levels that the world's first climate refugees can be found; however, they are victims of the lifestyles, production processes, and consumption patterns of others (Revkin, 2007). While the Standing Rock protest was occurring between 2016 and 2017, there are many "Standing Rocks" around the world, and there will be more.

In the future, as climate change and environmental damage increasingly affect nature and human and non-human populations, a public criminology must understand the local as global and vice versa. It must also recognize and draw attention to the persistence of current inequalities now exacerbated by new threats. For example, Wachholz (2007) argues that the predicted rise in natural disasters related to climate change is likely to be correlated with increases in violence against women within the regions that experience extreme weather events. There are various reasons why this may be so and also why there may be higher death rates for women as a result of natural disasters (IOM, 2009, p. 2). These reasons are directly linked to the socio-economic status of women in affected societies and to the economic and social rights available or denied to women. Statistically, natural disasters kill more women than men and kill women at a younger age than men—again, probably related to restrictions on their freedom of movement and behavior, to their poor or limited access to information and to availability of resources. Women are also often responsible for caring roles and tasks relating to others, such as children, older and wider family, for finding and bringing water, and for food farming. All these factors directly affect a woman's chances of survival in the face of crises like disaster, war, climate related problems and their aftermath. Again, without recognition of these variations in vulnerability and risk of victimization, a "public criminology" implies it has universal relevance and application. Instead, it requires sensitivity to local and contextualized understandings of circumstances and differences if it is to be fit to engage with the issues and challenges it needs to address.

How Does a Public Criminology Engage with Contemporary Issues and Enduring Challenges?

The criminological compass has been biased in directing attention away from some of the most important issues of our time. Nonetheless, there are some signs, including projects and methods, that can point us to new and helpful ways of thinking and working for a more public criminology. One example of a re-scaling analysis of criminological knowledge production is Lee and Laidler's (2013) discussion of contemporary Asian developments. Institutionally, criminology is generally under-recognized, under-resourced, and therefore under-developed in Asia. Administrative or governmental criminology remains an essential part of Asian statecraft. Asian states set narrowly defined research agendas and therefore regulate the production, direction and use of criminological knowledge. Academically, Asian criminology is dominated by the testing—and therefore reproduction—of particular Western paradigms, primarily testable U.S. theories on what they frame as conventional crime problems, such as juvenile delinquency. Lee and Laidler (2013, p. 150), however, suggest that there are signs of change "as new scholars, both locally and Northern trained, have become sensitive to the issues of the core and the periphery, and with new methodologies and new agendas, are beginning to shift the course of knowledge production." The challenge, then, is to understand the distinctiveness of the governmental rationalities, capacities, and practices of Asian states whilst using imaginative methods to produce locally grounded analysis and, equally importantly, a critical voice.

In the same spirit, we would argue that one of the urgent tasks for criminologists is to engage with the moral indifference and intolerance directed at migrants, providing informed and nuanced understandings of their criminalization and its devastating impact on their lives, particularly the most vulnerable ones, and documenting the complex set of conditions of precariousness to which migrants are exposed in everyday life. In this context, public criminology has much to learn from scholars in the growing subfield referred to as border criminologies, which interrogates Northern states' production of categories of "legal"/"illegal" aliens, "worthy"/"unworthy" migrants and directs their critical gaze at the "daily re-entrenchment of global inequalities through criminal justice" (Pickering, Bosworth, & Franko Aas, 2014, p. 390).

The methods developed by critical scholars in border criminologies have created an evidence base (as suggested in our model of public criminology) concerning human-centered border harms (Bowling, 2013) and are worth describing here as an example of a program of work that could be adapted. This approach has qualitatively and quantitatively mapped border-related deaths in Australia and beyond,[2] analyzing the human costs of border enforcement and irregular migration as "structural violence" rather than as "the product of risky personal choices" (Weber & Pickering, 2011, p. 198). They have measured the "quality of life" of immigration detainees and the way they cope with distress in the United Kingdom (Bosworth & Gerlach, 2017) and researched into the multiple perspectives and actions of enforcement agents and those who live in local border communities in Europe.[3]

But what counts as evidence? And whose way of seeing (and not seeing) is being privileged in this criminological knowledge production? There is a danger of public criminology reproducing epistemological norms and standards of Northern metropolitan states, asserting expert knowledge and professional routines in generating statistics and profiles of suspect migrants and expanding international intervention in social technologies of facilitation and capacitation through benchmarking, capacity building, and performance auditing (Andrijasevic & Walters, 2010; Lee, 2013). An alternative type of evidence takes the form of art produced by immigration detainees. The Immigration Detention Archive at the University of Oxford created by Mary Bosworth contains a range of material culture produced by and about detention, including several thousand bureaucratic documents, letters, photographs, drawings, sculptures, poems, fiction, sound recordings, and other art works and materials gathered during fieldwork and art workshops:

> Items produced in detention can be interpreted in many ways and can contribute evidence to research on mental health, effects of uncertainty, trauma, reasons for migrating to England, colonial legacies, art therapy, roles of gender and race, language, bureaucracy, paternalism and abuses of power.
>
> *(University of Oxford, 2016)*

This participatory action research project with immigration detainees also speaks to the possibilities (and dilemmas) of taking evidence and action "back to the people" in public criminology.

Developing methods to render the closed and secret more open and transparent is not an easy endeavor. Spaces of migration control, such as airports, refugee camps, temporary shelters, immigration detention and removal centers, and charter flights for deportation, are difficult places to access for researchers and activists alike. Criminologists need to find ways to offer a glimpse into, for example, migrants' worlds of emotions and experiences. Methods that may enable these insights might include working through art or different sorts of materials that show what detention is like and humanize those who are subject to this form of border control. In the United Kingdom, Detention Action's FreedVoices campaign and the Detention Forum's Unlocked tour of the detention estate via Twitter are two creative ways to open up these institutions.

Transparency also means connecting research questions to researched communities. As Ruggiero suggests, these efforts should be

> made in dialogue with communities affected by crime and crime control, rather than determined by institutional funding bodies. Dissemination of findings, in this case, would not be limited to the professional community, but would attempt to access public forums, thus reducing "servility", the chief pathological trait of academic research.
>
> *(Ruggiero, 2012, p. 154)*

This kind of approach might also be seen as a kind of "organic public criminology" (Stuart, 2017, p. 3), a "model of scholarship" that "prioritizes the co-production of knowledge, calling on scholars to develop research questions, collect data, and conduct analyses in dialogue with affected communities."

Such dialogue should take a public criminology in an applied direction. Ruggiero's (2012, p. 158) discussion of a public criminology draws on the "research-action" approach of Thomas Mathiesen as one providing the "tools, experiences and repertoires of action that help people engaged in conflict" and "struggles for reform." While many abolitionists and critical criminologists may rightly be skeptical about reform, and wary of the capacity of systems, states, and capital to incorporate critique, it should inform but not mean the rejection of calls for change.

The aim to achieve change for the good of those currently ill-served by the current distribution of life-chances and justice should be fundamental and central. This, Ruggiero (2012, p. 154) suggests, would contrast with the "calm, limited engagement" that might describe the kind of public criminology proposed by Loader and Sparks (2010a)—a position that could be taken to mean criminology can best serve "the public and the polity ... by doing pretty much what it is already doing" (Currie, 2011, p. 711). Instead, criminology can use its tools in the service of change, as, for example, through documenting concrete examples of development of human rights activism and politically challenging forms of solidarity in the Arctic border (Horsti, 2017). Rengifo (2017, pp. 3–4) notes the development of strategies for inclusive "public scholarship" and "co-production of knowledge, dissemination, and input into action or policy," with techniques that include filmmaking and journalism. Examples of this kind of "production and socialization of knowledge on crime and justice" include "award-winning work ... on topics ranging from patterns of injustice in Mexican criminal courts, to the quandary of reconciliation in the aftermath of Indonesia's 'dirty war', and the fragility of conservation work by park rangers in the Democratic Republic of Congo." New directions in criminological theory, methods, and empirical research have been diverse and exciting in recent years and should now be reflected in a public criminology.

Civic Missions, Post-Colonial Realities and Rethinking Public Criminology

In our initial article championing the idea of a public criminology, we concluded by emphasizing the importance of Mills's (1959) program for a sociological imagination, insisting that "his advocacy of paying attention to empirical evidence while developing critical theory" provided both inspiration and aspiration to our position (Carrabine, Lee, & South, 2000, p. 208). Mills (1959, p. 3) famously declared that neither "the life of an individual nor the history of a society can be understood without understanding both," yet the more radical implications of his argument over how the sociological imagination can offer liberation from oppressive conditions are largely forgotten.

Today, practically every introductory sociology textbook routinely invokes the first element of Mills's definition, that is, how individuals relate to society. They often ignore the second part, which uses the "concept to *overcome* the ties that bind us to social structure, *critique* the work of American sociologists who do not reach the same conclusions he did, and enable us to radically *transform* the status quo" (Goode, 2008, p. 239, emphasis in original). Something of this critical project can be seen in Young's (2011) attempt to subject criminology to the kind of withering attack that Mills delivered upon sociology over fifty years ago. He condemns the "abstract empiricism" of mainstream criminology, which he describes as one-dimensional, banal, technocratic and in the deadening grip of quantification, and discusses the aspiration to "grand theory" as similarly removed from social realities, thriving on trivial, ponderous obfuscation where "latter-day Foucauldians have taken an outrageous and iconoclastic thinker and turned his writings into some sort of Talmudic parody of contested interpretation" (Young, 2011, p. 6).

Mills initially identified these two contrasting tendencies in his scathing assessment of mid-century U.S. sociology, which, he argued, ignored the major issues of the day: how a post-war corporate economy led by a powerful elite which had forged alliances with the military machine, was corroding social structures and generating profound inequalities. Instead, the profession was content to produce timid, conservative, inaccessible work that lacked any sense of the big picture or the transformative politics required to change the social order for the better. Directing his critique at the leading representatives of each tendency he condemned "abstracted empiricism," exemplified in the work of Lazarsfeld, for how it mistakes technical sophistication in method for having something important to say, while the "grand theory" of Parsons is famously ridiculed for its lack of intelligibility and for evading urgent political questions surrounding the nature of power. In these different ways the emancipatory promise of sociology had become tragically distorted in the Cold War climate of the era.

Distancing himself from those "colleagues who were busy 'choosing the West,' otherwise giving aid and comfort to the witch-hunters, or neutering themselves by hiding behind the ideology of value-free scholarship" (Aronowitz, 2003, p. 5), Mills wanted sociology to rediscover the classic European thinkers of the nineteenth century who sought to comprehend the entire social condition. This ambition is not without its own problems, such that any attempt to simply apply Mills to the contemporary social science landscape is likely to end up reproducing the assumptions framing his initial critique (discussed in more detail in Carrabine, 2017). Others maintain that the routes to the sociological imagination advocated by Mills are no longer adequate to capture the complexities, "paradoxes, and challenges of reflexive modernity" (Beck, 1999, p. 134).

Nevertheless, Mills established a distinctly sociological diagnosis of the crisis in U.S. sociology and one that was crucial to the vision of public sociology later advocated by Burawoy (2005a) in his American Sociological Association presidential address that sparked considerable debate. He identified contemporary sociology's failure to engage sufficiently and critically with key public issues and contemporary challenges, contending there is a growing divide between an increasingly inward-looking professional ethos of the discipline and the world at large. The challenge then is one of developing a public sociology that is capable of engaging "multiple publics in multiple ways" (Burawoy, 2005a, p. 4). The intervention was one that struck a chord: inspiring allied calls for public philosophy, public history, public anthropology, as well as public criminology (Carrier, 2014). The issues raised get to the heart of the civic missions and the very roots of the social sciences.

The call for a public social science has a particular resonance in criminology, as it is a field organized around a social problem and is one "of acute interest to governments, justice practitioners, and citizens alike" (Loader & Sparks, 2010b, p. 771). Hughes (2007, pp. 201–208) was among the first to incorporate Burawoy's four-fold typology of professional, policy, critical, and public forms of intellectual production into criminology, taking care not to overstate the centrality of one form over another, nor viewing them as mutually exclusive roles, but rather representing specific aspects of academic life. In their book on the idea of a public criminology, Loader and Sparks (2010a) developed a five-fold taxonomy of ideal-typical criminologists: the scientific expert, the policy advisor, the observer-turned-player, the social movement theorist/activist, and the lonely prophet. Each of these stances suggests a distinctive kind of engagement, which they highlight in the text, before concluding that criminology, as a discipline, should conceive itself as a "democratic under-labourer" (a combination of some core elements of the ideal types), premised on an acceptance of methodological pluralism, respect for intellectual differences, the production of "reliable knowledge" and a kind of humility over what can be achieved—a "knowing of one's limits and one's place" (Loader & Sparks, 2010a, p. 132).

In this and other forms, the concept of public criminology quickly proved to be controversial. Although many welcomed the opportunity to think through the terms of political engagement, the exact ways in which this should happen are open to considerable contestation, and there is much doubt over whether a new term is needed to describe very old predicaments. These conflicts over public criminology are disputes over the very definition of criminology and are what Bourdieu (1992) would term a classification struggle. The hostilities are indicative of a deep investment in the stakes of this academic field. The rival positions are logics of practice, while classifying the classifiers helps shed light on the power dynamics involved in such sets of distinctions (see also Burawoy, 2009). Notably, for example, in a review symposium of their book, Walters (2011, p. 731) takes Loader and Sparks (2010a) to task for presenting a very Anglo-American focus, asking if the "title should have reflected that this really is *Public Criminology in Britain?* Many of the examples and content throughout the text are British. It does not cover, for example, recent developments in Australasia or mobilized scholarship in the sub-continent." Returning to the civic missions of the social sciences draws attention to their imperial origins in European modernity, highlighting how a range of anticolonial, feminist and postcolonial struggles have challenged their claims to universalism.

Conclusion

Burawoy (2005b, p. 508) noted that exposing the "parochialism of the social sciences" would be an important element of a progressive public sociology—or, for us, a progressive public criminology—but only as a "first step toward restructuring." In pursuit of this grander ambition, he advocated a *provincializing* of social science knowledge production. This idea connects to the emergence of Indigenous criminology in settler-colonial contexts, which can be seen as a critical response to systemic biases in crime control policy and the failure of mainstream criminology to reckon with its complicity in colonial violence (Cunneen & Tauri, 2016).

Progress, however, is slow. Criminology, especially of a sociological variety, has tended to be self-congratulatory about its awareness and championing of those who are "on the margins," disempowered, unvoiced, and unheard. For example, in an essay on "publicly-engaged criminology" for the newsletter of the American Society of Criminology, Rengifo repeats a familiar origin story about sociology when he observes:

> Many of the founding figures of crime, deviance and social welfare studies in the United States were first and foremost an eclectic bunch of organizers, activists, ... troublemakers and storytellers, from Jane Addams and Robert Park to E. Franklyn Frazier and W. E. B. Dubois.
>
> *(Rengifo, 2017, p. 3)*

Rengifo notes the need to diversify the range of participants, audiences, contributors, spaces, and activities that criminology should engage with but (perhaps unsurprisingly given where the essay is published) seems anchored to a worldview that places the United States at the center of any efforts to expand a public criminology. For all its grappling with the question of "whose side are you on?", the answers rarely take criminology far from its comfort zone. "Absences and amnesia" remain commonplace, limiting the vision and engagement of the field to repetition of the same old questions, investigated using the same old methods, and applicable to the same old centres of gravity in the mid-Atlantic and the global North. Rethinking a public criminology must ensure it engages with other points of the compass and addresses contemporary impacts on people and environments in a global context.

Notes

1 See Rodriguez et al. (Rodriguez, Mol, Brisman, & South, 2017; Rodriguez, Mol, South, & Brisman, 2017) for two collections that aim to mix academics and activists and translate Spanish writings into English and vice-versa.
2 For the latest annual report on border-related deaths from the Australian Border Deaths Database, see http://artsonline.monash.edu.au/thebordercrossingobservatory/. For a discussion of the quantity and quality of data on "missing migrants" in six different regions, see IOM (2017).
3 See http://europeanbordercommunities.eu/research/getting-to-the-core-of-crimmigration.

References

Amnesty International USA. (2008). *Jailed without justice: Immigration detention in the USA*. New York: Amnesty International.
Andrijasevic, R., & Walters, W. (2010). The international organization for migration and the international government of borders. *Environment and Planning D: Society and Space, 28*(6), 977–999.
Aronowitz, S. (2003). A Mills revival? *Logos, 2*(3), 1–27.
Beck, U. (1999). *World risk society*. Cambridge: Polity Press.
Bosworth, M., & Gerlach, A. (2017). *Quality of life in detention results from MQLD questionnaire data collected in IRC Heathrow (Harmondsworth)*. Oxford: Centre for Criminology. Criminal Justice, Borders and Citizenship Research Paper No. 3012171.
Bosworth, M., Parmar, A., & Vazquez, Y. (Eds.). (2018). *Race, criminal justice, and migration control*. Oxford: Oxford University Press.
Bosworth, M., & Turnbull, S. (2014). Immigration detention and the expansion of penal power in the UK.. In K. Reiter & A. Koenig (Eds.), *Extraordinary punishment: An empirical look at administrative black holes in the United States, the United Kingdom, and Canada* (pp. 50–67). London: Palgrave.
Bourdieu, P. (1992). *Distinction: A social critique of the judgement of taste*. London: Routledge.
Bowling, B. (2013). The borders of punishment: Toward a criminology of mobility. In K. Franko Aas & M. Bosworth (Eds.), *Migration and punishment: Citizenship, crime control, and social exclusion* (pp. 291–306). Oxford: Oxford University Press.
Burawoy, M. (2005a). For public sociology. *American Sociological Review, 70*(1), 4–28.
Burawoy, M. (2005b). Provincializing the social sciences. In G. Steinmetz (Ed.), *The politics of method in the human sciences* (pp. 508–525). Durham, NC: Duke University Press.
Burawoy, M. (2006). A public sociology for human rights. In J. Blau & K. E. I. Smith (Eds.), *Public sociologies reader* (pp. 1–18). New York: Rowman and Littlefield.
Burawoy, M. (2009). The public sociology wars. In V. Jeffries (Ed.), *Handbook of Public Sociology* (pp. 449–473). New York: Rowman and Littlefield.
Carrabine, E. (2017). *Crime and social theory*. London: Palgrave Macmillan.
Carrabine, E., Iganski, P., Lee, M., Plummer, K., & South, N. (2004). *Criminology: A sociological introduction*. London: Routledge.
Carrabine, E., Lee, M., & South, N. (2000). Social wrongs and human rights in late modern Britain: Social exclusion, crime control, and prospects for a public criminology. *Social Justice, 27*(2), 193–211.
Carrier, N. (2014). On some limits and paradoxes of academic orations on public criminology. *Radical Criminology, 4*(1), 85–114.
Chou, E. (2018, February 21). ICE makes 17 "collateral arrests" as part of weeklong immigration sweeps in Southern California that resulted in more than 200 detained. *Los Angeles Daily News*. Retrieved from www.dailynews.com/2018/02/16/ice-arrests-more-than-200-in-weeklong-immigration-sweeps-across-southern-california/.

Christie, N. (1986). Suitable enemy. In H. Bianchi & R. von Swaaningen (Eds.), *Abolitionism: Toward a non-repressive approach to crime*. Amsterdam: Free University Press.

Cohen, S. (2001). *States of denial: Knowing about atrocities and suffering*. Cambridge: Polity Press.

Cunneen, C., & Tauri, J. (2016). *Indigenous criminology*. Bristol: Policy Press.

Currie, E. (2011). Thinking about criminology. *British Journal of Criminology*, *51*(4), 710–713.

Dauvergne, C. (2008). *Making people illegal: What globalization means for migration and law*. Cambridge: Cambridge University Press.

The Economist (2018, April 5). Donald Trump Takes a Hard Turn on Immigration. Retrieved from www.economist.com/united-states/2018/04/05/donald-trumps-takes-a-hard-turn-on-immigration.

Flynn, M. (2014). *Why and how immigration detention crossed the globe*. Global Detention Project Working Paper No. 8, April 2014.

Franko Aas, K. (2012). "The earth is one but the world is not": Criminological theory and its geopolitical divisions. *Theoretical Criminology*, *16*(1), 5–20.

Franko Aas, K., & Bosworth, M. (Eds.). (2013). *The borders of punishment: Migration, citizenship, and social exclusion*. Oxford: Oxford University Press.

Frelick, B., Kysel, I. M., & Podkul, J. (2016). The impact of externalization of migration controls on the rights of asylum seekers and other migrants. *Journal of Migration and Human Security*, *4*(4), 190–220.

Global Detention Project. (2016). United States Immigration Detention Profile. Retrieved from www.globaldetentionproject.org/wp-content/uploads/2016/06/us_2016.pdf.

Goode, E. (2008). From the western to the murder mystery: The sociological imagination of C. Wright Mills. *Sociological Spectrum*, *28*(3), 237–253.

Harvey, D. (1996). *Justice, nature and the geography of difference*. Oxford: Blackwell.

Horsti, K. (2017). Solidarities in the Arctic Border. Retrieved from www.law.ox.ac.uk/research-subject-groups/centre-criminology/centreborder-criminologies/blog/2017/06/solidarities.

Hughes, G. (2007). *The politics of crime and community*. Basingstoke: Palgrave.

Human Rights Watch. (2017). *Systemic indifference: Dangerous and substandard medical care in US immigration detention*. New York: Author. Retrieved from www.hrw.org/report/2017/05/08/systemic-indifference/dangerous-substandard-medical-care-us-immigration-detention.

International Organization for Migration. (2009, May). *Migration, climate change and the environment* (Policy Brief). Geneva: Author.

International Organization for Migration. (2017). *Fatal journeys volume 3 part 2—Improving data on missing migrants*. Geneva: Author.

Lee, M. (2013). Human trafficking and border control in the Global South. In K. Franko Aas & M. Bosworth (Eds.), *Migration and punishment: Citizenship, crime control, and social exclusion*. Oxford: Oxford University Press.

Lee, M., & Laidler, K. (2013). Doing criminology from the periphery: Crime and punishment in Asia. *Theoretical Criminology*, *17*(2), 141–157.

Loader, I., & Sparks, R. (2010a). *Public Criminology?* London: Routledge.

Loader, I., & Sparks, R. (2010b). What is to be done with public criminology? *Criminology & Public Policy*, *9*(4), 771–781.

Mills, C. W. (1959). *The sociological imagination*. Oxford: Oxford University Press.

Mowforth, M. (2014, September 23). Indigenous people and the crisis over land and resources. *The Guardian*. www.theguardian.com/global-development/2014/sep/23/indigenous-people-crisis-land-resources.

Pickering, S., Bosworth, M., & Franko Aas, K. (2014). The criminology of mobility. In S. Pickering & J. Ham (Eds.), *The Routledge handbook on crime and international migration* (pp. 382–395). London: Routledge.

Rengifo, A. (2017). Local agendas meet global dilemmas: Publicly-engaged criminology in a testing world. *The Criminologist*, *42*(6), 1, 3–7.

Revkin, A. (2007 April 1). Poor nations to bear brunt as world warms. *New York Times*.

Rodríguez Goyes, D., Mol, H., Brisman, A., & South, N. (Eds.). (2017). *Environmental crime in Latin America: The theft of nature and the poisoning of the land*. London: Palgrave Macmillan.

Rodríguez Goyes, D., Mol, H., South, N., & Brisman, A. (Eds.). (2017). *Introducción a la Criminología Verde: Conceptos para la Comprensión de los Conflictos Socioambientales*. Bogota: Fondo Editorial de la Universidad Antonio Nariño.

Rodríguez Goyes, D., & South, N. (2017a). Green criminology before "Green Criminology": Amnesia and absences. *Critical Criminology*, *25*(2), 165–181.

Rodríguez Goyes, D., & South, N. (2017b). The injustices of policing, law and multinational monopolisation in the privatisation of natural diversity: Cases from Colombia and Latin America. In D. Rodríguez Goyes,

H. Mol, A. Brisman, & N. South (Eds.), *Environmental crime in Latin America: The theft of nature and the poisoning of the land* (pp. 187–212). London: Palgrave.

Ruggiero, V. (2012). How public is *Public Criminology*? *Crime, Media, Culture*, 8(2), 151–160.

Smith, L. T. (1999). *Decolonizing methodologies: Research and indigenous peoples*. London: Zed Books.

Stuart, F. (2017). Public criminology for whom? Bringing "organic" public scholarship out of the shadows. *The Criminologist*, 42(2), 1, 3–6.

Stumpf, J. (2006). The crimmigration crisis: Immigrants, crime, and sovereign power. *American University Law Review*, 56(2), 367–419.

Turner, B. S. (2004). *The Blackwell companion to social theory*. Oxford: Blackwell.

University of Oxford (2016). Immigration Detention Archive. Retrieved from www.law.ox.ac.uk/research-subject-groups/immigration-detention-archive.

Wachholz, S. (2007). "At risk": Climate change and its bearing on women's vulnerability to male violence. In P. Beirne & N. South (Eds.), *Issues in Green Criminology* (pp. 161–185). Cullompton: Willan.

Walters, R. (2011). Public or civic criminology: A critique of Loader and Sparks. *British Journal of Criminology*, 51(4), 730–734.

Weber, L. (2013). Visible and virtual borders: Saving lives by "seeing" sovereignty? *Griffith Law Review*, 22(3), 666–682.

Weber, L., & Pickering, S. (2011). *Globalization and borders: Death at the global frontier*. London: Palgrave Macmillan.

Whyte, K. P. (2016, September 16). Why the Native American pipeline resistance in North Dakota is about climate justice. *The Conversation*. Retrieved from https://theconversation.com/why-the-native-american-pipeline-resistance-in-north-dakota-is-about-climate-justice-64714.

Young, J. (2011). *The criminological imagination*. Cambridge: Polity Press.

3

WHERE IS THE PUBLIC IN PUBLIC CRIMINOLOGY?

Towards a Participatory Public Criminology

Stuart Henry

Introduction

What is public criminology? What is its scope? What makes a criminologist public? While acknowledging Inderbitzin's (2011) point that the multiple interpretations of both "criminology" and "public" means that "public criminology" should be reframed—perhaps as criminologies that engage multiple publics—Rock (2014, p. 414) says that to be considered "public," public criminology "must have something to do with ... audibility and visibility." Todd Clear said in his introduction to Uggen and Inderbitzen's "Public Criminologies," it "entails talking to, talking with, and talking about those publics in the production of criminological scholarship. Public criminologists situate their work in the so-called real world, and they orient their productivity to the way in which 'the real world' needs it in order to be able to use it" (Clear, 2010a, p. 722).

But the objective of engaging publics in the criminological enterprise is to stimulate their "criminological imagination" (Loader & Sparks, 2008, p. 19), "to critique existing approaches to questions of crime and justice," and to "facilitate the imagination and exploration of alternative ways of thinking and acting in relation to crime and justice" (Larsen & Deisman, 2013, para. 6). The key is to actively communicate with them in terms they can comprehend, while simultaneously listening to what they say and think. Thus, a necessary element of criminology's encounters with these various publics is communicability, without which being visibly loud in a contested space will make little substantive difference. Indeed, such a sentiment may have driven Barak's call for criminologists to directly engage the public through mass media, under the guise of "newsmaking criminology" (Barak, 1988, 1994). Barak defines newsmaking criminology as the "conscious efforts and activities of criminologists to interpret, influence or shape the representation of 'newsworthy' items about crime and justice" (2007, p. 191). Isn't this precisely what public criminologies do, regardless of whether their issues are newsworthy?

Barak provides insight into aspects of the four dimensions of public criminology: (1) the criminologists' purposes and method for doing public criminology; (2) the media's view of the public criminologist, and how far such engagement compromises or facilitates the criminological enterprise; (3) the government, specifically law enforcement agencies' views and whether partnerships with justice system practitioners serve public criminology's interests; and (4) the publics' views and roles in the process. Discussion of the last dimension is underdeveloped in the literature on public criminology which fails to address publics as knowledge producers with insight and experiential knowledge on the reality of crime, harm and justice. Thus, the publics' voices are ignored in the co-production of public criminology.

Here, I draw out the conception held of "the public" by stakeholders in the enterprise of public criminology. I then take a critical stance on the elitism of disciplinary hegemony in its appeal to do public good and to become policy relevant. Instead, I argue that the present state of public criminology not only competes with other elites for a commanding voice in civil society, but that it embodies exclusionary practices that weaken its potential effectiveness while reaffirming its claim to authority on matters of crime and justice. In doing so, academic criminology loses its "audience," allowing populist politicians to claim the space and create confusion through multiple truth claims and an anti-expert ideology. In allowing populist politicians to claim and control the public space based on the appeal that they are reflecting the thoughts of their publics, public criminologists cede to their framing of the many publics' voices that we have excluded from the realm of knowledge production.

There are parallels here to the argument made by interdisciplinarians and transdisciplinarians in their attempts to transcend the myopia of disciplines by integrating knowledge across disciplines. They ironically limit what counts as knowledge to what is produced through academic disciplines and ignore other knowledge formations, such as those of practitioners, or unorganized publics, groups, indigenous peoples, etc. (Carp, 2001). According to critics, transdisciplinarity should not be about constructing an overarching theoretical framework, as Nicolescu has argued (2010; de Freitas, Morin, & Nicolescu, 1994), but about the pragmatic practice of collaborative team building toward joint problem solving (Augsburg, 2014). Critics (Augsburg & Henry, 2016) state that rather than incorporating non-academics into the knowledge production process the non-academic's role is limited to feedback on proposed transdisciplinary solutions, as in the Zurich School's approach (Bernstein, 2015). In contrast, Klein identifies diverse forms of knowledge that include "system knowledge, target knowledge, and transformation knowledge, socially robust knowledge, contextualization, new social distribution of knowledge, science in society, co-production of knowledge [and] local, indigenous people's traditional forms of knowledge" (Klein, 2013, p. 194). Klein draws on the concept of "knowledge democracy" that contextualizes complex problems, such as crime and (in)justice within a public debate to emphasize the importance of recognizing lay perspectives and alternative knowledges. She says these bring a shift "from solely 'reliable scientific knowledge' to the inclusion of 'socially robust knowledge,' dismantling the academic expert/non-academic lay dichotomy" (Klein, 2013, p. 196).

Similarly, public criminology proposes "engaging" its various publics but not as active knowledge producers, problem framers, and problem solvers. In this chapter, I challenge public criminologists to recognize the publics' knowledge formations as integral to public criminology and later I discuss how this "knowledge democracy" might be accomplished in public criminology through the mechanism of participatory deliberative democracy (Canal, 2014; Chambers, 2003).

Criminologists' Purpose and Methods in Doing Public Criminology

Much of the discussion on "public-ology"[1] by social scientists is about what they do or do not do and what they should or should not do when engaging the public and about what constitutes the public role of the social sciences (notably as public sociology, public anthropology, and public criminology). The scope of their work remains primarily disciplinary and often involves applied research or policy analysis with a tendency toward hegemony of knowledge production. The scope of academic public sociology, for example, has been separated into professional sociology, policy sociology, public sociology, and critical sociology (Burawoy, 2005). The categories of criminological work are seen in a more dynamic and dialectical relationship such that "categories overlap" and "individuals may be involved in professional, critical, policy and public criminology to varying degrees" (Inderbitzin, 2011, para. 1; Uggen & Inderbitzin, 2010).

In this "public" work, are criminologists offering an "important service" to "the public" by feeding applied research findings into the "public debate" as correctives to myths and misconceptions, and as evaluations about the effectiveness of different correctional programs (Inderbitzin, 2011)? Are they forming institutes for criminal justice advocacy or policy as a strategy to target those powerful publics that make and implement policy? Are they targeting key politicians through lobbyists? Or, are they inserting themselves into the mass media as alternative newsmakers (Barak, 1988, 1994, 2007) to influence the "general public" or to specifically influence those who do "the country's professional level analytic and creative work" (Gans, 1989)? Are they on social media impacting popular culture or are they becoming part of the government (conservative, liberal, or socialist), assisting agencies in collaborative governance to work effectively to influence and implement government policies? And, in doing so, whose policies are they implementing? Moreover, how public should the work of criminologists be to call it public criminology?

What Is Public about Public Criminology?

Is criminology "public" if it develops and discusses criminal justice policy issues? Is it public if these discussions remain closeted in self-referential, specialized academic journals or academic monographs inaccessible to a lay audience, or even to sophisticated policy makers, politicians or legislators? What if the criminologists successfully respond to state or federal requests for research and accept public funding to conduct research, which is then reported back to the funding agency, and maybe to the city council, the state legislature, or to Congress or even the White House? What if these criminologists are hired by quasi-independent research institutes that receive their funding directly from the government with a purpose to channel criminological research toward the criminal justice aims of crime control and order maintenance? Such examples include New York's Vera Institute and the United Kingdom's Cambridge Institute for Criminology or its Home Office Research Unit, which were once the largest employers of criminologists in the U.K. (Rock, 2014, pp. 414–417). Are criminologists only public if they disseminate their publicly funded research through public channels? The Cambridge Institute certainly did that, with its criminologists also making regular appearances in national news media and being referenced as authoritative in the British Parliament (Rock, 2014, pp. 416–418).

If criminology must become part of public debate and even public life for it to be designated "public," how do we know when it is public enough? Does this involve forging relationships outside of academic criminology, and if so with whom: journalists; criminal justice agencies; the police; courts; the FBI? Is the resultant measure of criminological publicness doing television appearances?[2] Is it being featured in, or even writing articles on, criminological ideas, theories, and research in traditional media, such as newspapers or magazines (Barak, 1988)?

And what about criminologists' involvement in social media: the blogosphere, Facebook, social networks, political and activist groups, or posting their work on open access e-criminology internet sites with options for the public to comment? Some scholars have even argued that impacting future public officials while they are students under training in criminal justice, inside and outside the academy, is public criminology "in embryo" (Rock, 2014, p. 427). Students are "our first public, for they carry sociology [or criminology or anthropology] into all walks of life" (Burawoy, 2002, p. 7). Some criminologists have proposed a specific pedagogy to that effect (Hamilton, 2015). Does this mean that all criminologists teaching in criminology and criminal justice programs are public criminologists? What about teachers of criminal justice programs in high schools?

Indeed, reflecting on the criminologists of public criminologies, it is open to interpretation whether they are academic social scientists or pundits, "analysts, advisors, consultants, fact-finders, muckrakers, activists, or social critics" (Loader & Sparks, 2008, p. 18) or some of all of these things as they move in and out of the public realm (Burawoy, 2005). On one hand, almost everything a conventional academic criminologist does is, at least in some respects, public criminology. Only a small minority of "deviant" academic criminologists remain closeted in the university research laboratory in relative isolation from the public. So perhaps the issue is not what public criminologists do, but how directly, frequently, and explicitly criminologists engage the public and insert themselves in public debates on crime and justice issues for the purposes of bringing positive social change. As Larsen and Deisman state:

> public criminology at its best is a movement and a set of practices grounded in a commitment to informed and participatory democracy. It seeks to engage with a diversity of audiences through a variety of means, and to contribute to a wide range of criminological conversations.
>
> *(Larsen & Deisman, 2013, para. 6)*

Several commentaries in sociology, anthropology, and criminology ponder if we even need to declare some of what they do "public" since the content of what is described is similar, if not identical, to that which has been done for years (Loader & Sparks, 2010a, 2010b; Rock, 2014). The difference, however, is that the "public" designation highlights the explicit and intentional nature of the engagement. When criminology, sociology, or anthropology were publicly engaged in pre "public-ology" eras, there was no less determination to make change to improve society and its institutions based on the vision that things could be better. For example, in the late 1930s, Sutherland (1939, 1949), in his contribution to the debate over the question "what is crime?," argued that accepting the state definition of crime as strictly defined by law meant that equally harmful behavior would merely be an administrative rule violation, rather than white collar crime; its repeat offenders would be mere deviants rather than "habitual white-collar criminals." Sutherland argued for extending the legal definition of crime to include all offenses that are "socially injurious" or socially harmful.

Following Sutherland, critical criminologists argued that the definition of crime should be expanded to include the socially injurious activities of powerful groups against the powerless, as well as behavior that violates or intrudes upon others' human rights (Schwendinger & Schwendinger, 1970; Tifft & Sullivan, 2001). The Canadian government took up this charge in its deliberations culminating in the Canadian Law Commission's (2003) work *What is a Crime?* The critical question for our purposes is who were the audiences for these arguments for a new definition of crime, and how were these audiences engaged by the criminologists?

Audiences Targeted by Public Criminology

If the intended audience of policy-relevant research and analysis is the "general public," and if that is sufficient to make it "public criminology," then Sutherland and his followers seem to be doing public criminology. However, if this is not so and if the arguments are only made to other criminologists, or worse to a subset of criminologists, then their work is more a case of professional criminology than public criminology, even though it may have public implications. The arguments might be about public policy (what counts as crime), but they are not publicly communicated, do not, except by happenstance, impact legislators who, at least in Western democracies, make the laws that define some behavior as crime.

But what if critical criminologists, for example, write for public policy journals, such as *Criminology and Public Policy*? Surely, that is public criminology? Whether it is or not depends on who reads the journals. In sociology this issue is clear: Deflem says if it is "speaking only for and to itself, public sociology has no public. There is no debate with public sociology ... Public sociology allows no discussion with others. Public sociology cannot be spoken or heard except by itself" (Deflem, 2005, pp. 1, 7). Is the actual readership "the lay public"? Is it practicing politicians? Is it agents of governance? Is it legislators? To the extent that such a journal's central objective "is to strengthen the role of research findings in the formulation of crime and justice policy by publishing empirically based, policy focused articles" (American Society of Criminology, 2018, para. 1), it may be public criminology. But this objective alone does not make it public criminology, nor do criminologists whose articles are published in such a journal become public criminologists by the act of publication alone.

There used to be a naïve view among social scientists that publishing their work in academic journals and books contributed to the public debate—that by some process of osmosis their research filters up to inform the public and the policy makers The reality is that politicians, legislators, and commentators rarely read academic work (and if they do it is selectively and rarely, rather than systematically). Moreover, in some governance contexts (e.g., right-wing populism), academic research and analysis, even expert interpretation, and translation of academic work, is marginalized, if not completely condemned, as the knowledge of "elites" or as part of the ideological swamp of the liberal left and its intellectual class. At best, it is diluted "as one of many truths out there." The best that could be claimed for this level of policy research and analysis is that it has an indirect public presence but is too distal to have any direct impact on policy or practice, and, as a result, is not public criminology. To be public criminology, criminologists must engage "the public" and be open to the various publics engaging them.

Criminologists can be publicly engaged through those who communicate with the public and with those legislators who work with politicians. At a minimal level, albeit still indirect, public criminology can work through journalists in the mass media who report their research findings and critical analysis based on criminological work on crime, criminal justice, and public policy. However, the readership, listenership, or social media-ship of such journalistic outputs is increasingly dispersed into multiple, fragmented, and media-manipulated sources and sites, blogs and soundbites, such that the effective communication of its content is ultimately distorted if not debunked (Surette, 1998). Because of the framing of such issues by interest groups, journalistic practices, and media owners, some scholars have advocated for criminologists to become their own reporters and storywriters, following Barak's (1988, 1994, 2007) "newsmaking criminology." Newsmaking criminologists are at least prototype public criminologists, as noted by Loader and Sparks (2010a, p. 772). Since Barak made these observations, however, we have moved from traditional media to social media, the blogosphere, and internetworks. In turn, formats for outreach multiply and are fragmented into an infinite number of publics, each building their own multi-media infusion of sources of news and information about crime and justice. But even if criminological insights, research, and policy analysis leach out through these somewhat arbitrary and random-access ways, there remains the question of whether this form of public engagement is enough to warrant the term "public criminology."

To be public criminology, criminological knowledge infused into multiple publics must percolate up to policy makers and to criminal justice movers and shakers. Traditionally, this arguably occurred through public forums and town-hall meetings, but now it is more likely to be filtered through political lobbyists, political activists, and public image-makers. To be public criminology, criminologists must directly engage the agencies of governance who are shaping policy. One of the founders of "scientific" criminology, Enrico Ferri, was a public criminologist in accordance with the definitions developed here well before the concept was coined.

Ferri has been described as combining a "talent for assimilation and propaganda" in applying his research on crime and punishment "in the sociological and juridical field ... for the defense of society by direct and indirect methods of prevention and repression" (Gaspare, 1929, p. 179). He did so as criminologist, elected official, and member of the Italian Socialist Party. Perhaps Ferri was the first public criminologist? He certainly asserted the right of criminology to be a dominant voice in the competition for public persuasion.

Importantly, for our purposes, Ferri was politically active and publicly engaged, was elected to Italian Parliament in 1886, and later joined the Italian Socialist Party, edited their daily newspaper, and was re-elected as a Socialist Party Deputy in 1921. He was invited to implement his then "radical ideas" of multi-causality and multi-level criminal justice policy (Ferri (1901 [1884], 1917 [1894]) under Mussolini's fascist regime, and even though these ideas were eventually rejected by Mussolini for being too radical, the substance of Ferri's argument became the foundation of the Argentinian Penal Code of 1921 implemented in 1922 and was sustained subject a series of modifications through the late 1990s.

Subsequent developments in sociology and criminology have led to the establishment of numerous centers and institutes for public policy. Perhaps one of the most successful historical examples of public criminology in the 20th century by direct engagement in government was the research of Cloward and Ohlin (1960). Their research on delinquency and opportunity supported a major policy initiative by the Kennedy-Johnson era criminal justice reforms who drafted them to help devise a new federal policy for dealing with juvenile delinquency and that resulted in The Juvenile Delinquency Prevention and Control Act of 1961. From this public criminology collaborations emerged numerous social engineering programs, such as Mobilization for Youth, Head Start, Job Corps, Vista, Neighborhood Legal Services, and the Community Action Program. By the 1980s, most of Kennedy-Johnson's era programs had been dismantled, though several remain, and Kennedy's policies are a strong example of how direct public engagement by criminologists in government can open up the possibilities for social change.

The Government and the Media's View of the Public Criminologist

The government, specifically law enforcement agencies' views about whether there is a role for public criminologists, matters, since without such recognition, there is likely to be little available public space and even less policy influence. A related consideration for public criminology is whether partnerships with justice system practitioners serve public criminology's interests, let alone those of the discipline of criminology. Rock (2014) argues that public criminologists are "overshadowed by the real titans of the criminal justice system, the judiciary, police, and Bar" and that criminologists' "relative impotence" in claiming authoritative knowledge lacks both the support and cooperation of agencies of crime control, "for without them nothing can be done ... They have the power. Criminologists do not" (Rock, 2014, p. 424).

Although criminologists have "had to confront the embarrassing fact that in a society saturated with 'crime talk,' they have utmost difficulty in communicating with politicians, policy makers, professionals and the public" (Chancer & McLaughlin, 2007, p. 157). Why? It can be argued that collaboratively communicating with practitioners and other publics requires the opposite set of skills from those possessed by traditional criminologists. Such engagement often needs to be in the form of a succinctly presented argument focused on the small scale, with on-time availability, absent preamble and context, "unequivocal, clear and simple," quantitatively supported at a comprehendible level, "uncluttered by footnotes and endnotes, neologisms" and academic trappings, "empirically rather than theoretically grounded; pragmatic and practical" (Rock, 2014, p. 423). Not surprisingly this might scare off many criminologists from going public and subject those who do to ridicule and derogation.

An additional problem facing public criminology's ability to engage is that it can be subject to attack from the criminological conservative right. Indeed, some conservative criminologists have lambasted criminology, because, they claim, the academic profession is dominated by liberal-left criminologists [by 30 to 1], "mainly sociologists, trained in statistics and armed with theories" (Wright & DeLisi, 2017, para. 4). Criminologists are accused of lacking direct contact with offenders or victims, crime situations, and crime-ridden neighborhoods, "which invites misunderstandings about the reality of crime" and "fosters a romanticized view of criminals as victims, making it easier for criminologists to overlook the damage that lawbreakers cause—and to advocate for more lenient policies and treatment" (Wright & DeLisi, 2017, para. 5). This absence of real-world engagement and criminologists' liberal-radical orientation makes them prone to "grand pronouncements that don't often prove out in the real world" (Wright & DeLisi, 2017, para. 1). These critics argue that the "lack of ideological diversity in the social sciences" skews research in favor of leftist claims, which become guiding principles in many fields, resulting in unchecked content and tendentious claims of evidence as fact (Wright & DeLisi, 2017, para. 10).

At the same time, countervailing evidence receives much closer scrutiny and is suppressed. Wright and DeLisi (2017, para. 22) argue that criminology "has had a long history of suppressing evidence for expressly political reasons," particularly that informed by biological, genetic, and neurological research. They conclude by raising the fear of public criminology for its distorted conclusions and biases that impact ordinary people's lives in negative ways: "Public safety may be compromised, and valuable and limited resources may be squandered … the stakes are too high to accept research tainted by political bias" (Wright & DeLisi, 2017, para. 26).

So public criminology is fraught with all kinds of challenges, threats, and dangers, not just in relation to the community of academic criminologists but also from an alliance of the law, order and control ideology that prevails over law enforcement agencies. But, is public criminology necessarily compromised by collaborating with government and public agencies? If not, is that the threat conservative alliances fear? Is part of the problem actually public criminologies' limited conception of its publics and indeed those publics' perception of it?

Understanding the "Public" in Public Criminology and Publics' Perceptions of Criminology and Criminologists

What are the assumptions public criminologists make about "the public"? Are they passive consumers of evidence-based research, persuasive argument, expert knowledge, reasoned debate or uncritical observers of ideologically framed news? And which publics are we talking about? As discussed, some public criminologists recognize that there are not only multiple public criminologies (as Burawoy argued there are multiple sociologies), but also multiple publics (Inderbitzin, 2011).

Public-Ologies' Conception of the Public

The sociologist Herbert Gans, in his 1988 ASA Presidential address, stated that he was concerned with sociologists' "relations with America's non-sociologists, the lay public: both the very huge general public and the smaller well-educated one which does much of the country's professional level analytic and creative work" (Gans, 1989, p. 1). Gans then saw two publics of interest to the work of sociologists. His speech left unquestioned who these publics are; he seemed more interested in how sociology is seen or accepted by the mass media, whether sociologists are portrayed as caricatures in popular culture, and whether sociology is playing a valued role in the intellectual life of society.

These concerns are valid for criminologists because the media's view of public criminologists can affect whether or not and how successful they can be in their public engagement. If the media are skeptical of criminologists' value, it is unlikely criminologists will be invited to participate as experts. If Rock is right, gatekeepers controlling access to major media outlets see criminologists as

> little more than second or third ranked experts whose forms of knowing are inferior to those of people who can convey more immediate impressions of an event—victims, witnesses, practitioners and journalists [whose] experiential knowledge about egregious crime over and again trumps the disinterested and the scholarly in the public forum.
>
> (Rock, 2014, pp. 428–429)

For other voices in public criminology or public sociology, this does not mean one has to draw from a mainstream position that is quantitatively primed, narrowly specialized, and ready to reap the rewards of piecemeal social engineering. Rather, what is envisioned is a post-modern poetic sociology whose influence comes from the persuasion of its argument rather than the rigor of its research (Agger, 2007).

By the time of Burawoy's ASA Presidential Address in 2004, the conception of the public to be informed and engaged by a "transcendent sociology" had become more specified. In fact, an indication of Burawoy's later position on sociology's multiple publics is found in his personal statement for his ASA Presidential candidacy: "our potential publics are multiple, ranging from media audiences, to policy makers, from silenced minorities to social movements. They are local, global and national" (Burawoy, 2002, p. 7). Moreover, he describes a version of public sociology, which he calls "organic public sociology," as "the sociologist work[ing] in close connection with a visible, thick, active, local and often counter-public" (Burawoy, 2005, p. 7). Not only does Burawoy recognize multiple public sociologies and multiple publics, but he also notes that publics themselves are dynamic and changing: "We should not think of publics as fixed but in flux and that we can participate in their creation as well as their transformation" (2005, p. 8). Indeed, he advocates that "public sociology needs to develop a *sociology of publics* ... to better appreciate the possibilities and pitfalls of public sociology" (2005, p. 8). Similarly, we might argue that public criminologists need to understand, take seriously and appreciate the criminological imaginations of its multiple publics, from fearful community members, to victims of harm, by "street" or "suite" offenders, to the agencies of social control, and to the harm producers themselves, to the journalists who portray them and to the bloggers who rage against them. Without such understanding there will be limited engagement; without engagement there is no public criminology.

The Challenge of the Public as Knowledge Producers

As evident throughout this chapter, I believe that inclusion of a diversity of perspectives, described as "knowledge democracy," is vital to a sustained and positive criminological public engagement. Such inclusiveness is opposed to exclusion and marginalization and is particularly opposed to a selected public criminological elite monopolizing the power to influence crime and justice policy based on their narrow disciplinary interests, ideological position, or desire to be relevant. The history of the field is littered with the corpses of past public criminologists who "were belittled as not much more than administrative criminologists, voodoo criminologists, official criminologists … lickspittles and lackeys" (Rock, 2014 p. 424). Such disciplinary elitism, which denigrates would-be public criminologists, reflects the wider problem of disciplinary hegemony: one of the disciplines seeking to control knowledge domains by policing boundaries, excluding alternative thinking, disavowing experiential analysis, undermining interdisciplinary thinking, and negating anything applied, practical, or grounded in day-to-day practices (Augsburg & Henry, 2009; Henry, 2005).

Social sciences have always reflected an elitist hierarchical order of knowledge, with "pure" disciplinary knowledge and research often considered the prestigious pinnacle of this hierarchy. Beneath the pure are applied social scientists who are seen as somewhat contaminated, if not compromised by their engagement with the real world. As such, they are considered vulnerable to political and public interests, particularly by community and political groups who want to translate criminologists' academic research to serve their political ideological or cultural agendas. Indeed, Burawoy echoes others who see a cool reception of public sociology by those who, for example, "fear public involvement will corrupt science, threaten the legitimacy of the discipline as well as the material resources it will have at its disposal" (Burawoy, 2005, p. 15). Is a distinguished social science researcher who is invited to be part of a blue-ribbon commission or task force, one that contains multiple political and community stakeholders, "selling out" in the compromise over negotiated conclusions and recommendations? This position certainly is not something the "pure" researcher has to face. It is for this reason that those who are "co-opted" into the service of government or government agencies can be seen as "dirtied" by the experience. They, therefore, come to occupy the basement of the ivory tower and are of questionable value to the discipline as they risk compromising some of its purity. As a result, the disciplinary tribes of academic social science tend to separate, marginalize, or otherwise discredit those of their field who have deviated to the public sphere, seeing it as important to maintain a gap or distance between their disciplines and those outside their discipline, especially other disciplines (Becher & Trowler, 2001).

Related to the issues of disciplinary hegemony, hierarchies of knowledge, and whether "knowledge formations" can transcend the divide between passive consumers and active agents (Carp, 2001; Klein, 2013) is public criminologists' conception of the public as knowledge producers. This requires a recognition that there are multiple sites and sources of knowledge.

The point about acknowledging different sites of knowledge production and knowledge formations (Carp, 2001) is to (1) understand how they influence ideas, ideology and "sense and nonsense" about crime and public policy, (2) how they interact with other more formal sites of knowledge production, and (3) how they come together as part of the public debate, dialogue, policy, and practice that constitute the color and form of the policies and practices of the system of criminal justice that is emergent at any point of time. Are some of these forms of knowledge more active, or even more effective, when the political climate changes—say from rational and reasoned, evidenced-based, or fear and risk-oriented, or when swamped by a wave of populism? Are the publics co-producers of knowledge for solving complex problems, such as crime, or are they merely recipients of specialists' expertise, given little more than a token of respect?

The closest that public criminologists have come to recognizing this problem is Loader and Sparks' adaptation of Swift and White's (2008) "democratic underlaboring" (Loader & Sparks, 2010a, p. 776). As they explain, "To practice criminology as a democratic underlaborer is to be committed, first and foremost, to the generation of knowledge rather than (first and foremost) to scoring a point or winning a policy battle"

(Loader & Sparks, 2010a, p. 778). They describe a distinct role for public criminologist as democratic underlaborers who

> refuse to take the social world for granted or to accept received political "imperatives," ... [to] bring to public discussion a skepticism that refuses to treat at face value the categories, assumptions, and self-understandings that make up prevailing "common sense" about crime and its control.
>
> *(Loader & Sparks, 2010a, p. 778)*

Sparks and Loader argue that, as a democratic underlaborer, the public criminologists should "set forth alternative institutional arrangements for thinking about and responding to crime and to forge connections with groups in civil society (and not simply government) who are seeking to advance a better, or alternative, justice policy" (p. 778). They conclude that

> [t]he underlaboring conception of criminology is committed to participating within and to facilitating and extending institutional spaces that supplement representative politics with inclusive public deliberation about crime and justice matters, whether in local, state, or federal settings or across emergent transnational arenas.
>
> *(Loader & Sparks, 2010a, p. 779)*

A critical question I pose is whether Loader and Sparks go far enough, since their depiction of non-criminological publics as lacking a critical awareness of their own commonsense assumptions suggests again a hierarchy whereby criminological insight is more penetrating, more enlightened, and thereby more valuable. Should we, instead, adopt a more critical, transdisciplinarian position such as the one I described earlier in this chapter, that takes a democratic stance on knowledge production (see also Augsburg & Henry, 2016; Klein, 2013)? Is it enough to assume that "prevailing 'common sense' about crime and its control" is uncritical and is somehow less critical than the perspectives of the academic criminologist? Might that be because those expressing such knowledge are not trained in critical thinking or in articulating an argument about crime and justice in academic terms. Isn't part of the role of public criminology to treat its publics with the same respect that an anthropologist shows when trying to understand members of a non-industrial society; to tease out underlying assumptions and engage in deliberative dialog to better understand their views, and to see how and why they arrive at their commonsense knowledge, stereotypes, and stated positions? Ultimately, should public criminology engage in a partnership of problem solving with its multiple publics and, if so, how might that work in practice? One possibility for the underlaboring public criminologist is deliberative democracy.

From Knowledge Democracy to Public Criminology through Deliberative Democracy[3]

As indicated earlier, Larsen and Deisman's (2013) definition of deliberative democracy "requires the public criminologist to engage with a diversity of audiences through a variety of means, and to contribute to a wide range of criminological conversations." Extending these insights, we need to ask how public criminology engages with public knowledge producers in participatory democracy to produce criminal justice policy change. As opposed to "the public" being a passive recipient of criminological knowledge creation, a more progressive public engagement with criminology implies a conversation about crime and justice between criminologists and its various publics, where each learns about the other's perspective, assumptions and policy proposals. Thus, knowing about crime, criminology and criminal justice becomes part of the socio-political process of citizenship and involves the process of deliberative democracy (Elster, 1998).

Public deliberation is the "process through which deliberative democracy occurs" (Delli Carpini, Cook, & Jacobs, 2004, p. 317). Lindeman defines deliberation as "a cognitive process in which individuals form, alter, or reinforce their opinions as they weigh evidence and arguments from various points of view" (Lindeman, 2002, p. 199). For Gunderson, "Democratic deliberation occurs anytime a citizen either actively justifies her views (even to herself) or defends them against a challenge (even from herself)" (Gunderson, 1995, p. 199). In this process:

> deliberation is expected to lead to empathy with the other and a broadened sense of people's own interests through an egalitarian, open-minded and reciprocal process of reasoned argumentation. Following from this result are other benefits: citizens are more enlightened about their own and others' needs and experiences, can better resolve deep conflict, are more engaged in politics, place their faith in the basic tenets of democracy, perceive their political system as legitimate, and lead a healthier civic life.
>
> *(Mendelberg, 2002, pp. 153–154)*

The transformative effects of authentic deliberative engagement about knowledge transmission are significant. Indeed, Chambers (2003) notes that a central tenet of all deliberative theory is that deliberation can change minds and transform opinions and "under the right conditions will have a tendency to broaden perspectives, promote toleration and understanding between groups, and generally encourage a public-spirited attitude" (Chambers, 2003, p. 318).

A benefit of deliberation is that collective decisions can be "superior to individual ones because more information can be brought to bear" (Delli Carpini, Cook, & Jacobs, 2004, p. 327). However, evidence cautions that left alone "groups tend to use information that is already commonly shared, downplaying unique information held by specific individuals that could arguably improve the decision" (p. 328). Greater discussion can also increase the use of new, less commonly shared, information (Kelly & Karau, 1999) and in the process can improve the quality of the decisions reached by the group (Winquist & Larson, 1998). Communication in the deliberative engaged model involves a process of generating new, mutually acceptable knowledge, attitudes and practices. It is a dynamic exchange, as disparate groups find a way of sharing a single message (Gregory & Miller, 1998). Given that a deliberative model of communication incorporates an awareness of knowledge transformation, how does this translate into criminal justice policy making?

Deliberative Democracy, Public Criminology, and Lessons from Public Health Policy

As stated above, whether dialog among criminologists and its diverse range of publics makes a difference to criminal justice policy depends on how different knowledge formations are incorporated into the policy making process. Consistent with Bryant's (2002) work on public health policy, I argue that there has been a neglect by public criminologists of the political process that affects how different forms of criminological knowledge are accepted or rejected in the criminal justice policy formation process. In public health, Bryant says the kind of policy a government makes is affected by its own ideological influences but is also affected by the identity of its policy advocates. Bryant says that most valuable models in effecting health policy change are those that consider the knowledge activities of competing coalitions of private and public elite groups and organizations who lobby for change.

This point particularly applies to criminal justice policy, which is based on knowledge developed by experts, often lawyers, cause-based community members, and politically engaged groups or moral entrepreneurs. Some of these groups contain professional experts from research institutes and criminal justice agencies. These professional policy analysts produce objective instrumental knowledge developed through the application of the scientific process. Citizen activists who tend to be non-academic develop interactive or lay knowledge about crime and justice, which is shared among communities related to things that affect them personally, based on lived experience. Critical criminologists also mobilize on issues of criminal justice and tend to consider the influence of powerful socioeconomic forces that affect society and differentially impact some groups over others, and how these forces reinforce inequalities in criminal justice processing. What Bryant describes for health also applies to criminal justice: "Critical knowledge considers questions of right and wrong, analyses existing social conditions, and outlines what can be done to alter social conditions to improve quality of life" (Bryant, 2002, p. 93). Critical knowledge can be produced by forums, and meetings may draw from both the expert and the citizen community bringing them together in a collaborative deliberative discussion of the issues that increases the criminological awareness of citizens and educate justice policy experts about the social and political contexts of their knowledge.

For public health policy, Bryant's research found that anecdotal and "qualitative studies were more persuasive in influencing policy makers than instrumental knowledge," and that both professional policy analysts and citizens groups used anecdotal evidence as part of their communication strategy (Bryant, 2002, p. 95). However, Bryant also found that the socio-political identity of the actors who lobby policy makers was important in determining who got access to policy makers and what kinds of knowledge was acceptable: "Identity determined what constituted valid knowledge and evidence for government in its policy process" (p. 96). She further argues that "different types of knowledge are essential to building a case to achieve particular policy change outcomes" and that

> the political ideology of the government of the day and the political identity of the constituency influence the receptivity of government toward civil society actors and the ability of the actors to influence the policy change process … in the end, the government was willing only to heed knowledge and evidence that supported its ideological perspective.
>
> *(Bryant, 2002, pp. 96–97)*

Conclusion

I began this chapter with the argument that public criminology takes a privileged stance against other knowledge producers and assumes its knowledge and analyses are superior to those of non-academics in determining public policy. The presumption is that criminologists have difficulty influencing government unless they collaborate with government agencies, and that doing so risks compromising their perspective or, worse, they become agents of the state. A similar problem faces criminologists who work with the media. The solution to this challenge was seen by some criminologists as engaging in newsmaking or reframing crime and justice on their own terms to directly engage the public in their criminological ideas, research, and perspectives. However, this was not based on a theory of policy making, but on the assumption that criminological wisdom would counter media bias and its superficial and sensational coverage of crime, permeate to sections of the public and from there, to lawmakers and policymakers.

While engaging the public is more strategic than allowing criminological knowledge, evidence and insight to be filtered, channeled, and diffused, it is clear that the actions of special interests, lobbyists, and government agencies are what influences government policy. It is also clear that by assuming that the many publics of news and research are open to criminological ideas, even when engaged by public criminologists, overlooks the active agency and self-efficacy of members of these publics: that these publics have their own knowledge, insight and policy prescriptions for crime, crime control and justice. However, the reality is that public criminological "engagement" is really not so much engagement, as it further attempts to influence key publics, thus missing the opportunity to partner with these groups toward genuine social change. Public policy changes could be more effective if criminologists recognized the range of "criminological" knowledge producers outside of the academy and took a "knowledge democracy" position that sought to partner with these publics in an engaged participatory democracy.

Drawing on insights from health policy formation, this chapter suggests that participatory public democracy on matters of crime and justice would need partnerships of public criminologists with relevant publics to get their concerns to be embodied in the political process and to recognize the influence that anecdotal stories and personal accounts can have relative to empirical data in impacting politicians. But, even doing this successfully depends on the selective practices that serve the ideological position of governments in power. The sobering reality is that a public criminology based on participatory public democracy will likely have limited success, but likely be more transformational than the traditional models of policy change that do not articulate clear pathways through the existing political structures to implement change. Thus, to Rock's (2014) observation that public criminology is "audible and visible" we need to add that it needs to be strategically targeted through collaborative partnerships with its multiple publics to bring about positive social change.

Notes

1 "Public-ologies" is the term applied to those social sciences concerned with varieties of public engagement for their work.
2 But only if they "have the interest and the skills," according to Inderbitzin (2011).
3 Much of the following discussion was developed in Anastasia and Henry (2015) and has been applied here to public criminology.

References

Agger, B. (2007). *Public sociology: From social facts to literary acts* (2nd ed.). Lanham, MD: Rowman & Littlefield.
American Society of Criminology. (2018). Overview. *Crime and Public Policy*. Retrieved from https://onlinelibrary.wiley.com/page/journal/17459133/homepage/productinformation.html.
Anastasia, D. J. M., & Henry, S. (2015). A sociologically informed ethics of American science literacy: Toward a transdisciplinary understanding. *Sociology and Criminology*, 3(1), 1–8.
Augsburg, T. (2014). Becoming transdisciplinary: The emergence of the transdisciplinary individual. *World Futures: The Journal of Global Education*, 70(3–4), 233–247.
Augsburg, T., & Henry, S. (Eds.). (2009). *The politics of interdisciplinary studies: Essays on transformations in American undergraduate programs*. Jefferson, NC: McFarland.
Augsburg, T., & Henry, S. (2016). Expanding the scope of transdisciplinarity. *Colorado Critical Review*, 1(1), 86–113.
Barak, G. (1988). Newsmaking criminology: Reflections on the media, intellectuals, and crime. *Justice Quarterly*, 5(4), 565–585.
Barak, G. (Ed.). (1994). *Media, process and the social construction of crime: Studies in newsmaking criminology*. New York: Garland Publishing.

Barak, G. (2007). Doing newsmaking criminology from within the academy. *Theoretical Criminology, 11*(2), 191–209.

Becher, T., & Trowler, P. R. (2001). *Academic tribes and territories: Intellectual enquiry and the cultures of discipline* (2nd ed.). Philadelphia: Open University Press.

Bernstein, J. H. (2015). Transdisciplinarity: A review of its origins, development, and current issues. *Journal of Research Practice, 11*(1). Retrieved from http://jrp.icaap.org/index.php/jrp/article/view/510

Bryant, T. (2002). Role of knowledge in public health and health promotion policy change. *Health Promotion International, 17*(1), 89–98.

Burawoy, M. (2002). 2002–2003 candidates announced for ASA officers: President-Elect: Michael Burawoy. *ASA Footnotes, 30*(3), Retrieved from www.asanet.org/sites/default/files/march_2002.pdf

Burawoy, M. (2005). For public sociology. *American Sociological Review, 70*(1), 4–28.

Canadian Law Commission. (2003). *What is a crime? Defining criminal conduct in contemporary society*. Vancouver: University of British Columbia Press.

Canal, R. (2014). *Social inclusion and participatory democracy*. Barcelona: IGOP/UCLG/CGLU.

Carp, R. (2001). Integrative praxes: Learning from multiple knowledge formations. *Issues in Integrative Studies, 19*, 122–121.

Chambers, S. (2003). Deliberative democratic theory. *Annual Review of Political Science, 6*(1), 307–326.

Chancer, L., & McLaughlin, E. (2007). Public criminologies: Diverse perspectives on academia and policy. *Theoretical Criminology, 11*(2), 155–173.

Clear, T. (2010a). Editorial introduction to "public criminologies". *Criminology & Public Policy, 9*(4), 721–724.

Cloward, R., & Ohlin, L. (1960). *Delinquency and opportunity*. New York: Free Press.

de Freitas, L., Morin, E., & Nicolescu., B. (1994). *Charte de la transdisciplinarité [The charter of transdisciplinarity]*. Retrieved from http://ciret-transdisciplinarity.org/chart.php

Deflem, M. (2005). Public sociology, hot dogs, apple pie, and Chevrolet. *The Journal of Professional and Public Sociology, 1*(1). Retrieved from https://digitalcommons.kennesaw.edu/jpps/vol1/iss1/4/

Delli Carpini, M. X., Cook, F. L., & Jacobs, L. R. (2004). Public deliberations, discursive participation and citizen engagement: A review of the empirical literature. *Annual Review of Political Science, 7*(1), 315–344.

Ehrlich, E. (1979). Living law. In C. Campbell & P. Wiles (Eds.), *Law and society*. Oxford: Martin Robertson.

Elster, J. (1998). *Deliberative democracy*. Cambridge: Cambridge University Press.

Ferri, E. (1901)[1884]. *Criminal sociology*. New York, NY: D. Appleton.

Ferri, E. (1917) [1894]. *Socialism and positive science*. Chicago, IL: Charles H. Kerr.

Gans, H. J. (1989). Sociology in America: The discipline and the public, American Sociological Association, 1988 presidential address. *American Sociological Review, 54*(1), 1–16.

Gaspare, N. (1929). Enrico Ferri and criminal sociology. *Journal of Criminal Law and Criminology, 20*(2), 179–181.

Gunderson, A. (1995). *The environmental promise of democratic deliberation*. Madison: University of Wisconsin Press.

Gregory, J., & Miller, S. (1998). *Science in public: Communication, culture and credibility*. New York, NY: Plenum.

Hamilton, C. (2015). Towards a pedagogy of public criminology. *Enhancing Learning in the Social Sciences, 5*(2), 20–31.

Henry, S. (2005). Disciplinary hegemony meets interdisciplinary ascendancy: Can interdisciplinary/integrative studies survive and if so, how? *Issues in Integrative Studies, 23*, 1–37.

Inderbitzin, M. (2011). Public criminology. In *Oxford Bibliographies*. Oxford: Oxford University Press. Retrieved from www.oxfordbibliographies.com/view/document/obo-9780195396607/obo-9780195396607-0137.xml

Kelly, J. R., & Karau, S. J. (1999). Group decision making: The effects of initial preferences and time pressure. *Personality and Social Psychology Bulletin, 25*(11), 1342–1354.

Klein, J. T. (2013). The transdisciplinary moment(um). *Integral Review, 9*(2), 189–199.

Larsen, M., & Deisman, W. (2013). Notes on public criminology. *PoliceDeviance*. Retrieved from https://policedeviance.wordpress.com/public-criminology/

Lindeman, M. (2002). Opinion quality and policy preferences in deliberative research. In M. X. Delli Carpini, L. Huddy, & R. Shapiro (Eds.), *Research in micropolitics: Political decision-making, deliberation and participation* (pp. 195–221). Greenwich, CT: JAI Press.

Loader, I., & Sparks, R. (2008). What are we gonna do now? Revisiting the public roles of criminology. *Criminal Justice Matters, 72*(1), 18–19.

Loader, I., & Sparks, R. (2010a). What is to be done with public criminology? *Criminology and Public Policy, 9*(4), 771–781.

Loader, I., & Sparks, R. (2010b). *Public criminology*. London: Routledge.

Mendelberg, T. (2002). The deliberative citizen: Theory and evidence. In M. X. Delli Carpini, L. Huddy, & R. Shapiro (Eds.), *Research in micropolitics: Political decision-making, deliberation and participation* (pp. 151–193). Greenwich, CT: JAI Press.

Nicolescu, B. (2010). Transdisciplinarity: The hidden third, between the subject and object. *Human and Social Studies, 1*(l), 13–28.

Rock, P. (2014). The public faces of public criminology. *Criminology and Criminal Justice, 14*(4), 412–433.

Schwendinger, H., & Schwendinger, J. (1970). Defenders of order or guardians of human rights? *Issues in Criminology, 5*(2), 123–157.

Surette, R. (1998). *Media, crime and criminal justice: Images and realities* (2nd ed.). Belmont, CA: West/Wadsworth.

Sutherland, E.H. (1939). *Principles of criminology*. Philadelphia, PA: J. B. Lippincott & Co.

Sutherland, E.H. (1949). *White collar crime*. New York: Holt, Rinehart and Winston.

Swift, A., & White, S. (2008). Political theory, social science, and real politics. In D. Leopold & M. Sears (Eds.), *Political theory: Methods and approaches* (pp. 49–69). Oxford: Oxford University Press.

Tifft, L. L., & Sullivan, D. (2001). A needs-based, social harm definition of crime. In S. Henry & M. M. Lanier (Eds.), *What is crime? Controversies over the nature of crime and what to do about it* (pp. 179–206). Boulder, CO: Rowman & Littlefield.

Uggen, C., & Inderbitzin, M. (2010). Public criminologies. *Criminology & Public Policy, 9*(4), 725–750.

Winquist, J. R., & Larson, J. R. (1998). Information pooling: When it impacts group decision making. *Journal of Personality and Social Psychology, 74*(2), 371–377.

Wright, J. P., & DeLisi, M. (2017, Summer). What criminologists don't say, and why. *City Journal*. Retrieved from www.city-journal.org/html/what-criminologists-dont-say-and-why-15328.html

4
THE CHALLENGE OF TRANSFORMATIVE JUSTICE
Insurgent Knowledge and Public Criminology

Michelle Brown

Introduction: Imagining Public Criminology

In April 2018, the Legacy Museum and National Memorial for Peace and Justice opened deep in the American South of Montgomery, Alabama. The Legacy Museum, housed in a former slave warehouse in the heart of downtown, is the first of its kind in the United States, dedicated to exploring the U.S. legacy of slavery, racial terror, segregation, and, in an unprecedented move, mass incarceration. Similarly, the National Memorial for Peace and Justice, more popularly known as the lynching memorial, rises up on a hill just a short distance away. It is made up of over 800 six-foot monuments, suspended in air, that commemorate thousands of lynching victims, naming the counties and states where this racial terrorism took place. As you leave the memorial, a sculpture of young Black bodies encased in stone with hands up links the terror of the past to the brutality of contemporary policing.

Civil Rights lawyer Bryan Stevenson and the Equal Justice Initiative (EJI) are the authors of this project to memorialize the history of racial inequality and terror in the United States. They have visited hundreds of lynching sites, collected soil, and erected public markers in an effort to reshape the cultural landscape of the nation's memory. They continue to pull voices, images, and texts from the archives of slavery, Reconstruction, Jim Crow, and the Civil Rights eras. And they have studied the archives and prisons of mass incarceration. Only one criminologist is mentioned in the major timeline of the exhibition. His name is John DiIulio, a professor at Princeton University who coined the term "superpredator," predicting an unprecedented wave of violent racialized youth in the United States that never materialized. He later admitted that he was wrong, but not before his prediction, as well as the work of other criminologists, helped fuel a panic that led to dramatic increases in the sentencing and punishment of children, particularly Black and Brown children. I visited on the day that national protests against the detention and separation of immigrant families and children at the U.S.–Mexico border were taking place across the United States. Strange legacies of public criminology, indeed.

Public scholarship is imagined in a number of distinctive, often aspirational ways but always with a host of qualifications and references to its tragic "pitfalls," including the kind of dangerous intellectual grandstanding described above. An energetic and thoughtful debate in sociology and criminology has sought to remind us, against the performance aspects of public work, of the firmer connections between real-world social problems and the foundations of our disciplines—as well as the intellectual gap between (Burawoy, 2005; Clear, 2010; Loader & Sparks, 2011; Uggen & Inderbitzin, 2010). In this manner, public criminology is inevitably largely framed as a negative formation to the broader discipline of criminology, a necessary corrective or reconfiguration of the field itself—so much so that much of the dialogue about the public qualities of our work has been dominated by a "maybe we should, maybe we shouldn't, and if we do, then how?" approach. This suspension is captured quintessentially in the hanging question mark at the end of the key volume of criminologists Loader and Sparks (2011), *Public Criminology?*. Such discussions center upon anxieties related to relevance, but also necessarily, to the dangers of intervening in the kind of historical emergency the EJI seeks to address. In its worst forms, a reductive discussion, often about "taking sides," is configured against the kind of hypermasculine enactment that DiIulio performs, while in the backdrop, a much larger internal consensus marches to the beat of "keep calm and do better criminology." None of this (if ever) seems enough in the current moment.

I was struck at EJI by not only the complicity of criminology, but also by the manner in which criminology's role in producing important findings on mass incarceration was simply not a meaningful framework for understanding the history of the United States' largest crime: the ongoing racial terror of slavery and confinement. This kind of racial privilege can be accounted for a number of different ways. It is an important example of the distancing work criminology can be for those who are directly impacted by the carceral state (Piché, 2015). The obvious insularities and "hermetically sealed clusters" of the discipline—built around degrees, conferences, journals, and publications largely separate from the imaginary of crime and punishment—coincide, in Loader and Sparks's framing, "with a waning of influence over crime and penal policy that has come in recent decades to be driven more by popular emotion and political calculation than by reason and evidence" (2010, p. 772). The authors presciently link a longstanding criminological desire for intervention to a "heating up" of public crime discourse, one culminating in a volatile, unstable policy environment that "increasingly comes under the influence of mass media and 'public opinion' and at the mercy of ill-informed and sometimes actively whipped-up popular emotion" (p. 772).

In the wake of the Trump administration, Brexit, and the rise of the far right, Loader and Sparks' work now reads like prophetic guardedness. If a crisis was apparent then, just a few short years ago, the urgency of the current international political crisis reads as a calamity of legitimacy of new historic proportions for a variety of disciplines but with a heightened sense of accountability for criminology. As Piché (2015, p. 71) writes:

> If criminologists are concerned with trying to affect social change, how should they intervene at a time when there is notable resistance (e.g., people again taking to the streets in large numbers) to interpersonal and institutional violence, state impunity, and capitalism's excesses in Western democracies?

And, in the meantime, the directly impacted, like the staff at EJI, continue to organize and build their own histories, memorials, and survival strategies within and against the carceral state.

The nature of this public/criminology gap has a number of conventional preoccupations. It foundationally concerns breakdowns in a fairly unidirectional translation of criminological knowledge to a wider public audience and in a variety of forms. A particularly compelling way to think about public work is found in its construction as a unifying, holistic identity of the engaged criminologist, cutting across the pillars of academic life: research, teaching, and service. Uggen and Inderbitzin (2010) envision the fullness of this project as one that "embraces 'big ideas' and 'basic research,'" moves students out into communities by way of service-learning and internship opportunities, and constructs criminologists as expert witnesses, media consultants, and community-oriented researchers. No aspect of their work is untouched by the call to public-ness.

But the primary tendency has been to think of public criminology as policy-based applications. Public work is configured through a lexicon that centers "evidence-based" research, "applied," "practical" work, and a "disinterested," "objective" scholar who can self-moderate and astutely draw careful boundaries between the emotional life and biases of political engagement and the distanced rigor of an unaffected thinker. We hear disturbing echoes of Rock writing, "we all know ... how race and ethnicity became troublesome subjects for criminologists ... how some colleagues would not have any truck with the police or state" (2010, p. 757). Such work illuminates another focal point: advocacy for greater researcher presence within organizations that carry the power of the administration of justice, including police, courts, and penal institutions and a wide swathe of social service and nonprofit agencies. Public scholarship, in this manner, is often imagined as "bridging," but the substance and directionality of this joining is critically underdeveloped, begging the question of precisely what groups bear the spotlight (or the burden) of public criminology's focus.

One argument of this paper is that we might envision public work as just the opposite, working to undo the active role that criminology has often played as an intellectual prosthesis for the state, providing both material and ideological support and legitimacy for expansions and exercises of police power and mass imprisonment (Cohen, 1988; Seigel, 2018). Loader and Sparks (2010, 2011) advocate for the criminologist as "democratic underlaborer": a scholar who practices criminology first and foremost for the sake of generating rigorous knowledge "to be bearers and interpreters of knowledge" (2010, p. 778), but is also critical in their skepticism of the status quo and refusal to accept the ill-informed "common sense" ideologies that dominate public discussion, and commitment to theorizing alternative institutional arrangements. However, as Wacquant writes in his self-proclaimed "chastising" of Loader and Sparks, public criminology is romanticized in such a way in these accounts so as to ignore the fields of power within which the criminological domain exists, including:

> the neoliberal institutional ecology within which criminological knowledge is now being produced, validated and appropriated (or ignored) ... [which] at minimum include[s] discussion of the following items: the managerial makeover of the university and the generalized degradation of the conditions of employment, research and teaching on justice; increased dependency on external funding aimed at short-term technical issues; the growing weight of policy institutes on campus and the rise of "think tanks" off campus; the proliferation of paragovernmental outfits that foster and fabricate a bogus science plugged directly into the policymaking machine; the overt and covert intrusion of the concerns of politicians, themselves anxious to demonstrate their manly resolve to tame crime in synch with the demands and cycles of a media microcosm driven by the restless quest for audience ratings.
>
> *(Loader & Sparks, 2011, p. 442)*

The institutional contexts of public pursuits grow more challenging at the scene of the entrepreneurial, neoliberal university. Many of us have worked within various forms of public criminology for years only to find that our efforts have reified and reproduced the forms of power and sites of state violence our own research directs us to challenge (Brown & Schept, 2017). As Lumsden and Goode (2018) note in their research on efforts to work with police departments, the risks for co-optation are strong. Their findings navigate how police negotiate research roles in terms of their own needs and strategic priorities with "theoretical and methodological agendas ... likely to be set by the organization and while being researched" (2018, p. 252).

Furthermore, and echoing the concerns of feminist criminologists (Carlen, 2011; Nelund, 2014; Potter, 2013), the authors add that "the debate, thus far concerning 'public criminology' has been macho and of a relatively non-applied nature" (Lumsden & Goode, 2018, p. 244), eagerly intervening, generating performative discussion and controversy, and challenging public opinion and political discourse—all while warning of public intellectual overstepping and engineered outcomes with the other.

A prescription for action as non-action takes shape in such a space. Public criminology is not simply concerned with a kind of disciplinary insularity, but, even in its best forms, suffers from a kind of insularity itself, modeled after a sociological debate with similar flaws. One way in which to remedy this is through a more rigorous framing of advocacy, intervention, activism, and purpose, doing so through lenses of social justice (Carrabine, Lee, & South, 2000; Cohen, 1988; Currie, 2007).

Insurgent Knowledge and Activist Scholarship: Criminology on the Periphery

> I know only one criminological school which can claim to have always adopted a public stance. I am thinking of abolitionism ..."
>
> —*Vincenzo Ruggiero (2012, p. 157)*

Debates about public criminology, while important, have proceeded largely without engaging broader and deeper intellectual traditions of social justice. This has meant that criminologists have missed the work of a different kind of far more pervasive public criminology, one that occurs without any need for the construct itself. Other kinds of criminology and broader scholarship, quite simply, do the work. This is apparent, as one example, in how Rafter and I (2013) imagined the work of popular criminology, where film and media serve as a public space in which to work through meanings that enter collective memory, a site from which cultural actors assume, demand, and refuse responsibility in the representation of violence—a political and ethical encounter. In it, we view culture as an ever-present space of contestation in which popular criminological theorizing and meaning-making occurs.

But in this piece, I am pointing to a more engaged commitment that takes up other points of intersection, historical traditions, alternative questions, and urgent needs: A new wave of research grounded in insurgent knowledges and activist scholarship from various areas of thought.[1] This work spans race and ethnic studies, political and cultural geography, American Studies, critical prison and policing studies, and is in close dialogue with grassroots contexts that seek to disrupt the criminal justice system (Berger, Kaba, & Stein, 2017; Kaba, 2012). Its vanguard is largely made up of junior scholars whose vantage points emerge from Black feminist, anti-colonialist, Marxist, and queer theoretical horizons. Against institutional and structural disincentives (time, resources, discrimination, doxing, death threats, tenure denials, and career-ending efforts by their own departments, universities and the political right), these scholars pursue a public research that materializes in blogs, regular media columns, an active social media presence, and public statements and opinion pieces circulated across leading news sites. They do not expect nor are they waiting for their work to be recognized as teaching, service, or scholarship. Foundationally interdisciplinary, they may pull their focal points from multiple fields and disciplines, but they share commonality in their analysis of criminal justice and criminology through the vectors of racialization, intersectionality, Black radical study, and the combining of local and global lenses. As particularly celebrated examples, one need only think of the work of Rutgers University professor Brittney Cooper, co-founder of the popular blog Crunk Feminist Collective, or Yale University professor Claudia Rankine, author of the bestseller, *Citizen: An American Lyric*. But, there are many others at most universities.

In short, they pursue a kind of participatory research that reimagines "public" work and "publics" altogether and in an altogether new mediatized political and public landscape. Ruggiero (2012, p. 157) writes that public criminologists "seem to seek the help of experts working in adjacent areas and, while begging for their benevolence, try to improve the lives of others, namely nonexpert actors," what he calls a "missionary and paternalistic criminology, which is prepared to stand by the underdogs as far as they remain such." This approach not only makes little sense to insurgent scholars, but also leaves them vulnerable and unprotected by their own departments. Their work necessarily extends into the terrain of studying, researching, and organizing alongside of those directly impacted by the carceral state because, quite simply, they too are directly affected. While their work comes with great risk, it also is generative: their focus on the practical and emancipatory aspects of social struggle have led to burgeoning lecture circuits, new networks and solidarities, reinvented workshops and convergences, overflowing conference panel attendance, more publicly visible publications and media presence, and, finally and perhaps most importantly, organizing—so much so that prison and police abolition, once thought impossible, has entered the mainstream news cycle in the United States (Berger et al., 2017).

As criminologists Henne and Shah (2015, p. 105) make clear, it has been critical race scholars who "question the objective neutrality upon which much positivist social science rests, arguing that it masks how Whiteness underpins the normative purview of research design and findings." Here, we see how criminologists as "researchers can both neutralize and deny the multitude of ways that White privilege becomes articulated within their work—and to their benefit" (p. 106). Public criminology is a space in which, as with mainstream and critical criminologies, "Whiteness comes to shape approaches to the study of crime and findings about crime and deviance" (p. 105). At the center of these claims we continue to hear echoes of Hill Collins's haunting words:

> I found my training as a social scientist inadequate to the task of studying the subjugated knowledge of a Black women's standpoint … where we have long had to use alternative ways to create independent self-definitions and self-valuations and to rearticulate them through our own specialists … alternative ways of producing and validating knowledge.
>
> *(Hill Collins, 1990, p. 252)*

As critical race and intersectional studies (e.g., Potter, 2013) make clear, one cannot study power and oppression through the conventional tools or lenses of the past; they require different approaches, with attention not simply to vantage points but embodiment, attention to interlocking systems of oppression and how they generate everyday forms of resistance, and a clear commitment to accountability in knowledge claims that is interventionist at its core. And even as this knowledge resides in the body, it is never primarily about identity; it is about how social structures and knowledge production make certain identities the consequence of and the vehicle for vulnerability. When knowledge, including feminism and antiracism, are non-intersectional, they are not just neutral; they wind up reinforcing those very oppressions, adding up to failures that undermine our collective political capacities to shape more robust and inclusive sets of coalitions around social justice (Goodman, 2015).

As such, and with race as only one example of a vector of analysis in a much larger matrix of oppression, public criminology has been a myopic space from which to think about change, intervention, and transformation. In such contexts, we necessarily witness the insurrection of knowledge, the return and reappearance of what people know at a local level, those disqualified knowledges, following Foucault (1997), that made critique possible in the first place. Butler (2001, pp. 4–5), following this analysis of critique, insists

> Desubjugation happens when a mode of existence is risked which is unsupported by ... the regime of truth ... where one asks about the limits of ways of knowing because one has already run up against a crisis within the epistemological field in which one lives.

Insurgent knowledge is lived experience. It can therefore only act against the definitive public feature of criminology: the discipline's interdependence with the state agencies that comprise "criminal justice" and its close proximity to its prosthetic institutions (e.g., policing, prisons, detention, etc.).

Insurgent scholarship, in this way, is focused singularly on the transformative. Its constructs have emerged from a combination of activist scholarship and grassroots organizing searching for alternatives to standard criminal justice and criminological understandings of justice. Take, for instance, the term transformative justice. As with much of abolition practice, the concept derives from a lexicon developed largely by Black feminist survivor activists organizing on the ground in incredibly challenging contexts against gender-based violence. The California nonprofit Generation Five, dedicated to ending child sexual abuse, is generally credited by organizers for providing a usable definition of this practice: "Transformative justice [is] a liberatory approach to violence ... [which] seeks safety and accountability without relying on alienation, punishment, or State or systemic violence, including incarceration or policing" (Kaba, 2012; generationFIVE, 2017). Their work alerts us to a key way in which to understand the division between public criminology and the transformative: what distinguishes state managers, security advisors, media consultants, and expert witnesses from the transformative work of insurgent scholars who seek to dismantle the "criminal legal system," the carceral state, and end "mass criminalization"?[2]

As historian and American Studies scholar Robin D. G. Kelley writes in his volume *Freedom Dreams* (2002, p. 8), "Social movements generate new knowledge, new theories, new questions. The most radical ideas often grow out of a concrete intellectual engagement with the problems of aggrieved populations confronting systems of oppression." In this conceptualization, freedom and emancipation, not simply control and confinement, are essential conduits of pedagogic and research strategies. They require spaces from which organizers, educators, students, and community members who are struggling for progressive social change can gather and critically engage with historical materials that are often overlooked from earlier periods of political history and struggle. This is not simply a unidirectional extension of the university or a criminology department's "engagement" or "service" but a freedom school model. As Kelley (2016) explains, the freedom schools of the Civil Rights era "didn't want equal opportunity in a burning house; they wanted to build a new house."

Such work foregrounds the conscious production of understandings that challenge dominant or hegemonic "common sense" within, and about, various struggles. The terms specific to this mode of study are grounded knowledges rooted in mutual learning, participatory research, and solidarity. Insurgent research is relational, seeking to build enduring relationships of mutual interdependence. It focuses upon community building, witnessing and solidarity; it resides at the level of grassroots community action, not institutions or power elites; it merges highly intimate aspects of our lives—family, community, values, ethics, and commitments to change—with our research projects and pursuits. It pushes back against extraction research (Gaudry, 2011), the kind of colonizing work that removes knowledge from its immediate context, presents it to specialized groups of outsiders, and ignores the community needs from which it originates. Instead, it explicitly employs the worldviews of the directly impacted with the mandate that knowledge creation is for and by these insiders—that responsibility lies with the community and its participants (Gaudry, 2011, p. 114). It is, in this manner, the most rigorous of methodological approaches. Simplified versions of stories of oppression and oppression as variables are far more likely to reify neoliberal orders. In the carceral era, broad strokes, generalizations, and interpretive skills that are uninformed by the knowledges of the directly impacted do not simply erase lives. They reinforce their premature deaths.

Insurgency allows us to think through the dense articulation of global and local forces in relation to how scholars "think and act themselves into politics" (Holston, 2008, p. 23). Scholarship, like citizenship, becomes uncertain and emergent when intellectuals negotiate neoliberal forces in education and knowledge through ascribed identities of race, class, gender, sexuality, and beyond. It is catalytic, generative of new knowledges as "insurgence describes a process that is an acting counter, a counterpolitics, that destabilizes the present and renders it fragile, defamiliarizing the coherence with which it usually presents itself," using elements of the past, a bubbling up as opposed to a top down presence (Holston, 2008, p. 34). This is an active defamiliarization of what is taken for granted, the unexamined assumptions that accompany the status quo, in an effort to locate the conditions where projects of social justice have a better chance to take root and flourish. In this shift, "as dominant formulations of inclusion wear thin and the inequalities they cover become intolerable," (Holston, 2008, p. 275), a different kind of "heating up" takes place. "Increasingly exhausted," Holston explains, "incivility appears necessary as a public idiom of deep democratic change" (2008, p. 275).

Constructions of incivility lay claim to barriers against transformation. To unthink police and prisons is politically and structurally ascribed as rude business. Modeled in dialogue with abolition, insurgency tows a line, pushing back perpetually against non-reformist reforms, appropriation, and co-optation. It is a stoic politics of refusal that relentlessly reminds us of what foundational forms of violence make up the institutions of criminal justice. And it does so in order to remind us of the conditions of possibility for social, not criminal, justice, for emancipatory projects we have yet to know. The insurgent aspects of abolition privilege elements of disidentification (with crime, with the state, with naturalized, institutional meanings and assumptions); they value generativity (not simply reactive or defensive, deconstructive or destructive but critically practiced in thinking through alternative configurations); and they give primacy to locally determined practices that, regardless of their seeming inconsequentiality, alter the landscape of criminal justice. As McDowell writes:

> My use of the word "insurgency" is inspired by scholar activist Dylan Rodriguez's (2007, p. 16) call for a "politics that pushes beyond the defensive maneuvering of resistance." What our current political movements need, Rodriguez argues, are "grassroots pedagogies of radical disidentification with the state [...] that reorients a progressive identification with the creative possibilities of insurgency" (2007, p. 16, emphases in original). In contradistinction to carceral safety then, insurgent safety names locally determined anticapitalist ethics and practices that work within and against the racist carceral state to build a world where safety is not predicated on banishment, mass criminalization, or policing in any form.
>
> *(McDowell, 2019, pp. 8–9)*

Conclusion: Public Work in the Carceral Era

Much of the work discussed here takes shape against the intensification and the expansion of the carceral state, a formation that captures the cumulative effects of the interactions and processes of the entire justice system. This crisis is apparent in the very efforts to name the moment as we move past mass imprisonment to more specific usages. As Beckett (2018, p. 37) writes, "the term 'carceral state'" works

> to call attention to the expanding role of penal institutions, broadly defined, in the lives of the poor and in communities of color (e.g., Hernández et al., 2015). Scholarship showing that penal intervention matters even absent incarceration provides support for this conceptual framework.

Another way to think about this, however, is via the transformational knowledges of emergent subjects and insurgent encounters. For those directly impacted, "Love and rage constitute the organizing force behind this gathering coordinated during expanding wars. Love for community, freedom, and justice, for the incarcerated and for the "disappeared"—for those dying or surviving in war zones" (James, 2013, p. 208). Criminology, Ward (2015, p. 299) adds, is guilty of a "'slow violence', where victimization is attritional, dispersed, and hidden. Criminology is not merely compromised here—or limited in theoretical and empirical reach—but complicit, contributing to under-regulated racial violence rationalized in large part by the criminalization of race." As Black feminist Joy James insists in *Beloved Community* (2013), knowledge and organizing work is founded in resistance to violent and premature social and biological death, one in which no other space of existence—let alone academic role—is possible.

For those scholars and academics distanced from this lived experience, other forces are at work in the display of expertise. As feminist philosopher Nora Berenstain writes, "The nature of privilege is that it comes with a credibility surplus" (2016, p. 582). Expertise, its own kind of disciplinary apparatus, is more easily granted to some than others and in a manner that reflects the architecture of power. Much of the work of public scholarship on social and racial justice is designed to confound the institutional parameters of knowledge production and establish ways in which to confront oppressive ways of knowing. Berenstain offers a concise statement of the stakes of accountability in her elaboration of the term epistemic exploitation, a form of knowledge extraction at the heart of major disciplinary formations like philosophy, but also psychology, sociology, and criminology. Epistemic exploitation is related to forms of hermeneutical injustice where "the conceptual resources necessary to do the educational work already exist but the dominantly situated choose not to avail themselves of these resources" (Berenstain, 2016, p. 583). It is a kind of "willful hermeneutical ignorance" (p. 583) that reflects the "tendency of the dominantly situated to dismiss epistemic resources such as 'date rape' or 'heteronormativity' that make sense of the experiences and phenomena that are primarily discernible to the marginally situated" (Berenstain, 2016, p. 585). In its many forms, including White supremacy, patriarchy, carceral feminism, and others,

> It maintains structures of oppression by centering the needs and desires of dominant groups and exploiting the emotional and cognitive labor of members of marginalized groups who are required to do the unpaid and often unacknowledged work of providing information, resources, and evidence of oppression to privileged persons who demand it—and who benefit from those very oppressive systems about which they demand to be educated.
>
> *(Berenstain, 2016, p. 570)*

For the subjects of the carceral state who are also its insurgent scholars, criminology is only usable as a site of fugitive study, where, paraphrasing the famous adage of Harney and Moten (2013), one can only sneak in and steal what one can. Or, as Gilmore (2011, p. 263) writes, "Organize. Infiltrate what already exists and innovate what doesn't." In any discussion of public intellectual work, we have hard choices to make. But if we truly seek an intellectual life that is both public and emancipatory, as James writes, then necessarily,

> We seek spaces that constitute their own sites of struggle. So we leave academia to make connections with collectivities within which our very elitism is challenged and devalued. As radical rather than revolutionary subjects, we accept our engagement with the academic institutions while asserting our responsibility to be more than mere performers. Hence we offer ourselves, and encourage our students, to labor for justice.
>
> *(James, 2013, p. 221)*

Notes

1 See, for example, Camp (2016), Camp and Heatherton (2016), Choudry and Vally (2017), Collins (1990), Gilmore (2008, 2011), Johnson and Lubin (2017), Juris & Khasnabish, (2013), Kelley (2016), Koirala Azad & Fuentes (2009), McDowell (2019), Sudbury and Okazawa-Rey (2015), Schept (2015), Seigel (2018), and Vargas (2008).
2 What this work means at the level of practice is one that continues to be fleshed out across collectives nationwide, including Critical Resistance, CARA, Creative Interventions, Project South, Southerners on New Ground, INCITE! Women of Color Against Violence, the Bay Area TJ Collaborative, SpiritHouse, Project NIA and many more.

References

Beckett, K. (2018). The politics, promise, and peril of criminal justice reform in the context of mass incarceration. *Annual Review of Criminology*, *1*, 235–259.
Berenstain, N. (2016). Epistemic exploitation. *Ergo*, *3*(22), 569–590.
Berger, D., Kaba, M., & Stein, D. (2017, August 24). What abolitionists do. *Jacobin*. Retrieved from www.jacobinmag.com/2017/08/prison-abolition-reform-mass-incarceration
Brown, M., & Rafter, N. (2013). Genocide films, public criminology, collective memory. *British Journal of Criminology*, *53*(6), 1017–1032.
Brown, M., & Schept, J. (2017). New abolition, criminology, and a critical carceral studies. *Punishment & Society*, *19*(4), 440–462.
Burawoy, M. (2005). For public sociology. *American Sociological Review*, *70*(1), 4–28.
Butler, J. (2001, May). What is critique? An essay on Foucault's virtue. *Transversal*. Retrieved from http://eipcp.net/transversal/0806/butler/en
Camp, J. T. (2016). *Incarcerating the crisis: Freedom struggles and the rise of the neoliberal state*. Berkeley, CA: University of California Press.
Camp, J. T., & Heatherton, C. (Eds.). (2016). *Policing the planet: Why the policing crisis led to black lives matter*. New York: Verso Books.
Carlen, P. (2011). Criminological knowledge: Doing critique, doing politics. In S. Hall & S. Winlow (Eds.), *New directions in criminological theory* (pp. 35–47). London: Routledge.
Carrabine, E., Lee, M., & South, N. (2000). Social wrongs and human rights in late modern Britain: Social exclusion, crime control, and prospects for a public criminology. *Social Justice*, *27*(2), 193–211.
Choudry, A., & Vally, S. (2017). *Reflections on knowledge, learning and social movements: History's schools*. London: Routledge.
Clear, T. R. (2010). Editorial introduction to "Public Criminologies". *Criminology & Public Policy*, *9*(4), 721–724.
Cohen, S. (1988). *Against criminology*. New Brunswick, NJ: Transaction Books.
Collins, P. H. (1990). Black feminist thought in the matrix of domination. In *Feminist thought: Knowledge, consciousness, and the politics of empowerment* (pp. 221–238). Boston, MA: Unwin Hyman.
Currie, E. (2007). Against marginality: Arguments for a public criminology. *Theoretical Criminology*, *11*(2), 175–190.
Foucault, M. (1997). *The politics of truth*. (S. Lotringer & L. Hochroth, Eds.). New York: Semiotext(e).
Gaudry, A. J. (2011). Insurgent research. *Wicazo Sa Review*, *26*(1), 113–136.
generationFIVE. (2017). *A transformative justice handbook*. Retrieved May 15, 2018 from http://www.generationfive.org/wp-content/uploads/2017/06/Transformative-Justice-Handbook.pdf.

Gilmore, R. W. (2008). Forgotten places and the seeds of grassroots planning. In C. Hale (Ed.), *Engaging contradictions: Theory, politics, and methods of activist scholarship* (pp. 31–61). Berkeley, CA: University of California Press.

Gilmore, R. W. (2011). What is to be done? *American Quarterly, 63*(2), 245–265.

Goodman, A. (2015, December 16). Pt. 2: Black women at the intersection: Holtzclaw case links #BlackLivesMatter & anti-rape struggles. *Democracy Now!*. Retrieved from www.democracynow.org/2015/12/16/pt_2_black_women_at_the

Harney, S., & Moten, F. (2013). *The undercommons: Fugitive planning and black study*. Wivenhoe: Minor Compositions.

Henne, K., & Shah, R. (2015). Unveiling white logic in criminological research: An intertextual analysis. *Contemporary Justice Review, 18*(2), 105–120.

Hernández, K. L., Muhammad, K. G., & Ann Thompson, H. (2015). Introduction: Constructing the carceral state. *The Journal of American History, 102*(1), 18–24.

Holston, J. (2008). *Insurgent citizenship: Disjunctions of democracy and modernity in Brazil*. Princeton, NJ: Princeton University Press.

James, J. (2013). *Seeking the beloved community: A feminist race reader*. Albany, NY: State University of New York Press.

Johnson, G. T., & Lubin, A. (Eds.). (2017). *Futures of Black radicalism*. New York: Verso Books.

Juris, J. S., & Khasnabish, A. (2013). *Insurgent encounters: Transnational activism, ethnography, and the political*. Durham, NC: Duke University Press.

Kaba, M. (2012). Transformative justice. Retrieved May 15, 2018 from www.usprisonculture.com/blog/transformative-justice/

Kelley, R. D. (2002). *Freedom dreams: The black radical imagination*. Boston, MA: Beacon Press.

Kelley, R. D. (2016). Black study, black struggle. *Boston Review, 7*. http://bostonreview.net/forum/robin-d-g-kelley-black-study-black-struggle.

Koirala Azad, S., & Fuentes, E. (2009). Introduction: Activist scholarship—possibilities and constraints of participatory action research. *Social Justice, 36*(4), 1–5.

Loader, I., & Sparks, R. (2010). What is to be done with public criminology? *Criminology & Public Policy, 9*(4), 771–781.

Loader, I., & Sparks, R. (2011). *Public criminology?* London: Routledge.

Lumsden, K., & Goode, J. (2018). Public criminology, reflexivity and the enterprise university: Experiences of research, knowledge transfer work and co-option with police forces. *Theoretical Criminology, 22*(2), 243–257.

McDowell, M. G. (2019). Insurgent safety: Theorizing alternatives to state protection. *Theoretical Criminology, 23*(1), 43–59.

Nelund, A. (2014). Troubling publics: A feminist analysis of public criminology. *Radical Criminology, 4*, 67–84.

Piché, J. (2015). Assessing the boundaries of public criminology: On what does (not) count. *Social Justice, 42*(2), 70–90.

Potter, H. (2013). Intersectional criminology: Interrogating identity and power in criminological research and theory. *Critical Criminology, 21*(3), 305–318.

Rock, P. (2010). Comment on "public criminologies". *Criminology & Public Policy, 9*(4), 751–767.

Rodriguez, D. (2007). Warfare and the terms of engagement. In Southern California Library (Ed.), *Without Fear: Claiming Safe Communities without Sacrificing Ourselves* (pp. 9–18). Los Angeles, CA: Southern California Library for Social Studies and Research.

Ruggiero, V. (2012). How public is public criminology? *Crime, Media, Culture, 8*(2), 151–160.

Schept, J. (2015). *Progressive punishment: Job loss, jail growth, and the neoliberal logic of carceral expansion*. New York: New York University Press.

Seigel, M. (2018). *Violence work: State power and the limits of police*. Durham, NC: Duke University Press.

Sudbury, J., & Okazawa-Rey, M. (2015). *Activist scholarship: Antiracism, feminism, and social change*. New York: Routledge.

Uggen, C., & Inderbitzin, M. (2010). Public criminologies. *Criminology & Public Policy, 9*(4), 725–749.

Vargas, J. H. C. (2008). Activist scholarship: Limits and possibilities in times of black genocide. In C. R. Hale (Ed.), *Engaging contradictions: Theory, politics, and methods of activist scholarship* (pp. 62–87). Berkeley, CA: University of California Press.

Wacquant, L. (2011). From "public criminology" to the reflexive sociology of criminological production and consumption: A Review of *Public criminology?* by Ian Loader and Richard Sparks (London: Routledge, 2010). *British Journal of Criminology, 51*(2), 438–448.

Ward, G. (2015). The slow violence of state organized race crime. *Theoretical Criminology, 19*(3), 299–314.

5

ARTICULATION OF LIBERATION CRIMINOLOGIES AND PUBLIC CRIMINOLOGIES

Advancing a Countersystem Approach and Decolonization Paradigm

Biko Agozino and Kimberley Ducey

Introduction

Ever since Michael Burawoy presented *public sociologies* as the theme of the 2004 American Sociology Association's (ASA) annual general meeting when he served as ASA president, talk of *public sociology* has been all the rage among sociologists. Some criminologists, via *public criminologies*, have come to embrace many of the positions and themes championed by Burawoy. By public sociology, Burawoy (2005) means research in which practitioners engage directly in dialogue with some public, while remaining free to oppose a public's perspectives. Notably, in his 2004 address, Burawoy did not assess the destructive nature of key instrumental positivistic "true and tested methods" that overshadow professional sociology (2005).

For a myriad of reasons, we deeply appreciate Burawoy's vision, including his critical neo-Marxist perspective, his view that sociology has the potential to protect civil society against the marketplace and the nation-state, his acknowledgement that at times sociologists have been preoccupied with government and market concerns, and his recognition that in other parts of the world sociologists tend to lean towards critical and liberation-oriented goals (even though this is certainly not the trend in the United States). We especially welcome his optimism for a progressive public sociology that might ultimately find root in the United States, most likely generated by civil society organizations and social movements: "It will come when public sociology captures the imagination of sociologists," he said in his presidential address, "when sociologists recognize public sociology as important in its own right with its own rewards, and when sociologists then carry it forward as a social movement beyond the academy" (Burawoy, 2005, p. 25).

While we are indebted to Burawoy and to other scholars (e.g., Uggen & Inderbitzin, 2010) for their discussion of public criminology's connections to public sociology, our conception of liberation criminology more closely follows the approach outlined by Agger in *Public Sociology* (Agger, 2007). As Feagin, Vera, and Ducey (2014, p. 38) observed, "Nowhere in his presidential address does Burawoy acknowledge the earlier work of Ben Agger. This may be because Agger's public sociology is centrally a *critical* liberation sociology." As we show here, Agozino's decolonization paradigm corresponds well to Agger's ideas, as both models are unwaveringly faithful to progressive societal change—the kind of transformations expressed in the work of many progressive criminologists and sociologists.

Since 2004, the ASA has established a committee on public sociology and intermittently underscored the concept on its website. And yet, there is negligible indication of a substantial move away from instrumental positivism in mainstream sociology journals, educational curricula, or in the discipline more generally. Instrumental positivism and conventional quantitative methods dominate in criminology too. Importantly, Loader and Sparks (2008) have discussed the contradictory "successful failure" in criminology, in which the academic field of criminology is flourishing, while criminological expertise is generally sidelined in the public domain. Just as Agger's (2007) research on sociology led him to conclude that the discipline is still "training" younger sociologists "to be careerist civil servants and not ... public and activist intellectuals," the discipline of criminology is primarily training its next generation in the same manner.

This chapter puts forth a rethinking of criminology that is centered around liberation—one that we argue was pioneered by W. E. B. Du Bois and Ida B. Wells-Barnett in their public campaigns against lynching at a time that hundreds of laws against lynching failed to pass in the U.S. congress due to opposition to such laws mainly by Democratic Party members pejoratively called the Dixiecrats. Wells-Barnett started her campaign against lynching in 1892, but 46 years later Du Bois and the NAACP were still raising public awareness in opposition to lynching by flying a flag to proclaim that someone "was lynched today" (Karaim, 2012, pp. 50–55). The liberation criminology approach against injustice started with the struggle for the abolition of slavery and continued in the anti-colonial struggles around the world, the civil rights movement in the United States, the women's right to vote and to choose medical care movement, the anti-war movement, the anti-apartheid movement, the struggle against mass incarceration and the war on drugs, the struggle for immigration rights and for the abolition of capital punishment, and the struggle for same-sex relations.

We begin with a brief introduction to liberation sociology. Included in this account is the pioneering work of fourteenth-century Arab liberation criminologist and sociologist Ibn Khaldoun, as well as a discussion of the emergence of Eurocentric sociology four hundred years later. In the process, we show how European sociology has since its inception simultaneously contained the seeds of radical and conservative thought. We next turn to the question of "What is liberation criminology?" Drawing on *Liberation Sociology* (2014), we offer an overview of what constitutes liberation criminology and provide a comparison of the two emancipatory frameworks. We present several examples of liberation criminologists, including African American scholar-activists Du Bois and Wells-Barnett. Finally, we turn our attention to Agozino's decolonization paradigm in criminology, offering historical examples of White male elite sanctioned violence to illustrate this important countersystem model.

From New Catechism to a Countersystem Approach

Khaldoun (1332–1406) pioneered sociological research in North Africa as a methodology for explaining the cyclical conquest of city dwellers by rugged desert bands of warriors. Eurocentric sociology emerged four hundred years later, as seen in the work of France's Henri de Saint-Simone (1760–1825). Saint-Simone's work was based on the premise that the application of scientific principles could advance the pursuit of human happiness, a concept echoed in the U.S. Declaration of Independence (1776). Auguste Comte (1798–1857), who would become widely known as the father of sociology, followed in the footsteps of Saint-Simone, his teacher. His work emerged in stark contrast to the vision of continuous cycles of revolutionary change theorized by Khaldoun. Notwithstanding Comte's rejection of many progressive Enlightenment ideas, he was undoubtedly a child of the Enlightenment, and, as such, he believed in the power of reason to make sense of the world. Outlining his philosophies in the 1820s, he caught the attention of British philosopher, political economist, and civil servant John Stuart Mill (1806–1873). Mill unreservedly endorsed Comte's "positive philosophy."[1] As Comte (1965, p. 1332) saw it, he had discovered a fundamental law of the stages "through which the human mind has to pass, in every kind of speculation."

Comte believed sociology would become the ultimate science—what he termed *the queen of the sciences*. The discipline started as an ambitious science of reform and social harmony, with Comte rejecting the Enlightenment's idea that society should be changed to allow for the steady perfection of all people. He emphasized instead human adjustment to natural social laws and perceived individualism as a disease of Western civilization. For Comte, social order depended on moral consensus. Perhaps unsurprisingly then, the activist social scientist Karl Marx (1818–1883) noted that Comte was notorious among

> Paris workers as the prophet of personal dictatorship in politics, capitalist rule in political economy, hierarchy in all spheres of human activity, even in science, the creator of a new catechism, a new Pope, and new saints to replace old ones.
> *(Quoted in Manuel & Manuel, 1979, p. 717)*

Unlike Comte, Marx did not seek to anticipate the world for all time. Rather, he emphasized that social forces have the potential to bring about revolutionary change. In the spring of 1845, Marx (1962, p. 405) famously observed, "[T]he philosophers have only interpreted the world, in various ways; the point, however, is to change it." Criminologists concerned with human emancipation and genuine liberty-and-justice should take seriously this observation.

The overriding aim of liberation sociology is to research the social world and to promote the expansion of human rights, participatory democracy, and social justice. All liberation sociologists thus adopt what Sjoberg termed a *countersystem approach*. Feagin, Vera, and Ducey (2014, p. 1; see also Sjoberg & Cain, 1971) explain:

> A countersystem analyst consciously tries to step outside her or his own society to better view and critically assess it. A countersystem perspective often envisions a society where people have empathetic compassion for human suffering and a real commitment to reducing that suffering. It envisions research and analysis relevant to everyday human problems, particularly those of the socially oppressed. The countersystem standard is broader than that of a particular society or nation–state. Using a strong human rights standard, such as the UN Universal Declaration of Human Rights, the liberation social scientist accents broader societal and international contexts and assesses existing social institutions against a vision of more humane social arrangements.

Echoing the countersystem approach, Marx traced the tragic and farcical repetition of the history of oppression and revolution from communal societies, to slave societies, to feudalism, to capitalism. He concluded that the logic of modern capitalistic societies "made injustice, alienation, and exploitation inevitabilities rather than contingencies" (Wolin, 1969, p. 1080). But Marx also believed that just as enslaved persons would emancipate themselves, industrial wage slaves, and peasants would self-emancipate from injustice, alienation, and exploitation.[2]

In keeping with a liberation criminology perspective, with its concern for establishing more just and egalitarian societies, Marx opposed the death penalty because it was applied disproportionately to the poor and called for the abolition of vagrancy laws. He also recognized that European imperialist slavery systems formed the basis of the industrialized capitalistic system, writing,

> Direct slavery is as much the pivot upon which our present-day industrialism turns as are machinery, credit, etc. Without slavery there would be no cotton, without cotton there would be no modern industry. It is slavery which has given value to the colonies, it is the colonies which have created world trade, and world trade is the necessary condition for large-scale machine industry. ... [W]ipe North America off the map and you will get anarchy, the complete decay of trade and modern civilization. But to do away with slavery would be to wipe America off the map.
>
> (Letter to Pavel V. Annenkov, cited in Anderson, 2010, pp. 1157–1158)

African American scholar and human rights activist Du Bois supported the Marxist paradigm. He, like Marx, remarked that on the "bent and broken backs" of enslaved Black workers and other workers of color were laid "the founding stones of modern industry" (Du Bois, 1935, pp. 342–345). Du Bois, who wrote his doctoral dissertation on the suppression of the African slave trade, explained that the trans-Atlantic slave trade was restricted, and ultimately banned, by the White elite for fear that those enslaved might be so numerous as to successfully overthrow the White plantocracy (slavocracy). Du Bois also legendarily questioned why White workers failed to unite with Black workers against capitalist oppression, concluding that the White elite used a strategy of racial divide-and-conquer. White workers took lower than necessary salaries in exchange for a "public and psychological wage" of Whiteness (Du Bois, 1935, pp. 700–701), which established non-elite Whites as part of the prevailing racial hierarchy. Whites, for example, were admitted to public areas (e.g., segregated parks) and gatherings, from which racialized people were barred, supposedly because they were stereotyped as more crime-prone; whereas, poor whites also pay a hefty price for the authoritarian populism of white supremacy (see also, Agozino, 2018; Roediger, 1991).

What Is Liberation Criminology?

Drawing on *Liberation Sociology* (2014), we suggest that liberation criminologists share five common characteristics with liberation sociologists:

1. A liberation criminologist is staunchly committed to genuine democracy and liberty-and-justice.
2. A liberation criminologist represents the concerns and interests of those communities (e.g., women, racialized people, immigrants, the poor) who have historically and contemporarily been excluded from the political interests of the elite, and from the interests of most mainstream criminologists.
3. A decision to practice liberation criminology is a decision to take sides with the oppressed. Accordingly, a liberation criminologist is an activist.
4. A liberation criminologist does not neglect the experiences, realities, and concerns of those who are socially marginalized and oppressed.
5. A liberation criminologist is generally a major irritant for power elites.

Table 5.1 provides a comparison of the two emancipatory frameworks that underline the chapter.

Like liberation criminologist and sociologist Stanley Cohen, our preference is for a "skeptical" study of crime, deviance, and control as opposed to a statistically framed correctionalism. And, like Cohen, we are concerned about the ever-extending reach of the state into everyday life. In fact, Cohen's *Visions of Social Control* (1985), a dystopian analysis of how even seemingly nonthreatening reforms in the name of "the community" can give rise to even more pungent social controls, haunts us. Thus, like Cohen's *States of Denial: Knowing about Atrocities and Suffering* (2001), we combine our expertise in criminology

Table 5.1 A Comparison of Liberation Criminology and Liberation Sociology[3]

Liberation criminology	Liberation sociology
Concerned with establishing a more just and egalitarian criminal justice system and genuinely democratic laws.	Concerned with establishing more just and egalitarian societies.
Using a broader human rights standard, such as the UN's Universal Declaration of Human Rights, measures current criminal justice policies and intuitions against an image of more humane social standards.	Using a broader human rights standard, such as the UN's Universal Declaration of Human Rights, measures current social institutions against an image of more humane social standards.
Recognizes that the most reputable criminology is one that takes a position of apparent neutrality and is typically unmindful to its moral and political effects on humans and non-human animals.	Recognizes that the most reputable sociology is one that takes a position of apparent neutrality and is typically unmindful to its moral and political effects on other humans and non-human animals.
Liberation criminology takes an explicit moral position, which includes empathy for victims of an unjust criminal justice system, while liberation criminologists work for their emancipation.	Liberation sociology takes an explicit moral position, which includes empathy for victims of oppression, while liberation sociologists work for their emancipation.
Critically examines orthodox criminology as a "scientific discipline" that too often takes for granted state definitions of crime and criminals.	Critically examines orthodox sociology and promotes a self-reflective sociology that scrutinizes the current academic environment.
Engages in research to expose crimes of imperialism, colonialism, racism, sexism, transphobia, ableism, ageism, heterosexism, economic exploitation, and other oppressive corruptions.	Engages in research to expose imperialism, colonialism, racism, sexism, transphobia, ableism, ageism, heterosexism, economic exploitation, and other forms of oppression.
Favors multi- and interdisciplinary endeavors.	Favors multi- and interdisciplinary endeavors.
Eclectic in its approach and influenced by Enlightenment, modernist, and postmodernist theorists. The liberation theology of Latin America and Africa, and Neo-Marxist, feminist, antiracist, and anticolonial ideas influence liberation criminologists.	Eclectic in its approach and influenced by Enlightenment, modernist, and postmodernist theorists. The liberation theology of Latin America and Africa, and Neo-Marxist, feminist, antiracist, and anticolonial ideas influence liberation sociologists.
Committed to studying crimes of power and how such crimes are an outcome of unequal relations, while acknowledging that mainstream criminology generally focuses on crimes perpetrated by racialized, working-class, poor, or unemployed people.	Committed to the causes of the oppressed, exploited, and dominated, while acknowledging that mainstream sociology is more regularly committed to the vested interests of the status quo.

with a concern for human rights. Indeed, for some time now, Agozino has called on criminologists to show candid concern for human rights abuses, particularly crimes of colonization, and to include struggles for decolonization among the paradigms of criminology. He has argued elsewhere (Agozino, 1997) that the discipline of criminology emphasizes individual crimes, while ignoring state sanctioned violence. Indeed, much less theorized is the mass victimization of racialized people via the colonial guise of punitive expeditions and "in the name of and for the defense of a Superior Race born to rule the world" (Du Bois, [1945] 1965, p. 23).

Du Bois and Wells-Barnett are remarkable examples of liberation criminologists and sociologists who epitomize Agozino's paradigm. Of course, however, scholars do not have a monopoly on such ideas. An important contemporary liberation criminology movement, for example, is Black Lives Matter (BLM), created in 2013 by African American women activists Patricia Cullors, Opal Tometi, and Alicia Garza. Commencing at the community level as a reaction to abusive police behavior, particularly the killing of unarmed African American men, it is now global and intersectional (i.e., fighting anti-Black discrimination but also fighting discrimination against transgender and queer people of color). Encapsulating its significance, Ransby (2017, p. SR6) has stressed that BLM "is reinvigorating the 21st-century racial-justice movement." Similarly, Agozino (2018) has argued in "Black Lives Matter Otherwise All Lives Do Not Matter" that the police kill more White people in the United States than people of color who are killed disproportionately, hence the need for all to oppose White supremacy and support BLM as many White people do in solidarity with African Americans and in their own interests.

Pioneering African American Liberation Criminologists

Given the peculiar history of oppression that people of African descent have faced and survived through liberation struggles, any account of liberation criminology that fails to center the Africana paradigm will be incomplete. However, the Africana paradigm in liberation studies is also too vast to be completely summarized in one chapter. Therefore, we will be selective in highlighting the key exemplars of this tradition.

W. E. B. Du Bois

The doctoral dissertation of Du Bois at Harvard University, *The Suppression of the African Slave Trade in America*, was completed in 1896 and published as the foundational issue of the Harvard Historical Studies Series. From that study, which has been recognized as the founding text of human rights criminology (see Agozino, 2016), to his death in 1963, Du Bois dedicated his scholar-activism to the liberation of human society from various oppressions. His 1899 field study, published as *The Philadelphia Negro*, was the first such empirical exploration of African American urban life. Using mixed-methods, he blended historical analysis of the Philadelphia community and other qualitative data, with descriptive statistical analyses and survey methods. Additionally, he combined social-theoretical interpretations of his data with a human rights analysis—even before human rights were codified. Using survey questionnaires, he collected data that allowed him to chart conditions in which working-class and poor Black Philadelphians lived and worked.

The White men who commissioned the study were exceedingly distressed by the possibility that Whites could ultimately be engulfed by a pandemic of urban Black poor, whom they categorized as criminal and otherwise corrupt. The White funders thus gave Du Bois the following directions: "We want to know precisely how this class of people live … and to ascertain every fact which will throw light on this social problem."[4] Disregarding their directive as much as possible, Du Bois ([1899] 1973) spent countless hours in the field. His work resulted in approximately 2,500 household interviews. Although he recognized that his research and resulting publication had to be acceptable to the Whites who commissioned it, he managed to challenge White racism. Working inductively and historically (profiling the background of Philadelphia's Black population and their journey from the Southern United States), he weaved antiracist analyses into *The Philadelphia Negro*. For example, within its pages, he contrasted Black residents with White immigrants then entering Philadelphia, observing that they received many societal benefits not available to Blacks. He also courageously described in moralistic terms the poverty endured by many Black Philadelphians. In so doing, he offered what is arguably the first significant racial and class analysis of poverty and crime among Black urbanites (Du Bois, [1899] 1973).

Notably, in the final chapter of *The Philadelphia Negro*, Du Bois ([1899] 1973) delivered a strongly worded indictment of White racism, concluding it to be the fundamental cause for the troubled conditions in which the urban Black poor found themselves. He ended the 520-page tome with a section candidly titled "The Duty of Whites," daringly pronouncing that Whites may have

> a right to object to a race so poor and ignorant and inefficient as the mass of Negroes; but if their policy in the past is parent of much of this condition, and if today by shutting black boys and girls out of most avenues of decent employment they are increasing pauperism and vice, then they must hold themselves largely responsible for the deplorable results.
>
> *(Du Bois, [1899] 1973, p. 394)*

He included a further comment on the ethical duties of White Americans, writing (Du Bois, [1899] 1973, p. 394) that racism is "morally wrong, politically dangerous, industrially wasteful, and socially silly. It is the duty of Whites to stop it, and to do so primarily for their own sakes."

In his many other books, and as editor of the *Crisis*—the prominent National Association for the Advancement of Colored People (NAACP) journal—he was also a pioneering voice for genuine liberty-and-justice. And along with the likes of the scholar-activist Wells-Barnett discussed below, Du Bois signed the initial call for the NAACP, which was established in 1909. With like-minded activists, he used the NAACP to campaign against lynching, segregation, disenfranchisement, employment discrimination, warmongering, and genocide. In 1947, the NAACP remitted to the newly established United Nations (UN) a striking document titled "An Appeal to the World." Largely composed by Du Bois, it described the brutal White racist subjugation of people of color in the United States:

> A nation which boldly declared "All men equal," proceeded to build its economy on chattel slavery. ... Sectional strife over the vast profits of slave labor and conscientious revolt against making human beings real estate led to bloody civil war, and to a partial emancipation of slaves which nevertheless even to this day is not complete. Poverty, ignorance, disease, and crime have been forced on these unfortunate victims of greed. ... and a great nation, which today ought to be in the forefront of the march toward peace and democracy, finds itself continuously making common cause with race hate, prejudiced exploitation and oppression of the common man. ... Peoples of the World, we American Negroes appeal to you; our treatment in America is not merely an internal question of the United States. It is a basic problem of humanity; of democracy; of discrimination because of race and color; and as such it demands your attention and action.
>
> *(Du Bois et al., 1947, p. 45)*

Here again, Du Bois demonstrates a passionate faithfulness to authentic democracy, not to mention a shrewd international acuity. Alas, the leading White liberal Eleanor Roosevelt served on both the NAACP board and the U.S. delegation to the UN. She rebuffed any attempt to show the NAACP petition to the UN General Assembly for fear of damaging the image of the United States globally (Du Bois et al., 1947).

But nothing could dissuade Du Bois, not even the former First Lady. A mere four years after she blocked the first request for UN assistance, Du Bois and other African American leaders composed a much harsher condemnation of U.S. racism. The 1951 petition titled "We Charge Genocide: The Crime of Government Against the Negro People," meticulously described how the White U.S. elite bred and enacted Jim Crow racism against African Americans. The petition, which thoroughly documented the many genocidal crimes of legal segregation in the United States, read in part, as follows:

> The responsibility of being the first in history to charge the government of the United States of America with the crime of genocide is not one your petitioners take lightly. ... Your petitioners. ... submit evidence, tragically voluminous, of "acts committed with intent to destroy, in whole or in part, a national, ethical, racial or religious group as such"—in this case the 15,000,000 Negro people of the United States.
>
> (NAACP, 1951)

The petition was virtually ignored by the White-dominated media in the United States, but made headlines around the world. The U.S. delegation to the UN assailed and diminished the incontrovertible fact that the White controlled U.S. government had long engaged in genocide against African Americans. Consequently, the 1951 petition was rejected.

Du Bois paid dearly for his efforts in trying to push the United States towards genuine democracy. He had trouble securing research funds from corporate foundations. Irrespective of his long list of credentials (e.g., a Harvard PhD who studied abroad with leading social scientists like Max Weber and who completed major field research), the White establishment in the United States shunned him. As Agozino (quoted in Feagin et al., 2014, p. 267) has hauntingly put it,

> W. E. B. Du Bois was never tenured and was nearly jailed during the McCarthy era for trying to start a peace organization. We remember him, but few remember the cowards who got tenure and sold their sociological souls to the metaphorical devil.

In other words, being a liberation criminologist is worth all the risks because the paradigm makes you a better criminologist than the careerists who make no contribution to the advancement of human freedom.

Ida B. Wells-Barnett

Like Du Bois, Wells-Barnett should be listed among the great liberation criminologists. Her work epitomizes the potential of liberation criminology to defy injustice. She devoted her entire adult life to documenting and challenging White racism. Near the turn of the twentieth-century, she investigated and wrote diligently about White lynching of African Americans, using accounts from White newspapers to construct a database that she documented in her own newspaper so that no one would accuse her of peddling fake news. She approached the topic with an acute awareness of systemic racism in U.S. society. "The purpose of the pages which follow," she wrote,

> shall be to give the record which has been made, not by colored men, but that which is the result of the compilations made by white men, of reports sent over the civilized world by white men in the South. Out of their own mouths shall the murderers be condemned .
>
> (Wells-Barnett, 1895, pp. 150–165)

She openly contested the myth of the "Black male rapist," a popular idea among Whites then and now, alleging that Black men desired to rape White women.

At this early stage in the history of U.S. sociology, Wells-Barnett was already advancing sophisticated empirical and theoretical understandings of the links between gender and racial stratification. She helped construct a sociology from the standpoint of the oppressed and one dedicated to genuine social justice. Specifically, she risked her life and livelihood to campaign against the terrorism that was visited on her fellow citizens, including poor Whites, but predominantly against African Americans even when they were not suspected of doing anything wrong. She was among the first social scientists to examine data on the collective condition of African American men and women and poor Whites in terms of such important ideas as social repression, subordination, terrorization, and domination.

As is typical for liberation sociologists and criminologists, Wells-Barnett paid significant personal costs for her scholar-activism. For example, she narrowly avoided being murdered after suggesting that White men's sexual yearnings for Black women might be related to Whites' preoccupation with the rapist mythology. Her data showed that only about a third of those lynched were accused of rape, and yet the fear of rape was used as the main propaganda to support the lynching of Black men, women, and children. Her courage in standing up against what she called the American "horrors" of lynching represents an advanced strategy in liberation criminology by inviting scholar-activists to oppose injustice even when they are not personally targeted. As a woman, some feminists would have expected her to focus only on the oppression of women, but she was aware that the oppression of men and women was articulated or intersectional. As an African American woman, some may have expected her to only focus on the oppression of Black people, but she reported that many poor Whites were also lynched to reveal that she was doing race-class-gender articulation of intersectionality research long before it came into vogue.

White Male Elite Sanctioned Violence: Further Illustrating the Countersystem Model

The ideas and works of pathbreaking scholar-activists like Du Bois and Wells-Barnett—to mention but two of the giants whose research and commitment to a better world have shaped our society—helped to build a foundation that aligns with liberation criminology and its tenets. They refused to accept White racism as unproblematic and routine. They imagined a world with more democracy and a freer flow of information. They also thought about the way their research could bring about such a world.

The lynching of African Americans, who were alleged to have spoken in contradiction of a White oppressor, organized against Whites, committed a crime against Whites, or offended Whites in some other way, was vital to the bolstering of the emergent network of legal segregation in the United States. Between 1882 and 1927, lynchings of approximately 3,500 Black men and 76 Black women were recorded. Many more of these crimes remain undocumented. Between the Civil War and the mid-1980s, possibly as many as 6,000 lynchings of Black men and Black women had been committed in the southern United States, in border states, and in the North (Harris, 1984).

It is, of course, impossible to express just how inhumane lynchings were or how unsettling was the starkly ritualized atmosphere surrounding them. Perhaps only a description of a lynching could even remotely capture the suffering of Blacks at the hands of Whites. One such account from the 1940s concerned a Black man accused of attempting to rape a White woman (Harris, 1984, p. 10): "I ain't tellin' nobody just what we done to that nigger but we used a broken bottle just where it'd do the most damage," recalled one of the Whites who tortured and murdered the man. Following injuries from the broken bottle, the victim was soaked with kerosene and set ablaze. "[T]he groanin' got lower and lower and finely it was just little gasps and then it wasn't nothin' at all," explained the participant. Lastly, the victim was tied to a tree for his relatives to cut down.

Such gory rituals were preceded by the rape, torture, and mutilation of Africans and African Americans on slave ships, farms, and plantations. These historical facts are hidden like radioactive substances because "white supremacists and liberal racists … are invested in Whiteness as a type of racial innocence" (DeVega, 2015). White scholars are no exception. Racial innocence explains well why African American political commentator Chauncey DeVega was met with White rage (even from liberal Whites) when he daringly associated vicious lynchings and torture of Blacks between 1877 and 1950 with the disturbing 2015 murder by burning of a Jordanian pilot by the self-styled Islamic State of Iraq and Syria (ISIS). Another tyrannical example of White American male power occurred during slavery and under legal segregation. Black women and children routinely experienced sexual violence at the hands of White men. But even today this history does not warrant much attention from scholars, including criminologists. Yet, copious amounts of evidence for these ubiquitous crimes have long been available. Take for example the story of Robert Newsom and fourteen-year-old Celia (McLaurin, 1991). In 1850, the prosperous Missouri farmer, who was in his seventies, "purchased" Celia. He raped her continually over the next five years. She bore two of her predator's children. In 1855, Celia struck back, fatally wounding Newsom. She was convicted in a Missouri court of the "crime" and executed the same year.

Like other elite White men who routinely commit crimes against Black and Brown bodies, Newsom was considered a decent and reputable fellow. Certainly, the third president of the United States, Thomas Jefferson, is widely considered so. But he, too, was a rapist. He fathered at least one of Sally Hemings's children, a teenager he enslaved.[5] Pending DNA evidence, most White pundits and most of his White descendants vehemently denied that he had sexual relations with a Black woman (Associated Press, 2000; Finkelman, 1996).

Liberation criminology requires calling out these kinds of issues in past and contemporary criminology. Indeed, White racial innocence helps explain why criminology arose during the pinnacle of European global colonization and why present-day criminology is dominated by institutions in the former colonial countries, while being largely absent from institutions in the former colonial territories. That these facts are hardly ever acknowledged is at least in part due to White racial innocence. Renowned criminologist David Garland (1990) makes no mention, for example, of such patterns in his explanation of the emergence of British criminology in terms of the confluence between the governmental and the Lombrosian projects. There is no mention of the genocidal projects of imperialism and the paradigm shattering movement of decolonization in his work. Additionally, in the former colonial countries where criminology was long ago established, practically all the leading criminologists are people of White European descent. This pattern is not a coincidence either. It arises from a systemic and deliberate exclusion of racialized people, who play little or no role in the contest over control of the powerful technology that is criminology. And sadly, this White racist framing of Western criminology has slowed the collective progress of the discipline, which we explain with reference to the anti-colonial and anti-apartheid struggles in Africa.

It is difficult to imagine that Nelson Mandela remained on the terrorist watch list of the U.S. State Department until his name was removed from the list in 2008 by President George W. Bush, knowing that President Barack Obama was likely to stop that nonsense on day one (Dewey, 2013). Steve Biko and countless others, including school children, were murdered by the apartheid regime while the U.S. and the U.K. governments preferred a policy of constructive engagement in opposition to the cultural boycott of, and divestment from, apartheid South Africa. Samora Machel, the first President of Mozambique after the country's independence in 1975, used to joke that he was a terrorist too because that was how the brutal Portuguese colonizers portrayed him and the Mozambican Liberation Front (FRELIMO) fighters. Amilcar Cabral, one of Africa's foremost anti-colonial leaders, was also hunted down by the Portuguese and finally assassinated in Guinea for leading the struggle for national liberation from fascist Portuguese military dictators. Similarly, Angolan political and military leader Jonas Savimbi was welcomed as a hero by U.S. officials when he was colluding with the apartheid regime in South Africa to overthrow his country's independent government under the People's Movement for the Liberation of Angola (MPLA). Cuban troops responded to the call for help from Angola and contributed to the independence of Namibia and to the lifting of the ban on the African National Congress (ANC). In Algeria, Frantz Fanon used similar cases of colonialist violence to theorize that the foundation of such violence started at the international level with the 400 years of hunting and kidnapping of Africans for slavery by Europeans before giving way to the still international violence of colonialism during which Europeans tried to persuade Africans that they were superior by means of the napalm bomb. He called for reparations to be paid to Africans.

The Decolonization Paradigm in Criminology versus the Culture of Silence

The decolonization paradigm was first extensively explored in Agozino's 2003 book, *Counter-Colonial Criminology: A Critique of Imperialist Reason*, in which he argued that criminology is a *technology* designed to control human beings. Originally, those to be controlled were mainly the colonized and the poor in the metropoles. Women were dealt with primarily through the repressive technologies of patriarchal family institutions, constructed and maintained by the state as part of what Greek-French Marxist Poulantzas called the *ideological state apparatuses*.

Agozino's model brings to mind Du Bois's pioneering analyses of globalizing capitalism and imperialism. Writing about the years around 1900, Du Bois ([1920] 1999, p. 504) maintained:

> [W]hite supremacy was all but world-wide. Africa was dead, India conquered, Japan isolated, and China prostrate ... The using of men for the benefit of masters is no new invention of modern Europe ... But Europe proposed to apply it on a scale and with an elaborateness of detail of which no former world ever dreamed.

Examining Europe's colonization of Africa, Du Bois ([1945] 1965, p. 37) hauntingly expressed how the enormous poverty and deprivation endured by Africans were "a main cause of wealth and luxury in Europe. The results of this poverty were disease, ignorance, and crime. Yet these had to be represented as natural characteristics of backward peoples." And again echoing the spirit of the decolonization paradigm, in 1945, Du Bois ([1945] 1965, p. 23) summed up European imperialism and the damage it did to peoples of color around the globe: "There was no Nazi atrocity—concentration camps, wholesale maiming and murder, defilement of women and ghastly blasphemy of childhood—which the Christian civilization of Europe had not long been practicing against colored folk in all parts of the world."

Embracing Agozino's decolonization model as part of a broader liberation criminology perspective, modern criminologists have the potential to give effective voice to state sanctioned atrocities in Du Boisian fashion. By examining systemic racism, for example, we can better expose and illuminate the criminal victimization of people of color by elite and non-elite Whites. As a case in point, from the days of slavery, through colonialism, neocolonialism, and internal colonialism, history demonstrates that Blacks need not commit a crime to come under the authority and control of imperialistic White power. As Agozino has put it, rather than distort the nature of imperialism, we ought to encourage criminologists to devote at least one chapter in their fat textbooks to crimes of imperialism, which account for unprecedented levels of robberies, rapes, homicides, and other forms of violence around the world, but which criminologists expediently disregard in what Cohen (1993) called a "culture of silence" (see also, Schwendinger & Schwendinger, 1970).

Conclusion

Today as in the past, racialized and other oppressed peoples have lives imposed on them that are second-rate. Some of them are denied life itself. In search of the right to be, and in pursuit of genuine liberty-and-justice *for all*, we call on criminologists to give serious consideration to liberation criminology.[6] This project links directly to projects of so-called public social science.

To paraphrase and apply Burawoy's (2005) sociological insights to criminology, when liberation criminology seizes the imagination of criminologists and when criminologists accept liberation criminology as important in its own right with its own rewards, criminologists will carry it forward as a social movement beyond the academy. Like Burawoy (2005), we envision myriads of nodes, each forging collaborations of criminologists with their publics, flowing together into a single current. They will draw on a century of extensive research, elaborate theories, practical interventions, and critical thinking, reaching common understandings across multiple boundaries, not least but not only across national boundaries, and in so doing shedding insularities of old. Our angel of history will then spread her wings and soar above the storm.

Notes

1 *Positive* was a term selected by Comte to distinguish his ideas from what he saw as the *negative* philosophy of the German Hegelian system. While philosopher Georg Hegel (1770–1831) began from the errors made by philosophers who came before him, Comte held that one should depart from past errors with a positive statement of what is discovered through observation and comparison.
2 Importantly, Friedrich Engels—the long-time collaborator of Marx—added that a similar prediction could be made in connection to the oppression of women. Emerging within the family, private property, and the capitalist state, it too would wither away under communism to make way for the New Testament principle (i.e., to each according to their needs and from each according to their abilities).
3 We draw on a table previously published in Ducey, (2008).
4 Charles Harrison, Acting Provost of the University of Pennsylvania, as quoted in Lewis, (1994, p. 188; see also pp. 187–189).
5 Hemings was the half-sister of Jefferson's wife (Fresia, 1988; Smith & Wade, 2018).
6 We are indebted to Tatz (2003).

References

Agger, B. (2007). *Public sociology: From social facts to literary acts* (2nd ed.). Lanham, MD: Rowman and Littlefield.
Agozino, B. (1997). *Black women and the criminal justice system: Towards the decolonisation of victimisation*. Surrey: Ashgate Publishing.
Agozino, B. (2003). *Counter-colonial criminology: A critique of imperialist reason*. London: Pluto Press.
Agozino, B. (2016). The Africana paradigm: W. E. B. Du Bois as the founding father of human rights criminology. In L. Weber, E. Fishwick, & M. Marmo (Eds.), *Routledge international handbook of criminology and human rights* (pp. 40–49). London: Routledge.
Agozino, B. (2018). Black lives matter otherwise all lives do not matter. *African Journal of Criminology and Justice Studies*, 11(1), I-XI.
Anderson, K. (2010). *Marx at the margins: On nationalism, ethnicity, and non-western societies*. Chicago, IL: University of Chicago Press.
Associated Press (2000, May 7). Not all are welcome at Jefferson family reunion. *LA Times*. Retrieved from http://articles.latimes.com/2000/may/07/news/mn-27481.
Burawoy, M. (2005). For public sociology: 2004 American Sociological Association presidential. *American Sociological Review*, 70(1), 4–28.
Cohen, S. (1985). *Visions of social control: Crime, punishment and classification*. Cambridge: Polity.
Cohen, S. (1993). Human rights and crimes of the state: The culture of denial. *Australian and New Zealand Journal of Criminology*, 26(2), 97–115.
Cohen, S. (2001). *States of Denial: Knowing about atrocities and suffering*. Cambridge: Polity.

Comte, A. (1965). On the three stages of social evolution. In T. Parsons, E. Shils, K. D. Naegele, & J. R. Pitts (Eds.), *Theories of society: Foundations of modern sociological theory* (pp. 1332–1342). New York: Free Press.

DeVega, C. (2015, February 9). 20 things I learned about racism when I dared to talk about ISIS and the lynchings of black Americans. *We are respectable negroes*. Retrieved from www.chaunceydevega.com/2015/02/20-things-i-learned-about-racism-when-i.html.

Dewey, C. (2013, December 7). Why Nelson Mandela was on a terrorism watch list in 2008. *The Washington post*. Retrieved from www.washingtonpost.com/news/the-fix/wp/2013/12/07/why-nelson-mandela-was-on-a-terrorism-watch-list-in-2008/?noredirect=on&utm_term=.8f944ff35253.

Du Bois, W. E. B. (1935). *Black reconstruction in America 1860–1880*. New York: Harcourt, Brace and Co.

Du Bois, W. E. B. (Ed.). (1947). *An appeal to the world: A statement on the denial of human rights to minorities in the case of citizens of Negro descent in the United States of America and an appeal to the United Nations for redress*. Retrieved from www.aclu.org/appeal-world.

Du Bois, W. E. B. ([1899] 1973). *The Philadelphia negro*. Millwood, NY: Kraus-Thomson.

Du Bois, W. E. B. ([1920] 1999). *Darkwater: Voices from within the veil*. Mineola, NY: Dover Publications.

Du Bois, W. E. B. ([1945] 1965). *The world and Africa*. New York: International Publishers.

Ducey, K. (2008). Using the 1994 Rwanda genocide to integrate critical criminology and liberation sociology. *Critical Criminology, 16*(4), 293–302.

Feagin, J. R., Vera, H., & Ducey, K. (2014). *Liberation sociology* (3rd ed.). New York: Routledge.

Finkelman, P. (1996). *Slavery and the founders: Race and liberty in the age of Jefferson*. Armonk, NY: M. E. Sharpe.

Fresia, J. (1988). *Toward an American revolution: Exposing the constitution and other illusions*. Boston, MA: South End Press.

Garland, D. (1990). *Punishment and modern society: A study in social theory*. Oxford: Clarendon Press.

Harris, T. (1984). *Exorcising blackness: Historical and literary lynching and burning rituals*. Bloomington, IN: Indiana University Press.

Karaim, R. (2012). America's peculiar and horrifying tradition of vigilante justice. *American History, 46*(6), 50–55.

Lewis, D. L. (1994). *W. E. B. Du Bois, 1868–1919: Biography of a race*. New York: Henry Holt.

Loader, I., & Sparks, R. (2008). What are we gonna do now? Revisiting the public roles of criminology. *Criminal Justice Matters, 72*, 18–19.

Manuel, F. E., & Manuel, F. P. (1979). *Utopian thought in the western world*. Cambridge, MA: Harvard University Press.

Marx, K. (1962). Theses on Feuerbach. In K. Marx & F. Engels (Eds.), *Selected works* (Vol. 2). Moscow: Foreign Languages Publishing House.

McLaurin, M. A. (1991). *Celia: A slave*. Athens, GA: University of Georgia Press.

NAACP. (1951). We charge genocide. Petition to the United Nations. Retrieved from www.blackpast.org/.

Ransby, B. (2017, October 21). Black lives matter is democracy in action. *New York Times*. Retrieved from www.nytimes.com/2017/10/21/opinion/sunday/black-lives-matter-leadership.html.

Roediger, D. R. (1991). *The wages of whiteness: Race and the making of the American working class*. London and New York City: Verso Books.

Schwendinger, H., & Schwendinger, J. (1970). Defenders of order or guardians of human rights? *Issues in Criminology, 5*(2), 123–157.

Sjoberg, G., & Cain, L. D. (1971). Negative values, countersystem models, and the analysis of social systems. In H. Turk & R. L. Simpson (Eds.), *Institutions and social exchange: The sociologies of Talcott Parsons and George C. Homan*. Indianapolis, IN: Bobbs-Merrill.

Smith, D., & Wade, N. (2018, November 1). DNA evidence links Thomas Jefferson to slave's offspring. *Gainesville Sun*. p. 4A.

Tatz, C. (2003). *With intent to destroy. Reflecting on genocide*. London: Verso Books.

Uggen, C., & Inderbitzin, M. (2010). Public criminologies. *Criminology & Public Policy, 9*(4), 725–749.

Wells-Barnett, I. B. (1895). *A red record*. Chicago, IL: Donohue and Henneberry.

Wolin, S. S. (1969). Political theory as a vocation. *American Political Science Review, 63*(4), 1062–1082.

PART II
Engaging Publics

6

A REVOLUTION IN PROSECUTION

The Campaign to End Mass Incarceration in Philadelphia

Jill McCorkel

Introduction

In November 2017, voters in Philadelphia, Pennsylvania did what would have been unthinkable a year prior: we elected Larry Krasner, a veteran civil rights attorney and outspoken critic of mass incarceration, to be our next District Attorney (DA). He was the only candidate with no prior experience as a prosecutor and, notably, the only candidate who has sued the Philadelphia police department upward of 75 times. He won the election by a landslide and did so on a campaign platform that promised to end (among other things) cash bail, the prosecution of insignificant crimes such as possession of marijuana, the use of the death penalty, the over-incarceration of girls and young women, and unconstitutional stop and frisk. Considering that Pennsylvania's carceral system is among the largest in the United States and that the Philadelphia DA's Office is the largest in the state and among the largest in the country, Krasner's policies have the potential to make significant headway in addressing the wrongs of the War on Drugs and associated "get tough" prosecutorial practices.

Krasner is among a small but growing wave of progressive DAs across the country who were elected during the course of the Trump presidency. Journalists and political pundits often overlook the keys to their electoral success. Specifically, the revolution in prosecution is being waged through effective use of criminological and social science research. This was particularly evident in Krasner's campaign. Krasner argued that mass incarceration is the inevitable outcome of criminal justice policies and law enforcement practices that are *systemically racist*. It may be the first time that a winning candidate for the office of DA has used that language. It was certainly a first for a candidate in Pennsylvania. Although Philadelphia is a Democratic stronghold and a predominantly African American city, convincing voters that tough-on-crime policies are systemically racist presents a challenge. As every critical criminologist knows, it is not an argument that lends itself to quick sound bites and short-form tweets. To make the case, the campaign relied on a small but select group of social scientists to serve as advisors. I was one of those advisors. We drew on our professional expertise as researchers and academics to help the campaign develop effective talking points and advance meaningful policy platforms. Crucially, we mobilized research and theory to make the case that modest reforms would not appreciably counter the devastating social, political, and economic costs of mass incarceration. Ending mass incarceration demands a bolder vision—one that aims to fundamentally transform the relationship among prosecutors, police, victims, offenders, and the community.

In this chapter, I discuss my work on the Krasner campaign and the seemingly counterintuitive route by which I ended up there. Public criminology presents a number of challenges for scholars working in the academy, and I identify a few that are particularly relevant for criminologists. In spite of these hurdles, I argue that social scientists have an intellectual and civic obligation to use their expertise to inform public policy debates.

No Justice, No Peace, No Racist Police

My relationship with the Philadelphia DA's Office is now over two decades old. To describe it as "rocky" would be an understatement. For most of those twenty years, I was an outside agitator and a rather tenacious one at that. Throughout the mid-1990s, for example, I participated in weekly protests outside city hall that called attention to Philadelphia law enforcement's well-documented history of brutality, corruption, and racism. We held signs that read, "Jail Racist Killer Cops" and chanted, "No justice, No peace, No racist police." I walked in marches demanding an end to the death penalty and helped anti-death penalty organizations to compile research data on capital punishment. I sat in on hearings as a courtroom observer. I met with prisoners on death row and their families. I assisted incarcerated men and women with their legal filings and drafted *pro se* motions on their behalf. Additionally, I had a regime of letter writing—to the DA, Governor, court officials, and local news outlets—that rivaled that of a professional gadfly. When a local newspaper story mentioned me in their coverage of an appellate hearing for a well-known death row prisoner, I began receiving dozens of letters from incarcerated people sharing their experiences of police brutality, coerced confessions, bad plea deals, and wrongful convictions. Aside from similar patterns of police and prosecutorial misconduct that the letters revealed, I was particularly struck by the lack of resources, professional or otherwise, that were available to provide incarcerated people with research-related assistance. I wrote back to everyone and offered what I could. I did all of these things in the course of pursuing a Ph.D. in sociology and doing ethnographic research in a state prison for women.

Mine was certainly not the preferred route to take for someone who had an interest in working in an advisory capacity with the DA's office. For one thing, I am a sociologist and most advisors are current or former prosecutors, court officials, and law enforcement. For another, the organizational culture of the Philadelphia DA's office was, for the last thirty years, steeped in the law and order ideology of the War on Drugs. In this climate, career prosecutors were principally evaluated on two metrics: convictions and sentences. The higher the conviction rate and the more severe the sentences handed down, the better. Prosecutors did not get ahead by exhibiting concern for due process, the rights of the accused, or evidence-based evaluations of criminal justice policy. Indeed, the Philadelphia DA's Office was notorious for treating social science research with suspicion if not downright hostility. On the economics of the death penalty, for example, former DA Lynne Abraham was quoted as saying, "I don't care how many millions it costs … . Please don't tell me about costs when talking about the rights of the victim. It's of no interest to me" (Rosenberg, 1995, para. 14).

Given the political climate, I did not imagine that a collaborative relationship with the district attorney's office could result in meaningful criminal justice reform much less an end to mass incarceration. Indeed, I did not think a collaborative relationship was possible. Instead, I committed to my role as an outside agitator. In this, Larry Krasner and I shared a similar mindset. Following Krasner's graduation from Stanford law school in 1987, he spent a few years as a public defender in Philadelphia and then opened his own practice specializing in civil rights and police brutality cases. In a recent interview he recalled not ever wanting to work as a prosecutor in the DA's office because "Philly had a culture that was in love with the death penalty" (Sammon, 2017, para. 6). Lynne Abraham, dubbed "America's deadliest prosecutor" for her aggressive pursuit of the death penalty, won four terms between 1991 and 2010.

The consequences of her law-and-order style of prosecution quickly became evident. Among the ten largest cities in the United States, Philadelphia has consistently had some of the very highest rates of incarceration (Pew Charitable Trusts, 2011). These elevated rates of incarceration carry pronounced racial disparities that are disproportionately born by young, African American men and women and girls and boys (Nellis, 2016). Importantly, racial skews in the city's incarceration rate do not reflect real crime trends so much as an entrenched culture of racism and racial discrimination running through the ranks of the police department right up into the DA's office. Consider, for example, the 1997 release of video footage taken several years before of a training seminar for newly hired prosecutors. The tape showed a veteran prosecutor providing instruction on how to (unconstitutionally) exclude African Americans from juries. Jack McMahon, the prosecutor leading the session, was quoted as saying, "Young Black women are very bad [for juries] because they're downtrodden in two respects—they're women and they're black" (Abbott, 2001, para. 4).

In addition to these problems, the police department and DA's office have been plagued by ongoing misconduct and corruption scandals. A Human Rights Watch Report comparing police misconduct lawsuits across multiple jurisdictions found that during the mid-1990s Philadelphia was paying out some of the largest settlements among big cities (Human Rights Watch, 1998). This trend appears to have continued even after Abraham left the office. During the years 2011–2015, the city averaged just over $11 million per year in settling lawsuits triggered by police misconduct and abuse (Allyn, 2015). Beyond civil lawsuits, the police department has periodically come under investigation by the Department of Justice for brutality, witness intimidation, evidence tampering, corruption, and racial profiling. And it is not only Philadelphia's police force that has run afoul of the law. In 2017, a federal investigation into the district attorney's office resulted in a five-year prison term for Abraham's successor, Seth Williams. Williams pled guilty to bribery charges and, as part of that plea, admitted to the facts of 23 other charges against him, including fraud and extortion.

Despite the problems plaguing Philadelphia's criminal justice system, the community of activists who work exclusively and continuously on criminal justice related issues has been relatively small. This was particularly the case from 1995 through 2005. Although that period saw a groundswell of national and international support for Mumia Abu-Jamal, a prisoner on Pennsylvania's death row, it did not translate into support for other prisoners who had suffered from profound injustices or to interest in issues beyond Pennsylvania's use of the death penalty. The result is that most dedicated local activists know one another quite well.

When Krasner decided to run for office, I was not only quite familiar with his civil rights work, I also knew key members on his campaign team including Dustin Slaughter, a local freelance journalist who covered the criminal justice system and progressive social movements, and Oren Gur, a criminologist who worked on behalf of men and women on death row.[1] They were both familiar with my research and activism and both contacted me and invited me to get involved with the campaign. While my applied research and protest work earned me visibility and respect among the local community of activists, it did not endear me to police and prosecutors in Philadelphia, nor did it not win me any accolades in academia. It went largely unrecognized and unrewarded in my graduate program and in subsequent academic positions. On several occasions, faculty advisors warned that it was a distraction from "serious scholarship" and recommended that I not spend significant amounts of time pursuing it. This perspective, of course, is not unique to a particular graduate program or department, but it is consistent with broader disciplinary norms in the social sciences (Burawoy, 2005; Currie, 1999; Uggen & Inderbitzin, 2010). Although my activist scholarship was informed by my training in sociology and vice versa, I maintained a tidy (if troubled) split between activism and academia throughout the first half of my career. As I moved through graduate school and the tenure track, I endeavored to straddle the divide between the research I did to advance criminal justice reform in Philadelphia, and the work that counted as "serious" scholarship that advanced my academic career.

In the section that follows, I argue that this divide between activism and academia is largely artificial. It occurs when academic disciplines value one kind of knowledge production over another. While it is appropriate and necessary to distinguish the quality of the knowledge produced, distinctions based on the ends to which that knowledge are put are of dubious merit. Ultimately, my activist scholarship makes use of all the same methodologies and theoretical frameworks that inform my broader research efforts. A reinvigorated notion of public criminology, one that is informed by intersectional feminism, offers criminologists a way out of this divide and carries the promise of scholarship that operates in service of democratic ideals and the public good.

Public Criminology and the Promise of Intersectional Feminism

Although policy work and activist scholarship is often not rewarded in academia, many of us nonetheless feel compelled to do it by a sense of civic obligation, moral commitment, or a combination of both. In an effort to explain why he engaged politically after previously critiquing such endeavors, sociologist Pierre Bourdieu (1998, p. vii) wrote, "I would not have engaged in public position-taking if I had not, each time, had the—perhaps illusory—sense of being forced into it by a kind of legitimate rage, sometimes close to something like a sense of duty." As a discipline, sociology has had a much longer and more vibrant history of politically engaged scholarship than its disciplinary offshoot, criminology. It is worth emphasizing that sociology's founders, from Marx and Weber in Europe to DuBois and Addams in the United States, were on a mission to change the world. Their scholarship engaged directly with the troubles and issues that plagued individuals and communities. It also necessarily engaged multiple audiences and aimed to directly intervene in discrete aspects of social life. It is not until the post-World War Two era that a "pure science" model emerged that challenged sociology's public commitments.

In his presidential address at the 2004 meetings of the American Sociological Association, Burawoy (2005) argues that contemporary sociology produces four types of knowledge that, although they are not equally valued, mutually reinforce and complement one another. They are professional sociology, critical sociology, policy sociology, and public sociology. Professional sociology is that which is intended for an academic audience. It offers the theoretical frameworks, analytical schemes, methodological processes, and repositories of knowledge that constitute the discipline as a whole. Critical sociology, directed at the same audience, interrogates the field's assumptions, protocols, direction, and canon of knowledge. Policy sociology involves research and analyses that are undertaken on behalf of a particular client like a government agency or business. The client defines the question to be studied and decides the ends to which the research is put. In the case of public sociology, scholarship is done in dialogue with a broader public and through this dialogue both sociologist and public adjust to one another with the goal of producing knowledge that is both sociologically informed and socially relevant. Burawoy's (2005) presidential address concludes with a strong push for sociologists to take up the difficult work of public sociology and to fight to expand its institutional legitimacy.

While criminology does not share sociology's more radical origins, it is a discipline that has strong roots in applied research and, in this sense, has always had a public, rather than exclusively professional, face. Consider, for example, early research done by Sheldon and Eleanor Glueck (1950) that aimed to detect and predict future delinquency in juveniles as young as six years old. This research was not only designed to test discrete theories of delinquency but also to propose specific interventions. In the case of the Gluecks, this included sentencing that was based on the individual character of the defendant rather than on the particular crime. Even Lombroso, 19th century founder of the positivist school of criminology, used his research measuring human skulls and bodies to advance particular policy platforms, most notably life imprisonment and the death penalty (Lombroso, [1911] 1968).

However, as these examples make clear, criminology's public face is one that is strongly influenced by its relationship to state structures and the criminal justice system. This is much more the case with respect to criminology than sociology. Criminology's *raison d'être* is measuring crime and identifying its sources. In this sense, mainstream criminology necessarily adopts the perspective of the state which holds that crime (a) is a real and identifiable phenomenon; (b) is problematic and disruptive to the social order; and (c) demands state intervention (see Quinney, 1970, 1974). Research done by Lombroso, the Gluecks, and many other mainstream criminologists uncritically proceeds from these tenets. The political implications are deeply troubling even when they do not involve executing people designated as "evolutionary throwbacks" (in the case of Lombroso) or preemptively labeling children as delinquents (in the case of the Gluecks).

In an effort to legitimize public criminology in the discipline, Uggen and Inderbitzin (2010) modify Burawoy's (2005) typology to differentiate professional criminology (analogous to professional sociology), critical criminology (analogous to critical sociology), policy criminology, and public criminology. Policy criminology involves the application of criminological theories to prevent crime, as well as the use of evaluation studies and evidence-based policy recommendations. Public criminology also traffics in evidence-based policy recommendations, but it does so through a much broader set of dialogic engagements. Its audience is not limited to lawmakers, criminal justice organizations, and funding agencies. Public criminology aims to identify social problems that may not receive adequate attention and to consider the scientific, moral, and practical implications of proposed solutions to these problems. Uggen and Inderbitzin's (2010) article offers a useful start for thinking about public criminology. However, it does not adequately disentangle and problematize the ways that definitions of crime and criminals reflect the interests of the state and market; nor does their definition consider how the control of crime is a form of governance that institutionalizes social inequality. To responsibly engage in public criminology, we must ask the question famously posed by Becker (1967), "Whose side are we on?"

If renewed interest in public sociology is, as Burawoy (2005, p. 7) posits, "a reaction and response to the privatization of everything," then public criminology must necessarily be a reaction and response to the mass incarceration of entire communities and publics. Mass incarceration is a principle engine of race, class, and gender inequality. It is both an ideology and a set of institutionalized practices that rely on definitions of and assumptions about crime that are not politically neutral, empirically justifiable, or epistemologically sound. For this reason, public criminology has a much greater responsibility to itself and to its commitment to building a just and safe world than to merely engage in dialogue with what Clear (2010, p. 722) refers to as "crime/justice consumer publics"—that is, the people who make the policies and the people who are impacted by them. It is crucial that public criminologists recognize real differences in power and resources that discrete publics command, as well as the different stakes that each has in the outcome of research studies and policy changes. As Foucault (2003) noted, subjugated knowledge reveals what official knowledge obscures through its definitions, categories, institutions, and archives. In other words, the kind of knowledge that public criminologists produce cannot aim to balance the perspectives of multiple publics without falling prey to a sort of guileful relativism. It is here where intersectional feminism offers a useful set of guideposts for practicing a truly public criminology.

Intersectional feminism critiques scientific positivism and structures of knowledge production that privilege the interests and perspectives of elites, Whites, and men (Collins, 2000; Crenshaw, 1989, 1991; Smith, 1987). As Collins (2000) and Smith (1987) argue, science does not proceed from an Archimedean point of nowhere. All scientific projects begin with the formulation of a problem to be studied. It is here where culture, politics, race, gender, and economics influence the structure, process, validation, and legitimacy of scientific research. Positivism obscures the social situatedness of research projects by failing to adequately acknowledge or investigate the context of discovery—specifically, the ways in which the researcher's social and institutional positionality, political biases, and cultural assumptions shape the articulation of the research question, among other things (Harding, 1991; McCorkel & Myers, 2003). Similar mechanisms are at work when we fail to acknowledge the relationship between criminology and state governance (Quinney, 1974). Crenshaw (1989, 1991) develops a parallel critique of Western law and jurisprudence. Her research on anti-discrimination law demonstrates how juridical assumptions about race and gender inequity work to prioritize the gender discrimination claims of White women and the racial discrimination claims of Black men while disadvantaging Black women who experience both forms of discrimination simultaneously. Although neither the law or positivist criminology are free from bias, both proceed institutionally as if they are. This, in turn, poses a significant challenge for the practice of public criminology.

The split that I encountered between the intellectual work that went into my early activism and the intellectual work that I did to advance my career encapsulates the problem. The source of the split involves the institutional structure of academe as well as the hegemony of scientific positivism (McCorkel & Myers, 2003). The former privileges research that is externally funded and validated by elite gatekeepers. The latter mistakenly conflates political neutrality with scientific objectivity (Harding, 1991). In this case, research that proceeds from dominant institutional perspectives can appear to be politically neutral. This type of scholarship often escapes scrutiny because it is (wrongly) assumed to be objective, while research that challenges a particular policy or institutional practice is treated as scientifically suspect. In reality, both projects demand that researchers scrutinize data collection and analysis, as well as the context of discovery (Harding, 1991; McCorkel & Myers, 2003). Taken together, both the institutional structure of academe and the hegemony of scientific positivism not only minimize the number of collaborative opportunities between researchers and disenfranchised communities, they artificially dampen the intellectual and institutional significance of public scholarship, particularly public criminology.

Further, investing in public scholarship is essential for ensuring the scientific integrity of professional sociology and criminology. For example, my activist work afforded me access to a broad social network of community organizers, public defenders, civil rights lawyers, and current and formerly incarcerated men and women, and their families. Through this network I became increasingly aware of the large gap between research in sociology and criminology during the early years of the drug war and the questions being raised in African American, Latinx, and marginalized communities regarding drug war policies. At the time, a number of sociologists and criminologists (including myself) were actively engaged in policy research—that is, research that aimed to answer discrete, policy-oriented questions such as whether one particular drug treatment modality was more effective at reducing relapse and recidivism than another. However, this scholarship too often proceeded from the assumptions, perspectives, and needs of the carceral system (McCorkel, 2007; McCorkel & Myers, 2003). Further, it all but ignored the impact of mass incarceration on women and families.

The oversights and limitations of this scholarship are attributable to the fact that it was not grounded in the concerns of the people and the communities who were directly and indirectly impacted by changes in sentencing policy, more aggressive styles of policing, expanded use of pretrial detention, and increasingly punitive prison regimes. These communities were asking very different kinds of questions. Women incarcerated in the prison I was collecting evaluation data at, for example, asked me pointed questions regarding the experimental drug treatment program I was studying that went well beyond concern for recidivism and relapse. They asked why they were in prison at all, whether they were being "brainwashed" in drug treatment, and what the consequences were for their identities and family relationships (McCorkel, 2013; McCorkel & Myers, 2003). The issues they raised offered important insights about gendered shifts in punishment and rehabilitation that were not being addressed in either policy or professional scholarship on gender inequality and mass incarceration. It was only through pursuing answers to these questions that my scholarly research was able to break new theoretical ground on gendered forms of punishment and control (see McCorkel, 2003). Further, it is through this line of research that I was able to develop a set of specific, empirically grounded policy recommendations that served to inform Larry Krasner's campaign platform.

Advocating for Women, Girls, and Families

When I was approached to serve as an advisor to the Krasner campaign during spring 2017, I leapt at the opportunity. I was familiar with Krasner's civil rights work, most notably his litigation on behalf of victims of police brutality and corruption. His campaign was already up and running in advance of the democratic primaries when I agreed to serve. I was excited at the prospect of utilizing the office of prosecutor as a key site from which to dismantle mass incarceration and Krasner offered a progressive and visionary platform. He had the respect and support of most of the activists, organizers, family members, and current and former inmates I had worked with over the years.

However, the campaign lacked an analysis of how gender shaped the conditions and consequences of mass incarceration, and there were no policy recommendations specifically aimed at women and girls. As one formerly incarcerated woman said to me, "I want to support him but when is he going to deal with what's happening to us [incarcerated women]?" These were serious oversights and ones that I was well suited to address. In my initial discussions with the campaign team, we talked about whether my advising work would focus principally on issues involving wrongful conviction and commutations or on gender disparities and the impact of criminal justice policies on families. I chose the latter. I did so because I was aware of a number of local academics, activists, and lawyers who would bring their considerable expertise to bear on issues involving wrongful conviction and commutation. There are not nearly as many people or organizations dedicated to issues facing incarcerated women or families.

I agreed to develop a set of concrete policy recommendations targeting gender and family issues. Each recommendation included a summary of relevant research and a forecast of the anticipated outcome. They were informed by the research literature as well as my ongoing conversations with current and formerly incarcerated women and members of their social networks. My primary focus was on drastically reducing the number of incarcerated women and girls, accompanied by suggestions regarding the DA's handling of sexual assault, domestic violence, and stalking cases.[2] In the interests of space, I will confine my summary here to those recommendations directed at reducing the number of women Philadelphia incarcerates.

Ending the Mass Incarceration of Women in Philadelphia

By 2016, most states, including Pennsylvania, had succeeded in reducing the size of their prison populations (some more so than others). Aggregate incarceration data, however, masked a troubling gender issue. Since 2009, almost all of the reductions in state prison populations have been men (Sawyer, 2018). Further, women's incarceration rate has continued to rise. Much of this increase has occurred within local jail populations where 60% of confined women have not been convicted of a crime (Sawyer, 2018). Indeed, women in jail are now the fastest growing correctional population in the United States (Swavola, Riley, & Subramanian, 2016).

Philadelphia is no exception to this trend. In 1980, the jail incarceration rate for women in Philadelphia was 20 per 100,000 residents between the ages of 15 and 64. By 2015, the rate was 120.2 per 100,000 (Vera Institute of Justice, 2018). Notably, this increase was not due to substantial changes in women's crime participation. Women did not, over the course of three decades, engage in more serious and/or more violent types of offenses. In fact, women's actual crime participation changed very little over the period (Britton, Jacobsen, & Howard, 2017; Kruttschnitt, 2013). Compared to men, women tend to be nonviolent offenders charged and/or convicted of less serious crimes. In light of this point, women should be the demographic group seeing the greatest reductions in their incarceration.

Women have not benefited from criminal justice reform for several reasons. First, they are frequently overlooked in both public policy and criminology. Among other things, this contributes to the fact that incarcerated women have fewer community-based options like halfway houses and reentry centers in which to serve out a portion of their sentences (McCorkel, 2013, 2018). Second, incarcerated women (and those facing incarceration) are particularly socially vulnerable. Poverty renders the majority economically vulnerable. Unable to post bail, they end up serving time despite not having been convicted of a crime (Harris, Evans, & Beckett, 2010). Motherhood and caretaking responsibilities create added pressure on women to accept disadvantageous guilty pleas as well as various juridical stipulations that they are otherwise constitutionally entitled to challenge (Kopf & Rubuy, 2015; McCampbell, 2005). Third, police, prosecutors, and court officials are unable to accurately identify victims of human trafficking (many of whom are women). Instead, trafficking victims are charged with criminal offenses even when their participation was the result of force, fraud, and/or coercion (Dempsey, 2015). Fourth, women are particularly hard hit by the sentencing policies of the War on Drugs, particularly mandatory minimums (McCorkel, 2013). These policies fail to distinguish an individual's role in a drug crime; instead, sentences are primarily set based on the volume of the drug. Thus, it is entirely possible that a drug seller and a drug lookout receive the same sanction despite the fact the latter plays a modest and considerably less lucrative part in the crime. Given the gender hierarchies that structure labor and consumption in illicit drug economies, women routinely find themselves relegated to minor roles that are high risk and low reward. Nonetheless, the sentences they receive are not reflective of the limited nature of their participation. The result is that today many women are doing time for crimes that, in the past, would have resulted in more modest sanctions including probation, suspended sentences, and community-based alternatives.

As deeply distressing as this situation is, there are several straightforward remedies that prosecutors can pursue to substantially improve it. I recommended that the campaign pledge to implement three policies that would not only provide immediate relief to women and families, but they would also reverse the longer-term trend of women's over-incarceration. They are: (1) eliminate cash bail, (2) end the practice of "up charging," and (3) distinguish degrees of culpability in commercial sex offenses and improve methods of identifying victims of human trafficking. The first two suggestions are likely not a surprise to readers familiar with criminal justice reform. While both policies are gender neutral and benefit multiple constituencies, they have particularly important implications for women. Over a third of defendants in Philadelphia are incarcerated because they cannot afford bail (Mattew, 2018). Among women this percentage is even greater. Although most women are not charged with serious crimes and do not present a flight risk, they end up in jail for months and sometimes years awaiting trial. For many women, this is untenable given their responsibilities as primary caretakers of children and family members. Many respond to this dilemma by taking disadvantageous guilty pleas. These limit time away from children, families, and jobs, but pose substantial legal consequences including lifetime felony records. Clearly, neither option serves women defendants, nor does it enhance community safety or public order. It is also worth noting that bail reform benefits those women and children who are not facing legal sanction. Studies show that in general bail and pretrial detention have adverse effects on families—contributing to an increased likelihood of poverty, financial instability, residential mobility, homelessness, and child trauma (Aiello & McCorkel, 2018; De Claire & Dixon, 2015; Foster & Hagan, 2015). Eliminating cash bail benefits defendants, families, and communities, and promises to substantially reduce the number of women in jail.

The other significant contributor to women's high rate of incarceration is prosecutorial charging decisions, particularly in the context of drug war sentencing policies. In numerous jurisdictions including Philadelphia, prosecutors are incentivized to up charge defendants, particularly when the possibility exists for a drug conviction (Bush-Baskette, 2000). This practice hits women particularly hard. In an earlier study I did with incarcerated women, many explained that although their primary offense was linked to participation in the commercial sex trade, the crimes they were actually charged with were drug crimes. In many cases, they were only tangentially linked to drugs (such as when drugs were found in their place of business or on their Johns) (McCorkel, 2013). For prosecutors, drug convictions carry an occupational currency that commercial sex offenses do not. Given the high penalties stipulated to most drug crimes, there is added pressure on defendants to plead guilty. The result is that women who otherwise would not be serving prison or jail sentences for their actual offenses end up doing so to avoid even lengthier mandatory minimums on drug charges. Ending the practice of up charging, particularly with respect to drug offenses, promises to substantially reduce the number of incarcerated women. Indeed, approximately one third of women in jail and prison are there due to drug charges and/or convictions (Kajstura, 2017).

Public order offenses, including prostitution, account for another 20% of women incarcerated in jail and 10% of those in prison (Kajstura, 2017). These numbers can also be substantially reduced through improvements in prosecutorial charging practices. Specifically, prosecutors need training and evidence-based mechanisms for identifying victims of human trafficking. All too often, trafficking victims are prosecuted and punished for crimes associated with the commercial sex trade when their participation was a product of force, fraud, and/or coercion (Dempsey, 2015). Preliminary research suggests that this is primarily due to a lack of knowledge and adequate training of law enforcement and prosecutors rather than ill intent (Anchan, 2016). Establishing degrees of culpability for commercial sex trade offenses also improves the accuracy of charging and avoids unduly penalizing the women who are the most vulnerable and powerless.

These policy recommendations were well received by Krasner and the campaign team and resonated with the suggestions of other advisors and local advocacy organizations. Although the experience of working as an "insider" on a campaign was new to me, I was not particularly surprised by the warm reception of my work. Krasner had more than earned his stripes among progressive activists in Philadelphia and was committed to running a campaign that utilized social science evidence to inform criminal justice policy. Krasner wanted to hear from social scientists and encouraged creative, community-based solutions to the myriad problems of mass incarceration. As a dedicated outside agitator, I would not have agreed to serve as an advisor to a candidate with anything less than a progressive vision of the DA's Office as a vehicle for social, rather than simply criminal, justice.

Conclusion

Although it is a cliché in U.S. politics that campaigns make promises they cannot or will not deliver on, this does not appear to be the case with Larry Krasner. Since assuming office in January 2018, he has instructed prosecutors not to bring charges for marijuana-related offenses, expanded the use of diversion programs, significantly shortened probation sentences, and eliminated cash bail for a list of 25 crimes including prostitution and retail theft. Regarding the gender-specific recommendations I made, he has required that prosecutors make plea offers at the bottom end of sentencing guidelines (thereby eliminating some of the most egregious aspects of up charging) and has issued a "do not charge" order on most prostitution-related offenses. All of these changes will significantly reduce the number of women coming into the penal system.

But what of the thousands of women who are already doing time? Krasner is pursuing two innovations that are quite promising. First, he is in the process of setting up the country's first sentencing review unit. The unit will examine whether an applicant's original sentence is proportionate relative to both the crime and to the needs of the community. The unit will explicitly consider the cost of an individual's incarceration as well as the seriousness of their criminal participation. This will have a significant impact on women, for all the reasons discussed above. Second, in August 2018 the Philadelphia DA's Office announced that it is partnering with the Vera Institute of Justice to substantially reduce the number of girls and young women in the juvenile justice system. The partnership will draw on social science research to generate gender-specific policies and programmatic innovations to keep young women and girls out of the system altogether.

The speed with which Larry Krasner has been able to overhaul the law and order policies of the Philadelphia DA's office is remarkable. It reflects the power of the political will of the electorate, the vast majority of whom demanded an immediate end to policies associated with mass incarceration and the drug war, and an end to police and prosecutorial corruption. It also reflects the power of social science research and public criminology. Krasner's critique of the criminal justice system as an engine of racial and economic inequality was substantiated and legitimized by overwhelming social science evidence. Further, the solutions he is pursuing to dismantle mass incarceration have been developed in coordination with public criminologists—social scientists with long histories of working with multiple constituencies to develop policies that are democratic, just, and effective. Public criminology offers social scientists the opportunity to do work that is not only personally fulfilling, but is also critical to the integrity of the research enterprise and to the health of democracy.

Notes

1 Following Krasner's election, Slaughter agreed to serve as Communications Deputy and Gur became Director of Research for the DA's Office.
2 For example, in 2016, there were approximately 1,300 rape kits in Philadelphia awaiting testing (Pennsylvania Auditor General, 2016). While Philadelphia has improved its response to sexual assault cases since the 1990s, it still has a long way to go to ensuring that these crimes are taken seriously. Although the District Attorney's office is not primarily responsible for testing, it is an issue that the district attorney can exert considerable influence over.

References

Abbott, K. (2001, April 25). Racial profiling jurors? Guilty! *Philadelphia Weekly*. Retrieved from www.philadelphiaweekly.com/news/racial-profiling-of-jurors-guilty/article_d265914b-0f77-5080-991e-eebfa4a6317d.html

Aiello, B. L., & McCorkel, J. A. (2018). 'It will crush you like a bug': Maternal incarceration, secondary prisonization, and children's visitation. *Punishment & Society, 20*(3), 351–374.

Allyn, B. (2015, July 16). Philadelphia spends millions every year to settle claims of police misconduct. *WHYY*. Retrieved from https://whyy.org/articles/philadelphia-spends-millions-every-year-to-settle-claims-of-police-misconduct/

Anchan, C. (2016). Protecting the imperfect victim: Expanding safe harbors to adult victims of sex trafficking. *William & Mary Journal of Women and the Law, 23*(1), 117–139.

Becker, H. (1967). Whose side are we on? *Social Problems, 14*(3), 239–247.

Bourdieu, P. (1998). *Acts of resistance: Against the new myths of our time*. New York: Polity Press.

Britton, D., Jacobsen, S. K., & Howard, G. E. (2017). *The gender of crime*. New York: Rowman & Littlefield.

Burawoy, M. (2005). For public sociology. *American Sociological Review, 70*(1), 4–28.

Bush-Baskette, S. (2000). The war on drugs and the incarceration of mothers. *Journal of Drug Issues, 30*(4), 919–928.

Clear, T. (2010). Editorial introduction to "public criminologies". *Criminology & Public Policy, 9*(4), 721–724.

Collins, P. H. (2000). *Black feminist thought*. New York: Routledge.

Crenshaw, K. (1989). Demarginalizing the intersection of race and sex: A black feminist critique of antidiscrimination doctrine, feminist theory, and antiracist politics. *University of Chicago Legal Forum, 1989*(1), 139–167.

Crenshaw, K. (1991). Mapping the margins: Intersectionality, identity politics, and violence against women of color. *Stanford Law Review, 43*(6), 1241–1299.

Currie, E. (1999). Reflections on crime and criminology at the millennium. *Western Criminology Review, 2*(1), 1–14.

De Claire, K., & Dixon, L. (2015). The effects of prison visits on family members well being, prison rule breaking, and recidivism: A review of the research since 1991. *Trauma, Violence, and Abuse, 18*(2), 185–199.

Dempsey, M. (2015). Decriminalizing victims of sex trafficking. *American Criminal Law Review, 52*(2), 207–229.

Foster, H., & Hagan, J. (2015). Punishment regimes and the multilevel effects of parental incarceration. *Annual Review of Sociology, 41*, 135–158.

Foucault, M. (2003). *Society must be defended: Lectures at the College de France, 1975–1976*. (D. Macey, Trans). New York: Picador.

Glueck, S., & Glueck, E. (1950). Unraveling juvenile delinquency. *Juvenile Court Judges Journal, 2*, 32.

Harding, S. (1991). *Whose science? What knowledge?* Ithaca, NY: Cornell University Press.

Harris, A., Evans, H., & Beckett, K. (2010). Drawing blood from stones: Legal debt and social inequality in the contemporary United States. *American Journal of Sociology, 115*(6), 1753–1799.

Human Rights Watch. (1998). *Civil remedies*. Retrieved from www.hrw.org/legacy/reports/reports98/police/uspo30.htm

Kajstura, A. (2017). Women's mass incarceration: The whole pie. *Prison Policy Initiative*. Retrieved from www.prisonpolicy.org/reports/pie2017women.html

Kopf, D., & Rubuy, B. (2015). Prisons of poverty: Uncovering the pre-incarceration incomes of the imprisoned. *Prison Policy Initiative*. Retrieved from www.prisonpolicy.org/reports/income.html

Kruttschnitt, C. (2013). Gender and crime. *Annual Review of Sociology, 39*, 291–308.

Lombroso, C. ([1911] 1968). *Crime: Its causes and remedies*. Montclair, NJ: Patterson Smith.

Mattew, T. (2018). Bail reform takes flight in Philly. *Citylab*. Retrieved from www.citylab.com/equity/2018/02/bail-reform-takes-flight-in-philly/552212/

McCampbell, S. (2005). *The gender-responsive strategies project: Jail applications*. Washington, DC: Department of Justice.

McCorkel, J. (2003). Embodied surveillance and the gendering of punishment. *Contemporary Ethnography, 32*(1), 41–76.

McCorkel, J. (2007). When the stakes are life and death: The promise and peril of public sociology in capital cases. In S. Miller (Ed.), *Criminal justice research and practice* (pp. 76–91). Boston, MA: Northeastern University Press.

McCorkel, J. (2013). *Breaking women: Gender, race, and the new politics of imprisonment*. New York: New York University Press.

McCorkel, J. (2018). Banking on rehab: Private prison vendors and the reconfiguration of mass incarceration. *Studies in Law, Politics, & Society, 77*, 351–374.

McCorkel, J., & Myers, K. (2003). What difference does difference make? Position and privilege in the field. *Qualitative Sociology, 26*(2), 199–231.

Nellis, A. (2016). *The color of justice: Racial and ethnic disparity in state prisons*. Washington, DC: The Sentencing Project.

Pennsylvania Auditor General. (2016). *Untested rape kits: A special report*. Retrieved from www.paauditor.gov/Media/Default/Reports/RPT_Untested_rape_kits_FINAL.pdf

Pew Charitable Trusts. (2011). *Philadelphia's crowded, costly jails: The search for safe solutions*. Philadelphia, PA: Author.

Quinney, R. (1970). *The social reality of crime*. Boston, MA: Little, Brown.

Quinney, R. (1974). *Critique of legal order*. Boston, MA: Little, Brown.

Rosenberg, T. (1995, July 16). The deadliest D.A. *New York Times*. Retrieved from www.nytimes.com/1995/07/16/magazine/the-deadliest-da.html

Sammon, A. (2017, May 12). After a career suing cops, this lawyer wants to be Philly's next district attorney. *Mother Jones*. Retrieved from www.motherjones.com/politics/2017/05/larry-krasner-district-attorney-philadelphia-reformer/

Sawyer, W. (2018). The gender divide: Tracking women's state prison growth. *Prison Policy Initiative*. Retrieved from www.prisonpolicy.org/reports/women_overtime.html

Smith, D. (1987). *The everyday world as problematic*. Boston, MA: Northeastern University Press.

Swavola, E., Riley, K., & Subramanian, R. (2016). *Overlooked: Women and jails in an era of reform*. New York: Vera Institute of Justice.

Uggen, C., & Inderbitzin, M. (2010). Public criminologies. *Criminology & Public Policy, 9*(4), 725–749.

Vera Institute of Justice. (2018). People in prison. Retrieved from www.vera.org/publications/people-in-prison-2017

7

REFLECTIONS FROM AN ACCIDENTAL PUBLIC SCHOLAR

Peter B. Kraska

Introduction: Becoming an Accidental Public Scholar

In early June 1997, I was playing with my daughter at home when I received a phone call from William Booth at the *Washington Post*. A colleague told him about an "alarming" article in the journal *Social Problems*, which I had co-written. He asked if I had a few minutes to talk. I said sure, and we talked for two hours about my research. His final question surprised me: "Do you have tenure?" I did not. Joel Best, the editor of *Social Problems*, posed the same question to me the year before when finalizing mine and Vic Kappeler's publication, "Militarizing American Police: The Rise and Normalizaton of Paramilitary Units" (Kraska & Kappeler, 1997).

A few days later an acquaintance of mine at the National Institute of Justice (NIJ) in Washington, DC, called to let me know that my research was featured on the front page of the *Washington Post*. He also said that his bosses at NIJ were grumbling about the article, given that I linked the rise of militarized policing with community policing. (The U.S. Department of Justice was in the midst of generously funding community policing reform efforts.) I had no idea William Booth (1997) was going to write and publish, "Exploding Number of SWAT Teams Sets Off Alarms." That same day I had 15 requests for interviews with television (TV), radio, and print media outlets. With zero experience, I decided to call two journalists back: Eric Silverman from National Public Radio (NPR), and Jeffrey Kaye at the Jim Lehr News Hour (PBS). Both of them were consummate professionals and did excellent pieces on the police militarization trend. The flow of requests did not abate for 20 years, and, since 1997, I have helped put together at least 2,000 print, TV, radio, and Internet media stories.

What "alarmed" the *Washington Post* were the definitive and steep trend lines documenting the police marching rapidly down the militarization continuum. A wealth of qualitative data and theoretical analysis was incorporated as well, depicting a large and growing segment of police relying heavily on the military model—materially, culturally, organizationally, and operationally. Today, most police analysts concede that police institutions are replete with the trappings of military special operations culture, and routinely engage those living in socio-economically disadvantaged areas as a militarized occupying force.

What alarmed some of my colleagues and administrators at Eastern Kentucky University (EKU) was the attention I garnered for being "anti-police." The concern about my tenure status from Boothe and Best was well founded. Some co-workers (and a few police academics outside EKU) claimed that I fabricated my data because they simply were not believable, some expressed concern over how I was wasting my time talking to the media, and others were openly hostile about what they saw as politically-charged scholarship. Even one of my closest academic allies expressed open skepticism to me (and others) about the legitimacy of my work and the appropriateness of me talking about my research to the media. It did not help that during that same time period, some research on police sexual violence (on-duty police officers sexually assaulting female citizens) started to receive widespread media attention (*ABC News*, 1997; Kraska & Kappeler, 1995). This derision ultimately led to a long, contentious, face-to-face conversation with EKU's Provost about whether I should be denied tenure. There were of course no grounds for any of these accusations and I was awarded tenure during my third year of employment at EKU.

Despite the blowback I encountered, the media attention has led to some other unique opportunities. I have done expert witness testimony work, most of which has been pro-bono on particularly outrageous instances of police violence related to police militarization. I have also agreed to work on some high-profile legal cases involving police militarization (including *U.S. Government vs. Timothy McVeigh*[1] and a case involving the Royal Canadian Mounted Police). Some of this work has led to direct activist work for the families and the communities impacted. Other types of public scholarship included consulting with a U.S. White House commission after the Ferguson tragedy, testifying at the U.S. Senate on the issue of police militarization, working on numerous state commissions, and doing lots of guest-speaking for activist groups and at Universities in the U.S. and abroad. Most recently, I have begun to write public essays on various incidents/issues revolving around policing and police militarization (Kraska, 2018).

This chapter will focus only on my work with print and television media, drawing primarily on my experience from the last 22 years. Its four objectives are: (1) to make the connection between public scholarship and public theory; (2) to highlight some key drawbacks and benefits for academe and individual academics in doing this type of public scholarship; (3) to outline some lessons learned over my years of doing this line of work; and (4) to warn critical criminologists about the real danger in the idea of public criminology being coopted and exploited by those with a regressive political agenda.

Public Scholarship and Public Theory

My involvement with print and television media was inspired by Gregg Barak's call for criminologists to participate in newsmaking criminology. I first read Barak's foundational piece on scholars engaging with the media in the mid-1990s. For him, "newsmaking criminology refers to the conscious efforts of criminologists and others to participate in the presentation of 'newsworthy' items about crime and justice" (Barak, 1988, p. 37). This simple idea, and the acknowledgement of what I had been doing for years, helped me recognize the importance of participating in the social construction of media narratives about the police and state violence. However, it was not until 2008 that I fully realized two things: first, how insular and counterproductive criminology as a discipline was with regard to engaging with the media; and second, the significant potential of criminologists to shape and frame public narratives about the nature of crime and crime control. With regard to the first point, I grew tired of hearing the unsubstantiated claim at conferences that journalists were poor sources of information and that academics produced the only legitimate forms of knowledge. This bias—and the notion of superiority underpinning it—led to much of the academic community keeping journalists at an arm's length, which meant the knowledge we did produce made little impact outside academe.

At one point, in an effort to encourage other academics to work with the media, I began writing a "tips and techniques" article for academics who might want to share their work with the public. However, given the reaction of my colleagues noted above, I eventually surmised that academics doing public scholarship would prefer to stay under the radar. It simply was not worth the professional risk. As this volume demonstrates, I was thankfully wrong, and much of the social science academic world has since begun to embrace public scholarship and activism as legitimate, perhaps even merit-worthy, academic work.

It should be fairly obvious that doing public criminology constitutes an attempt by academics to influence the public's knowledge and perceptions about crime and justice phenomena and issues (Currie, 2007). As noted in this volume, many scholars simply do what we do best—teach, except they do so to the general public via the media. The aspect that I find most interesting, and potentially consequential, is teaching the public *why*. It is no doubt essential to teach them descriptive information—for example, no-knock and quick-knock contraband raids carried out by police paramilitary units on people's private residence has increased by 1,900% since the early 1980s. However, impacting the public's theoretical narratives—that is, why have we seen a 1,900% increase in these police paramilitary raids—is a poorly understood and rarely discussed activity within the academy.

Part of the reason is that many academics would never acknowledge that a public theoretical narrative exists. And, if they did, they would not bestow on it the sacred label of "theory." The social science community has constructed a disciplinary straitjacket around the notion of theory—an entity and phenomenon owned and used exclusively by academics and generally for other academics (this is particularly true for exclusively quantitative researchers). Even among critical scholars, attempts at theorizing that fall outside the halls of academe often do not constitute a legitimate form of theory at all. Instead, we refer to it as merely "ideology" or sometimes "public consciousness." By monopolizing theory, we separate it from everyday thinking. Not only is this an untenable position—most, if not all, social science theory emanates from real-world thinking and ideas—it ignores the fact that "public theorizing" is of far more consequence than what we do in academe. Indeed, criminology and justice studies tend to lose sight of what ought to be the ultimate goal of academic theory: influencing and shaping public thinking, or what I refer to as "public theory."

Good public scholarship, then, attempts to influence public theory. The stakes in doing so are high. Consider, for example, the research on climate change:[2] the public's accurate theoretical understanding is of paramount importance to the survival of humankind. Similarly, making accurate theoretical sense of national and global inequality is crucial to meaningful social, political, and economic change. The media obviously plays a large role in molding public theory, and in our field of study, it is often governmental officials and politicians who spoon-feed the media theoretical narratives. Just a simple organizing concept repeated again and again by academics—like "police militarization"—can go a long way toward guiding public explanations.

For example, when I testified at the U.S. Senate, I was invited to talk about military weapons transference programs to local police departments (the 1033 program). The entire format revolved around the unquestioned assumption, made by journalists and politicians, that military weaponry and gear caused police militarization. It was tempting to go along with this public theory because I certainly would have liked to see the elimination of the 1033 program. However, I felt compelled to spell out a host of far more influential causal factors, including a racially charged war on drugs, a well-funded post-9/11 Department of Homeland Security grant program, the rapid rise of a deep militaristic culture (militarism) in contemporary policing, and the aggressive pursuit of property and money by the police under civil asset forfeiture programs (EKU College of Justice and Society, 2014). It is worth noting, that my extensive experience talking about these theories in an accessible manner with the media prepared me for doing the same in front of the U.S. Senate.

Benefits and Drawbacks for Public Scholars

Impacting how the public understands and explains police killings, police sexual violence against women, the war on drugs, and state violence against racial minorities has been probably the most rewarding aspect of my public criminological work. As public criminology begins to become normalized in our field, we need to consider its potential benefits and drawbacks, particularly in relation to the individual choosing to engage in this activity. The following draws from numerous observations and experiences.

Benefits

Public scholarly activity is a tangible demonstration of the power of research and scholarship to make a difference. For critical criminologists, it realizes the hope of critical social science (Kraska & Neuman, 2012, p. 57):

> The purpose of critical research is not simply to study the social world but to change it. Critical social science (CSS) researchers conduct research to critique and transform inhibiting social conditions by revealing the underlying sources of these conditions and empowering people, especially less powerful people. More specifically, they uncover deep-seated ideologies, reveal hidden truths, and help people to change the world for themselves. In CSS, the purpose is "to explain a social order in such a way that it becomes itself the catalyst which leads to the transformation of this social order."
>
> *(Fay, 1987, p. 27)*

Drawing media attention to one's research has potential to yield professional benefits, including greater likelihood of guest-speaking invitations in academe and in political activist circles, as well as book publishers being more likely to be receptive to proposals. It also increases the chance of being asked to do consulting and expert witness legal work, a higher standing or profile in one's university, and a greater personal sense that one's work is making a difference. In sum, at least for me, my public criminological work has been rewarding and worthwhile. However, it definitely has quite a few potential drawbacks.

Drawbacks

Engaging as a public scholar could yield little to nothing with regard to one's career or impacting the public. Several factors enter into this possibility. Media coverage, even national media coverage, does not mean that anyone will seriously pay attention or care. Most media stories are little more than background noise and filler (particularly true for television and radio media). They could lead to a few tweets or reader comments, but most are ignored. Many factors play a role in whether one's work gets noticed: the political appeal of the subject matter; the quality of the research and scholarship conducted; whether this scholarship fits into an appealing or controversial sound-bite (e.g., police militarization); and, the extent to which the public scholar puts serious effort into influencing the tone and nature of the media coverage.

This work is uncompensated labor. From the thousands of hours I have worked for for-profit and non-profit media outlets, I have never received any compensation. Working on a media story often involves up to eight hours on the phone with the primary journalist answering questions and attempting to frame the story in a way that will result in critical (in the social theory sense) coverage of the topic. This can also include putting together documents, doing some primary research, giving the journalists leads for other people to talk to, and working with a fact-checker at the end of the process. I have received travel and expenses to fly to a location for a documentary or TV spot, but no honorarium or payment for my time and expertise. Of course, academics are accustomed to working for free (e.g., writing student letters of recommendation, journal article and book reviews, external tenure review work), so perhaps this kind of work is just another category of "service." However, this type of service is intensely time-consuming, and the immediate rewards overall are limited.

I am an accidental public scholar in the sense that I fell into a timely research topic and a course of events with little aforethought and no desire to work with the media (Layton, 2016). I had to do virtually nothing (at least initially) beyond agreeing to interviews to make it happen. I cannot imagine how difficult and time-consuming it would be to proactively seek out this type of scholarly activity. A serious drawback, then, would be the arduous process of disseminating one's scholarship in a public forum without being solicited by the media.

Derision from the academy, co-workers, and the university is still a serious concern, especially for criminologists who are communicating critical messages. Our research topics can be polarizing and difficult to understand. Moreover, especially in the contemporary moment in the United States, there are right-wing watchdog groups that keep track of critical scholars' work and comments.

Also do not assume that national media attention will result in academic attention. While my own research is well cited in other disciplines, criminology has mostly ignored this research until recently. I have to admit that years ago I found it peculiar and frustrating to have my work sought after and be publicized locally, nationally, and internationally, yet criminology—the venue where I most wanted to establish my reputation as a serious scholar—did not pay much attention. And almost comically, now that my work is more recognized in criminology (due mainly to the police militarization phenomenon taking center stage in recent critiques of the criminal justice system), I now care far more about influencing the public than I do the academy.

Lessons Learned

If an academic weighs the benefits and drawbacks and then decides to engage with the media, the following section includes a few bits of advice for doing so:

- Never assume print journalists are poor or uninformed researchers. The academic snobbery about journalists not understanding research, from my experience, is totally unfounded. In criminology, we tend to forget that journalists have conducted the initial research that has led to a lot of cutting-edge academic research (e.g., police killings).
- Most journalists are hardworking and well prepared. Some, however, hope that you (the academic) will do their leg work for them, guide them through your work without reading it, and will even ask you for leads and documents that they could easily obtain themselves. Encourage journalists to read your work before being interviewed.
- Live TV appearances require a particular personality type. I tried a few times and found the experience unpleasant. One has to be completely at ease with themselves in front of a live camera in order to think out loud in a clear and brief manner. A taped interview can be stopped or edited afterwards. Nothing said live can be recanted. I found it intimidating. I can, however, pretty effectively do an hour of live radio (perhaps because I am not worried about how I appear on camera).
- Police militarization is a fairly easy sell for most journalists. It ranks on the sensibilities of those on the left and right, therefore making it easier to guide the framing of the story. Other topics, such as prison or police abolition, would be much more difficult. One solution for critical criminologists is to focus primarily on leftist media outlets.
- Do not be guided by their questions alone. Take an active role in framing the discussion. Sometimes journalists will not ask questions that are theoretical in nature; provide the answers anyway.
- Numerous media outlets are open to publishing original public essays by academics. This is a good way to publicize ideas and recent research. *The Huffington Post*, *The Nation*, and

Alternet are good examples; outlets like *The Atlantic* are often far more difficult to get into, but worthwhile.
- Try not to get too invested in the importance of public scholarship. The reality is even a front-page feature in a leading outlet is likely to end up as another digital blip in a massive media landscape. University bureaucracies generally do not give credit, and academic colleagues oftentimes either do not care about or can even resent this kind of work. The goal of educating the public is laudable, but it is difficult to get a tangible sense of its impact.
- This is all unpaid public service work. It is free labor. I personally have not found this problematic, except when working with wealthy media giants like CNN, NBC, and CBS.
- Be cautious of unethical journalism or distortions of what you have said. While I have found this to be uncommon, it does happen. For example, I had a two-hour lunch meeting with a high-end journalist from the *New York Times* a few years ago. We talked at length about a discovery I made and had been tracking for years: the phenomenon of police Warrior training conducted by ex-military soldiers and its connection to police killings. A few months later this journalist ran a full featured piece on this exact topic and never asked for an interview or attributed any of the discovery to my hard work. I contacted him and diplomatically tried to get a sense of why he did this. His response was defensive and evasive, indicating he clearly knew what he had done. It angered me, but I pursued it no further. (I would be happy to share his name through email if anyone reading this wants to avoid him).
- Public engagement with the media takes skill, preparedness, diplomacy, and time to help journalists construct their story in a way that best captures your ideas or research. The most important element I have found is to be down-to-earth and candid.
- Public criminology is a serious time commitment with few tangible rewards. The ego-bump of seeing your name in print or having friends and relatives impressed you were on TV is short-lived. The drive to do public criminology must come from realizing the important potential benefit from teaching others (the public) on such a massive scale.

Warning: It Cuts both Ways

Public criminological scholarship does have an appeal for most critical criminologists. We research, teach, and write hoping to make a difference—not to merely contribute to the discipline. The surface appeal, however, masks a serious risk: public criminology can be just as easily used for regressive ends.

Consider the decades-long push by critical criminologists to legitimize ethnographic field research and qualitative research in general. Robust and brilliant critical ethnographies have exposed gendered, racial, and class oppression while pointing to structural impediments and needed changes. These same critical ethnographies have provided grounded theoretical insights into the "why" of crime and crime control. Much of this work has been summarily dismissed by mainstream academic criminologists as mere subjective musings devoid of rigor and research legitimacy. Over the past 15 years, though, qualitative research has been increasingly acknowledged as legitimate research. This mainstream approval, however, has come with a steep price. The growing number of qualitatively oriented studies funded by the NIJ, and those conducted by mainstream criminologists, are predictably quite conservative in their approach and findings. They have merely upheld the status quo and raised few substantive questions about the larger political, economic, and cultural context of the social issues they have researched. One could view this apparent victory, therefore, as in some ways a failure—particularly given the way in which qualitative methods are rapidly being coopted and used for regressive purposes.[3]

Public criminology runs the same risk. A host of "blue-blood" criminologists have for a long time fully embraced the role of public scholar (as well as the significant financial benefits). These folks are, in many ways, activist scholars, in that they actively promote punitive crime control policies and activities. Leftist public scholars such Elliott Currie, Bernard Harcourt, and Jonathan Simon have been exposing the fallacies and questionable work of these types of conservative (sometimes mainstream liberal) activist criminologists for decades.

Imagine these same types of scholars today, unleashed in greater numbers due to the fashionable trend of public scholarship. The story of the police reform movement, and simultaneous rise of police militarization, is a solid case in point (Kraska, 2016). The steep growth in the number and activities of police paramilitary teams coincided with a steep increase in community policing funds and reforms. The high-profile blue-blood scholars advocating for police as a viable entity for controlling crime ultimately resulted in a police-induced debacle. "Fixing broken windows" morphed into massive state resource extraction from the poor (and into the pockets of local police and prosecutors). "Weed and seed" type programs devolved rapidly into police paramilitary squads occupying neighborhoods using proactive techniques of punitive control such as no-knock raids and stop-and-frisk. It was activist academic criminologists, such as David Weisburd, Lawrence Sherman, James Q. Wilson, and George Kelling, that led the way in conceptualizing and assisting in the enactment of this catastrophic and cynical reform campaign. The point here is that critical criminologists, just as with critically engaged ethnographers, need to be aware of the very real danger of cooptation—and, as we do best, hold those that will exploit it for questionable ends to account.

Conclusion

The academic world has been taken to task for residing in their own bubbles, generating self-referential knowledge for the purpose of furthering the careers of those working in these bubbles. Many have come to realize that scholars, especially in fields such as criminology and justice studies, should actively engage the public sphere in order to further the public good. It is assumed that academics have a level of expertise, one that stems from rigorous research and careful study, that is useful for alleviating suffering and perhaps helping to bring about substantive structural and macro-cultural change. The truth needs public advocates.

I stumbled into this line of work in the late 1990s. I am slowly stumbling out of it. I have put in a lot of time and energy, and my interest is somewhat waning. I have, however, started the process of writing a series of public essays that I eventually plan on incorporating into a book. Public essays are more appealing at this juncture because they mean I am not relying on a journalist to get the story right. Rather, I can write my own stories and theoretical narratives.

My next public essay (tentatively titled "Police Militarization Camouflaged"), interestingly, is how the media's interest in police militarization, which hit a peak in 2014 and 2015 after the Ferguson protests following the police shooting unarmed Black teenager Michael Brown to death, has diminished to almost non-existent. This is fascinating and worthy of public discussion and theorizing. Part of the reason for this growing lack of interest could be similar to why I have lost some interest in the topic: the increasing awareness of police killings and punitive police practices has led to a larger concern, beyond police militarization, with what we might call "mass policing." In other words, police militarization is only one component, albeit a central one, to the larger phenomenon of mass policing.[4]

A more cynical possibility is that the proverbial frog has been boiled: 25 years of incremental growth in police militarization has conditioned journalists, and the general population, to view militarized policing as normal and routine. While the militaristic images of police during the Ferguson civil unrest did stir up outrage, this same imagery had already become a mainstream and accepted part of the cultural landscape. Perhaps the police marching down the militarization continuum, particularly now during the spectacle of the Trump administration, has been normalized to the extent that the media no longer views it as having any shock value. In media circles, the truth is that which sells. "If it ain't selling, it must not be true" (Kraska, 2003).

Notes

1 *United States v. McVeigh*, 918 F. Sup. 1467 (W.D. Okla. 1996).
2 While I use "climate change" here, some media outlets use "climate crisis," a move that reflects how many advocates and experts describe the issue.
3 The list of recent ethnographies that fit this description is extensive. I will not list them explicitly to avoid the blowback for doing so. I do plan to write a paper on this problem where I will lay out several key examples (e.g., Decker & Pyrooz, 2012). I would like a co-author if anyone is interested.
4 I find it fascinating that U.S. criminology has focused untold amount of attention to mass incarceration, yet has arguably given the massive growth in punitive, intrusive, and large-scale policing a free-pass. It is as if the entire field forgot that it takes mass policing to realize mass incarceration. The obvious explanation is that U.S. criminology has, to a large extent, left the study of policing to police academics who tend focus on conservative pursuits such as evaluations and how to reduce crime.

References

ABC News. (1997). Betrayed by the badge. 20/20.
Barak, G. (1988). Newsmaking criminology: Reflections of the media, intellectuals, and crime. *Justice Quarterly*, 5(4), 565–587.
Booth, W. (1997, June 17). Exploding number of SWAT teams sets off alarms. *Washington Post*. Retrieved from www.washingtonpost.com/archive/politics/1997/06/17/exploding-number-of-swat-teams-sets-off-alarms/898513be-cc10-43d2-a9d7-e55232f55836
Currie, E. (2007). Against marginality: Arguments for a public criminology. *Theoretical Criminology*, 11(2), 175–190.
Decker, S. H., & Pyrooz, D. C. (2012). Contemporary gang ethnographies. In F. T. Cullen & P. Wilcox (Eds.), *Handbook on criminological theory* (pp. 274–293). Oxford: Oxford University Press.
EKU College of Justice and Society. (2014, October 21). *Dr. Peter Kraska: Senate hearing - police use of military equipment* [Video file]. Retrieved from www.youtube.com/watch?v=AT79zyQ_3Vo
Fay, B. (1987). *Critical social science: Liberation and its limits*. Cambridge: Polity Press.
Kraska, P. B. (2003). Quote from a personal interview with a major TV producer.
Kraska, P. B. (2016). *Academic complicity in police militarization*. Paper presented at the University of London and the London School of Economics.
Kraska, P. B. (2018, February 4). State theft and police militarization: Cops and prosecutors routinely steal cash from poor people accused of crimes. *Alternet*. Retrieved from www.alternet.org/2018/02/state-theft-and-police-militarization-cops-and-prosecutors-routinely-steal-cash-poor/
Kraska, P. B., & Kappeler, V. E. (1995). To serve and pursue: Exploring police sexual violence against women. *Justice Quarterly*, 12(1), 85–111.
Kraska, P. B., & Kappeler, V. E. (1997). Militarizing American police: The rise and normalization of paramilitary units. *Social Problems*, 44(1), 1–18.
Kraska, P. B., & Neuman, L. (2012). *Criminal justice and criminology research methods* (2nd ed.). Boston, MA: Pearson Publishing.
Layton, R. A. (2016). The accidental scholar, by Jagdish N. Sheth with John Yow, Sage Publications, 2014. *Journal of Business-to-Business Marketing*, 23(1), 81–84.

8

ENGAGING THE PUBLIC

Access to Justice for Those Most Vulnerable

Emily I. Troshynski

"How Can You Do This?" An Illustration of Local Civil Justice

In the spring of 2013, a video documenting a 2011 family court hearing was released to the public. A young woman, accompanied by her young child, enters a civil courtroom. She is seeking to vacate a temporary protection order (TPO) that her ex-husband filed. She does not have a lawyer present. The ex-husband is also not present. Interactions that occurred next would later make local and national news.

According to reports, as this woman was leaving the hearing, a court marshal ordered her into a waiting room for an unexplained drug search.[1] She asked for a female witness to be present during this search. Immediately following, the women returned to the same courtroom with her young child. She told the judge that, after she entered the separate room, the marshal ignored her request for a female witness, asked her to lift up her shirt, and touched her breasts and buttocks. The video shows the judge ignoring the woman. The same marshal searches through the woman's purse. A law enforcement officer starts to question her. The young child runs over to the judge sitting at her bench. The judge faces away from the young woman and, instead, interacts with the child. The woman becomes increasingly distressed as the cop and marshal proceed to handcuff and arrest her for making false allegations.[2] During these exchanges, the judge remains silent and never intervenes. Instead, she continues to interact with the child. The video shows them playing with a large stuffed animal. Eventually, the child walks back over to her mother as she's being arrested. The woman starts crying and pleads for help saying to the judge, "*How can you do this?*" Her little girl begs the marshal and cop not to take her mother away. Her young voice repeats, "*Leave her alone.*"

Shortly after this video goes viral, a federal lawsuit filed against the marshal, law enforcement officer, judge, and court claimed civil rights violations, battery, false imprisonment, defamation, and negligence. Main complaints included wrongful conduct of the marshal accused of sexually assaulting the young woman as well as wrongful conduct of the judge as exhibiting "reckless, callous and deliberate indifference to plaintiff's federally protected rights" (see German, 2013). During the summer of 2013, this judge stepped down. Even though the marshal denied the sexual assault allegations, he was later fired. The young woman's charge of making false allegations was reduced to misdemeanor disorderly conduct to which she pled no contest. Lawsuits were finally settled during the summer of 2014.

This case was the impetus for a collaborative and interdisciplinary research project aimed at better understanding domestic violence (DV) issues, including victims' experiences with civil justice systems and those "gatekeepers" (i.e., judges, marshals, advocates, lawyers, and court staff) that work within them. It occurred in a court that oversees anywhere between 8,000 to 11,000 civil protection order hearings annually. This civil court is located in a diverse metropolitan city, with over 600,000 residents. Half of the population speaks English and a quarter (25%) speaks Spanish. This city is located in a U.S. state that has one of the highest rates of domestic violence incidents annually and consistently ranks in the top five—and in recent years, first—for homicide among female victims murdered by males in single victim/single offender incidents (Violence Policy Center, 2017).

First, this chapter discusses the importance in researching access to justice particularly for those most marginalized. Then, it reflects on prior research dedicated to DV victims' experiences with civil court systems, which documents numerous barriers. After highlighting barriers to access to justice in civil courts, this chapter summarizes a collaborative and interdisciplinary research project addressing similar concerns. Preliminary findings chart a range of barriers encountered by DV victims. What becomes clear is that inconsistencies in treatment and remedies available, as well as a range of injustices do occur. Notes on pursuing justice outcomes through public criminological commitments are offered as well as some thoughts on doing public criminological methods and praxis. The chapter concludes with a reflection on overall impacts.

The Public Importance of Access to Justice

As the example in the introduction demonstrates, victims seeking help from civil court systems can experience a range of barriers and injustices; some are as severe as assault and arrest. This illustration brings to mind questions about access to justice, particularly the notion of "equal justice under law," a hallmark of the U.S. legal system. Even though all humans are supposed to be equal in dignity and rights (United Nations, 1948), scholars highlight the reality that millions of humans lack any access to justice, let alone equitable access, particularly when their dignity and their rights are infringed upon. When justice systems do not ensure equitable access, those most vulnerable become even more defenseless and further marginalized (Golub, 2003; Rhode, 2004). These questions of justice and of rights are common amongst criminologists. Yet, as a discipline, criminology has largely failed to engage with important access to justice queries, particularly in the civil justice realm.

Criminology has traditionally focused on juvenile delinquency, violent crime, street crime, and issues associated with policing, criminal courts, and corrections. The majority of these studies include secondary data sets and analyses that test for theoretical hypotheses. Public criminology suggests that, despite criminology's accumulation of these theoretical and empirical works, not much impact has been made on public discourse that addresses the realities of crime as well as justice responses (Currie, 2007). Thus, public criminology, as proposed by Loader and Sparks (2013), seeks to (1) produce knowledge pertaining to crime and criminal justice policy; (2) increase the regard for this knowledge among media and policy outlets; and (3) unearth the significance of the crime question within contemporary society. Just as research on access to justice for individuals, groups, and communities has been overlooked by the discipline of criminology, public criminology has also barely attended to these involvements. Even so, there are important justice-centered synergies across critical, feminist, and public criminological commitments, which I discuss further here.

For example, for those of us trained as, influenced by, and working within a feminist and/or critical criminological tradition, there is an ethos and responsibility to document and highlight harms perpetuated and normalized by those in power. This often includes analysis of institutions, legal systems, and governmental actions at the local, state, federal, and international level. Indeed, feminist and critical criminologists have long engaged in research that attends to state and corporate crime; sexist, racist, and classist violence; and human rights abuses. These works are particularly compatible with a public criminological agenda. As Loader and Sparks (2013, p. 34) note,

> We also see it as our task to place criminological knowledge (or counter-knowledge), together with our research skills, at the service of those marginalized on the basis of their class, gender, ethnicity, sexuality, or age, and have joined with social movements and campaigns to end discrimination and advance social justice.

This chapter reflects on these shared commitments in relation to research on victims' accessing civil legal spaces post abuse episodes.

If we are to place our criminological knowledge at the service of those most marginalized, research on and about access to justice is helpful in that it challenges public criminology to identify, understand, and advocate for disadvantaged persons and groups that come in contact with civil court systems of justice. Additionally, access to justice work challenges us to collaborate with members of institutions that may or may not participate in reproducing inequality (i.e., willingly or unknowingly). This balancing act requires recognition that those most knowledgeable are the ones experiencing justice systems as victim/applicant, abuser/defendant, and practitioner/judge. Thus, both clients and employees know the obstacles they face; they also have ideas about strategies to mitigate them. In the pages that follow, analyses of civil remedies are considered as action items that can contribute to the production of alternative ways of thinking about and distributing justice, particularly for those most marginalized. Importantly, such remedies align well with key tenets of critical, feminist, and public criminologies.

Civil Protection Orders (CPOs) and Barriers to Access to Justice

Criminologists, specifically feminist and critical criminologists, have long been devoted to researching the experiences and consequences of DV. Yet, as Dragiewicz (2014, p. 122) notes, these conversations have "rarely broached the subject of family law and domestic violence." Recently, some have documented victims' help-seeking behaviors associated with formal criminal and civil justice systems (Durfee, 2008; Durfee & Messing, 2012; Jordan, 2004). Others have documented the effectiveness of civil legal remedies available (Bell, Perez, Goodman, & Dutton, 2011; Burgess-Proctor, 2003; DeJong & Burgess-Proctor, 2006).

Understanding civil protection orders as well as barriers to accessing civil courts is important given that, since the passing of the Violence Against Women Act (VAWA; Title IV of Public Law 103-322), DV victims have increasingly utilized CPOs as a means of legal protection against their abusers (Keilitz, Hannaford, & Efkeman, 1997; Tjaden & Thoennes, 2000). In fact, recent studies document that over 1.5 million protection orders are issued within the United States each year (Fleury-Steiner, Miller, Maloney, & Postel, 2016; Logan, Shannon, Walker, & Faragher, 2006) rendering them one of the most commonly sought remedies for DV, second only to calling 911 (Goldfarb, 2007; Jordan, 2004). Every day, thousands of women experiencing DV apply for a CPO via their local civil court system; the majority initiate these orders *pro se*[3] and without legal counsel (Bejinariu, 2016; Bell et al., 2011).

When a victim documents and discusses publicly their DV experiences and is granted a CPO, they are also told *criminal* penalties will ensue if the identified offender is ever in violation of the order. Even with these sanctioned criminal punishments, research has shown that offenders do violate at high rates (Keilitz et al., 1997; Logan & Walker, 2009, 2010). This is due to perceptions of seriousness associated with civil remedies (compared to criminal justice system responses), victim's failing to report when an offender violates a standing CPO, lack of enforcement via adequate police responses to violations, and/or criminal prosecutors' offices failing to file criminal charges post violation. Additionally, CPO violations occur because of some need for ongoing contact between parties, primarily those who share children in common. Despite the emphasis to criminalize CPO violations, states have not assumed responsibility to protect victims of DV and have not been held accountable/liable for any failure to protect (*Castle Rock v Gonzales,* 545, U.S., 748, 2005).

CPOs are important because they serve over 1 million domestic violence victims annually in the United States[4]; these victims are especially vulnerable, marginalized on multiple intersecting grounds inclusive of gender, race and/or ethnicity, class, citizenship, and language identities (MacDowell, 2013; Sandefur, 2008). Data from one western U.S. state found that 63% to 95% of victims' successfully obtaining a CPO self-identified as ethnic minorities. The largest constituency was Latina women. Most lacked a high school education and lived below federal poverty guidelines, while 25% were monolingual in Spanish (Engler, 2010; Hannaford-Agor & Mott, 2003). These state data run parallel to national statistics, which also reveal that the majority of individuals accessing the civil court system have low incomes, experience relatively low levels of formal education, and are racial and ethnic minorities (National Center for the State Courts, n.d.). Research on victimization, help-seeking, and access to justice demonstrates that experiences with DV and the protection order process are inconsistent, complex, and influenced by a range of intersectional experiences.

Understanding DV Victims' Barriers to Access to Justice

Barriers to DV victims' access to justice are contextual and would benefit from further comparative and intersectional theorizing. Public criminology's commitments to ethical reflections via human rights and social justice suggests that, in researching domestic violence, we should endeavor to understand the role of civil justice in the lives of these relegated victims.

First, women face gender barriers associated with affordability of and accessibility to the legal system. Further, whether or not the victim resides in an urban or rural location impacts accessibility to CPOs (Logan & Walker, 2009) as does living in a "victim friendly" state with comprehensive protection order statutes (Burgess-Proctor, 2003; DeJong & Burgess-Proctor, 2006). Since the vast majority of women seeking CPOs are mothers, additional concerns include a worry that children will witness abuse, become victims, or will be used as manipulation/intimidation (Fleury-Steiner et al., 2016; Hamby, 2014). Many women applying for CPOs have histories of abuse that are complicated if they were pregnant during the DV episode (Bacchus, Mezey, & Bewley, 2004; Jasinski, 2004). Prior experiences with justice systems also impacts access to future help-seeking as does perceptions of CPO effectiveness (Bell et al., 2011; Logan & Walker, 2010). Even when women do access civil courts for a CPO, only 20% to 63% successfully obtain one (Holt, Kernic, Lumley, Wolf, & Rivara, 2002; Logan & Walker, 2009). These findings demonstrate how justice barriers are based on multiple realities whereas the successful issuance of a CPO is impacted by gender via socio-economic status, location, histories of abuse, having children, pregnancy status, and prior experiences with justice systems.

Women from all backgrounds and identities are victims of domestic violence. Yet, research on racial and/or ethnic barriers to access to justice show there are variances. First, compared to White women, African American women are more likely to seek out a CPO (Flicker et al., 2011). This is due, in part, to educational and socioeconomic positions as well as perceptions of civil court helpfulness (Bell et al., 2011). In the United States, African American victims are often poor and undereducated and do not view the criminal justice system as "trustworthy" as White women do (Potter, 2006). African American women, who are young, divorced or separated, poor, and residing in urban spaces are the *most frequent victims* of DV (Honeycutt, Marshall, & Weston, 2001). Also, compared to White women, they experience four times the rate of DV (Buzawa & Stark, 2017). Married Black women, for instance, often face unique cultural and socio-economic challenges when they leave their abusers and/or their homes. These include protecting children and other family members as well as finding/securing affordable housing (Potter, 2008; Richie, 1996). Furthermore, Black women have an increased risk of experiencing victimization post issuance of a CPO (Benitez, McNiel, & Binder, 2010; McFarlane et al., 2004). Even with these stark realities, research dedicated to Black and African American victims' experiences with CPOs are limited.

Second, research on Latina and Hispanic[5] women's access to justice is also minimal. Compared to other Latina and Hispanic groups, Mexican DV victims have disproportionately lower educational attainment scores and encompass some of the lowest socio-economic strata within the U.S. (Gonzalez-Barrera & Lopez, 2013; Lopez, Gonzalez-Barrera, & Cuddington, 2013; Sabina, Cuevas, & Schally, 2015). Compared to Cuban American women, Puerto Rican, Mexican, and Mexican-born women have higher rates of DV (Frias & Angel, 2005; Torres et al., 2000). Compared to White women, Mexican American women have an increased likelihood of experiencing any type of DV (i.e., threat, stalking, physical, and sexual) and Mexican-born women report higher rates of DV overall (Buzawa et al., 2017; Sabina et al., 2015). Even though research on Latina and Hispanic victims' experiences with CPOs is almost absent from the literature, findings suggest that they are more likely to seek out informal support via family members and that their knowledge of CPOs depends on access to social services as well as their immigration status (Flicker et al., 2011; Messing, Vega, & Durfee, 2017).

Third, immigration and acculturation impact rates of DV as well as victims' access to civil courts for obtaining a protection order. For example, current research finds that Latinas with higher levels of acculturation report higher levels of DV. These victims also use formal justice services more than Latinas with less acculturation experiences (Sabina, Cuevas, & Schally, 2012, 2013; Sabina et al., 2015). Immigration status impacts DV primarily due to unique barriers associated with victims' fear of deportation (Messing et al., 2017; Reina, Lohman, & Maldonado, 2014). Studies have noted how immigrant Latina women, specifically, are less likely to seek formal help (Messing et al., 2017; Rizo & Macy, 2011). Given that the Hispanic population is the fastest growing within the United States, more research is needed.

Lastly, current figures suggest that, each year, more English as Second Language (ESL) and Limited English Proficiency (LEP) individuals access the civil court system. Similarly, they do so *pro se* and without the help of a lawyer. Even though ESL/LEP victims request the use of court-employed interpreters, the reality is that justice systems still fail to accommodate. In a recent study of 35 U.S. state courts (Abel, 2010), 46% failed to provide interpreters in all types of civil cases, 80% failed to guarantee that the courts will pay for interpreters for indigent litigants, and 37% failed to require the use of credentialed interpreters trained to interpret in a specialized courtroom setting, even when such interpreters were available. Additionally, many ESL/LEP individuals lived in states that did not ensure that court-employed interpreters could speak English proficiently, speak the language to be interpreted, or know how to interpret in a specialized courtroom setting. For ESL/LEP victims, the framing of requests for protection depends on access to legal counsel, victim advocates, other court personnel, *and* interpreters (Durfee, 2008; Durfee & Messing, 2012; Messing, Vega, & Durfee, 2017). Thus, DV victims' barriers to access to justice are multiplicative and include experiences based on gender, race and/or ethnicity, acculturation, immigration status, and language.

Observing a Civil Protection Order Court

This section reflects on a collaborative and interdisciplinary research project aimed at documenting victims' experiences with the civil protection order process. Beginning in the spring of 2012 and ending in the fall of 2015, the goal of the project was to better understand DV victims' experiences within CPO courts as well as with gatekeepers working within civil court systems. Thus, semi-structured ethnographic interviews were conducted with a range of actors affiliated with legal aid and other self-help center personnel. Judges, marshals, and victim advocates were also interviewed. Additionally, protection order cases were observed and transcribed while "official" court data was made available. Other secondary materials were collected, and archival and legislative research also occurred. Some preliminary findings are discussed below and underscore rates and realities associated with access.

During the first year of observations, 7,382 CPO filings occurred, and 8,837 CPO hearings were held. Seventy-four percent of all filings were a request to extend a temporary protection order (TPO), 10% were denied a hearing, 4.7% were requests to modify or dissolve a TPO, and 2.9% were to show contempt of court. Of the filings that received a hearing, 65% were granted a protection order. Close to 80% of all victims were women while 20% were men.[6] The average age for female victims was between 30 and 44. Over half (54%) were employed full-time, 17% were employed part-time, and 26% were unemployed. These victims were 55% White, 33% Black, 7% Asian/Pacific Islander, 3.5% Other, and 0.8% Native American.[7] Approximately 148 women (or 3.3%) disclosed that they were pregnant during the time of filing.

The total amount of CPO hearings observed included 303 cases. These were comparable to all hearings held where 65% of cases resulted in a protection order granted. Eighty-four percent included a woman as the victim/applicant. When race and ethnicity was made known to the research team, a third of cases included White victims (33%). Compared to official court data, observations made it possible to document those who showed up to CPO hearings. Forty percent of the cases included the presence of a *pro se* victim only. Both a *pro se* victim and unrepresented offender were present in another 36% of cases. Other courtroom actors that were present included a friend or family member for the victim (21%), a victim advocate for the victim (17%), and legal counsel for victim (11%). The use of a court-employed translator occurred in 10% of cases observed.

In analyzing the effectiveness of courtroom actors, findings suggest that whether or not a victim successfully obtains a CPO, and for how long, depends on what harms are articulated in court as well as who is present with her in court (Bejinariu, 2016). For instance, even though protection order courts are designed to allow victims to file and proceed without legal counsel, findings evoke that, when a victim shows up to court *with* a lawyer, her chances of successfully obtaining a CPO increase. In contrast, when an offender shows up to court with a lawyer, the likelihood of the victim receiving a CPO decreases (Bejinariu, Troshynski, & Miethe, 2019).

In observing *pro se* victims' interactions, findings note how civil court staff and other employees would dispense legal assistance incompatibly and in non-neutral ways. Legal information provided to victims was found to be inconsistent (i.e., some received information, others did not), and, when provided, information about legal remedies available was also inconsistent, where some received narrow interpretations while others received broad explanations. Examples include staff members failing to assist victims with applications for financial restitution as well as with applications for child and/or spousal support—requests that are available to victims in DV CPO cases (MacDowell, 2016).

In observing examples of staff and marshal interactions with victims, additional barriers included a lack of understanding the delivery of protection orders. Victims articulated how it was difficult to serve their offender. Directions about the servicing process, receiving contact information for third party and/or law enforcement service, were complicated and inconsistent. Some victims also described how law enforcement officials failed to serve their offender.

Since two research team members were individuals for whom English is their second language, observations of 32 ESL/LEP cases, where the victim required a court-employed translator, provided insights on additional barriers. First, a lack of requested interpreters resulted in (1) ESL/LEP hearings continuing with the use of "informal translators" (i.e., a friend or family member of the victim that would translate conversations between the judge and the victim) or (2) rescheduling ESL/LEP cases. Even when ESL/LEP victims secured legal representation, if a court-employed interpreter was unavailable, hearings were rescheduled. These differences and delays of protection order cases are barriers specific to ESL/LEP victims.

Second, interactions between the judge and ESL/LEP victims were unique with or without a court-employed interpreter. It was common for judges to ask victims supplemental questions about English language spelling and grammar errors found in CPO paperwork. Once filed, these become official applications and are used to assess abuse experienced as well as to understand risk of future violence. ESL/LEP victims experienced additional barriers associated with understanding English language legal documents, forms, and courtroom procedures. This resulted in supplementary questioning from the bench.

Third, when examining the effectiveness of language services provided, irregularities in translation styles occurred. Interpreters differed in terms of when they translated victim's testimony to the judge: some would wait and translate after the victim finished talking while others would translate while the victim was talking. There were also differences in what information was actually translated in court: some would translate everything the victim said verbatim while others would summarize or paraphrase the victim's testimony. These findings suggest that court-employed translators have a range of interpretation styles that are inconsistent and that abuse experiences, as articulated by ESL/LEP victims, are sometimes lost in translation.

Of the 30 cases where the victim was a battered immigrant applicant, observations revealed that their safety concerns did include a worry about their life as well as the life of their children (Bejinariu et al., 2019). These victims would also discuss worries about the offender, often the father of their child/children, would abduct and kidnap the child/children across country borders. Immigrant women were also concerned about their safety in retrieving important legal immigration paperwork from their abusers and/or places of residence. Some also feared threats and realities of deportation. Consequently, the overlapping nature of battered immigrant women's experiences with CPOs demonstrates complex intersections inclusive of immigration status concerns.

What becomes clear is that a range of actors (staff, marshals, lawyers, interpreters, and judges) act as gatekeepers to a complex civil legal system originally designed to be easily accessible to those requiring assistance. These individuals play central roles in the construction of deservingness for DV victims. Understandings of safety, rights, and remedies available for victims depend upon interactions with a range of actors. Thus, access to justice, here access to CPOs, is complex and barriers are multiple. A number of important questions regarding the importance of identifying impacts on access to justice systemically arise and comparative research dedicated to understanding the involvements of victims' accessing other protection order courts are necessary. Given the millions of victims who apply for CPOs annually, are their experiences similarly laden with these inconsistencies and barriers?

Doing Public Criminological Methodologies and Praxis

The ways in which we incorporated public criminological methodologies and praxis occurred throughout this project is key. First, a commitment to understanding DV victims' experiences rendered a topic of criminological interest, but the focus on victims' experiences with civil courts was distinct. In recognizing that empowerment is at the heart of public criminology, methodology and praxis noted herein emphasized an "empowerment-oriented public criminology" as imperative (Carrabine, Lee, & South, 2000, p. 207). Engaging in research for individuals and communities, rather than for "narrow political interests" was key. In other words, this project was a commitment to be a part of an interdisciplinary research team that emphasized social justice and human rights first and foremost.

Second, in keeping with how a public criminology might help to nurture "a better politics of crime and, ultimately, stronger democratic publics" (Loader & Sparks, 2011, p. 5), researching access to justice helps to raise "important questions about the purpose of criminology and its engagements with social and political worlds" (Brown & Rafter, 2013, p. 1017). Specifically, this project highlights not only the significance of understanding marginalized and unrepresented experiences with crime and victimization, but it also illuminates the wider range of justice system responses to violence. Thus, research that attends to victims' access to justice via civil systems remains unique in that they are touted as providing a myriad of protections for victims of domestic violence which can be tailored to each individual's needs. Protections often include, but are not limited to prohibiting contact, removing abuser from shared residence, ordering temporary custody of children, ordering abuser into counseling, and providing economic relief—all without the use of the criminal justice system.

Third, as a method of working towards social justice and human rights, a "practice-orientation" model was also adopted, which means that something practical should always come of the research that we carry out. These practical outcomes should further promote and improve the quality of life and well-being for the poorest and most vulnerable (Carrabine et al., 2000, p. 208). Since DV victims are some of the most marginalized, experiencing frequent and complex barriers that are sometimes interrelated with criminal legal problems, practice-orientations should attend to a myriad of arrangements and can include interdisciplinarity, training of students, advocates, and practitioners. Embracing a commitment to interdisciplinarity and student training (Uggen & Inderbitzen, 2010) is albeit one version of practice-orientation and, in effect, represents public outreach as well as criminological training of the public along these justice-centered and/or justice-focused concerns.

To demonstrate, during the duration of this project, research team members included four JD students and four MA graduate students. Out of the eight (1 male, 7 female), three were African-American, one was Central American, one was Asian Pacific Islander, two acknowledged English as their second language (ESL), one self-identified as a "religious minority," and one was a White cisgender man.[8] Every year of the project, two undergraduate students were also trained and participated in on-going research activities.[9] These engagements provided a living example of interdisciplinary "on-the-ground" research including investigations between "Law" and "Social Science" disciplines. The fact that the local law school is the only law school in the state, and that a large percentage of law graduates stay and practice locally, made the importance of—and need for—this unique interdisciplinary research and training opportunity evident.

Accordingly, training was considered a form of public outreach as well as a way to provide criminological and legal training to the public—or at least those who would be involved in the justice system. Calling these types of activities a "public criminology in embryo," Rock (2014, p. 427) acknowledges that criminologists have a history of teaching and training practitioners both inside and outside of the discipline and academy. Yet, not much is known about the actual impacts of these practice-orientation models. These considerations are imperative because our understanding of human rights, due process, the rule of law and "associated tenets of liberal legalism informs, motivates, and frames much contemporary criminological research and writing" (see Loader & Sparks, 2013, p. 86). For future projects, the paradoxes and challenges associated with doing public criminology should include conversations about the impacts of such empowerment- and practice-orientations.

Impacts from Engaging Particular Publics

As mentioned, many criminologists rarely participate in scholarship that includes outreach, policy engagement, and research on or about the civil justice system. Even fewer have engaged with questions of access to justice through empirical and theoretical endeavors. This chapter provides albeit one example that sought to conceptualize and understand access to justice, particularly for DV victims seeking help from civil courts, so that they can be made more effective.

In terms of pursuing practical solutions, inconsistencies and barriers observed can be addressed by improving training for self-help and civil court staff, court-employed translators, and judges. As intended by the design of the study, findings from this research are useful in creating and implementing evaluations of civil legal service projects (i.e., self-help centers, anti- and non-violence programs) as well as DV victim services at the local level. Relatedly, it points to the necessity of legislation and policies geared towards bettering civil court facilities and improving prevention programs that address gender inequality as well as those root causes of violence. Changes in legislation, as well as the creation and the promotion of services for those living with violence, are essential. Moreover, educational and public outreach training that brings awareness of legal protections and rights for *all* victims of DV, including immigrant and ESL/LEP victims, is necessary. For example, economic relief provisions could be updated (if they already exist) or included in state statutes (when they do not already exist). These protection provisions should also be widely publicized. Further, this research demonstrates that many victims still seek out informal support. Thus, knowledge of public health and social services that focus on physical and mental health consequences of DV should be cultivated and also widely publicized, as should services that promote inclusivity, cultural competency, and sensitivity training of staff and practitioners.

This collaborative experience pointed to how interdisciplinary projects that include academics, undergraduate, graduate, and law student researchers, and DV advocates within the community can help to facilitate partnerships with existing institutions (e.g., schools, social service and public health facilities, criminal justice facilities) as well as with the media. Although this project has ended, public engagement is ongoing and relevant to note as examples of continued public impact. They are enabled by the project's commitments to developing interdisciplinary research groups, training a range of students, and building relationships with local and state legislators, non-profits, advocates, and other DV courts.

These relationships have enabled a harnessing of networks for further public criminological engagements. Becoming a member of the state's Attorney General task force to end DV has proven to be extremely educational and productive in terms of understanding current training modules (of law enforcement and legal actors), educational outreach programs, and legislation. Invitations to present research to county commissioners, district attorneys, civil justice system judges, and victim advocates maintain ongoing communications and future prospects. Additionally, becoming a member of local and state antiviolence organizations have facilitated ongoing research on access to justice as well as work on training and educational initiatives focused on prevention. Becoming an affiliated professor of the university's School of Medicine has provided opportunities to engage with and alongside medical, public, and mental health students, professors, and practitioners, shedding light on additional dimensions of health and well-being issues underpinning victims, survivors, and offenders' experience with DV. These opportunities, in part an outgrowth of the research, continue to promote collaborative relationships with community members and legislators.

Research, advocacy, and activism around DV are already part of criminology, particularly for feminist and critical criminologist. As discussed throughout, to participate in a collaborative and interdisciplinary research project that is relevant and geared towards having an impact both within and outside of academia makes a difference in "how people think and feel about criminological objects, and how sovereign power is exercised upon them" (Carrier, 2014, p. 86). Due to the fact that more DV victims seek help from civil court systems, researchers should focus their attention on these populations as well as those dealing with criminal courts. In so doing, we would have a better understanding of the many obstacles to accessing existing services as well as practitioners', service providers', and victims' perspectives on the creation of new avenues for needed service. Thus, the focus on civil court responses to crime-related phenomena, such as DV, pushes criminology to become even more public.

Future public criminological musings on access to justice must empirically and theoretically help to uncover the nature and extent of unmet legal and justice needs. There is a need to query the impact of these evaded needs on individuals, marginalized social groups, rural and urban communities, states, and countries. At the very least, doing so would cultivate an understanding and critique of the overall effectiveness of specific models of legal assistance in meeting a range of personal needs. These critiques would also help articulate an understanding of the many similarities and differences associated with DV victims' involvements with civil and/or criminal justice systems.[10] If public criminology seeks to commit to placing social justice and human rights "at the heart of theoretical and applied interventions that seek to make a difference and bring about change" (Carrabine et al., 2000, p. 207), then doing research on access to justice for those most marginalized is a necessary—and overdue—project.

Notes

1. Links to internal reports are available at https://abovethelaw.com/2013/06/horrifying-video-of-alleged-sexual-assault-while-family-court-judge-literally-looks-the-other-way/
2. Video available at the Encyclopedia of American Politics website: https://ballotpedia.org/Patricia_Doninger
3. The right to act without a lawyer by proceeding *pro se*, meaning "for oneself" or "on one's own behalf," is an established tenet in State and Federal law (*Faretta v. California*, 422 U.S. 806, 1975).
4. This figure is based on FBI reporting. See Wider Opportunities for Women (WOW) annual report entitled, "Protection Orders and Survivors" for updated figures as well as recommendations and innovative state policies available at https://iwpr.org/wp-content/uploads/2017/01/Protection-Orders-and-Survivors.pdf
5. These terms refer to ethnicities that originate from North, Central, and South America, the Caribbean, and Europe. Categories, such as Latinx and Hispanic, should not be treated as monolithic descriptors, as they capture groups of diverse people. Doing so ignores important historical, cultural, and demographic differences (see Sabina et al., 2015).
6. The majority of offenders (76%) were men; 53% were unemployed; 37% employed full-time; and 1.2% employed part-time. They were White (39.7%), Hispanic (26.4%), Black (26.2%), Asian/Pacific Islander (4.4%), Other (2.9%), and Native American (0.4%).
7. This total of 125.3% is due to victims selecting multiple categories (and thus self-identifying as bi- or multiracial).
8. Four successfully obtained their MA and continued on to PhD programs; another four successfully completed their JD where one graduated and began work as a Clerk to the State Supreme Court.
9. Five undergraduate students participated; four identified as women of color and one was a White woman. All five went on to graduate and/or law school programs.
10. Currently, projects that compare/contrast DV victims' experiences with civil and criminal legal systems (i.e., experiences with dedicated DV courts, specialized DV dockets, and general criminal courts) are needed.

References

Abel, L. (2010). *Language access in state courts*. New York: New York University School of Law, Brennan Center for Justice.

Bacchus, L., Mezey, G., & Bewley, S. (2004). Domestic violence: Prevalence in pregnant women and associations with physical and psychological health. *European Journal of Obstetrics and Gynecology and Reproductive Biology, 113*(1), 6–11.

Bejinariu, A., Troshynski, E. I., & Miethe, T. D. (2019). Civil protection orders and their courtroom context: The impact of gatekeepers on legal decisions. *Journal of Family Violence, 34*(3), 231–243.

Bejinariu, E. A. (2016). Judicial differences in protective orders issuance rates: An examination of courtroom actors, case aspects, and individual characteristics (Master's thesis, University of Nevada, Las Vegas, Las Vegas, USA). Retrieved from http://digitalscholarship.unlv.edu/cgi/viewcontent.cgi?article=3637&context=thesesdissertations

Bell, M. E., Perez, S., Goodman, L. A., & Dutton, M. A. (2011). Battered women's perceptions of civil and criminal court helpfulness: The role of court outcome and process. *Violence against Women, 17,* 71–88.

Benitez, C. T., McNiel, D. E., & Binder, R. L. (2010). Do protection orders protect? *Journal of the American Academy of Psychiatry and the Law Online, 38*(3), 376–385.

Brown, M., & Rafter, N. (2013). Genocide films, public criminology, collective memory. *British Journal of Criminology, 53*(6), 1017–1032.

Burgess-Proctor, A. (2003). Evaluating the efficacy of protection orders for victims of domestic violence. *Women & Criminal Justice, 15*(1), 33–54.

Buzawa, E. S., Buzawa, C. G., & Stark, E. (2017). *Responding to domestic violence: The integration of criminal justice and human services* (5th ed.). Thousand Oaks, CA: Sage.

Carrabine, E., Lee, M., & South, N. (2000). Social wrongs and human rights in late modern Britain: Social exclusion, crime control, and prospects for a public criminology. *Social Justice, 27*(2 (80), 193–211.

Carrier, N. (2014). On some limits and paradoxes of academic orations on public criminology. *Radical Criminology,* (4), 85–114.

Currie, E. (2007). Against marginality: Arguments for a public criminology. *Theoretical Criminology, 11*(2), 175–190.

DeJong, C., & Burgess-Proctor, A. (2006). A summary of personal protection order statutes in the United States. *Violence against Women, 12*(1), 68–88.

Dragiewicz, M. (2014). Domestic violence and family law: Criminological concerns. *International Journal for Crime, Justice and Social Democracy, 3*(1), 121–134.

Durfee, A. (2008). Victim narratives, legal representation, and domestic violence civil protection orders. *Feminist Criminology, 4,* 7–31.

Durfee, A., & Messing, J. T. (2012). Characteristics related to protection order use among victims of intimate partner violence. *Violence against Women, 18,* 701–710.

Engler, R. (2010). Connecting self-representation to civil Gideon: What existing data reveal about when counsel is most needed. *Fordham Urban Law Journal, 37*(1/2), 37–92.

Fleury-Steiner, R. E., Miller, S. L., Maloney, S., & Postel, E. B. (2016). "No contact, except …" Visitation decisions in protection orders for intimate partner abuse. *Feminist Criminology, 11,* 3–22.

Flicker, S. M., Cerulli, C., Zhao, X., Tang, W., Watts, A., Xia, Y., & Talbot, N. L. (2011). Concomitant forms of abuse and help-seeking behavior among White, African American, and Latina women who experience intimate partner violence. *Violence against Women, 17*(8), 1067–1085.

Frias, S. M., & Angel, R. J. (2005). The risk of partner violence among low-income Hispanic subgroups. *Journal of Marriage and Family, 67,* 552–564.

German, J. (2013, April 6). Victim of Family Court groping incident files federal lawsuit. *Las Vegas Review-Journal.* Retrieved from www.reviewjournal.com/crime/courts/victim-of-family-court-groping-incident-files-federal-lawsuit/

Golub, S. (2003). Access to human rights: Obstacles and issues. International Council on Human Rights Policy. Retrieved from www.international-council.org/ac/excerpts/133.doc

Goldfarb, S. F. (2007). Reconceiving civil protection orders for domestic violence: Can law help end the abuse without ending the relationship. *Cardozo L. Rev., 29,* 1487.

Gonzalez-Barrera, A., & Lopez, M. H. (2013). *A demographic portrait of Mexican-origin Hispanics in the United States.* Washington, DC: Pew Research Center.

Hamby, S. (2014). *Battered women's protective strategies: Stronger than you know.* New York: Oxford University Press.

Hannaford-Agor, P., & Mott, N. (2003). Research on self-represented litigation: Preliminary results and methodological considerations. *Justice System Journal, 24,* 163–181.

Holt, V., Kernic, M., Lumley, T., Wolf, M., & Rivara, F. (2002). Civil protection orders and risk of subsequent police-reported violence. *Journal of the American Medical Association, 288,* 589–594.

Honeycutt, T. C., Marshall, L. L., & Weston, R. (2001). Toward ethnically specific models of employment, public assistance, and victimization. *Violence against Women, 7,* 126–140.

Jasinski, J. L. (2004). Pregnancy and domestic violence: A review of the literature. *Trauma, Violence, & Abuse, 5*(1), 47–64.

Jordan, C. E. (2004). Intimate partner violence and the justice system: An examination of the interface. *Journal of Interpersonal Violence, 19,* 1412–1434.

Keilitz, S. L., Hannaford, P. L., & Efkeman, H. S. (1997). *Civil protection orders: The benefits and limitations for victims of domestic violence.* Williamsburg, VA: National Center for State Courts.

Loader, I., & Sparks, R. (2011). *Public criminology?* New York: Routledge.

Loader, I., & Sparks, R. (2013). *Public criminology?* New York: Routledge.

Logan, T. K., Shannon, L., Walker, R., & Faragher, T. M. (2006). Protective orders: Questions and conundrums. *Trauma, Violence, & Abuse, 17*, 175–205.

Logan, T. K., & Walker, R. (2009). Civil protective order outcomes: Violations and perceptions of effectiveness. *Journal of Interpersonal Violence, 24*(4), 675–692.

Logan, T. K., & Walker, R. (2010). Civil protective order effectiveness: Justice or just a piece of paper? *Violence and Victims, 25*(3), 332.

Lopez, M. H., Gonzalez-Barrera, A., & Cuddington, D. (2013). *Diverse origins: The nation's 14 largest Hispanic-origin groups*. Washington, DC: Pew Research Center.

MacDowell, E. L. (2013). Theorizing from particularity: Perpetrators and intersectional theory about domestic violence. *Journal of Gender, Race & Justice, 16*, 531–576.

MacDowell, E. L. (2016). Domestic violence and the politics of self-help. *William & Mary Journal of Women & the Law, 22*, 203–256.

McFarlane, J., Malecha, A., Gist, J., Watson, K., Batten, E., Hall, I., & Smith, S. (2004). Protection orders and intimate partner violence: An 18-month study of 150 Black, Hispanic, and White women. *American Journal of Public Health, 94*(4), 613–618.

Messing, J. T., Vega, S., & Durfee, A. (2017). Protection order use among Latina survivors of intimate partner violence. *Feminist Criminology, 12*(3), 199–223.

National Center for State Courts. (n.d.). National Center for State Courts. Retrieved from www.ncsc.org/

Potter, H. (2006). An argument for black feminist criminology: Understanding African American women's experiences with intimate partner abuse using an integrated approach. *Feminist Criminology, 1*(2), 106–124.

Potter, H. (2008). *Battle cries: Black women and intimate partner abuse*. New York: New York University Press.

Reina, A. S., Lohman, B. J., & Maldonado, M. M. (2014). "He said they'd deport me": Factors influencing domestic violence help-seeking practices among Latina immigrants. *Journal of Interpersonal Violence, 29*(4), 593–615.

Rhode, D. L. (2004). *Access to justice*. New York: Oxford University Press.

Richie, B. (1996). *Compelled to crime: The gender entrapment of battered Black women*. New York: Routledge.

Rizo, C. F., & Macy, R. J. (2011). Help seeking and barriers of Hispanic partner violence survivors: A systematic review of the literature. *Aggression and Violent Behavior, 16*, 250–264.

Rock, P. (2014). The public faces of public criminology. *Criminology & Criminal Justice, 14*(4), 412–433.

Sabina, C., Cuevas, C. A., & Schally, J. L. (2012). The cultural influences on help-seeking among a national sample of victimized Latino women. *American Journal of Community Psychology, 49*(3–4), 347–363.

Sabina, C., Cuevas, C. A., & Schally, J. L. (2013). The effect of immigration and acculturation on victimization among a national sample of Latino women. *Cultural Diversity and Ethnic Minority Psychology, 19*(1), 13–26.

Sabina, C., Cuevas, C. A., & Schally, J. L. (2015). The influence of ethnic group variation on victimization and help seeking among Latino women. *Cultural Diversity and Ethnic Minority Psychology, 21*(1), 19.

Sandefur, R. L. (2008). Access to civil justice and race, class, and gender inequality. *Annual Review of Sociology, 34*, 339–358.

Tjaden, P., & Thoennes, N. (2000). *Extent, nature and consequences of intimate partner violence (NCJ 181867)*. Washington, DC: U.S. Department of Justice, National Institute of Justice.

Torres, S., Campbell, J., Campbell, D. W., Ryan, J., King, C., & Price, P. (2000). Abuse during and before pregnancy: Prevalence and cultural correlates. *Violence and Victims, 15*(3), 303–321.

Uggen, C., & Inderbitzin, M. (2010). Public criminologies. *Criminology & Public Policy, 9*(4), 725–749.

United Nations. (1948). Universal declaration of human rights. General Assembly Resolution 217 A (III) of 10 December, Article 1, New York.

Violence Policy Center. (2017). *When men murder women: An analysis of 2015 homicide data*. Washington DC: Author.

9

PUBLIC FEMINIST CRIMINOLOGIES

Reflections on the Activist-Scholar in Violence against Women Policy

Anastasia Powell and Ruth Liston

Introduction

In the week that we finalized this book chapter, a man raped and murdered a young woman, 22-year-old comedian Eurydice Dixon, in a public park in inner Melbourne, Australia. Eurydice was attacked just a few hundred meters from her home, having walked back from a night-time performance. Speaking to the media in the aftermath of the crime, a Victoria Police Superintendent stated (Sullivan, 2018):

> The message we would provide to all members of the community is to take responsibility for your safety ... this is an area of high community activity ... so just make sure you have situational awareness, that you're aware of your surroundings.

Less than 24 hours later, a Victoria Police homicide detective repeated a similar message: "People need to be aware of their own personal security. That's everywhere. If people have any concerns at any time, call triple-0. We would much rather have too many calls than too few" (Sullivan, 2018). These statements, with their clear inference that women could avoid rape and murder if only they took more responsibility for their own safety, was roundly criticized as victim-blaming by activists, academics, and the wider community (Sullivan, 2018).

This sexual homicide, and our responses to it, gave us pause in real time to reflect on our multiple roles and responses as feminist criminologists to violence against women (VAW). As women who live, work, and socialize in the same neighborhoods as Eurydice, we were (and indeed remain) saddened and outraged at another tragic act of violence against a woman in our city. We reached out to our friends and colleagues to offer empathy and support in the face of a crime which felt somehow simultaneously distant and yet close to home. In our role as criminologists, we gave media interviews making the links between individual acts of violence against women, and the broader social and structural factors that create the conditions for that violence (Touhy, 2018). One of our colleagues wrote an article for *The Conversation* (Fileborn, 2018), and many others in our scholarly network gave interviews highlighting the need to continue efforts to address sexual violence in our communities. As policy advocates, we consulted with our contacts in the anti-violence sector about joint responses to the crime and assisted in forming public statements. As feminist activists, we reached out through social media to contribute to community-led discussions about the crime, and to critique both the police and media responses for their victim-blaming narratives. Another of our colleagues was involved in organizing a vigil for Eurydice, which we attended along with thousands of Melburnians. And finally, we write this chapter. We expect that many more feminist criminologists will also publish about this case, as they will about countless others that prompt public discussion and policy change on violence against women.

How could we not respond to this crime in these multiple ways? Engaging with the public and seeking to influence policy on behalf of women who experience violence is an integral part of our work as feminist criminologists, and indeed as human and humane women who are both scholars and activists in this field. In this chapter, we reflect upon and examine our role as public feminist criminologists seeking to address, and ultimately to prevent, violence against women. In so doing, we draw on specific examples from within our own work and experience. As such, our reflections are partial and situated within our own fields of expertise and influence. Yet the themes within these reflections are, we suggest, indicative of a set of inherent tensions for the public feminist criminologist. We suggest that feminist criminology is not, and can never be, a dispassionate and "neutral" science, but rather that as activist-scholars we engage in a "conscious partiality" (Gelsthorpe, 1990, cited in Gelsthorpe, 2009, p. 188) wherein even our most quantitative and seemingly value-free endeavors (e.g., measuring crime) are rooted in a desire for a better world for women. For feminist criminologists, as with those from minority and working-class communities (Sprague & Laube, 2009), our connection to our public—namely, to other women—is a given (Nelund, 2014). As Nelund (2014, p. 77) points out, "The assumption that we can choose to engage with different publics and do not have established ties problematically reinforces the idea of … the academic from nowhere." Indeed, feminist scholarship actually "emerged from the groundbreaking insight that academic practice and activism can and must inform each other" (do Mar Pereira, 2016, p. 100).

In the following sections of this chapter, we explore the experience of being public feminist criminologists, as well as the multiple roles or identities that we hold as such, and indeed the tensions and challenges that we must navigate in the course of our work in violence against women policy. First, we discuss the nature of public engagements and impact of feminist criminologies on violence against women policy. Then, we consider the opportunities and problematics of emotional appeals in violence against women policy activism, which can easily be co-opted to support conservative, penal populist policy agendas. Next, we discuss the challenges of backlash, which is increasingly apparent in response to public feminist criminologies (as indeed it is for other public feminists). Finally, we consider a further potential identity of the public feminist criminologist, that of the survivor-scholar. Though of course we acknowledge that many "malestream" criminologists engage publicly and may similarly identify with the public for whom they advocate, we argue that there are nonetheless experiences inherent to the feminist criminologist working on violence against women that are markedly different from many other policy advocacy fields in criminology.

Feminist Criminologies and Violence against Women (VAW)

Within criminology, and increasingly in the public domain, there is recognition of the scale of the problem of men's violence. In Australia, the figures are similar to other comparable nation states: one woman a week dies as a result of violence from her male partner or ex-partner (Bryant & Bricknell, 2017). One in five women experience sexual violence in their lifetime (Cox, 2015). One in three women will experience physical violence in their lifetime, most commonly at the hands of an intimate partner, ex-partner or other known man, and most often in a private home (Cox, 2015). And while one in two men will experience violence in their lifetime (Australian Bureau of Statistics, 2017), it is overwhelmingly at the hands of other men and in public space—often, it is even thought to be the sign of a "top night out" (Tomsen, 1997; Waitt, Jessop, & Gorman-Murray, 2011). Men's violence against women, and indeed against other men, is a significant social and policy problem.

There can be little doubt that feminist criminologies have had an observable impact on exposing this nature of men's violence, and on shaping law and justice policies in response to it. As Chesney-Lind explains:

> Turning back the clock, one can recall that prior to the path-breaking feminist works on sexual assault, sexual harassment, and wife abuse, these forms of gender violence were ignored, minimized, and trivialized ... In retrospect, the naming of the types and dimensions of female victimization had a significant impact on public policy, and it is arguably the most tangible accomplishment of both feminist criminology and grassroots feminists concerned about gender, crime, and justice.
>
> *(Chesney-Lind, 2006, p. 7)*

Arguably, feminist criminologists were the original "public criminologists." From the earliest criminological work on men's violence against women, feminist criminologists have had to navigate their roles as publicly engaged activist-scholars, both outside, and indeed within, the academy. Even researching men's violence against women within criminology (or women's offending, though there is not room to reflect further on this here) was by definition an activist act, whereby feminist scholars sought to—and continue to seek to—challenge and displace traditional "malestream" definitions of crime, violence, and justice (see also Risman, 2006).

There are many repertoires of political action that have been, and continue to be, undertaken by public feminist criminologists seeking to influence policy concerning men's violence against women. Akchurin and Lee (2013) describe three broad forms of women's activist repertoires that provide a useful context to the reflections on public feminist criminologies here. Drawing on the example of gender pay parity, they suggest that women's strategies differ according to whether they are (1) professionalized women's activism, (2) labor/unionized women's activism, or (3) popular women's activism (Akchurin & Lee, 2013). Informed by the Australian context, one might add a fourth more particular type of professionalized women's activism—that of "femocrats" (feminist bureaucrats) who advocate specifically from within the government and/or political policy machinery (see Chappell, 2002; Eisenstein, 1996). These repertoires might differ in the key agents of change that are involved from, for example, politicians, to policymakers, to corporate executives, to union leaders, to individual direct participation through civil society. They may also differ in the specific strategies used, from lobbying in closed meetings and consultations, to providing expert evidence in public inquiries, to boardroom negotiations, to the consciousness-raising that comes with truth telling, to protests and demonstrations both online and in the streets. Yet it is not in isolation, but rather, collectively that these activist repertoires are most likely to impact on policy, law and justice for violence against women.

Each of these activist repertoires represent varied roles for the public feminist criminologist. Foremost is the role of the objective, dispassionate expert: the professional criminologist who is called upon to present evidence of the extent and nature of men's violence against women to a range of audiences and stakeholders (such as media and government). Through our participation as union members and our roles as women academics we also advocate *within* the academy. Working alongside femocrats and translating our research for uptake in the policy advocacy work of others' is a further vital role for the feminist criminologist. Finally, as feminist activists in our own personal lives, we are engaged with other forms of public activism such as via social media, street demonstrations, and petitions as well as everyday difficult discussions on violence against women.

To consider one example, over the last seven years the phenomenon referred to colloquially as "revenge pornography" (where nude or otherwise intimate photos or videos are distributed without the consent of the person depicted) has escalated first as a subgenre of pornography, and in turn as a salacious news story, to now increasingly recognized as a harmful practice and, in some jurisdictions, a criminal offense.[1] The work of feminist criminologists and legal scholars has been enormously influential in challenging the mainstream media representations of the issue of "revenge pornography," and advocating that police and other government agencies understand and respond to the issue as related to other forms of sexual violence, harassment, stalking, and partner violence. Notably key to legal and policy reform in their countries since 2013, has been the work of the following academics: Clare McGlynn (Durham University, U.K.), Erika Rackley (Birmingham University, U.K.), Mary-Anne Franks (University of Miami, U.S.A.), Nicola Gavey, (University of Auckland, New Zealand), and an Australian team of researchers comprising Nicola Henry (RMIT University), Asher Flynn (Monash University), and Anastasia Powell (RMIT University).

Generating research on the extent and nature of revenge pornography, however, is a small part of the advocacy and activism that has influenced policy reform on this issue. Reflecting on the Australian experience, one of the early challenges one of the authors and her collaborators faced was representing the issue not as an acceptable subgenre of pornography, nor as the "just desserts" directed towards an ex-partner who ends a relationship, but rather as a form of *image-based abuse*. Indeed, Powell and Henry first coined the term image-based abuse in a 2015 media interview (Marriner, 2015) and article for *The Conversation* (Powell & Henry, 2015), using it in subsequent research reports and scholarly articles (Henry & Powell, 2016; Henry, Powell, & Flynn, 2017; Powell & Henry, 2017). It has since gained traction as the preferred term in Australian public policy having been adopted by the Office of the e-Safety Commissioner[2] and Australian support services,[3] as well as in legislation,[4] parliamentary inquiries,[5] and public debates on the issue.[6] Similarly in the United Kingdom and United States, a related term "image based sexual abuse," has since been used by McGlynn and Rackley among others to further highlight the harms associated with the non-consensual taking, distributing, and threatening to distribute intimate images without consent (see DeKeseredy & Schwartz, 2016; McGlynn & Rackley, 2016, 2017).

The re-framing of revenge pornography as image-based abuse has been vital to subsequent policy advocacy and legislative reform work. It was not research evidence alone, but rather a multitude of reinforcing actions that engendered this change. In addition to academic scholarly publications, the research team has published summary research reports for more general audiences, written for *The Conversation*, made submissions to law reform and parliamentary inquiries, met with politicians and policy advisors, provided expert commentary for news media, participated in advisory groups for government, delivered professional development seminars and webinars, signed and circulated online petitions, and have blogged, tweeted, and "Facebooked" about the issue. The team worked collaboratively with non-government organizations (NGOs), government departments, and survivor-advocates in both making their research available for use in policy and reform advocacy, as well as co-designing a range of potential reform and service provision options in response to image-based abuse. In developing recommendations for reform, the research team remained in consultation with non-government agencies who provide direct services to victims of image-based abuse, to ensure that the advocacy continues to be grounded in the harms and justice needs experienced by victims themselves. Over and above all of these efforts, it cannot be underestimated that one of the features of the "success" of this reform campaign was the use of research expertise to elucidate the damaging effects experienced by victims of this emerging form of harassment and abuse. In short, there is an affective element to the impact of public feminist criminologies.

Activist-scholars: Engaging with the Public while Avoiding Populist Punitivism

As a result of the unfortunate surfeit of stories about women's victimization and death at the hands of men in the media, VAW activist-scholars are arguably readily able to elicit public sympathy than those attempting to engage with the public around less overtly emotive issues, for example sentencing reform. Certainly, as activist-scholars, an ability to engage with the public on an emotional level about violence against women can be a useful strategy (Mopas & Moore, 2012). Increased public awareness can have its pitfalls, however. For example, the tendency for the media to focus on physical relationship-based violence against so-called "ideal victims" (White, straight, cisgender women and their children) may mean that the experiences of others, for example LGBTIQ+ victim/survivors, racial and ethnic minorities, and sex workers, are ignored (see Thompson & Louise, 2014). Likewise, less obvious violence, such as controlling behavior and verbal or image-based abuse, may not be as readily viewed as being problematic. There is also an ever-present risk that penal populists may co-opt that public concern, promoting their narrow focus on punishment and deterrence as solutions.

As criminologists, we are acutely aware that the law and criminal justice systems are, at times, instruments of violence, and that both can "play key roles in eroding the rights of both women and people of color" (Chesney-Lind, 2006, p. 10). In engaging with the public, activist-scholars must be careful to avoid being too seduced by the promises of a "victimological turn" in crime policy, especially because a focus on justice for victims is commonly a bedfellow of punitive populism (Garland, 2001). For decades, feminist legal scholars and criminologists have debated the relative merits of either harnessing, abandoning, modifying, or revolutionizing legal responses to violence against women (Lewis, Dobash, Dobash, & Cavanagh, 2001). While Smart (1989, p. 160) urged us to "avoid the siren call of law," others have acknowledged that in our current system it is unavoidably a "tool of necessity" (Matsuda, 1989, p. 9). While recognizing the symbolic role of law, and the practical and vital function of the criminal justice system for many victims, policies that prioritize deterrence through punitiveness to solve the problem of violence against women are limited in complexity and effectiveness and may result in unintended negative consequences (Lewis et al., 2001).

This kind of punitive impulse was apparent in the public response to the death of Eurydice Dixon (discussed above), as well as other local "signal crimes" (Innes & Fielding, 2002). Five years earlier, for instance, the rape and murder of another Melbourne woman, Jill Meager, engendered public outrage, which in turn spurned a series of popular punitive reforms, including substantial investment in CCTV and restrictions to Victoria's parole system (Bartels, 2013; Milivojevic & McGovern, 2014; Powell, Overington, & Hamilton, 2018). Further afield, the use of pro-arrest policies in response to domestic violence in some jurisdictions has resulted in substantial increases in dual arrests, including in situations where victims of domestic violence have acted in self-defense (Finn & Bettis, 2006). At the same time, policies that require police to identify a "primary aggressor" have had the unintended effect of reducing overall arrest rates (Hirschel, McCormack, & Buzawa, 2017). Meanwhile, problematic claims about protecting women from men's violence have featured prominently in policy statements seeking to restrict transgender women's access to women's bathrooms (Schilt & Westbrook, 2015; Stones, 2017).

How, then, do we maintain our desire as feminist activists for violence against women to be taken seriously, especially given our understanding of the flawed nature of the criminal justice system? For some, the answer is legal alternatives, such as restorative, innovative, or civil society justice (Daly & Stubbs, 2006; McGlynn, Downes, & Westmarland, 2017; Powell, 2015). For others, the authors included, it is engaging in actions that counter the key drivers of gendered violence, namely primary prevention efforts that aim to improve gender equality. The joint efforts of academics, policy advocates, femocrats, and activists have gained traction for this approach in Australian public policy over the last ten years. Indeed, it was 2007 when the Victorian Health Promotion Foundation (VicHealth) launched a ground-breaking framework for the primary prevention of violence against women. The framework, *Preventing Violence Before It Occurs*, on which one of the authors was a contributing researcher, set the scene for ten years of policy, research, and program development that has focused on addressing the underlying unequal gender roles, stereotypes, and behaviors that contribute both to gender inequality and violence against women in our community. Fast-forward to 2018 and Australia now has a national framework for primary prevention that has been endorsed by the Council of Australian Governments (COAG), and features in the National Plan to Reduce Violence Against Women and their Children (Commonwealth of Australia, 2011; Our Watch, ANROWS and VicHealth, 2015). The framework is grounded in research evidence that links institutional and societal level markers of gender inequality as the core drivers, and as such, the oft-neglected aspects of our policy efforts to address violence against women. Indeed, while retribution was on the minds of many in the public after Eurydice Dixon's death, it was heartening to us that the focus from many public commentators and the news media was primarily on how we as a society—and men in particular—needed to change to prevent violence against women from happening in the first place: evidence that, at the level of public and to some extent mainstream media discourse, there is growing recognition in Australia that gender inequality is the key driver of men's violence against women. Indeed, it is our feeling that activist strategies must look beyond the law to engender change; it is by highlighting the socio-cultural and socio-structural causes of men's violence that we can resist the co-option by populist politicians that would see increased punitiveness against individuals as the ready-made solution to this problem.

Activist-scholars: Countering Backlash

Backlash can start early for the feminist criminologist who engages publicly. For one of us, it was in the year after graduating from doctoral studies. The public engagement was an online opinion article, a joint piece with another early career colleague. The latest romantic comedy film, we thought at the time, offered a great hook into writing about how modern dating and intimate relationships continued to be underscored by "unwritten rules" based in gender inequality. It got some traction; we had published it in an open-access online site, and it was re-published by national media, after which we were invited to do radio interviews about modern dating rules. It was among the first of a series of experiences of public backlash in response to questioning men's and women's roles in the negotiation of sex and relationships (and not, sadly, the last). From feminazis, to old dried-up witches who should get on their brooms and fly out of town, to silly girls, to man-haters, to questions about whether we just hate sex and have penis envy: that level of sexist abuse, we would learn, was to be expected whenever we spoke publicly about feminist issues. But it does not always end there for the public feminist criminologist. We also received personal emails attacking us, including speculation that we were bitter because we could not land a man, and suggesting (in more colorful terms) that what we really needed was to get laid. It was eight months before we would both gathered ourselves up and were ready to take on public commentary again.

Almost 10 years later, one of the authors was doing a breakfast radio interview about image-based abuse. Just prior to going on air, the male radio host shook hands, leaned in, and initiated the conversation in the following way:

Host: So, did you bring me any?
Author: Any what?
Host: Any pics. Did you bring me any nudes?

With nothing more than a glance of silent apology from his female staffer, the interview went to air. Whether or not it was the overt intention of the host, his comment had the effect of both rattling the author and undermining the interview. Every subsequent on-air question he posed about harmless flirting, or where such images are typically available, confirmed his apparent views that the issue was merely a salacious crowd-pleaser and not a matter of abuse at all.

While sexism and harassment as a response to our public engagements as feminist criminologists on these issues might be (unfortunately) anticipated, further challenges are presented by facing sexism and harassment within academia itself; and we have both experienced more than our fair share over the last ten years. In one particularly pertinent example, one of the authors was presenting at a conference, only to be alerted afterwards by some colleagues that one of the attendees had been video recording the presentation and had been seen zooming the image onto our breasts and legs as well as those of other women in the room, before sending the video to someone else via email. The voyeur in question left the session early and before being confronted by those who had witnessed the incident. In another instance, as a female scholar was accepting a prize at a criminology conference, a male professor casually remarked to his colleagues, "Oh, she's just another Barbie doll criminologist," presumably the implication being that her substantive contribution to her field was as a pretty or sexualized object, rather than anything of intellectual substance. It seemed apparent to him, and his nodding male colleagues were in agreement, that a young woman surely was not being awarded a professional prize for her intellectual contribution. (Side note: having overheard the comment, we did ask the professor in question whether he had actually read the award-winning article. He had not.)

There is then a double burden for the public feminist criminologist who faces sexist backlash from without the academy whenever speaking publicly and who within the academy is required to navigate an imposed identity as a female object, rather than equal colleague, in the eyes of many of our fellow (male) academics. Our experiences as feminist criminologists point to few safe spaces to discuss and develop our research: from our feminist research being devalued compared to more "mainstream" criminological research to assumptions being made that we are the note-taker rather than an academic representative for departmental meetings with senior management to comments about our physical appearance making it "more enjoyable" to work with us to being described as a "lovely girl" by our male colleagues or the "rose among the thorns" in a male-dominated committee to being called "ma'am" by a male colleague in his email reply to a repeated request for overdue work[7] to the unwanted sexual approaches that occur at annual academic conferences to rejecting invitations to "collaborate" with senior men in their hotel rooms or over "a late drink" rather than in a meeting room or public space to rape jokes being made by men in the departmental morning tea room.

Emerging research suggests that these examples are far from isolated incidents, but rather that a wide spectrum of sexist harassment, abuse, and threats are increasingly common experiences for women researchers who engage publicly, both from outside and within the academy (see Cole, 2015; Cole & Hassel, 2017; Jane, 2018; Liu, 2019; Sang, 2018; Vera-Gray, 2017). For feminist criminologists who frequently advocate for reform on policy issues such as sexual violence, domestic violence, harassment and stalking, our public criminologies expose us to both private and public backlash in ways that target us through our gender, our bodies, and our sexuality. In effect, the abuse received by public feminist criminologists replicates the forms of violence and discrimination against women that we are so often advocating to change. In this sense, public feminist criminologists are often putting themselves personally on the line in ways that are quite unlike malestream public criminologists (as are our anti-racist and queer criminology colleagues). That is not to say that men speaking about mainstream crime and justice issues do not receive backlash, including online abuse; rather, it is to say that it takes a less personalized form, and less directly replicates violence and abuse that they themselves have routinely experienced.

The Personal Is Political: Public Criminology and "Survivor-Scholar" Identity

A further way in which the personal can be political for the feminist criminologist is as survivor-scholars themselves. Many academic women working on issues of men's violence against women will have experiences of sexism, gender-based discrimination, sexual harassment, and/or violence in their own lives—or they will certainly know a woman who has. Who among our readers of this chapter did not feel something of a familiar sting in the anecdotes of everyday sexism, harassment, and abuse that we have related above? At the very least, for many feminist criminologists, the nature of their research work means that it is inevitable that they will invest themselves personally and emotionally, for example, when interviewing victim/survivors of sexual assault (Campbell, 2013). Herein lies the triple-burden of the public feminist criminologist.

While even a basic appreciation of the high rate of violence against women in society would suggest that many activist-scholars have themselves been victims of gendered violence and abuse, comparatively few reveal that identity. Perhaps this is because there may be professional costs associated with disclosing subjective experience, lest our public and scholarly "expert" status be discredited. For some, to assume or reveal the identity of victim, or even to engage in an overtly emotional way with their area of expertise, is to further discredit and diminish their position as neutral, objective researchers. As Ahmed (2013, p. 170) writes, "Feminists who speak out against established 'truths' are often constructed as emotional, as failing the very standards of reason and impartiality that are assumed to form the basis of 'good judgment.'"

Her point speaks to the historical devaluation of feminist research within the academy as part of the hierarchy between ivory tower positivist academic criminology and feminist research (and related activism) (Nelund, 2014). Put simply, the neoliberal academy does not yet sufficiently recognize or value the importance of much of the work carried out by feminist criminologists. Take, for example, research examining the role of emotions in crime. The "scientization" of criminology as a positivist discipline in its nascency, featuring the self-styling of (mostly male) criminologists as dispassionate and rational technicians, resulted in the neglect of consideration of the role played by emotions in the commission of, and responses to, deviant and criminal behavior (Gelsthorpe, 2009). More recently, deeper consideration of the affective and symbolic dimensions of crime and punishment has been considered a key factor in understanding the "foreground" of offending (Ferrell, 1997; Katz, 1988; Lyng, 2004) and in attempts to counter the appeal of populist punitiveness (Freiberg, 2001). Despite this, top journals are less likely to publish qualitative feminist research (Gonzalez & Nunez, 2014 cited in Fraser & Taylor, 2016), while funding still strongly favors work that is positivist in nature. Measures of success do not sufficiently account for public engagement; rationality and conformity are rewarded, as is keeping one's politics to oneself (Giroux, 2014 cited in Fraser & Taylor, 2016). Notably, this chapter is most likely the only contribution that we have made in the wake of the rape and murder of Eurydice Dixon that will "count" towards our "research output," despite the other activities we listed at the start of this chapter being as—if not more—important for us personally and for the women in our city. In short, a market driven university devalues feminist research and activist-scholarship because they do not "produce" in prescribed ways (Fraser & Taylor, 2016, p. 6).

Too often as feminist criminologists we conceal our personal experiences of violence, harassment, and sexism. Perhaps we feel our work, whether it is in the service sector, or in government policy, or in academic research, or as a caring friend or family member, will be dismissed as too biased, too emotional—or too feminist. We are reluctant to speak with emotion, lest we be cast aside as not rational, not scientific, not *academic*. Yet we have every right to stand with survivors, to be emotional—passionately resolute, motivated by anger, even furious—in the face of the systemic violence and injustices experienced by women. We have every right to work collectively towards a society in which women not only live free from violence and the fear of violence but are also able to go about their lives autonomously and as equals. These are the aims of a feminist movement against men's violence—both within and without the academy—and our experiences of violent victimization do not, by default, make us any more prone to bias than are our gender-blind colleagues. As Ahmed (2013, p. 170) suggests:

> The response to the dismissal of feminists as emotional should not then be to claim that feminism is rational rather than emotional. Such a claim would be misguided as it would accept the very opposition between emotions and rational thought that is crucial to the subordination of femininity as well as feminism. Instead, we need to contest this understanding of emotion as "the unthought," just as we need to contest the assumption that "rational thought" is unemotional, or that it does not involve being moved by others.

We argue, then, that rather than refusing to be emotional, we should consider being emotional as a personal act of activism. It is something that separates us from a narrow understanding of criminology as technical and devoid of political agenda. There are a number among us in the feminist academy who successfully navigate this public identity as a survivor-scholar, relating their own experiences of domestic violence, sexual violence, sexual harassment, sexism and abuse, alongside their research and advocacy for reform on these issues. Among them are Alisa Ackerman-Acklin (2018), Nina Funnell (2017), Winnie Li (2017), and Bri Lee (2018). In that spirit, and inspired by these colleagues, this chapter has included some of our own personal reflections. To paraphrase feminist journalist Jill Filipovic (2012): sharing our experiences without anyone else's approval or endorsement is what initially brought men's violence against women out of the shadows. Continuing to speak the truth is what keeps the light on.

Conclusion

Throughout this chapter we have sought to connect our own personal reflections and experiences of public engagement, backlash, sexism, and harassment with the broader scholarship and practice of public feminist criminologies. Such experiences, though partial and situated, are at the same time not uncommon for the public feminist criminologist working on violence against women, and they are markedly different from many other policy advocacy fields within "malestream" criminology. In effect, there is a triple-burden facing the public feminist criminologist: she is simultaneously engaging on issues of gendered violence and inequality publicly, as well as often within the academy itself, while also having either direct or indirect experience of gendered violence and inequality in her personal life. There is a risk, or perhaps fear, that navigating this triple-burden might undermine our scholarly and public reputation, particularly because others will only deem us as credible in our role as impartial "experts," and as such we must carry the burden of our own experiences alone.

Yet, as criminologists, we are all too aware that affect and values cannot be disentangled from crime nor from our community and system responses to it. Arguably feminist criminologists working on violence against women and its prevention are successful in their public engagements at least in part due to this capacity to harness emotion in response to the experiences of victim survivors. At the same time there are risks and tensions in doing so, the most notable being the co-option by punitive politics which would harness that same emotion to justify greater imprisonment. Activist-scholars must perform a fine balancing act to ensure that the outcomes of their public work contribute to a better society for all, not just victim survivors.

There is personal risk, too, when engaging publicly on an issue, and in asking men in particular to relinquish some of their privilege, as a means of changing the structures, practices, and norms that contribute to the high levels of violence against women in society. The backlash that feminist criminologists face both within and outside of academia is one such unfortunate outcome. That it exists, though, should suggest that our message is getting through. And its effect on us is contrary to its intended purpose; rather than diminishing us and our work, it is the very thing that convinces us that we need to keep going.

Acknowledgements

Many of the experiences and reflections related here present a rather bleak picture of the everyday life of the public feminist criminologist. We have tried here not to shy away from some of the very real tensions and challenges that we have not only experienced ourselves but have observed in their lives of many of our fellow feminist criminologists. We are grateful to our wonderful feminist colleagues who provide both informal debriefing and mutual support in what can be a disheartening and vicariously, and at times directly, traumatizing job.

We are also particularly grateful to many male mentors and colleagues who have supported us and collaborated with us on an equal and respectful basis. When you invite us to lead (not to follow), when you open a space for our voice (not talk over us), when you acknowledge our contributions (not undermine or take credit for them), when you encourage us to be bold (not warn us against it), when you challenge your male peers (not nod along in silence), your collegiality is also feminist activism, and frankly, we need more of it—and from many more academic men like you.

Notes

1. Image-based abuse refers to the non-consensual creation, distribution, and/or threats to distribute a nude or intimate image without the consent of the person depicted. While sometimes the images are sometimes distributed in order to humiliate or harass the victim, in other cases of image-based abuse the motivations of perpetrators are less about direct harm to the victim and more so related to the perpetrators' gaining of status, credibility, or even money in online spaces and communities (Powell & Henry, 2017; Henry, Powell, & Flynn, 2017). There are numerous websites, image-sharing boards, forums, and social media that serve as platforms for (mainly) men to trade in images, with men competing with each other to provide the "win" shots and often identifying or sexually commenting about the women depicted.
2. See www.esafety.gov.au/image-based-abuse.
3. See www.1800respect.org.au/violence-and-abuse/image-based-abuse.
4. See www.aph.gov.au/Parliamentary_Business/Bills_Legislation/bd/bd1718a/18bd074.
5. See https://parliament.nt.gov.au/__data/assets/pdf_file/0005/488921/38-2017-Inquiry-into-the-Criminal-Code-Amendment-Intimate-Images-Bill-2017.pdf.
6. See www.parliament.nsw.gov.au/bill/files/3396/2R%20Crimes.pdf.

7 In fact, the full phrase used was "No Ma'am," a thinly veiled reference to the anti-feminist men's rights organization in the U.S. television show *Married with Children*, "NO MA'AM," otherwise known as the "National Organization of Men Against Amazonian Masterhood."

References

Ackerman-Acklin, A. (2018). *There is a better way* [blog]. Retrieved from www.alissaackerman.com/blog/

Ahmed, S. (2013). *The cultural politics of emotion*. New York: Routledge.

Akchurin, M., & Lee, C. S. (2013). Pathways to empowerment: Repertoires of women's activism and gender earnings equality. *American Sociological Review*, 78(4), 679–701.

Australian Bureau of Statistics. (2017). *Personal safety survey, 2016*. Cat no: 4906.0. Retrieved from www.abs.gov.au/ausstats/abs@.nsf/mf/4906.0

Bartels, L. (2013). Parole and parole authorities in Australia: A system in crisis? *Criminal Law Journal*, 37, 357–376.

Bryant, W., & Bricknell, S. (2017). *Statistical reports no. 2: Homicide in Australia 2012–13 to 2013–14: National Homicide Monitoring Program report*. Canberra: Australian Institute of Criminology. Retrieved from https://aic.gov.au/publications/sr/sr002

Campbell, R. (2013). *Emotionally involved: The impact of researching rape*. New York: Routledge.

Chappell, L. (2002). The "femocrat" strategy: Expanding the repertoire of feminist activists. *Parliamentary Affairs*, 55(1), 85–98.

Chesney-Lind, M. (2006). Patriarchy, crime, and justice: Feminist criminology in an era of backlash. *Feminist Criminology*, 1(1), 6–26.

Cole, K., & Hassel, H. (2017). *Surviving sexism in academia: Strategies for feminist leadership*. New York: Routledge.

Cole, K. K. (2015). "It's like she's eager to be verbally abused": Twitter, trolls, and (en)gendering disciplinary rhetoric. *Feminist Media Studies*, 15(2), 356–358.

Commonwealth of Australia. (2011). *The national plan to reduce violence against women and their children 2010–2022*. Canberra: Author.

Cox, P. (2015). *Horizons research report, issue 1: Violence against women: Additional analysis of the Australian Bureau of Statistics' personal safety survey 2012*. Australia's National Research Organisation for Women's Safety (ANROWS), Sydney: ANROWS.

Daly, K., & Stubbs, J. (2006). Feminist engagement with restorative justice. *Theoretical Criminology*, 10(1), 9–28.

DeKeseredy, W. S., & Schwartz, M. D. (2016). Thinking sociologically about image-based sexual abuse: The contribution of male peer support theory. *Sexualization, Media, & Society*, 2(4), 1–8.

do Mar Pereira, M. (2016). Struggling within and beyond the performative university: Articulating activism and work in an "academia without walls". *Women's Studies International Forum*, 54, 100–110.

Eisenstein, H. (1996). *Inside agitators: Australian femocrats and the state*. Philadelphia, PA: Temple University Press.

Ferrell, J. (1997). Criminological verstehen: Inside the immediacy of crime. *Justice Quarterly*, 14(1), 3–23.

Fileborn, B. (2018, June 15). "Stay safe:" Why women are enraged by advice to steer clear of violent men. *The Conversation*. Retrieved from https://theconversation.com/stay-safe-why-women-are-enraged-by-advice-to-steer-clear-of-violent-men-98338

Filipovic, J. (2012, November 10). The ethics of outing your rapist. *The Guardian*. Retrieved from www.theguardian.com/commentisfree/2012/nov/09/ethics-of-outing-rapist

Finn, M. A., & Bettis, P. (2006). Punitive action or gentle persuasion: Exploring police officers' justifications for using dual arrest in domestic violence cases. *Violence Against Women*, 12(3), 268–287.

Fraser, H., & Taylor, N. (2016). *Neoliberalization, universities and the public intellectual: Species, gender and class and the production of knowledge*. London: Springer.

Freiberg, A. (2001). Affective versus effective justice: Instrumentalism and emotionalism in criminal justice. *Punishment & Society*, 3(2), 265–278.

Funnell, N. (2017). I believe you. In J. Caro (Ed.), *Unbreakable: Women share stories of resilience and hope* (pp. 1–24). Brisbane: University of Queensland Press.

Garland, D. (2001). *The culture of control*. Oxford: Oxford University Press.

Gelsthorpe, L. (2009). Emotions and contemporary developments in criminology. In S. D. Sclater, D. W. Jones, H. Price, & C. Yates (Eds.), *Emotion: New psychological perspectives* (pp. 183–196). London: Palgrave Macmillan.

Henry, N., & Powell, A. (2016). Sexual violence in the digital age: The scope and limits of criminal law. *Social & Legal Studies*, 25(4), 397–418.

Henry, N., Powell, A., & Flynn, A. (2017). *Not just "revenge pornography": Australians' experiences of image-based abuse: A summary report*. Melbourne: RMIT University.

Hirschel, D., McCormack, P. D., & Buzawa, E. (2017). A 10-year study of the impact of intimate partner violence primary aggressor laws on single and dual arrest. *Journal of Interpersonal Violence*. doi:10886260517739290

Innes, M., & Fielding, N. (2002). From community to communicative policing: "Signal crimes" and the problem of public reassurance. *Sociological Research Online*, 7(2), 1–12.

Jane, E. A. (2018). Gendered cyberhate as workplace harassment and economic vandalism. *Feminist Media Studies*, 18(4), 575–591.

Katz, J. (1988). *Seductions of crime: Moral and sensual attractions in doing evil*. New York: Basic Books.

Lee, B. (2018). *Eggshell skull*. Sydney: Allen & Unwin.

Lewis, R., Dobash, R. E., Dobash, R. P., & Cavanagh, K. (2001). Law's progressive potential: The value of engagement with the law for domestic violence. *Social & Legal Studies*, 10(1), 105–130.

Li, W. (2017). *Dark chapter*. London: Legend Press.

Liu, H. (2019). An embarrassment of riches: The seduction of postfeminism in the academy. *Organization*, 26(1), 20–37.

Lyng, S. (2004). *Edgework: The sociology of risk-taking*. New York: Routledge.

Marriner, C. (2015, September 30). Revenge porn: Government urged to make it illegal. *The Sydney Morning Herald*. Retrieved from: www.smh.com.au/national/government-urged-to-outlaw-revenge-porn-20150926-gjvod5.html

Matsuda, M. J. (1989). When the first quail calls: Multiple consciousness as jurisprudential method. *Women's Rights Law Reporter*, 11, 7.

McGlynn, C., Downes, J., & Westmarland, N. (2017). Seeking justice for survivors of sexual violence: Recognition, voice and consequences. In E. Zinsstag & M. Keenan (Eds.), *Restorative responses to sexual violence* (pp. 179–191). New York: Routledge.

McGlynn, C., & Rackley, E. (2016, March 9). *Not "revenge porn," but abuse: Let's call it image-based sexual abuse by @McGlynnClare & @erikarackley*. Retrieved from http://everydayvictimblaming.com/media-complaints/not-revenge-porn-but-abuse-lets-call-it-image-based-sexual-abuse-by-%e2%80%8fmcglynnclare-erikarackley/

McGlynn, C., & Rackley, E. (2017). Image-based sexual abuse. *Oxford Journal of Legal Studies*, 37(3), 534–561.

Milivojevic, S., & McGovern, A. (2014). The death of Jill Meagher: Crime and punishment on social media. *International Journal for Crime, Justice and Social Democracy*, 3(3), 22–39.

Mopas, M., & Moore, D. (2012). Talking heads and bleeding hearts: Newsmaking, emotion and public criminology in the wake of a sexual assault. *Critical Criminology*, 20(2), 183–196.

Nelund, A. (2014). Troubling publics: A feminist analysis of public criminology. *Radical Criminology*, 4, 67–84.

Our Watch, ANROWS and VicHealth. (2015). *Change the story: A shared framework for the primary prevention of violence against women*. Melbourne: Our Watch.

Powell, A. (2015). Seeking rape justice: Formal and informal responses to sexual violence through technosocial counter-publics. *Theoretical Criminology*, 19(4), 571–588.

Powell, A., & Henry, N. (2015, October 4). How can we stem the tide of online harassment and abuse? *The Conversation*. Retrieved from: https://theconversation.com/how-can-we-stem-the-tide-of-online-harassment-and-abuse-48387

Powell, A., & Henry, N. (2017). *Sexual violence in a digital age*. London: Springer.

Powell, A., Overington, C., & Hamilton, G. (2018). Following #JillMeagher: Collective meaning-making in response to crime events via social media. *Crime, Media, Culture*, 14(3), 409–428.

Risman, B. (2006). Feminist strategies for public sociology. In J. R. Blau & K. E. I. Smith (Eds.), *Public sociologies reader* (pp. 281–292). Lanham, MD: Rowman & Littlefield.

Sang, K. J. (2018). Gender, ethnicity and feminism: An intersectional analysis of the lived experiences feminist academic women in UK higher education. *Journal of Gender Studies*, 27(2), 192–206.

Schilt, K., & Westbrook, L. (2015). Bathroom battlegrounds and penis panics. *Contexts*, 14(3), 26–31.

Smart, C. (1989). *Feminism and the power of law*. New York: Routledge.

Sprague, J., & Laube, H. (2009). Institutional barriers to doing public sociology: Experiences of feminists in the academy. *The American Sociologist*, 40(4), 249.

Stones, R. J. (2017). Which gender is more concerned about transgender women in female bathrooms? *Gender Issues*, 34(3), 275–291.

Sullivan, R. (2018, June 15). The post about #EurydiceDixon Australian women are sharing on social media. *News.com.au*. Retrieved from www.news.com.au/lifestyle/real-life/news-life/the-post-about-eurydice-dixon-australian-women-are-sharing-on-social-media/news-story/5131bf8ff310bd2fd0fe600c888e5295

Thompson, J. D., & Louise, R. (2014). Sexed violence and its (dis)appearances: Media coverage surrounding the murders of Jill Meagher and Johanna Martin. *Outskirts*, 31(1). Retrieved from www.outskirts.arts.uwa.edu.au/volumes/volume-31/jay-daniel-thompson-and-rebecca-louise

Tomsen, S. (1997). A top night: Social protest, masculinity and the culture of drinking violence. *The British Journal of Criminology, 37*(1), 90–102.

Touhy, W. (2018, June 19). We must end epidemic of violence against women. *Herald Sun*. Retrieved from www.heraldsun.com.au/news/opinion/wendy-tuohy/news-story/344fc445d967ec49794bde51a6a69751

Vera-Gray, F. (2017). "Talk about a cunt with too much idle time": Trolling feminist research. *Feminist Review, 115*(1), 61–78.

Waitt, G., Jessop, L., & Gorman-Murray, A. (2011). "The guys in there just expect to be laid": Embodied and gendered socio-spatial practices of a "night out" in Wollongong, Australia. *Gender, Place and Culture, 18*(2), 255–275.

10
LIBERATING ABORTION PILLS IN LEGALLY RESTRICTED SETTINGS[1]
Activism as Public Criminology

Mariana Prandini Assis

Introduction

The first weekend of August 2018 was an important one for Brazilian feminists who, for decades now, have mobilized against the criminalization of abortion. The Supreme Court held a public hearing of medical and legal experts, social movements' representatives, religious authorities, and legal practitioners in the context of a lawsuit aiming to declare the criminalization of abortion unconstitutional. During that weekend, activists from all over the country gathered in the capital, Brasília, for a Festival for Women's Lives where we discussed issues ranging from reproductive justice to holistic security in abortion activism. Among the participants were activists from Argentina and Uruguay who shared the history and most recent developments of the struggle for legalizing abortion in their countries. While Uruguay, in 2012, became the first country in South America to make abortion on demand legal up until twelve weeks of gestation, Argentina has a very active network of feminists, known as *Socorristas en Red*,[2] who publicly help women accessing accurate information and medication that can safely and effectively end a pregnancy in the privacy of their homes.

The discovery of pills that can end an unwanted pregnancy was a watershed in access to abortion worldwide. Medication abortion—as the use of drugs to terminate a pregnancy is usually known[3]—is an effective and safe abortion method that can be used outside of the clinical setting (Ramos, Romero, & Aizenberg, 2014), and without the involvement of a healthcare provider (Gerdts, Jayaweera, Baum, & Hudaya, 2018). When performed with medication that is self-sourced and self-used and outside of a clinical context, the procedure is known as self-managed abortion (Erdman, Jelinska, & Yanow, 2018).

After decades of documenting evidence and gradually recognizing the relevance of abortion with medication for addressing inequities in access, the World Health Organization (WHO) has issued a comprehensive guideline on medical management of abortion (WHO, 2018). This guideline (WHO, 2018, p. vii) not only acknowledges that medication abortion "plays a crucial role in providing access to safe, effective and acceptable abortion care," but also recommends this as a safe method for abortion after the first trimester. While currently the medical profession increasingly recognizes the benefits of medication abortion, the discovery of the pills' wonders was not the deed of physicians or researchers. Brazilian women, with the help of pharmacists and drugstore workers, were the ones who identified the abortive effect of a drug initially prescribed to treat gastric ulcer in the 1980s—Cytotec, the commercial name for misoprostol in the country. And yet, today, women in Brazil are denied access to a technological innovation that they introduced to the world.

In a stark contrast, misoprostol has not been restricted in Argentina to the same extent as in Brazil. Such factual condition has enabled a favorable environment for the development of a network of activists, part of a strand of feminist abortion mobilization that openly provides information and accompaniment to women getting medical abortions. This network has been operating for a decade now, working alongside two other tracks of activism for abortion rights: The National Campaign for Free, Safe and Legal Abortion and the rights and public health strategy pursued by feminist lawyers and public health professionals (Ruibal & Fernandez Anderson, 2018). The positive synergy of these three strands of activism—"political mobilization, public health and rights strategy and direct action and service provision" (p. 4)—has paved the way for the 2018 massive demonstrations in favor of a proposed bill decriminalizing abortion. As abortion advocates chose a green handkerchief as a symbol, their extensive protests became known as *La Marea Verde* (the Green Wave) in the region.

That said, existing criminal restrictions to the medication in Brazil mean that accessing it often entails dealing with the illegal drugs market (Diniz & Madeiro, 2012), an individualized endeavor that may also become perilous. Criminalization endangers access to an essential medicine and poses additional costs to collective action. Contrasting to Argentina, where the three activist strands described above have flourished side by side, public activism for abortion in Brazil has remained largely focused on legal mobilization in its narrow sense (Ruibal & Fernandez Anderson, 2018), amounting to high profile litigation and campaigns targeting the legislature, both aiming at gradual legalization.[4] Unfortunately, there is no clear evidence regarding the specific interests behind the changes in the Brazilian regulation of misoprostol or how exactly these changes came about, leading to its total ban in the formal market.[5] Evident, nonetheless, are the harmful effects of the ban on women's reproductive freedom.

In this chapter, I argue that the criminalization of misoprostol has had damaging effects on abortion activism in Brazil, because it has created grave obstacles to forms of direct action that appropriate a technological discovery to circumvent the effects of criminal restrictions on abortion. The case discussed in this chapter gives a close view into how criminal law works to produce harm (Erdman, 2018), particularly when it is instrumentalized for social and sexual control. While activists in Brazil continue to pursue abortion legalization by fighting the restrictions of the penal code, the ban of the medication deny women and pregnant people access to one of the safest, effective, and most autonomous methods to end an unwanted pregnancy.

Even if unintendedly, through the strong hand of criminal law combined with seemingly protective sanitary regulation, Brazilian authorities have succeeded in forcing public abortion activism to remain tied to an outdated frame of the abortion clinic. This, in turn, moves into the deepest underground any attempt of direct action through harm reduction practices such as medical abortion accompaniment, counseling, and informational hotlines, as has been publicly happening in Argentina. Rather than focusing on the specific prohibition of abortion as stated in criminal law, this chapter focuses on criminalization as a broader set of legal acts with effects specific to self-managed abortion and direct-action strategy.

As such, this chapter is an attempt to develop what I call "grounded public criminology." Much of the work done by scholars engaged in public criminology is set out as a well-intentioned move to bring their "work 'back to the people' (Carrabine, Lee, & South, 2000) by explaining [their] work to the public (Uggen & Inderbitzin, 2010)" (as cited in Nelund, 2014, p. 76). As such, public criminology often operates as a benevolent act of teaching extra-academic publics what academia has learnt about crime control and punishment. This chapter takes a different approach: it deploys academic skills to address a problem that emerged from within activism for abortion decriminalization in Brazil. The critiques of criminalization articulated here are based on experiencing it on an every-day basis as an activist scholar. They constitute thus an attempt to speak to my partners within the movements and tell them we might be targeting the wrong enemy. But they also address our academic allies and urge them to learn from the struggle, rather than the usual attempt to teach to struggle.

In order to do so, I look back at the historical developments in Brazil regarding medication abortion, from the discovery of the abortive uses of misoprostol by Brazilian women to our current context, marked by a strong criminalization of not only of abortion *per se* but also of any action related to the medication. I compare the Brazilian case to the Argentine one, where criminal laws regulating abortion are similar, but the medication is available in pharmacies with no criminal offense attached to them. My aim with the comparison is to trace the impact of criminalization of the abortion pill—and not abortion *per se*—on social movement building and direct-action activism.

What is novel about the Brazilian case is how criminalization of reproductive freedom has effectively been achieved, in a time of technological advancement, through the production of a legal architecture, rather than a single criminal prohibition. A complicated scheme of sanitary regulations combined with criminal law, supposedly enacted to protect public health and medicine consumers, is in fact doing the opposite. The prohibition is barring women and pregnant people from accessing the safest method to end an unwanted pregnancy, while also criminalizing movement building in an indirect way.

Being a reflexive exercise of how medico-criminal architecture impact both the exercise of women and pregnant people's rights—to health, to innovation, and to information—and the strategies adopted by abortion activists, this chapter is an example of a public criminology that disrupts the "unidirectional transmission of knowledge implied in the public criminology literature" (Nelund, 2014, p. 78). If public criminology is about criminology's engagement with social justice issues, it is time to recognize both the knowledge and actions of activists engaging with criminal law as an integral and equal part of the field, as I intend to do in this chapter.

Discovering the Pill … Outlawing the Pill … Liberating the Pill … the Fate of Abortion Activism in Brazil and Argentina in 200mcg

Abortion is restricted in similar ways in Argentina and Brazil. Both countries outlaw the procedure in their penal codes, charging providers and women who cause or consent to an abortion to imprisonment that ranges from one to four years.[6] There are a few circumstances in which, if performed by a licensed physician, abortion is not to be punished. In both countries, there is an exception for when the pregnancy is the result of rape or when it poses risk to the woman's life. In Argentina, there is also the exception of risk to the "mother's health,"[7] and in Brazil, a physician can also perform the procedure if the fetus is anencephalic.[8] Research shows that abortion remains difficult to access in both countries, even in the narrow circumstances where it is legal (Madeiro & Diniz, 2016; Zurbriggen, Keefe-Oates, & Gerdts, 2018).

Nonetheless, evidence from around the world demonstrates that criminalization does not stop women and pregnant people from procuring an abortion; it, does, however, impact its safety and timing (Zurbriggen et al., 2018). The Guttmacher Institute shows that South America and the Caribbean, which are among the regions with the most restrictive laws on abortion in the world, also had the highest annual rates of abortion in 2010–2014. In the Caribbean, the abortion rate was estimated at 59 per 1,000 women of reproductive age, followed by South America, at 48 (Guttmacher Institute, 2018). Historically, women have resorted to every mean available in order to circumvent restrictive abortion laws and exercise their reproductive freedom, from herbal teas to clandestine clinics. It was in this messy underground world of social experimentation and criminalization that Brazilian women discovered the use of misoprostol alone to induce an abortion as early as the 1980s (Coeytaux & Wells, 2013).

Cytotec was introduced in Brazil in 1986 for treating gastric and duodenal ulcers, and its use as an abortifacient quickly spread by word of mouth. Cytotec is the commercial name for misoprostol, a synthetic analogue of prostaglandin E,[9] developed by G. D. Searle & Company. In 1988, Biolab, a Brazilian laboratory, began marketing the drug (Barbosa & Arilha, 1993). The pill was inexpensive and easily obtainable in pharmacies all over the country, allowing women to safely and privately end an unwanted pregnancy, without the assistance of a medical professional. In addition, if used buccally or sublingually, misoprostol cannot be detected by the time contractions begin. This means that an induced and a spontaneous miscarriage cannot be distinguished by bodily symptoms, making it nearly impossible for an induced abortion to be prosecuted as such.[10]

By 1991, Cytotec was widely known as an abortifacient throughout Brazil.[11] Knowledge was spread through an informal network that included pharmacists, doctors, the manufacturer, the media and women themselves (Barbosa & Arilha, 1993). Studies show that in the 1980s, when Cytotec was largely available, the number of women reaching the public health system due to complications from induced miscarriage fell drastically (Faúndes, 2010, p. 33) as medical abortion is not only easy, but also effective and safe.[12]

As the drug gained notoriety as an abortifacient, a public controversy followed, and two main public positions on the issue gained traction. Groups and institutions linked with medical surveillance demanded that Cytotec be withdrawn from the market as it was solely being used for inducing abortion. Gynecologists, on the other hand, argued that the drug should remain available as it rendered illegal abortion less risky and unsafe (Barbosa & Arilha, 1993).

Following the public outcry, in 1991, the Ministry of Health altered the regulation under which the drug was marketed, establishing that it could only be sold in authorized drugstores, upon retention of a doctor's prescription (Pazello, 2010). The laboratory reduced the drug's monthly production as part of an agreement reached with the Minister of Health to control its use (Barbosa & Arilha, 1993).

Interviews conducted with Brazilian women in 1992 showed that they had enough knowledge about medication abortion and consciously chose the procedure with Cytotec for three main reasons. First, the drug had a very low cost,[13] especially when compared to other methods, such as surgical abortion. Second, the procedure itself was seen as an easy one because the drug is administered in privacy, it requires less (or even no) outside intervention and is perceived as less traumatizing than other methods. Finally, women saw medication abortion as a safer method, "one that does not kill women" (Barbosa & Arilha, 1993, pp. 238–239).

Interestingly, the first scientific study about the use of misoprostol for obstetric purposes was conducted by a Brazilian professor and published in a scientific journal in 1987 (Faúndes, 2010). Four years later, another study conducted by two Argentine doctors was published in the Lancet (Faúndes, 2010). From then on, there was a rapid diffusion of the use of misoprostol in obstetrics and gynecology, followed by hundreds of publications in the most respected area journals (Faúndes, 2010). Today, misoprostol is recognized as the drug for women: used in abortion, miscarriage management, labor induction, prevention and treatment of postpartum hemorrhage, and cervical dilation in gynecological interventions, it is a game changer for maternal and reproductive health. In 2005, the WHO added misoprostol to its List of Essential Medicines for countries where abortion is not against the law. In 2009, misoprostol was also included for the treatment of incomplete abortion (Zamberlin, Romero, & Ramos, 2012). In 2018, the WHO issued an extensive guideline on medication abortion.

Despite all these progressive developments worldwide, in Brazil, the regulation of misoprostol has continued moving backwards. The controversy over the medication, which led to the aforementioned regulatory change in 1991, grew stronger when, in the same decade, a group of researchers suggested that misoprostol could have teratogenic effects on the fetus if the dosage was not sufficient to induce abortion (Diniz, 2008). Throughout the next ten years, several clinical research reports attempting to establish a correlation between the use of misoprostol during pregnancy and fetal malformation were published (Diniz, 2008), with the Moebius Syndrome—a very rare congenital neurological disorder—being the alleged most severe outcome.

These studies led to an ever-increased public attention to the "underground" practice of misoprostol use for inducing miscarriage. In 1998, as negative publicity about the medication grew, the newly established National Sanitary Agency adopted a regulation on "substances and medications subjected to special control" (Administrative Rule no. 344/1998) as one of its first regulatory actions. Misoprostol was included on the list.[14] According to Administrative Rule no. 344/1998, Article 2, a special authorization from the Sanitary Agency is mandatory in order "to extract, produce, fabricate, distribute, transport, prepare, manipulate, import, export, transform, pack, or repack the substance and its improved versions, or the medications that contain it." Today, there is only one authorized producer of misoprostol in Brazil, which is distributed under the brand name Prostokos.[15] In addition, misoprostol can only the bought and used in healthcare facilities authorized by the Sanitary Agency, and it is obligatory that any medicine containing the substance include a warning about the risk for pregnant women in its package. More recent Administrative Rules have attempted to regulate not only its commerce, but also any form of publicity or dissemination of related information on its use available on the internet and any social media (Administrative Rules no. 911/2006 and 1050/2006, updated by Administrative Rule no. 1534/2011).

If these were the only regulations, violations would be an administrative offense and the consequences would not be so serious. However, the aforementioned sanitary regulation is linked to a specific crime against public health, specified in article 273 of the Penal Code. The crime consists in "importing, selling, exposing, having in deposit to sell, or distributing or delivering to consumption" a medicine that is on the list of "substances and medications subjected to special control" issued by the National Sanitary Agency (Administrative Rule no. 344/1998). The penalty for this crime, which is intended to protect public health and medicine consumers' safety, can range from a minimum of 10 to a maximum of 15 years in jail. Currently, some Brazilian judges, understanding that the penalty is evidently unreasonable based on the offense, have charged people dealing misoprostol with the penalty for drug trafficking, which carries a minimum of 5 and a maximum of 15 years in jail, allowing, therefore, for lower sentences if the circumstances are favorable for the accused.[16] In very few cases, when Courts identify that the drug had been produced in a foreign laboratory and was illegally brought into the country, the charge is contraband, which carries 3 to 5 years in jail.[17]

All of the three criminal offenses applied to all actions related to misoprostol—carrying, having in deposit, selling, giving away, distributing, to mention but a few—have no direct relationship to abortion. One is drug trafficking; another is a crime against public health; and the other is contraband. Therefore, the fact that misoprostol can be used for inducing a miscarriage should not be in the purview of judges deciding on the fate of the medication. Nonetheless, case law shows that the judiciary finds it relevant to mention, and therefore a more reprehensible action, that the illegally sold or contrabanded medication is used for the purpose of inducing a miscarriage. Such line of judicial reasoning evokes the idea that the definition and interpretation of crimes are directed by ideologies and moralities: "almost all aspects of the definition of a 'good' person in society are bound up in constituting crime, criminal law, and the criminal" (Miller, Roseman, & Rizvi, 2019, p. 2). Someone whom in any way may help a woman to have an abortion is not a good person, in these judges' view. Misoprostol, differently from all the other hundreds of drugs included in the list annexed to Administrative Rule no. 344/1998, carries with it a stigma for being "the abortion pill."

While lay people, including women using misoprostol and activists campaigning for the decriminalization of abortion, do not know the intricate and uncertain legal architecture described above, it is widely known that dealing, using, or distributing misoprostol is a crime. Such knowledge creates a number of barriers for women and pregnant people to access the medication: they usually get the pills in the clandestine market, being thus unable to verify the quality of the product; and they pay much more than if the drug was legalized. On the other hand, pro-choice activists who may access the drug through solidarity networks in other countries often fear being caught with the medication, since the penalties are so high. In addition, the criminalization of the medicine creates a feeling of insecurity amongst activists themselves: no one is ever sure about whom they can trust and even talking publicly about abortion with medication, following the WHO guidelines, becomes a risky endeavor.[18] This chilling effect caused by criminalization of misoprostol—and not of abortion *per se*—contributes to misinformation, further violating human rights standards and, particularly, the right to information.

Thirty years later, the use of misoprostol for abortion, which began in Brazil as a natural public health experiment, has been validated by rigorous clinical studies and recommendations of the WHO.[19] Meanwhile, women continue to spread the word. Medication abortion first made it to the international headlines with the work developed by the organization Women on Waves. In June 2001, Women on Waves set out from a Dutch port in a rented ship to provide women with pills that induce miscarriage in countries where abortion is illegal (Bazelon, 2014). Today, at least two large international feminist organizations—Women on Web and Women Help Women—are dedicated to delivering abortion pills and information to women's and pregnant people's hands, no matter where they are, and assisting them throughout the process of self-managed abortion.

In Latin America, in contexts of restrictive and resistant-to-change abortion laws, local activist groups have had a central role in promoting medication abortion as a safer choice for women (Mc-Reynolds-Pérez, 2017), through telephone and internet hotlines, and in-person accompaniment. Argentina is a good example of successful mobilization, where young activists have turned to direct action and service provision since the late 2000s (Mc-Reynolds-Pérez, 2017, p. 362). Such strategy is one of the three strands of abortion mobilization in the country, one that understands its "practices as complying with legal norms", even when it is "indeed defying the official interpretation of the current [criminal] law" (Ruibal & Fernandez Anderson, 2018, p. 8).

One such group is *Socorristas en Red*, a network of feminist activists that provide information, medication, and support to women seeking abortion. Since its foundation in 2010, the network has quickly grown and currently includes 39 collectives from across the country (Zurbriggen et al., 2018). The model of *Socorrista* action encompasses: (1) a telephone hotline; (2) in-person group meetings; (3) telephone support throughout the process of home abortion; (4) in-person accompaniment, especially in second-trimester cases, including the provision of misoprostol or the full course of pharmaceutical abortion drugs, acquired through transnational activist contacts (Mc-Reynolds-Pérez, 2016); and (5) post-abortion medical treatment. The network has also developed extensive informational material on how to use abortion medication, which has a large distribution beyond Argentine borders.

Most *Socorristas* do not have formal medical training, but they undergo intensive feminist guidance on principles and medical guidelines to be able to fully support women and pregnant people. As such, *Socorristas* not only challenge the privileges of expert knowledge, but by appropriating and subverting it, they also question criminal regulation of abortion, which includes practicing medicine without a license. As the *Socorristas* (Zurbriggen et al., 2018, p. 109) have described their training:

> This training consists of studying materials that describe safe medication abortion practices, shadowing and being supported by other *Socorristas* who have more experience accompanying abortions, training by other regional and international organizations that

provide medication abortion, and contact with medical professionals who help train *Socorristas* to identify when and how women should seek medical care if necessary.

Particularly important for these activists is to stress that they are providing women and pregnant people something qualitatively different from any kind of care they could access elsewhere; it is a feminist model of care that will remain in place even if abortion is legalized (Ruibal & Fernandez Anderson, 2018). As such, *Socorrismo* is a direct confrontation with "a patriarchal society by guaranteeing that women are not forced to become mothers if they choose not to" (Zurbriggen et al., 2018, p. 113), while it is also a disruption of existing interpretations about abortion laws.

There is no doubt that *Socorristas en Red* are a brave group of women willing to put themselves at risk through direct action that has completely changed the landscape of abortion care in Argentina. It is important to acknowledge though that the women and pregnant people they accompany and counsel, as well as themselves, have easy access to the means of controlling a safe and effective abortion experience. The pill is the game changer (Mc-Reynolds-Pérez, 2017, pp. 358–359), which make the criminalization of abortion contained in the penal code completely outdated:

> I especially want to underscore that the direct-action misoprostol activist strategy that I describe could not have become so widespread without the availability of the drug itself. Misoprostol allows Argentine activists to facilitate abortion while maintaining a distance from the actual procedure. The pill allows women to be the agents of their own abortions, with activists advising and "accompanying" them, but at a distance through the hotline and Internet-based communication. The distance created by both the pharmaceutical and telecommunications technology allows the activists to avoid prosecution, since they really are only providing information and not abortions. It also makes it possible to provide these services over long distances, not just to a population within the same metropolitan area as the activists.

For a long time, misoprostol was sold in Argentina mixed with diclofenac under the brand name Oxaprost, a medicine officially prescribed for stomach issues (Booth, 2018). Women could have access to this drug in pharmacies with a specific medical prescription that would be kept by the retailer and controlled by the sanitary authority. In October 2018, the Argentine feminist movement won another victory. The National Administration for Medication, Food and Technology (ANMAT) authorized[20] the sale of misoprostol in pharmacies for the purpose of legal abortion. The procedure for accessing the drug is uncomplicated: The doctor prescribes misoprostol to their patient for a legal abortion, and the prescription is retained by the pharmacy. With the growth of self-managed abortion rates in the country and the social legitimacy the discourse of reproductive rights has acquired as shown by the popular adherence to the *Marea Verde*, this latest step taken by Argentine institutions amounts to decriminalization through other means.[21]

In the case of Argentina, social decriminalization was achieved through the everyday work of activists who were doing "public criminology" even though they did not frame it in those terms. Activists' ongoing commitment to ensure that women and pregnant people have access to safe and autonomous abortion without fearing criminal persecution, while at the same time, changing drastically public opinion about reproductive freedom, is an exercise of public criminology at its core.

It is true that "the use of criminal law to regulate sex, gender, and reproduction is decidedly not new; such regulation has been the hallmark of the modern state" (Miller et al., 2019, p. 2). What is novel about the Brazilian case, however, and in contrast to the Argentine one, is how criminalization of reproduction has been achieved through a complicated scheme of sanitary regulations combined with criminal law supposedly enacted to protect public health and medicine consumption. Technology has played a transformative role in defining how much a person seeking an abortion needs to interact with the state or other institutional actors. Medical abortion pills mean that the individual is sovereign in their decision and does not need to interact either with state institutions or the medical profession. And yet, this transformative role can be blocked by simply placing a criminal wall between the person (or their supporters) and the pill.

While in several other countries, including Argentina, "women's health advocates have utilized a harm-reduction model to combat mortality and morbidity from unsafe abortion by providing women with counselling and information about early medication abortion (<12 weeks' gestation) through websites, hotlines, and social media platforms" (Gerdts et al., 2018, p. 2), such actions are much riskier in Brazil. Facing charges of a criminal offense that may lead to incarceration for fifteen years might not be an activist choice for many, particularly in a country with a highly class and racially selective criminal justice system.

Such fears create barriers even to the production and dissemination of knowledge such as the one represented in this chapter. Even if we see the engagement with the criminalization of misoprostol in Brazil as a public criminology exercise, we are afraid that the public exposure of it might lead to actual enforcement of existing laws, further jeopardizing the work of activists. But the realization of the barriers created by fear should actually work to transform silence into language and action (Lorde, 1984). This is where I see a grounded public criminology taking shape: silence is not an option, nor a protection; speaking and acting is a necessity in order to move forward.

Producing Political and Embodied Harm through Medico-Criminal Regulation

Abortion criminalization worldwide is a relatively recent phenomenon, dating back to the 19th century. Criminalization of many social practices is usually justified through hegemonic frameworks that suggest a public values' defense, and critiques of such criminalization often rest on pointing out the inefficacy of criminal laws. In the case of medical/social issues, however, the critique to criminalization should go a step further. It is essential to attend to how existing inequalities interact with these criminal shifts, creating uneven effects upon particular sectors of the population.

In the case of criminal abortion laws, these disproportionate effects are evident. The fact that access to abortion or, most importantly for this chapter, to misoprostol is a crime in Brazil does not mean that women stopped seeking abortion. Women still look for ways to terminate an unwanted pregnancy, but criminalization often pulls them towards lesser safe methods. Data from the Ministry of Health show that, every year, an average of 250,000 women visit public hospitals to undergo curettage after an unsafe abortion procedure (Arilha, 2012). The fact that most of these women are young, poor, and Black exposes how access to abortion in legally restrictive settings is a social justice issue, one that sits at the intersection of law, poverty and race.

A dual system of clandestine abortion is a common feature of countries where the procedure is illegal: Upper-class women can quietly access abortion in private, often expensive clinics run by trained physicians or travel overseas to have the procedure. Poor and working-class women risk their lives when having back-alley procedures, which include unsafe clinical procedures, the use of all kinds of herbs, and even the introduction of objects in their bodies. For this reason, Black feminists in Brazil, in similar ways as in the United States and other parts of the world, have claimed that the struggle must be framed around the notion of reproductive justice, which also addresses other vectors of structural inequality and not only reproductive rights. For them, decriminalization efforts entail fighting structural racism that criminalizes Black lives as such: they want to be able to end an unwanted pregnancy as much as they want to be mothers and raise their children without fearing they will be assassinated by the police.

Misoprostol has changed the landscape of reproductive justice as a technological discovery. Brazil and Argentina are no exception. Today, with medication abortion, clandestine practices do not need to be unsafe. However, the histories of public abortion activism in Argentina and Brazil took very different paths, in part due to the regulation of access to abortion medication. In Argentina, feminist groups are actively engaged in an open and visible direct-action strategy, which paved the way for the legislative reform debated in parliament in 2018; in Brazil, direct action is hidden and underground, marked by fear and insecurity.

If it is true that "the widespread use of Cytotec in Brazil highlights contradictions of the illegal situation of abortion and has, at the same time, generated a favorable atmosphere in which to promote discussion of the need to legalize abortion" (Barbosa & Arilha, 1993, p. 239), the criminalization of the drug has also produced what I call political and social harm. As we learn early on in law school, criminal law is a regime that allows the state to use force against actions that it deems harmful enough to justify the imposition of criminal consequences (Erdman, 2019).

In the case of the criminalization of abortion pills, this is happening the other way around. It is criminal law, through the condemnation of the medication, that is creating "its own order of harm more real and certain than any it seeks to prevent" (Erdman, 2019, p. 249).

The two cases discussed in this chapter show that the kinds of intricate, indirect harm produced by criminal law can only be captured through grounded forms of public criminology, which I use to make visible the knowledge produced by everyday experiences against criminalization. While criminalization attempts to silence activists, a grounded public criminology perspective recognizes that such silence does not mean protection. As such, it is necessary to turn silence into language and action.

Notes

1 This work was supported by the Canadian Institutes of Health Research [grant number 153012], to which I am grateful. I also thank Sara Larrea, Susan Yanow, Kinga Jelinska, and Joanna Erdman for their helpful comments. My acknowledgment goes to the feminist activists for reproductive justice in Latin America who are making this world more liveable for us all.
2 While *Socorristas en Red* is only one of the various groups engaging in direct action and service provision in the context of abortion activism in Argentina (Ruibal & Fernandez Anderson, 2018), they have become widely influential throughout the region by spreading their political vision, known as *socorrismo*. As such, *socorrismo* aims not only to provide women with access to safe abortion right now, but also to de-stigmatize and demystify the practice, centering it around women, their needs and their desires (Ruibal & Fernandez Anderson, 2018). *Socorristas* see themselves continuing the political work they do even after (and if) abortion is legalized in the country, as one of their members told me in a workshop.
3 Other terminologies, such as medical abortion or abortion with pills, are also used.
4 Here, it is important to make the distinction between legalization and decriminalization. The former entails keeping abortion in criminal law while identifying the grounds on which it is allowed. The latter means removing all the existing criminal sanctions against abortion from the books (Berer, 2017). Even though the definitions seem to be clear enough, activists still struggle with them, and often use one for the other. Up until today, Canada is the only country in the world that has decriminalized abortion, through a Supreme Court decision.
5 From conversations that I have had with activists and researchers who lived through the changes, I learned that three events in the 1990s intersected to produce the extremely restrictive regulation of misoprostol now in place in Brazil. First, the publication of various clinical case reports associating the use of misoprostol during pregnancy and the development of Moebius Syndrome, a very rare congenital neurological disorder (Corrêa & Mastrella, 2012). Second, the ecofeminist condemnation of the pharmaceutical control over women's bodies, particularly during the United Nations Meeting on the Environment in Rio, known as Eco 92. Finally, the need of newly established National Sanitary Agency to assert its power by regulating restrictions on specific substances.

6   Abortion is criminalized in articles 85–88 of the Argentine Penal Code and articles 124–127 of the Brazilian Penal Code. Both penal codes, as one would expect, employ a highly gendered language: the person who undergoes an abortion is a woman and/or a mother.
7   The health exception has been widely explored by the public health and rights strategy in Argentina, where activists achieved the important outcome of having the Minister of Health issue a guide explaining how to interpret article 86 of the penal code. This guide embraced the WHO's comprehensive definition of health, including psychological health, and established the woman's decision over the risk she would be willing to take as the decisive factor to request a legal abortion (Ruibal & Fernandez Anderson, 2018).
8   This exception was introduced by a Supreme Court decision, in 2012.
9   Misoprostol causes the cervix to soften and the uterus to contract, resulting in the expulsion of the uterine contents. The physical process that the body undergoes is the same as natural birth or miscarriage. First trimester medical abortion is a highly safe and effective procedure. Up to 9 weeks gestation, the effectiveness of the misoprostol alone regime is between 75% and 90%.
10 What happens though is that women who induce an abortion with misoprostol and seek post-abortion care in health facilities are often psychologically and physically tortured to confess they had used the pill. Cases like these are common in the Brazilian healthcare system, and even though in violation of basic patient's rights, such as the right of professional secrecy, lead to the women's criminal persecution.
11 One study from the mid-1990s shows that among the women hospitalized for abortion, 76.1% had knowledge of misoprostol or of a medication for inducing abortion whose name they could remember (Diniz, 2008, p. 29).
12 One study conducted in the 1990s established a correlation between the three phases of misoprostol commercialization in Brazil and the number of women reaching the public health system for complications with induced miscarriage. These three phases were the beginning of commercialization in pharmacies, the peak of diffusion of the information on the abortifacient property of the drug and the period immediately after the prohibition of commerce. The study shows that there was an increase of nearly 50% in infectious and hemorrhagic complications between the period of the peak of the drug's commercialization and the prohibition (Diniz, 2008, p. 24).
13 One study conducted in the 1990s showed that the medium price for misoprostol was US$6.00, while an abortion in private clinic cost US$144.00 (Diniz, 2008).
14 In a seemingly contradictory move, the National Sanitary Agency has listed misoprostol in the National List of Essential Medicines since 2010.
15 Interestingly, Brazil was one of the pioneer countries in the independent production of drugs containing misoprostol for obstetric purposes (Faúndes, 2010), under the brand name ®Prostokos.
16 Article 33 of Federal Act no. 11.343/06.
17 Article 334-A of the Penal Code.
18 In August 2019, a group of activists in Southern Brazil who distributed pamphlets containing the WHO guidelines for medication abortion was notified by the local public prosecutor to explain their actions. These activists were obviously exercising their constitutional right to information but, in the prosecutor's view, they were advertising abortion.
19 WHO recommends a combination of the drugs misoprostol and mifepristone for medical abortion or, where mifepristone is not available, misoprostol alone. It is important to notice, though, that it was very recently when the Organization showed interest about informal use of misoprostol outside the clinical setting or the telemedicine paradigm.
20 Regulation no. 946, from October 12, 2018.
21 The Argentine case of abortion is a paradigmatic example of social decriminalization achieved through "transformative illegality". The term has been coined by Enright and Cloatre (2018) to describe the long-term illegal distribution of condoms in Ireland by activists, which has led to their transformation into a different legal object—"from abject to commonplace, challenging existing restrictive laws" (p. 283). Similarly, in Argentina, feminist direct-action strategy has attacked and de-stabilized existing understandings about abortion, "replacing them with more liveable alternatives" (p. 279) that connect to actual women's reproductive experiences.

References

Arilha, M. M. (2012). Misoprostol: Percursos, mediações e redes sociais para o acesso ao aborto medicamentoso em contextos de ilegalidade no Estado de São Paulo. *Ciência e Saúde Coletiva, 17*(7), 1785–1794.

Barbosa, R. M., & Arilha, M. (1993). The Brazilian experience with Cytotec. *Studies in Family Planning, 24*(4), 236–240.

Bazelon, E. (2014, August 31). The dawn of the post-clinic abortion. *The New Times Magazine.* Retrieved from www.nytimes.com/2014/08/31/magazine/the-dawn-of-the-post-clinic-abortion.html

Berer, M. (2017). Abortion law and policy around the world: In search of decriminalization. *Health and Human Rights Journal, 19*(1), 13–27.

Booth, A. (2018, June 25). The drug that's transforming abortion in Argentina. *Medium.* Retrieved from https://medium.com/s/story/the-drug-thats-transforming-abortion-in-argentina-182189d48b39

Carrabine, E., Lee, M., & South, N. (2000). Social wrongs and human rights in late modern Britain: Social exclusion, crime control, and prospects for a public criminology. *Social Justice, 27*(2 (80), 193–211.

Coeytaux, F., & Wells, E. (2013, May 28). Misoprostol is a game-changer for safe abortion and maternal health care. Why isn't it more widely available? *Rewire News.* Retrieved from https://rewire.news/article/2013/05/28/why-arent-we-taking-advantage-of-the-potentially-game-changing-drug-misoprostol

Corrêa, M. C. D. V., & Mastrella, M. (2012). Aborto e misoprostol: usos médicos, práticas de saúde e controvérsia científica. *Ciência & Saúde Coletiva, 17*(7), 1777–1784.

Diniz, D. (2008). *Aborto e saúde pública: 20 anos de pesquisas no Brasil.* Rio de Janeiro: UERJ. Brasília: UnB.

Diniz, D., & Madeiro, A. (2012). Cytotec e aborto: a polícia, os vendedores e as mulheres. *Ciência & Saúde Coletiva, 17*(1), 1795–1804.

Enright, M., & Cloatre, E. (2018). Transformative illegality: How condoms "became legal" in Ireland, 1991–1993. *Feminist Legal Studies, 26,* 261–284.

Erdman, J. N. (2019). Harm production: An argument for decriminalization. In A. M. Miller & M. J. Roseman (Eds.), *Beyond virtue and vice: Rethinking human rights and criminal law* (pp. 248–267). Philadelphia, PA: University of Pennsylvania Press.

Erdman, J. N., Jelinska, K., & Yanow, S. (2018). Understandings of self-managed abortion as health inequity, harm reduction and social change. *Reproductive Health Matters, 26*(54), 13–19.

Faúndes, A. (2010). O uso do misoprostol no Brasil. In M. Arilha, T. Lapa, & T. Pisaneschi (Eds.), *Aborto medicamentoso no Brasil* (pp. 9–22). São Paulo: Oficina Editorial.

Gerdts, C., Jayaweera, R. T., Baum, S. E., & Hudaya, I. (2018). Second-trimester medication abortion outside the clinic setting: An analysis of electronic client records from a safe abortion hotline in Indonesia. *BMJ Sexual & Reproductive Health, 44*(4), 286–291.

Guttmacher Institute. (2018). *Induced abortion worldwide.* Retrieved from www.guttmacher.org/sites/default/files/factsheet/fb_iaw.pdf

Lorde, A. (1984). The transformation of silence into language and action. In A. Lorde (Ed.), *Sister outsider: Essays and speeches* (pp. 40–44). Berkeley, CA: Crossing Press.

Madeiro, A. P., & Diniz, D. (2016). Serviços de aborto legal no Brasil – um estudo nacional. *Ciência & Saúde Coletiva, 21*(2), 563–572.

Mc-Reynolds-Pérez, J. (2016). Argentina's abortion activism in the age of misoprostol. *Global Dialogue, 6*(4). Retrieved from http://globaldialogue.isa-sociology.org/argentinas-abortion-activism-in-the-age-of-misoprostol/

Mc-Reynolds-Pérez, J. (2017). No doctors required: Lay activist expertise and pharmaceutical abortion in Argentina. *Signs, 42*(2), 349–375.

Miller, A. M., Roseman, M. E., & Rizvi, Z. (2019). Introduction. In A. M. Miller & M. J. Roseman (Eds.), *Beyond virtue and vice: Rethinking human rights and criminal law* (pp. 1–14). Philadelphia, PA: University of Pennsylvania Press.

Nelund, A. (2014). Troubling publics: A feminist analysis of public criminology. *Radical Criminology, 4,* 67–84.

Pazello, M. (2010). Internet, restrição de informações e acesso ao misoprostol. In M. Arilha, T. Lapa, & T. Pisaneschi (Eds.), *Aborto medicamentoso no Brasil* (pp. 81–119). São Paulo: Oficina Editorial.

Ramos, S., Romero, M., & Aizenberg, L. (2014). Women´s experiences with the use of medical abortion in a legally restricted context: The case of Argentina. *Reproductive Health Matters, 43*(supp44), 4–15.

Ruibal, A., & Fernandez Anderson, C. (2018). Legal obstacles and social change: Strategies of the abortion rights movement in Argentina. *Politics, Groups, and Identities.* Advanced online publication. doi:10.1080/21565503.2018.1541418

World Health Organization (WHO). (2018). *Medical management of abortion.* Geneva: Author.

Zamberlin, N., Romero, M., & Ramos, S. (2012). Latin American women's experiences with medical abortion in settings where abortion is legally restricted. *Reproductive Health, 9*(1), 34.

Zurbriggen, R., Keefe-Oates, B., & Gerdts, C. (2018). Accompaniment of second-trimester abortions: The model of the feminist Socorrista network of Argentina. *Contraception, 97*(2), 108–115.

PART III
Barriers and Challenges

11
STRANGERS WITHIN
Carving Out a Role for Engaged Scholarship in the University Space

Monique Marks

Introduction

My university life did not begin as an academic. It began as a student in the midst of two States of Emergency in apartheid South Africa. Being a student at this time meant making a choice: to focus solely on attaining a degree or to become a change agent while studying. This choice is not as binary as might seem. For many who chose the first option, it was with the belief that in gaining a degree or certification the possibilities for impacting positively would be enhanced. This is not to deny that a significant number of students—generally from privileged backgrounds—turned a blind eye to the harsh realities of apartheid or did not want to deal with the discomforts of gross inequality, state brutality, and a complete absence of social justice. For the second cohort, university life provided a platform for praxis, for not just thinking but also for enacting change. New ideas, particularly for those of us in the humanities, provided us with insights about our social context and how to transform it. This was particularly the case at the "liberal" universities such as the University of the Witwatersrand (Wits) where I gained my first three degrees. The Wits Sociology department was a hub of social activism. Lecturers were committed Marxists who not only taught about class struggle, dialectics, and praxis, but also lived their teachings through being active members of mass democratic organizations. They were leaders in the anti-apartheid movement organizations, including the trade unions. They led the marches on campus, protecting students from the generally violent police response to the voices of change.

   I do not claim that this student experience was the sole reason for my strong belief in and commitment to engaged scholarship, but there is no doubt that it contributed hugely to it. What I learned as a Wits student was that it is not possible to be a sociologist or a social worker (my initial training) without the university being a permeable space rather than purely a place of abstraction. I came to understand that while theorization and research on its own is important, the very point of making sense of the world in which we live is to ensure that these activities are geared toward impacting the everyday lived experience. This point, I believe, is the fundamental role of the university and should be integrated into our teaching and our research. It is not to say that all academics (and students) should be activists. Rather, that the endeavors that university-based communities embark on should be with a broad consciousness of the connection between academe and the world outside of it. Engaged learning and scholarship is arguably the best route for universities to provide public goods in ways that are relevant and required. It would be both naïve and misleading not to acknowledge that universities are elite institutions.

This chapter talks to one engagement project that forms part of the center that I head in Durban, namely the Urban Futures Centre (UFC) at the Durban University of Technology. I use this project as a lens for making sense of what engaged scholarship is and what its benefits are. I also reflect on the various challenges associated with being involved in such endeavors as a scholar whose experiences and stances have been shaped fundamentally by my university life.

Bringing Hope to Street Level Heroin Users in Durban

In 2014 a moral panic of sorts erupted in Durban, focused on a large group of heroin users who had congregated and were living in a public park in the center of the city. The vast majority of people who formed part of this community used a drug called "whoonga," which is essentially low-grade heroin combined with a range of different bulking agents. The whoonga users who lived in the park, for the most part, hustled to make enough money to prevent the horrendous withdrawals associated with the cessation of any form of heroin. Hustling took a number of forms ranging from car guarding, to begging, and also to petty theft. Having been kicked out of their homes and being labeled as "parasites," the whoonga users formed a strong community with roughly 400 people living in the park at any given time. Businesses and residents in the areas surrounding the park, believing that this community of people presented a public health and public safety risk, began to engage in what can be thought of as rough justice. And, while a number of departments in local government tried (ineffectively) to reintegrate the whoonga users into society, the police disrupted this community by using scorched earth tactics. The results of the police intervention were the disruption of a functional community, the spread of a public health problem and the opening up of drug markets in parts of the city that had not previously been exposed. An enforcement approach, though widely supported by Durban residents and business owners, did nothing to reduce heroin use or to shut down drug dealing. Policing became even more complex as the whoonga community started to live in much smaller groupings throughout the city.

In April 2014, four months after the UFC was launched, I received a phone call from a civilian member of an inner-city community policing forum. He asked if I could attend a meeting to discuss ways to get the broader public to view the whoonga users as humans rather than as delinquent parasites. He felt that the UFC could play a key role in this endeavor. I went to the meeting comprised of five people: two from civic groupings, two from faith-based organizations, and an off-duty cop. All five, including the cop, were concerned about the degrading manner in which the whoonga users were being treated by Durban citizens and by the police. They wanted to create a public dialogue where police, whoonga users, local residents, and business owners could come together to talk about anxieties and their perceptions of the problem. It was agreed that this public dialogue would be held on the university campus, organized by the UFC. On the evening of the event, the venue was packed with more than 100 people coming onto the university campus to engage in civic and civil dialogue.

At this forum, a whoonga user had the opportunity to talk about her pathway into drug use, and a police officer spoke about what the police mandate is and how this impacts their approach to street level drug users. Business and residential representatives also had opportunity to express their fear of drug users, issues of petty theft, and concerns about minor public disorder that they believed the whoonga users were responsible for. This forum was not meant to create a solution, but rather to allow groupings that otherwise would not meet up to dialogue and deliberate. Through this small initiative, the university opened its doors for knowledge exchange and for peace making. The large turn-out was partly due to the belief that the university is a safe and neutral space to hold such conversations. Hosting this event, while a form of engagement, did not feel sufficient. More needed to be done to make sense of the pathways into street-level heroin use and into ways of ameliorating the public health and safety problems associated with drug use disorders from the perspective of users, their family, and the broader community.

As someone whose research work has focused on the police for many years, I decided to explore, in an ethnographic manner, the policing of street-level drug users. What became evident to me was that police had very little regard for this vulnerable group of people. Rough policing was the order of the day. From the back of the police van, I observed the disregard for basic rights and the complete lack of care for the limited life chances available to people who use drugs that are from resource poor backgrounds.

But more than this observation, I heard time and again how heroin users talked of the need for access to an opioid substitute medication. The one referred to most on the street was methadone, which was only available on the black market. Most users we encountered on the streets felt unsafe using this medication as it was provided without any supervision from the medical practitioners (both pharmacists and doctors) that were selling methadone in the city and without any training or adherence to pharmaceutical protocols.

It was then that I decided that any future attempts to address the needs of street-level drug users required proper access to a medication that is not yet on the South African essential medicine list. I began to read up about harm reduction and networking with the very small group of harm reduction activists in South Africa to craft out a solution to this existing deficit. The result, following consultation with national and international drug policy experts, was the establishment of the first low threshold opioid substitution therapy (OST) demonstration project in the country. The objective of this project was not simply to provide this medication to those with a heroin use disorder, but also to demonstrate to government that OST has a tangible and positive impact on quality of life of local heroin users. A second objective was to demonstrate to health practitioners in the public and private sector as to how to do OST in line with international best practice that is evidence based. The first beneficiary of this project was initiated in April 2017; within a few months, 50 low-income heroin users were initiated onto the project.

The results have been remarkable. Heroin users who had felt helpless and disconnected began to feel, for the first time, that there was hope of normalizing their lives. They started to reconnect with family members; take care of their health and personal hygiene; returned to secondary and tertiary educational institutions; and found mechanisms for being part of community project such as feeding schemes. Getting to this point took significant time and emotional energy. Developing a set of protocols to guide practice and providing psycho-social interventions was incredibly complex. But the impact has been significant not only for the daily lives of the beneficiaries themselves but also for the future of drug policy and treatment. The Department of Health at provincial and national levels is now turning to the Durban OST Demonstration Project in devising new policies and in spurring a move to have opioid substitutes on the Essential Medicine List. This has been widely reported in the written press, on radio, and even on South Africa's most lauded investigative television programs (*Carte Blanche*). The public attention has been advantageous to the project beneficiaries who were given a platform to share their life pathways, to the university who was portrayed as doing engaged research, and for the advocacy campaign given the reporting of the positive life changes as a result of OST.

The Benefits of a Supportive University

This engagement project would not have been possible had the Durban University of Technology (DUT) not provided me with support from the get-go. Ethical clearance for the project was provided in a very short space of time. Members of the ethics committee recognized the need for the project. Their usual caution was lessened by the fact that this project was guided by a very considered medical and psycho-social infrastructure put in place to frame it. Given the publicity around whoonga use, it appeared evident that the university could be at the forefront of bringing new knowledge and practice into the public realm in regard to a vexing social problem.

University leaders at the DUT have not questioned the resources (personnel, financial commitments, and time) required to get this project up and running and sustained. They have engaged with this project as a critical intervention with the possibility of generating locally based evidence and bringing the outside community into the thinking space of the university. While not the mainstream at this university, public intellectuals are viewed as a source of creativity, making the business of theorizing accessible and relevant. As a technical university, innovation is valued highly and to innovate means taking risks and forging unexpected partnerships. Linking with a non-governmental organization (NGO), civic groupings, and state departments (including the police) made this project networked, in line with the initial vision of the UFC which was established as Vice Chancellor project.

In a country whose legislation regarding drug use and drug markets is principally prohibition and abstinence based, supporting a harm reduction innovation was risky. Yet resources were provided (financial and in-kind) to generate public support for the project. Events linked to the demonstration project such as a Support Don't Punish campaign was made possible because of the active involvement of the Corporate Affairs office of the university. Support Don't Punish is a global campaign geared toward more humane drug policy, including the decriminalization of drugs. On June 26, over 200 cities across the world celebrate Support Don't Punish. Two-thousand and sixteen was the first time this campaign was celebrated in Durban, and without the financial assistance of the Corporate Affairs Office at DUT, it would have been a difficult event to organize. But, perhaps more significantly than the financial contribution that came in the form of catering and printing T-shirts with the "Support Don't Punish" slogan, the university also took a risk in the policing of this event so as to indicate its permeability to the "outside" community.

Prior to the event, which was held on our city campus, I met with campus security and the public police. Together, we devised a strategy where the police had little visibility and did not search people who use drugs that were attending the event. Even more radically, it was agreed that campus security would turn a blind eye to (illicit) drug use on that day unless there was an outburst of violence or conflict that emerged as a result of drug use on campus premises. We agreed to it in the spirit of "Support Don't Punish," but there was also a research agenda. This research agenda was to establish whether people who use drugs, let to their own devices, would self-regulate and self-police if given the opportunity to do so. As it turns out, not a single incident of interpersonal conflict or violence occurred during that event much to the surprise of the various security agencies. I know of no other university that would allow for this type of experimentation. Very few South African universities would be prepared to support a fairly radical harm reduction event, as it could place them at odds with various government departments and industries.

Is This a Romantic Tale by an Engaged Scholar?

There is more to tell about this story. Much depends on how one measures success and how one defines engaged scholarship. The OST Demonstration Project itself can be measured in various ways. If abstinence is a way of measuring success, then the outcome is not absolute. Many of the beneficiaries have experienced "relapses" (their own words) and have used heroin while being on methadone. The vast majority use marijuana to stabilize their moods and to assist with sleeping in the absence of heroin. In the harm reduction view, this outcome is not a failure but rather part of a broader learning experience. More importantly, our goal is not abstinence, but rather normalization. It is for this reason that quality-of-life indicators are more important than closely observing drug use. For those who have significantly reduced their drug use, thus reducing the harm that their drug use has brought to them, it is a success. The same can be said for those who once felt that they were leading abnormal lives, being on the streets disconnected from past friend and from family. Reconnecting, taking care of their bodies, doing physical exercise, and returning to studies are all indicators of normalization leading to de-stigmatization and reintegration. Each individual has set their own goals. It is by that self-determined objective that success needs to be measured. The final outcomes in this regard are to be evaluated at the end of the demonstration project, which is 18 months after initiating onto OST.

Bringing hope to one of the most marginalized and vulnerable groups of people in itself is significant for engaged scholars. Doing research to promote the rights of people who use drugs and medication to deal with what could be conceived of as a chronic relapsing brain disease is also important—so too is the radical reduction in the negative contact that this cohort have with the criminal justice system. While a minority of participants have been arrested and held in custody for possession of illicit drugs while being part of the demonstration project, the vast majority have not experienced the revolving door of life on the streets and life in prison or holding cells. As is the case globally, being on OST does reduce criminalization, which is a large part of the story that beneficiaries tell when asked about their experience of being part of the OST demonstration project. For the university, the success lies in using scientific knowledge to improve the lives of the most marginalized.

More importantly, perhaps, we should unpack why DUT supported this evidence-based project. In the first instance, the fact that the project was led by a full professor with a strong research track record was definitely key to the support provided. Had a similar project been proposed by a lecturer or by an early career scholar, it is highly unlikely that the same resources would have been mobilized. What this point says is that scholars have to prove themselves in traditional ways prior to being able to have the latitude to have "time out" to do this kind of work and to use the name of the university in forging partnerships and networks. Engagement is not viewed, in and of itself, as a means for gaining status or privilege within university contexts. The ethos of the university as a permeable institution with a mission to improve daily lived experiences came from the top. The Vice Chancellor at the time was a visionary with a similar (although far richer) activist record. His ethos permeated downstream into faculties, departments, and support staff, and this is precisely what this project enacted. This dynamic is often not the case, which can be disastrous for those scholars who aim to be engaged and recognized as valued members of the university community.

Prior to joining DUT, for example, I was employed at the University of KwaZulu-Natal. At this traditional academic university, I felt far more limited in my ability to be an engaged scholar. My research activities, which have primarily been participatory and often ethnographic, were never curtailed or questioned. This allowed for my ongoing engagement with practitioners, such as the police, and more "subversive" groups such as those involved in self-policing (what some would call vigilante) activities. Yet, strangely at this university, there was little scope for bringing outsiders into the university realm without having to follow a series of bureaucratic processes. Public dialogues such as the one held in 2014 at DUT were extremely difficult to convene if they were not viewed as part of a more formalized (and usually timetabled) occasion generally organized by senior academics or their support staff. More concerning was this university's preoccupation with research outputs and teaching, despite its stated commitment to what is called "community engagement." UKZN provided no university resources—financial or in-kind—for such activities. The link between strong, embedded research and engagement seemed to elude those in management positions from the very top to middle management. Even more concerning was the actual derailing of engaged work by academic members of staff and students.

Indeed, the barriers to being an engaged scholar were a catalyst for my resigning from this university. The sparking moment came when students who had been part of a photo-voice project with "at risk" high school kids, were informed that they could not participate in a presentation to the university management about the project because they had to attend a formal research methods class. The students' exclusion from this platform upset them greatly, as they believed they had learned more from doing engaged research than from classroom learning. They wanted to be able to showcase the results of their commitment to giving voice to young people who had largely been written-off by their school and sometimes even their families. This project was conducted jointly by a team from Virginia Commonwealth University (VCU) and the University of KwaZulu-Natal, yet only the VCU students had the opportunity to showcase their work. This event took place on a Friday morning. On the Friday afternoon, UKZN students came to talk to me about their frustration and disappointment at the bureaucratic inertia and lack of responsiveness of academic staff in the School. The following Monday I resigned from the university after having joined 17 years previously.

My recounting of these events is not the full story of UKZN either. Community engagement was not well supported, but at no point was I curtailed in participatory (primarily ethnographic) research. My extensive time spent outside of the university, often in spaces considered dodgy or dangerous, was never questioned so long as I fulfilled my teaching and administration commitments. Academic freedom, which is highly valued at UKZN, meant that there were few barriers to how research was done. Having said this, the University relied on performance management instruments to measure output with regard to teaching, research, and (in theory) community engagement. Research was by far the most important output, and the number of peer reviewed articles published was more closely monitored for promotion purposes than for the other performance outputs. Knowledge gain at this university was bounded by the very strong stipulations on publishing in the "right" journals. What some then viewed as a balancing act on my part—that is, publishing and engaging—has always been inextricably bound and seamless. The depth of my understanding of my research subjects and their social contexts comes from ongoing engagement, which allowed for unbounded knowledge exchange.

Engagement as part of my scholarly endeavors has never just focused on disadvantaged communities. I have always viewed the police—actors with authority and power—as experts in both security and the rhythm of urban life. Without their insight, my ability to write and sense make would have been greatly compromised. In return, the police made use of my resources in furthering their studies and even in planning operations. Uniformed officers often come into my office, no doubt causing great concern from those who had no knowledge of my research work. Even though they were "strangers within," nobody questioned my invitation to the police to make use of my personal academic resources or those of the Department in which I was based. University managers or administrators never curtailed my field trips with graduate students into the world of the police despite the somewhat precarious circumstances of these trips, such as joining the public order police on their daily operations. In these respects—that is, of academic freedom and of a flow of people and knowledge between field and the university—"boundless knowledge" has been a feature of my life at these two universities; however, the infrastructural support needed for knowledge building in more risky domains has been far more available in the technical university space. Having said this, the need to respond immediately to crisis situations, or to cover unexpected costs that emerge while in praxis, is severely limited by university structures and processes, which are designed for more linear and predictable research programs.

What was and is not available at either of these universities—and as far as I am aware this is the case for most other universities globally—is emotional support from peers and supervisors. Engaged scholarship, particularly with vulnerable groups or groupings engaged in acts of violence (which could include the police), is often highly emotive. My daily interactions with the beneficiaries of the OST Demonstration Project have been taxing. Most have experienced trauma and disconnect, which is often vocalized or expressed in other forms in conversations or group sessions. Engaging with support persons of the beneficiaries creates inner turmoil. These support persons live with the dilemmas of wanting to be supportive of their kin while at the same time being anxious of being targets of theft and angry outbursts by the people they are supporting through this process.

Engaging in this field means working with conflicting feelings that are raw and manifest. Participating with the police in their working lives can also be grueling. Aside from placing ourselves in precarious situations in doing fieldwork with the police, particularly as ethnographers, the actions of the police can be ruthless, leaving the researcher with complex emotions to process about whistleblowing, loyalties, and knowing what is best practice given the reality of slippery research ethics. At the very least, what is required for some engaged scholars is a forum to debrief about the knowledge generated and how it was done. At best, what should exist are peer support groups to discuss moral dilemmas and secondary trauma, and supervisors need to recognize their role in the process of debriefing students and early career scholars. The richness of engaged research comes at an emotional cost, which is almost never accounted for or recovered.

Untangling the Notion of "Engaged Scholarship"

The idea of engaged scholarship is fluid, as it has to be understood contextually (in time and space). Engaged scholarship for some—like for those at the University of Witwatersrand in the 1980s—means being politically aligned in doing research and being part of civic organizations that activate a particular change agenda. For others, engaged scholarship talks primarily to ensuring that knowledge generation is boundless and geared toward the improvement of the human condition in ways that are understood to be universally good (and therefore not politicized).

However, what ties together all scholars that consider themselves to be engaged is the belief that relevance is critical. Abstracted, bounded knowledge created in the bubble of academe is viewed as antithetical to all engaged scholars, regardless of the detail of their political or social agendas. Engaging means having clarity about what knowledge is required to improve the human and planetary condition, and ensuring that knowledge flows between academic researchers, practitioners, and planetary actors. Understood in this way in relation to the field of criminology takes us not only into far more ethnographic and participatory ways of doing research, but it also pushes us beyond the usual criminological research focus on crime and social control. It is not strange, therefore, that criminologists are now engaging with the idea of the Anthropocene and are finding ways of getting humans to be more mindful in their actions toward all living beings and even to things. The boundaries of doing engaged research grow, rather than constrict, when we prioritize relevance and interconnected flows.

Yet the engaged scholar does remain a stranger within. Universities are, for the most part, not equipped for the permeability required for ongoing engagement with what is outside of the university perimeters. Their elitism is their mark of "excellence" and so scholars who opt for research in dodgy and unpredictable environments are placed under more pressure than most to demonstrate the rigor and quality of their research outputs. An added challenge is that many peer-reviewed journals (criminology included) tend to prioritize more abstracted and measurable research outcomes, rather than research that is embedded and often normative. Things are slowly beginning to change though. The onus is on engaged scholars to continue to demonstrate that true public intellectualism comes from being engaged at all stages of the knowledge-building process.

It is my view that being an engaged scholar is inextricably linked to public intellectualism. Public intellectuals focus on issues (in this case social issues) that resonate with the dilemmas of everyday life. It is the role of public intellectuals to bring ideas to the fore that help in making sense of these issues and in finding ways to solve vexing problems in ways that are comprehensible to those most affected by them. In so doing, public intellectuals are able to create knowledge in partnership with those who are most affected by "burning" social issues and find ways to resolve them. This they do by mobilizing the skills, knowledge, and resources of a network of partners to play a key role in facilitating change processes. Through being engaged, public intellectuals are able to tap into community knowledge and sensibilities about what key social issues are and generate concern and an impulse for praxis.

Senior scholars have greater leverage within the university system and are therefore able to carve out time and resources to do engaged scholarship with an implicit understanding that this will generate scholarly publications. University leaders and managers are also aware that engaged scholarship by senior academics augments the reputation of the institution as responsive and innovative. This ability to leverage based on an established record is critical. Junior or emerging scholars, however, should not feel disillusioned. They are often the members of the university that have closer links to community groupings and networks and are well placed to ignite engaged research programs. Strategic young scholars will bring on board established public intellectuals early on in the engagement process, particularly in the co-production of knowledge, and in its dissemination in ways that demonstrate a commitment to public intellectualism and to praxis. Engaged scholarship brought about through the lens of public intellectualism positions both emerging and established scholars to do what it seems to me is our occupational mandate. Knowledge production is at its richest when embedded in the field that is to be sense-made, and when it is geared toward an enhanced planetary existence that is brought about as understandings underpin collaborative change processes. In demonstrating that engagement and intellectualism are fundamentally linked, the current stranger in the university is well placed to become a guiding confrère.

12
THE PUSH AND PULL OF GOING "PUBLIC"
Barriers and Risks to Mobilizing Criminological Knowledge

Krystle Shore

Introduction: Public Criminology and Activism in the Knowledge Mobilization Era

Activist scholarship is not a new phenomenon. For decades social scientists have taken on community activist roles, using their knowledge as a tool to effect positive social change. Yet it was Michael Burawoy's (2005) call for "public sociology" that articulated scholars' moral obligation to help the publics around them and to protect civil society as a whole, the latter of which Burawoy described as being "colonized and co-opted by markets and states" (2005, p. 288). Following this sentiment, "public criminology" is now a widely recognized term to denote the efforts of criminologists to bring discussions of crime, justice, and security outside of the walls of the academy (Loader & Sparks, 2010). Like public sociology, public criminology can take many different forms and involve many different publics. Some scholars engage in public criminology by sharing their research findings with policy makers in order to improve crime and security policy. Others may choose to form partnerships with corporate or community organizations. Some scholars prefer more organic and activist-based forms of public engagement and work with individuals or communities at a grassroots level in order to pursue social justice. And still others may opt for multiple or other forms of public criminology activities. In other words, while scholars engaging in public criminology all recognize the value of working with public groups, the ways they choose to do so by no means constitute a homogeneous set of activities.

Though public criminologists could be differentiated by which public realms they choose to enter, a more astute distinction can be made according to whether or not their audience has a vested interest in maintaining existing power disparities. The field of criminology—and positivistic strands of criminology in particular—has long been criticized as prone to co-option and misuse by hegemonic entities (Taylor, Walton, & Young, 1973). As knowledge producers in a domain so intimately tied to political interests, criminologists are often subject to having their work usurped to push hegemonic agendas. In relation to public criminology, political or economic elites (e.g., politicians and CEOs) not only have the power to define the questions being asked of the "expert" criminologist—thus having significant input into shaping the type of research being conducted in the first place—but also retain the ability to "pick and choose from [the findings] those parts which they can interpret in some way which 'helps' them, as they see it, to construct their intended course of practical action" (Douglas, 1970, p. 267, as cited in Taylor et al., 1973). Research findings can become distorted through this process, either by losing context or by being bent to suit political goals. Public criminology is thus vulnerable to becoming a product that is consumed and (re)packaged to uphold or even extend hegemonic interests.

How, then, does an activist public criminologist dedicated to disrupting hegemony work against the co-optation of their research? It could, for example, entail working less as an expert and more as an ally with publics, community groups, or grassroots organizations that share the desire to dismantle societal power imbalances. Doing so more closely answers Burawoy's (2005) call to defend civil society from imperialist pressures and inequality, though such work is not easy, particularly when considered alongside the broader institutional pressures that academics face. Concurrent with the increasing interest in public criminology (of all forms) is the growing emphasis that universities are placing on knowledge or research partnerships between their faculty and communities. More specifically, the past decade has borne increasing pressure for faculty to demonstrate "knowledge mobilization" (KMb)[1] or "research impact"—that is, to make transparent how they plan to disseminate research findings to wide audiences, including the public.

The institutional shift toward KMb is largely attributable to the neoliberalization of the university (Cain, Shore, Weston, & Sanders, 2018). It is widely accepted that the academy has undergone a major transformation since the embrace of market values beginning in the 1980s, particularly in the Global North (Delanty, 2001; Horn, 2000; Hyslop-Margison & Leonard, 2012; Walker, 2008). Now operating in a corporatized climate, post-secondary institutions are continually required to demonstrate their public relevance in order to maintain both funding and their position as institutions of knowledge. To do this, many universities in North America are incorporating KMb rhetoric into their mission statements and pushing faculty to commercialize their outputs or to demonstrate how they will share knowledge with the broader community, whether through policy work, corporate or community partnerships, or some other form of public engagement (Cain et al., 2018). Federal granting bodies are also requiring researchers to explicitly state how they will engage in these KMb activities.

For many criminologists, KMb activities may take the form of public criminological pursuits, though there is an important distinction to be made between critically-oriented activist forms of public criminology and KMb initiatives. While the former can serve to counter the erosion of civil society by hegemonic and neoliberal forces, engaging in KMb reflects the institutional acquiescence of these same forces. Thus, KMb initiatives (and, as discussed above, some forms of public criminology) can bolster the status quo by producing knowledge that aligns with hegemonic interests. In contrast, while activist-based public criminology activities may "count" as KMb in terms of university metrics, their impetus is not university-driven but rather often stem from a moral commitment to social change.

The pressure to engage in KMb has been felt by academics across the globe and has important implications for the ways in which knowledge is being produced. As KMb initiatives exist to protect the interests of the academy, they can operate as an oppressive force against activist public criminologists who are often critical of the very structures that KMb serves. As will be discussed throughout this chapter, the push for KMb can privilege scholarship that aligns with existing power dynamics in the academy while suppressing more critical forms of scholarship, and thus KMb processes can put activist public criminologists at a distinct disadvantage compared to their colleagues. The negative implications of this disparity are compounded for faculty members who are women, racialized minorities, or at early stages in their career, since these groups already experience systematic discrimination within the academy (Matthew, 2016; Wijesingha & Ramos, 2017). Having outlined the tensions of public criminology in the knowledge mobilization era, the remainder of this chapter examines how the institutional push for KMb can be understood as an extension of broader neoliberal and hegemonic trends and is evidence of the "repressive state apparatus" (Hyslop-Margison & Leonard, 2012) operating within the university. Specific attention will be paid to the individual and institutional risks associated with making counter-hegemonic knowledge public. The argument will be made that KMb initiatives—operating within a socio-political climate characterized by anti-intellectualism, hostility, and the repressive state apparatus—ultimately privilege scholarship that bolsters the status quo while contributing to the suppression of critical scholars and their work.

Institutional Governance and Rhetorical Exercises

Regardless of the form of public engagement, scholars face many obstacles when entering the public sphere (Feilzer, 2009; Mopas & Moore, 2012; Uggen & Inderbitzin, 2010; Young, 2012). First, doing so requires access to a particular public group (e.g., policy makers, corporations, community groups), which some academics can find difficult to gain. It also requires translating academic work into outputs that are meaningful and digestible to the public. It is here that the researcher runs the risk of having their findings misunderstood, or—worse—misused, as can be the case when policymakers "cherry pick" research findings that most suit their particular political agenda. Finally, the overall act of engaging the public requires time, which scholars often lack due to institutional demands to produce traditional research outputs, such as publishing their work in peer-reviewed journals, attending academic conferences, and securing grant funding. Further, many scholars face additional time constraints from other required academic work, such as teaching, supervision, and service duties.

In addition to access, translation, and time restraints, many universities lack meaningful internal reward mechanisms for scholars engaging the public. The lack of incentive to do so has pushed KMb-related work into the category of unrecognized labor, which can have particularly negative implications for marginalized faculty (Moten & Harney, 2013). While all faculty face time restraints that can bar them from pursuing KMb, marginalized faculty face compounded time restraints because of other forms of unrecognized service labor often required of them (discussed further later in the chapter).

The obstacles outlined above can dissuade or prevent even the most well-intentioned scholar from engaging public groups (Cain et al., 2018), and while many universities have the capacity to mitigate these obstacles, support for faculty engaging in KMb is considerably low (Cooper, Rodway, & Read, 2018). Additionally, although faculty members may feel high institutional pressure to engage in KMb, they also identify a notable lack of follow through. For example, in our work[2] in Canada (Cain et al., 2018), faculty members explained that, while they were often required to identify potential KMb activities on grant applications, there was no incentive to carry out such activities and no accountability measures after submission. Academic perceptions of the institutional pressure to do KMb activities and subsequent lack of institutional support has led many scholars to frame KMb as a form of institutional governance and to perceive their engagement with KMb as little more than a rhetorical exercise (Cain et al., 2018).

Since the institutional push for KMb appears to be more rhetorical than tangible, it can be understood as a function of the academy's adoption of neoliberal market values. Requiring scholars to adopt KMb language in their research practices allows the institution to demonstrate continued public relevancy, regardless of whether public engagement actually occurs. As one participant in our study explained, "I think that people who can write really well about it get the money. But then it doesn't actually mean that it happens. I think that knowledge transfer and knowledge mobilization become little tick boxes to tick off" (Cain et al., 2018, p. 47). In the end, most participants in the study viewed KMb as a "buzzword" that aligned well with the current demand for universities to demonstrate relevance but had little meaning to faculty beyond obtaining grants (Cain et al., 2018).

Importantly, participants in our study did not refer to public engagement in general as problematic, but rather highlighted the fact that institutional pressure for KMb is part of a broader shift toward the institutional governance of faculty. The push for KMb in academia therefore emerges as a form of "regulatory ritualism," whereby ever-increasing institutional regulations are adopted ceremoniously and have little bearing on day-to-day activities (Braithwaite, Makkai, & Braithwaite, 2007; Heimer & Gazley, 2012). By incorporating KMb rhetoric into grant applications, scholars appear to comply with university practices without having to expend the (often unavailable) time and effort required of most KMb activities. Through regulatory ritualism, any institutional value of KMb becomes merely symbolic; scholars' use of KMb language alone is enough to count as public engagement. In the process, more meaningful forms of public engagement, like activist forms of public criminology, become unrecognized and therefore devalued while still appearing to be incentivized by the university.

Increasing Institutional Support for Knowledge Mobilization

I would be remiss not to acknowledge that, while institutional support efforts for faculty engaging in KMb is often low, there are a considerable number of post-secondary institutions attempting to address this problem. Many universities in North America now have specific KMb services available to faculty. Some Canadian universities have gone as far as to create dedicated KMb centers, like York University's Knowledge Mobilization Unit and Carlton University's Knowledge Mobilization Hub. Yet despite these efforts, research suggests that KMb support does not match institutional demand, and that the KMb facilities and services that do exist remain largely unused by researchers (Cooper et al., 2018). Moreover, the fact that there are rarely institutional rewards for KMb practices signals that attempts at institutional support remain only partial (Cain et al., 2018).

In their review of current KMb support, Cooper et al. (2018) recommend embedding institutional support initiatives by formalizing the value of KMb activities within promotion structures (e.g., tenure) and hiring faculty positions who are dedicated to KMb practices and will assist other researchers in their departments with their own KMb efforts. They also suggest that universities hire "intermediaries" who can serve as a liaison between the researcher and their targeted audience and note that doing so will alleviate some of the barriers that academics face when disseminating their research to the public (e.g., issues with access). Lastly, Cooper et al. (2018) suggest that funding agencies, like the Social Science and Humanities Research Council (SSHRC), the Natural Science and Engineering Research Council (NSERC), and the Canadian Institution of Health Research (CIHR) in Canada, or the National Science Foundation (NSF) in the United States, be responsible for training researchers to effectively engage in KMb practices.

While recommendations such as those noted above certainly have merit, they are not without issue, nor do they escape the neoliberal trends inherent in KMb initiatives. Since the push for KMb is more about retaining institutional legitimacy within a market-driven climate than it is about public enlightenment, increasing institutional support for KMb may deepen the entrenchment of hegemonic interests in the academy while ignoring important facets of individualized risk faced by faculty engaging the public (discussed in depth later in the chapter). For instance, intermediaries hired by universities to serve as a bridge between faculty and communities during KMb practices would likely succumb to the institutional pressure to keep research partnerships with the community non-controversial, suppressing more critical research in the process. Embedding KMb capacity could also formalize faculty discrimination. For example, including KMb initiatives as part of the tenure process could discriminate against researchers who face extended obstacles when engaging publics, such as those whose research topics are controversial and those who are racialized, female, queer[3], and/or junior faculty members. Finally, handing over training capacity to federal funding agencies would only strengthen state interests currently imbued in KMb initiatives. Overall, recommendations such as those from Cooper et al. (2018) have the capacity to strengthen the hegemonic forces behind KMb initiatives and to reify existing power disparities among faculty. As a prominent feature of the neoliberal transformation of the academy is the offloading of unrecognized labor onto marginalized groups, reinforcing initiatives that uphold this transformation would privilege faculty whose work is non-controversial. In the process, more critical forms of public intellectualism are devalued and silenced, and marginalized faculty conducting this work are pushed deep into what Moten and Harney (2013) call the "undercommons"[4] of the university: a space "not the opposite of a prison, since they are both involved in their way with the reduction and command of the social individual" (p. 42).

Critical Public Criminology as Risky Business

Any scholar interested in going public with their research faces certain obstacles, such as the aforementioned concerns of access, translation, and time, and these obstacles are augmented by minority status within the university. Engaging in public criminology, however, poses an additional set of challenges, as topics of criminological research have a unique ability to become contentious issues within the public sphere (Loader & Sparks, 2010). In North America, the current politicization and polarization of many crime and social justice issues, such as the proliferation of inaccuracies about increasing crime rates used by politicians in order to gain public support for tough-on-crime initiatives, constitute what Loader and Sparks (2010) call a "hot climate" for public criminology. Since critical scholars have the ability to dispel public misconceptions and to expose the hegemonic forces propping them up, scholars entering into pubic discussions of politically contentious issues are likely to face considerable pushback from those with vested interests in maintaining the status quo, like the politician who benefits from public misconceptions about crime.

In addition to political pushback, critical scholars may also face rebuke from their own institution. Seeking to discredit or dismantle hegemonic structures—as is often the goal of critical scholarship—can mean discrediting or dismantling the very structures that fund the university. To avoid losing credibility with powerful funding agencies, institutional risk is often offloaded from the university onto the individual researcher. Government, corporate, or public backlash toward particularly controversial research may translate into pressure on the university to respond to the researcher with negative repercussions, such as the denial of tenure or even the loss of a job. To illustrate, consider Jasbir Puar, a Professor of Women's and Gender Studies at Rutgers University: After speaking critically and publicly in 2016 about the power dynamics driving Israel's use of live ammunition on Palestinian civilians,[5] Puar received an onslaught of public (and academic) criticism. Many called for her dismissal from the university, while others went as far as to threaten her with violence. While Puar's position as a faculty member at Rutgers was ultimately protected through her institution's stance on academic freedom of speech,[6] her Faculty Union made clear that they could not protect her from the individualized and violent threats she received.

While there are examples of universities publicly defending their critical scholars, such as Rutgers' defense of Jasbir Puar, our study on faculty perceptions of KMb found that—as was true for Puar—those engaging in public criminology perceive considerable personal risk associated with such scholarship, particularly if the topic is critical in nature (Cain et al., 2018). Participants, including both faculty and research administrators, noted that criminological topics that are "too critical or revolutionary" (Cain et al., 2018, p. 18) had the potential to bring harm to the academic establishment by jeopardizing public legitimacy and funding. As such, participants felt such research was discouraged. In contrast, topics that brought positive press to the university through KMb channels were encouraged. As one research facilitator in the study astutely surmised,

> One of our metrics is bringing in money and bringing in good PR [public relations] for the university and creating positive community connections, and our media and public affairs people would prefer that we stick with stories about research around Rubik's Cubes, and things like anthropomorphizing recycling bins … of course if you are bringing out information that is embarrassing to a corporate partner at the university… and of course, is posing problems to the government, or involves attacking a government program, then the university—that same university—becomes skittish of the publicity because they don't want to bite the hand that feeds them.
>
> *(Interview quote, in Cain et al., 2018, p. 19)*

Negative consequences for faculty engaging in activist public criminology are not an absolute guarantee, but the perception that they exist has important implications. Even if these risks are not directly experienced, they can influence the type of criminological research being produced. As best said by Turner (2013), "what emerges as 'knowledge' at any given time, in any given place, is contingent upon the context within which such knowledge is produced" (p. 162, as quoted in Cain et al., 2018). The lack of support and perceived personal risk associated with anti-establishment knowledge can deter scholars from engaging in such research, or at the very least, deter scholars from engaging in such work publicly. In some instances, universities may refrain from hiring critical faculty altogether because of the potential harm they could bring the institution. The institutional pressure for KMb can thus quell critical scholarship, while knowledge that does not challenge hegemonic structures becomes privileged both inside and outside of the academy through overt and discursive means. Scholars who do opt to engage in activist public criminology do so at great personal risk, as was evident by the threats Jasbir Puar received after speaking out against the Israeli Defense Force. Undoubtedly, this risk is compounded for the marginalized academic, as discussed in the next section of this chapter.

A Note about Intersectionality

Up to this point, this chapter has demonstrated that criminologists, particularly those whose work is critical in nature, can face distinct barriers to engaging the public beyond those faced by anyone undertaking KMb initiatives. It is imperative, though, to mention that individual scholars can face additional barriers and risks depending on their personal characteristics. Labeled as "intersectionality" by Crenshaw (1991), marginalized axes of one's identity (e.g., race, class, gender, disability, sexual orientation, etc.) have important implications for social experiences, and have particular influence on existing power dynamics. Barriers such as race, gender, and position within the academy (among other "axes," of course) can dictate or exacerbate the negative consequences experienced by particular groups of public scholars.

Research has consistently identified that racialized faculty face systemic discrimination within the academy (Weinberg, 2008; Wijesingha & Ramos, 2017). For example, Canadian research shows that, although many racialized faculty members tend to produce higher levels of traditional research outputs (i.e., writing peer-reviewed articles and securing grants) than their non-racialized counterparts, they also tend to receive tenure and promotions at a comparatively lower rates (Wijesingha & Ramos, 2017). Additionally, racialized faculty report that their research topics and chosen career paths are often devalued by colleagues, especially if the topics and choices differ from mainstream academia (Baez, 1998). On the other hand, researchers who pursue Eurocentric topics receive more rewards (i.e., are published in higher impact journals, receive more and larger grants, and receive tenure at a higher rate) than those whose topics are not Eurocentric in nature (Henry & Tator, 2012). Since controversial public criminology endeavors also have the potential to negatively impact a researcher's career, members of racialized groups who engage in such endeavors likely experience a particularly heightened sense of risk. The adverse implications for racialized activism map onto a much larger trope of racial discrimination in academia, such as the propensity for labor by racialized faculty to go unrecognized, or even punished, by the institution. As suggested by Matthew (2016), this discrimination can be difficult for other faculty to see at the surface level, especially as many universities profess to embrace diversity. Even so, it is clearly persistent and deeply problematic for the faculty who experience it.

Female faculty members also face systemic discrimination and do significant unrecognized labor in their workplace. They are more likely to be given onerous teaching and service burdens and are more likely to have to balance work with familial responsibilities when compared to non-female faculty members (Perna, 2005). It is thus not surprising that female faculty tend to have lower traditional research outputs and receive tenure and promotion at a lower rate compared to their counterparts (Wijesingha & Ramos, 2017). Again, researchers in this group are also likely to experience a particularly heightened sense of risk with regard to their career trajectory when engaging in controversial public criminology. Of course, women of color and women who experience other facets of marginalized identity (e.g., queer women or nonbinary persons of color) occupy a distinctly marginalized space in the academy.

Finally, while less discussed in the literature, academic rank is arguably another important factor to consider when examining one's experience with public criminology or KMb activities. Scholars in the very early stages of their career, such as graduate students or recent graduates entering the job market, are particularly vulnerable to the risks associated with activist forms of public intellectualism; participating in research that is critical of hegemonic structures may make them less desirable to hiring committees. Additionally, those scholars engaging in critical research publicly may find difficulty gaining access to research sites, as gatekeepers will likely see them as a potential threat and be hesitant to grant them entry. This is particularly problematic for junior scholars who have yet to establish themselves as experts in a particular field, and who may have limited research connections to help them facilitate site access.

The point being made here is that the risks associated with making controversial research public are less for the tenured and non-marginalized professor, as they are less vulnerable to negative repercussions compared to non-tenured faculty[7] due to greater job security. Tenured faculty may also find themselves with more time to engage in the academic endeavors of their choice, including public criminology, as they do not face the same level of pressure to produce traditional outputs compared to those who are pre-tenure. Further, tenured faculty who do produce outputs at a high rate may still have an easier time engaging the public, as they are more likely to have well-established research connections and less research and service burdens. Cooper et al. (2018) note with optimism that "researchers with the most academic outputs also had the most non-academic output" (p. 16), as they argued that this indicated that academic work like publishing in peer-reviewed journals did not serve as a barrier to KMb activity. However, the authors fail to link this point to the fact that 91% of their sample was tenured faculty and had 10 or more years of experience in academia since receiving their doctoral degree. Scholars in such a secure career position are far less susceptible to the negative repercussions associated with public engagement outlined above. Again, this underscores the neoliberal and hegemonic undercurrents at work in the academy, as tenured faculty are celebrated for their ability to engage the public while the experiences of marginalized faculty are rendered invisible. Findings like those reported by Cooper et al. (2018)—that ignore the experiences and implications of intersectional identities in academia when assessing KMb—can bolster the privilege experienced by some faculty while pushing marginalized others deeper into the undercommons.

Public Criminology and Anti-Intellectualism within a Repressive State Apparatus

Due to the contentious nature of most criminological discussions, public criminologists—to varying degrees, depending on their individual identities—face a certain level of individualized risk when engaging the public. Government tropes of anti-intellectualism currently proliferating across many nations have exacerbated these risks and contribute to a particularly hostile public. The rise of anti-intellectualism is a global phenomenon, but nowhere is it more observable than in North America, where political leaders like Donald Trump are capitalizing from the ease with which they can dispute scholarly knowledge, threatening the position of scholars as society's knowledge producers.

Criminologists in particular have indicated that the blatant disregard for research that occurs through government anti-intellectualism is especially constraining in terms of their public engagement (Cain et al., 2018). Notably, findings from our 2018 study came from faculty working at Canadian post-secondary institutions during a time when the conservative federal government was particularly vocal about the irrelevance of criminological research (Cain et al., 2018). For example, in 2013, then-Prime Minister Stephen Harper responded to his political opponent's emphasis on the importance of investigating root causes of terrorism by infamously saying that "now is not the time to *commit* sociology" (Cohen, 2013 as cited in Cain et al., 2018, emphasis added). Using terminology to liken academic research with criminal activity no doubt signaled to Canadian criminologists and their institutions that research critical of the establishment would not be tolerated (Cain et al., 2018).

The power that state and corporate interests exude over both academic and public spheres can censor activist scholarship, and while the anti-intellectual sentiment put forward by the Harper Administration in Canada was perceived as constraining to critical academic voices, the current Trump Administration in the United States is downright stifling. Since his inauguration in 2017, President Trump has unleashed an overt attack on intellectualism that includes the drastic reduction of budgets for national research institutions (i.e., the National Science Foundation, the Center for Disease Control, and the National Institute of Health), the replacement of scientists from research-based government positions (e.g., the head of the Environmental Protection Agency) with corporate leaders, and the use of moral panic tactics to promote false information that serves a political agenda. No longer is the criminologist at risk of having their findings bent to serve political will; they are being removed from the conversation altogether.

Anti-intellectual sentiment has permeated beyond politicians, cultivating a particularly hostile public with which activist public criminologists must contend. The rise of social media, and with it the rise of "fake news" and "alternative facts," has given the public access to unprecedented amounts of (often problematic) information. Public scholars who wish to circumvent political agendas may still encounter public groups who, like the government, are armed with information to suit their position on a topic and that can be used to object to scholarly claims of the contrary. To illustrate, consider climate change deniers' use of "alternative facts[8]" to lobby against environmental protection, which then prevents important environmental knowledge from being translated into action across North America.

This current socio-political climate, characterized by anti-intellectualism and hostility, can be linked to a broader shift away from the subverted hegemonic forces typical of the neoliberal era and toward much more overt exertions of imperial power. This reflects what Hyslop-Margison and Leonard (2012) warn of in their discussion of the growing "repressive state apparatus,"[9] a term used to describe the aggressive and militaristic state tactics employed to protect hegemonic interests and to extinguish any forum for public dissent. The authors claim that, in this shift toward autocratic governance, the repressive state apparatus will specifically target post-secondary institutions since, as they are important discursive sites for critical thought, they pose a significant threat to the status quo. However, while Hyslop-Margison and Leonard (2012) posit that academic institutions in general will face an increasing attack from the repressive state apparatus, the argument has been made throughout this chapter that, through institutional forms of governance, any such attack has been redirected away from the university and toward the individual scholar. Thus, while anti-intellectualism threatens academia as an institution, this will surely translate—through subverted neoliberal mechanisms like regulatory ritualism—into an amplification of the risks faced by critical activist scholars. Academic institutions will subvert any attack by their continued embrace of hegemonic processes; they will retain legitimacy by, for example, placing further pressure on researchers to engage in non-controversial public scholarship. In the process, scholars who tend to be privileged within the academy (e.g., non-racialized and tenured faculty) will see their status ratified, while scholars whose research is anti-establishment will risk increasing marginalization, or, perhaps, be silenced altogether.

As Hyslop-Margison and Leonard (2012) suggest, the trend toward the suppression of critical research and voices within the academy will likely continue and that "under post neo-liberalism we should expect to witness continued and more forceful challenges to universities as potential sites for democratic critique" (p. 9). It is therefore reasonable to expect that, as we continue down this trajectory of repressive conditions within which North American scholarship is produced, the individual risk faced by the activist public criminologist will only increase. Yet this is a time where, more than ever, public forum for critical discussion is necessary in order to counter the hate and injustice coursing through our society. Recognizing the oppressive nature of the institutional push for KMb is therefore an imperative first step in protecting these important critical and activist voices that are currently at risk of being silenced both inside and outside the walls of the academy.

Conclusion

Scholars and their institutions are now operating in a post-neoliberal era characterized by palpable anti-intellectualism and hostility. The repressive state apparatus is increasingly targeting any potential sites of discursion, including post-secondary institutions. Having already adopted market values, universities are responding to this attack by pushing their scholars toward KMb activities in order to demonstrate their public relevance and legitimacy as an institution. Yet the push toward KMb is not equal for all scholars. Importantly, KMb initiatives serve the university as an institution and work to elevate scholars whose work is non-controversial, while silencing more critical scholars like the activist public criminologist. Through this, any risk the repressive state apparatus poses to the university is offloaded onto individual faculty. This amplifies the individualized risk facing critical scholars who wish to make their work public, especially if they are scholars who hold marginalized positions within the university. The result is an elevation of privilege within the academy and a potential silencing of critical scholarly dissent.

This chapter has differentiated public intellectualism according to whether the scholarship is motivated by hegemonic or counter-hegemonic dimensions. Recognizing the oppressive nature some aspects of public intellectualism, like institutional push for KMb, is an imperative first step in protecting critical and activist voices that are currently at risk of being silenced by the academy. It is also important to recognize that the suppression of scholarly voices is not a new phenomenon; many groups of scholars have endured marginalization within the academy since its inception. Racialized faculty have withstood a long history of oppression in academe and can offer valuable guidance for critical public criminologist. For instance, writing on the topic of marginalized voices within the university, Grace Kyungwon Hong (2008) acknowledges how the academy is "implicated in the specific processes of racialization and gendering in the contemporary moment" through "norms governing what can be validated as scholarly knowledge" (p. 98). The solution to this dilemma, according to Hong (2008), is to change the parameters of what constitutes knowledge production. Thus, rather than simply increasing the number of marginalized bodies in academia—as is the case with so many institutional diversity initiatives—the academy must work to elevate knowledge produced by these scholars. This requires a profound change in what is considered academic "excellence"—a change beyond the addition of public scholarship to institutional metrics and toward a release of the blind faith in "ostensibly neutral criteria [that] not only regulate[s] *what* gets said but ... also determines *who* can say it" (Hong, 2008, discussing the work of Christian, 1994, emphasis in original). Perhaps, then, it would be appropriate to close the chapter by revisiting a charge first put forth by critical criminologist scholars in 1973: that we—as public criminologists—take up the task

> not merely to "penetrate" [social] problems ... or to act as carriers of "alternative phenomenological realities". The task [instead] is to create a society in which the facts of human diversity, whether personal, organic, or social, are not subject to the power to criminalize.
>
> *(Taylor et al., 1973)*

Notes

1 Note that, while KMb is a widely recognized term among North American universities, it is not universally used. For example, it can also be referred to as "knowledge transfer" and "knowledge utilization."
2 This empirical work sought to understand the perceived impact of KMb on the production and dissemination of criminological research by conducting in-depth interviews with Canadian academics, university administrators, and research facilitators.
3 I use queer in relation to politics, sexuality, and gender (as in genderqueer), noting there is a much wider range of orientations and identities than I address in the body of the text.
4 In this brief discussion of the "undercommons," I realize that I give the impression that its inhabitants are powerless; this is not the case. As Moten and Harney (2013) make clear, inhabitants of the undercommons are like those of maroon communities, where the "revolution is still [B]lack, still strong" (p. 26).
5 Puar has since published some of this work in a book (Puar, 2017).
6 Visit www.rutgersaaup.org/news/executive-council/defense-professor-jasbir-puars-academic-freedom to see Rutgers' full statement in support of Jasbir Puar's academic freedom.
7 While a comparison is being made between tenured and non-tenured faculty, class disparity in academia extends beyond tenure-track professors and includes lecturers/adjuncts and non-tenure-track employees who can be fired at will for their public work.
8 Many climate change deniers use reports that claim that there is no evidence that humans are responsible for climate change, or that the Earth's climate is not significantly changing, as a base for their arguments; such reports are typically produced and promoted by right-wing think tanks.
9 While I use the interpretation of the "repressive state apparatus" put forth by Hyslop-Margison and Leonard (2012), the authors acknowledge that the term is largely based on Althusser's (1971) concept of the "ideological state apparatus".

References

Althusser, L. (1971). *Lenin and philosophy and other essays.* New York: Monthly Review Press.
Baez, B. (1998). *Negotiating and resisting racism: How faculty of color construct promotion and tenure.* Retrieved from https://files.eric.ed.gov/fulltext/ED430420.pdf
Baez, B., & Boyles, D. (2009). *The politics of inquiry: Education research and the "culture of science."* Oxford: Oxford University Press.

Braithwaite, J., Makkai, T., & Braithwaite, V. (2007). *Regulating aged care: Ritualism and the new pyramid*. Cheltenham: Edward Elgar.

Burawoy, M. (2005). For public sociology. *American Sociological Review, 70*(1), 4–28.

Cain, K., Shore, K., Weston, C., & Sanders, C. (2018). Knowledge mobilization as a tool of institutional governance: Exploring academics' perceptions of "going public." *Canadian Journal of Higher Education, 48*(2), 39–54.

Christian, B. (1994). Diminishing returns: Can black feminism(s) survive the academy? In D. T. Goldberg (Ed.), *Multiculturalism: A critical reader* (pp. 168–179). Boston, MA: Blackwell Publishers.

Cohen, T. (2013, April 25). String of terror incidents no reason to "commit sociology." *National Post*. Retrieved from http://news.nationalpost.com/news/canada/politics/string-of-terror-incidents-noreason-to-commit-sociology-stephen-harper

Cooper, A., Rodway, J., & Read, R. (2018). Knowledge mobilization practices of educational researchers across Canada. *Canadian Journal of Higher Education, 48*(1), 1–21.

Crenshaw, K. (1991). Mapping the margins: Intersectionality, identity politics and violence against women of color. *Standford Law Review, 43*, 1241–1299.

Delanty, G. (2001). *Challenging knowledge: The university in the knowledge society*. Buckingham: Open University Press and Society for Research in Higher Education.

Douglas, J. D. (1970). The impact of the social sciences. In J. D. Douglas (Ed.), *The impact of sociology* (pp. 250–281). New York: Appleton-Century-Crofts.

Feilzer, M. (2009). The importance of telling a good story: An experiment in public criminology. *The Howard Journal, 48*(5), 472–484.

Heimer, C. A., & Gazley, J. L. (2012). Performing regulation: Transcending regulatory ritualism in HIV clinics. *Law & Society Review, 46*(4), 853–887.

Henry, F., & Tator, C. (2012). Interviews with racialized faculty members in Canadian universities. *Canadian Ethnic Studies, 44*(2), 75–99.

Hong, G. K. (2008). The future of our worlds: Black feminism and the politics of knowledge in the university under globalization. *Meridians: Feminism, Race, Transnationalism, 8*(2), 95–115.

Horn, M. (2000). "The wood beyond": Reflections on academic freedom, past and present. *Canadian Journal of Higher Education, 30*(3), 157–178.

Hyslop-Margison, E. J., & Leonard, H. A. (2012). Post neo-liberalism and the humanities: What the repressive state apparatus means for universities. *Canadian Journal of Higher Education, 42*(2), 1–12.

Loader, I., & Sparks, R. (2010). *Public criminology?* London: Routledge.

Matthew, P. A. (2016). Written/unwritten: The gap between theory and practice. In P. A. Mathew (Ed.), *Written/unwritten: Diversity and the hidden truths of tenure* (pp. 1–25). Chapel Hill, NC: University of North Carolina Press.

Mopas, M., & Moore, D. (2012). Talking heads and bleeding hearts: Newsmaking, emotion, and public criminology in the wake of a sexual assault. *Critical Criminology, 20*(2), 183–196.

Moten, F., & Harney, S. (2013). *The undercommons: Fugitive planning and black study*. Wivenhoe: Minor Compositions.

Perna, L. W. (2005). Sex differences in faculty tenure and promotion: The contribution of family ties. *Research in Higher Education, 46*(3), 277–307.

Puar, J. K. (2017). *The right to maim: Debility, capacity, disability*. Durham, NC: Duke University Press.

Taylor, I., Walton, P., & Young, J. (1973). *The new criminology: For a social theory of deviance*. London: Routledge.

Turner, E. (2013). Beyond "facts" and "values": Rethinking some recent debates about the public role of criminology. *British Journal of Criminology, 53*(1), 149–166.

Uggen, C., & Inderbitzin, M. (2010). Public criminologies. *Criminology & Public Policy, 9*(4), 725–749.

Walker, J. (2008). Social/corporate accountability: A university's "trek" towards excellence. *Canadian Journal of Higher Education, 38*(2), 45–71.

Weinberg, S. L. (2008). Monitoring faculty diversity: The need for a more granular approach. *Journal of Higher Education, 79*, 365–387.

Wijesingha, R., & Ramos, H. (2017). Human capital or cultural taxation: What accounts for differences in tenure and promotion of racialized and female faculty? *Canadian Journal of Higher Education, 47*(3), 54–75.

Young, J. (2012). *The criminological imagination*. Cambridge, MA: Polity Press.

13
PUBLIC CRIMINOLOGY IN CHINA
Neither Public nor Criminology

Jianhua Xu and Weidi Liu

Introduction

We begin this chapter by sharing some of the first author's personal experiences in China. Over the past decade, he has encountered tens, if not hundreds, of ordinary citizens in China with a friendly curiosity about his occupation. When hearing the term "criminology," the typical comments that follow are something like, "Wow, you study criminal psychology." These responses are not unique. An online focus group discussion conducted by the first author with fourteen criminologists in China in May 2018 revealed that most of them had similar experiences and observations. For a lay Chinese audience, criminology is often thought of as the study of criminal psychology. While psychological disposition of criminals is certainly worth studying, criminology as a discipline covers topics far beyond criminal psychology.

In this chapter, we scrutinize the common belief among ordinary Chinese citizens that "criminology equals criminal psychology." We examine the current status of the production of criminological knowledge (professional criminology), the dissemination of such knowledge to the public (public criminology or criminologists as public intellectuals), and how the unique Chinese context affects the production and dissemination of criminological knowledge in China. In doing so, we explore the opportunities and challenges for the development of public criminology in China.

The Call for Public Criminology in the World

Criminology has a long tradition of engaging with the public. One of the early examples is Clifford R. Shaw, the founder of the classic social disorganization theory, who actively shared his findings with the citizens he studied in the Chicago neighborhood in the 1920s. As an institutional response, he also founded the Chicago Area Project to improve the living conditions that contributed to the high crime and delinquency problems in the area (Uggen & Inderbitzin, 2010). The tradition of active public engagement of criminologists continued both in the United Kingdom and the United States into the 1970s (Currie, 2007; Rock, 2010). However, with the increasing professionalization of the discipline, criminologists' presence in the public discourse and their role in the making of criminal justice policy declined in many Western countries. At the same time, the need for such knowledge proved to be more urgent than ever before as higher crime rates became a new norm alongside fundamental transformations in crime control (Garland, 2001). Indeed, some scholars have observed that criminology is facing the paradox of being a "successful failure": the popularity of the discipline has increased in universities, but its policy relevance has actually declined (Loader & Sparks, 2011). The advocacy for public criminology has gained momentum against this backdrop (Clear, 2010), following in the footsteps of the powerful call for more active engagement of sociologists in public policy and social movements through public sociology (Burawoy, 2005).

Elliott Currie, a long-time advocate for public criminology in the United States, argues that criminology as a discipline has generated much knowledge over the past half century, but, unfortunately, this knowledge has not been effectively disseminated to the public or had notable impact on public policy. On the contrary, the making of criminal justice policy is largely influenced by populism and ungrounded arguments. One of the most significant examples is the rise of mass incarceration in the United States, which is an accepted (yet arguably failed) crime-control policy despite significant criminological evidence showing its counter-productive consequences (Currie, 2011). If criminologists who know best about crime and criminal justice do not have their voices heard in educating the public or in the making of public policy, the public perception of crime and the making of criminal justice policy become disproportionally influenced by criminal justice practitioners, politicians, and (often biased) media reporting (Chancer & McLaughlin, 2007).

Many advocates for public criminology believe that the balance between the production of criminological knowledge and dissemination of such knowledge is biased towards the former (Currie, 2007). In response, criminologists should increase their roles as experts in the realm of crime and justice by communicating their peer-reviewed evidence through clear points and plain language (Uggen & Inderbitzin, 2010). Some practitioners have echoed that criminal justice is too important to leave it to lawyers and politicians. The voices from criminologists should be heard loudly (Kennedy, 2011).

The call for public criminology in the United States has been enthusiastically echoed by some scholars in other parts of the world (Loader & Sparks, 2011), despite some scholars being more cautious (Rock, 2014) or even opposing such a development (Wacquant, 2011). Most research and debate surrounding public criminology focus on the United States and the United Kingdom where two pre-conditions for developing public criminology are sufficiently met. On the one hand, public criminology must be based on significant knowledge accumulation in professional criminology. Without creditable knowledge based on scientific research, the development of public criminology is arguably groundless. On the other hand, an open public sphere must exist to allow the dissemination of professional and critical criminological knowledge. Without the freedom of expression and proper development of civil society, the production of professional criminology will not only be difficult, but the dissemination of such knowledge will also be extremely challenging. However, the two prerequisites for developing public criminology vary from country to country. In this chapter, we examine the current status of public criminology and corresponding factors affecting its development in China.

Professional Criminology in and of China: A Discipline in Its Early Childhood

The production of criminological knowledge is affected by social and political factors in a particular society (Radzinowicz, 1994). China is no exception. In Mao's China, the social sciences were abolished to facilitate the totalitarian control of the Party state. It was not until the 1980s, when China started its economic reform and developed policies more open to the international engagement, that sociology, the oft-regarded mother discipline of criminology, started to be rehabilitated. Despite the significant development of sociology as a discipline over the past three decades, Chinese sociologists are slow in turning their attention to the study of crime because of overall political conservativeness in the society (Xu, 2016). As a result, the empirical study of crime and its control is very underdeveloped despite some progress in recent years (Cao & Hebenton, 2018; Scoggins, 2018).

In China, criminology as a research field has been institutionally located within the discipline of criminal law (Hebenton & Jou, 2010). A good illustration is that in 2018, the official newsletter of the annual meeting of Chinese Society of Criminology (CSC) stated that close to 200 "*legal scholars* and representatives from criminal justice departments" participated in this one and a half day meeting (Quanzhou Net, 2018). It did not recognize scholars who work on crime as criminologists, but as legal scholars. In addition, the CSC is more a bureaucratic institution than many professional and academic associations; it has one president, one executive vice-president, eighteen vice-presidents, one secretary-in-general, and five deputy secretaries-in general, along with 147 board members, 67 of whom are executive board members (Cao & Hebenton, 2018). Its annual conference remains a small, but highly political event. For instance, there were only 151 papers presented in its 2018 annual conference. The conference welcome remarks were given by several senior government officials (rather than scholars) from various levels including China's CCP Committee Member of the Supreme People's Procuratorate and Vice Procurator-General Tong Jianming; the CCP Standing Committee Member and the Secretary-General of Political-Legal Committee of Fujian Province Wang Hongxiang; the CCP Secretary-General and Procurator-General of Fujian Province Huo Min; and CCP Secretary-General of Quanzhou City Kang Tao. Conference themes were also politically-driven, including, for example, ones that are relevant to the Xi Jingping's "one-belt-one road" initiatives (Quanzhou Net, 2018). One Chinese criminologist in the United States cynically remarked that there was probably "not a single qualified criminologist" in the meeting (focus group discussion, October 2018). Generally speaking, criminology as a discipline in China remains "still in its infancy" (Hebenton & Jou, 2018, p. 377); criminological research largely focuses on general discussions or speculations without sound theoretical frameworks and empirical evidence (Zhang, 2011).

While criminology within China has made slow progress in terms of establishing itself as a valid discipline, substantial progress has been achieved by international scholars who are interested in the empirical study of crime and its control in China. Over the past two decades, criminological publications in English have increased dramatically (see Cao, Hebenton, & Sun, 2014). Various journals have also featured special issues on crime in China, including leading publications such as *The British Journal of Criminology* (2002) and *The Journal of Research in Crime and Delinquency* (2017). The establishment of the Association of Chinese Criminology and Criminal Justice in the United States in 2010 is another example of increasing interest in criminology of China. In 2018, ACCCJ reached a milestone with over one hundred paid members.

Indeed, one of the main reasons for the increasing criminological research about China is the expanding force of overseas Chinese criminologists. In the past three decades, more and more Chinese students have pursued their doctoral training in criminology and criminal justice in other countries. While some of them return to mainland China after graduation, many of them find positions at universities in the United States, the United Kingdom, Canada, Australia, Hong Kong, and Macau. These overseas-based Chinese criminologists enjoy a hybrid identity of both insiders and outsiders. On the one hand, their overseas training equips them with better skills in conducting empirical criminological research. Their cultural capital and knowledge about Chinese society, including connections in the country, also facilitate their empirical data collection. On the other hand, their location overseas reduces active censorship and self-censorship when conducing criminological research (Xu, Laidler, & Lee, 2013). Their insider/outsider status has not, however, successfully contributed to the dissemination of professional and critical criminological knowledge to the Chinese public due to various constraints there.

Considering the criminological knowledge produced by Chinese scholars within China and international scholars (both overseas Chinese and non-Chinese), it might be reasonable to argue that there has been moderate accumulation of professional criminological knowledge about China in the world. Although criminology *inside* China may still be in its "infancy," criminology *about* China has "approach[ed] a critical mass" (Scoggins, 2018, p. 82) and reached its early childhood. The life stage of criminology in and about China has direct bearing about the development of public criminology in China.

The Public Faces of Criminologists in China: The Case of Professor Li Meijin

The development of public criminology requires not only significant development of professional criminology, but also a public sphere in which criminologists can find a venue to have their critical voices heard. Unfortunately, Chinese media is heavily controlled and censored (King, Pan, & Roberts, 2014, 2017; Xu, 2015). Compared to democratic countries, the development of public criminology in China faces what might be thought of as double obstacles: both the lack of sufficient professional criminological knowledge and the existence of censorship. Despite the decent accumulation of professional criminology about China in the English language literature, international scholars are slow in promoting such knowledge to the Chinese public. Two kinds of censorship arguably contribute to its slow dissemination: (1) active censorship from the Chinese government, and (2) self-censorship among scholars fearing that a critical approach may further endanger their limited opportunities to conduct empirical criminological research in China (Xu, 2016). As a result, the overall development of public criminology in China is rather limited. Figure 13.1 shows the mentioning of criminologists and sociologists in the Chinese newspaper database Wisenews.[1] Generally speaking, out of all mentions of criminologists and sociologists in Chinese media, criminologists are mentioned only around *two* percent of the time.

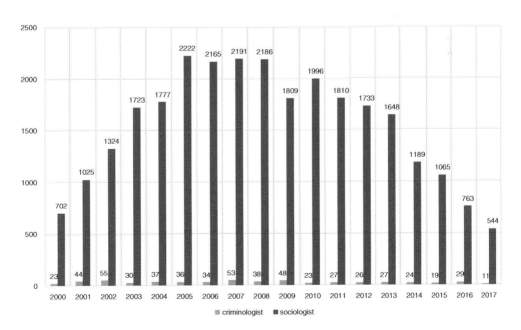

Figure 13.1 Mentions of "Criminologist" and "Sociologist" in China's Newspapers

We do not mean to say there is no demand for public opinions from criminologists in China. With the increasing commercialization of Chinese media since the 1990s (Shirk, 2011), crime has become a hot topic for media consumption. Experts are often invited to comment on some high-profile crime cases in the mass media. Rather than adopting a critical perspective to examine how social and structural factors—such as anomie, inequality, demography, transitional factors, discrimination, and social exclusion in China's unprecedented process of urbanization and modernization (Bakken, 2018)—contribute to crimes, criminologists who enjoy high media publicity often emphasize how individual and psychological features affect the occurrence of specific crimes. Accordingly, the development of the Chinese version of public criminology tends to individualize crime and not bring attention to structural forces, which goes against what many criminologists would desire.

For example, Professor Li Meijin (李玫瑾) enjoys the highest publicity in Chinese mass media among all alleged criminologists. Li works in the School of Criminology at People's Public Security University, the only department/school with criminology in its official name in China (Cao & Hebenton, 2018). She frequently gives comments on crimes in various TV programs in China Central Television (CCTV, the mouthpiece of the Party-state and the most watched TV in China) and various newspaper articles. A Baidu[2] search in November 2018 generated 280,000 items about Professor Li. In comparison, only 2,710 items could be found in Baidu for Professor Wang Mu (王牧), the former president (2002–2012) and current honorary president for the Chinese Society of Criminology. Li is self-identified and publicly recognized as a criminal psychologist. Her influence in Chinese media could further be illustrated by the fact that all top news about criminal psychologists in China's cyberspace are about her (Figure 13.2).

Figure 13.2 Screenshot of Baidu Search about Criminal Psychologists

However, Li and her comments on crime often tend to focus on individual's psychology without mentioning social structural reasons. Although the most well-known public criminologist, Li's approach on crime has been very controversial. She has been involved in commenting on several high-profile cases in China. In 2004, a university student Ma Jiajie from Yunnan University killed four of his classmates after they accused Ma of cheating in playing cards with them. Ma confessed during police interrogation that he had long been looked down upon and discriminated by his classmates because he came from a very poor family. Sometimes, and even when he made efforts to become friends with them by making some jokes, the only response he received was further laughter and ridicule. Thus, the accusation of cheating at cards triggered an anger response so strong that he killed his card-playing classmates. While some commentators emphasized how poverty and exclusion had been elements leading to his violent acts, Li argued that such explanations were misleading. The "real" reasons, she argued, lay in his strong but suppressed emotional features, distorted opinions about life, and a "self-centered character deficit" (Li, 2004). In addition, Li (2004) framed his criminal psychology and reasons for offending as related to his low IQ.

In 2006, Li was involved in commenting on another controversial serial killing: the Qiu Xinhua case. Suspecting his wife was having an affair with a Daoist monk in a temple, Qiu killed the monk and nine others on July 14, 2006. Qiu also brutally cut out the monk's heart and lungs, cut them into pieces, fried them, and put them on a plate. He killed another victim on the road while on the run. On August 29, 2006, Qiu was arrested. Before the first trial, Li asked a journalist from CCTV to pass on two questionnaires to Qiu. Based on the answers provided by Qiu, Li concluded that "Qiu was completely aware of what he was doing and knew the consequence, having clear self-protection consciousness and behaviors" (Morning News, 2006, p. 5). Li's comments on the case were widely publicized in the media. Based on Qiu's abnormal behavior, many psychiatrists and legal scholars in China called for a forensic mental status evaluation for Qiu by the court. In contrast, Li insisted that Qiu's mental status was stable.

Four months after his arrest, and only four days before the Supreme People's Court reclaimed the power to review all death penalty cases, Qiu was swiftly executed on December 28, 2006, without any professional forensic mental status evaluation by the Shanxi Provincial High Court. Professor Li was widely criticized as "facilitating the execution of a possible innocent" and mentally ill perpetrator (Morning News, 2006, p. 5). As a self-described criminologist, Li's public commenting on crimes has life or death consequences even if she alone may not shape the outcome.

The third and probably most controversial case in which Professor Li Meijin was involved is the Yao Jiaxin case. Yao was a university student from Xi'an College of Music. On the night of October 20, 2010, Yao hit and wounded a rural woman, Zhang Miao, while driving a car. Afraid that the victim might remember his car plate number and demand a high compensation, Yao stabbed her eight times with a knife, killed her, and then fled from the scene. Three days later, Yao was arrested. While commenting on this case, Professor Li remarked on CCTV that Yao's killing was out of a "mechanic movement of playing piano." Facing criticism from other scholars as well as the media, Li defended her comments on CCTV forcefully again. In particular, critics of Li claimed she defended the rich, sarcastically calling her a "brick person" (zhuanjia 砖家) instead of an expert, playing on the same pronunciation of the character zhuan, meaning both "brick" (砖) and "expert" (专) (Beijing Daily, 2011).

Despite the high profile of Professor Li in China's mass media and her public comments on crimes, many observers begin to question her qualifications as a criminologist. Li's highest level of education is a bachelor's degree in philosophy from People's University of China, which she earned in 1982. She subsequently spent all of her career in People's Public Security University teaching criminal psychology. While she may benefit from extensive communication with frontline police officers, her lack of advanced training in any discipline, let alone in criminology or criminal psychology, constrains her capacity to act as a qualified scholar. Indeed, most of Li's publications could hardly be regarded as serious academic writings. A search for her journal articles included in the China Academic Journal Network Publishing Database (中国学术期刊网) in November 2018 revealed that among her 31 first-authored or single-authored publications in 33 years (1985–2018), the average number of references is 5.63. Excluding newspaper articles from the citation count, the average academic references were as low as 3.87 per paper—an arguably low output indeed and not that of a country's most celebrated scholar. When there is a lack of public engagement from professional criminologists, the spillover effect is that some unqualified scholars may meet the market demand by providing unprofessional criminological knowledge.

Indeed, unlike different roles played by criminologists in developed countries such as scientific experts, policy advisors, observer-turned players, social movement theorists/activists or the occasional lonely prophet (Loader & Sparks, 2011), Li could be best described as playing the role of a pro-establishment intellectual to the Chinese Party-state (Hao & Guo, 2016), proactively and passively following the party line by blaming the individual while ignoring the social structural reasons for crimes. As a further demonstration of the Chinese Party-state's preference for individual and psychological approaches in explaining crimes, the keyword "criminal psychologist" sometimes enjoys more popularity than "criminologist" in Chinese mass media (Figure 13.3) following the political conservative turn in China since 2012.

Although criminology in general and public criminology in particular are very much underdeveloped in China, the case of Professor Li provides a good example of the current situation and the factors affecting the status quo. It demonstrates how public engagement around crime is often nothing more than populist and tabloid media-hype about crime rather than a scholarly debate on the cases of crime. Unfortunately, the events around Li also show that this trend has

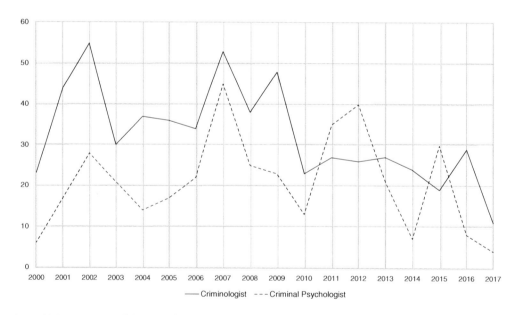

Figure 13.3 Mentions of "Criminologist" and "Criminal Psychologist" in China's Newspapers

notable implications: with the active promotion from the Chinese Party-state in general and the engagement of pro-establishment scholars in particular, crimes are often regarded as an individual's problem while social structure reasons are underexplored in China.

Concluding Remarks: Neither Public nor Criminology

We conclude by contextualizing the state of Chinese public engagement about issues of crime within wider discussions and debates about public criminology. Specifically, we critically reflect on various concerns about the development of public criminology. Some concerns are universally shared while others are particular to Chinese criminology.

Although the call for public criminology has been applauded by some scholars internationally, others are more cautious—and for various reasons. The first concern relates to the actual knowledge of professional criminology. Although advocates for public criminology argue that as a discipline "we in fact *know* a lot" (Currie, 2007, p. 176), some scholars do not share this perspective. They argue that we may not know as much as we claim (Chancer & McLaughlin, 2007; Rock, 2010). For instance, despite substantive research, criminologists were not able to predict a fundamental transformation of the overall crime situation: the great decline of crime rates occurring in developed countries since the 1990s. Further, when it occurred, criminology did not offer explanations for the drop (Zimring, 2007). The second concern is about the possibility of promoting controversial, and even wrong, knowledge by public criminologists. In sociology and criminology, critics argue what we think we know today may prove to be the contrary of what we may think tomorrow (Tittle, 2004). Additionally, some criminological research is ideologically oriented or methodologically flawed. Rock (2014, p. 425) has reminded us that many once popular criminological arguments, such as "property crime is a progressive tax on the bourgeoisie" and "criminals and the prisoner are primitive rebels," have since been discredited.

Moreover, some contemporary criminological research appears obsessed with methodological fetishism—that is, the modern version of "abstracted empiricism" criticized by C. Wright Mills (1959). We see this trend most clearly in relation to some poorly conducted quantitative-oriented research. To some extent, the so-called professional criminology becomes the collection of "works of people who carry statistical hammers and look for database nails to hit" (Tonry, 2010, p. 784), as for them "the telescope becomes of greater importance than the sky" (Young, 2011, p. viii). A further and related concern is the possible endangering of legitimacy for criminology as an academic discipline. When public criminology advocates for an agenda, criminologists themselves might become an interest group, something which may affect their neutrality and credibility in producing professional knowledge (Rock, 2010; Tittle, 2004). In this sense, public criminology faces the dilemma of the Gordian knot: the more it develops, the more it endangers the promise it can provide a good to the public (Ruggiero, 2012). Indeed, it is hard to reach a consensus among criminologists, and it is often the case that "for every established scholar who advocates for a given new policy, it seems there is an equally well established scholar who will argue against it" (Clear, 2010, p. 721).

In addition to the above-mentioned concerns, the development of public criminology in Western countries is also hampered by institutional obstacles, such as over-rewarding the production of professional criminological outputs and under-valuing the activities to disseminate such knowledge to the public (Currie, 2007). The promotion of public criminology in authoritarian countries such as China may face some further challenges despite the fact that there is a great need for such an approach (McCaffree, 2018). Civil society provides the soil for the development of a critical knowledge in the social sciences (Burawoy, 2005). In China, civil society is underdeveloped (Bakken, 2018). Given the authoritarian nature of the Chinese Party-state, the production of academic knowledge is often constrained, and what is presented as public criminology may not be described as criminology at all.

If criminology as a discipline runs the risks of becoming a tool of social control in Western democracies (Henne & Shah, 2015; Jacques & Wright, 2010), this concern is particularly relevant—and to a much larger extent—in authoritarian China. People's perceptions are largely shaped by the mass media. As scholars are important claim-makers in the construction of social problems, they can influence ordinary citizens' perceptions about social reality when they engage publicly (Berger & Luckmann, 1967). In China, the media is often censored, and robust scholarship is seldom presented in the media. The phenomenon that "criminology equals criminal psychology" has its roots both in the lack of the development of professional criminology as a discipline and in the political drive to blame individuals rather than acknowledge deeper social structural reasons.

All in all, the production of professional criminology in China is rather limited and could be regarded as at best in its early childhood. The dissemination of professional and critical criminological knowledge also faces the constraint of an underdeveloped civil society and its corresponding public sphere. In this sense, the future development of public criminology is particularly difficult and challenging in China. Nils Christie et al. (2011) once argued that experts are sometimes dangerous people, as they are often captured by ideas but sometimes blind to the side effects. In promoting public criminology in China, we may have to keep his wisdom in mind.

We conclude this chapter on public criminology in China by quoting the sarcastic remark made by Mahatma Gandhi when asked what he thought about Western civilization: "I think it would be a good idea" (O'Toole, 2013). Indeed, public criminology would have been a good idea had it existed in China. However, for criminology to be relevant to Chinese society, some basic questions need to be addressed, such as the consequences of unprecedented levels of urbanization, the crime rise in cities, the victimization of rural-to-urban migrant workers, the galloping inequality in Chinese society, the criminogenic settings emerging from almost three hundred million rural-to-urban migrants, and the more than 60 million "left-behind" children growing up without appropriate parenting—just to name a few crucial examples. In addition to these concerns, public criminology should also turn its gaze to the state. The state itself is the agent of social control in relation to a range of issues, from the recent nationwide hard-strike campaign on organized crimes (saohei chu'e 打黑除恶)—the so-called crackdown on "black evil"—to the increasing securitization and control in China. There are few ways to describe such incidents as "criminal psychology." Certainly, they exceed that scope.

Notes

1 Wisenews is a database containing around 2000 newspapers published in China.
2 Chinese version of Google.

References

Bakken, B. (2018). *Crime and the Chinese dream*. Hong Kong: Hong Kong University Press.
Beijing Daily (2011, April 19). Li Mei Jin: Jie shou pi ping bu jie shou wai qu (Li Meijin: I accept criticism but not distortion). 19.
Berger, P. L., & Luckmann, T. (1967). *The social construction of reality: A treatise in the sociology of knowledge*. London: Penguin.
Burawoy, M. (2005). For public sociology. *American Sociological Review*, 70(1), 4–28.

Cao, L., & Hebenton, B. (2018). Criminology in China: Taking stock (again). *The Criminologist, 43*(2), 1–9.

Cao, L., Hebenton, B., & Sun, I. Y. (2014). *The Routledge handbook of Chinese criminology*. Abingdon, Oxon: Routledge.

Chancer, L., & McLaughlin, E. (2007). Public criminologies: Diverse perspectives on academia and policy. *Theoretical Criminology, 11*(2), 155–173.

Christie, N., Currie, E., Kennedy, H., Morgan, R., Laycock, G., Sim, J., ... & Walters, R. (2011). A symposium of reviews of "public criminology?". *British Journal of Public Criminology, 51*(4), 707–738.

Clear, T. (2010). Editorial introduction to "public criminologies". *Criminology & Public Policy, 9*(4), 721–724.

Currie, E. (2007). Against marginality: Arguments for a public criminology. *Theoretical Criminology, 11*(2), 175–190.

Currie, E. (2011). Thinking about crime. *British Journal of Criminology, 51*(4), 710–713.

Garland, D. (2001). *The culture of control: Crime and social order in contemporary society*. Oxford: Oxford University Press.

Hao, Z., & Guo, Z. (2016). Professors as intellectuals in China: Political identities and roles in a Provincial University. *The China Quarterly, 228*, 1039–1060.

Hebenton, B., & Jou, S. (2010). Criminology in and of China: Discipline and power. *Journal of Contemporary Criminal Justice, 26*(1), 7–19.

Hebenton, B., & Jou, S. (2018). Criminology in China. In R. Triplett (Ed.), *The handbook of the history and philosophy of criminology* (pp. 377–391). Oxford: Wiley-Blackwell.

Henne, K., & Shah, R. (2015). Unveiling White logic in criminological research: An intertextual analysis. *Contemporary Justice Review, 18*(2), 105–120.

Jacques, S., & Wright, R. (2010). Criminology as social control: Discriminatory research & its role in the reproduction of social inequalities and crime. *Crime, Law and Social Change, 53*(4), 383–396.

Kennedy, H. (2011). Public criminology? *British Journal of Criminology, 51*(4), 713–716.

King, G., Pan, J., & Roberts, M. E. (2014). Reverse-engineering censorship in China: Randomized experimentation and participant observation. *Science, 345*(6199), 1–10.

King, G., Pan, J., & Roberts, M. E. (2017). How the Chinese government fabricates social media posts for strategic distraction, not engaged argument. *American Political Science Review, 111*(3), 484–501.

Li, M. (2004). Ma Jia Jue fan zui xin li fen xi (the criminal psychology analysis of Ma Jiajue). *Journal of Chinese People's Public Security University, 109*(3), 110–115.

Loader, I., & Sparks, R. (2011). *Public criminology? Criminological politics in the twenty-first century*. London: Routledge.

McCaffree, K. (2018). The growth of Chinese think tanks and the question of crime. *East Asia, 35*(1), 43–58.

Mills, C. W. (1959). *The sociological imagination*. New York: Oxford University Press.

Morning News. (2006, December 22). Qiu Xing Hua an bu fen da juan du jia gong kai (the exclusive publicity of some answers to Qiu Xinghua's questionnaires). *xin wen chen bao. Morning News*. 5.

O'Toole, G. (2013). "What do you think of western civilization?" "I think it would be a good idea". Retrieved from https://quoteinvestigator.com/2013/04/23/good-idea/

Quanzhou Net. (2018). Zhong Guo Fan Zui Xue Xue Hui Di Er Shi Qi Jie Xue Shu Yan Tao Hui Zai Quan Zhou Ju Hang (the 27th Annual Meeting of Chinese Society of Criminology Was Upheld in Quanzhou). Retrieved from www.qzwb.com/gb/content/2018-10/20/content_5886162.htm

Radzinowicz, L. (1994). Reflections on the state of British criminology. *British Journal of Criminology, 34*(2), 99–104.

Rock, P. (2010). Comment on "public criminologies." *Criminology & Public Policy, 9*(4), 751–767.

Rock, P. (2014). The public faces of public criminology. *Criminology & Criminal Justice, 14*(4), 412–4423.

Ruggiero, V. (2012). How public is public criminology? *Crime, Media, Culture: An International Journal, 8*(2), 151–160.

Scoggins, S. (2018). Policing modern China. *China Law and Society Review, 3*(2), 79–117.

Shirk, S. L. (2011). *Changing media, changing China*. New York: Oxford University Press.

Tittle, C. (2004). The arrogance of public sociology. *Social Forces, 82*(4), 1639–1643.

Tonry, M. (2010). Public criminology and evidence-based policy. *Criminology & Public Policy, 9*(4), 783–797.

Uggen, C., & Inderbitzin, M. (2010). Public criminologies. *Criminology & Public Policy, 9*(4), 725–749.

Wacquant, L. (2011). From "public criminology" to the reflexive sociology of criminological production and consumption: A review of *Public Criminology?* By Ian Loader and Richard Sparks (London: Routledge, 2010). *British Journal of Criminology, 51*(2), 438–448.

Xu, J. (2015). Claims-makers versus non-issue-makers: Media and the social construction of motorcycle ban problems in China. *Qualitative Sociology Review, 11*(2), 122–141.

Xu, J. (2016). Criminologizing everyday life and doing policing ethnography in China. In M. Adorjan & R. Ricciardelli (Eds.), *Engaging with ethics in international criminological research* (pp. 154–172). London and New York: Routledge.

Xu, J., Laidler, K. J., & Lee, M. (2013). Doing criminological ethnography in China: Opportunities and challenges. *Theoretical Criminology*, 17(2), 271–279.

Young, J. (2011). *The criminological imagination*. Cambridge: Polity.

Zhang, L. (2011). Transferring western theory: A comparative and culture-sensitive perspective of crime research in China. In C. Smith, X. Sheldon, & R. Barberet (Eds.), *Routledge handbook of international criminology: An international perspective* (pp. 77–86). London and New York: Routledge.

Zimring, F. E. (2007). *The great American crime decline*. New York: Oxford University Press.

14

A CASE FOR A PUBLIC PACIFIC CRIMINOLOGY?

Miranda Forsyth, Sinclair Dinnen, and Fiona Hukula

Introduction

Recent debates around the public role of criminology in the global North acknowledge the discrepancy between the discipline's robust health as a field of academic study and its limited impact on policy and reform processes (McLaughlin & Chancer, 2007). Many policy responses to crime fly in the face of compelling criminological research findings, including the continuing reliance on punitive measures and the significant expansion of incarceration associated with populist "law and order" politics. While the instrumentalization of "law and order" is by no means confined to political actors in highly industrialized countries, criminology as a discipline has a distinctly lower profile in the global South. This reflects, in part, the very different material conditions under which academic and research work typically occurs, not least being severe resource constraints. It is also the case that the criminological enterprise, in terms of its origins, orientation, and institutional development, has been dominated by Northern-based scholarship, as pointed out many years ago by Stanley Cohen (1982) and as highlighted again in recent discussions about Southern criminology (e.g., Carrington, Hogg, & Sozzo, 2016).

Although criminology courses and research are flourishing in Australia and New Zealand, as in Europe and North America, there has been little interest in extending the purview to the neighboring Pacific Islands. This is despite the obvious geographic proximity, shared history, and significant development engagement by Australia and New Zealand in the Pacific Islands, as well as serious concerns about crime, violence, and conflict in parts of the region. Such considerations have led prominent Australian scholar John Braithwaite (2013) to call for a Pacific criminology, noting that Australia's location and vibrant criminological community provides a unique opportunity to learn from the most socio-linguistically diverse region in the world, and one with many rich indigenous justice traditions. Braithwaite's call has remained largely unheeded.

Just as criminal justice policy has tended to disregard criminological scholarship about the limitations of populist law and order approaches to crime in the global North, criminal justice policy in the Pacific Islands has paid little attention to regular observations in reports and scholarship about the need for meaningful engagement with indigenous justice and social control traditions and institutions. This neglect of Indigenous justice traditions has been reinforced by the administrative and development-oriented nature of contemporary research and policy engagement with crime and violence in the region. High levels of crime and violence have often been represented as an inevitable pathology of rapid modernization (e.g., Goddard, 1995), while research and development initiatives have adopted a narrow focus on state institutions such as the police and the courts, and on ways to replicate processes and outcomes attributed to similar institutions in

Australia and other parts of the global North. If the Pacific Islands, which are almost devoid of criminology, have a "public criminology" challenge, perhaps it is in the form of these institutional issues.

In this chapter we draw on our experiences as researchers working on issues of crime, justice, and regulation in the Pacific region in order to reflect on the case for a public Pacific criminology. We acknowledge the practical (among other) difficulties of such an aspiration, as well as the grounds for pursuing it as worthy and desirable goal. We are wary of setting out any agenda that might be construed as the latest "shiny criminological brand" (Loader & Sparks, 2011), and are not seeking to transplant yet another discipline from the Northern academy into the region. At the same time, we do see real value in highlighting the potential contribution of a new site of transdisciplinary and inclusive criminological scholarship in and for the Pacific. It would be a criminology that draws from all parts of social science (Braithwaite, 2005) and one that develops organically, a public criminology that embraces the distinctive types of scholarship and praxis already existing in the region, as illustrated by the examples discussed below. We embrace a vision of an emergent public criminology that would create institutional spaces for open interrogation about fundamental questions such as:

- What constitutes crime and insecurity in the context of the region?
- Who decides on these categories and how?
- Who are the providers of security and justice in the region?
- How is knowledge about crime and justice produced?

Many current unexamined answers to these questions are based on tired assumptions about the role of the state and the political economy of countries in the region that need to be broken down and scrutinized. In sum, we see a public Pacific criminology not just interested in "What works?" but also in "What is broken and who decides what to 'fix'?"

The Pacific Islands region today comprises 22 distinct political entities scattered across a vast expanse of ocean. Despite originating in the imperial mapping of an earlier era of European exploration and colonization, the sub-division of the Pacific Islands into three broad cultural areas or sub-regions has endured, with Melanesia to the southwest, Polynesia to the east, and Micronesia to the northwest (see Figure 14.1). Our focus in this chapter is on the independent Melanesian states, primarily Papua New Guinea (PNG) and Vanuatu, as this is where the authors have lived and worked, as well as being the most densely populated part of the region with the most significant concentration of crime and violence.

One very relevant question for Pacific criminology as a future area of intellectual focus—which we raise here but do not conclusively answer—concerns the conditions in which it is productive for comparative research within and across the larger Pacific region. Unifying contextual features that suggest there is value in a comparative approach are the shared histories of pre-colonial, small-scale, self-regulating societies; relatively short periods of European colonialism (primarily British, French, German and Australian); the widespread and enthusiastic adoption of Christianity; the largely peaceful transitions to independence in the 1970s and 1980s;[1] and the continued relevance of customary and other non-state institutions in responding to social disorder, wrongdoing and everyday security. However, we note that caution is required given the significant social, historical, and geographic variations across the region and confine our discussion below to selected Melanesian contexts.

Our chapter is structured as follows. First, we discuss the repeated studies that show the failures of the formal police service in PNG, taking this as an exemplar of the larger failures or perceived failures of the state criminal justice system in Melanesia more broadly. Second, we discuss three examples from our work as interdisciplinary scholars, using them to illustrate the diversity of justice and policing forms that coexist in the region's complex social landscapes. Third, we

A Case for a Public Pacific Criminology?

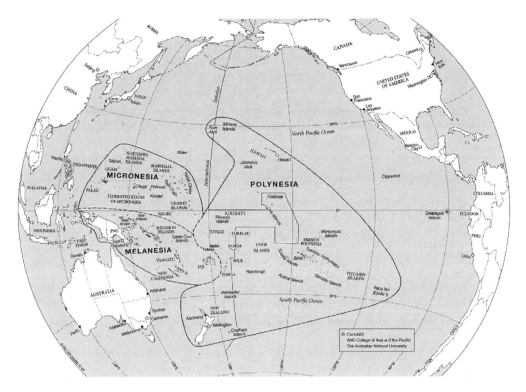

Figure 14.1 The Sub-Division of the Pacific Islands into Three Broad Cultural Areas or Sub-Regions of the Pacific

reflect on what agenda a public Pacific criminology should pursue, and the types of practices and ethics it would need to embody, as well as discussing some concerns about the future possibilities such a framing might produce.

Policing in Postcolonial Papua New Guinea

Crime and policing have become prominent issues in the larger independent Melanesian countries, particularly in PNG and Solomon Islands and, to a lesser extent, in Fiji and Vanuatu. Rapid socio-economic change, including population growth, urbanization, limited economic opportunities and growing inequalities, informs the broader context for rising crime and social disorder. PNG, the region's largest and most populous country with distinct development challenges, has experienced the most serious of these problems. Pervasive concerns over security and "law and order" throughout the country's post-independence history have highlighted the limited effectiveness and, for many citizens, the questionable relevance of its national police organization.

Institutionalized policing originated in PNG as a key instrument of colonial pacification and administration. Early police work included suppressing indigenous resistance to colonial incursion, ending fighting between local groups, protecting European interests, and collecting the head tax that was introduced to compel a plantation labor force. The territory's large size and challenging topography led to a distinct form of frontier policing based on patrols led by European district officials, known as *kiaps*, aimed at extending and consolidating colonial authority among a widely dispersed indigenous population (Dinnen & Braithwaite, 2009). This kind of policing was coercive and often violent, oriented more towards order maintenance than the prevention or control of crime.

Decolonization entailed an intensive period of institutional modernization as part of the transition to independence from Australia in 1975. It included the establishment of the Royal Papua New Guinea Constabulary (RPNGC) and the national justice system. Concerns about a growing urban crime problem in PNG increased in the 1960s and 1970s as the population of the capital, Port Moresby, rapidly expanded. Rising crime rates contributed to mounting concerns about deteriorating "law and order." Youth gangs, known locally as *raskols*, provided the folk devils in an escalating moral panic around urban insecurity. Throughout the 1980s and 1990s, Port Moresby experienced cyclical patterns of crime waves followed by special crime control measures, often involving curfews and other emergency measures, and invariably entailing heavy-handed special policing operations directed at the informal urban settlements viewed as the incubators of *raskolism* (see Dinnen, 2001). While bringing some temporary relief, this reliance on transplanted "law and order" solutions ultimately served to accentuate the grievances of many of the city's most marginalized groups, thereby perpetuating further cycles of lawlessness and militaristic policing. A much more promising development in the 1990s was the emergence of criminal gang surrenders, an incipient restorative justice institution that sought to link the negotiated exit from crime of self-declared *raskols* to accessing legitimate economic and livelihood opportunities instead (Dinnen, 1995). Occurring on the periphery of official policing and justice responses to crime, gang surrenders were not a transplanted solution but rather represented a unique and organic Melanesian institution.

Rural security concerns revolved around the resurgence of "tribal fighting" in parts of the Highlands from the 1960s. The introduction of firearms dramatically altered the ground rules and fueled escalating cycles of conflict that proved difficult to resolve through either policing interventions or more "traditional" peacekeeping approaches. Tribal conflict has since been accentuated by intensified competitiveness associated with elections, as well as violent contestation around the unequal distribution of local benefits from large-scale resource extraction projects. Such projects are typically located in rural areas where government presence and essential services are often minimal and where few other development opportunities exist.[2] While militarized policing responses tended to aggravate rather than resolve such conflicts, more positive outcomes have resulted from locally devised and culturally inflected peacemaking initiatives in a number of conflict-affected Highlands provinces that have drawn on the resources of multiple local stakeholders. These include the innovative peacemaking practices of Village Courts and Operation *Mekim Save* in Enga (Pupu & Wiessner, 2018) and those of the District Peace Management Teams in the Eastern Highlands (Allen & Monson, 2014).

Violence against women and girls, including rape and other forms of sexual abuse, remains an enormous problem throughout PNG. For example, Human Rights Watch has recently claimed that gender violence has reached "emergency" levels, with more than two-thirds of women experiencing some form of it and, in some areas, 80% of men admitting to committing sexual violence against their partners (Human Rights Watch, 2015). An ongoing epidemic of sorcery-related violence, often targeting women, has precipitated a concerted campaign of law reform, awareness, and other interventions by government, NGOs, churches, and donors (Forsyth & Eves, 2015).

The shortcomings of the RPNGC have long been viewed as a significant contributor to PNG's problems of insecurity. Police numbers have failed to keep up with a population that has almost quadrupled in size since independence. RPNGC leaders have sought to supplement their limited resources by relying on auxiliary and reserve police, although lack of adequate supervision has also led to regular allegations of abuse against them. Even where accessible, the RPNGC is widely viewed as unresponsive to requests for assistance, often demanding payment before responding. Inadequate funding and poor financial management have encouraged some officers to resort to illicit rent-seeking opportunities. Limited public confidence in the police has, if anything, declined further in recent years, with many citizens viewing the organization as beset by endemic levels of criminality, corruption, and brutality. Legacies of colonial policing persist, with many citizens suspicious—if not afraid—of the national police and reluctant to engage with them. These perceptions appear to have been little affected by decades of external assistance from Australia, which has been providing capacity-building support to the RPNGC since the late 1980s. The results from these efforts have been disappointing, to say the least. Donor engagement with the RPNGC has also tended to obscure the significant role of non-state policing in PNG, an oversight also repeated in its Melanesian neighbors (see Dinnen & Mcleod, 2009). More positive outcomes have been associated with New Zealand assistance to a distinct form of community policing in post-conflict Bougainville that has involved supporting strong linkages with existing community governance and leadership structures (Dinnen & Peake, 2013).

In light of the multiple and continued limitations of the state police and other justice institutions, community-based approaches to dispute resolution and security remain prevalent throughout PNG and other Melanesian countries. While profoundly affected by the changes wrought by colonialism, existing socially embedded local mechanisms and processes were not displaced. Rather, older, traditional kinds of self-policing and dispute resolution adapted and continue to prevail at local levels. The next section turns to look at a number of these in greater detail, drawing out their contribution to security and the local framing of crime and justice.

Justice, Security, and Social Control above, beside and below the State

While there has been extensive research on the pluralizing effects of marketization for policing and security in the global North (e.g., Abrahamsen & Williams, 2011; Loader & Walker, 2007), the literature from the global South on this and other drivers of pluralization is sparse. The related field of legal pluralism, which investigates the coexistence and interplay between different legal orders, often in colonial or postcolonial settings, has generally been more concerned with dispute resolution than policing or security (see Kyed, 2011). This section outlines the pluralized security landscape in PNG and Vanuatu, where high levels of insecurity and the deficiencies of the state police have driven a deepening pluralization in recent years. The complex realities of diverse and overlapping configurations of policing and security actors underline the limitations of state-centric conceptions of security provision, both in terms of the failure to understand how security and policing actually work in places like PNG, as well as the reluctance to recognize both the potential benefits and the risks, of working with pluralism in addressing today's security challenges.

Rather than being tethered to a predetermined institutional form, this section argues for a broader conception of "policing" and "justice" that can accommodate the plural realities of policing and security provision in contemporary Melanesia. Donors, governments, and other stakeholders committed to improving security outcomes would be better served by acknowledging this pluralism as the starting point for developing more networked and problem-solving approaches to current security challenges. Adopting Baker's inclusive definition of policing as "any organized activity, whether by state or non-state groups, that seeks to ensure the maintenance of communal order, security and peace" (Baker, 2008, p. 23), it is evident that multiple providers operate in complex postcolonial social landscapes, such as those in Melanesia. In addition to state police, these include "traditional" leaders, church groups, human rights defenders, NGOs, settlement committees (*komitis*), gangs, market associations, neighborhood watch schemes and, in recent decades, a rapidly expanding commercial security sector. Localized outbreaks of violence in some rural parts of PNG have led to the establishment of unofficial "police," such as in Domil in Jiwaka province and Gor in Simbu province. In the latter case, local leaders responded to prolonged tribal conflict and sorcery-related violence by setting up their own "community police" with the tacit approval of provincial authorities (Bal, 2015). These initiatives in remote rural areas of PNG bear similarities to successful policing schemes in remote Aboriginal communities in Australia, such as night patrols, some of which have appeared in influential recent discussions in Northern criminology (see, for example, Sharkey, 2018).

The arguments made in this section about the importance of "the local" and of pluralism are far from new. For example, the Clifford report in 1984 documented the shortcomings of individual agencies and was critical of the weakness of planning and budgeting across the sector in PNG. A distinguishing feature of the Clifford report was its emphasis on the need to reduce the perceived gap between the realm of formal state justice and the myriad informal institutions of social control at community levels across the country. In this regard, the report recommended a gradual shift in policy toward one that sought to incorporate informal (non-state) mechanisms in the maintenance of order and dispute resolution, while gradually reducing what it viewed as over-reliance on formal (state) structures. Commenting on the shortcomings of the formal agencies, the report (Clifford, Morauta, & Stuart, 1984, p. 125) stated that:

> [T]he possibility that existing services may be defective or inefficient—not because they are starved of resources but because they are either irrelevant to the situation in Papua New Guinea or refusing to work with communities—does not seem to have detained people long.

Despite the passage of almost thirty-five years, these comments remain equally valid today.

Example 1: Order Making in Urban Settlements in PNG

Increasing urbanization in the Pacific Islands has come with many challenges. Port Moresby has been described as one of the 10 most unlivable cities in the world (Fitzmaurice, 2017), and is known for its crime and disorder. Home to more than half a million people, Port Moresby is often described as a mini Papua New Guinea because people from the country's over 800 language groups converge here in search of access to better social services and employment opportunities. Due to lack of affordable housing, many of its residents live in informal settlements where utilities such as water and electricity are often unavailable. While long depicted as a breeding ground for criminals, settlements are home to a varied population of private sector and government workers, as well as those dependent on the informal economy. Whether domestic, ethnic, or land related, disputes are a normal feature of urban life in the national capital. The deficiencies discussed above of the RPNGC mean that social disorder and crime tend to be addressed through informal mechanisms. Many urban residents, like most rural citizens, rely on extended family, kinship and ethnic networks, and other community-based approaches for their everyday policing needs. These often entail informal links with regular police and other state agencies, for example through relationships with individual officers, magistrates or other officials. Diverse institutional arrangements regulate everyday disputation and safety in the burgeoning settlements where the bulk of the urban population live. However, these generally have little visibility beyond the immediate locality and often involve community-initiated governance processes entailing *komitis*, leadership networks and widespread use of mediation (see Craig & Porter, 2018).

The following description of how disputes are settled is based on fieldwork by one of the authors in a Port Moresby settlement made up of residents who are predominantly from a particular province in PNG.[3] Residents in urban settlements, such as those residing at Morobe

Blok in Nine Mile, where the fieldwork was undertaken, use a variety of different mechanisms to address disputes.

In Morobe Blok there is a local governance structure in place, also known as a settlement *komiti*. The role of the *komiti* is to represent the interests of the settlers at public meetings and also to provide leadership for the residents. The *komiti* (Porter, Craig, & Hukula, 2016; see also Evans, Goddard, & Patterson, 2010; Hukula 2013) has a number of sub-committees, such as a water *komiti* and a law and order *komiti*. At Morobe Blok, the law and order *komiti* has the task of mediating disputes between parties, with the aim of reaching an amicable solution. *Komiti* members can also play other roles within the community, such as being a leader within their church or ethnic group. As an informal mechanism, a *komiti* does not have "legal" authority to make decisions regarding disputes, but has sufficient authority within the community to bring disputing parties together to address problems. In other words, its convening power is a significant part of the overall regulatory landscape. At Morobe Blok, the local *komiti* convenes meetings as and when necessary, but most "kot" (court) hearings are on weekends when more people are free to attend. A *komiti* hearing involves both parties presenting their case to the *komiti* members and the members of the *komiti* deliberating to come up with an outcome based on the evidence provided by both parties. If one or both parties do not agree with the decision, then they are advised to take the case to the nearest village courts.[4]

The *komiti* at Morobe Blok is known as the Morobe Community Goroac Juju, formerly known as the Morobe Community Development Association. The name of the association reflects the Morobean origins of the settlers, thus the use of words in the Yabim and Kote languages of the Morobe province. The word Goroac means "the people" in Yabim language and the word Juju means "good life" in Kote language. At first settlement in the 1990s, residents physically settled according to electoral boundaries. Although the evidence of settlement in electoral boundaries is less clear now, this settlement pattern is still somewhat evident with respect to people from the different electorates living in close proximity to each other and, in some cases, in clusters of houses of close kin. It also gives an impression of manageability, familiarity and exclusiveness; by living within electoral boundaries, people are able to easily access local leaders, live among people they know and, in some sense, isolate themselves from those whom they do not wish to live among. *Komiti* members are then appointed to represent the different electorates from the province.

Daily security concerns in Port Moresby focus on street harassment and petty crime, such as bag snatching and stealing. Two other pressing issues are the high levels of domestic and public violence against women and the violence arising out of excessive alcohol consumption. In a city where a large portion of the population generates its income through the informal economy, low levels of education and few job opportunities lead some residents to resort to crime as a means of earning a living.

However, findings from the Port Moresby Community Crime Survey revealed that life within squatter settlements was no more violent than in non-settlement areas (Guthrie, 2013), and that people in low-income suburbs of Port Moresby often felt safer than those living in other parts of Port Moresby. There are a number of potential explanations for such a finding. First, settlement residents tend to live among people they know, within their ethnic grouping. Second, security of tenancy is assured because landlords tend to rent out rooms rather than a whole house, which means that the landlords are often living in the same place as the tenants. Third, with limited trust and confidence in the police, people turn to their own communities to resolve disputes. This means that instead of apportioning blame and seeking punishment through the criminal justice system, serious cases are often resolved through informal mediation focused on restoring the relations between the two parties.

As this example shows, a public Pacific criminology would need to be highly attentive to insider perceptions of insecurity and localized sources of security. From the outside, Port

Moresby's squatter settlements are considered dangerous and violent, but from the inside, security is perceived quite differently. While "crime" in the sense understood by criminologists from the global North is a cause for concern, lack of secure tenancy agreements that threatens the vital geographic co-location of ethnic and tribal groups creates far greater insecurity. In addition to understanding this, public Pacific criminology needs to highlight the roles of local structures such as *komitis*, as well as their relationship with state justice agencies, in co-producing order within these communities. A critical role for scholars therefore is to investigate how these potentially empowering, community-led approaches might also reinforce existing imbalances of power and divisions along lines of gender, age, or status. This would recognize the reality that local power brokers can capture poorly regulated and unaccountable responses and use them as instruments of discrimination against and oppression of vulnerable groups.

Example 2: Private Security Provision

This second example—private security—is also concerned with a response to the inadequacies of the state police, albeit one resorted to by a very different socio-economic segment of the population. The corporate and business sector has been a major driver of the dramatic growth of private security in recent decades, both as consumers and as suppliers of security services. Serious crime problems have long been viewed as a major additional cost of doing business in PNG. For example, in a 2012 business survey, 80% of respondents reported that crime had affected their business and investment decisions and they had little confidence in the police and judicial system (Institute of National Affairs and Asia Development Bank, 2012). As well as providing extra security for employees and property, businesses pay high insurance premiums and claim to have difficulties in attracting international staff. World Bank research indicates that concern with crime and violence among the PNG business community is more than four times the regional average in East Asia and the Pacific (Lakhani & Wilman, 2014). Violence in PNG is considered comparable with countries like El Salvador, Venezuela, and the Democratic Republic of Congo, although objectively the violence is more deadly in these places. The same research indicates that business investment in security personnel and infrastructure, at around 84% of all companies surveyed, is significantly higher than the average for the East Asia and Pacific, Sub-Saharan Africa, and Latin American regions.

According to PNG's Security Industries Authority (SIA), which issues licenses to security companies, the number of licensed security companies increased from 173 in 2006 to 464 in 2016, with a total workforce of around 30,000 security guards (Isari, 2017). These figures do not include unlicensed companies and personnel, conservatively estimated by the SIA to be around 219 companies and 7,649 guards in 2016 but popularly believed to be much higher. The number of licensed guards is still over three times that of serving police and exceeds the combined strength of PNG's three "disciplined" services (police, defense, and corrections). Some have speculated that the industry is now the country's third largest employer. Companies range from transnational security corporations with global reach, large locally owned firms, through to numerous smaller and often short-lived informal operators.

Security companies are most visible in the expanding urban centers where government, business, and private wealth are concentrated. They also operate in the rural areas where major resource development projects are located, including the Southern Highlands, Hela, and Enga provinces. The larger mining companies often have significant in-house security capabilities. For example, Barrick Gold, the Canadian operator of the Porgera mine in Enga, had around 450 security personnel in its asset protection department in 2010 (Human Rights Watch, 2011). Australia's controversial offshore refugee detention facilities on Manus island have provided lucrative employment for a succession of security companies, while PNG's hosting of APEC in 2018 provided another, albeit temporary, boost to the industry. The security services offered include protection of infrastructure at mines and plantations, as well as security for government buildings, shopping centers, airports, hospitals, schools and private residences. Additional services include personal protection, security training, emergency evacuations, and installing of electronic surveillance systems and security fencing.

The Security (Protection) Industry Act 2004 established the SIA as the industry regulator with responsibility for issuing and revoking licenses, and for setting and enforcing industry standards. Chaired by the RPNGC Commissioner, the SIA has representatives from the security, insurance, mining, agriculture and manufacturing industries, as well as from churches and trade unions. Its effectiveness is hampered by limited resources and the rapidity with which the industry is growing. Clear guidelines for issuing and cancelling licenses are still lacking, while other challenges include the large number of unlicensed operators, discipline problems with security guards, underpayment of guards, and the provision of unapproved (and therefore potentially inappropriate) training courses by some operators.

An increasingly interdependent relationship exists between the private and public security sectors. While this might be viewed as a potential opportunity for assisting the under-resourced police, it is also a potential risk to the integrity of the latter as providers of a public service. Both sets of providers share the same challenging operating environment and, in the case of the larger companies, undertake many of the same activities. The SIA website states that security companies "play an important secondary role as a quasi-law enforcing agency beside the Police force" (Security Industries Authority, 2013, para. 5). Strong informal networks exist, with many senior industry employees having previous police (or military) experience in PNG or from overseas. These links are reinforced through having the police commissioner chair the SIA, upon which private providers depend for their operating licenses. Larger companies, such as Guard Dog Security, regularly assist their RPNGC colleagues by, for example, providing fuel and tires for vehicles, while informal networks facilitate intelligence sharing. Superior resources available to the high-end of the private market include communications, surveillance and satellite tracking systems that are unavailable to the RPNGC.

Collaboration between the police and the business community has a long history in PNG. This includes special police services provided to logging and mining projects operating in remote locations. Such arrangements are sometimes covered by formal agreements or memoranda of understanding (MoUs) between the parties and often include the payment of allowances, transport costs, and provision of meals and accommodation. There have also been frequent allegations of serving officers moonlighting as security for private clients, often while wearing police uniforms and using police equipment.

Extensive interaction serves to blur the lines between public and private policing. Concerns have been regularly aired about the potentially corrosive impacts of the burgeoning private sector on the performance and standing of the police. These include sensitivities about private providers encroaching on areas that police believe should remain their exclusive preserve, notably the enforcement of state law. There are also concerns that the growing prominence of private providers diverts attention away from the need to adequately resource and support the public police, as well as perceptions that some public-private security collaborations privilege powerful business over the security interests of ordinary citizens (see Government of Papua New Guinea, 2013).

While reliable data is hard to come by, it is popularly believed that there have been growing levels of investment by PNG's business and political elite (often one and the same) in private security companies, in part fueled by windfalls from PNG's booming resources sector. As well as concerns about vulnerability to corruption, significant elite investment risks creating disincentives for political decision-makers to support and strengthen struggling public security agencies such as the police. This could weaken state security further, particularly for the vast majority of Papua

New Guineans who cannot afford private security, including the most at-risk groups, such as women, whose reliance on community-based and other forms of informal policing would be reinforced.

A public Pacific criminology will need to highlight and analyze the risks and potential benefits associated with PNG's pluralized security landscape. It needs to be sensitive to the variety of interests, assumptions and priorities of different security actors, particularly as to how these might potentially influence sources of funding for research, convening, and dialogue. For example, much current funding comes through donors who have demonstrated an enduring loyalty to particular kinds of policing and security provision, and conversely, blindness or antipathy toward other institutional forms.

Additionally, a public Pacific criminology will need to account for the relative prominence of privatized criminological thought, security markets in service of the elite, which is more important in the Pacific Islands than in the four main registers of sociological/criminological research distinguished by Burawoy (2005) and subsequently refined by Loader and Sparks (2011)—public, professional, critical, and policy (see also Braithwaite, 2005). Significant parts of the region at different times have been captured by private security providers. For example, the Pacific was the setting for the dramatic failure of the British private military contractor, Sandline International, with its attempted intervention in the Bougainville civil war in 1997 (Dinnen, May, & Regan, 1997). The rebellion by the PNG Defense Force and broader public played an important role in bankrupting one of the two largest private military corporations in the world at the time. These developments in the Pacific Islands, as well as the debacles involving Mark Thatcher and others in central Africa, helped to revitalize the anti-mercenary norm. In subsequent years, former members of Fiji's military flocked to Iraq to serve a new private security model that was more akin to an adjunct to NATO forces, and less a militarized entrepreneur of lucrative takeovers of diamond, copper or gold reserves in conflict-affected regions of the global South.

There is a privatization of the public in parts of the Pacific that is important to acknowledge, but also of note is a publicization of the private (Freeman, 2003). The latter is most evident in the significant investment by transnational mining corporations in community security initiatives in remote areas with a limited public security presence where they typically operate (e.g., see Whayman, 2015).

Example 3: Community Rule Making and Security Provision in Vanuatu

The example above suggested that privatized criminology is perhaps a more important category than the original Burawoy (2005) and Loader and Sparks (2011) distinctions among public, professional, policy, and critical sociology/criminology. This next example illustrates how distinctions between public, professional, policy, and critical sociology/criminology may also be less important in the Pacific than distinctions between a publicized imaginary of law and a customary imaginary. Yet, as will become evident, both scholarship and praxis (as well as filmmaking: see Johnson, Dean, & Butler, 2015) reveal how these distinctions are eroded through the hybrid practices that emerge as individuals navigate between different regulatory regimes and institutions of order-making.

The third example comes from Vanuatu, another country in Melanesia but with a different geography and context from PNG. Vanuatu is significantly smaller, with a population of only 250,000 spread over 65 inhabited islands. It is a country of diverse customary leadership and governance structures, with hereditary chiefs, elected chiefs, and "big man" style leadership based on grade-taking ceremonies (allowing for a rise in status) all in active operation. The state justice system operates predominantly on just two of the islands (Efate and Santo), with only a small number of magistrates, corrections officers and police dispersed between the other islands, many of which have no permanent state justice presence. In such a context, the categories of crime and criminality, the sources of insecurity, and the provision of justice and security needs are extremely diverse (see Forsyth, 2009).

A flavor of this diversity can be gleaned from looking at some of the written local community laws. Across Vanuatu, many communities have engaged in the process of writing their own by-laws or local constitutions for a variety of reasons, including to bolster the legitimacy of the chiefs, to strengthen community cohesion, and to make customary justice systems more valid in the eyes of the state. While the written product is not likely to be any more than a loose representation of local and cultural perceptions of wrongdoing at a particular point in time, it offers important insights into sets of priorities and moral orientation that are not congruent with the state criminal law. For example, the by-laws of one community have five sections that broadly encompass the criminal space.[5] The first is a long section on diverse environmental crimes, including burning and cutting of bush and killing immature marine species, and also crimes related to destroying graves or culturally significant stones. The second is a section on sexual offenses, covering rape of an underage girl, a boy or girl having sex without being married, provisions for child maintenance if a boy does make a girl pregnant, marrying one's sister, a single boy having sex with a married woman, homosexual acts, and a man or woman performing some sexual act with an animal. There is then a section on upholding culture, which covers killing someone through the use of black magic and women not being allowed to wear short shorts or drink kava in public. Fourth is a generic category of misconduct including fighting and stealing. The final category covers murder and the by-law provides that the local chiefly authority cannot deal with these cases but must give them to the state to deal with. In all other cases, the penalty provided is a monetary fine to be paid either to chiefs or to the victim, sometimes with objects of cultural significance such as a finely woven mat (two different grades are specified) or a pig.

This overview of "crimes" is instructive. It demonstrates the centrality of relationships, both with regard to sexual offences, where the relationship between the victim and perpetrator is critical, and also relationships with the natural environment and with cultural heritage. Justice is achieved primarily through the payment of compensation to victims, directly addressing their fractured relationship, rather than through imprisonment. It is therefore restorative in orientation, although in certain places it has punitive inflections and corporal punishment is used. The state criminal legislation presents a far more typically Western set of crimes that does not include damage to the natural environment per se or adultery, and in which sentences are predominantly in the form of fines paid to the state or imprisonment, supplemented by orders for supervision and community work. The influence of Christianity is quite clear in regard to community proscribed crimes such as adultery and others concerned with the sanctity of marriage, although customary marriage is also an important institution. The by-laws also show interesting penetrations of the state justice system into local conceptions of justice, such as in the provisions for child maintenance. It is notable that clear limits are envisaged on the jurisdiction of local authority: murder goes to the state; the rest can be dealt with locally. Again, such a vision is at odds with official policy, whereby the state has jurisdiction over all crimes, although it may accurately reflect actual practice. Finally, gender is central to most of the ways in which crimes are conceptualized, often forming an element of the crime itself and sometimes also of the sentence. The by-laws enable the local authority to assert regulation over women through specifying what they may wear and where they may be, justified through the upholding of custom.

Many of the tensions and debates around non-justice systems in Vanuatu, and indeed in the Pacific more broadly, can be seen from this brief overview of just one of the countless numbers of local laws throughout the country. The first is the treatment of women by non-state justice systems. There has been a long and determined push by many activists within Vanuatu to address the high rates of gender-based violence in Vanuatu (Vanuatu National Statistics Office, 2009) through identifying problematic customary practices such as bride price and the normalization of violence against women. Concerns over physical and sexual violence against women and girls has manifested in a focus on the state criminal justice system and the adoption of the criminalization agenda developed over the past two decades in the global North (United Nations Women, 2016). There have been extensive legislative reforms, including the passage of family violence protection laws, and the imposition of increasingly lengthy terms of imprisonment (Jowitt, 2015). While important work has been done in the state justice space, looking forward it is vital that public Pacific criminology opens up more creatively to engagement with customary and Christian institutions. For reasons of geographical and cultural contiguity, they provide the overwhelming majority of justice services and security provision to women throughout the country, and this is unlikely to change in the near to medium future.

The second theme is the relationship of non-state justice systems with international human rights norms and the human rights principles in the state Constitution (Merry, 2006; New Zealand Law Commission, 2006). This theme arises in relation to provisions relating to equality of treatment between men and women, but also in relation to a wide variety of other issues, such as the exercise of the freedom of religion and freedom of movement. One example concerning the freedom of movement comes from persistent attempts by customary councils established within urban areas to regulate their ethnic communities through "sending back" transgressors of hybridized urban custom to their originating island. This example identifies the fluid and dynamic way in which custom adapts to new forms of social organization (such as urban squatter settlements), creating new conceptions of wrongdoing and new forms of sanction and assertions of authority as needed. Rather than conceptualizing the tensions between human rights norms and customary norms as zero-sum games, it is more helpful for public Pacific criminology to start with a realization of the transformative possibilities that emerge from recognizing change, tensions, and contestations within and between these different socio-legal orders. A focus on the actual practices of key actors involved in both state and customary justice provision as they navigate the everyday tensions between the different systems, in addition to the more usual focus on institutional structures and norms, will be of great value.

The third theme is the instrumental interpretation and use of custom and culture by male leaders to entrench their authority in an oppressive and patriarchal manner. While this has been noted by a series of scholars primarily in relation to land law (McDonnell, 2016), and the payment of bride-price (Jolly, 1992), it is also highly relevant for criminology more broadly. It demonstrates the critical importance of scholars and practitioners in drilling below amorphous categories such as "communities" and claims to represent "custom" in order to interrogate power dynamics at a range of different scales. In so doing, it is critical to pay particular attention to generational, ethnic, class, religious and gendered divides.

A Public Pacific Criminology?

We start this section by acknowledging that we are wary of the proliferation of new and regional criminologies, such as Southern criminology and Asian criminology, and are conscious of a number of problems with the notion of introducing a new public Pacific criminology. In particular, we reject any notion to present the region as exceptional, or one that cannot engage with and learn from decades of established criminological knowledge and theories from the global North. At the same time, however, the discourses and excitement surrounding the new criminologies play an important role in highlighting the need for criminology as a discipline to be more open to innovations and knowledge from all places, including the Pacific, that have to date been largely excluded from the core of criminological scholarship and praxis. It is critical also to note that we do not see our tentative embrace of public Pacific criminology as requiring any new wholesale commitment to the discipline, such as the establishment of new departments in universities already stretched to their limits. Rather, we see it as a way to extend and cross-fertilize existing intellectual traditions from a range of disciplines around the cross-cutting themes of crime, security, justice, violence, restoration and punishment. This approach is more likely to drive the type of "cross-category, theory-driven innovation" that Braithwaite (2005, p. 347) posits will open "new horizons of social theory."

If a public Pacific criminology does take shape, it should contain the following characteristics. First, it must be an interdisciplinary and transdisciplinary endeavor genuinely committed to involving scholars from backgrounds such as law, anthropology, psychology, social work, sociology, development studies and peacebuilding, as well as those who work within state and non-state criminal justice and security provision institutions. Critically, it must also involve the victims and survivors of crime and violence. We see public Pacific criminology as grounded in local research partnerships between academics, police officers, village leaders, the private sector, and local civil society organizations, who collaboratively design and undertake research on priorities identified by those impacted by crime and violence.[6] This will naturally have profound methodological and theoretical consequences that are likely to have relevance and application far beyond the region itself. For now, these types of developments are just starting to crystallize: the RPNGC has recently established a research and development unit and the Department of Justice and Attorney General is looking to set up PNG's first ever crime and justice research unit.

Second, a public Pacific criminology should have a strong ethical foundation, and it is in this regard that the "public" dimension becomes apparent. Our experience has overwhelmingly been that research subjects share their stories *in order to* inform policy-making in the hope and expectation that this will lead to improvements in their lives and those of their children. This places significant responsibility on criminologists to ensure the data collected is presented in ways that can meaningfully contribute to national and local debates on policy. This obliges researchers to go beyond writing reports and policy briefings, to actually engaging in communicating empirical and normative insights through creative arts, social media, radio, and other generally accessible modes of communication. Furthermore, in order to be useful in the Pacific context, criminology must be less captured by professional criminology expectations and instead be more public in a very broad Pacific understanding of that term, by including tribes, clans, and local churches, as well as civil society.

Third, a public Pacific criminology must be founded on an awareness of plurality and recognition of variations in the configurations of different actors in security and justice landscapes across time and space. In such a dynamic and fluid context, it is not surprising that the singular focus on one institutional form that has characterized donor and government efforts to date has met with such limited success. If we start with the plural and networked reality of security and justice governance in the region, a more promising approach emerges, one that involves understanding the strengths and weaknesses of different forms and approaches in particular settings, enabling efforts to be concentrated on building the former while minimizing the latter.

In conclusion, our somewhat muted yet well-founded call for a public Pacific criminology is oriented toward highlighting a worthwhile direction for future scholarship and praxis. There is a need for greater support for Pacific Islands research institutions and practitioners to engage in criminological research, and to develop new methodological and theoretical tools to enable more sustained and relevant solutions to the provision of justice and security for the region. The beneficiaries will not just be the Pacific region but the discipline writ large, as the region is exceptionally rich in innovative thinking and traditions that have much to offer criminology.

Acknowledgments

The authors would like to thank Professor John Braithwaite for his insightful comments and suggestions to improve this chapter.

Notes

1 Except for the Francophone countries that remain colonized; West Papua, which remains colonized (see Hernawan, Chapter 18, this volume); and Tonga, which was never colonized.
2 The development challenges associated with PNG's resource economy, including issues of conflict and violence, are well covered in the *2014 National Human Development Report—Papua New Guinea*, UNDP.
3 Fieldwork was carried out over 15 months in 2009–2010 at Morobe Block in the capital of Port Moresby.
4 The village courts in PNG are the only officially recognized local level dispute resolution entity. There are 27 village courts throughout Port Moresby. Village courts are mandated to hear cases regarding disputes within communities. There is an overlap between the work of the village court and *komiti*. For example, a *komiti* can convene a hearing and follow the same procedures as a village court sitting; however, any orders or decisions made are not recognized officially like those of a village court. *Komiti* decisions and meetings work only if there is a level of trust in the work of the *komiti* to solve disputes. In some instances, where cases are being heard, village court officials are invited to participate as observers at a mediation conducted by *komiti*.
5 These by-laws were gathered by a colleague anthropologist on a fieldtrip to the island several years ago and shared with the author. The author has a large collection of similar by-laws either gathered personally or shared by colleagues. The writing of by-laws was the subject of an international conference in 2018, the proceedings of which are available here: http://regnet.anu.edu.au/news-events/events/7159/codification-and-creation-community-customary-laws-south-pacific-and-beyond?tb=general_information#tab.
6 The burgeoning literature on inclusive and participative Pacific research methodologies is highly relevant here (e.g., Baba, Mahina, Williams, & Nabobo-Baba, 2004; Vaioleti, 2006).

References

Abrahamsen, R., & Williams, M. C. (2011). *Security beyond the state. Private security in international politics*. Cambridge: Cambridge University Press.
Allen, M., & Monson, R. (2014). Land and conflict in Papua New Guinea: The role of land mediation. *Security Challenges*, 10(2), 1–14.
Baba, T., Mahina, O., Williams, N., & Nabobo-Baba, U. (Eds.). (2004). *Researching the Pacific and indigenous peoples*. Auckland: University of Auckland.
Baker, B. (2008). *Multi-choice policing in Africa*. Uppsala: Nordiska Afrikainstituter.
Bal, C. (2015). Kumo Koimbo: Accounts and responses to witchcraft in Gor, Simbu Province. In M. Forsyth & R. Eves (Eds.), *Talking it through: Responses to sorcery and witchcraft beliefs and practices in Melanesia* (pp. 299–307). Canberra: ANU Press.
Braithwaite, J. (2005). For public social science. *British Journal of Sociology*, 56(3), 345–353.
Braithwaite, J. (2013). One retrospective of Pacific criminology. *Australia & New Zealand Journal of Criminology*, 46(1), 3–11.
Burawoy, M. (2005). For public sociology. *British Journal of Sociology*, 56(2), 259–294.
Carrington, K., Hogg, R., & Sozzo, M. (2016). Southern criminology. *British Journal of Criminology*, 56(1), 1–20.
Clifford, W., Morauta, L., & Stuart, B. (1984). *Law and order in Papua New Guinea* (Clifford Report). Port Moresby: Institute of National Affairs and Institute of Applied Social and Economic Research.
Cohen, S. (1982). Western crime control models in the third world: Benign or malignant? In S. Spitzer & R. Simon (Eds.), *Research in law, deviance and social control* (Vol. 4, pp. 85–119). Greenwich: JAI Press.
Craig, D., & Porter, D. (2018). *Safety and security at the edges of the state: Local regulation in Papua New Guinea's urban settlements*. Washington, DC: World Bank.
Dinnen, S. (1995). Praise the Lord and pass the ammunition—Criminal group surrender in Papua New Guinea. *Oceania*, 66(2), 103–118.
Dinnen, S. (2001). *Law and order in a weak state: Crime and politics in Papua New Guinea*. Honolulu: University of Hawai'i Press.

Dinnen, S., & Braithwaite, J. (2009). Reinventing policing through the prism of the colonial kiap. *Policing & Society, 19*(2), 161–173.

Dinnen, S., May, R., & Regan, A. J. (Eds.). (1997). *Challenging the state: The sandline affair in Papua New Guinea*. Canberra, ACT: National Centre for Development Studies, Research School of Pacific Studies, The Australian National University.

Dinnen, S., & Mcleod, A. (2009). Policing Melanesia: International expectations and local realities. *Policing & Society, 19*(4), 333–353.

Dinnen, S., & Peake, G. (2013). More than just policing: Police reform in post-conflict Bougainville. *International Peacekeeping, 20*(5), 570–584.

Evans, D., Goddard, M., & Patterson, D. (2010). The hybrid courts of Melanesia: A comparative analysis of village courts of Papua New Guinea, island courts of Vanuatu, and local courts of Solomon Islands. Justice and development working paper series, no. 13. Washington, DC: World Bank.

Fitzmaurice, R. (2017, August 17). The 10 least liveable cities in the world in 2017. *Business Insider*. Retrieved from www.businessinsider.com/the-worst-places-to-live-in-the-world-2017-8/?r=AU&IR=T/#10-kiev-ukraine-478100-points-kiev-is-the-only-european-city-in-the-12-that-scored-below-50-points-in-terms-of-liveability-1.

Forsyth, M. (2009). *A bird that flies with two wings: Kastom and state justice systems in Vanuatu*. Canberra: ANU Press.

Forsyth, M., & Eves, R. (Eds.). (2015). *Talking it through: Responses to sorcery and witchcraft beliefs and practices in Melanesia*. Canberra: ANU Press.

Freeman, J. (2003). Extending public law norms through privatization. *Harvard Law Review, 116*(5), 1285–1352.

Goddard, M. (1995). The rascal road: Crime, prestige, and development in Papua New Guinea. *The Contemporary Pacific, 7*(1), 55–80.

Government of Papua New Guinea. (2013). *National security policy*. Retrieved from www.aspistrategist.org.au/wp-content/uploads/2014/08/2013-PNG-National-Security-Policy.pdf.

Guthrie, G. (2013). Social factors affecting violent crime victimization in urban households. *Contemporary PNG Studies: DWU Research Journal, 18*, 35–54.

Hukula, F. (2013). Blok Laif: An ethnography of a Mosbi settlement. Unpublished Thesis, University of St Andrews.

Human Rights Watch. (2011). *Gold's costly dividend: Human rights impacts of Papua New Guinea's Porgera Gold Mine*. Retrieved from: www.hrw.org/report/2011/02/01/golds-costly-dividend/human-rights-impacts-papua-new-guineas-porgera-gold-mine.

Human Rights Watch. (2015). *Bashed-up: Family violence in PNG*. Retrieved from www.hrw.org/report/2015/11/04/bashed/family-violence-papua-new-guinea.

Institute of National Affairs and Asia Development Bank. (2012). *The challenges of doing business in Papua New Guinea*. Retrieved from www.adb.org/publications/challenges-doing-business-papua-new-guinea-2014.

Isari, P. K. (2017). *Information paper on the security industry in PNG*. Port Moresby: Security Industries Authority. Unpublished paper (mimeo) provided to one of the authors (Dinnen).

Johnson, C., Dean, B., & Butler, M. (Producer and Director). (2015). *Tanna* [Motion Picture]. Australia: Lightyear Entertainment.

Jolly, M. (1992). Specters of inauthenticity. *Contemporary Pacific, 4*(1), 49–72.

Jowitt, A. (2015). Sentencing for sexual offences: A comment on Wenu V Public Prosecutor [2015] VUCA 51. *Journal of South Pacific Law, 2015*(2). Retrieved from https://home.heinonline.org/titles/Law-Journal-Library/Journal-of-South-Pacific-Law/Vol_2015/.

Kyed, H. M. (2011). Introduction to the special issue: Legal pluralism and international development interventions. *Journal of Legal Pluralism, 43*(63), 1–23.

Lakhani, S., & Wilman, A. M. (2014). *Gates, hired guns and mistrust: Business as unusual*. Washington, DC: World Bank.

Loader, I., & Sparks, R. (2011). *Public criminology?* Abingdon: Routledge.

Loader, I., & Walker, N. (2007). *Civilizing security*. Cambridge: Cambridge University Press.

McDonnell, S. (2016). *My land my life: Property, power and identity in land transformations in Vanuatu* (unpublished doctoral dissertation). Canberra: Australia National University.

McLaughlin, E., & Chancer, L. (2007). Public criminologies: Diverse perspectives on academia and policy. *Theoretical Criminology, 11*(2), 155–173.

Merry, S. E. (2006). *Human rights and gender violence: Translating international law into local justice*. Chicago, IL: The University of Chicago Press.

New Zealand Law Commission. (2006). *Converging currents: Custom and human rights in the Pacific*. Wellington: Author.

Porter, D., Craig, D., & Hukula, F. (2016). *Come and see the system in place: Mediation capabilities in Papua New Guinea's urban settlements.* Washington, DC: World Bank.

Pupu, N., & Wiessner, P. (2018). *The challenges of village courts and operation Mekim Save among the Enga of Papua New Guinea today: A view from the inside.* Department of Pacific Affairs, Discussion Paper 2018/1. 1–19. Canberra: Australian National University.

Security Industries Authority (SIA). (2013). *Current status of the security business in PNG.* Retrieved from www.sia.gov.pg/seccomps.html.

Sharkey, P. (2018). *Uneasy peace: The great crime decline, the renewal of city life, and the next war on violence.* New York: W.W. Norton & Company, Inc.

United Nations Women. (2016). *Women and children's access to the formal justice system in Vanuatu.* New York: UN Women.

Vaioleti, T. M. (2006). Talanoa research methodology: A developing position on Pacific research. *Waikato Journal of Education, 12,* 21–34.

Vanuatu National Statistics Office. (2009). *Vanuatu national survey on women's lives and family relationships.* Vanuatu: Author.

Whayman, J. (2015, June 5). A public-private partnership tackling law and order in PNG. [web log comment]. Retrieved from www.devpolicy.org/a-public-private-partnership-tackling-law-and-order-in-png-20150605/.

15

THE CHALLENGES OF ACADEMICS ENGAGING IN ENVIRONMENTAL JUSTICE ACTIVISM

Joshua Ozymy and Melissa Jarrell

Public criminologists typically express a strong desire to apply their skills and knowledge towards social justice activism (Belknap, 2015). This activism can be in the form of research that has a public voice and speaks to issues of injustice theoretically or empirically (Kramer, 2014, 2016; Petrossian, 2015; Stretesky & Lynch, 1999). Such activism can also use academic research to draw on the researcher's own experiences to illuminate a particular issue of social injustice in their local community and draw it into the broader literature in criminology (Jarrell, 2009; Jarrell, Ozymy, & McGurrin, 2012). Simply put, public criminologists have an excellent opportunity to create a synergy between their own moral and social causes and the research they undertake.

Yet, academic environments with risk-averse administrators trying to please boards, legislators, community members, and donors (many of whom are not sympathetic to the free exchange of sensitive ideas or grassroots political organization) are oftentimes not the best environments to engage people in direct action on behalf of social injustices in their own community. Public criminologists, as with any academics speaking to or engaging political issues, can risk censure or punishment at work, but often persist in their actions on behalf of just causes. If public criminologists derive their research from their activism or generate social justice-oriented research independent of their own activist experiences, they can in both cases illuminate public causes. In doing so, they keep with the spirit of creating and nurturing a public criminology.

One area of public criminology that intersects with economics, political science, sociology, environmental science, and many other fields is environmental justice (EJ), or the study of the prevalence and causes of the undue environmental harm faced by low-income, communities of color in the United States and abroad. Arguably the primary goal of this movement is to remove people from harm. Emerging from over a decade of work in this area, both creating research and engaging in direct, grassroots action to rid our community of environmental injustices, we are now in a position to pose questions in this article that were almost impossible to consider years ago and never seemed to warrant serious deliberation at the outset: What if you get what you want? What happens if your direct actions actually lead to the best outcome in your area in that people actually get "bought out" and get to move away from the industrial facilities that are slowly killing them?

Our goal in this chapter is to reflect back on these questions and turn an eye towards the difficulties and challenges of exerting a significant amount of time doing environmental justice work and actually getting what you want. We wish to focus in on the difficulties of doing EJ work and the sometimes-conditional victories one achieves even when you are more successful than you imagined at the outset. Our hope is to provide honest examples for other academics and public criminologists wishing to engage in EJ work with an eye towards the practical realities involved. The article is arranged on the theme of collaborating with different groups in this process. We start with a brief introduction to our local community and discuss our work with other activists, public officials, and victims of environmental crime.

Background

Corpus Christi is a city of approximately 300,000 on the Texas Gulf Coast. Hemmed in by six refineries, related chemical manufactures, natural gas processors, and one of the country's largest petrochemical ports, the city fans out from the shipping channel along Corpus Christi Bay. Three fenceline communities are located extremely close to heavy industry: Oak Park, Hillcrest, and Dona Park. In the 1990s, activists formed People Against Contaminated Environments (PACE) to address EJ issues in their community. Building on a longer tradition of civil rights groups formed in the area, such as the American GI Forum and the League of United Latin American Citizens (LULAC), PACE worked with LULAC, the Sierra Club and other groups to orchestrate a significant buyout of Oak Park. This left residents of Hillcrest and Dona Park to continue to face undue environmental burdens from being located too close to heavy industry. Like many EJ communities, all of these areas pre-dated the expansion of the refineries and chemical corridor. Hillcrest used to be the first country club area of the city prior to White flight in the mid-20th century and Dona Park was a small, bedroom community located minutes from downtown Corpus Christi.

Research shows that minority groups face a disproportionate share of environmental burdens from hazardous waste sites, industrial facilities, and chemical pollution (Bullard, 1983; Mohai & Bryant, 1992; United Church of Christ, 1987). Arguably the ultimate goal of environmental justice activists and academics engaging in this area of research would be to move people away from harm or buy them out. Although not an EJ community, the classic U.S. case would be the work of activist Lois Gibbs and the buyout associated with Love Canal in upstate New York. This case brought national attention to the danger of siting neighborhood chemical waste dumps (as was the case in Love Canal) or near industrial sources of pollution. Public attention focused on the Love Canal disaster resulted in the passage of the Comprehensive Environmental Response, Compensation and Liability Act (CERCLA), better known as the Superfund Act.

In the time between Love Canal and the passage of the Superfund, other academics and activists started to pose another related set of questions related to living near industrial sources of pollution: Where are these sources located in the United States? Who bears the greatest burden? What can be done about these injustices?

Early work by Bob Bullard comes to mind here as one of the intellectual forbearers of the academic movement to study environmental justice both theoretically and empirically (Bullard, 1983, 1990, 1994). Outside of his academic work, Dr. Bullard is well-known for his activism on behalf of ending the disproportionate environmental harm faced by certain groups in society. Admittedly Bullard is somewhat of an intellectual hero and example for the authors. His work has both academic and practical implications that have resulted in positive changes, both to the academy and society, traits that fulfill the wider promise of public criminology. This example is what inspired us, the authors,[1] to get involved in EJ work in our own community. In the next section, we discuss our involvement with different groups in this process, including activists, public officials, and environmental crime victims, leading to a final discussion of how these actions culminated in buyouts.

Working with Activists

Our initial work started by becoming part of Citizens for Environmental Justice (CFEJ). Working with other activists locally via CFEJ helped to provide a venue for meeting and collaborating. At first it could be quite enthralling as we wanted to get attention. We got students involved on campus, started staging protests of the refineries, put on a community theatre production highlighting these problems in our community, made friends with reporters and got on the local news, were featured in the local paper, *The Caller Times*, started a blog, debated angry conservatives and industry sympathizers on talk radio, and even went on public access television. At the time, the latter was mortifying for many reasons, but particularly because the shirts we purchased for the event misspelled our name Citizens for Environmental "Jusice" and we had to cover up the missing "t" on air.

All of these actions started to get attention and then we were able to work with other groups that became interested in our work and were helpful in gathering scientific data to further study the severity of the air and water pollution problems at the refineries. Dr. Neil Carman was an excellent advocate who worked for the Lone Star Chapter of the Sierra Club. He was very good at understanding technical regulations surrounding air permits and had been involved in the PACE buyout decades earlier. Through him and others we learned the value of collecting our own data and using it to draw attention to our cause. Eric Schaeffer and the Environmental Integrity Project (EIP) were also extremely helpful in working to illuminate the problems of air monitoring and aggregating state data on air pollution in Texas. We were able to team up with Denny Larson of Global Community Monitor to help start a Bucket Brigade program to help us measure air pollution ourselves. We even had an opportunity to measure air quality in real time with a Cerex Hound Multi-gas Analyzer (a very expensive mobile air monitoring system).

Working in the community helped us to become a point for environmental activism locally and to connect to other actors in the state. Keeping up media attention kept these issues alive locally and helped us locate ourselves within the greater narratives national environmental groups were trying to pursue across the country. All of these connections started to coalesce in 2008, when a group of concerned citizens created the Clean Economy Coalition, and in February 2009 hundreds marched along the Bayfront protesting the $3 billion petroleum coke processing plant being proposed for the area titled the Las Brisas Energy Center (LBEC). At the time, Texas was proposing an expansion of coal-fired power plants and both Public Citizen and Sierra Club as part of their Beyond Coal campaign came to Corpus Christi and helped activists access the media and government, gain publicity, and ultimately hold up its air permit in court. By 2013, the plant was cancelled after a long political fight. This was an extremely rare instance in Texas. Arguably, many of the refineries, while they would have benefitted from the facility, did not come out in force supporting it. Perhaps it had something to do with its real potential to put Corpus Christi in non-attainment status under the Clean Air Act (CAA), which would have required a series of pollution control measures on the area, such as stricter permitting, reformulated gasoline, emissions offsetting, and potential loss of highway funding (U.S. Chamber of Commerce, 2010).

Our experience of working with other environmental groups was decidedly positive. The difficulties involve trying to tie your issue into what state or national-level groups are doing. When the two collide then your work can have real benefit to the community if other groups are willing to render aid. The best way to contextualize our role in linking local to national issues is simply to do your best to make your issue salient and make relationships with other people within your policy network. Since our issue was EJ and the problems of people living near heavy industry, we made sure to connect to local reporters, sympathetic writers at the *Texas Tribune* and the *Texas Observer*, other activists working for national environmental groups located in our state, such as the Lone Star Chapter of the Sierra Club, Public Citizen and the Environmental Integrity Project, and to make contacts in government at the state and federal level in the EPA and Department of Justice. In this vein you can become a source of information for reporters working on environmental or human rights pieces or become enmeshed in broader policy programs of environmental groups if the pieces fit. Ultimately, in either case you are working to bring salience to your issue within these spheres.

A good example of this working well, as we discuss below, is when Public Citizen and others were promoting a nationwide anti-coal campaign, Texas became front and center when the state wanted to issue a handful of permits to new coal-fired power plants. When the Las Brisas petroleum coke processing plant was seeking an air permit, our relationships help to center local, state, and national attention on the issue, and it became a focusing event for the anti-coal campaign waged by national environmental groups. We worked with them on the ground to organize local opposition and it was their organizational, human, and financial resources that helped stall the plant's permit out in court so that it was never built. This was a big win for everyone in Corpus Christi in health terms and was made possible by keeping our issues salient and when the opportunity arrived, linking it to what larger, better-funded groups were doing and helping to make it a flashpoint for them. We did the same with the *U.S. v. Citgo* case[2] when we worked with state and local officials during the investigation, prosecution, and sentencing phase of the trial. During the case we helped the government gather information, find witnesses, mobilized local constituencies to get involved, spoke with various media outlets, and generally helped bring attention to the case. Later we assisted in sentencing with helping to identify and mobilize victims to appear in court to read victim impact statements.

Our own university was somewhat less sympathetic. Maybe it is the CITGO observatory on campus or the scholarship donations, but early on one of us was taken aside by our Dean and told that in private they support us, but in public to stop protesting the refineries. Our next Dean was a bit more sympathetic, finding a few hundred dollars to help when Lois Gibbs agreed to speak at our university. We were fortunate enough to meet her in our comings and goings while attending the 30th anniversary of Love Canal in Upstate New York as well. We can only hope with the expansion of the Port due to the boom in natural gas fracking, and new related facilities, our own university will not become even more sympathetic to these industries, given their political and economic power in the community.

It bears mentioning that we benefitted from involvement with other academics outside our university quite a bit. Dr. K. C. Donnelly from Texas A&M University helped us fund and implement a bio-monitoring study in the community, which was very helpful in shedding light on blood benzene levels in residents. Kelly Haragan, the Director of the Environmental Law Clinic at The University of Texas at Austin, worked tirelessly on challenging a variety of air permits and engaging in much technical, legal maneuvering over the years to help residents. The former head of the Environmental Protection Agency's (EPA) Region 6 office, Dr. Al Armendariz (also a former professor at SMU), was a very helpful presence in our community. Dr. Neil Carman was an ex-academic who early on transferred his skills to a career in environmental activism and was always an excellent friend and colleague. In the next section, we turn to our experiences with public officials to show how our local work was able to get caught up in a larger legal case with national implications that helped us to foster direct change in the community.

Working with Public Officials

Being professors at the local university gave us social legitimacy when working with different groups, but we came to realize that trying to access government involves a lot of technical details, legal jargon, and knowledge and funds that national-level groups possess and we did not. Without them we could not have taken the next step, which was to foster change in the policy process. Over time we came to learn the real-world language of environmental regulation and enforcement, which means understanding how language is used by scientists, lawyers, and bureaucrats to often exclude people from the conversation. We realized, however, that having a Ph.D., a policy and statistical background, and generally higher social status as a professor offers social access to these arenas in a way low-income, communities of color could never have initially. In both cases, you have to earn a place at the table, but it became rather obvious we could expedite this process and in a way this gave us value as a link between the community and those that sought to change it or simply do nothing. We continued this role as a conduit, working between these groups throughout our tenure in these policy circles and still feel it is a solid place for a well-intentioned academic to place themselves.

Our work with public officials began to coalesce with the criminal investigation of CITGO Petroleum by the EPA, Department of Justice (DOJ), and other federal and state agencies. CITGO owns two of the six refineries in the area along with Valero and Flint Hills Resources. The case started as the Texas Commission on Environmental Quality (TCEQ) sent an investigator to the site and she felt ill afterwards. Migratory birds were also dying near two oil-water separator tanks. The tanks were kept open, but were found to illegally contain benzene, a dangerous volatile organic compound that was likely released into the atmosphere in large amounts over time. While the refinery had been fined for a variety of offenses over the years, which is not uncommon for a large industrial facility, the DOJ brought criminal charges against the company. This culminated in the 2007 federal court case *U.S. vs. CITGO*; at that time, it was the first criminal case involving an oil refinery and the Clean Air Act (CAA).

We were fortunate to be able to attend the court proceedings, hear from witnesses, take copious notes, and follow the entire case in the courtroom and the media. We used our contacts to help the prosecution get in touch with and to organize residents living near the facility. We found out that what you don't see in regulatory data collected by the federal government is that most cases against large corporations are civil fines or consent decrees agreed to by both parties, rather than criminal cases. It is very expensive, technical, and time consuming to charge a large company with criminal charges and hard to make them stick. CITGO was charged under the CAA, as well as the federal Migratory Bird Treaty Act. For these cases to be successful, you need a federal prosecutor to agree to bring charges either from the U.S. Attorneys or the DOJ's Environmental Crimes Section (ECS). Those prosecutors then work with state regulators, in this case the Texas Commission on Environmental Quality, EPA, TCEQ, Texas Parks and Wildlife, U.S. Fish and Wildlife, and the Federal Bureau of Investigation (FBI). For these multi-year cases to be successful a coalition of public officials needs to form to make it successful. We feel that given the costs of these prosecutions, there is a good likelihood they only come after years of state-level penalties, warnings, and other measures that finally leads to a criminal prosecution.

As one of the only point groups, CFEJ was allowed to act as a conduit to help make sure certain residents were involved in the process. This ensured that public hearings had to occur, typically in Hillcrest at the Oveal Williams Senior Center, and that residents could testify in court. This provided a good forum for residents to air grievances and be heard and it also helped to keep them coalesced around the issue: If CITGO was poisoning them and was at fault, should the company be required to buy them out? This question helped mobilize residents.

During this process we realized how hard many public officials work on behalf of fenceline communities. Ultimately, regulatory agencies are not usually in the business of buying people out, but of reducing harm through deterrence-based measures, such as civil penalties or criminal sanctions or through the negotiated or mandated adoption of pollution-reducing technologies. Given the difficulties of oversight and prosecution of facilities, federal regulatory agencies often focus on getting companies, through law or through enforcement actions, to adopt better technology to ensure compliance. We learned that on-the-ground monitoring of industrial facilities is difficult, often lax, and mostly left to state agencies. At the time of the CITGO case there was only one enforcement agent for the TCEQ in the area and the EPA criminal investigator was housed in Houston.

We found it interesting that if a person is stealing a car, robbing a gas station, breaking into your house, or just playing loud music, you can call 911 and generally get a pretty quick response; however, if residents of a fenceline community are passing out from noxious fumes, a refinery stack is flaring bright into the night, or other environmental harms are taking place, there was one person to call and there was not much they could do. Most complaints were left on voicemail and if you were lucky, you might get a call back several days later. An actual real time response was only guaranteed if something were to blow up. To put things into perspective, real-time monitoring and response to industrialized environmental crimes is almost non-existent and measurements for the level of pollution are arguably greatly underestimated. At the local, state, and federal level there is no environmental enforcement apparatus to protect residents in real time. We found this situation quite troubling and residents let us know time and again this is the kind of life you lived in Dona Park or Hillcrest; you came to expect it. We came to have great admiration for the lead DOJ prosecutor Howard Stewart, whose tenacity and political wrangling kept the case alive to sentencing for seven long years. Local and state officials, while some were hard working and conscientious, often played a negligible role in this fight on a daily basis. It was only the federal presence that gave the case the media attention, resources, and organization to persist.

Working with Environmental Crime Victims

The CITGO case took an astonishing seven years to reach sentencing. What made the case unique was not the criminal trial, but the outcome during sentencing. Working with other attorneys with victim expertise, we worked to organize victims and helped them to file motions that they be considered victims of CITGO's crimes under the federal Crime Victims Rights Act (CVRA). This was a unique legal strategy put forward by former federal court judge Paul Cassel, who represented some of the victims in the motion (after we convinced him to help us with this case). In a surprising twist, the judge, while not awarding any compensation, granted them victim status under the CVRA. This was the first case of its kind to recognize victims in a fenceline community as victims of an environmental crime. Our role was to help identify crime victims, assist them in getting legal recognition, and act as an on-the-ground resource for their legal team to allow them to file the appropriate motions on their behalf. These are things that could have been done without us, but our knowledge of the local community, situation, and trust we possessed therein facilitated a much speedier process. What was interesting to us in this particular case was that Cassel was actually a conservative federal court judge. Like the Victims Rights Movement in the U.S. in general, our relationship paired a legal team that likely had diametrically opposed views on many issues to center on the idea that EJ communities can be victims of environmental crime and should have certain protections under a law, which probably did not come with that original intent when passed by Congress.

We feel that everyone who lives next to or near heavy industry is a victim of environmental crime, but it is rarely the case that the courts acknowledge this fact. With CITGO, we helped organize potential victims for the Cassel legal team since they did not live in Corpus Christi. A select group was able to testify in court about what it is like to live near heavy industry and the pain and suffering they endured in terms of the respiratory illnesses and high cancer rates in their families. Spending time in Dona Park or Hillcrest even for an hour or two will help to validate these concerns. You can see heavy industry from their homes, refinery stacks blazing at night, air pollution being released constantly, and your eyes and throat will burn. On multiple occasions, residents would record pollutants saturating their cars and anything left outside in their yards. On at least a few occasions residents showed us vouchers they were given by industry for free car washes. More troubling was when residents would show us an oily substance oozing from trees. Looking over state groundwater maps where thousands of geo-probes are sunk in the ground demonstrate the extremely high level of groundwater contamination in the area as well. These victim impact statements are quite interesting to read and are available on the public record.

Our work with victims in many respects came full circle when, in the course of contesting air permits, Kelly Harrigan was able to secure over $2 million in funding to help orchestrate a buyout of individuals in Dona Park. The resulting discussions resulted in the creation of the Environmental Justice Housing Fund (EJHF) and a landmark opportunity for academic activists to actually spend a large sum of money with the goal of action causing direct change: buying people out. This example is so rare there was little for us to draw upon.

EJHF was incorporated as a non-profit with a governing board deciding rules on the buyout. We focused on contacting residents, getting lists together for how long they had lived in the neighborhood, verifying information, and deciding how we would orchestrate the buyout. We held a community meeting that was well-attended. Unfortunately, it broke down into a melee of yelling and misunderstanding. Many residents felt we were working for the government and they should get to decide how the funds were spent. This, of course, would have been a colossal mistake and conflict of interest. Some residents shouted Kelly and the other board members down, as well as us, and it was overall an awful experience. It can be challenging to help victims of environmental crime when they are suspicious of your intentions. It is hard for some people to believe that we wanted to help and did not have any ulterior motives. We did form a community committee to help verify facts and suggest plans for a buyout.

We had gained trust with many in the local community from our years of attending community meetings, going to their homes, working on the CITGO case, working the Las Brisas fight, and other events. This gave us credibility more generally and trust more specifically for those we knew in greater depth. What we learned from the EJHF buyout is these elements only mattered to a minor degree when it came to money. Once money was involved it changed the dynamic. While we were helping and doing so at great personal time cost without pay, we were going to be in a position, as an organization and the board running the organization, to become landlords and buy real property. Once this occurred the issues quickly revolved around who, when, and how much.

Homes here have no real market value, because most people do not want to pay much to live in a fenceline community. We set generous rates of what it would cost to buy a home of similar size in a better area of the community, along with sufficient moving costs and time to move. Ultimately, we tried to buyout residents that lived in Dona Park the longest and were able to purchase twenty properties in total. The real "fun" part was that many of the residents were still rude or suspicious of us, even those we knew for years. If there was some naivety about the generosity one expected or at least the graciousness offered for one's time (it is important to note all of this was done as a volunteer effort without pay), those hopes were quickly dashed when these became business transactions and EJHF became a property owner.

Once the properties were acquired and residents moved, we were left with a couple dozen properties. What do you do with twenty houses that you cannot sell to other people or industry on principle? What do you do when you would like to expand these purchases to create larger buffer zone? The answer to the former has been to bulldoze the houses and pay to keep up the lots. The problem here is that residents now use them to park cars, dump trash, or leave other items on the board's property. In a strange twist there are twenty, mostly non-contiguous green spaces in the neighborhood.

To answer the latter question may involve collaboration with the city or companies to buy and bulldoze more properties to increase the buffer zone. The catch here is that if you knocked down many of the houses the neighborhood would start to look worse. It would take on an eerie quality you find when you drive through the Oak Park Triangle that was bought out and leveled in the 1990s. There are a few houses scattered around, but that area is mostly an open field now; for those that never knew of its existence, it is so close to the refineries that it really makes sense that it looks like a buffer zone.

Our work with victims in the CITGO case and in the EJHF buyout was incredibly rewarding, if not frustrating at times. The paradox of EJ in practice is that given the choice, even being offered generous funds to move, many people, knowing the health costs, still would choose not to do so for a variety of reasons. Some people essentially ask for what amounts to extortion payouts to move. Some people like the area or downplay the costs. Some people simply cannot imagine moving anywhere else, having lived on the fenceline for decades, if not their entire lives. You come to realize there are so many motivations and situations it is almost impossible to orchestrate a full-scale buyout of an area on a voluntary basis. We cannot help but feel that some of the activists that lived in and were involved in the long-term fight for Dona Park had their entire identities wrapped up in being activists, having little else to fall back on, so being bought out wasn't necessarily a good thing in the long run. Money may help you to move, but it does not necessarily buy community or identity. People may come to find it more intrinsically rewarding to suffer from living near heavy industry and fighting against those wrongs than actually winning and just being a resident of another anonymous neighborhood of which you have no standing or purpose related to that location. We did not feel that it was our job to discern these motivations or to pass value judgments on them, just to give people the choice to move as we were able. Even with all of the known harms of living near heavy industry our example is not unique; today people have even built homes near Love Canal and other sites close to industry.

Our hope for Corpus Christi is that buyouts continue in both Dona Park and Hillcrest. We would like to see all these people moved out of harm's way. Whether this will be possible remains unknown, but it is unlikely that all would move voluntarily even if they recognize the health costs and were given sufficient compensation to relocate. Thus is the nature of any human endeavor that you rarely get universal agreement on a course of action no matter the cost being borne by those involved. For our own stake in the matter, we feel our efforts have been well worth the cost and the intrinsic benefits numerous. We hope readers will find some value in this chapter when exploring options for doing similarly situated work in their own community. The important takeaway is that there are many actions you can take to help your community in this regard and they can do a lot of good. This experience taught us that given time and concentrated effort academics do not have to be unrealistic do-gooders but can use their skillsets and knowledge in practical ways for the betterment of others.

Conclusion

There were many victories over the years (i.e., organizing coalitions, garnering significant media attention, getting regulators to install better monitoring equipment, succeeding in challenging air permits, winning fights against the sitting of new toxic facilities, getting health-effects studies undertaken, making government pay attention and generally learning a lot about politics and government). Arguably, the three most impactful victories were our involvement in the *U.S. vs. Citgo*, the creation of EJHF, and the fight against the LBEC. In these cases, we were able to do our best work collaborating with other groups to have a direct impact in our community. We hope to have elaborated herein on how working with activists, public officials, and victims helped to produce fruitful results for the community, even if it was often challenging, intrinsically rewarding, and the results, while extremely positive, are also quite conditional.

We feel this work has fully embraced the spirit of public criminology in that it has a direct impact on social-justice oriented causes in our community. This work has come full circle as it has informed our research, as well as our research informing our activism (see the following for examples: Jarrell, 2009; Jarrell et al., 2012; Ozymy & Jarrell, 2012, 2015). As the Harbor Bridge buyout is ongoing, we see the expansion of the facilities near the Shipping Channel, such as: $15 billion Cheniere natural gas liquefaction plant expansion (Acosta, 2018), the $1 billion M&G plastics facility argued to potentially be the largest in the United States (Plastics.com, 2018), the $700 million Voestalpine facility that processes iron pellets into steel (Freeman, 2016), and the world's largest ethylene cracker plant being built by ExxonMobil at a cost of almost $10 billion (Ramirez, 2017). These events tell us the EJ fight in Corpus Christi is not only likely to get worse, but also different. Many of these new facilities are in Portland, Texas, right across the Bay, and are extremely close to a range of residents. The ExxonMobil facility in particular is being constructed with a few miles of a school and a solidly middle-class neighborhood. Further down the bay, residents of Ingleside and Ingleside on the Bay have contacted us multiple times to discuss fighting the expansion of these facilities.

These fights will be long and against very difficult odds, but have already expanded the fight beyond low-income, communities of color to the broader community. In these cases, our experience tells us that if well-organized local opposition coordinates with other state and national groups, tries to place themselves within the larger narrative of what they are fighting for, utilizes the legal and regulatory system, and gets lucky, they may be able to beat this back to a degree. The fact that it is still culturally and legally acceptable for heavy industry to expand or locate itself near any existing community is the larger and broader fight that must still be won.

Embracing social justice causes as a public criminologist can be very rewarding. Doing EJ work for over a decade, we have experienced the full range of what can happen when you get involved in grassroots activism and it would be hard to expect much better results. We participated in community organizing, mobilization, health studies, fought off a billion-dollar company, watched the legal process unfold for prosecuting a multi-national company with an endless budget, had fenceline victims recognized under the law, and even managed a buyout. This work greatly informed our research and understanding of the policy process, grassroots organization, politics, and the paradox of EJ itself.

Corpus Christi is unique in that it has three EJ communities and two (Oak Park and Dona Park) have now experienced buyouts (the latter was less complete because of funding limitations). Currently, the Harbor Bridge that crosses Corpus Christi Bay and connects Corpus Christi to Portland is set to displace many residents in the Hillcrest Neighborhood. As a result, the Port of Corpus Christi and the Texas Department of Transportation have orchestrated a buyout of the area to make way for the bridge (Port of Corpus Christi, 2016). While this is not a complete buyout, it shows that by different means and intents, all three fenceline communities experienced buyouts, which is quite rare. Many residents have already left and driving through Hillcrest today is strange, as homes of people we knew are now abandoned or torn down. The area has a temporary, transitional feeling, which is what Oak Park must have felt like before it mostly became a buffer zone. What is likely to occur is the density of the buyouts will inadvertently correspond to the closeness of the neighborhoods to the refineries: Oak Park, Hillcrest, and Dona Park. What has to be kept alive as the first two become fields with a smattering of older, mostly dilapidated houses here and there, is the collective memory of the area and why this happened in the first place. While we have no long-term plans to memorialize this fight outside of our academic writing, it would be a fruitful avenue for public criminologists to create a long-term, digital warehouse of these fights online. The archive of case studies by the University of Michigan (2004) was a great example but needs updating and would be a good example to institutionalize among public criminologists to develop a public archive and collective history for the world.

Notes

1 The chapter refers to the authors generically for purposes of exposition throughout in reference to our experience, instead of referring to the first or second author in particular instances.
2 *United States v. CITGO Petroleum Corp.*, No. 14–40,128 (5th Cir. 2015)

References

Acosta, T. (2018, August 30). Cheniere may ship LNG from port of Corpus Christi by end of 2018. *Corpus Christi Caller Times*. Retrieved from www.caller.com/story/news/local/2018/08/30/cheniere-may-ship-lng-port-corpus-christi-end-2018/1148913002/

Belknap, J. (2015). Activist criminology: Criminologists' responsibility to advocate for focial and legal justice. *Criminology*, 53(1), 1–22.

Bullard, R. D. (1983). Solid waste sites and the Houston Black community. *Sociological Inquiry*, 53(2-3), 273–284.

Bullard, R. D. (1990). *Dumping in dixie: Race, class, and environmental quality*. Boulder, CO: Westview Press.

Bullard, R. D. (1994). *Unequal protection: Environmental justice and communities of color*. San Francisco, CA: Sierra Club Books.

Freeman, S. (2016, May 5). Voestalpine Corpus Christi begins testing new plant. *Corpus Christi Business News*. Retrieved from www.ccbiznews.com/4734

Jarrell, M. L. (2009). Environmental crime and injustice: Media coverage of a landmark environmental crime case. *Southwest Journal of Criminal Justice*, 6(1), 25–44.

Jarrell, M. L., Ozymy, J., & McGurrin, D. (2012). How to encourage conflict in the environmental decision-making process: Imparting lessons from civic environmentalism to local policymakers. *Local Environment*, 18(2), 184–200.

Kramer, R. (2014). Climate change: A state-corporate crime perspective. In T. Spapens, R. White, & M. Kluin (Eds.), *Environmental crime and its victims: Perspectives within green criminology* (pp. 22–39). New York: Routledge.

Kramer, R. (2016). State crime, the prohetic voice and public criminology activism. *Critical Criminology*, 24(4), 519–532.

Mohai, P., & Bryant, B. (1992). Environmental racism: Reviewing the evidence. In B. Bryant & P. Mohai (Eds.), *Race and the incidence of environmental hazards: A time for discourse* (pp. 163–175). Boulder, CO: Westview Press.

Ozymy, J., & Jarrell, M. L. (2012). Upset events, policy drift, and the regulation of air emissions at industrial facilities in the United States. *Environmental Politics*, 21(3), 451–466.

Ozymy, J., & Jarrell, M. L. (2015). Wielding the green stick: An examination of criminal enforcement at the EPA under the Bush and Obama administrations. *Environmental Politics*, 24(1), 38–56.

Petrossian, G. A. (2015). Preventing illegal, unreported and unregulated (IUU) fishing: A situational approach. *Biological Conservation*, 189(2), 39–48.

Plastics.com. (2018). Joint venture "Corpus Christi Polymers" purchases Texas M&G plant. Retrieved from https://plastics.com/joint-venture-purchase-mg

Port of Corpus Christi. (2016). Hillcrest/Washington-Coles voluntary acquisition and relocation program. Retrieved from http://ccharborbridgerelocation.com/index.php

Ramirez, C. (2017, April 19). ExxonMobil corp: World's largest ethylene cracker plant with be in South Texas. Retrieved from www.caller.com/story/money/business/local/2017/04/19/exxon-mobil-corp-worlds-largest-ethylene-cracker-plant-south-texas/98820232/

Stretesky, P. B., & Lynch, M. J. (1999). Corporate environmental violence and racism. *Crime, Law and Social Change, 30*(2), 163–184.

U.S. Chamber of Commerce. (2010). Consequences of non-attainment. Retrieved from www.uschamber.com/consequences-non-attainment

United Church of Christ. (1987). *Toxic wastes and race: A national report on the racial and socio-economic characteristics of communities with hazardous waste sites.* New York: Author.

University of Michigan. (2004). Environmental justice case studies. Retrieved from http://umich.edu/~snre492/cases.html

PART IV

Critiques and Critical Reflections

16

YOU'RE A CRIMINOLOGIST? WHAT CAN YOU OFFER US?

Interrogating Criminological Expertise in the Context of White Collar Crime

Fiona Haines

The term "white collar crime" is a stroke of genius. By coining this term, E. H. Sutherland established a strong criminological presence in calling attention to the crimes and harms of business. It makes a criminological analysis unique. Hence, it is not surprising the call for heavier sanctions and criminal penalties remains strong in the field. This chapter critically analyses this call and highlights the dilemmas involved. Firstly, criminalization can be a conservative not a progressive strategy in responding to white collar crime. Secondly, when criminologists venture beyond this sphere, they must contend with multiple strands of expertise and the relevance of our analysis can be challenged. The combination of these two dilemmas risk a criminological analysis of white collar crime being accused on the one hand of being reactionary and superficial and on the other of being swamped by analyses that might distract from the radical potential that criminological analyses contain.

How, then, should we as criminologists respond to this problem? One possibility favored by many is to continue to demand greater criminalization and enforcement of criminal penalties. Yet, for others this demand appears as a distraction from understanding the systemic reasons why law and law enforcement more often supports the activities of business rather than controlling it. An alternative response is to interrogate the possibilities within broader regulatory controls: some legal, some relational, some physical. This approach can be effective, but a regulatory focus also can blunt efforts to draw attention to fundamental structural problems that generate ongoing problems, even as small gains might be made. Further, in the world of regulation, criminological knowledge competes with law, economics, and political science for relevance. We are then confronted with questions about the nature of our expertise and the rigor of our analysis. In the process, our world becomes more complex even as our public message on what to do require clarity and parsimony.

One solution to this problem is a more systematic interrogation of the demand to criminalize: to understand when, and under what conditions, it might be a critical strategy to change the rules of the game around business conduct and when it might be a way of deflecting attention from more systemic problems. A useful theoretical tool to assist in this work is to understand the demand for criminalization as occurring within a *field of struggle* where attention is directed towards the different actors who are calling for and resisting the call to criminalize as well as the specific strategies and reforms that are associated with both.

That is to locate the demand for criminalization within a specific context (or field) to assess whether the call is associated either with changes to more far reaching rules that govern business conduct or is a discrete effort that leaves standard business practices intact. In this chapter, I argue that both the concept itself and the debates on what actually constitutes a field of struggle provide a way for criminological analysis to take context seriously and to value close, critical, and theoretically informed empirical work that goes well beyond "mindless empiricism."

Criminalization and the Call to Arms

Criminological foray into the crimes and harms of the powerful began with throwing down the gauntlet: we had been looking the wrong way—to the crimes of the powerless rather than the powerful! Perhaps one of the enduring legacies of criminology is Sutherland's (1940) term itself: white collar crime. It captured a sentiment and a reality that significant and damaging crimes can be committed by those in positions of influence, and without sanction beyond what might appear a slap on the wrist. Sutherland's 1939 address announcing this insight to the American Sociological Association made the newspaper headlines of the day (Odum, 1951). Since 1939, its use has grown and the names applied to white collar crime have proliferated—from corporate crime (Clinard & Yeager, 1980) to occupational crime to state corporate crime (Kramer, Michalowski, & Kauzlarich, 2002) or simply crimes of the powerful (Pearce, 1976; Rothe & Kauzlarich, 2016). Terminology has generated a significant criminological legacy for looking at the powerful if you wish to understand white collar crime.[1]

Terminology aside, why does a criminological *analysis* matter? Does its primary strength lie in its capacity to act as a rallying cry—a way of giving voice to the idea of crime as a social and political problem, not simply a legal property (Higgins, Short, & South, 2013; White & Kramer, 2015)? That we determine what is criminal and what should be done about it? For my colleague Adam Sutton this was a profoundly conservative and ultimately misguided effort.[2] It simply deflected attention from the deep structural imbalances that lay at the heart of white collar harm. Taking his cue from Aubert (1952), the problem to be uncovered was one of unravelling ambiguity; why was the law structured, and enforced, in the way it was? What was it about the nature of the activity that meant that even if successful a prosecution against a single white collar criminal (or several) would hardly spell the death knell of white collar crime? An alternative view was put by Kit Carson in his inaugural lecture as Professor of Criminology at La Trobe University in 1983 (Carson, 1993). For him, the call for criminalization and for use of the criminal law was political, a strategy to enable greater social change. For the purposes of political expediency, ambiguity needed to be dispensed with. There is considerable value in careful thought about what the call for criminalization can and cannot do in ensuring business acts in the public interest.

This task of ensuring business acts in the public interest is now more complex than ever. It is no longer sufficient to castigate businesses and business executives for their role in financial collapse, miserable wages and conditions and countless deaths and injuries. The human toll of business practice, including a rise in new forms of slavery, is now met by alarming environmental damage, not only from climate change, but critical biodiversity loss, nitrogen depletion in soils, ocean acidification, plastic pollution, and much more. Industries and their constituent businesses are part and parcel of this damage (Haines & Parker, 2018). Are there any progressive possibilities that remain in a call to criminalize individual examples of business harm? Can criminalization tackle the deeply intertwined social and environmental damage wrought by current business practices?

Criminalization or Crime Prevention? Entering the Regulatory Debate

Many argue that a first step is to look beyond the criminal law to a suite of strategies of control of business conduct. Prevention—crime prevention if you will—for many has the primary role to play in the control of white collar crime (Laufer, 2006). This takes analysis into the world of regulation where the focus is as much on stopping the harm from arising in first place rather than enforcing for a breach after the damage is done. There has been a proliferation of writing in the area of regulation (for a recent extensive collection of writing, see Drahos, 2017). Delving into the multiple ways of control of business is important (Larsson, 2012), but there is a criminological ambivalence towards this scholarship, arguing it underplays the nature of power that leads to an undermining of the need for strong enforcement of the criminal law (Tombs, 2002). Yet, key components of law beyond criminal law have always had an important role to play. Car safety, design of roads, freedom of association laws, and so on form some of the basic conditions under which businesses compete (Freiberg, 2010). They can be understood as part and parcel of the conditions of trade or the rules of the market. The struggle over the content of these laws, and innovating ways of ensuring compliance, is as important to the control of white collar crime as the use of criminal statutes or the infliction of criminal penalties. There is a complementarity here, where breach of the underlying regulations might well be met with stronger criminal penalties—but attention needs to be paid across the spectrum from law enforcement, including criminalization, to the actual content of the legal and regulatory regime and its consequences for how businesses ply their trade.

Details and Actuarial Risks

An assessment of the law's content though brings with it significant challenges. The first is in understanding what legal provisions and regulatory approaches might assist in reducing harm. This requires both knowledge of the law and knowledge of the technical area involved in the harm itself (major hazards, occupational health and safety, corporate collapse, etc.). That is, to venture into the territory of the lawyer, and of the engineer, the actuary, the accountant and so on. Hence, any criminologist who ventures into this terrain must become a bit of a Jill of all trades or a Jack of multiple professions. In my own work, an early challenge was in understanding engineering—at least to a passable extent of ensuring that I understood enough of the technical challenges of major hazard facilities (at least as a knowledgeable observer) to ensure that my writing could at least garner some respect from technical audiences.

In each area of business harm, one challenge is to understand what might be considered technical knowledge and to try to distinguish this from the very human and social dynamics that pertain to the social construction of that knowledge. To be sure, there is value in a primary focus on interrogation of the economic, political and social dynamics around a particular form of harm (e.g., Douglas, 1992). For me, though, a sole focus on this dimension ultimately proved unsatisfactory. A main concern I developed in my work was around what I labelled actuarial risk—that is the impact and probability that a particular hazard will be realized (Haines, 2011). My paradigmatic case was the industrial disaster. Irrespective of the social construction of the risk, the political influences and so on was the reality that, if the assessment was wrong and the right controls not in place the industrial plant would at some point explode. Without at least some understanding of the industrial processes in place, it was almost impossible to make any sensible comment on the degree to which a governance regime will, or will not, be sufficient to prevent the next disaster. But it was equally misguided to ignore the economic, social and political influences that shape not only the nature of the risk assessment, but also the development of the laws and regulations, and the nature of compliance and enforcement in any particular place and time.

A key lesson from this work was that the actuarial risks that constitute white collar crime and harm are not all the same. In particular, the most material of elements, money and its representation in a set of accounts, proved to be the most elusive in terms of undertaking an assessment of what constituted the actuarial risk of corporate collapse. The comparison between such an assessment and one centered on the risk of an explosion at a major hazard facility was stark. In both there was complexity to be sure. But accounts and money are themselves a social, economic, and political construct in a manner that an explosion that emerges from an ignition source and a flammable gas is not. Engineering is not accounting. The figures on a balance sheet and the number on the coin or note are meaningless if the confidence is lacking that the figures do indeed have meaning. The circulation of money, replete with numerical denomination of worth, itself rests on a confidence trick. The (im)materiality of money is socially constructed; it is simply a means of distributing value across space and over time (Haines, 2011, 2014).

The conclusion from *The Paradox of Regulation* (Haines, 2011) was, not surprisingly, that the content of the harm matters and the economic and political context within which the regulatory regime emerges matters. Returning to the criminal enforcement, then, it matters greatly whether you have a law that is worth enforcing. To know that, you need to dig deeper. In ignorance, call for greater criminal enforcement and accountability (even against white collar criminals) may simply fail to reduce the carnage, since compliance may not reduce harm if the specific rules embedded within law and regulation mean that compliance and harm reduction are not compatible.

Finding a Way Back to Understanding Systemic Problems: Riffs on State-corporate Crime

There is an essential truth to maintaining the unity in the call for criminalization. It is a call for justice for an equal share, an equal opportunity, and equal chance to be protected from the harms that businesses perpetrate. There is, in delving into the complexity of individual regulatory arenas and devouring different forms of technical knowledge, a trap. Namely, in subjecting each specific harm in the detail and rigor it requires, it is possible to overlook the connections between them.

There is a need to go beyond detail to understand the *commonalities* that lie behind why business is regulated the way it is. The first step here is to recognize a key social and legal assumption that is made—namely that business is beneficial to society. Businesses are seen as the fundamental way our lives are ordered. They bring significant benefits, through goods and services, jobs and a sense of meaning value and worth. It follows then, that business activity should be supported, and it is, through laws (such as corporate law, licensing, planning, employment laws and so on). This aspect of law has recently been usefully developed by Whyte (2014) in his concept of "regimes of permission" to capture the extensive legal infrastructure that provides the basis for businesses to ply their trade.

Regulation and the control of business harm is measured against the benefits businesses are argued to bring (Carroll, 2008). Each area, each actuarial risk replete with its specific governance regime (occupational health and safety, major hazards, pollution control, unsafe products, fraud of various kinds) acts as a check, an attempt at discipline on business behavior and the behavior of those who control the business. So, understanding the specific nature of the controls remains important, but so too is understanding the general nature of support for business together with this specific legal infrastructure. Regulation, then, can be understood as "instrumental law" (Teubner, 1998).

What then should we make of the call to criminalize? In addition to the problem of demanding compliance with and enforcement of laws when breached being ineffective in stemming the harm is the problem that criminalization in one specific area of concern might deflect attention from the way that regimes of permission, in and of themselves, order and facilitate harm. Whyte (2014, p. 241) argues, "even the most punitive and invasive regulatory agencies do little more than marginally re-distribute the burdens of cost and responsibility for corporate harms." From this lens, the call to criminalize seems even less likely to engender progressive change.

Yet, perhaps this is too sweeping a claim. There are two separate considerations here. Firstly, is to interrogate the nature of business benefit and secondly to ask the key political science question regarding the conditions under which more, or less, harmful business practices emerge. In terms of business benefit, clearly much of the criminological literature focuses on the harms. The benefits are not subject to the same level of discussion. Sutherland, when asked about the definition of white collar crime and what all the different offences had in common responded that their commonality lay in their breach of American values—of the value of competition, and essentially good clean business practice. There was no sense in his work of a systemic problem of the nature of the capitalist enterprise. Many criminologists would disagree and would point to the fundamental problems associated with, in particular, private for profit corporations embedded within a capitalist economy (Glasbeek, 2002; Tombs & Whyte, 2015).

Perhaps it is helpful to think at a less lofty level at the embedded nature of harm within benefit. Many (but certainly not all) of the daily necessities, those of us in the industrialized North consume, come to us through capitalist industrial processes. To that extent, they provide benefit. They also provide employment for a significant proportion of many people (again, though not all). They also provide revenue to government through taxes (not only corporate taxes but also payroll taxes of various kinds, income tax from workers, royalties, and so on). To an extent, then, it is helpful to understand the harms of white collar crime as embedded within these benefits (or, if you prefer, the benefits embedded in the harms). Critically, these benefits provide significant political purchase—implicit or explicit threats to governments that if controls are too onerous, benefits will not flow.

A focus on the relationship between business and the state is central to criminological writing on state-corporate crime and the debates on the use of the term (Kramer et al., 2002; Whyte, 2014). Through the lens of state-corporate crime, the relationship between the state and business is brought center stage. It allows us to understand how harm emerges from this relationship, for example where poor resourcing of regulatory agencies lies behind an incapacity to enforce business laws and regulation properly. But categorizing and classifying different harms that emerge from the relationship between business and state is one thing; understanding why is another. This is where understanding benefits can come in—in teasing out the pull of business on the state to ensure the benefits keep flowing. Tombs (2002) and Whyte (2014) draw on Gramsci to provide some theoretical heft here. They point to the "interventionist state" that is the fundamental role of the capitalist state in managing an "ethical" relationship between business and government to maintain social order. In carrying out this role and in managing these social relations the state engages in a "complex disciplinary process" (Whyte, 2014, p. 240). Through this process the state must maintain its legitimacy and to do so it needs to exert at least some control over business harm. My own framing of a similar dynamic draws from a Habermassian base, where regulation is understood to emerge from a state concern with maintaining the conditions for capital accumulation (and its own revenue) whilst also reassuring the population of its security (Haines, 2011). These different theoretical traditions help explain both why regulatory regimes emerge (to reassure the citizenry of their security) whilst they are also subject to complaints by the business of "red tape" and the need to deregulate and reduce the "regulatory burden" as a drag on business.

This theoretical focus on the relationship between business and the state helps explain why a call to criminalize business activity (either in statute or through enforcement) is mostly rebuffed, occasionally acceded to but always shaped in context specific ways. Criminalization of corporate harm and white collar crime requires a specific set of political circumstances for it to emerge. Even under these political circumstances, analysis of industrial manslaughter over many decades points to the challenges in developing laws that can actually target those with the greatest responsibility in generating harm (Gobert, 2008). Literature on the conventionalization of white collar crime shows how criminal laws focusing on business practice are transformed into something less than criminal: they are tamed and made palatable to those who hold the reins of power (Carson, 1980; Johnstone, 2007). Small business is an easier target for such initiatives that leave the large end of town untouched (Parker, 2012). The letter of the law, the resources for enforcement and the resources of the accused all conspire to defeat many attempts to hold white collar offenders to account.

Criminalization remains publicly powerful, though. It reassures the public that they have been heard. When criminal penalties have not been applied there is strong condemnation, as in the condemnation of the lack of prosecutions of senior financial executives in the United States following the financial crisis (Calathes & Yeager, 2016; Pontell, Black, & Geis, 2014). The significant penalties that followed the savings and loans crisis in the U.S. are recalled with fondness. The jailing of Enron and WorldCom executives are also noted. Bernie Madoff is sentenced to 150 years. What has been the success of these? Detailed research in the U.S. context needs to be done, not so much on the criminality and complicity of executives that are involved in such scandals, nor on the success or otherwise of the trials, but rather on the impact of specific criminal sentences on subsequent corporate and political action and the impact of vociferous calls to criminalize. Anecdotally, the levels of imprisonment following the Savings and Loans crisis did not appear to ameliorate the impact of the Global Financial Crisis. This would suggest that criminalization as a simple head count of who is behind bars and for how long is a poor indicator of success.

Recent scholarship on the Madoff case is particularly illuminating. In *Bernie Madoff and the Crisis*, Eren (2017) outlines in careful detail how this significant sentence came about. Her thesis is convincing: namely that the complexity of financial dealings that led to the crisis formed a lightning rod for the identification of a single villain. This is despite the crime not being instrumental in the crisis itself. Rather, the enormity of the harm, the complexity of the collapse (and indeed the crisis) combined with a human drama where a clear villain was identified. Eren (2017) carefully teases out why this sentence cannot be seen as part of a broader strategy of challenging and changing the dominant nature of U.S. capitalism.

An alternative outcome from the call to criminalize is possible. In my own work on the Longford Gas Disaster in 1998 in Victoria, Australia, I traced the aftermath of that disaster in terms of legislative change and practice on the ground (Haines, 2011). Here, I found strong pressure to introduce industrial manslaughter laws in the wake of the disaster. It was taken up by the then Labor government who introduced an industrial manslaughter bill into the parliament in in 2001. However, facing a tight election in 2002 an under criticism from the opposition they dropped the bill as part of their effort to retain control over the Senate and win a further term in government. This might be seen as a failure—and to an extent it was. However, intense scrutiny of the 2002 Labor government remained, and they needed to reassure the public that there would be no repeat disaster. Industrial manslaughter as the way to ensure this was no longer viable, so they opted instead for radical changes to major hazards legislation together with increasing the capacity of the regulator to enable it to manage and enforce the new law. These changes had a significant impact on major hazard facilities (chemical plants and oil refineries), improving their practices. In this way, the *call* to criminalize was part of a series of events that led to successful and effective reform.

These two examples suggest there may be a different way to tease out more carefully across different contexts whether the call to criminalize, as well as actual criminal prosecutions, do or do not lead to helpful reform. That is to place prosecution as well as the call to criminalize as part of a *field of struggle*. In this way, it is possible to analyze methodically and in place whether the demand for criminalization, criminal prosecution, and the activism and activity that revolves around it represents only isolated pockets of accountability or can be understood as part of systemic change.

At its most straight forward, a field of struggle is defined by actors in relation to one another acting intentionally and strategically to gain greater influence by shaping the rules that govern the field (Fligstein & McAdam, 2011). When seen as part of a field of struggle, criminalization can be understood in part as a set of rules within a field, but also the call itself a strategy to reshape relationships within the field itself. The purpose of criminalization is to change the relative influence that actors have within the field—and with that to change "the rules of the game" under which businesses act.

One of the first lessons from the fields of struggle literature is that effects within the field are best explained, at least in the first instance, by close attention to the field itself (Levi Martin, 2003). That is, the specific context or field within which a call for criminalization occurs is critically important. The impact of the call—or indeed the impact of a specific criminal penalty—can only be assessed by looking in a detailed fashion at the place itself, and tracing how these events shape subsequent controls on business (and indeed business behavior itself). Only on this basis can we understand whether significantly higher penalties in the United States (or indeed in Iceland) are important when compared with Germany, Indonesia, or China.

Debates within the fields of struggle literature contain further insights. One such debate centers on whether there is one set of rules or a struggle over which rules apply. Fligstein and McAdam (2011) argue that a single set of rules that are explicit within a field with actors acting intentionally to try to gain advantage by drawing on those rules. The rules have general agreement (even from "challengers" who receive less of the gains and more the harms within the field) because of the stability afforded by agreed rules. Others disagree, arguing that part of the struggle is about *which* rules apply (Emirbayer & Johnson, 2008; Goldstone & Useem, 2012; Swartz, 2008, 2014). The latter makes sense. In its simplest terms, the debate that is often seen around whether civil or criminal law applies in the case of business harm is precisely one of which rules count in this case. But this can be taken more broadly. The call for a "social license" to govern business activity rather than simply a legal mandate is another example of struggles around mining, oil, and gas exploration that are precisely about what the rules of the game should be (Curran, 2017).

Rules are significant in another way. In a strict legal sense, appeal to law requires standing before the law. In other words, action against businesses by regulators, or indeed by communities claiming redress requires that they have the requisite legislative mandate to be able to do so. Hence the problem arises with multi-national companies and legislation that cannot cross jurisdictional boundaries. However, activism can cross borders and in very real ways can have an impact on the rules by which multi-national businesses act and behave. But, whether the rules of the game are, or are not, shaped by activism around a given case of corporate damage (e.g., deforestation due to palm oil) requires careful empirical scholarship. The impact of activism can be blunted, too, by host country efforts such as in India and Indonesia curtailing the capacity of foreign actors to support local activist groups (Balaton-Chrimes, 2015; Balaton-Chrimes & Macdonald, 2015) that again shapes the legitimacy of actors in the field.

In terms of assessing the impact of criminalization, understanding criminalization as a constituent element of the rules themselves in specific field suggests further insight. Namely, does a call for criminalization lead to changes in the rules themselves allowing criminal sanctions to be used? If so, does it change the rules of the game? That is, does criminalization in its many social and legal guises act, within a specific context, as an integral component that ensures businesses in that location act in the public interest?

The call for criminalization might also be seen not as a constituent element of the rules but rather a strategy. The conceptualization of criminalization as social property suggests that the claim is critically part of a strategy of those who wish to see a change in a specific field of struggle. Utilizing a criminal prosecution too might also be understood as a strategy. It is here that the purpose of a criminal sanction becomes critically important to understand. If the purpose of a criminal penalty is accountability, then perhaps prosecutions are more likely to be an end in themselves independently of the broader impact they have. They act to reassure that the rules of the game are, after all, fair. But, to be true to the fields' perspective the proof of this depends on context and the nature of a specific field. Emirbayer and Johnson (2008) point to a basic feature of the fields literature, namely that strategies are used by both those who wield significant influence in a field and those who do not. Strategies such as criminalization can be used to conserve the status quo or to subvert it.

Understanding which strategies are influential and why is also important. Those drawing from a Bourdieusian base within the fields of struggle literature, understand actors as drawing on their economic, cultural and symbolic capital (that they may bring from different fields) to argue for influence within a particular field (Emirbayer & Johnson, 2008). Not surprisingly, they use the capital with which they are best endowed either the challenge or to conserve power. Criminalization is redolent with symbolic power. In contrast to understanding criminalization as a constituent element of the rules, understanding and tracing its symbolic influence as a strategy might yield further insights. The call to criminalize is a form of symbolic capital, which can be widely dispersed. On the other hand, access to technical capital is not distributed in the same way. That the public response to corporate harm is often one of criminalization is then not surprising. What its impact is, though, depends on dynamics within the specific field of struggle within which it located.

Conclusion

This chapter has used criminalization of white collar crime as an anchor to understanding criminology's contribution in the public sphere. It is here that criminology makes its most unique contribution to the field of business harm and crime. To be sure, criminological contributions extend well beyond this, into the range of possible strategies that can be used to control business, insightful analyses of the underlying dynamics that shape business behavior and the need to pay close attention to the specific harm, or actuarial risk itself. Attention to detail and gaining at least a semblance of expertise in different areas is important but is both a challenge and a paradox. In these broader fields, criminological knowledge is joined, and to some extent competes with, a range of other perspectives and finding a distinct voice can be harder.

This is not to suggest that scholarship should be confined to what makes criminology unique. Far from it. But it might make it more understandable why the demand for harsher penalties and in particular criminal penalties against individual business actors remains such a prominent part of the criminological cannon in the white collar crime literature. However, the focus on criminalization might be a way to explore in a more nuanced way the connectedness between different forms of business harm. To do so, however, the chapter has argued there is a need for a more reflexive framing to understand the role played both by criminalization by state agencies and by activists and the broader public. Understanding criminalization as part of a field of struggle, either one that is a constituent element of the rules of the game or a strategy, has much to offer. It is here that we might understand the multiple and different roles criminalization can play both in conserving the status quo that supports continuing and chronic levels of harm by business and how, and under what circumstances, it is the way systemic change can arise. A detailed empirical exploration is required to assess whether a call to criminalize remains a narrow and misguided form of accountability or part of a suite of change that is systemically capable of ensuring businesses act in a socially and environmentally just way. The answer to this cannot be answered in the abstract. Rather, it is to be found in critical engagement with the places where we undertake our research, act in concert with others, teach our students, and write our papers.

Notes

1 For the purposes of this chapter, and for reasons I have explained elsewhere (Haines & Sutton, 2012), I use the term white collar crime to encompass the crimes and harms perpetrated by business actors and business people.
2 Adam and I taught *Corporate and White Collar Crime* together at the University of Melbourne together for 15 years. One of his main lessons for students was to highlight the futility of criminalization absent from broader changes. He is no longer with us, but in a real sense this chapter can be considered a virtual conversation with him.

References

Aubert, W. (1952). White collar crime and social structure. *American Journal of Sociology, 58*(3), 263–271.
Balaton-Chrimes, S. (2015). POSCO's Odisha project: OECD national contact point complaints and a decade of resistance. *Corporate Accountability Research*. Retrieved from http://corporateaccountabilityresearch.net/njm-report-v-posco-odisha
Balaton-Chrimes, S., & Macdonald, K. (2015). Wilmar. *Corporate Accountability Research*. Retrieved from http://corporateaccountabilityresearch.net/njm-report-viii-wilmar
Calathes, W., & Yeager, M. G. (2016). Sweetheart settlements, the financial crisis, and impunity: A case study of SEC v. Citigroup Global Markets, Inc. *Social Justice, 42*(1), 53–69.
Carroll, P. (2008). Rethinking regulation. In P. Carroll, R. Deighton-Smith, H. Silver, & C. Walker (Eds.), *Minding the gap: The promise and performance of regulatory reform in Australia* (pp. 73–88). Canberra: ANU E-Press and the Australian and New Zealand School of Government.
Carson, W. G. (1993, September). *The challenge of white collar crime*. Presented at the Inaugural lecture, Department of Legal Studies, La Trobe University.
Carson, W. G. (1980). The institutionalization of ambiguity: Early British factory acts. In E. Stotland & G. Geis (Eds.), *White collar crime: Theory and research* (pp. 142–173). Beverly Hills, CA: Sage.
Clinard, M. B., & Yeager, P. C. (1980). *Corporate crime*. New York: Free Press.
Curran, G. (2017). Social licence, corporate social responsibility, and coal seam gas: Framing the new political dynamics of contestation. *Energy Policy, 101*, 427–435.
Douglas, M. (1992). *Risk and blame: Essays in cultural theory*. London: Routledge.
Drahos, P. (Ed.). (2017). *Regulatory theory*. Canberra: ANU Press. doi:10.22459/RT.02.2017
Emirbayer, M., & Johnson, V. (2008). Bourdieu and organizational analysis. *Theory and Society, 37*(1), 1–44.
Eren, C. P. (2017). *Bernie Madoff and the crisis: The public trial of capitalism*. Stanford, CA: Stanford University Press.
Fligstein, N., & McAdam, D. (2011). Toward a general theory of strategic action fields. *Sociological Theory, 29*(1), 1–26.
Freiberg, A. (2010). *The tools of regulation*. Annandale: The Federation Press.
Glasbeek, H. (2002). *Wealth by stealth: Corporate crime, corporate law, and the perversion of democracy*. Toronto, Canada: Between the Lines.
Gobert, J. (2008). The corporate manslaughter and Corporate Homicide Act 2007—Thirteen years in the making but was it worth the wait? *The Modern Law Review, 71*(3), 413–433.

Goldstone, J. A., & Useem, B. (2012). Putting values and institutions back into the theory of strategic action fields. *Sociological Theory, 30*(1), 37–47.

Haines, F. (2011). *Paradox of regulation: What regulation can achieve and what it cannot.* Cheltenham, UK: Edward Elgar.

Haines, F. (2014). Corporate fraud as misplaced confidence? Exploring ambiguity in the accuracy of accounts and the materiality of money. *Theoretical Criminology, 18*(1), 20–37.

Haines, F., & Parker, C. (2018). Moving towards ecological regulation: The role of criminalisation. In C. Holley & C. Shearing (Eds.), *Criminology and the anthropocene* (pp. 81–108). New York: Routledge.

Haines, F., & Sutton, A. (2012). White collar and corporate crime. In M. Marmo, W. de Lint, & D. Palmer (Eds.), *Crime and justice: A guide to criminology* (4th ed., pp. 191–209). Pyrmont, NSW: Lawbook Co.

Higgins, P., Short, D., & South, N. (2013). Protecting the planet: A proposal for a law of ecocide. *Crime, Law and Social Change, 59*(3), 251–266.

Johnstone, R. (2007). Are occupational health and safety crimes a hostage to history? An Australian perspective. In A. Brannigan & G. Pavlich (Eds.), *Governance and regulation in social life (Essays in honour of W. G. (Kit) Carson* (pp. pp. 33–54). London: Cavendish-Routledge.

Kramer, R. C., Michalowski, R. J., & Kauzlarich, D. (2002). The origins and development of the concept and theory of state-corporate crime. *Crime & Delinquency, 48*(2), 263–282.

Larsson, P. (2012). Regulating corporate crime: From punishment to self-regulation. *Journal of Scandinavian Studies in Criminology and Crime Prevention, 13*(supp. 1), 31–46.

Laufer, W. (2006). *Corporate bodies and guilty minds: The failure of corporate criminal liability.* Chicago, IL: University of Chicago Press.

Levi Martin, J. (2003). What is field theory? *American Journal of Sociology, 109*(1), 1–49.

Odum, H. W. (1951). *American sociology: The story of sociology in the United States through 1950.* New York: Longmans, Green and Co. Retrieved from www.asanet.org/edwin-h-sutherland

Parker, C. (2012). Economic rationalities of governance and ambiguity in the criminalization of cartels. *British Journal of Criminology, 52*(5), 974–996.

Pearce, F. (1976). *Crimes of the powerful: Marxism, crime and deviance.* London: Pluto Press.

Pontell, H., Black, W., & Geis, G. (2014). Too big to fail, too powerful to jail? On the absence of criminal prosecutions after the 2008 financial meltdown. *Crime, Law & Social Change, 61*(1), 1–13.

Rothe, D. L., & Kauzlarich, D. (2016). *Crimes of the powerful: An introduction.* Abingdon, UK: Routledge.

Sutherland, E. H. (1940). White-collar criminality. *American Sociological Review, 5*(1), 1–12.

Swartz, D. L. (2008). Bringing Bourdieu's master concepts into organizational analysis. *Theory and Society, 37*(1), 45–52.

Swartz, D. L. (2014). Theorizing fields. *Theory and Society, 43*(6), 675–682.

Teubner, G. (1998). Juridification: Concepts, aspects, limits, solutions. In R. Baldwin, C. Scott, & C. Hood (Eds.), *A reader on regulation.* Oxford: Oxford University Press.

Tombs, S. (2002). Understanding regulation? *Social & Legal Studies, 11*(1), 113–133.

Tombs, S., & Whyte, D. (2015). *The corporate criminal: Why corporations must be abolished.* Oxford: Routledge.

White, R., & Kramer, R. C. (2015). Critical criminology and the struggle against climate change ecocide. *Critical Criminology, 23*(4), 383–399.

Whyte, D. (2014). Regimes of permission and state-corporate crime. *State Crime Journal, 3*(2), 237–246.

17

OUR NORTH IS THE SOUTH

Lessons from Researching Police-Community Encounters in São Paulo and Los Angeles

Sebastian Sclofsky

Conducting research in Los Angeles and São Paulo unearthed two events that, despite taking place thousands of miles away from each other, reveal striking similarities. As recounted by Nicole:[1]

> I remember we had just finished school and on our way home some friends and I decided to hang out in one of the corners near the school. Suddenly two cops came from nowhere. They ordered us against the wall and told us to put our hands on our heads and began to frisk us. I didn't know back then that male cops cannot search girls. I felt violated, we were just kids doing stupid things, but we were not doing anything dangerous or criminal.
>
> *(Nicole, Los Angeles, May 2015)*

Similar negative encounters occur in São Paulo, as the story of Samuel and his daughter shows:

> My daughter had her cellphone stolen and we went to the station to file a complaint. The officer behind the desk began looking at my daughter in an inappropriate manner. My daughter is sixteen years old, and this officer was staring at her. He started asking her all these personal questions. My daughter was embarrassed. I felt terrible, ashamed that I couldn't do anything. I knew that if I reacted or said something things could get worse, so I did nothing. My daughter cried all the way back home. I held my tears, but I wanted to cry, too. You feel like you are nothing.
>
> *(São Paulo, October 2015)*

What struck me from Samuel's story is how this type of behavior is not simply inappropriate; it is gendered abuse. It is a way in which the police exert its power over those who are powerless—in these cases, people who are considered not simply as "Others," but as nobodies deprived of rights. In the context of the development of the carceral state in these two global cities, non-White residents of low-income communities share similar negative experiences with the police.

Here, I juxtapose research conducted in Los Angeles and São Paulo in order to illustrate effects of policing, in the context of the carceral state, in the lives of non-White residents of low-income communities in two global cities. I will argue that the deployment of these new policing methods has contributed to the erosion of democracy in both cities, and, following Todd Clear's (2010, p. 14) plea, I attempt to develop a dialogue that can "enable us to imagine new and potent strategies for improving justice." This consideration is especially important as scholars studying violence in Latin America in general and Brazil in particular implicitly posit the United States as a policing model to follow (Tulchin, Frühling, & Golding, 2003; Tulchin & Ruthenburg, 2006; UNOCD, 2011). In the context of São Paulo, newer, U.S.-inspired policing strategies and accountability mechanisms have not brought much change to the daily violence and killings committed by police officers. Instead, they have added new legalized modes that contribute to the systematic violation of rights in the city's periphery.

An important goal of public criminology has been to close the gap between knowledge and policy and to promote the adoption of new strategies to reduce violence and increase justice that are based on solid research and in dialogue with the communities most affected by the deployment of crime and social control programs. Yet, as Wacquant (2011) warns us, since the 1970s, several U.S. think tanks have promoted ideas that favored their economic and political interests, buffering decision-makers from alternative points of view and limiting the ability of the public to participate in the decision-making process. For instance, the Manhattan Institute played a central role in validating and exporting the "broken windows theory" to Europe and Latin America, producing the same negative effects it produced in places such as Los Angeles (Wacquant, 2011). More importantly, it has insulated the strategies from the open and public discussion that public criminology is supposed to promote in order to enhance justice and democracy.

Furthermore, while police violence and abuse continues to take place across the United States and Latin America, one of the effects produced by the development of the carceral state has been the rationalization and legalization of police violations of rights. Much of the negative experiences that the residents of south Los Angeles and São Paulo's periphery have with the police are not produced through violent encounters, but rather by seemingly benign and legal police practices. Examining them illuminates authoritarian enclaves in different democratic contexts and how the police produces and reproduces these authoritarian practices. If we are to develop a public criminology that is responsive to these problems, we must first understand policing practices and effects in context. In addition, focusing on the experiences of local residents aids in learning how the police has had a strong influence in the construction of racial identities among residents of south Los Angeles and São Paulo's periphery, and, in turn, how they develop a sense of second-class citizenship.

Understanding policing through the experiences of those who suffer the most by it can serve to promote the necessary dialogue that can bring change and enhance justice. It can support public criminology, for, as Uggen and Inderbitzin (2010) suggest, public criminology is committed to engaging communities—and, in this case, reaching out to neglected audiences and contributing to improve their democratic experience. Further, it supports a more nuanced picture of policing and its effects, especially as much of the literature on police violence in Brazil has focused on police killings (Brinks, 2008; Chevigny, 1990, 1995; Trindade Maranhão, 2004). While police killings can be considered the most egregious violation state agents commit, they are only part of the complex picture of abuse and violation of rights that take place in São Paulo.

Policing in the Context of the Carceral State

The carceral state has changed the way policing, prosecuting, sentencing, and penal sanctioning is done (Garland, 2001). It has developed new rationales of social control in which social problems are dealt through law and order frameworks, assuming that tougher punishments, longer sentences, tighter and widespread mechanisms of control, and more aggressive policing, in particular against minor offenses, can enforce and assure social order. The rise of the carceral state in the

United States has emerged through a series of political decisions made against the backdrop of unintended consequences of social movements and socio-economic changes associated with the fall of the New Deal and the rise of neoliberalism, as well as the reaction by conservative politicians against the advancements of the civil rights movement (Beckett & Herbert, 2010; Gottschalk, 2006, 2015; Lerman & Weaver, 2014; Murakawa, 2014; Schoenfeld, 2018).

A well-known effect of the carceral state has been the increase in incarceration, which retains significant racial disparities in terms of imprisonment rates. Scholars have highlighted how the carceral state has diminished the democratic experience of African Americans in the United States (Alexander, 2012; Beckett & Murakawa, 2012; Clear, 2007; Gottschalk, 2014; Lerman & Weaver, 2014; Tonry, 2011; Wacquant, 2008, 2009). In order to understand the ways in which the carceral state has affected the lives of residents of low-income communities of color, it is important to consider the development of new policing strategies in the context of the carceral state, how these policing strategies have rationalized and even legalized the surveillance, control, discrimination, and oppression of non-White communities, thereby reinforcing the existing racial and socio-economic inequalities.

The significant, arguably central, role of the police in the contemporary carceral state is linked to crime control practices that developed in the 1970s and early 1980s, which conceived of crime as a consequence of inadequate controls. Of particular importance is Broken Windows theory, which would guide policing in this new era. Kelling and Wilson (1982) advocated for a zero-tolerance policy for any behavior considered as deviant. This approach to crime control combined well with the development of community-policing strategies across the United States, which attempts to actively shape the community norms and standards in coordination with some members of the community, in particular older, wealthier, and more conservative members (see Roussell, 2015).

Through the lens of frameworks like broken-windows theory, the problems low-income communities face are assumed not to be a product of the socio-economic or racial structure, but a product of a lack of control and deterrence. It is the police that need to develop strategies to increase control and deterrence by shaping communal norms, by expelling "strangers," and becoming community leaders, social workers, mental health workers, neighborhood conflict mediators, and educators. Rebranded as "quality-of-life" policing, police departments continue to follow the same premises established in the broken windows theory. Stop and frisk, zero tolerance, investigatory stops, increased surveillance, the creation of new laws, rules and regulations, are all tactics used by the police in the quality-of-life approach.

Although the carceral state took shape in the United States, Latin American countries imported its rationale and policing strategies, particularly in Brazil. In 1998, Mexican President, Ernesto Zedillo, launched a "National Crusade against Crime," with a series of tough-on-crime measures with the goal "to imitate programs like 'zero tolerance' in New York City" (cited in Wacquant, 2009, p. 20). In 2002, a group of businessmen, with the support of local politicians, hired Rudy Giuliani and his consultant team to come to Mexico City, investigate the causes of crime, in particular in the downtown area, and developed a program to reduce criminal activity (D. E. Davis, 2007). In 1997, William Bratton, a firm proponent of zero tolerance and broken windows, was offering his expertise in Brazil (Goodman, 2013). Twelve years later, the Giuliani Security and Safety consultant company formed a partnership with the Investigative Management Group, led by former DEA agent and Giuliani campaign advisor Robert Strang, and began working in Rio de Janeiro in preparations for the 2016 Olympic Games hosted at that city (Lasusa, 2015). Accordingly, broken-windows and zero tolerance, the campaigning on tough-on-crime platforms, the enactment of more stringent sentencing laws, the construction of prisons, and the expansion of the prison population—the main components of the carceral state—have spread across Latin America since the 1990s.

Policing strategies developed in the United States, exported to Latin America, and adopted by local police departments become promoted as the panacea to solve the problems of violence in the region. Global cities, such as São Paulo and Los Angeles, are not simply connected by the new strategic role they play in the organization of the world economy (Sassen, 2014); they are connected by a logic of expulsion. Through austerity programs and the deregulation of labor and capital markets as a result of global and national financial crises, people are expelled from employment, housing, and social protections (Sassen, 2014). Alongside luxurious office buildings and expensive gated communities, a planet of slums continues to grow (M. Davis, 2006). The construction of walls, the privatization of public spaces, and the proliferation of surveillance technologies are transformations affecting many global cities (see Caldeira, 2000). In fact, beyond policing, many of the instruments used to enforce segregation in cities around the world, including São Paulo, first developed in Los Angeles (Caldeira, 2000). In doing so, spaces such as the peripheries of south Los Angeles and São Paulo share experiences of segregation, expulsion, surveillance, and control—even though they are contextually distinct. In the era of the carceral state, they emerge as authoritarian enclaves in which state agents can systematically violate residents' rights, sometimes through violent actions, but more often through seemingly non-violent and legal actions. The fact that these actions are seemingly non-violent and legal obscures the erosion of democracy and civic rights they produce; hence, criminologists need to make the link between these types of police actions and the violation of rights clearer.

The Development of Authoritarian Enclaves and the Rationalization of Violence

Political scientists have defined authoritarian enclaves as spaces in which, despite the existence of a democratic regime at the national level, democratic political rights are limited or inexistent—as observed, for example, in the southern United States during the Jim Crow era and some regions in Latin America (Benton, 2012; Gibson, 2012; Giraudy, 2010; Mickey, 2015). However, by focusing almost exclusively on political rights, they fail to consider the different ways in which state agents produce and reproduce the second-class citizenship status of residents of low-income communities of color, where political rights exist, but civic rights are systematically violated.

These authoritarian enclaves take shape through violent actions that range from police killings to police beatings and others abuses of power. The killings, beatings, and abuse suffered by residents at the hands of the police have become part of the daily life for non-White residents of low-income communities in both south Los Angeles and São Paulo. Further, it is also important to acknowledge and address the most common encounters these residents have with the police, which are not physically violent and often conducted in legal manners. In many instances, the police end up reproducing the residents' perception that they have no rights. "Legal inequality," Fischer (2008, p. 5) argues, "has to be sought not in the letter of the law but instead in the practices of the law."

As Epp and his colleagues (2014) have illustrated, we need to look at those instances in which the police, acting legally, shape the construction of a second-class citizenship among residents of south Los Angeles and São Paulo's periphery. These seemingly benign experiences influence the way people perceive their civic status. We see them reinscribed through U.S.-style policing tactics: in a police stop, the person stopped is arrested for the duration of the stop, she is not free to leave, and is sometimes subjected to thorough interrogations. Residents interviewed in south Los Angeles and São Paulo's periphery describe similar patterns to these stops. Police pull them over, officers ask for their documents, and they request (often politely) that drivers get out of the car.

They are sometimes handcuffed while they wait, sitting on the curb and even patted-down. Officers obtain consent for searching the car, they then search the car, and most of the time the driver is released with an apology for the time wasted. With the exception of the handcuffs, these practices often do not include any physical violence; they are legal and civil. Nonetheless, for those who go through these kinds of stops regularly, they generate a feeling of being under constant surveillance, a sense of fear and resentment of the prospect of state violence.

Take, for example, Randall, an African-American lawyer in his mid-thirties, resident of Southwest Los Angeles:

> There was a month that almost every morning they would pull me over. They said they had information regarding drugs or gang activity, or whatever, and that's why they would pull you over. The funny thing is that I never saw a white driver being stopped. They would ask for my documents, they then would ask me to get out of the car, most of the times they would ask me to sit in the curb and sometimes they would handcuff me. And then they would ask to search the car, and once they were done searching they would apologize and let me go.
>
> (Randall, Los Angeles, June 2015)

When we spoke, I asked Randall why he allowed the police to search his car. "You can't say no," he replied. "I once said no, and they handcuffed me, sat me on the curb, and I waited for two hours while dogs sniffed the outside of the car," Randall explained further. "If you say no," he continued, "you'll have to wait there for two hours. You say yes, it'll take thirty minutes. I have nothing illegal in the car, so I say yes and thirty minutes later I'm on my way to work."

Legally, Randall had the right to refuse the police request to search his car; however, this would have meant that he would have been under temporary "arrest" for a longer period of time. Hence, one could ask if he actually had the right to refuse the police request. From Randall's perspective that right exists only in theory; police officers create the conditions that force you, in practice, to give consent to their requests, doing so through a legal, non-violent, and seemingly benign way. As mentioned above, these seemingly benign actions obscure the ways in which the rights of residents of these areas are systematically violated. Residents feel that they are under siege, increasing the hostility between the police and the communities they are bound to serve.

The situation in São Paulo is comparatively not much different. Being stopped regularly by police and identified as a suspect is part of the daily life of many of São Paulo's periphery residents. In conversations with young residents in both cities, they shared their annoyance about being considered as suspect. "I don't know what else to do," a young kid from Osasco told me regarding how to act when he sees a police officer.

> If I lower my head, they think I'm avoiding them, so they stop me. If I look them straight, they say I'm being disrespectful and they stop me. If I walk slowly they stop me. If I walk quickly they stop me; I don't know what the fuck should I do!

These testimonies show part of the daily life for many residents of south Los Angeles and São Paulo's periphery. There is violence and abuse, and, in São Paulo in particular, police killings continue to take place. Also notable, though, is how policing strategies developed under the carceral state render the systematic violation of enshrined notions of individual rights into something benign and legally permissible. Police actions reinforce residents' racial identities and their second-class civic status, limiting the possibility of asserting their rights. The fact that these violations take place under the mantle of legality makes them harder to contest. While police abuse and violence can be easily seen as illegitimate, comprehending how legal actions erode civic rights and democracy generates a greater challenge. Only after we observe and scrutinize how these actions, done regularly against non-White residents, contribute to a second-class citizenship status can we appreciate the way they erode residents' democratic experience.

Producing and Reproducing Racial Identities

The expansion of the carceral state, including the aforementioned policing strategies, took place parallel to the development of a colorblind ideology, which attempts to hide the influence of race in the production of public policy and state practices. Colorblind ideology, as explained by Bonilla-Silva (2006), is a mode of perpetuating the hierarchical racial structure without any direct reference to race, blaming the victim of racism for their own perils, and assuming that racism is the action of a few individuals rather than the result of the social structure. Analyzing the ways in which the carceral state has reproduced and reinforced racial hierarchies is a fundamental endeavor to the promotion of democratic values and racial justice that public criminology attempts to do. Although the striking down of Jim Crow laws meant a formal end to many forms of legal segregation and discrimination, racism continues to exist in the United States, and policing practices sustain racial hierarchies. As many scholars (Alexander, 2012; Bonilla-Silva, 2006; Cole, 1999; Epp et al., 2014; Tonry, 2011) have explored these tensions in depth, I turn to Brazil, as an important site to examine how racial hierarchies inform state practices. I then argue for the need to expand this dialogue as a way of challenging these racialized and authoritarian state practices.

The ideology of racial democracy, Brazil's brand of colorblindness, developed almost 100 years ago by Gilberto Freyre (2003 [1933]), argued that the particular characteristics of the Portuguese plantation system, the close proximity of Black people and White people prior to emancipation, and the long process of miscegenation prevented the formation of strict racial categories and racial discrimination. Although criticized and debunked by many Brazilian sociologists, in particular Bastide and Fernandes (2008 [1959]), racial democracy became Brazil's official ideology during the military dictatorship. Only in the late 1990s and early 2000s did Brazilian scholars once again began rejecting this myth.

During my time in the field in São Paulo, my fieldwork helped me to appreciate how policing reproduces Brazil's racial hierarchies. The vast majority of people killed by the police are Black, and the negative experiences residents of São Paulo's periphery have with the police affect the way they identify racially. Marcelo, a resident of São Paulo's southern periphery, born and raised in one of the favelas in the region, shared the following story:

> Os homens[2] came in the middle of the night. They were looking for a suspect in the area and they thought he may be at my house. It was around midnight and we were all sleeping. My wife was pregnant at that time with our second child, and my four-year old son was sleeping in the next room. They broke in with full force, kicking and pushing everything in their way. They pointed their machine guns at me and shoved me out of my bed, slapping and kicking me. My son came running to our room. My wife hugged him tight, both of them crying. At the beginning the officers thought I was the suspect they were looking for. When they realized I wasn't him, they kept slapping me and asking where that person was. At gunpoint, they ordered me out of the house. When the neighbors heard all the confusion, they came out, too. They shouted at the officers that I was a "worker" and not a "bandit" and asked them to let me go. The commotion was such that the officers decided to let me go.
>
> *(Marcelo, São Paulo, September 2015)*

I asked Marcelo: "If you were not the suspect and the officers knew you didn't know anything about the suspect, why did they keep beating you?" He answered, "Because for them I was just another Black bastard," and, as I could ascertain from his comments, a Black person has no rights in São Paulo's racial hierarchy.

This story, which exemplifies an aspect of the daily life in São Paulo's periphery, may not present anything novel, except for the fact that from a visual perspective Marcelo does not appear Black. From an outsider's perspective, such as mine, Marcelo could easily be categorized as White. However, his experiences with the police as a favela-born man living in São Paulo's periphery lead him to identify himself as Black. In Brazil's ambivalent definition of race, constructing racial identities is as much an internal process as it is one shaped by external forces. In this context, policing becomes a central element in the construction of race; as the popular expression in São Paulo goes, "if you want to know who is Black, just ask the police." The police, as Penglase (2014) indicates, connect socioeconomic, racial, and spatial markers of difference. In doing so, they give meaning to race. Thus, as the Brazilian case shows, the lack of legally defined racial categories does not eliminate the informal categorization of race, which situates non-Whites in general, and Blacks in particular, in lower echelons of the social structure (Bastide & Fernandes, 2008 [1959]; Haney López, 2006). Police violence and abuse over Black bodies is not accidental, but central to the maintenance of White supremacy (Alves, 2014).

In 1954, Oracy Nogueira examined the differences in racial prejudice between Brazil and the United States. He characterized Brazil as having a prejudice based on mark or color, while the United States had a prejudice based on origin. A prejudice of mark, according to Nogueira (2006 [1954]), is based on the physical traits of the individual or phenotype and is more flexible, allowing Afro-Brazilians who may look White, or have special abilities to move up in the social ladder, although they are exceptional cases. In the case of prejudice of origin, exemplified by the one-drop-of-blood rule, the stratification system is more rigid. These ideal types defined by Nogueira have become less appropriate in examining the ways racial prejudice works, although certain elements remain in place. Penglase (2014) adds a third category: the prejudice of crime or criminal spaces by which the police misrecognize the way racial dynamics function in periphery spaces and treat Black residents of those spaces as criminals. Blackness and criminalization overlap: sometimes Blackness is seen as a sign of criminality, but in other instances it is police treatment of an individual or a space as criminal that renders an individual or space as Black (Penglase, 2014, p. 159). This type of racial prejudice in United States and Brazil have similarities, but they are nonetheless still influenced by the legacies of their own past and the different expressions of their racialized structures.

The negative and mostly violent encounters with the police do not only affect the way individuals define themselves racially, but they also give content to the meaning of being Black or Brown. The criminalization of Blackness, particularly the halo of suspicion that surround Black bodies, has deep historical roots in Eurocentric science, political thought, and the development of disciplines, such as criminology, both in the United States and in Brazil. Police actions reinforce images that posit Black bodies as threats. While the influence of the prejudice of mark and origin still play an important role, my research in Los Angeles and São Paulo points to a convergence: Certain racialized groups are criminalized because of the spaces they inhabit, because of the way they look, dress, talk, or walk. This criminalization process is used to justify police surveillance and control over Black bodies, reinforces their second-class citizenship status, and strengthens the hierarchical racial structure, which posits non-Whites as nobodies. Our task, as public criminologists, is to unearth this complex process, because it is a necessary first step in challenging these police strategies and practices in particular and the racial hierarchical structure in general.

In making this point, I do not mean to allude to non-White residents as passive subjects on which their racial identity is imposed. Resistance to state violence, specifically police violence, takes place in Los Angeles and São Paulo, both individually and collectively. For example, when Marcelo proudly defined himself as *pobre, preto, e periférico*,[3] he is not simply establishing his belonging to an economic, racial, and spatial category. He sees himself as being part of a larger, arguably imagined community, one who sees the belonging to these categories as a symbol of pride and resistance. In both cities, residents resist through organized collective action, through street art and music, through protests and demonstrations, and also through the development of small survival tactics in an attempt to avoid the law and its enforcers (Sclofsky, 2016). Residents of these communities have created different grassroots organizations and forums to challenge police practices, in doing so they have developed a space for activist criminology, which examines policing through their own experiences, and attempts to bring down the authoritarian practices that take place in their communities.

Conclusions

Uggen and Inderbitzin (2010) suggest that public criminologists should develop research in dialogue with communities and generate an open dialogue, which would allow us to imagine new strategies to improve justice. To do so, we need to pay careful attention to how communities experience crime and crime control interventions. Rather than simply accepting U.S. policing strategies as the model for Latin American cities, I suggest, following Uggen and Inderbitzin (2010), that we engage in a critical comparison between these places, focusing on the lived experiences of those most affected by the expansion of the carceral state. In particular, I have attempted to show how U.S. policing strategies exported to Latin America have produced similar kinds of negative consequences for residents of low-income communities of color.

These policing strategies, which are at the center of the carceral state, have rationalized and legalized what, at least in other contexts, is understood as clear violations of rights. In doing so, they support the creation of authoritarian enclaves across different urban landscapes. The deployment of community policing, based on the broken windows theory, does not reduce police abuse and violence. It does, however, make some of its features more complex. As discussed here, the regular, legal, and seemingly benign police stops reinforce the sense of second-class citizenship that many residents of São Paulo's periphery had already felt. Further, negative and mostly violent experiences with the police affect the way in which residents' racialized identities take shape. It also informs different modes of resistance, which call not only for immediate police reform, but attempt to address the social, racial, economic, and political conditions that enabled the importation of the carceral state mechanisms and the (re)production of authoritarian enclaves. In these authoritarian contexts, when, then, is the obligation of public criminology?

One key task, as public criminologists, is to help recover democratic practice by engaging the communities that most suffer from the policing practices described in this chapter. It is especially important when we consider Wacquant's observations that think-tanks, such as the Manhattan Institute, have "turned police chiefs George Kelling and William Bratton into global experts in urban security, who, disguised as semi-scholars … wield more influence on policing debates than thousands of criminologists rolled together" (2011, p. 443). His arguably dramatized statement should be taken as a wake-up call for those of us social scientists who are engaged in public criminology: we must continue to foster critical dialogues with communities affected by policies that support the formation of authoritarian enclaves in order to devise strategies to change them.

Notes

1 The names and places of residence of participants have been changed for their protection.
2 *Os homens* ("the men") is the way in which periphery residents of São Paulo generally refer to the police, especially the Military Police.
3 *Preto, pobre, e periférico* translates to "Black, poor, and from the periphery."

References

Alexander, M. (2012). *The new Jim Crow: Mass incarceration in the age of colorblindness*. New York: New Press.

Alves, J. A. (2014). From necropolis to blackpolis: Necropolitical governance and black spatial praxis in São Paulo, Brazil. *Antipode, 46*(2), 323–339.

Bastide, R., & Fernandes, F. (2008 [1959]). *Brancos e negros em São Paulo* (4th ed.). São Paulo, Brazil: Global Editora.

Beckett, K., & Herbert, S. (2010). *Banished: The new social control in urban America*. New York: Oxford University Press.

Beckett, K., & Murakawa, N. (2012). Mapping the shadow carceral state: Toward an institutionally capacious approach to punishment. *Theoretical Criminology, 16*(2), 221–244.

Benton, A. L. (2012). Bottom-up challenges to national democracy: Mexico's (legal) subnational authoritarian enclaves. *Comparative Politics, 44*(3), 253–271.

Bonilla-Silva, E. (2006). *Racism without racists: Color-blind racism and the persistence of racial inequality in the United States* (2nd ed.). New York: Rowman & Littlefield.

Brinks, D. M. (2008). *The judicial response to police killings in Latin America: Inequality and the rule of law*. New York: Cambridge University Press.

Caldeira, T. P. R. (2000). *City of walls: Crime, segregation, and citizenship in São Paulo*. Los Angeles, CA: University of California Press.

Chevigny, P. G. (1990). Police deadly force as social control: Jamaica, Argentina, and Brazil. *Criminal Law Forum, 1*(3), 389–425.

Chevigny, P. G. (1995). *Edge of the knife: Police violence in the Americas*. New York: New Press.

Clear, T. (2007). *Imprisoning communities: How mass incarceration makes disadvantaged neighborhoods worse*. New York: Oxford University Press.

Clear, T. (2010). Policy and evidence: The challenge to the American Society of Criminology: 2009 presidential address to the American Society of Criminology. *Criminology, 48*(1), 1–25.

Cole, D. (1999). *No equal justice: Race and class in the American criminal justice system*. New York: New Press.

Davis, D. E. (2007). El factor Giuliani: Delincuencia, la "cero tolerancia" en el trabajo policiaco y la transformación de la esfera pública en el centro de la ciudad de México. *Estudios Sociológicos, 25*(75), 639–681.

Davis, M. (2006). *Planet of slums*. New York: Verso.

Epp, C. R., Maynard-Moody, S., & Haider-Markel, D. (2014). *Pulled over: How police stops define race and citizenship*. Chicago, IL: University of Chicago Press.

Fischer, B. (2008). *A poverty of rights: Citizenship and inequality in twentieth century Rio de Janeiro*. Stanford, CA: Stanford University Press.

Freyre, G. (2003 [1933]). *Casa Grande e Senzala*. São Paulo, Brazil: Global Editora.

Garland, D. (2001). *The culture of control: Crime and social order in contemporary society*. Chicago, IL: University of Chicago Press.

Gibson, E. L. (2012). *Boundary control: Subnational authoritarianism in federal democracies*. New York: Cambridge University Press.

Giraudy, A. (2010). The politics of subnational undemocratic regime reproduction in Argentina and Mexico. *Journal of Politics in Latin America, 2*(2), 53–84.

Goodman, J. D. (2013, December 24). Bratton gives revolving door one more Spin. *New York Times*. Retrieved from www.nytimes.com/2013/12/24/nyregion/bratton-tries-to-untangle-his-corporate-ties.html

Gottschalk, M. (2006). *The prison and the gallows: The politics of mass incarceration in America*. New York: Cambridge University Press.

Gottschalk, M. (2014). Democracy and the carceral state in America. *Annals of the American Academy of Political and Social Science, 651*(1), 288–295.

Gottschalk, M. (2015). *Caught: The prison state and the lockdown of American politics*. Princeton, NJ: Princeton University Press.

Haney López, I. (2006). *White by law: The legal construction of race*. New York: New York University Press.

Kelling, G. L., & Wilson, J. Q. (1982, March). Broken windows. *The Atlantic*. Retrieved from www.theatlantic.com/magazine/archive/1982/03/broken-windows/304465/

Lasusa, M. (2015, October). Giuliani in Rio. *Jacobin*. Retrieved from www.jacobinmag.com/2015/10/giuliani-mayor-dinkins-mexico-city-el-salvador-policing/

Lerman, A. E., & Weaver, V. M. (2014). *Arresting citizenship: The democratic consequences of American crime control*. Chicago, IL: University of Chicago Press.

Mickey, R. (2015). *Paths out of dixie: The democratization of authoritarian enclaves in America's deep South 1944–1972*. Princeton, NJ: Princeton University Press.

Murakawa, N. (2014). *The first civil right: How liberals built prison America*. New York: Oxford University Press.

Nogueira, O. (2006 [1954]). Preconceito racial de marca e preconceito racial de origem: Sugestão de um quadro de referência para a interpretação do material sobre relações raciais no Brasil. *Tempo Social, 19*(1), 287–308.

Penglase, R. B. (2014). *Living with insecurity in a Brazilian favela: Urban violence and daily life*. New Brunswick, NJ: Rutgers University Press.

Roussell, A. (2015). Policing the anticommunity: Race, deterritorialization, and labor market reorganization in south Los Angeles. *Law & Society Review, 49*(4), 813–845.

Sassen, S. (2014). *Expulsions: Brutality and complexity in the global economy*. Cambridge, MA: Harvard University Press.

Schoenfeld, H. (2018). *Building the prison state: Race and the politics of mass incarceration*. Chicago, IL: University of Chicago Press.

Sclofsky, S. (2016). Policing in two cities: From necropolitical governance to imagined communities. *Journal of Social Justice, 6*, 1–24.

Tonry, M. H. (2011). *Punishing race: A continuing American dilemma* (Kindle ed.). New York: Oxford University Press.

Trindade Maranhão, C. A. (2004). *Entre a lei e a ordem: Violência e reforma nas polícias do Rio de Janeiro e Nova York*. Rio de Janeiro, Brazil: FGV editora.

Tulchin, J. S., Frühling, H. H., & Golding, H. (2003). *Crime and violence in Latin America: Citizen security, democracy, and the state* (J. S. Tulchin, H. H. Frühling, & H. Golding, Eds.). Washington, DC: Woodrow Wilson Center Press.

Tulchin, J. S., & Ruthenburg, M. (2006). *Toward a society under law: Citizens and their police in Latin America* (J. S. Tulchin & M. Ruthenburg, Eds.). Washington, DC: Woodrow Wilson Center Press.

Uggen, C., & Inderbitzin, M. (2010). Public criminologies. *Criminology & Public Policy, 9*(4), 725–749.

United Nations Office on Crime and Drugs. (2011). *Introductory handbook on policing urban space*. Retrieved from www.unodc.org/pdf/criminal_justice/Introductory_Handbook_on_Policing_Urban_Space.pdf

Wacquant, L. (2008). *Urban outcasts: A comparative sociology of advanced marginality*. Cambridge, UK: Polity Press.

Wacquant, L. (2009). *Punishing the poor: The neoliberal government of social insecurity* (English ed.). Durham, NC: Duke University Press.

Wacquant, L. (2011). From "public criminology" to the reflexive sociology of criminological production and consumption. *The British Journal of Criminology, 51*(2), 438–448.

18
CONFRONTING POLITICS OF DEATH IN PAPUA

Budi Hernawan

In July 2018, Amnesty International's Indonesian Office released a new report on the on-going problem of summary execution in Papua[1] entitled, "*Sudah, kasi tinggal dia mati*" ("Don't bother, let him die"). It states that Indonesian authorities have committed 95 summary executions in the last eight years without any accountability. The conflict derives from the ongoing Papuan armed and political resistance against Indonesian regime since the 1960s, which has been met with heavy-handed measures of the Indonesian security forces. During Suharto's military dictatorship, the Indonesian military acted with almost complete impunity for more than three decades (1967–1998), but it has changed little in post-Suharto's Indonesia. The report reaffirms that the problem remains unresolved even though Indonesia transitioned to a democracy 20 years ago. Perhaps not surprisingly, Indonesian authorities publicly dismissed the report by questioning its validity. Moeldoko, the Chief of Staff, insisted that Amnesty International should be more balanced in its reporting on the situation in Papua (Stefanie, 2018), and the Indonesian military framed the report as a baseless accusation.

The Amnesty International report is a single moment that cannot capture the broader, much more complex picture of the unresolved problem of state crime in Papua. Indigenous Papuans have raised a series of concerns: the deprivation of their ancestry land, the influx of non-indigenous Papuans, the unavailability of adequate health and education services, corruption, the denial of their freedom of expression, and racism that many Papuan students experience in their campuses in major cities across Indonesia. Their range of grievances, I argue, reflects what Mbembe describes as necropolitics, which concerns "the power and the capacity to dictate who may live and who must die" (2003, p. 11). Drawing on Foucault's concept of biopower, Schmitt's state of exception, and the state of siege, Mbembe examines the relationship between politics and death. Understanding such politics as the work of death is effective in explaining the ongoing pattern of impunity that has systematically undermined Papua for decades. This chapter explains the importance of understanding these politics, particularly their postcolonial context and implications, before embarking on attempts at public criminological engagement. Thus, rather than advocate for public criminology, I want to highlight the need to better understand how state crime and other forms of politics of death continues with impunity and how some forms of resistance to the politics of death already reflect public criminological commitments.

Drawing largely on my personal and professional experience in Papua over the last two decades, I highlight how these criminological concerns, which are public in nature, reveal deeper logics of governance, which are necessary to attend to when developing strategies to confront them (see Uggen & Inderbitzin, 2010). The chapter discusses the relevance of necropolitics in the Papua context before going into a description of how they have deeply shaped the contemporary governance of Papua. It covers four key areas: (1) the patterns of basic service delivery that affect Papuans' everyday life; (2) extractive industry and land grabbing; (3) penetration of *wahhabism*, which promotes the puritanical stream of Islam, and (4) state violence. I then reflect on two types of Papuan resistance (violent and non-violent) to Indonesian necropolitics. The chapter concludes with final remarks that illustrate some public criminological insights gleaned from this case.

Making Sense of Necropolitics: The Politics of Death as Part of Life in Papua

Literature on state violence in Papua (Tim SKP Jayapura, 2006; Tapol, 1983; Hernawan & Indarti, 2007; Komnas Perempuan, 2010) generally addresses issues of state violence from the human rights perspective. Although scholars of peacebuilding (Braithwaite, Braithwaite, Cookson, & Dunn, 2010; Hernawan, 2018; McLeod, 2015; Siregar, Mustafa, Conoras, & Sipla, 2013; Widjojo, 2010) address the ways to deal with the impact and consequences of state violence, the discussion of Papua, at least through the lens of state crime is limited, with the exception of work by Stanley (2014). Drawing on Mbembe's work on the postcolony, we can conceive of Papua as an example of "societies recently emerging from the experience of colonization and violence" (2001, p. 102). To understand these dynamics, let us first consider the history of Papua.

Papuans officially became part of the modern state in 1969 when the territory was incorporated into the nation-state of Indonesia through the United Nations-supervised plebiscite, The Act of Free Choice (Departemen Dalam Negeri, 1969). Under the 1962 New York Agreement between the Netherlands and Indonesia, the plebiscite was to determine whether the Papuans would join Indonesia or establish a newly independent state. Historical accounts indicate there was systematic coercion by Indonesian authorities, which affected the outcome of the vote (Drooglever, 2009; Saltford, 2003). For example, one of the members of Papua Representatives for Pepera (*Dewan Musyawarah Pepera*; DMP[2]) testified that the Indonesian Military held her for a month prior to the date of the plebiscite, prompting her to publicly declare that she joined Indonesia, even though it was against her conscience (Hernawan, 2018, p. 58). Indonesian military allies in the DMP emerged as part of the necropolitics in Papua, as their use of torture ensured that many indigenous Papuans were unable to exercise their rights to self-determination. In fact, the state did not hesitate to display their broken bodies to the public (Hernawan, 2016b).

The United Nations (UN) nonetheless voted to accept the result of the public consultation, which led to a declaration for Papua to join Indonesia (Saltford, 2003). There are at least three key issues worth highlighting here: First, not a single UN member state voted against the resolution. Most of them voted in favor, including the Netherlands, the former colonizer of Indonesia (though there were thirty abstentions). Second, the UN language uses the term "take note," suggesting that it did not fully endorse the Act, but no one had articulated a reason to argue against it. Third, as a consequence, the UN was instrumental in formally ending Papua's dispute over its rights to self-determination.

This outcome was not surprising, given the spirit of the decolonization of the 1960s and the geopolitics of the time. These two major factors have contributed to the incorporation of Papua to Indonesia. Prior to the implementation of the Act of Free Choice, Indonesia had hosted the 1955 Bandung Conference, where newly independent Asian and African nations expressed overwhelming support for Indonesia over its dispute with the Netherlands over Papua. The Conference communique treated Papua as an issue that should be solved to end the era of colonization of Indonesia by the Netherlands altogether. The Conference, however, overlooked the Papuans' voices. As a result, it opened a new chapter of unfinished decolonization in which the indigenous Papuans have had to fight for self-determination (Hernawan, 2016a, p. 175). As the legacy of the unfinished decolonization remains unresolved, Papua deserves our full attention, for it represents the status of "the frontiers" (or colonies). This term, Mbembe (2003) argues, refers to zones characterized by war and disorder: "the colonies are the location par excellence where the controls and guarantees of judicial order can be suspended—the zone where the violence of the state of exception is deemed to operate in the service of 'civilization'" (p. 24). The following sections analyze the conditions of Papua to illustrate its status as "the frontier."

Public Service Provision in Papua

As the easternmost province of Indonesia, the provinces of Papua and West Papua have suffered under-development in the last fifty years. Their rankings in the 2017 Indonesian Human Development Index (HDI) remain at the bottom. Papua is at 59.09 and West Papua is at 62.99 whereas the Indonesian national index is at 70.81 (see Table 18.1). In comparison to other provinces, which have improved in the last seven years, the Papuan provinces have not changed to the same extent—despite dramatic budget increases provided for the Papua provinces under the Special Autonomy scheme since 2001.

Table 18.1 The Indonesian Human Development Index

Province	2010	2011	2012	2013	2014	2015	2016	2017
Aceh	67.09	67.45	67.81	68.30	68.81	69.45	70	70.60
Sumatera Utara	67.09	67.34	67.74	68.36	68.87	69.51	70	70.57
Sumatera Barat	67.25	67.81	68.36	68.91	69.36	69.98	70.73	71.24
Riau	68.65	68.90	69.15	69.91	70.33	70.84	71.20	71.79
Jambi	65.39	66.14	66.94	67.76	68.24	68.89	69.62	69.99
Sumatera Selatan	64.44	65.12	65.79	66.16	66.75	67.46	68.24	68.86
Bengkulu	65.35	65.96	66.61	67.50	68.06	68.59	69.33	69.95
Lampung	63.71	64.20	64.87	65.73	66.42	66.95	67.65	68.25
Kep. Bangka Belitung	66.02	66.59	67.21	67.92	68.27	69.05	69.55	69.99
Kep. Riau	71.13	71.61	72.36	73.02	73.40	73.75	73.99	74.45
Dki Jakarta	76.31	76.98	77.53	78.08	78.39	78.99	79.60	80.06
Jawa Barat	66.15	66.67	67.32	68.25	68.80	69.50	70.05	70.69
Jawa Tengah	66.08	66.64	67.21	68.02	68.78	69.49	69.98	70.52
Di Yogyakarta	75.37	75.93	76.15	76.44	76.81	77.59	78.38	78.89
Jawa Timur	65.36	66.06	66.74	67.55	68.14	68.95	69.74	70.27
Banten	67.54	68.22	68.92	69.47	69.89	70.27	70.96	71.42
Bali	70.10	70.87	71.62	72.09	72.48	73.27	73.65	74.30
Nusa Tenggara Barat	61.16	62.14	62.98	63.76	64.31	65.19	65.81	66.58
Nusa Tenggara Timur	59.21	60.24	60.81	61.68	62.26	62.67	63.13	63.73
Kalimantan Barat	61.97	62.35	63.41	64.30	64.89	65.59	65.88	66.26
Kalimantan Tengah	65.96	66.38	66.66	67.41	67.77	68.53	69.13	69.79
Kalimantan Selatan	65.20	65.89	66.68	67.17	67.63	68.38	69.05	69.65
Kalimantan Timur	71.31	72.02	72.62	73.21	73.82	74.17	74.59	75.12
Kalimantan Utara	–	–	–	67.99	68.64	68.76	69.20	69.84
Sulawesi Utara	67.83	68.31	69.04	69.49	69.96	70.39	71.05	71.66
Sulawesi Tengah	63.29	64.27	65	65.79	66.43	66.76	67.47	68.11

(*Continued*)

Table 18.1 (Cont.)

Province	Human Development Index							
	2010	2011	2012	2013	2014	2015	2016	2017
Sulawesi Selatan	66	66.65	67.26	67.92	68.49	69.15	69.76	70.34
Sulawesi Tenggara	65.99	66.52	67.07	67.55	68.07	68.75	69.31	69.86
Gorontalo	62.65	63.48	64.16	64.70	65.17	65.86	66.29	67.01
Sulawesi Barat	59.74	60.63	61.01	61.53	62.24	62.96	63.60	64.30
Maluku	64.27	64.75	65.43	66.09	66.74	67.05	67.60	68.19
Maluku Utara	62.79	63.19	63.93	64.78	65.18	65.91	66.63	67.20
Papua Barat	59.60	59.90	60.30	60.91	61.28	61.73	62.21	62.99
Papua	54.45	55.01	55.55	56.25	56.75	57.25	58.05	59.09
Indonesia	66.53	67.09	67.70	68.31	68.90	69.55	70.18	70.81

Source: Indonesian Bureau of Statistics (n.d.)

Economist Budhi Resosudarmo and his team of researchers (2009) have drawn attention to how the emphasis of government development is in the urban centers, which are predominantly inhabited by non-indigenous Papuans; indigenous Papuans live in rural areas, especially in the central highlands, the swampy areas in the Southern Papua, and small islands in the North or the bird-head areas. As a result, the indigenous community receives less access to government services. The low quality of government services in health, education and economy sectors have contributed to the low level of HDI achievement. *Bappenas*, the Indonesian Ministry for National Development Planning (Hanafi, 2018), has acknowledged that the interior of the Papuan provinces, which fall under category of the area of difficult access (*daerah sulit*), receives only 14% of the whole development project budget.

While the statistics illustrate aspects of the indigenous Papuans' livelihoods, the figures can easily hide real human faces and experiences. In 2018, the Indonesian public was shocked with stunting and malnutrition problem in Asmat area and the measles outbreak in Korowai, South Papua. Long-term malnutrition in the swampy area of Asmat is a particular concern, as the area relies completely on food supply from outside. Measles, on the other hand, is "one of the leading causes of death for young children," according to the World Health Organization (WHO) (2017), although it is rare and preventable by vaccine. The WHO Indonesia office (ibid.) has noted that Papua was not the priority of 2017 when the outbreak occurred, so its actions (or lack thereof) might have contributed to the incident.

Connections to Resource Extraction

The encroachment of extractive industries across Papua is another characteristic of the frontier. While many smaller-scale industry actors have impacted Papuans' existence, I analyze Freeport Indonesia, as this particular international corporation best illustrates the work of necropolitics. Scholars (Droogle-ver, 2009; McKenna, 2015; Poulgrain, 2015; Stanley, 2014) tend to agree that the starting point of Freeport Indonesia in 1967 was problematic. Why? Because Papua was officially incorporated to Indonesia in 1969, two years after Freeport CEO and then President Suharto signed the Contract of Work (CoW), it is questionable as to whether the first CoW was entirely legal.

Poulgrain (2015) has investigated whether the world's largest gold deposit played a role in the incorporation of Papua into Indonesia. The gold deposit, first identified by Dutch geologist Dozy and his team during an expedition, amounted to a "concentration of gold was 15 grams/ton. For comparison the Witwatersrand (South Africa) underground goldmine was 7.5 grams/ton and the richest in the world in 1936" (Poulgrain, 2015, p. 37). There was a complex power struggle between the world's major players of the time, including the United States and Soviet Union, as well as other players, including the Netherlands and Indonesia. Given the immense gold deposit, the Dutch, according to Poulgrain (2015), concealed the findings, as it coincided with its dispute with Indonesia over Papua in the 1960s. In fact, the Dutch proposed to the UN that Papuans had to determine their own fate under their trusteeship until they could exercise their own rights to self-determination. Had their argument prevailed, the Dutch would have had sufficient time to mine and exploit the gold deposit. In other words, it was all about the gold, not about the Papuans, which Dutch Foreign Minister Joseph Luns later acknowledged (Poulgrain, 2015, p. 33). The gold deposit thus contributed to the Dutch decision reason to retain Papua, even though they ultimately failed to do so.

When a team led by Wilson reassessed the gold deposit in 1960, they discovered more. Wilson then secured contract from Suharto in 1967 and completed exploration in 1968. In 1969, when the Act of Free Choice was implemented in Papua, a feasibility study by Bechtel-Pomeroy was completed, Freeport began its operation in 1970 (Poulgrain, 2015, p. 41). It was therefore not a coincidence that CoW was signed in 1967 or why Indonesia's leaders were determined to make sure the Act of Free Choice favored Indonesia.

For more than fifty years, Freeport Indonesia[3] has enjoyed state-provided privileges, such as military protection[4] and legal provision (Ballard, 2002; Global Witness, 2005; Leith, 2003). It is only in 2017 that the Indonesian authority managed to persuade Freeport to comply with a new Indonesian law on mining that requires the company to divest its shares. In 2018, the Jokowi government took one step further by controlling majority shares of Freeport Indonesia and buying shares of Rio Tinto Indonesia. Although critics still express discontent, it is a landmark decision as Indonesia gained a full control over the company which had never happened before.

The deal does not solve the problems of the extractive industry, which are manifestations of necropolitics. Apart from mining, the ongoing expansion of oil palm plantation across Papua has already caused both devastating social and environmental impacts, especially in the Southern Papua, since it has given a leeway to grab land of indigenous communities (Hernawan, 2017a). In 2015, Jakarta-based environmental non-governmental organization (NGO), the Pusaka Foundation, published *Peta Sawit Papua* ("A Map of Oil Palm in Papua") (Franky & Morgan, 2015, pp. 59–62), which outlines the investments of palm oil companies across Papua and shows the quantity of land grabbing in Papua. The report documented 87 permits for 87 companies that occupy 2.1 million hectares (approx. 21,000 sq km) of Papua—approximately 13 times the size of the city of London. This finding resonates with Stanley's analysis that "Indonesian power in West Papua has consistently reflected and reinforced multinational corporate interests, land appropriation and resource extraction" (Stanley, 2014, p. 85).

The Penetration of Wahhabism

The third issue is the penetration of Wahhabism to Papua. Unlike traditional Islam, Wahhabism adopts a spirit of purification in relation to Islam across Indonesia, including Papua (see Al-Rasheed, 2007). In contrast to widespread beliefs that religion is not an issue in Papua, the Tolikara incident in 2015 demonstrates tensions that implicate Christian-Muslim relations (Al-Makassary, 2017). During this incident, the majority Christian community, which held their gathering in the highland city of Karubaga, attacked members of the Muslim community who were praying in a soccer field. Some police officers, who were at the prayer fired at the Christian crowd, hurting them. The mob burned the market where non-Papuans who are Muslim often go. A small mosque attached to the market coincidentally burned. The incident prompted a national response, as a delegation of cabinet ministers arrived in Tolikara within days. The national government provided funding to support rebuilding the mosque.

The incident not only represents the resentment between the two communities, but it also invited outside Wahabi groups from Java to operate more intensively within Papua. The late Ja'far Umar Thalib, the commander of *Laskar Jihad* who led the Muslim paramilitary groups during the Ambon conflict (Hasan, 2005), arrived and settled in the vicinity of the provincial capital of Jayapura. Despite the rejection of his presence by the Muslim organizations in Papua in 2016, he remained, even when the late Regent of Keerom officially asked him to leave. Instead, he insisted that he was a free man doing *dakwah* (proselytism) in Papua.[5] This claim of merely doing *dakwah* was questionable, though, as evinced by his attack on a Papuan family in February 2019. The incident not only threatened the life of the family but also flared the fury of the whole community against his action regardless of their religious background. The police acted quickly by arresting Jafar and his group as well as detaining them with criminal charges (Arnaz & Bisara, 2019).

In a similar vein, Fadlan Garamatan, an indigenous Muslim preacher from Fak-fak, promotes his *dakwah* by claiming that Papuans are still non-believers. In a March 2018 public statement, Garamatan accused Christian missionaries of introducing alcohol to Papua and training indigenous Papuans to rub pork fat over their bodies as a form of taking a bath. His activities and public statements caused strong reactions from both Christian and Muslim leaders in Papua who reported him to the police for insulting their identity. Garamatan then apologized to the Chair of Papuan Muslim Council, not to the Papuan community or the Christian community, and was never prosecuted.

The Indonesian state continues to take little to no action against the penetration of a puritan stream of Islam that has threatened the existing social and cultural cohesion. The lack of response communicates a tolerance of individuals with violent backgrounds and seriously undermines the long-established peaceful coexistence of various faiths in Papua. In other words, the state reinforces its dominating power over death and lives over Papuans, reflecting what Mbembe argues as the power of the state to co-opt opponents.

State Violence

The Indonesian National Commission on Human Rights (Komnas HAM), among other NGOs, has documented cases of gross violations of human rights that are still pending prosecution, including the perpetrators of the Wasior incident of 2001 and Wamena incident of 2003 (Komnas Ham, 2014). These cases entail extrajudicial killings, torture, rape, and destruction of civilians' property by Indonesian police and military in the island of Wasior and the city of Wamena, respectively. Komnas HAM has also investigated the case of killings of students in the Central Highlands in 2014, but there is no follow-up.

In retrospect, we see that the protracted conflicts in Papua have changed little in the last five decades. Authorities' heavy-handed approach is not simply against Papuans inside Papua's jurisdiction; rather, it has become a common pattern for the police to target Papuan communities and their solidarity supports across the Indonesian archipelago. Furthermore, racism has become more overt: members of the public no longer hesitate to call Papuan students outside Papua names like as "black monkey," "primitive," and "savage." These dehumanizing labels towards Papuans not only affirm postcolonial inequalities, but they also reveal how the Indonesian state tolerates the public mistreatment over Papuans.

The state authorities also make use of proxies in targeting Papuan communities, such as *Front Pembela Islam* (Islamic Defender Front/FPI), the Pancasila Youth (PP), Community Forum for Sons and Daughters of the Police and Armed Forces (FKPPI) and the Association of Sons and Daughters of Army Families (Hipakad). Although the involvement of proxies in handling security matters in Indonesia is not novel (Aspinall & Van Klinken, 2011), their deployment in dealing with Papuan students is a new development. If we take a closer look at these organizations, however, we see they do not operate as one front. Rather, they compete and even oppose each other based on their conflicting interests and affiliations. For instance, FPI are well-known in campaigning on an Islamist agenda, such as implementation of Sharia law, raiding places of worship of religious minorities, as well as leading protests against the former Governor of Jakarta Basuki Tjahaja Purnama for blasphemy, which made its involvement against Papuans and advocating for a nationalist agenda stand out. It does show, though, the chaotic nature of the postcolony as Mbembe suggests.

The International Coalition for Papua (ICP) (2019) documented ten most common pattern of human rights violation in 2018 to demonstrate the latest status of Papua's human rights situation. The report identifies three highest numbers are as follows: the highest number of cases is related to political arrests where the police arrested at least 1201 individuals in relation to political events. The second is 648 cases of violation of victims' health, and the third is 80 cases of torture (International Coalition for Papua, 2019). The personal account of prominent ex-Papuan political prisoner Filep Karma (2014) offers a powerful illustration of what these statistics represent. Entitled "*Seakan kitorang setengah binatang*" (As if we are half beast), his narrative demonstrates the Papuan experience of being denied, humiliated, and subject to state violence with impunity. My own research (Hernawan, 2016d, 2018) on torture in Papua over the last five decades further explores—and confirms—this observation. It reveals how the Indonesian state renders Indigenous Papuans as abject characterized by non-existence. As citizens, Papuans are subject to claims by the Indonesian state, which demonstrates its sovereignty through control over their life and death.

Confronting Necropolitics

In response to embedded necropolitics, indigenous Papuans and their solidarity networks have long resisted. Resistance in this case refers to myriad elements, such as non-violent struggle (Karma, 2014), violent struggle, passive or active, hidden or open, verbal or physical, spontaneous or strategic, local or global, and frequently a combination of some or all (Braithwaite et al., 2010; Chenoweth & Stephan, 2011; McLeod, 2012; Tebay, 2009). Resistance can be an effective way to defeat an oppressive regime in the long run, including arguably in Papua. We can trace Papuan resistance in its different forms historically, categorizing them in two major camps: violent and non-violent. The source, intensity, targets and impact of these two methods of resistance are remarkably different and dynamic.

Violent Resistance

The Papuans organised *Tentara Pembebasan Nasional Papua Barat* (the Papuan National Liberation Army/TPNPB) as the military wing of the broader umbrella *Organisasi Papua Merdeka* (Free Papua Movement/OPM). The late Otto Ondawame, a member of ULMWP, detailed the evolution of TPN in his book, *One People, One Soul* (2010), which was developed from his doctoral thesis and offers an insider's analysis. The struggle, however, exclusively responds to Indonesian state violence but does not deal with basic needs, corporation or penetration of Wahhabism.

Ondawame (2010, p. 65) begins his account by emphasizing that TPN was not born as a reaction to the Indonesian oppression; rather, it had been conceived by Papua nationalism since Dutch colonial rule. The TPN, he writes, came into existence when it launched its first attacks on 26 July 1965 and declared an independent Papuan state (p. 67). Two brothers, Loedwik and Barren Mandatjan, led a group of ex-PVK (Papuan battalion) to attack an Indonesian military outpost in Kebar, Manokwari. Two days later, Ferry Awom attacked another outpost of the Infantry Batalion 641 in Arfak, Manokwari, and seized 1000 arms. The attacks were not only recorded in academic literature, but also in the official documentation of the Indonesian military. The latter records the significance of the attacks, as it took months for the Indonesian military to regain control—and even then it was not a great success (Pusat Sejarah Dan Tradisi TNI, 2000, p. 126). These attacks show three important points: (1) the armed resistance has been part of the Papuan resistance movement, (2) the Indonesian military do not always prevail easily as a widespread belief, and (3) the attacks have been recorded in a popular lyric that the younger Papuan generation sings during their public demonstration (see Hernawan, 2018, p. 55).

The attacks did not stop in the Manokwari area; other attacks in Paniai, Makbon, Sausapor, Anggi, Merauke, Ubrub, Pyramid, North Biak, West Biak, and Sorong followed. In other words, many parts of Papua, except the Southern part, fostered armed resistance against the Indonesian military, which demonstrated that they strongly opposed Indonesia's presence. The armed resistance, however, did not last very long, as Indonesian forces suppressed them. The armed resistance retains its spirit, though, with guerilla struggle continuing. Some pocket areas in the Central Highlands of Papua, such as the Districts of Puncak, Puncak Jaya, and Lani Jaya, are sites where the TPN targets military and police stations as well as civilians who are accused of collaborating with the Indonesian state apparatus. Random attacks can occur at any time in the Central Highlands.[6] While it is rare, attacks can be deadly.

TPN organized their headquarters, *Markas Victoria*, in the border area between Papua and Papua New Guinea. The TPN leaders structured their resistance into five commands (KODAM) to challenge the structure of Indonesia military. The unity did not last very long when Jacob Pray and Seth Rumkorem had an irreconcilable argument on March 13, 1976, due to different personality and internal power struggle (Ondawame, 2010, pp. 80–81). The split of leadership caused serious consequences, with Victoria no longer serving as the central command and sharing power with a new one established by Jacob Pray in Ubrub.

Ondawame explains that TPN adopted three strategies: decentralization of power, mass mobilization, and internationalization. Decentralization of power entails the principle of "giving the masses an opportunity to take responsibility" (Ondawame, 2010, p. 88). Accordingly, TPN was organized into five commands. Three of territorial command structures are located in the Central Highlands of Papua, only one covers the low land area around Jayapura, and one is in the South, a structure that reveals the concentration of the Papuan armed resistance is in the Central Highlands. The next two principles work hand in hand. Mass mobilization aims to create "an effective underground network in towns by mobilizing all revolutionary forces—trade unions, students, women, workers, intellectuals, police and army personnel, public servants, churches, political parties and domestic bourgeoisie" (Ondawame, 2010, p. 89). While the aim is tactical, not all elements identified here exist in the Papuan context today. For example, trade unions and domestic bourgeoisie do not really exist in Papua. The third principle, internationalization, refers to any campaigns to put Papua on the global radar by increasing public awareness and working with the solidarity movements (p. 91). These latter two principles are crucial and have been effective to mobilize support inside and outside Papua to date. The solidarity movement for Papua operates both inside and outside Papua, and it cannot be separated from the idea of armed resistance to Indonesian authorities.

Furthermore, with regard to the third principle, Ondawame notes that TPN adopted new tactics in 1970s and 1980s by taking hostages and through aggressive political and military campaigns. He acknowledged that "taking hostage in particular is inhumane," but he claimed that

> this tactic has many advantages to gain material equipment, to draw international attention to the issue of West Papua, to force the parties to the peace negotiation table, and finally to press for the withdrawal of the Indonesian military from the border region.
>
> *(Ondawame, 2010, p. 94)*

A number of hostage cases included the kidnapping of Colonel Ismail and other Indonesian officers in 1978 (Samsudin, 1995), the kidnaping of an international team of scientists in Mapduma in 1996 (Saraswati, 1997; Start, 1997), and kidnapping of road workers in Merauke area in 1996. It is questionable, however, whether the tactic meets the objective. Not only is taking hostage is a serious breach of the international humanitarian law (International Committee of the Red Cross, n.d.), parties to armed conflict should make a clear distinction between combatants who are legitimate targets and civilians who should be protected by all parties at all time. Targeting civilians also generates bad publicity among international community. Notwithstanding, the practice of targeting civilians has changed little. In fact, in June 2018, TPN killed three civilians, including a woman and a minor, in the District Capital of Keneyam in the Central Highlands of Papua. They were accused of working with the military intelligence (Mambor, 2018).

By the end of 2018, the Papuan armed resistance renewed its operation in the Papua Central Highland of Nduga. Led by Egianus Kogoya, TPN-PB killed 19 road workers of PT Istaka Karya who were working on construction work in the area (Tehusijarana, 2018). In a press release, Sebby Sambom, the spokesperson of TPN-PB, explained that the attack had been planned three months in advance and claimed responsibility (Hadi & Ayu, 2018). The attack sparked national reaction, as it constituted the highest number of civilian casualties. As a result, the government immediately deployed troops to track down TPN-PB. The fight between the government troops and TPN forced the villagers to leave their homes and take refuge in neighboring areas. Four months later, at the time of this writing, the situation remains unresolved according to a joint investigation between Papua and Jakarta NGOs (Halim, 2019). The continuing cycle of violence shows that the Indonesian authorities prefer to resort to military than legal responses. This approach invites TPN-PB to respond in an equally militaristic way.

Non-violent Resistance

While the arms struggle has gained little public sympathy, the non-violent resistance has received more support nationally and internationally. In the last two decades, for instance, solidarity networks for Papua inside and outside Indonesia have grown exponentially and have been effective in confronting necropolitics in all forms. The networks mobilize a variety of actors, including lawyers, religious figures, journalists, academics, activists, students, and politicians across the globe as TPN aspires. We can divide them into three categories with different goals and approaches.

First, at the local level, we can identify two types of civil society organizations. One group promotes a rights agenda while the other advocates for political negotiations. The former is represented by FOKER LSM Papua (the Papua NGOs' Forum) and Church-based NGOs, whereas the latter is represented by JDP. Although FOKER LSM Papua was established in 1991, it grew from Papua civil society movement that established *Kelompok Kerja Oikumene* (the Ecumenical Team Work/KKO), a loose-structure of individuals concerned with social justice issues in December 1980. KKO was concerned with the policy and practice of the New Order government, which seized indigenous land to resettle migrants from outside Papua under the transmigration policy and enacted a high level of state-sponsored violence against Papuans under the policy of *Daerah Operasi Militer* (Zone of Military Operation/DOM).[7]

As Septer Manufandu, former Executive Secretary of FOKER, recalls:

> One of the reasons behind the establishment of FOKER was to anticipate the go-east government policy. There was strong concern that the development policy would marginalize the people. So FOKER was founded in order to amplify the voice of the people.[8]

Sixty-eight NGOs joined FOKER to advocate for the mining and the environment conservation, legal aid, women rights, rural development, health issues, civil and political rights as well as micro-economic empowerment. The breath of issues represents the complexity of the lives of the indigenous Papuans. Although less active in the last few years due to the leadership issue, FOKER's members still advocate for the rights of indigenous Papuans in various sectors. In fact, in its 25th anniversary, FOKER published a reflection on the work of its members, entitled *Perlawanan Kaki Telanjang: 25 tahun Gerakan Masyarakat Sipil di Papua* ("Struggle with barefoot: 25 year of the civil society movement in Papua"). The title precisely captures the essence of this network, which realizes its limitations as represented by "barefoot" in front of major challenges of issues and powerful actors especially the state, international corporations and their own donors. All of these actors influence strongly, if not dictate, the work of the NGOs in Papua as well as the lives of Papuans themselves.

In conjunction with FOKER LSM Papua, the Papua Churches established NGOs to promote human rights and social justice across Papua. The Catholic Diocese of Jayapura was pioneering in this social justice arena by establishing *Sekretariat Keadilan dan Perdamaian Keuskupan Jayapura* (SKP Jayapura) or the Office for Justice and Peace of the Catholic Diocese of Jayapura in July 1998. SKP Jayapura has been instrumental in monitoring, documenting and advocating for the rights of indigenous Papuans, especially in the interior where most Papuans have much less access to legal aid. The Synod of the Christian Evangelical Church in Tanah Papua (GKI) has a similar office under the name of *Sekretariat Keadilan, Perdamaian dan Keutuhan Ciptaan Gereja Kristen Injili di Tanah Papua* (SKPKC GKI) or the Justice and Peace office of the Christian Evangelical Church in Tanah Papua. This office works under the direct guidance of the largest Christian denomination in Papua and has an extensive network that goes to village level to monitor and advocate for the human rights of indigenous Papuans.[9]

On the political dialogue side, it took almost fifty years before Papuan civil society established *Jaringan Damai Papua* (Papua Peace Network/JDP) in 2010 (Jaringan Damai Papua, 2010). JDP only has one agenda "Papua Road Map" (LIPI, 2008), namely promoting dialogue between the government and indigenous Papuans in order to solve conflict in Papua. In implementing this agenda and with the support of Humanitarian Dialogue Centre, JDP organized a series of public consultation (Elisabeth et al., 2015) with the indigenous Papuans and the migrants (Siregar et al., 2013) who live in Papua in separate occasions. It also holds close door sessions with top government officials, senior police and military officials in order to persuade the government to take steps in opening up dialogue with Papuans. After almost a decade of lobbying Indonesian authorities, none of Indonesian administrations take their proposal seriously.

Other key organizations that promote political negotiations are Papuan student organizations, namely *Komite Nasional Papua Barat* (KNPB) and *Aliansi Mahasiswa Papua* (AMP). They have broad and strong networks both inside and outside Papua to promote Paupans' right to self-determination. It is also in part why Indonesian security apparatus target them (Davidson, 2019). Police have suppressed their activities, and some of the key KNPB leaders were found dead in gruesome conditions (Hernawan, 2017b). In fact, some cases of extra-judicial executions documented by Amnesty International has included their leaders and members.

Secondly, solidarity networks established during the Suharto's military dictatorship, such as YLBHI, ELSAM, and Walhi, still exist at the national level.[10] They are among the oldest NGOs, which opposed the encroachment of necropolitics against Papua and Indonesia as a whole in the forms of state violence and encroachment of corporations. Along with NGOs, solidarity network was also developed in the 1990s, especially the Human Rights Advocacy Team for Irian Jaya. When the Team was no longer active, other groups were established a decade later, such as National Papua Solidarity (NAPAS) and #PapuaItuKita (PIK). As loose networks that operate on a voluntary basis, their activities are ebb and flow depending on the availability of their members.

Nevertheless, we should pay attention to a newly established leftist solidarity group called *Front Rakyat Indonesia* (FRI), which explicitly advocates for the rights to self-determination for Papuans. This political approach has attracted repercussion from the Indonesian authorities, prompting harsh police responses to many FRI activities (BBC News, 2018).

Finally, at the international level, we find two types of resistance movements: United Liberation Movement for West Papua (ULMWP), a Papuan representative body, and the solidarity networks in Europe and Australasia that adopt various names, such as the International Coalition for Papua, Australia West Papua Association, and a West Papua Solidarity "desk" in New Zealand. The two types have different foci, strategies, and approaches. ULMWP is the only Papuan political organization that represents and is accepted by all Papuan political factions (United Liberation Movement for West Papua, 2015). Declared in 2014 with the strong support from Vanuatu elders and government, ULMWP has been effective in promoting the Papuan political agenda at the international diplomatic fora (Hernawan, 2016c). The effectiveness of their campaign can be seen from the responses of Indonesian government: authorities often take immediate and strong reaction to any ULMWP statements or actions, but not to NGOs' statements, journalists' reports, or research publications. To date, ULMWP specifically responds to state violence committed by Indonesian authorities.

The other types of resistance outside Indonesia's jurisdiction are solidarity networks for Papuans. In the last decade, the ICP has published bi-annual reports on the situation of Papua from the human rights perspective. Not only are their reports important, but ICP also represents a joining of forces between civil society organizations in Indonesia and international solidarity networks worldwide. The network aims to address politics of death in various forms. I have the privilege to be among the co-founders when it began as the Faith-based Network for Papua, which consisted of European faith-based organizations that have historical networks with counterparts in Papua. ICP's contribution to confronting the necropolitics cannot be overestimated, as the network has survived internal dynamics, external pressure, and lack of funding since its establishment in 2003.[11]

While both violent and non-violent resistance has exposed the impacts and consequences of the politics of death, they are not on equal footing with major actors, such as the state, corporations, and religious entities. They may confront the politics of death, but they are still unable to dismantle it. Empirically, scholars of peacebuilding (e.g., Chenoweth & Stephan, 2011; Human Security Research Group, 2014; McLeod, 2015) have found that non-violent resistance is more effective in exposing the logic of the politics of death and at some point, dismantle it through so-called "people's power." The power of the weak can win if they are able to consolidate their struggle, as in the case of Timor Leste (Braithwaite, Charlesworth, & Soares, 2012).

In contrast to the peacebuilding scholars who frame the Papuan context as a binary opposition, Mbembe describes the relation between the ruling with the ruled in the postcolonial context as an intimate tyranny often marked by conviviality. That is, both sides are interconnected in more fluid and ambiguous ways than it may appear on the surface. This pattern fits into the analysis of illegality and state exemption in the broader context of Indonesian politics, where the state and resistance movements co-opt each other for their own benefits. This does not mean that they collaborate but rather, they simply make use of each other.

Conclusion

In the postcolonial context of Papua, the politics of death may seem unstoppable, as they have operated through state, corporate, and religious modes for the last five decades. They have been met with strong resistance in the form of both violent and non-violent methods. The confrontation, however, is not symmetric, as resistance efforts occupy a more fragile position. Although state domination remains incontestable, it is not necessarily absolute. The fact that Papua resistance movement exists—and even continues to grow—demonstrates that there is sufficient space to maneuver. Both violent and non-violent resistance engages different publics and promote consciousness raising in order to challenge the domination of Indonesian state. Exposing the violent and illegal nature of the Indonesian state domination is at the core of the Papuan resistance, which involves strategy, networking, public communication, and mass mobilization to do so.

In this context, public criminology might be able to contribute to advancing the Papuan issue, but they would have to account for the postcolonial conditions of Papua as a frontier—which I have done here. Analyzing Papua through the lens of necropolitics reveals the postcolonial conditions of Papua, which otherwise remain under-researched. Specifically, it aids in illuminating the economic, social, political and religious conditions of Papua. Applying necropolitics here reminds us that while social scientists may aim to engage broader audience, they should not abandon important conceptual tools when they seek wider engagement. With these insights in mind, the contribution of public criminology could be valuable in terms of dissecting and explaining how the Papuan frontier has emerged from and responds to state crime, which is arguably a form of unpunished and long-term state violence. It could support a more radical project by, as Piché (2015, p. 71) explains, helping "to affect social change" and "intervene at a time when there is notable resistance." But, if public criminology were to do this work, it, like the Papuan resistance, must struggle against being co-opted by the state.

Notes

1 For Indigenous residents, the word "Papua" refers to the western half of the island of New Guinea. It has had various names: The Dutch called it Nieuw-Guinea, the first Indonesian President Sukarno renamed it Irian Barat before the second president Suharto changed it to Irian Jaya, and the fourth President Abdurahman Wahid restored its Indigenous name Papua in 2000. Many English speakers use "West Papua," which activists have adopted. The Indonesian government administration divides the territory into two provinces: Papua Barat and Papua. I use the word "Papua" to reflect what Indigenous Papuans use.
2 DMP was selected by the Indonesian military to represent the Papuan community for the implementation of the Act of Free Choice. During the plebiscite, under the gunpoint, DMP declared unanimously and publicly that they opted for integration with Indonesia.
3 This company occupies 2.6 million hectares of land (26,000 square km), which is 33 times larger than the size of New York City (784 square km).
4 An investigative report by the New York Times in 2005, for instance, revealed the company paid some US$35 million per year for military infrastructure and US$20 million per year to military and police between 1998 and 2004.
5 In a letter to the late Regent of Keerom dated September 20, 2017, the late Ja'far Umar Thalib questioned the plan of the local government to close his Islamic boarding school (*pesantren*) and return his students to Java.
6 My recent fieldwork to the Central Highlands in May 2018 confirms an active movement of the Papuan armed group in the District of Lani Jaya.
7 Personal communication with the author on September 21, 2018.
8 Personal communication with the author on October 4, 2018.
9 These Church-based organizations have been instrumental in helping establish a strategic alliance of civil society organizations called *Koalisi HAM Papua*, the Alliance for Human Rights of Papua. The Alliance is a network of key human rights organizations based in Jayapura. These include *Sekretariat Keadilan, Perdamaian dan Keutuhan Ciptaan Fransiskan Papua* (SKPKC-FP), the Justice and Peace of the Franciscans Order, SKPKC of the GKI, LBH Papua, Jubi, Jerat, ELSHAM Papua, Kontras Papua, FOKER, and Tiki Papua.
10 *Yayasan Lembaga Bantuan Hukum Indonesia* (YLBHI) is one of the oldest legal aid foundations in Indonesia. It established its Papua-branch office in the late 1980s to deal with the land-grabbing problems. ELSAM is one of the oldest human rights NGOs in the country which sued Freeport McMoran in the US court in the 1990s. Walhi is Indonesia's oldest environmental NGOs which has monitored the destruction of the environment across Indonesia, especially Papua.

11 The network has grown significantly and geographically, now including non-faith-based organization, so it has been renamed as the International Coalition for Papua to reflect the diversity of its members (see www.humanrightspapua.org/).

References

Al-Makassary, R. (2017). *Insiden Tolikara & Ja'far Umar Thalib: Kontroversi Mushalla yang "dibakar" dan Drama Jihad di Tanah Papua*. Jakarta: Kementrian Agama Provinsi Papua.

Al-Rasheed, M. (2007). *Contesting the Saudi state, Islamic voices from a new generation*. Cambridge: Cambridge University Press.

Arnaz, F., & Bisara, D. (2019, March 1). Police name former Laskar jihad leader a suspect in religious charged assault case in Papua. *Jakarta Globe*. Retrieved on March 30, 2019 from https://jakartaglobe.id/context/police-name-former-laskar-jihad-leader-a-suspect-in-religiously-charged-assault-case-in-papua.

Aspinall, E., & Van Klinken, G. (2011). *The state and illegality in Indonesia*. Leiden: KITLV Press.

Ballard, C. (2002). The signature of terror: Violence, memory and landscape at freeport. In D. Bruno & M. Wilson (Eds.), *Inscribed landscapes: Marking and making place* (pp. 13–26). Honolulu: University of Hawai'i Press.

Braithwaite, J., Braithwaite, V., Cookson, M., & Dunn, L. (2010). *Anomie and violence: Non-truth and reconciliation in Indonesian peacebuilding*. Canberra, ACT: ANU Press.

Braithwaite, J., Charlesworth, H., & Soares, A. (2012). *Networked governance of freedom and tyranny: Peace in Timor Leste*. Canberra, ACT: ANU Press.

Chenoweth, E., & Stephan, M. J. (2011). *Why civil resistance works: The strategic logic of nonviolent conflict*. New York: Columbia University Press.

Davidson, H. (2019, January 8). "New chapter of persecution": Indonesia cracks down on West Papua separatists. *The Guardian*. Retrieved March 30, 2019, from www.theguardian.com/world/2019/jan/08/new-chapter-of-persecution-indonesia-cracks-down-on-west-papua-separatists.

Departmen Dalam Negeri. (1969). *West Irian: Implementation of the act of free choice* (July 14–August 2, 2nd ed.). Jakarta: Departemen Dalam Negeri.

Drooglever, P. (2009). *An act of free choice: Decolonization and the right to self-determination in West Papua*. Oxford: One Word.

Elisabeth, A., Tebay, N., Sumule, A., Sudrajat, Pamungkas, C., Siregar, L. A., & Manufandu, S. (2015). *Bersama-sama Membangun Papua Damai*. Jakarta: Lembaga Ilmu Pengetahuan Indonesia dan Jaringan Damai Papua.

Franky, Y. L., & Morgan, S. (2015). *Atlas Sawit Papua, Di Bawah Kendali Penguasa Modal*. Jakarta: Pusaka.

Global Witness. (2005). *Paying for protection: The Freeport mine and the Indonesian security forces*. Washington, DC: Global Witness.

Hadi, S., & Ayu, M. (2018, December 6). OPM admits deadly attack, demand independence. *Tempo*. Retrieved March 30, 2019, from http://en.tempo.co/read/924057/opm-admits-deadly-attack-demand-independence.

Halim, D. (2019, March 29). Ungkap Temuan di Nduga, Tim Investigasi Minta Pemerintah Evaluasi Operasi Pengejaran KKB. *Kompas*. Retrieved March 30, 2019, from https://nasional.kompas.com/read/2019/03/29/17342481/ungkap-temuan-di-nduga-tim-investigasi-minta-pemerintah-evaluasi-operasi.

Komnas Ham. (2014). *Ringkasan Eksekutif Laporan Penyelidikan Pelanggaran Hak Asasi Manusia Berat*. Jakarta: Komisi Nasional Hak Asasi Manusia.

Hanafi, T. (2018). *Instruksi Presiden Republik Indonesia Nomor 9 Tahun 2017 tentang Percepatan Pembangunan Provinsi Papua dan Provinsi Papua BArat*. Jakarta: Desk Papua Kementrian PPN/Bappenas.

Hasan, N. (2005). *Laskar Jihad, Islam, Militancy and the Quest for Identity in Post-New Order Indonesia*. PhD thesis, University of Utrecht.

Hernawan, B. (2016a). *Papua and bandung: A contest between decolonial and postcolonial question*. New York: Rowman & Littlefield.

Hernawan, B. (2016b). Torture as theatre in Papua. *International Journal of Conflict and Violence*, 10, 77–92.

Hernawan, B. (2016c, December). ULMWP and the insurgent Papua. *Live Encounter*. https://liveencounters.net/2016-le-mag/12-december-2016/1-dr-budi-hernawan-ulmwp-and-the-insurgent-papua.

Hernawan, B. (2016d). Torture as theatre in Papua. *International Journal of Conflict and Violence (IJCV)*, 10(1), 77–92.

Hernawan, B. (2017a). Papua. *The Contemporary Pacific*, 29, 347–354.

Hernawan, B. (2017b) Why does Indonesia kill us? Political assassination of KNPB activists in Papua. *Kyoto Review of Southeast Asia*.

Hernawan, B. (2018). *Torture and Peacebuilding in Indonesia, the case of Papua*. London: Routledge.

Hernawan, B., & Indarti, P. (2007). *The practice of torture in Aceh and Papua 1998–2007 with an annex on the situation of human rights in Timor Leste.* Jakarta: SKP Jayapura.

Human Security Research Group. (2014). Human security report 2013: The decline in global violence: Evidence, explanation, and contestation. Vancouver, BC.

Indonesian Bureau of Statistics. (n.d.) *Indeks pembangunan manusia menurut provinsi (Metode Baru), 2010–2018.* Retrieved September 25, 2018, from www.bps.go.id/dynamictable/2016/06/16/1211/indeks-pembangunan-manusia-menurut-provinsi-2010-2017-metode-baru-.html.

International Coalition for Papua. (2019). *Human rights update West Papua—October 2019.* Retrieved from http://humanrightspapua.org/images/docs/Human%20Rights%20Update%20West%20Papua%20October%202019.pdf

International Committee of the Red Cross. (n.d.) Rule 96. hostage-taking. Retrieved October 15, 2018, from https://ihl-databases.icrc.org/customary-ihl/eng/docs/v1_rul_rule96.

Karma, F. (2014). *Seakan Kitorang Setengah Binatang: Rasialisme Indonesia di Tanah Papua.* Jayapura: Deiyai.

Leith, D. (2003). *The politics of power: Freeport in Suharto's Indonesia.* Honolulu: University of Hawai'i Press.

LIPI. (2008). *Papua road map.* Jakarta: Author.

Mambor, V. (2018, June 25). Indonesia: Gunmen shoot at plane, kill 3 civilians at Papua airport. *BenarNews.* Retrieved October 13, 2018, from www.benarnews.org/english/news/indonesian/plane-attack-06252018161455.html.

Mbembe, A. (2001). *On the Postcolony.* Berkeley, CA: University of California Press.

Mbembe, A. (2003). Necropolitics. *Public Culture, 15*, 11–40.

McKenna, K. (2015). *Corporate social responsibility and natural resource conflict.* London: Routledge.

McLeod, J. (2012). *Civil resistance in West Papua (Perlawanan tanpa kekerasan di Tanah Papua).* PhD thesis, University of Queensland.

McLeod, J. (2015). *Merdeka and the morning star: Civil resistance in West Papua.* Brisbane: University of Queensland.

BBC News. (2018, December 1). Peringati 1 Desember Papua, organisasi proPapua merdeka: Hampir 600 orang ditangkap di berbagai kota. *BBC News Indonesia.* Retrieved March 30, 2019, from www.bbc.com/indonesia/indonesia-46411149.

Ondawame, O. (2010). *'One people, one soul': West Papuan Nationalism and the Organisasi Papua Merdeka.* Adelaide: Crawford House.

Papua, J. D. (2010). *Tawaran Konsep Dialog Jakarta-Papua.* Jayapura: Jaringan Damai Papua.

Komnas Perempuan. (2010). *Stop Sudah! Kesaksian Perempuan Papua Korban Kekerasan dan Pelanggaran HAM 1963–2009.* Jakarta: Komisi Nasional Anti Kekerasan terhadap Perempuan, Majelis Rakyat Papua, ICTJ.

Piché, J. (2015). Assessing the boundaries of public criminology: On what does (not) count. *Social Justice, 42*(2), 70–90.

Poulgrain, G. (2015). *The incubus of intervention.* Petaling Jaya: Strategic Information and Research Development Centre.

Pusat Sejarah Dan Tradisi TNI. (2000). *Sejarah TNI Jilid IV (1966–1983).* Jakarta: Author.

Resosudarmo, B. P., Napitupulu, L., & Manning, C. (2009). Papua II: Challenges for public administration and economic policy under special autonomy. In B. P. Resosudarmo, & F. Jotzo (Eds.), *Working with nature against poverty.* Singapore: Institute of Southeast Asian Studies.

Saltford, J. (2003). *The United Nations and the Indonesian takeover of West Papua, 1962–1969: The anatomy of betrayal.* London: Routledge Curzon.

Samsudin. (1995). *Pergolakan di Perbatasan: Operasi Pembebasan Sandera Tanpa Pertumpahan Darah.* Jakarta: Gramedia Pustaka Utama.

Saraswati, A. (1997). *Sandera, 130 Hari Terperangkap di Mapnduma.* Jakarta: Pustaka Sinar Harapan.

Siregar, L. A., Mustafa, H., Conoras, Y., & Sipla, C. (2013). *Menuju Papua Tanah Damai: Perspektif Non Papua.* Jayapura: Aliansi Demokrasi untuk Papua.

Stanley, E. (2014). Resistance to state-corporate crimes in West Papua. In E. Stanley & J. McCulloch (Eds.), *State crime and resistance.* London: Routledge.

Start, D. (1997). *The open cage the ordeal of the Irian Jaya hostages.* London: Harper Collins.

Stefanie, C. (2018, February 7). Istana respons laporan Amnesty International soal Papua. *CNN Indonesia.* Retrieved on October 13, 2018 from: www.cnnindonesia.com/nasional/20180702191057-20-310885/istana-respons-laporan-amnesty-international-soal-papua.

Tapol. (1983). *West Papua: The obliteration of a people.* London: Author.

Tebay, N. (2009). *Dialog Jakarta-Papua: Sebuah Perspektif Papua.* Jayapura: Sekretariat Keadilan dan Perdamaian, Keuskupan Jayapura.

Tehusijarana, K. (2018, December 7). Papua mass killing: What happened. *The Jakarta Post.* Retrieved March 30, 2019, from www.thejakartapost.com/news/2018/12/07/papua-mass-killing-what-happened.html.

Tim SKP Jayapura. (2006). *Memoria passionis di Papua: Potret sosial, politik, dan HAM sepanjang 2004*. Jayapura: Sekretariat Keadilan dan Perdamaian Keuskupan Jayapura.

Uggen, C., & Inderbitzin, M. (2010). Public criminologies. *Criminology & Public Policy, 9*, 725–749.

United Liberation Movement for West Papua. (2015). *ULMWP Sebuah Profil: Persatuan dan Rekonsialiasi Bangsa Melanesia di Papua Barat*. Jayapura, Tim: ULMWP.

Widjojo, M. S. (ed.). (2010). *Papua road map: Negotiating the past, improving the present, and securing the future*. Jakarta: Kerja sama LIPI, Yayasan Tifa, dan Yayasan Obor Indonesia.

World Heath Organization Indonesia. (2017). *Measles rubella immunization campaign in Java Island on Aug-Sep 2017*. Retrieved from www.searo.who.int/indonesia/topics/immunization/MR_CAMPAIGN/en.

19
RETHINKING HOW "THE PUBLIC" COUNTS IN PUBLIC CRIMINOLOGY

David A. Maldonado

The "public" in public criminology is often assumed to be separate from, but in conversation with, academia. Discussions of public criminology also often assume experts in the university are reaching out to the public(s): They often start from the premise that public criminology reaches outward from the university, often failing to interrogate the university as a space that itself requires engagement. In doing so, they also often fail to examine these social relations as constitutive, missing an opportunity to interrogate how changing societal dynamics inform the state-university nexus. In this chapter, I examine the university as a contested public, ask how it serves as a gatekeeper to who is considered part of "the public" and who has a say in public discourse, and discuss the implications for public criminology. I argue that not only is the university a "public," it is a space in which we see contradictions of violence and carcerality persist.

Here, drawing on my position in the university as a formerly incarcerated graduate student and activist at the University of California, Berkeley (hereafter "UC Berkeley"), I consider critically how some of us come to be "in but not of" the university (Harney & Moten, 2013, p. 26). As subversive intellectuals, many of us find ourselves "in" the university, but we reject the university's framing of education as a linear process that conceptualizes study as emanating exclusively from the classroom. Such conceptualizations often frame studying as merely a means of professionalization (Harney & Moten, 2013), thus reproducing capitalism's ends. Rather, study is what we already do together,

> talking and walking around with other people, working, dancing, suffering, some irreducible convergence of all three, held under the name of speculative practice ... The point of calling it "study" is to mark that the incessant and irreversible intellectuality of these activities is already present.
>
> *(Harney & Moten, 2013, p. 110)*

While UC Berkeley promotes a vision of the university pursuing enlightenment through education, its integration of the liberal subject into its "public" masks its deeper commitment to a recuperative marketing of itself that displaces alternative modes of study (Harney & Moten, 2013; Meyerhoff, 2019).

As the authors of the undercommons remind us, "it cannot be denied that the university is a place of refuge, and it cannot be accepted that the university is a place of enlightenment" (Harney & Moten, 2013, p. 26). Kelley (2016) helps us understand that this, at least in principle, means the university will never cease being sexist, racist, xenophobic, Islamophobic, or heteronormative, and we should therefore *not* look for selective inclusion of darker faces (or "worthy" dispossessed subjects) as a means to transform the university. We should instead call for its reimagining. In fact, we already bring modes of knowledge to the university that speculates an elsewhere, right here, an end to the university-as-such (Undercommoning, 2016).

I begin this chapter with a reflection on how the university is carceral, reflecting on moments in UC Berkeley's history, as well as my own experience, to illustrate its violence. I draw heavily from scholarship associated with the field of critical university studies, which aids in understanding the cultural and economic shifts that have informed changes in higher education. I then explain how public criminology rarely attends to these concerns, thus failing to recognize how it, as a project, can become a commodity that does not account for how university conditions are constitutively linked to wider social, economic, cultural, and punitive trends. In doing so, these forms of public criminology inevitably work in the interests of state and threaten to perpetuate carceral logics.

Carceral Shifts and the University

One of the aims of this chapter is to reflect on how the university is an arm of the state, one that draws on logics employed to secure state legitimacy, particularly during moments of crisis. This relationship is worthy of a conjunctural analysis. Drawing on the work of Hall and Massey (2010), conjunctural analysis exposes the particular contradictions in a capitalist liberal democratic society during a historical moment—especially when those contradictions can no longer reproduce themselves. By this Gramscian logic, during a crisis in hegemony, the historical bloc has to reconfigure the equilibrium between the state and civil society, forcing a readjustment of consent and coercion (Gramsci, 1971).

We can see these maneuvers in UC Berkeley's history. For example, its closing of the criminology school—often referred to simply as "The Berkeley School"—revealed a disdain for attempts at a critically engaged public criminology. Then Governor Reagan and the UC Regents questioned the academic standards of the school despite its rigor and ability to draw on expert voices from the community. These politically-driven attacks stemmed in large part from the radical faculty's interest in questioning U.S. military involvement in Vietnam and the rise of carceral logics (Schwendinger & Schwendinger, 2014). Perhaps not surprisingly, the Regents (which contained only one educator) and their associates seemingly "owned and operated the State of California" in that members also sat on corporate boards, owned media outlets, and directed corporate military interest (p. 12). They also managed the university crisis with tactics that drew on McCarthyite rhetoric. They ultimately closed what was perhaps one of criminology's most radical chapters by suppressing dissenters as a function of securing hegemony. That is, overwhelmingly, state forces, including and especially the university, maintained what counts as public by securing hegemony during a crisis moment.

The U.S. carceral state has a history of similarly securing legitimacy during crises of hegemony: it reconfigures repressive governance by hardening ideological commitments, often using crime and criminalized persons to do so. For example, Hall, Critcher, Jefferson, Clarke, and Roberts (2013) have shown with incredible precision how the British state manufactured a moral panic by targeting and demonizing the "Black mugger"—a racialized folk devil—in the maintenance of authority. In doing so, it supports the production of anti-Blackness while also producing "illegality/criminality of non-Black bodies" as a function of carceral expansion and expropriation (paperson, 2017, p. 12). More recently, crises in public surpluses have informed the spike in carcerality and targeted criminalization that ushered in mass incarceration. Gilmore (2007) has shown how California used prison building to manage the various crises left by agribusiness, surplus labor, public spending, and state legitimacy. Gilmore's seminal work performs a conjunctural analysis of prisons that is instructive of state responses to crises more generally and California more specifically.

The rise of Supermax prisons and solitary special housing units (SHU) also occurred in the shadow of a state-sponsored project to manage the crises of the Attica prison uprising and the death of George Jackson (Berger, 2016; Thompson, 2017). When collectives of radical prisoners pushed back against racist prisons and prison guards, the state answered with increased violence and repression. This critical historical conjuncture occurred when support for prisons was waning, when radical prisoners were organizing, and the crime rate was dropping. The state managed the contradictions by convincing people that prisons contained an undeserving dangerous Other that should be locked away forever (Berger, 2016; Thompson, 2017).

The same counterinsurgent logics emerge across timelines: During the 2011 California prison hunger strikes, solitary confinement prisoners from "rival" racial groups came together and organized a mass hunger strike. Through legal and political action, the men from Pelican Bay's SHU brought changes to solitary practices and importantly also created the mandate to end racial hostilities. These men's actions reflect an abolition geography that is

> capacious (it isn't only by, for or about Black people) and specific (it's a guide to action for both understanding and rethinking how we combine our labor with each other and the earth). [It] takes feeling and agency to be constitutive of, no less than constrained by, structure. In other words, it's a way of studying, and doing political organizing, and of being in the world, and of worlding ourselves.
>
> *(Gilmore, 2007, p. 238)*

In short, abolition, like Harney and Moten's (2013) commentary on study, involves doing and thinking together.

When radical collectives come together to expose state violence and related contradictions, the state often responds with counterinsurgent attempts to manipulate public opinion by constructing a folk devil. For instance, in response to the California prison strikes, the state answered with thinly veiled attempts to convince the public that California prisons are full of dangerous "gang members" instead of implementing meaningful educational opportunities, changing the brutal conditions in prison, or re-evaluating the "gang validation" process. Guards at Corcoran State Prison resumed the practice of orchestrating "gladiator fights" between the few groups that still have on-site conflict by releasing small numbers of select groups onto a yard simultaneously. They are also "integrating" protective custody people back into main yards, which promotes conflict (Sonenstein, 2019). The politics of integrating protective custody people back into main yards requires rejecting relative innocence as part of an abolitionist praxis (Gilmore, 2017; Wang, 2018), which rejects sorting and confining people at all. These reintegration and sorting tactics reveal the state's motives: After the legal victories achieved by California prisoners and activists, the state wishes to convince the public that all the prison's repressive measures, including solitary confinement, are necessary, that everyone locked up is a danger, and that authorities told us so.

These conditions affect the university, as the state's project of sorting incarcerated people influences how incarcerated people can access education. The bifurcation between conviction typologies (violent/nonviolent) influences who can access certain programs (again read, the relatively innocent) and informs how formerly incarcerated students are asked to perform once they are "in" the university. We are asked to share our stories of trauma, because it fits a narrative of overcoming conditions that does not touch the underlying power relations that caused this trauma and criminalization. It also renders alternative forms of education as illegible at the site of the university.

Similar tensions emerge in mainstream criminology, which has long recognized problems with the carceral state but tends to focus on large data sets and naming the problems of racial disproportionality without properly theorizing underlining concerns linked to the state apparatus, such as anti-Blackness and settler colonialism. Even though anti-Blackness is operationalized as a foundational carceral logic (paperson, 2017), criminology for the most part fails to engage what this means—that is, beyond the mere counting of racialized bodies (see Henne & Shah, 2015)— and thus ultimately fails to reckon with carcerality. Following an abolition framing, which is not the norm within criminology, requires a deep meditation on the ways that selective incorporation into restrictive enrollment institutions (Harkins & Meiners, 2017), actually extends the life, scale, and scope of the carceral possibilities of the prison—and the university.

Carcerality is not confined to the prison. For instance, the university can actually expand carceral logics, including the policing of dissent, as it absorbs the "responsibilized" student of color presumed to be a criminalized risk into its reformed image of civil society. Furthermore, by operationalizing keywords like diversity and inclusion, the university participates in what Sexton (2010) considers "people-of-color-blindness," which flattens concerns particular to Blackness by reducing wider race issues to "Black" issues. Even more problematically, claims that include gains for people of color often reproduce anti-Blackness by failing to adequately theorize Black suffering. The worst form of this involves non-Black people of color misrepresenting or ignoring the specificity of anti-Blackness in their political gains.[1] This framing reinforces a selective kind of inclusion into the university or invites participation in a form of Black capitalism that is irreconcilable with demands for a different university (Ferguson, 2017). The university disperses these constitutive logics in its epistemology, especially in disciplines such as criminology. Criminology manages conjunctural crises by studying crime, and sometimes race, as if both categories are natural features of a social formation. Criminology pays inadequate attention to the ways that anti-Blackness and the political economy are imbricated in targeted criminalization. Unpacking this dynamic concedes that a Black futurity means we are all free—a core abolitionist tenet.

Navigating the University as a (Public) Carceral Space

Although this chapter illustrates how the university is a problematic space, I acknowledge it is a place where subversives can find each other and organize in modes of fugitive futurity—that is, those imaginations that see abolition and decolonization as projects to be launched in the undercommons (Harney & Moten, 2013). For the formerly incarcerated, fugitivity is often lived in the paradoxes caused by the shadow of state supervision but also simultaneously in the daylight of subversive solidarity against the university machine.

I recall being reminded of that fugitivity one day as I was walking across the campus to join a strike action when I heard a commotion. As a graduate student instructor, I had canceled class to join the mainly Black and Brown service workers striking to protest the stagnant wages, the racial and gender pay gap, and the outsourcing of their jobs. When I arrived, my comrades told me that UC Berkeley campus police just brutalized a protester: a Black service worker. What mainstream media coverage did not adequately cover is that the protester was almost hit by a White motorist while blocking the busy Telegraph Avenue intersection. To protect himself from getting hit, he slammed his sign on the hood of the car. The driver immediately told a campus police officer he had been the victim of what the police later called vandalism, essentially weaponizing his Whiteness in order to use the police as violence against Black people. The protester's Blackness marked his body as subject to criminalization and open to gratuitous violence. Whiteness, in contrast, emerges as a property and is thus deputized to shoot, maim, kill, or in this case, run down Black people with seeming impunity (Harris, 1993; Mirpuri, 2017; Reinstein, 2019).

As a result, the protestor blocking the intersection was open to be hit by an angry White motorist. Instead of coming to his defense or attempting to understand the situation, the campus police brutalized and arrested him for vandalism and resisting arrest. His criminality was assigned a priori, residing in his Blackness, as criminal, immutable, and pathological. The university's militarized policing of service workers' strikes revealed carceral logics coalescing—quite literally—in and through the elbows and fists of the campus police officers as they tore the protestors' flesh across the pavement of the campus quad. This particular moment is part of the university's carceral cycle, which renders many laborers precarious, polices their resistance, and drives them from the surrounding community.

I remember that as an undergraduate I was similarly welcomed to the campus by the arrest of my fellow formerly incarcerated comrade during protests associated with the Occupy Movement. He was arrested during a protest that happened days after the campus police stormed tents and violently removed the campus occupiers at three o'clock in the morning and just days after the UC Davis police pepper-sprayed a group of sitting protesters. On this day, the UC Berkeley police jammed a Billy-club into my Brown comrade's stomach and then arrested him, eventually leading to a probation violation and county jail time for him. Although much of the exchange was caught on cell phone cameras, no police were disciplined, and my comrade sat in a jail cell. More recently, during some of the alt-right visits to UC Berkeley, a heavily tattooed Latinx comrade of mine was racially profiled, searched, and then arrested for walking while formerly incarcerated: for possessing a pocketknife.

The message in this through line was clear: UC Berkeley celebrates itself as the "number one public university in the world" while advancing neoliberal market values, policing resistance to this market violence, and distancing itself from the surrounding community—all signifying values that are seemingly far from being part of the many communities that make up "the public." These practices cannot be separated from UC Berkeley's longer history of counterinsurgency and repression of radical movements, including the closing of its School of Criminology. The "public" university can—and does—maintain carceral logics. We should therefore express a deep wariness about the epistemologies and imaginations evoked when universities use the term "public." They are not necessarily just.

It is important to note that the university not only disperses modes of carcerality, but it is also neoliberal (Ferguson, 2012). Neoliberal ideology often evokes terms like public housing, public benefits, public transportation, and public space in ways that selectively apply to racialized and gendered populations who become framed as "underserving" people. Such neoliberal logics, when embraced by the university, constitute what Harney and Moten (2013) consider the university's "negligence", which has disproportionate effects. In particular, their work shows us how the university maintains silos to accommodate wealthy, tuition-paying students and new debtors (Harkins & Meiners, 2017; Harney & Moten, 2013). The university's rigid division of labor, including precarious academic faculty positions, underpaid and overworked graduate students, and exploited service workers, maintains the university's carceral political economy. As the surrounding housing markets adjust to accommodate wealthier groups (especially out-of-state tuition paying students), not only are local residents displaced as they suffer from precarity, but they are also more likely to be criminalized. University policing then aids in repressing demands for justice, including efforts that call for tuition-free colleges and labor strikes. These precarious populations are not simply subject to the harsh edge of the university's carceral political economy; they do not come to count as valued members of the public at or in the university.

In contrast, the academy often holds up the idea of the public as analogous to the ideals of democracy and pluralism, and as invested in searching for an ever-evolving universal knowledges that will improve human(ist) understanding. It assumes an idealized version of the public that is capable of critiquing itself. This critique claims to advance the university along the humanist lines of enlightenment discourses of reason. Kant (1998, p. 643), as one of reason's primary proponents and defenders, argued that "freedom" depends on "no dictatorial authority" and is constitutive of "agreement of free citizens, each of whom must be able to express his reservations, indeed even his veto, without holding back" (see also Kant, 2000). Therefore, reason must have a robust notion of the public, free from forms of censure, with a strong public sphere to achieve its unitary function (Arendt, 1989). Kant's notion of subjective universality, from his aesthetic theory, can be thought of as providing emancipatory notions of human equality by showing that the common human experience of aesthetic judgment, especially the judgment of beauty, is not reserved just for elites (Kant, 2000). Further, the argument goes, if we all have this capability of judging without interest and persuading others, we can build upon it so as to create a bridge to a shared politics and public sphere (Arendt, 1989; Heller, 2018). However, Kant is suggesting a public sphere with epistemological contours shaped by Whiteness (Moten, 2018).

Important work on the public gives a hopeful reading of a public sphere, depicting it as a discursive arena that mediates between the state and civil society towards a consensus ideal (Habermas, 1991). This is emblematic of the liberal imagination of the university. This notion of the public arguably invokes liberal fantasies of the meritocratic possibilities of education. Many universities actively deploy the term, "public," to defend their institutional existence. Does the qualifier change, however, when we use the term to refer to declining social wages and support? To public benefits? Or public space? This is the type of public that public criminology has trouble imagining. To understand how these dynamics manifest, let us consider the contemporary conditions in which the so-called public university exists.

Neoliberal Multiculturalism as Reordering of University

Struggles affecting the university are not—and have never been—race neutral in the United States. Over time, however, the university has long folded and accounted for notions of difference (Ferguson, 2012). The reordered formation of the contemporary university constitutes what Melamed (2006) considers "neoliberal multiculturalism," which creates an official discourse that displaces more radical anti-racisms with ones that are more liberal—and often assimilationist—in nature (Ferguson, 2012; Melamed, 2006, 2011). For example, postwar racial liberalism emerged as a rhetorical strategy that positions the state as officially anti-racist in the pursuit of U.S. nationalism (Melamed, 2011). This rhetoric cannot be separated from contemporary neoliberalism, which is often characterized as a retreat from the welfare state and a belief in market logics, the privatization of public goods, and global economic hegemony across borders (Harvey, 2007). Thus, neoliberal multiculturalism exists within a context of growing inequality and capital accumulation, even though it articulates an official anti-racist stance.

At its best, multiculturalism challenges White norms and racism, especially through wider non-White representation; however, it also arguably reflects a watering down of civil rights claims. Its progressive detractors note the ways "multiculturalism became a byword for a kind of accommodation that replaced a focus on substantive political and economic goals with an emphasis on cultural diversity" (Melamed, 2006, p. 16). Consumption thus often becomes the mode of pursuing and appreciating this greater diversity. For the cosmopolitan citizen, this often means learning a second language or consuming Black culture, particularly hip-hop culture, as if it were a kind of enlightened capital accumulation and pursuit of a more global freedom. For poor individuals and people of color, it often means radical antiracist claims are now seen as threats to economic freedoms and its attending opportunities:

> neoliberal multiculturalism sutures official antiracism to state policy in a manner that prevents the calling into question of global capitalism. However, it deracializes official

antiracism to an unprecedented degree, turning (deracialized) racial reference into a series of rhetorical gestures of ethical right and certainty.

(Melamed, 2006, p. 18)

On one hand, the university opens its doors to some alterative perspectives, but, on the other hand, it valorizes capital and invites oppressed individuals to participate selectively as a way of tempering radical forms of critical thought. The university, in turn, can be officially "anti-carceral" in the same way it is officially "anti-racist": by pointing to select course offerings and the acceptance of some activities by formerly incarcerated people, while simultaneously rejecting the surrounding community most affected by the university's excess and carcerality.

For the formerly incarcerated students, neoliberal multiculturalism shapes our relationship to the university by limiting the claims we can make against it. Because personal responsibility is contained within the politics of neoliberal success, critiques of both the overtly repressive aspects of the state apparatus, such as the prison, and those that seem more ideological, such as schooling (Althusser, 2001), are obscured in favor of the politics of inclusion and the market logics of access. We, therefore, should not be surprised that this progressive form of neoliberalism operates at the level of representation, while eliding the material project of redistribution (Fraser, 2019; Fraser & Honneth, 2004). In sum, the tensions of neoliberal multiculturalism are embedded in the university, and formerly incarcerated students are embodied agents who both understand and must navigate its violence.

Implications for Public Criminology

Public Criminology, insofar as it can exist, needs to reckon with the ways state formations produce value logics through carcerality. Here, I have sought to explore the dynamics of the university to open up possibilities for questioning the logics of selective inclusion and value. Simply put, the university reserves value for those that "deserve" their place at the university, those that seemingly *choose* to be entrepreneurial and creative in their pursuit of *accessing* human capital. At an ideological level, according to this neoliberal logic, the truly undeserving—the "dangerous, violent, queer, non-citizen, etc."—and those who did not *personally choose* redemption through education, emerge as seemingly deserving of punishment and criminalization—that is, to be locked out of public discourse (Cacho, 2012). In short, the university is not only a carceral space; but it also can figure into justifying carceral practices of exclusion.

Criminology too often fails to acknowledge these underlying tensions and instead focuses on narrow reforms that reward the relatively innocent (Gilmore, 2017; Wang, 2018), especially persons with seemingly non-violent conviction histories, while throwing the book at persons whose conviction histories are framed as violent. This dichotomy impacts who is and who is not deserving of meaningful engagement. Market logics suggest that personally responsible people can access education in a fair system and those who avoided "serious" trouble (again because of personal responsibility) can still find redemption in higher education. Beyond creating a deserving/undeserving binary, which is itself problematic, this trope reinforces individually reductive logics that ignore the structural violence that creates carcerality and targeted criminalization, often along racialized lines.

By failing to interrogate these constitutive relations, public criminology arguably operates from an irreconcilable position of conjoining the "public" and "criminology" as if university and community interests were always aligned. As Zou (2019) points out, however:

> for university to be part of a community, instead of standing apart, the university must also open itself up to the same agitation and transformation that it engages beyond its walls. If the architectural logic of incarceration, of border separation, is walls, then the

architecture of decarceration must at the very least identify places where conceptual and physical walls between the university and its surrounding community become porous.

In other words, calls for the university and criminology to engage the public should mean taking seriously community engaged scholarship that listens to the voices of the dispossessed—those who come to embody the folk devil—as prototypical targets of criminalization.

The field must query the university's assertions of enlightenment and untangle its own relationship to the political economy of the university, a university that disciplines labor at every level from the classrooms to the dining halls. It means moving beyond simplistic understandings and analyses of race to uncover the anti-Black and settler colonial logics that undergird practices of criminalization and dispossession. It is important to understand that the "settler" is not an identity but represents relations of power with respect to land. The settler is "the idealized juridical space of exceptional rights granted to normative settler citizens and the idealized exceptionalism by which the settler state exerts its sovereignty … a site of exception from which whiteness emerges" (paperson, 2017, p. 10). Making space for an abolition geography involves disrupting the settler fantasy of enclosure by transforming places, "destroying the geography of slavery" with "Reconstruction place-making" that establishes a new social order (Gilmore, 2017, p. 231). It, in turn, means making room to hire and support faculty who may not practice mainstream criminology but are committed primarily to abolition and decolonization. We have to imagine cluster hires that represent the publics they claim to serve, especially along the lines of intersectionality and previous incarceration. When we appreciate the constitutive relationships of the university as a public, we understand these actions are themselves contributing to a form of public criminology. Further, they contribute to larger, potentially transformational aims, for as Grande (2018, p. 48) reminds us, "what is at stake is a fundamental condition, a structure [settler colonialism]—and not a momentary crisis or incident—an event."

Although public criminology begins from a promising premise of linking the university to discourses and imaginations from outside its walls, it is perhaps not surprising it has had limited success breaking from the contradictions that the university manages in securing hegemony. Criminology as discipline rarely invites those who are most targeted by criminalization to participate in the conversation (an important dimension of the public). Although the figure of the "folk devil" changes depending on the historical moment, the processes of criminalization and enclosure remain. In other words, the demonization of the Black mugger, the racialized prison group member, the radical criminologist, the dissident student, and the protestor all contribute to the continuum of a carceral logic. Traditional articulations of public criminology fail to be meaningful interventions, because they, too, fail to question how the university—and much of the knowledge generated in it—is part of the carceral political economy.

Notes

1 Afropessimists remind us that Blackness has no analogue; it is positioned as fundamental antagonism (Dumas, 2016; Sexton, 2010; Wilderson, 2003). For them, the Black subject is positioned outside of civil society, in the position of social and political death, and importantly, open to gratuitous violence as constitutive foundational feature. While risking the ire of Afropessimists, I follow Wang (2018) in believing that both logics, racial capitalist theory (exploitability) and the logics of anti-Blackness (disposability), can occur simultaneously.

References

Althusser, L. (2001). *Lenin and philosophy and other essays*. New York: Monthly Review Press.
Arendt, H. (1989). *Lectures on Kant's political philosophy*. (R. Beiner, Ed.). Chicago, IL: University of Chicago Press.

Berger, D. (2016). *Captive nation: Black prison organizing in the civil rights era* (reprint ed.). Chapel Hill, NC: The University of North Carolina Press.

Cacho, L. M. (2012). *Social death: Racialized rightlessness and the criminalization of the unprotected.* New York: New York University Press.

Dumas, M. J. (2016). Against the dark: Antiblackness in education policy and discourse. *Theory Into Practice, 55*(1), 11–19.

Ferguson, R. A. (2012). *The reorder of things.* Retrieved from www.upress.umn.edu/book-division/books/the-reorder-of-things.

Ferguson, R. A. (2017). *We demand: The university and student protests.* Oakland, CA: University of California Press.

Fraser, N. (2019). *The old is dying and the new cannot be born: From progressive neoliberalism to Trump and beyond.* London and New York: Verso.

Fraser, N., & Honneth, A. (2004). *Redistribution or recognition? A political-philosophical exchange* (J. Golb, J. Ingram, & C. Wilke Eds., Trans.). London and New York: Verso.

Gilmore, R. W. (2007). *Golden gulag: Prisons, surplus, crisis, and opposition in globalizing California.* Berkeley, CA: University of California Press.

Gilmore, R. W. (2017). Abolition geography and the problem of innocence. In G. T. Johnson & A. Lubin (Eds.), *Futures of black radicalism.* London and New York: Verso.

Gramsci, A. (1971). *Selections from the prison notebooks.* (trans. Q. Hoare & G. N. Smith). New York: International Publishers Co.

Grande, S. (2018). Refusing the university. In E. Tuck & K. W. Yang (Eds.), *Toward what justice? Describing diverse dreams of justice in education* (pp. 47–66). New York: Routledge.

Habermas, J. (1991). *The structural transformation of the public sphere: An inquiry into a category of bourgeois society* (6th ed.). Cambridge, MA: The MIT Press.

Hall, S., & Massey, D. (2010). Interpreting the crisis. *Sounds, 44,* 57–71.

Hall, S., Critcher, C., Jefferson, T., Clarke, J., & Roberts, B. (2013). *Policing the crisis: Mugging, the state and law and order* (2nd ed.). Basingstoke: Palgrave Macmillan.

Harkins, G., & Meiners, E. R. (2017). Beyond crisis: College in prison through the abolition undercommons. *Lateral, 3.* Retrieved from https://csalateral.org/issue/3/college-in-prison-abolition-undercommons-harkins-meiners/.

Harney, S., & Moten, F. (2013). *The undercommons: Fugitive planning and black study.* Brooklyn: Autonomedia.

Harris, C. I. (1993). Whiteness as property. *Harvard Law Review, 106*(8), 1707–1791.

Harvey, D. (2007). *A brief history of neoliberalism.* Oxford: Oxford University Press.

Heller, A. (2018). Freedom, equality and fraternity in Kant's. *Critique of Judgement. Critical Horizons, 19*(3), 187–197.

Henne, K., & Shah, R. (2015). Unveiling white logic in criminological research: An intertextual analysis. *Contemporary Justice Review, 18*(2), 105–120.

Kant, I. (1998). *Critique of pure reason.* (Trans. P. Guyer & A. W. Wood). New York: Cambridge University Press.

Kant, I. (2000). *Critique of the Power of Judgment* (Trans. P. Guyer & E. Matthews). New York: Cambridge University Press.

Kelley, R. D. G. (2016, March 7). Black study, Black struggle. *Boston Review.* Retrieved from http://bostonreview.net/forum/robin-d-g-kelley-black-study-black-struggle.

Melamed, J. (2006). The spirit of neoliberalism: From racial liberalism to neoliberal multiculturalism. *Social Text, 24*(4), 1–24.

Melamed, J. (2011). *Represent and destroy: Rationalizing violence in the new racial capitalism.* Minneapolis, MN: University of Minnesota Press.

Meyerhoff, E. (2019). *Beyond education: Radical studying for another world.* Minneapolis, MN: University of Minnesota Press.

Mirpuri, A. (2017). Racial violence, mass shootings, and the U.S. neoliberal state. *Critical Ethnic Studies, 2*(1), 73–106.

Moten, F. (2018). *Stolen life.* Durham: Duke University Press Books.

paperson, l. (2017). *A third university is possible.* Minneapolis, MN: University of Minnesota Press.

Reinstein, J. (2019, August 15). A prison guard drove a truck through a group of Jewish ice protesters, injuring several. *BuzzFeed News.* Retrieved from www.buzzfeednews.com/article/juliareinstein/ice-prison-guard-never-again-action-drove-truck-jewish-ice.

Schwendinger, H., & Schwendinger, J. R. (2014). *Who killed the Berkeley school? Struggles over radical criminology.* Surrey: Thought Crimes Press.

Sexton, J. (2010). People-of-color-blindness: Notes on the afterlife of slavery. *Social Text, 28*(2), 31–56.

Sonenstein, B. (2019, February 15). Torture in corcoran: Endless lockdown and gladiator fights, again. *San Francisco Bay View*. Retrieved from https://sfbayview.com/2019/02/torture-in-corcoran-endless-lockdown-and-gladiator-fights-again/.

Thompson, H. A. (2017). *Blood in the water: The attica prison uprising of 1971 and its legacy* (reprint ed.). New York: Vintage.

Undercommoning. (2016, June 4). Undercommoning within, against and beyond the university-as-such. Retrieved August 26, 2019, from http://undercommoning.org/undercommoning-within-against-and-beyond/.

Wang, J. (2018). *Carceral capitalism*. South Pasadena, CA: Semiotext.

Wilderson, F. (2003). Gramsci's Black Marx: Whither the slave in civil society? *Social Identities, 9*(2), 225–240.

Zou, C. (2019). Against the carceral logic of the university. *Public: A Journal of Imagining America, 5*(2). Retrieved from http://public.imaginingamerica.org/blog/article/against-the-carceral-logic-of-the-university/.

20
DOES THE PUBLIC NEED CRIMINOLOGY?

Vincenzo Ruggiero

Introduction

According to the well-known philosopheme posed first by Francois-René Chateaubriand, then by Honoré de Balzac, and then again by Karl Polanyi later (Brie, 2017), we are given a magic gift by which, through simply pressing a button, every wish we utter can be granted immediately. However, it comes at a price: every time we press the button, one Chinese person dies. How many people would refrain from pushing that magic button? This enduring question points to a notion of the "public" that incorporates an obligation to assume responsibility for the lives of others, protects society as a whole, and, as Immanuel Kant put it, embraces a form of world patriotism. This contribution sets off by explaining how difficult it is for criminology as an academic discipline to accept such an obligation. It highlights three sets of difficulties: first, those experienced by criminologists; second, those suffered by the public; and third, those challenging public action and social movements.

Criminologists in the Marketplace

In many countries, criminologists are witnessing a decline of universities, which are now structured as enterprises under the control of managers. The power of the latter is due less to their intellectual strength in some specific area of knowledge than to their expertise in managing any business, be that a financial institution or a supermarket. Universities, as a consequence, tend to jettison critical thinking and adopt a view of themselves as organs of the marketplace. Academics are required to gear their research to the boosting of the economy and to translate their findings into new opportunities for business, even though there is a high probability that many businesses will then end up hiding their profits in Panama. Students are charged scandalous fees and encouraged to convert their desire to learn into an expectation for high grades in the name of their sacred rights as customers. And, while the prevailing economic doctrines determine the gloomy prospects of graduates, universities are required to address "employability," implying perhaps that they should train students to accept zero-hour contracts.

When academic staff members are moved into new premises, the space to keep books into their minuscule shared offices is limited: "the dream of our boneheaded administrators," writes Eagleton (2016, p. 153), "is of a bookless and paperless environment, books and paper being messy, crumply stuff incompatible with a gleaming neo-capitalist wasteland consisting of nothing but machines, bureaucrats and security guards." Finally, vanity, envy, and petty competition, which often connote academic life, are exacerbated by this new climate, making universities "cribs of the selfish gene"

(Eagleton, 2016, p. 153), where the pursuit of success leads to mere self-interested action. Against this background, it is hard to establish what type of contribution academic disciplines might make to the "public."

The process that embedded criminology in the marketplace, however, cannot be solely imputed to political external forces. There is an endogenous mechanism within the development of criminology as a discipline, more precisely as an "independent" discipline, that makes its attempt to "go public" extremely difficult. In order to claim its own scientific uniqueness, criminology has always been tempted to delimit its field of study, often to distance itself from the very mother discipline that gave it birth. I am alluding here to classical sociology and social theory, which contain notions of public action and conceptual traces of "social movement," though such traces form a vague corollary to its central concern around conflict and social change. Often, both the concept of "movement" and that of "change" are hidden behind, and coalesce with, notions of instability and incumbent menace. Exclusive attention to the latter notions was part of the cost criminology had to pay for its ambition to independence. Disciplinary independence, in other words, grew out of the ambivalent nature of the social forces bringing change, their unpredictability and presumed irrationality. Ultimately, confronted with unprecedented industrial and urban development, criminology alimented its independence with what I would term a deep sociological "fear of living together" (see Ruggiero, 2001, 2003). As such, concepts such as "social change" and "collective action," which imply public commitment are less useful to the expansion of criminology. As a consequence, transitional zones and criminal areas became central scenes of inquiry, with the sociological gaze being diverted from more general conflicts.

Let us remind ourselves that the major concerns of sociological theory in general have always been conflict, movements, and social change. Durkheim (1960) explains how an unwanted division of labor in society leads to movements trying to modify that division of labor (right to combat). Of course, for a sociologist *avant la lettre* like Marx, conflict, movement, and social change are the core, if not the exclusive issues, on which any theorizing should be based. Weber (1947) describes "class action" and includes in his reasoning a crucial element of subjectivity: collective action requires not only a distinctly recognizable condition of social injustice, but also an awareness that such injustice is unacceptable, because based on an arbitrary distribution of resources and power. Finally, Simmel's (1978) notion of fluidity and movement describes a feeling of dizziness but also one of perpetual change. In his *Philosophy of Money*, one perceives a constant conflict between the objectivity of technological production and financial exchange on the one hand, and the subjectivity of individuals and groups making choices in their daily life on the other. In brief, the founders of sociological thought are concerned with the variables and concepts that are central to the study of public action. Criminology forgoes these concepts when claiming its academic and scientific independence. Its mission—and not only among mainstream representatives of the discipline—consists in devising a social technology, one which can be applied in response to synchronic, immediate, and urgent situations. This sense of urgency hinders the understanding of the historical dimensions of social action, while limiting the criminological horizon to immediate contingencies.

Public criminology encounters a similar Gordian knot: the more it talks about itself, the more it has to distance itself from social theories: even when "conflict" and the "allocation of resources" are brought into the equation, only risible conflicts can be addressed, and negligible degrees of redistribution achieved. In this sense, the arrogance detected by Tittle (2004) in public sociology denotes, in fact, most criminology, a discipline, which needs informants, not peers—a type of social inquiry that needs to teach others in what contexts they are situated, which the others presumably ignore. Criminologists (Olympian observers) believe they can see the whole picture. "The excuse for occupying such a bird's eye view is usually that scientists are doing reflexively what the informants are doing unwittingly" (Latour, 2005, p. 33). Lack of proximity, in this context, makes criminology unaware of change, movement, of how individuals and groups shift from one form of association to another, in brief, how they engage in the reassembling of the collective. As Bauman (2011, p. 163) has contended, our objects of study are not dumb by nature, but in order to retain our status "and to secure the sovereign authority of our pronouncements, the objects to which our pronouncements refer need first to be made dumb."

This "dumbness" emerges even when re-reading the classical texts of new, radical, criminology, where the topics of conflict and collective action constitute an extraordinary omission in the range of deviant acts and crimes, which allegedly contribute to human liberation (Taylor, Walton, & Young, 1973). Deviant hedonistic activity, vandalism ("kicking back at a rejecting society"), forms of individual industrial sabotage ("working at one's pace"), and even "some sex crimes," are all included among the subjective choices to challenge "the social structure and the structure of power" (Ruggiero, 2006, p. 96). And yet, organized collective action, which often utilizes deviant methods to challenge structures of power, is surprisingly excluded. The suspicion arises that such omission is due to the very organized nature of collective action, which may turn violent, and express too high a degree of subjectivity even for new criminologists to handle. In other words, when faced with socially vulnerable actors, it is always possible for criminologists to optimistically detect a form of rebellious agency in those actors and offer an interpretation of their conduct in the form of sympathy, whether or not those adopting such conduct explicitly request or welcome such sympathy. This is part of the propensity of some criminologists to study marginalized communities with a missionary zeal and a honeyed paternalism that derive from traditional philanthropy. Similarly, criminologists need their objects of study more than they need criminologists but become disoriented when the strong subjectivity of those they study makes their patronizing attitude inopportune. Ultimately, the only forms of political action with which the new criminologists seem analytically comfortable are those embryonic forms of social dissent, or even those "unconscious," "pre-political" elements of contention that one could read in conventional criminal acts. In this case, at least, criminologists can fulfill their mandate by unveiling the "conscious" meaning behind such acts, while their role tends to wither away when consciously organized conducts prove that, at times, actors have nothing to learn from those interpreting them.

With new developments (e.g., the emergence of cultural criminology) little appears to change. Crime is located in everyday life, a site of drama, tragedy and joy, and it is captured as a holistic phenomenon, with "its adrenaline, its pleasure and panic, its excitement, and its anger, rage and humiliation, its desperation and its edgework" (Young, 2011, p. 84). But again, all of this describes transgressive acts which remain pre-political in nature, while it is left to criminologists to detect in those acts a desire for social change of which the "dumb" actors are supposed not to be aware.

The Eclipse of the Public

It is time to revisit "the public," namely the context into which criminologists are expected to bring their action. Democracies are successful when they celebrate the public and allow it to flourish, when they produce individuals and groups capable of acting as the whole community of which they are a part (Blumer, 1998; Mead, 1934). By contrast, they are unsuccessful when they inspire individuals and groups to pursue completely different social orders. I would like to describe such unsuccessful democracies as "off-shore democracies" that seem to be shaped by a crisis of hegemony, leading them to suspend the rules to which they, nevertheless, claim loyalty.

Secrecy characterizes many operations conducted by contemporary global elites, in the economic as well as in the political realm (Urry, 2014). The term "off-shore," applied to the range of financial irregularities that allow the hiding of wealth (Ruggiero, 2017), can also describe contemporary mechanisms of democratic decision-making and practices, which, in turn, are increasingly hidden from public scrutiny. Let us delineate this process.

Empirical theories of democracy tend to focus on existing models, so that they end up endorsing the status quo as the most preferable arrangement. Inspired by a sense of realism, such theories jettison suggestions of improvement, let alone of alternative models, treating them as idealistic, empirically inadequate or "unreal" (Held, 2006). However, the performance of "real" democratic systems cannot be dissociated from the evaluation expressed by those who experience the functioning of such systems. Civil society, for instance, may not limit its action to the periodical expression of voting preferences, but is likely to put forward demands and, in so doing, exercise a form of surveillance or vigilance over institutional decisions. A public sphere distinct from the state apparatus, in other words, constitutes a key component of what we ought to understand for democracy. Democratic decision making, in brief, can be accomplished through political action from below:

> In the historical evolution of democratic regimes, a circuit of surveillance, anchored outside state institutions, has developed side by side with the institutions of electoral accountability … democracy develops with the permanent contestation of power.
>
> *(Della Porta, 2013, p. 5)*

Non-state aggregations, including independent media and professionals, pressure groups, non-governmental organizations and social movements have traditionally played such a surveillance function. The latter, in particular, as relevant actors and purveyors of collective needs and sentiments, express implicit judgments on elites and their activity. What distinguishes democratic systems is their specific capacity to respond to such judgments or, to put it differently, their ability to deal with contentious politics.

Not all politics is contentious, as it commonly consists of elections, consultation, ceremony and bureaucratic process (McAdam, Tarrow, & Tilly, 2001). Social movements, instead, do express contentious politics when they make "contained" and/or "transgressive" claims, namely when demands are put forward through well-established and/or through innovative means. Ultimately, democracy distinguishes itself from other regimes in that its elected political agents should be able to interact with challengers, with new political entities and their innovative collective action (Tilly, 2004, 2007). Democracies, in brief, can be classified on the basis of the elasticity of their structures and the degree to which they encourage political processes and social dynamism leading to change (Ruggiero & Montagna, 2008).

This classification was proposed by some among the very founders of classical political thought, with Machiavelli (1970), for instance, identifying as corrupt those systems that proved unable to deal with tumults and other forms of troubling dissent. Contention, including violent contention, Machiavelli argued, causes no harm, particularly when the elite, through changes in social arrangements and legislation, defeats the corrupt elements within itself. Livy's history suggests that the absence of corruption was the reason why the numerous tumults that took place in Rome "did no harm, but, on the contrary, were an advantage to that republic" (Bull, 2016, p. 35).

Democracies can claim that they are concerned with the pursuit of harmony and public well-being, but as Dewey (1954) argued, they can hardly claim that their acts are always socially beneficial. For instance, one of the most regular activities of democracies is waging war:

> Even the most bellicose of militarists will hardly contend that all wars have been socially helpful, or deny that some have been so destructive of social values that it would have been infinitely better if they had not been waged.
>
> *(Dewey, 1954, p. 14)*

Democratic political acts, therefore, may be presented as socially beneficial, even when their anti-social nature prevails. This is why citizens, Dewey warned, should be cautious in identifying their community and its interests with politically organized institutions and theirs. While launching this warning, Dewey approached an embryonic notion of social movement, stressing that the recognition of the harm caused by states on behalf of the public leads the public itself to institute its own sphere of action with the purpose of conserving and expanding its interests. Democracies striving to achieve unity, on the other hand, may do so only by imposing intellectual uniformity and "a standardization favorable to mediocrity" (p. 115). They tend to regiment opinions and respond to difference with astonishment or punishment: mass production is not confined to the factory but covers ideas, an argument that led Dewey to identify a process of "eclipse of the public." While the political candidate, with "his firm jaw and his lovely wife and children" (p. 115), prepares to make decisions, he also breeds indifference if not contempt. We are faced, here, with a crisis of politics as perceived around a century ago, when the public grew apathetic, bewildered, barred from expressing its opinion or dissent.

In brief, off-shore democracies are unable to deal with political contention, to interact with challengers, to accept contestation, and to submit choices to collective assessment and deliberation. They are incapable of appreciating the role of "the public," thus testifying to a crisis of politics that pushes them in the direction of increasing secrecy. Crucial decisions affecting all are made in closed enclaves impervious to popular control.

Intolerance and Political De-skilling

Intolerance towards public dissent constitutes one of the major manifestations of today's crisis of politics, which hampers the possibility of collective action, denies space for negotiation between rulers and ruled, and ultimately prevents human communities from representing themselves as agents of their own history (Balibar, 2016). In this sense, the very notion of citizenship is "under siege and reduced to impotence," while democratic systems take on a "pure" form, namely they become capable of dealing exclusively with their own logic and the mechanisms of their own reproduction (Balibar, 2016, p. 12). Individuals and groups, as a consequence, are expelled from their public place (Sassen, 2014).

While reducing the opportunities for participatory forms of action, contemporary democracies simultaneously expand the sphere of delegation. Thus, the electoral process becomes increasingly influenced by private interests expressed through the initiative of donors and lobbyists. Soliciting bribes is now termed "fundraising" and bribery itself "lobbying," while bank lobbyists "shape or even write the legislation that is supposed to regulate their banks" (Graeber, 2013, p. 114). While participation is discouraged, enclaves of political and economic power become increasingly unreceptive to the moods and needs of the public. Hidden from the public, such enclaves lead a process of political de-skilling of the public, who grows impotent, disillusioned and, again, apathetic.

Lack of participation marks the simultaneous decline of deliberative practices, namely those processes leading to the formation of opinions in interaction with others. These practices characterize social movements and the way in which their horizontal communication produces tolerance for the other and acceptance of diversity. The shift in institutional responses to social movements, looking at purely technical factors, proves how this communicative process is being hampered. Protest raises military responses, aided by crowd-control techniques such as "kettling" or "corralling." The former is a metaphor likening the containment of protesters to the containment of heat and steam within a kettle and consists in the encircling of demonstrators and their subjugation through forced immobility. To avoid allusions to military confrontation, however, the latter term is used, which refers to the practice of enclosing animals and restricting the territory they occupy. Demonstrators so "kettled" or "corralled," being denied access to food, water and toilet facilities, are unlikely to fight and defy batons or electrified "battle-prods." Often, growing tired after hours of being surrounded, they may just ask to go home. In some cases, the "kettling" takes place well before the agreed location is even reached by protesters, who are blocked at bus or train stations and physically prevented from joining the demonstration. Regarded as a violation of human rights, these techniques and their military corollary increase the cost of protest, eliciting feelings of injustice, and, therefore, at times strengthening the willingness to participate.

Certainly, the militarization of crowd control is perhaps a constant feature of democracies, which have often found it particularly hard to recognize the right to demonstrate and to negotiate with demonstrators. This feature, however, has gained novel prominence with the transformation of public into private space, whereby demonstrators are seen as perturbers of the smooth running of business, enemies of consumers and deniers of their "human right" to shop. Idle demonstrators had better evacuate private spaces, because they do not count, they are neither consumers nor labor force. The philosophy behind this shift is found in the paradoxical idea that, in countries where dissent is permitted, there is no need to dissent: on the contrary, it is in countries where opposition is banned that protest is justified. Hence, the disingenuous claim that regime change, carried out through the invasion of undemocratic countries, is aimed at providing their inhabitants with the right to protest.

Revitalizing the Public

The argument presented so far is that, as forms of government become increasingly elitist and circles and networks of power grow impervious to external needs and demands, they are led to dismiss negotiation with any public force. It is unlikely that criminology can restore or energize social forces. Rather, the revitalization of the public can be achieved through the revitalization of social movements, which would raise the density of communication among individuals and groups and contribute to the development of cosmopolitan identities (Della Porta, 2013). In this sense, criminology cannot go public unless social groups restore a public sphere and include all, criminologists among them, who could attempt through public participation to allay their selfish gene.

Restoring the public sphere may lead to collective action, although the modality and protagonists of such action depend on the underlying philosophy inspiring it. Traditional social movements take inspiration from specific sectors of society (e.g., the industrial working class), their needs and demands, which are deemed the core source of contentious action. Contemporary social movements, however, may not elect any specific sector of society as its vanguard, but rather base their activity on a plurality of forces present in the public sphere. The concept of multitude may help identify such social movements, as the multitude possesses diverse wills and desires and is composed of individuals who constitute a threat to the monopoly of political decision making. "The challenge posed by the concept of multitude is for a social multiplicity to manage to communicate and act in common while remaining internally different" (Hardt & Negri, 2004, p. xiv). Multitudes produce communication, relationships, forms of life, images, ideas, and affects. They mark a shift from centralized forms of political contention, while their networked structure is adaptable to a diversity of struggles. It is in this networked structure that, among other actors, criminologists may find space. This is possible if a distinct conception of social change is embraced.

Some conceptions of the social world and visions of history see "structures," guided by "laws" and animated by "forces," while seeing "the public" as fundamentally determined in its action by those structures, laws and forces (Boltanski & Chiapello, 2018). The volition of those participating in public action, according to such conceptions, does not affect social change or, for that matter, the direction their contentious politics will give to the course of history. Public action, in this perspective, is inscribed in a pre-determined design indicating the inevitable trajectory of social arrangements, their development, and ultimate decline. Revolution is on the agenda of history, not in the plans of those fighting for it. In these conceptions, intellectuals, such as criminologists, may or may not have a place: they may if they follow the leadership of the subjects chosen for carrying out the inevitable outcome of their historical mandate-mission; they may not if they claim independence from that leadership and claim loyalty to their own professional identity. These conceptions, which we may well describe as positivist, require that those participating remain in the closest possible contact with the core protagonists of public action, namely the sectors of the working population that, according to the historical period, suffers more or less the humiliation, exploitation and, in general terms, the most stringent contradictions of the systems that will be superseded.

Positivist conceptions require scientific analyses not only of concrete conditions and historical trends, but also of the values and ideas harbored by social and political actors. Because structures, laws, and forces are supposedly beyond their control, their consciousness is also determined by the position they occupy in society and in the productive system. Therefore, ideas that do not coincide with those involved in contentious action are deemed ideologies.

The conundrum of criminologists, as a consequence, becomes evident. Criminologists may choose to unveil the lies represented by ideologies and clarify to subjects the "real" values and principles that they should hold, admonishing them that their beliefs constitute false consciousness that helps them survive in an unjust system. In this case, a patronizing attitude will be put in place that can be rejected by the subjects addressed—who might legitimately claim that they never dreamed of appointing criminologists (of all people) as their representatives or political vanguards. Another choice for criminologists could consist in the recognition of their own ideology, namely the hypocritical cover that allows them to make sense of their role and position. In this case, however, a relentless work of reflectivity and self-analysis would be required to which not many criminologists are inured.

Distancing themselves from positivist conceptions, participants in public action can see people's choices as the outcomes of will rather than the results of ready-made programs inscribed in structures. Action, from this perspective, becomes intentional; it signals the willingness of participants to assume risk and to pursue their own normative principles. Criminologists, in this case, have to compare their own principles with those held by actors involved in the public arena and verify whether risks may be jointly taken with them. This does not mean that values and principles constitute the only realm in which criminologists can engage, as the material sphere is essential for the development of the public. It is, in fact, when material precariousness diminishes that critique can be revived. This is what we learn, for instance, from resource mobilization theory in the sociology of social movements, which hypothesizes that not scarcity, but availability of concrete and symbolic tools offers social groups opportunities for action. Mobilization, it could be argued, is not just the result of frustration and discontent, but also of strength and resources. They include anything from infrastructures to funds, from the capacity to deliver services to non-material items such as authority, moral commitment, trust, skills, and camaraderie (Ruggiero & Montagna, 2008). Mobilization therefore is a process by which aggrieved groups marshal and utilize resources for the pursuit of specific sets of goals. It may be determined by the strength of pre-existing organization, networks and resources, but it is certainly also propelled by collective solidarity, ideological commitment and shared identity. The difficulty remains, however, when we attempt to ascertain to what extent criminologists are prepared to marshal their resources and moral commitment alongside aggrieved groups.

A public criminology may establish an alliance with powerless groups and expose and fight the crimes of the powerful. The difficulty here is finding out how many criminologists pay attention to this type of criminality, particularly within a discipline that is still predominantly focused on conventional deviance and the crimes of the excluded. Public criminologists may also be guided by the indignation they prove when faced with the conditions of others. Without this emotional reaction, critique is hard to develop, although emotions may prove insufficient to produce action for change. Giving voice to the excluded while translating their needs into terms that refer to the common good may be a solution, but it must be recognized that public criminologists instead tend to choose their interlocutors among the included. In this sense, something esoteric and elitist still remains in the description of public criminology as we find it in relevant texts (e.g., Loader & Sparks, 2010). In some such texts, it seems that experts working in academia seek the help of experts working in adjacent areas and, while begging for their benevolence, try to improve the lives of others, namely non-expert actors.

This "plea to be nice" addressed to policy-makers displays yet another element of what earlier I have described as missionary and paternalistic criminology, which is prepared to stand by the underdogs as far as they remain such (Ruggiero, 2012). This type of criminology echoes the call for *dementia* that Seneca (2009) addressed to Nero, elevating clemency (not justice) as the ruler's cardinal virtue. Seneca supported autocracy as a virtuous form of government, and clemency, namely the capacity to grant mercy or pardon, as the prime prerogative of autocrats. Academics acting as mere mediators between the socially excluded and the authorities perpetuate mechanisms of dominance enacted through the expropriation of speech. Unwittingly, such mediators may "destroy the communicative infrastructure that constitutes the basis for a cooperative mobilization and elaboration of feelings of injustice" (Honneth, 2007, p. 88). Public criminology, without involving those who suffer, does not refer to the common good, but to its own good, namely the criminal justice apparatus that gives it an occupational context and an academic identity.

Conclusion

The difficulties highlighted in this contribution pertain to the current state of academic criminology, the harsh conditions encountered by the public action, and the obstacles preventing the development of collective action. These three sets of difficulties can be referred to the dichotomy included-excluded as we observe it in national as well as international contexts. "Included are those who are connected, linked to others—people of higher-level bodies such as public services, families, firms, policymakers—by a multiplicity and diversity of bonds" (Boltanski & Chiapello, 2018, p. 348). By contrast, the excluded are those whose ties binding them to others have been severed, those who have thus been relegated to the fringes of the social system, where needs are either invisible or interpreted as problems. These are the disaffiliated, persons whose connections have been successively broken and whose existence is regarded as extraneous to the social fabric (Castel, 2008). Criminologists have a world of work to do before providing the excluded with an alternative source of affiliation.

References

Balibar, E. (2016). Critique in the 21st century. *Radical Philosophy*, 200, 11–21.
Bauman, Z. (2011). *Collateral damage: Social inequalities in a global age*. Cambridge: Polity Press.
Blumer, H. (1998). *Symbolic interactionism*. Berkeley, CA: University of California Press.
Boltanski, L, & Chiapello, E. (2018). *The new spirit of capitalism* (translated by G. Elliott). London: Verso Books.
Brie, M. (2017). *Karl Polanyi in dialogue*. Montreal: Black Rose Books.
Bull, M. (2016). Softening up the state. *New Left Review*, 100, 33–51.

Castel, R. (2008). The roads to disaffiliation: Insecure work and vulnerable relationships. *International Journal of Urban and Regional Research, 24*(3), 519–535.
Della Porta, D. (2013). *Can democracy be saved?* Cambridge: Polity Press.
Dewey, J. (1954). *The public and its problems.* Columbus, OH: Ohio University Press.
Durkheim, E. (1960). *The division of labour in society.* Glencoe: The Free Press.
Eagleton, T. (2016). *Culture.* New Haven, CT and London: Yale University Press.
Graeber, D. (2013). *The democracy project.* London: Penguin Books.
Hardt, M., & Negri, A. (2004). *Multitude.* London: Penguin Books.
Held, D. (2006). *Models of democracy* (3rd ed.). Cambridge: Polity Press.
Honneth, A. (2007). *Disrespect: The normative foundations of critical theory.* Cambridge: Polity Press.
Latour, B. (2005). *Reassembling the social: An introduction to actor-network-theory.* Oxford: Oxford University Press.
Loader, I., & Sparks, R. (2010). *Public criminology?* London: Routledge.
Machiavelli, N. (1970). *The Discourses.* Harmondsworth: Penguin.
McAdam, D., Tarrow, S., & Tilly, C. (2001). *Dynamics of contention.* Cambridge: Cambridge University Press.
Mead, G. H. (1934). *Mind, self, and society.* Chicago, IL: University of Chicago Press.
Ruggiero, V. (2001). *Movements in the city.* New York: Prentice Hall.
Ruggiero, V. (2003). Fear and change in the city. *CITY: Analysis of Urban Trends, Culture, Theory, Policy, Action, 7*(1), 45–55.
Ruggiero, V. (2006). *Understanding political violence: A criminological analysis.* New York: Open University Press.
Ruggiero, V. (2012). How public is public criminology? *Crime, Media, Culture, 8*(2), 151–160.
Ruggiero, V. (2017). *Dirty money. On financial delinquency.* Oxford: Oxford University Press.
Ruggiero, V., & Montagna, N. (Eds.). (2008). *Social movements: A reader.* London: Routledge.
Sassen, S. (2014). *Expulsions: Brutality and complexity in the global economy.* Cambridge, MA: Harvard University Press.
Seneca. (2009). *De clementia.* Oxford: Oxford University Press.
Simmel, G. (1978). *The philosophy of money.* London: Routledge & Kegan Paul.
Taylor, I., Walton, P., & Young, J. (1973). *The new criminology: For a social theory of crime.* London: Routledge & Kegan Paul.
Tilly, C. (2004). *Social movements.* Boulder, CO: Paradigm.
Tilly, C. (2007). *Democracy.* New York: Cambridge University Press.
Tittle, C. R. (2004). The arrogance of public sociology. *Social Forces, 82,* 1639–1643.
Urry, J. (2014). *Offshoring.* Cambridge: Polity Press.
Weber, M. (1947). *The theory of social and economic organisation.* New York: The Free Press.
Young, J. (2011). *The criminological imagination.* Cambridge: Polity Press.

PART V
Future Trajectories

21
STARTING THE CONVERSATION IN THE CLASSROOM
Pedagogy as Public Criminology

Lori Sexton

Introduction: On Public Criminology, Questions, and Answers

Over the past few decades, public criminology has been discussed as a way of bringing criminological knowledge to the attention of broader audiences, with the goal of informing people, perspectives, and policies. From Merton and Merton's (1968) "public-minded researcher" to Burawoy's "public sociologist" (2004), academics who engage with broader publics play the role of "bearers and interpreters of … knowledge" (Loader & Sparks, 2010, p. 778; see also Currie, 2007; Uggen & Inderbitzin, 2010). All of these permutations of public criminology position us (criminologists) as the experts and envision a unidirectional flow of more or less objective information from expert to layperson.

This common formulation of public criminology is problematic for a number of reasons. First and foremost, it reifies a boundary between "academic" and "public" in terms of criminologies, audiences, and ways of knowing. Knowledge and its transmission are assumed to be the exclusive purview of academic experts, while the undifferentiated "public" is cast as an empty vessel waiting to be (or sometimes resisting being) filled with our valuable knowledge. Further, in order to occupy the status of academic expertise, our knowledge must be of a certain type: empirical, positivist, and generally quantitative. These types of knowledge production are well-suited for public criminology, as they come cloaked in a veneer of objectivity that belies their normative, ideological, and political dimensions. Qualitative, interpretive, and theoretical forms of knowledge are relegated to the periphery of public criminology (after all, they are too fuzzy and wishy-washy to be distilled into talking points), and other ways of knowing and forms of knowledge beyond standard empirical research are eclipsed entirely. Because the public—which is comprised of many practitioners who are intimately involved in the day-to-day imposition of crime control and an even larger number of people with lived experience of that imposition—does not produce the correct forms of evidence, their native knowledge is given no standing in public criminology, thus foreclosing the opportunity for reciprocal paths of knowledge transmission *into* the academy as well as out from it. This does a disservice to criminology; as Turner (2013, p. 154) notes, "criminological knowledge should and must compete with other discourses on crime and justice—it does not have any automatic right to guide or influence policy."

It is this ultimate goal of guiding and influencing policy that necessarily narrows the scope of public criminology. Thus construed, public criminology demands that we bring to the table answers, not questions. This chapter upends that assumption by considering the following questions: Where is the place of inquiry in public criminology? Where is the place for dialogue, rather than lecture? Where is the place to grapple with competing concerns born of values and ideology? Can classrooms provide this space? And to what end shall we use them?

Loader and Sparks (2010, p. 778) have called for a public criminology that engages in a process of "generating controversy, opening up and extending debate, as well as challenging and provoking received public 'opinion' and political postures, not closing such discourse down." The place that I propose we begin engaging in this dialogic, dynamic form of public criminology is one with which we are well acquainted: the classroom. To quote an adage often attributed to Helen Keller, "A well-educated mind will always have more questions than answers." To the extent that public criminology is about educating the broader public, we need to start valuing our questions more than our answers and viewing our primary site of pedagogy as an important site of public criminology as well. We must not fall into the trap described by Rock (2014, pp. 427–428) in which the work we do as "criminologists teach[ing] and train[ing] practitioners and officials inside and outside the academy" is treated as nothing more than a "side-engagement or a shadow activity that runs in parallel to our real and more solid professional lives."

Public Criminology and Teaching: An Artificial Divide

To the extent that public criminology is about educating the public, it has always been about teaching. When we, as criminologists, bring our knowledge to people who do not have ready access to it, that is teaching. When we use translational language to make criminology accessible to broader audiences, that is teaching. But our most quintessential form of teaching—classroom teaching—is an important form of public criminology as well. First and foremost, students are part of the public. As tertiary education has democratized—a process that is unfortunately eroding as public funding of colleges and universities diminishes and the cost of tuition skyrockets—our classrooms have begun to resemble the broader public in important demographic ways. Today's undergraduates at U.S. colleges and universities are increasingly diverse. In terms of race and ethnicity, U.S. resident undergraduates are 56% White, 18% Hispanic, 14% Black, 7% API, 1% American Indian or Alaska Native, and 4% mixed race (National Center for Education Statistics, 2017). International students account for 5% of undergraduates at U.S. colleges and universities (National Center for Education Statistics, 2017). More than a third (34%) of undergraduates are first-generation college students, with figures varying by race: 25% of white and Asian students are first-generation compared to 41% of Black students and 61% of Latinx students (National Center for Education Statistics, 2017).

Criminology students are not just part of the public; they are a particularly important part: a segment of the public who has self-selected into courses and degree programs that focus on the study of crime, crime control, and matters of justice. Oftentimes, they are students who have had experiences with harm and victimization that inspired their interest in criminology, or students who have had involvement with the criminal justice system in some form or another. n my classrooms at an urban-serving, public university in the middle of the United States, these students generally fall into at least one of the two following groups: (1) students who are positioned to staff the criminal justice system and related agencies of crime control, and (2) students who find themselves ensnared within those same systems of control. Overlap exists between these groups when prior experience with system involvement leads students to aspire to be criminal justice practitioners in their own right, but both groups bring to the classroom a wealth of experience and expertise in matters of crime and justice.

With the professionalization of criminal justice practice, criminal justice and criminology programs at colleges and universities have proliferated, and academics have found that their workplaces are less a longstanding ivory tower than a haphazardly constructed school-to-practitioner pipeline. The public-minded among us have embraced this opportunity to educate future and current criminal justice practitioners, but this education has somehow escaped categorization as public criminology (Rock, 2014). When many of our students graduate, they will go on to fill the ranks of our law enforcement agencies, staff our prisons, and run our courts. They will sentence people to prison, collect their urine samples, and administer actuarial risk assessments. As criminologists, we will study their performance and bemoan the disconnect between their practice and our "best practices." We will call for more training designed and implemented by academics in the name of public criminology. When we evaluate the effect of this training and find that the status quo has been more or less unaffected, we will lament that training is "too little, too late." In order to interrupt this dysfunctional and ineffective cycle, we need not do anything different—just orient to what we already do in a different way. If training is too little too late, well, university teaching is just enough, at the perfect time. We have the powerful opportunity to provide rigorous, critical, social science education to practitioners before they are indoctrinated into institutions of social control, insulating against the effects of institutional groupthink and emboldening them to use alternative frames (e.g., legitimacy, justice, anti-racism) to view their work (Holsinger & Sexton, 2017). This opportunity runs both ways: we also have available to us a wealth of insight into the native knowledge of practitioners, including what they know about their work on the ground and the lenses through which this knowledge is filtered.

Another important segment of the public sits alongside current and future practitioners in our classrooms: students who find themselves on the wrong side of the criminal justice system, constrained by its reach and subject to its strictures and the lasting repercussions thereof. These are students whose lives have been shaped by the matters we study as criminologists: crime, efforts at crime control, poverty, racism, and inequality writ large. These students are perfectly situated to utilize academic tools to critically understand the world around them. They need no education on the lived realities of poverty, racism, and criminalization; in fact, they are often in a position to educate us on those realities. What they do need is theoretical and empirical frameworks that help make sense of their lives by relating their personal experiences to larger social issues and laying bare the institutions and power structures that shape them. It is important not to cast these students as victims making sense of their own victimization, however. The same students who experience the business end of the criminal justice system are those who are best positioned to create change in our criminal justice system from without. While future practitioners can strive to effect change from within, students who are accustomed to finding avenues around the criminal justice system might discover that these same avenues can be used to challenge, change, or eliminate entirely the more harmful elements of the system. In order to embrace the value that these students bring to the classroom, Ruggiero (2010, p. 208) urges us to move beyond our current "missionary and paternalistic criminology, which is prepared to stand by the underdogs so far as they remain such." Instead, we must embrace an inclusive criminology that runs the risk of rendering itself obsolete.

The Praxis of Public Criminology in the Classroom

If we are to reinvent our classrooms as spaces for an inclusive public criminology, it is essential that our pedagogy be guided by principles of critical constructionism and that we reimagine what it means for professors to "profess." Teaching from a place of critical constructionism requires acknowledgement that there is no objective standpoint from which to evaluate knowledge claims (McMillan, 2015). For our teaching to be guided by critical constructionism, we must ask our students to relate not only to the "facts" of crime and crime control (a fraught term to begin with), but also to the values that undergird and suffuse these same phenomena and our approach to their study. Criminological facts bear the mantle of objectivity though not the substance, having been constructed through the active but often invisible definitional and measurement choices *made by people* (Rafter, 1990). Even absent changes in definition and measurement, the facts that structure our discipline change over time. Crime trends up or down, crime control epochs wax and wane, and societal circumstances shift (for some more than others). By the time students graduate, or even finish a course, crime rates will have risen or fallen, and our hodgepodge societal repertoire of crime control measures may have been recomposed. But an awareness of how to find and evaluate evidence, and most importantly, the broader schema with which we must understand that evidence and put it to use, will be the enduring lessons of public criminology in the classroom.

An important part of this broader schema is our values. Many students come to our classrooms having fully bought into the positivist paradigm of criminology as an objective body of theory and evidence that sheds light on absolute truth (Rafter, 1990). We must dispel this misconception from the beginning. Our knowledge is constructed, contingent, and situated (Henry & Milovanovic, 1991; Rafter, 1990), and our pedagogy must follow suit. One way to achieve this is through the constant consideration and discussion of values—the sometimes contradictory values that suffuse our criminal justice system, the broader values that structure our society, the values inherent in our epistemological approaches to criminology, and the values that we wish to encourage in our public, including the people who staff the criminal justice system and the people whose lives are structured by it. This latter set of values includes inquiry, critical thinking, and an understanding of different types of evidence and ways of knowing. A classroom that emphasizes these values can bolster our defenses against the enduring appeal of positivism's simplicity, and engender conversations and thought processes that embrace nuance, lend themselves to critical inquiry, and produce contextualized understandings informed by a variety of forms of knowledge.

An unflagging attentiveness to values will help students understand and evaluate the broader context in which their discipline is situated, even as it shifts around them over time and as they move from place to place. As Simon (2014, p. 21) reminds us, there exists a "considerable nexus between penal policies and social structures of inequality and injustice." The goal of critical pedagogy, then,

> is not to induct students into an ideology or social justice value system but rather to introduce them to data that indicate the links between social inequality and crime/punishment together with the theory which may assist them to interpret this data.
>
> *(Hamilton, 2013, p. 25)*

With the development of critical thinking skills and an understanding of different types of evidence and ways of knowing, students will be able to dynamically adapt their understandings to fit ever-changing contexts while remaining attentive to the inequalities that structure our society.

The normative dimension of teaching makes many a criminologist uncomfortable. Indeed, the normative dimension of *criminology* makes some of us uncomfortable. Nonetheless, it is time to cast off the constraining myth of objectivity that is holding us back from educating people about crime and justice in a way that is valid, useful and potentially transformative. It is time to realize that teaching criminology from a truly value-neutral standpoint is simply not achievable (Hamilton, 2013).

There are three key reasons for this. First, teaching is inherently subjective. As teachers, we come to the classroom with our own perspectives serving as a lens through which information is filtered. We bring our whole selves to the classroom whether we endeavor to or not. Just as qualitative researchers use reflexive processes to understand and account for subjectivity in their research, teachers must recognize the role that our identities, ideologies, and positionalities play in education. It is important to acknowledge that our students, too, are "whole human beings with complex lives and experiences rather than simply ... seekers after compartmentalized bits of knowledge" (hooks, 2014, p. 15). As active participants in their education, students' lenses inform their education as much as their professors' lenses do.

Once we acknowledge the role that our identities, ideologies and positionalities play in our teaching, and thus in our public criminology, we can no longer feign objectivity. We can no longer subscribe to the banking model of education in which teaching is nothing more than the process of professors depositing information into students' brains, where it will be stored until a time at which it is useful again (Freire, 2000). We must remember that "education consists in acts of cognition, not transferrals of information" (Bartholomae, Petrovsky, & Waite, 2014, p. 217). The process of inquiring, of asking questions of both the data and the producers of the data, is a crucial part of education—and our students must be active participants in this questioning.

Second, beyond the inherent subjectivity of teaching, there is subjectivity built into the fabric of our discipline. Crime is socially constructed: behaviors are not inherently criminal; they are made criminal by laws that proscribe them (Rafter, 1990). These laws are guided by ideology and informed by values; they are products of normative assessments and expectations of behavior imposed unevenly on marginalized groups (e.g., indigenous peoples, people of color, immigrants, poor people). Our criminology cannot be value neutral because crime is not value neutral. And our engagement in public criminology in the classroom must be a means toward liberation. We must connect our knowledge to our larger social struggles—struggles in pursuit of decolonizing agendas, against racism, and toward justice as we define it (hooks, 2014). It is imperative that criminological education not "reinscribe practices of domination" (hooks, 2014, p. 10) like colonialism, racism, classism, sexism, and homophobia; rather, it must teach students to critically interrogate such practices and model how to engage and dismantle them.

Thus, we must add to the list of values that structure our teaching and which we wish to nurture in our students: material (rather than metaphorical) decolonization (Tuck & Yang, 2012), anti-racism, and a nuanced understanding of privilege and oppression. In practice, this can take many forms. We can decolonize our syllabi by ensuring that they represent perspectives and epistemologies that actively counter hegemonic narratives, and that they foreground works by indigenous authors and authors of color. We can model anti-racism and decolonization for our students through the continuous incorporation of explicit discussions of racism and colonialism, both historical and contemporary, into our teaching on crime and justice. We can pay unflagging attention to privilege and oppression as they play out in our classrooms by managing how speaking time in the classroom is distributed across students, in order to ensure that certain voices are not heard louder and more often than others.

Third, and perhaps most pragmatically, our students would simply not stand for "objective" discussions of crime and crime control that disregard their values (and rightfully so). They would bristle at the suggestion, to borrow an example from Braithwaite (2011), that we should boil offenders in oil should it prove an effective deterrent. Criminology professors would be hard-pressed to propose this means of crime control to students, and students would be unlikely to support it. Tonry (2010) makes the same point with more mundane realism, noting the reluctance (or inability) of people to separate criminological facts from values and ideology with regard to their views of the death penalty as a whole. Even short of suggesting that we boil people in oil, the public (including our students) is simply not basing their views of the death penalty on assessments of efficacy; they are instead informed by the normative and ideological dimensions of the matter.

For these reasons, we must teach students to engage in discussions that consider theory and evidence in light of the full array of applicable normative and ideological considerations. This is what the conversation requires, and this is what the job should entail. If we are to teach our students from a perspective of blind adherence to best practices or "what works" in a social vacuum, we are further concealing the inherent subjectivity of the phenomena that we study and asking our students to engage with them in ways that are artificial at best, and harmful at worst.

If our education is to truly be public criminology, we must encourage students to find their own criminological voices, in both class discussions and their writing. We must invite them to be part of the conversation. Many students struggle with the realization that they have standing in a criminological conversation. They have been professed to far too often and prompted to ask questions guided by their own interests and insights far too seldom. One way to help students find their criminological voices is by encouraging them to use "I" statements. The use of first-person pronouns helps make it clear to students (and others) that they are active participants in a dialogue about matters of crime and justice. As in any dialogue, students are positioned to both ask and answer questions, to co-create knowledge and reflect on that knowledge creation. Criminological dialogue in particular calls upon them to assemble and assess evidence, weigh competing values and normative ideals, engage in analysis that is both nuanced and transparent, and perhaps most importantly, consider the effects of their positionality in how they create and assemble all of these elements of their own nascent criminology. These skills are carried with them outside of the classroom, into their work (in the criminal justice system or elsewhere), their conversations with friends and family, and their approach to the social world writ large. In short, this type of criminological thinking informs them as a public in their interactions with other, even broader publics.

Pedagogy as Public Criminology: Challenges and Opportunities

In his critique of the narrowness of dominant conceptions of public criminology, Piché (2015) notes that public criminology is generally the purview of adherents to reformist rather than abolitionist paradigms. In the reformist model of public criminology, researchers engage primarily with practitioners and policymakers in order to extract from (positivist) criminological evidence implications for criminal justice policy and practice. In doing so, they necessarily use "language that reifies and reproduces dominant constructions of 'crime' and justice" (Piché, 2015, p. 71; see also De Giorgi, 2014). In contrast, public criminology is seldom seen as the work of criminologists with a more critical or abolitionist bent, by virtue of the incompatibility of their radical perspectives with the "real world" in which the public lives: a world in which crime is a social fact, prisons appear as seemingly permanent fixtures of the landscape (Davis, 2003), and concerns with security and crime control overshadow civil liberties. Radical criminologists themselves are often "disinclined to enter into a compact with Leviathan or strengthen what they defined as an oppressive system" (Piché, 2015, p. 84), and thus are foreclosed from participating in public criminology narrowly construed.

The classroom, by contrast, can serve as a space for such abolitionist scholars to engage in public criminology. As hooks (2014, p. 12) reminds us, "The classroom remains the most radical space of possibility in the academy." While many forms of public criminology take reform to the current system as their raison d'être, this is not the case with pedagogy. Thus, the classroom can be a space in which abolitionist ideas have breathing room. Students can be prompted to engage with dominant conceptions of crime and justice from a counter-hegemonic standpoint and pushed to interrogate the systems through which we create, control, and respond to crime and to reimagine public life without them.

While the classroom certainly provides space for such a radical perspective, it is important to acknowledge that this perspective is one of many that our students will hold. Our classrooms contain fledgling adherents to both reformist and abolitionist models. Given that criminology classrooms are increasingly populated with current or aspiring criminal justice practitioners, the "real world" perspective of reformism is strong among criminology students. Students who are studying criminology in order to become better criminal justice agents—whether that be a police officer or a prison guard—are not in it to tear down the system. They are in our classes to expand their knowledge base and skill set in order to prepare them for a job as an effective agent of the state. It is our duty not to convert them to a radical agenda, nor to reconcile their reformist paradigm with a more radical or abolitionist perspective, but rather to bring the two into dialogue with one another. Evidence abounds that the problematic nature of our criminal justice system lies in more than just superficial characteristics that can be tweaked or tinkered with (a reformist approach); its flaws are foundational, and efforts toward justice must attack them at their source. But we must still be mindful of the multiplicity of publics in our classrooms, including criminal justice practitioners who have no interest in (and minimal agency to achieve) the dismantling of criminal justice as we know it. Exposing these students to abolitionist perspectives will expand their worldviews and prompt them to juxtapose their own frames with those of others, thus engaging with the field (and their future careers in criminal justice) on a more critical level.

Our students are diverse in more ways than just their orientation to the criminal justice system. They come from a range of backgrounds and hold a myriad of identities; moreover, they have interactions with the criminal justice system that are patterned based on these factors. The public in our classrooms is as heterogeneous as the larger public, and given the current state of politics worldwide, that means that there are widely divergent (and often passionately held) political ideologies at play in our class discussions. It is our responsibility as educators and public criminologists to actively engage with those political ideologies rather than wishing them away. The classroom will always be a political space, inasmuch as the world around us is political. As hooks helpfully reminds us, while our politics are often invisible, they are omnipresent; a White, male professor who assigns works from only White, male authors is making a political decision, albeit one that is camouflaged against the backdrop of societal patriarchy and white supremacy (hooks, 2014). It is our duty as teachers not to exile politics from our classrooms, but to render those politics visible.

In order to engage in critical pedagogy, we must also ensure that those politics are counter-hegemonic. To do so, we must reject politics of colonialism, racism, sexism, classism, ableism, and homophobia so that our classrooms may be places of liberation and learning, rather than spaces that reinforce the status quo. How do we begin this ambitious agenda? We can start by recognizing the political ideologies that pattern our values. Our values—from those that structure our criminal justice system and our discipline, to those that we wish to cultivate in our students—are thoroughly steeped in and reflective of political ideologies. If our public criminology in the classroom is to model for our students how to engage with facts and values simultaneously, we must not eclipse their politics (or ours). Our students are political, and we must allow them to be. We as professors are political as well and must continue to be so in the classroom. By explicitly acknowledging the political dimensions of crime, criminal justice, and criminology, and reflexively considering how our own political viewpoints impact our understandings of them, we can engage in meaningful discussion of the full complexity of criminology. If classroom discussions and debates are to provide a template for how students will engage in criminological discussions elsewhere (or even make criminal justice related decisions as practitioners and policymakers), it is important to dwell in the grey area where contrasting sets of values are part and parcel of knowledge. By explicitly identifying our politics and reflexively examining their influence, and by encouraging students to do the same with their own diverse political viewpoints, we can "model for [our] students productive civic discourse" (Bahls, 2018, n.p.).

This is becoming ever more challenging. There are echoes of the 1980s' politicization of criminal justice in the recent politicization of tertiary education. College campuses are regularly (and unfairly) derided in the media and by the larger public as incubators of politically correct groupthink, havens for overly sensitive liberals, and hostile environments for students who dare to espouse conservative political ideologies (Phillips-Fein, 2019). Faculty are being penalized for allowing politics to enter their classrooms (as if there were any choice) and for their political activities outside the classroom, off campus, and even online. As academic freedom has been abridged, tenured and tenure-track faculty find themselves in a newly precarious position, and contingent faculty remain unprotected altogether. Outside the United States, in Hungary, Turkey, Venezuela, and elsewhere, academic freedom is being curtailed even more sharply, with professors losing their jobs for speaking out against the government.

The state of affairs in the United States prompted the American Council of Trustees and Alumni to write a report entitled "Building a culture of free expression on the American college campus" (Malcolm, 2018). In pursuit of the "unfettered pursuit of truth" (Malcolm, 2018, p. 2)—a positivist claim if ever there was one—the report declares "safe spaces" a cover for liberal campus orthodoxies and unproblematically valorizes free speech as though all speech were created equal and all speakers equally situated and protected. Despite the heralding of free speech, the report sharply criticizes faculty who exercise theirs by accusing them of "use[ing] the classroom to present their personal political views" (Malcolm, 2018, p. 14). The irony of an academic organization calling for censorship of its own faculty in order to (ostensibly) make the classroom a freer place for students is inescapable (Bahls, 2018).

In this climate, it is all the more important for our classrooms to be spaces for public criminology. We must challenge ourselves to

> make intelligible contributions to public debate and policy formation in this more politicized environment—an environment in which *all* knowledge claims potentially also become politicized and controversial, all the more so when they address major cleavages of world view and ideological commitment (as criminology typically does).
>
> *(Loader & Sparks, 2010, p. 774)*

To achieve this in the classroom, we need a more comfortably activist academy. The appearance of impartiality bolsters a dangerous status quo in criminology—a status quo with the illusion of objectivity where information masquerades as knowledge. As Green (2018, n.p.) notes, "calling for more advocacy from within the academy will make many people nervous. The legitimacy of the university as an institution rests on the reputation of scholars as impartial researchers." She goes on to explain that "the production of knowledge is necessarily political and cannot be otherwise. Choosing to ignore this reality has diminished the influence of [social] scientists in the public sphere" (Green, 2018, n.p.).

In order for criminologists to freely engage in the bold and disruptive public criminology that is called for in the classroom, the existing reward and penalty structures of academia must be reconfigured. Current structures of job security and advancement (i.e., promotion and tenure for those who have it) undervalue—or worse yet, sanction—earnest public engagement in many forms, while the compartmentalizing of our jobs into the triad of research-teaching-service disregards completely the classroom as a site of engagement with the public. The use of student evaluations (metrics with the full weight of promotion and tenure or contract renewal decisions behind them) to measure teaching performance renders problematic any approaches to teaching that allow professors to be their full selves, and challenge students to do the same, politics and all. As tertiary education responds to political pressures through constraint and constriction, narrowing its reach and limiting its efficacy, the promise of public criminology in the classroom is stifled.

Conclusion

In spite of these constraints, academic freedom provides us a *relatively* uncompromised space to engage in public criminology. This is exceedingly rare, as most forms of public criminology are inherently an exercise in compromise, rendering us unable to "speak truth to power in our own untrammeled tongue ... and without a deference to standards imposed by those whose interests, modes of thinking and priorities were not our own" (Rock, 2014, p. 423). Pedagogy as public criminology provides a welcome respite from these constraints. In the classroom, we need not contort our criminology into soundbites or policy briefs (although we must, of course, tailor our language to our student audience and be aware of professional landmines); standards are imposed largely on our own terms, with academic rigor and attention to various epistemological paradigms; and our modes of thinking and priorities can be our own, in furtherance of the values of inquiry, critical thinking, respect for different forms of evidence, and actively countering the hegemony that we identify as problematic in the larger social world.

As we reorient to teaching as public criminology, it is crucial that we assess and address the ways in which our criminology, public and otherwise, may be "reinforcing a discipline that, in its administrative and managerial forms, is integral to the maintenance of a punitive status quo" (Piché, 2015, p. 74). To present and analyze the normative and ideological dimensions of criminology without addressing our own complicity in many of the harms that the criminal justice system has wrought would be self-serving and naive. For this reason, our public criminology in the classroom must be radical and transgressive, and it must simultaneously empower and challenge our students to become public criminologists in their own right—staking their claim in the criminological conversation and holding their own with the tools we have provided them.

References

Bahls, S. (2018, May 18). FIRE, aim, ready! *Inside Higher Ed*. Retrieved on July 15, 2018 from www.insidehighered.com/views/2018/05/31/weakness-recent-report-free-speech-american-council-trustees-and-alumni-opinion.
Bartholomae, D., Petrovsky, A., & Waite, S. (2014). *Ways with words* (10th ed.). Boston, MA: Bedford/St. Martin.
Burawoy, M. (2004). Public sociologies: Contradictions, dilemmas, and possibilities. *Social Forces*, 82(4), 1603–1618.
Currie, E. (2007). Against marginality: Arguments for a public criminology. *Theoretical Criminology*, 11(2), 175–190.
Davis, A. Y. (2003). *Are prisons obsolete?* New York: Free Press.
De Giorgi, A. (2014). Reform or revolution: Thoughts on liberal and radical criminologies. *Social Justice*, 40(1-2), 24–31.
Freire, P. (2000). *Pedagogy of the oppressed* (30th anniversary ed.). New York: Continuum.
Green, J. F. (2018, July 15). Why we need a more activist academy. *The Chronicle of Higher Education*. Retrieved from www.chronicle.com/article/Why-Wee-Need-a-More-Activist/243924/.
Hamilton, C. (2013). Towards a pedagogy of public criminology. *Enhancing Learning in the Social Sciences*, 5(2), 20–31.
Henry, S., & Milovanovic, D. (1991). Constitutive criminology: The maturation of critical theory. *Criminology*, 29(2), 293–316.
Holsinger, K., & Sexton, L. (2017). *Toward justice: Broadening the study of criminal justice*. New York: Routledge.
hooks, b. (2014). *Teaching to transgress*. New York: Routledge.

Loader, I., & Sparks, R. (2010). What is to be done with public criminology?. *Criminology & Public Policy, 9*(4), 771–781.

Malcolm, J. L. (2018). *Building a culture of free expression on the American college campus: Challenges & solutions.* Report by the American Council of Trustees and Alumni Institute for Effective Governance. Retrieved August 1, 2018 from www.goacta.org/images/download/building-a-campus-culture-of-free-expression.pdf.

McMillan, C. (2015). Pedagogy of the impossible: Žižek in the classroom. *Educational Theory, 65*(5), 545–562.

Merton, R. K., & Merton, R. C. (1968). *Social theory and social structure: 1968 enlarged edition.* New York: Free Press.

National Center for Education Statistics (2017). Digest of education statistics, 2016. Retrieved on January 5, 2018 from https://nces.ed.gov/programs/digest/d17/index.asp.

Phillips-Fein, K. (2019, January 31). How the right learned to loathe higher education. *Chronicle of Higher Education.* Retrieved from www.chronicle.com/article/How-the-Right-Learned-to/245580.

Piché, J. (2015). Assessing the boundaries of public criminology: On what does (not) count. *Social Justice, 42* (2), 70–90.

Rafter, N. (1990). The social construction of crime and crime control. *Journal of Research in Crime and Delinquency, 27*, 376–389.

Rock, P. (2014). The public faces of public criminology. *Criminology & Criminal Justice, 14*(4), 412–433.

Ruggiero, V. (2010). *Penal abolitionism.* Oxford: Oxford University Press.

Simon, J. (2014). A radical need for criminology. *Radical Criminology, 1*, 37–66.

Tonry, M. (2010). "Public criminology" and evidence-based policy. *Criminology & Public Policy, 9*(4), 783–797.

Tuck, E., & Yang, K. W. (2012). Decolonization is not a metaphor. *Decolonization: Indigeneity, Education and Society, 1*(1), 1–40.

Turner, E. (2013). Beyond "facts" and "values": Rethinking some recent debates about the public role of criminology. *The British Journal of Criminology, 53*(1), 149–166.

Uggen, C., & Inderbitzin, M. (2010). Public criminologies. *Criminology & Public Policy, 9*(4), 725–749.

22

YOU ARE ON INDIGENOUS LAND

Acknowledgment and Action in Criminology

Lisa Monchalin

The message is clear, they wanted us to disappear, but we're still here.
—JB The First Lady, 2017, from her song "Still Here" on her album *Meant to Be*

Excuse Me, Criminology, We Are Still Here

Public criminology questions and calls for ways in which criminological work and research can have greater public reach and impact. It queries how to put this work into the public arena and how to get criminological knowledge to play a larger role in shaping policy (Currie, 2007; Loader & Sparks, 2011). Those who engage in or practice public criminology actively pursue public engagement on criminological knowledge and research. They work towards ways of achieving greater social impact from their criminological work, including having it inform and shape public policy. Many, however, also note the hurdles in trying to achieve such undertakings, and the roadblocks to getting this knowledge heard and used in the public sphere (Currie, 2007).

When it comes to attempting public engagement in relation to Indigenous perspectives of crime and justice, there is an added hurdle, as the public are largely colonized—with deeply entrenched colonial attitudes and beliefs pervading and guiding discourses on crime and justice. While key scholars of public criminology speak to the importance of, as well as strategies for, getting the "collective voice" within criminology heard (Currie, 2007, p. 190), the reality is that this "collective voice" largely excludes Indigenous perspectives and truths regarding crime and justice. As such, engaging in mainstream forms of public criminology will not make a productive intervention, as the colonial discourse needs to be first exposed and challenged. We need to think through and take steps towards anti-colonial politics in everyday life, which includes working towards changing the discipline of criminology to be more reflective of Indigenous realities and truths and having them come to be a part of the discipline's "collective voice." Only after this achievement can more mainstream understandings of public criminology be utilized to make a productive impact on reducing injustices facing Indigenous peoples today.

There must be widespread education on Indigenous realities and truths across Turtle Island (North America). There must be a consciousness raising of Indigenous perspectives, histories, and experiences if justice is to be realized. To achieve this greater public awareness, systems of education must change. A good starting point is criminology itself, as many students who take criminology go on to work within the criminal justice system or in a justice related field. These next generations are the public and can play a role in shifting thinking within the justice realm, which can spearhead real action over time. These efforts require the voices, experience, and engagement of Indigenous peoples and communities.

Education is therefore my activism. As academics we must not lose sight of our capacities as educators, and attempt change with students in our very classrooms. In Anishinaabe traditions, we are told to always consider the next seven generations in everything we do. This chapter in itself is using my capacity as an educator to create change. I call for criminology as a whole to incorporate Indigenous peoples' histories and realities into the discipline to a much larger extent. In terms of Indigenous peoples within criminology, it has largely been outsiders looking in, and attempting to explain Indigenous peoples' relation to "crime" through a fundamentally colonizing lens. Engaging Indigenous communities and peoples is key in order to reduce the gross injustices impacting people today. This means that peoples and communities must not be left to the margins, or "studied" or spoken about without being accurately and respectfully reflected, included, and acknowledged within the discipline. Māori scholar Linda Tuhiwai Smith has noted the continual Western obsession with studying the so-called "Indigenous problem," which has been "a recurrent theme in all imperial and colonial attempts to deal with Indigenous peoples" (Smith, 2012, pp. 94–95). Thus, as a start, we must stop being looked at as a "problem" population that is in need of "research" or "saving." Instead, to engage Indigenous peoples and communities, and to have Indigenous justice perspectives enter the public sphere, a first step is to consider how Indigenous voices, histories, and truths can—and *should*—be accurately reflected within the discipline. Trying to achieve widespread public influence and recognition of Indigenous justice is a lot more challenging if Indigenous perspectives remain at the margins of criminology.

Criminology is a field that not only largely ignores Indigenous peoples, histories, and perspectives, but also tends to mostly focus on Indigenous disparities and overrepresentation in prisons without accounting for colonial legacies contributing to them. Indigenous peoples are the most overrepresented in prisons in Canada, representing 27 percent of admissions to federal custody and 28 percent of admissions to provincial territorial custody while representing just over 4 percent of the adult population in Canada (Malakieh, 2018). In the United States, the number of Indigenous persons incarcerated in state and federal prisons per capita is about 38 percent above the national average (Lakota People's Law Project, 2015). This pattern should not go unnoticed. It should be acted on—it must be—and we need public engagement on this crisis; however, if the only lens criminology offers to the public sphere is to view Indigenous peoples as a "problem," then the same results shall continue. For true public engagement to happen, criminologists need to acknowledge that Indigenous peoples and their experiences in Turtle Island are much more nuanced and complex than the recognition of disparities. For instance, despite genocide we are still here due to our resiliency, stemming from our rich cultures and traditions. Additionally, Indigenous peoples have had their own various "criminologies" that have been in place long before the arrival of the colonizers. These "criminologies" include various strategies relating to justice and how to live in a good way, which has sustained communities since time immemorial.

This chapter is a call to criminologists. Those interested in making a real impact in the public sphere can start by using their power as educators to inform the next generations on Indigenous truths by upholding and supporting Indigenous voices and perspectives. Notably, when discussing Indigenous overrepresentation in terms of incarceration, victimization, and their interrelated factors, it must not be separated from the context of past and ongoing colonialism. This is a big problem with criminology; historical context and colonialism are either glossed over or ignored in discussions of disparities and overrepresentation. For instance, as Cain (2000) explains, Western criminology is orientalist and occidentalist, wherein it fetishizes the Other, while completely disregarding the possibility of difference, or seeks to explain it away. This continued lack of acknowledgement reinforces the false notion of the "vanishing Indian," which has been propagated in films, literature, media, and news outlets. This false conception tries to frame Indigenous peoples as something of the past, almost non-existent. The discipline of criminology largely does the same thing, and public policy reflects this tendency. These untruths, which are widespread and repeated throughout Canada and the United States, include misleading arguments or false assumptions, such as the notion that Indigenous peoples had no laws or governance before the arrival of colonizers. This belief is entirely not true.

It is time for criminology and criminologists alike to remember and acknowledge that we are still here. This ignorance is not due to Indigenous peoples being silent. There are many vocal Indigenous peoples, communities, organizations, and more. Because of the deeply engrained colonial discourse and agenda—many times, Indigenous voices come to be ignored. As such, this chapter begins by outlining colonialism, the roots of Indigenous injustice. Given that within criminology we are largely examined in terms of disparities, I link and explain how and why such discussions must not be separated from a discussion of past and ongoing colonialism. I then outline, and set the record straight, on some of the colonial lies regarding Indigenous peoples, speaking to what I call, "the real criminology"—that is, the real criminologies of Native America, the criminologies of the lands which we are on. The focus then shifts to exploring how to engage Indigenous peoples and communities in criminology and why this emphasis is important if we want to see a move towards justice. The chapter concludes by highlighting change-makers, challenging colonial falsehoods, underscoring the important reality that people live on stolen Indigenous lands, and raising awareness of violence against Indigenous women and girls through dance.

Reminder, We Are Not "The Problem"

Criminological research and education delivered throughout institutions on Turtle Island must stop spreading colonial falsehoods, which is rhetoric that upholds colonial agendas and thus perpetuates disparities. These untruths have been spread throughout Canadian and U.S. histories, literature, film, media, and many modes of popular culture depictions. All largely give precedence to Eurocentric goals and interests, while undermining Indigenous territories, communities, and peoples. Through the continued propagation of such falsehoods, or even an ignorance of Indigenous histories or realities, the population maintains their deliberate ignorance. With the dominant population ignorant to truths, stereotypes, and assumptions are then made and continually upheld, and the status quo continues. Unfortunately, criminology, including textbooks, curriculum, and research, has generally followed along with this status quo.

This discourse continues because of the continued grip of colonialism. Tsalagi scholar Corntassel (2012) explains how colonialism aims to extinguish Indigenous peoples collective and individual confidence through the distortion of Indigenous histories and domination. One form of colonialism is settler colonialism, which involves foreign peoples who view themselves as being racially superior (Bonds & Inwood, 2016). They come to lands not of their own with the goal to steal, exploit, dislocate, and disconnect the original peoples of those lands—all for their own personal gains and benefits. It encompasses efforts to eliminate and control populations in order to claim legitimacy to Indigenous territories. Many different tactics are used to achieve such goals, such as the continual spreading of colonial falsehoods about Indigenous peoples. This is done not only to convince settlers, but Indigenous peoples as well, that we are a supposed "inferior" race and a "problem population" to be handled, regulated, and managed. Institutions and modes of governance then come to have these goals built into their operations—including universities and their various academic disciplines.

Criminology—even that which is critical—has not escaped the onslaught of colonialism. In a content analysis of the most popular 31 introductory criminal justice and criminology textbooks published between 2004 and 2010, Martin (2014) found that American Indian and Alaskan Native peoples were greatly underrepresented in the texts. This means that books being used in universities and colleges on Indigenous lands barely speak about the peoples whose lands they are on—as if we do not exist. In doing so, Indigenous justice perspectives remain at the margins of the discipline. Along the same lines, by way of illustration, much of the public continues to support "Columbus Day," which is still a federal holiday and celebrated in many states and cities in the United States. Some major cities close the streets for parades, many people get the day off of work, and many universities cancel classes. Such celebrations go on even though Columbus carried out genocide against Indigenous people and never set foot in mainland North America. He landed in what is known today as the Dominican Republic and Haiti (Dunbar-Ortiz, 2014; Wanjek, 2011). Upon his arrival, he met Indigenous peoples from area, including the Taino, Arawak, and Lucayan peoples, which he wrote in his journals as being giving, welcoming, and friendly peoples. Rather than return kindness, his own writings show that he went on to enslave and exploit peoples. He brutalized, imprisoned, tortured, and murdered. During his second voyage, he went from island to island in the Caribbean looking for gold, and forcing children and women to be his and his crews' sex slaves (Zinn, 2012). Yet, many young people in the Americas today still receive and internalize a fabricated story of the "discovery of America" (Bigelow & Peterson, 1998) in which White people came from their developed and advanced country to largely empty lands where they found "uncivilized" people who needed to be "saved."

This exploitative spirit of Columbus lives on, as many people throughout Canada and the United States give little recognition to the fact that these places are on stolen land (Bigelow & Peterson, 1998). For example, Canada celebrated its 150th Anniversary in 2017, which for many Indigenous peoples can sound ridiculous. Or, for some, it is offensive, given that the last 150 years has not really been something to celebrate, due to the genocide and seven generations of imprisonment in residential schools. These celebrations, and the incomplete stories they convey, point to how colonialism is still ongoing and that the heart of the colonial project remains the achievement of Indigenous territory.

At the same time, the public have been slowly waking up to the realities of Columbus. In particular, some cities in recent years have replaced Columbus Day with Indigenous Peoples Day, including Olympia, Washington, and Traverse City, Michigan, among others. Some grassroots peoples and organizations also put on their own Indigenous Peoples Day in cities where Columbus Day is still celebrated. For the 150th celebrations in Canada, some Indigenous peoples boycotted them while others reclaimed and remade them to celebrate 150 years of resistance and survival.

But what are criminologists doing when some of their own universities cancel classes to celebrate genocide? If criminologists want to engage Indigenous peoples and communities, and thus make real impacts in terms of reducing crime and injustice, then perhaps we should begin by advising students of colonial realities. Many settler celebrations increase injustices, as they are a complete disregard of truths, which further the colonial agenda that aims to silence, eliminate, and assimilate. If criminology is to have an actual, comprehensible role to the public sphere, then it must begin to acknowledge Indigenous ancestral lands. It must be remembered that we are still here and not a fantasy people of the past. As Dion (Lenape/Potawatami) explains, educators must "take a critical look at how the image of First Nations people as romantic, mythical Others is reproduced in schools and to consider strategies to challenge it" (Dion, 2009, p. 8).

The colonial project continually spreads propaganda in the public sphere, promoting falsehoods in the minds of future generations. This historical amnesia does not bring justice or change. Criminology must not ignore harsh truths, such as the realities of Indian legislation and Indian boarding and residential schools intended to push Indigenous peoples out of existence. For instance, criminology largely ignores original treaty agreements that outlined how things were supposed to move forward in these lands upon the arrival of the colonizers. They must be told and shared widely. One primary example is the Two Row Wampum agreement. This agreement was initially made between the Haudenosaunee and Dutch in 1613, known as the *Kaswentha* (King, 2007). A belt with two rows of purple beads that run parallel to each other, each representing two paths, represents this codified agreement. One path symbolizes the Haudenosaunee canoe, and their "language, their culture, their customs and their ways." And the other path symbolizes the Dutch ship, and "their own language, culture, customs and ways" (Boots, 1989, p. 37). And while these paths remain parallel, they never interfere with one another. They are to never try to steer the other's boat. Between these parallel purple rows are three rows of white beads that symbolize the continued relationship of "peace, respect, and friendship," an agreement to live together side-by-side, but to never interfere in each other's way of life or governance (King, 2007, p. 460). Yet this treaty has not been adhered to by Canada or the United States, and such a violation is in itself a crime.

This agreement of peace, friendship, and non-interference has been communicated by Indigenous nations to settler peoples since their initial arrival and still is today. In 1764, the Two Row Wampum was presented by more than twenty-four nations to the British colonial government during the Treaty of Niagara, a meeting which served to ratify the Royal Proclamation of 1763 (Gehl, 2014). Sir William Johnson, the superintendent of Indian Affairs at the time, reaffirmed and accepted this relationship with the approximately 2000 Indigenous leaders who were present at negotiations (Borrows, 2002). Negotiated agreements of peace and friendship such as this one continues to be brought forward, as these agreements are not forgotten in Indigenous peoples' histories.

Unfortunately, instead of following through with agreements, governments instead tried to eliminate Indigenous presence. In Canada, the government instituted Indian legislation as a tool of elimination. A case in point is the Indian Act of 1867, which imposed a series of provisions to regulate First Nations peoples and lands. Under this Act it was made illegal for First Nations people to partake in traditional dancing, or practice and engage in cultures, including any ceremonies. People could be imprisoned for doing do, including having any cultural items confiscated. There were also restrictions on First Nations peoples' ability to engage in agricultural trade. Additionally, no one, First Nations or otherwise, was allowed to advance land claims, or to gather to discuss land claims; anyone found doing so would be liable to imprisonment. Some of the worst restrictions of this act were lifted in 1951 with another major amendment in 1985; however, it still remains very discriminatory, oppressive, and paternalistic, with goals unchanged from its early years. Federal law continues to regulate First Nations people's lands and identities. It maintains an Indian registry, defining who is legally an "Indian" based on a government system of registration, and still enforces and controls governance in First Nations communities with imposed Band Councils (Monchalin, 2016).

Like Indian legislation, the realities of residential schools and Indian boarding schools must not go unspoken as part of a legacy connected to Indigenous peoples' overrepresentation in the criminal justice system. For example, U.S. Army Captain Richard Henry Pratt established Indian Boarding Schools. In 1875, Pratt ran a jail in St. Augustine, Florida for Indigenous persons taken as prisoners during the Plains Wars. Prisoners were shackled, starved, abused, shamed, and humiliated. The only hope for release was if prisoners were to forgo being "Indian" and assimilate. This included never speaking their language or practicing any aspects of their cultures and traditions (Lookingbill, 2006; Molin, 1988; O'Connor & O'Neal, 2010).

In 1879, Pratt expanded those measures, establishing the first off-reservation residential school in the United States: the Carlisle Indian Industrial School in Pennsylvania. He persuaded the federal government that this "school" would train Indigenous children to accept the White man's ways. Throughout its tenure, over 10,500 Indigenous children were taken from their homes across the United States and relocated to this institution where they were subject to horrible abuses in an attempt to "Kill the Indian. Save the Man" (Fear-Segal & Rose, 2016). Upon arrival, children had their hair chopped off and their names changed to "White" names. They were forbidden to speak their language, and if caught could face a range of sanctions, including confinement, food deprivation, and corporal punishment (Bowker, 2007).

Canada looked to this model of assimilation being practiced in the United States and under the direction of their first prime minister, Sir John A. Macdonald, implemented it to "solve" their so-called "Indian Problem." In Canada, these institutions were financed by the federal government, and operated by Christian churches (Cote & Schissel, 2008). By 1920, it became mandatory by law that all Indigenous children attend and they reached their peak with over 80 in operation across Canada by 1931 (Fournier & Crey, 2006; Kelly, 2008). They were purposely far distances from children's homes to break family ties so that children would not be influenced by their culture. Like the institutions in the United States, children were forbidden to speak their language, and could face extreme punishments for doing so. Such punishments included needles pushed through their tongues and left for extended periods of time or having their mouths scrubbed out with Ajax, a toxic household cleaner (Chansonneuve, 2005; Chrisjohn & Young, 2006).

The physical, sexual, emotional, and psychological abuses that went on in Residential Schools are well documented (Truth and Reconciliation Commission of Canada, 2015). In the 1990s, survivors of these institutions began legal challenges against the churches and government for the abuse they endured. In 2006, the largest class-action settlement in Canadian history set in motion a comprehensive resolution to the residential schools' legacy, known as The Indian Residential Schools Settlement Agreement. It included the establishment of the Truth and Reconciliation Commission, which collected testimonies from over 6,000 people, the majority of whom were survivors (Truth and Reconciliation Commission of Canada, 2015). In their final report they note the extensive abuses and how the government deliberately separated Indigenous children from their families in order to weaken and diminish kinship and cultural connections and to purposely brainwash children to accept Euro-Christian culture. As Nehiyaw scholar Tamara Starblanket (2018) elaborates, these extensive abuses, and forced policies of extermination by governments, equates to the crime of genocide.

If you are teaching or doing research on Indigenous over-incarceration or Indigenous peoples and the criminal justice system, but do not recognize past and ongoing colonialism, then you are perpetuating injustice—thus, foreclosing the possibility of engagement and action with many Indigenous peoples and communities. The colonial context must be acknowledged, especially since government-imposed harm has not stopped. Instead, it has become reframed and normalized as an "Indian problem," rather than as "the colonial problem" it is. Residential schools caused immense trauma in survivors as well as intergenerational trauma that has had cumulative adverse impacts that continue to negatively affect survivors' children and grandchildren's well-being still today (Bombay, Matheson, & Anisman, 2014). The large majority of those incarcerated are imprisoned due to the structurally racist system or are criminalized for their trauma. At the same time, though, while Indigenous peoples may have inherited trauma, we have also inherited resilience. It must also not be forgotten that Indigenous peoples have survived and continue to persevere through this genocide.

The Real Criminology

Another truth that must be told is the fact that Indigenous peoples had, and still have, methods of dealing with crime and justice long before the arrival of the colonizers. They are *real criminologies*, or Indigenous criminologies. They are not those brought over and imposed by a foreign colonial entity. In contrast, the dominant systems of justice currently operating in Turtle Island today are foreign imports brought over from the colonizers. Consider even what the Canadian parliament hill in Ottawa resembles. It is not of this land. You can find a very similar structure in London, England. Not only is that government structure in Ottawa not of these lands, but it is built right over top of an ancient Algonquin burial ground (Gehl, 2014). In many ways, it can be understood as a complete disregard of Indigenous peoples as human beings. And, since colonizers could not recognize Indigenous people as persons, they also did not recognize Indigenous systems of justice.

As explained by Robert Yazzie (Chief Justice Emeritus of the Navajo Nation), the European colonists did not recognize Indigenous systems of justice because to them they did not exist, as "they couldn't see police; they didn't find courts; they didn't see uniforms, jails and all the trappings of power" (Yazzie, 2005, p. 122). If this discipline is to make a measurable difference to crime, it must pull back the colonial veil. As Indigenous peoples have very advanced laws and methods for dealing with crime. While some argue that such knowledge is lost (Widdowson & Howard, 2008), it is clear that the many vast cultures, knowledges, and models of governance and justice, including knowledge keepers, remain. As Stó:lō scholar Wenona Victor states, "To think that Indigenous concepts of justice do not exist is Eurocentric thought" (Victor, 2007, p. 13). While they might not be the exact same as they were before colonization, they are still in existence and have adapted overtime with changing conditions and environments. Like any living tradition, they do not stay fixed, or in their original state, and certainly undergo changes over time (Friedland, 2014).

There is a vast array of Indigenous criminologies across Turtle Island. Just as nations have their own languages, cultures, and traditions, they also have their own distinct laws, and their own ways of dealing with harms and resolving conflicts. A study examining six Indigenous legal traditions across Canada: Coast Salish, Tsilhqot'in, Northern Secwepemc, Cree, Anishinabek, and Mi'kmaq highlights their diversity in approaches to justice (Friedland, 2014). While several legal traditions share a strong emphasis on reconciliation, healing, harmony, and forgiveness across several legal traditions, they do not have simple, standalone responses to conflict or harm. Rather, there is a range in how different nations implement these principles. For instance, a Mi'kmaq Elder explained how the concept of *abeksikdawaebegik* (reconciliation) is central in the Mi'kmaq legal tradition. To achieve reconciliation, a person who committed harm must take responsibility for their actions. To do this, they must offer restitution, as well as advance empathy, to those they harmed. In the Cree legal tradition, the healing of the offender is a central response, even in the case of extreme harms. For example, if someone had turned *wetiko*, which is a Cree concept describing a person who is very dangerous and harmful, they must still be seen as family members, and the proper response is to try and heal the person. At the same time, while healing is central in the Cree tradition, it does not mean that healing is implemented without recognition of keeping people safe. While waiting for someone to go through their healing process, separation or avoidance may be necessary to maintain safety (Friedland, 2014).

Similarly, Hansen (member of the Opaskwayak Cree Nation) interviewed six Omushkegowuk (Swampy Cree) Elders from northern Manitoba on concepts of justice, finding that an *Inninew* (Cree) approach to justice is one that is much more focused on healing rather than punishment (Hansen, 2012). As he explains, when someone causes harm, there is a conflict resolution process. This process involves having the person who committed a wrongdoing learn about the impact of the harm they have caused, take actions to assure harm does not reoccur, and repair the harm caused. The community is included in this justice process, and would come together to deal with it, because the view is that the harm of one is the harm of all.

In Blackfoot justice, what is typically considered to be a "crime" is something that disrupts "the harmonious working of their society" (Peat, 1997, p. 570). Opposed to the Canadian system, which follows an adversarial trial model of establishing proof, guilt, and then imposing punishment, Elders gather in a circle with the person harmed and the person who did the harm. In this circle, it is not so much about trying to determine the facts of what happened, but rather, the focus is on how to restore the balance. Thus, the person who caused harm might be asked to suggest an action that would fulfil and satisfy those who had been impacted. Once everyone involved in the incident has established their relationship back to one of balance, their decision is shared publicly with the whole of the community (Peat, 1997).

The various approaches to dealing with harm or crime throughout Turtle Island sustained communities since time immemorial. According to Mohawk scholar Patricia Monture-Angus (1998, p. 363), "there were few problems of crime and disorder among Aboriginal populations at time of contact and for some years after." Her point is not to say that crime was non-existent in Indigenous communities or that we lived in perfect harmony. Instead, it suggests that crime in Indigenous communities was not a considerable or substantial issue before colonization, yet with the arrival of the colonizers, an increase in crime, disruption, and disorder eventually followed. As Huron-Wendat historian Georges Sioui (1992, p. 42) tells us, there is archeological evidence that has proven that Indigenous peoples did not "experience significant conflicts." As Mi'kmaq author and Elder Daniel N. Paul (2006) explained, of course, all people throughout the world have among them those who are capable of committing horrendous crimes. And Indigenous peoples are not exempt from this. As Paul continues, however, cruelty was not a practice that was endorsed or supported within Indigenous societies.

The array of approaches to maintaining justice in Indigenous communities across Turtle Island must not go unacknowledged. The neglect of Indigenous systems of justice perpetuates the continual disregard of Indigenous peoples, including histories, territories, and even existence. At the core, this ignorance and neglect is a stratagem of colonialism that seeks erasure of Indigenous peoples to reach its continued central goal of the attainment of Indigenous territories.

Listening, Truth-telling, and Supporting Indigenous Peoples and Perspectives

Public criminology's quest for how to best engage and change public policy is not something new to Indigenous peoples—as Indigenous communities and organizations have continued their attempts to influence public policy since the initial arrival of settlers and their governments. Real meaningful consultation with Indigenous persons regarding policies, even those policies directly concerning Indigenous persons, is often lacking, both historically and still today. A major roadblock to achieving governmental and policy change is the entrenched colonial system that was set-up to actively eliminate Indigenous presence, and the public's continual acceptance and ignorance of what this colonial system continues to perpetrate. Thus, the sense of frustration felt by criminologists attempting to enter the public sphere is also experienced by Indigenous communities and organizations. If the discipline of criminology can better align with Indigenous voices, then perhaps Indigenous organizations and communities—and criminology—can work together in efforts towards shaping public policy. As such, Indigenous perspectives of crime and justice must be reflected within the discipline of criminology and become part of the discipline's "collective voice" rather than remaining at the margins. Only then can public criminology take steps to effectively achieve real change in reducing Indigenous injustice on Turtle Island.

To do this, it is essential for criminology to draw on the voices, experiences, and perspectives of Indigenous peoples and communities in order for change and justice to be realized. A strategy of colonialism has been to separate Indigenous persons from knowledge and research regarding Indigenous peoples and, instead, make us "topics" of study without any significant engagement or input. Thus, as a first step, criminologists must engage Indigenous peoples as partners and support Indigenous peoples in their quests for justice and truth. It means listening to Indigenous communities: hear Indigenous stories, support Indigenous voices, and act on the words Indigenous peoples are saying. There must be a bridging of the gaps between truths and criminology, which includes exposing colonial falsehoods, telling Indigenous histories, and reflecting on the real criminologies of these lands.

We must keep in mind that the education system has historically been a central tool of colonialism (Cote-Meek, 2014). As teachers, we have a duty not to perpetuate these legacies. We have a duty to assure that the learning environment is a safe space for everyone—not just the dominant groups in the classroom. It means being sure not to further objectify Indigenous students or perpetuate colonial violence and trauma in the classroom (Cote-Meek, 2014). To avoid doing so, it is imperative to incorporate works of Indigenous authors, leaders, organizations, and academics in the classroom. Read and teach works by Indigenous scholars and bring in local Indigenous peoples, such as Elders, grassroots organizations, artists, and knowledge keepers into the classroom.

Inclusivity can also occur at conferences. Begin with a land acknowledgment in the opening of criminology conferences. Consult with the local nation to whose land the conference is on and seek their consent, as this is showing respect and recognition. Ask if they would like to be involved, and if so, how. Reach out to a local Elder or knowledge keeper who might be interested in opening the conference, or to share truths of their land. When reaching out, follow the local protocols of the land. For instance, the offering of tobacco when asking for someone's time is common in many places in Turtle Island. When asking an Elder, knowledge keeper, or artist for their talents, skills, and knowledge, people often provide an honorarium for their time. While it is important to be inclusive, it is also important to be mindful not to simply take, or proceed in disrespectful ways, or in ways that continue to marginalize.

There are also many Indigenous peoples who are making change and spreading awareness through the arts. Reach out, listen, and support these artists and their messages. In her research on Indigenous hip-hop and historical trauma, Sheffield (2011) highlights how hip-hop is an outlet for many to voice their resistance to oppression and genocide, while at the same time, serving as a platform for expressing identities with pride. As Navarro (2014, p. 102) notes, since hip-hop's beginnings, it has "responded to various forms of racism, class inequities, and systemic state violence." While there is a popularized strain that objectifies women and focuses on acquiring material wealth—with some Indigenous hip-hop not exempt from this—it is not what makes up all of Indigenous hip-hop. In fact, there is an incredible amount of Indigenous hip-hop that is positive and focused on educating. JB the First Lady (Nuxalk and Onondaga Nations), quoted at the start of this chapter, is a prime example. She has continued to incite change, inspire, educate, and empower people through her music. She has been a leader in this movement of positive change-making hip-hop, as she has been cited as stating, "My music is political, but it's positive, it's about love" (CBC News, 2014).

Bring these artists who have messages to share into criminology classrooms or to criminology conferences. Listen to the voices of the people who are putting themselves out there to educate and inspire. Create space for people to tell their stories and share their gifts. For instance, I have brought JB into my classroom to present and share with criminology students. She came as part of an Indigenous Community Justice Lecture Series I put on in fall 2017, where I brought in 17 Indigenous knowledge keepers, educators, and artists throughout the term. They included Lekeyten, Kwantlen First Nation Elder and the Elder in Residence at our university who shared teachings of the lands to which our university is located. It also included artist Brandon Gabriel from Kwantlen First Nation who educates and creates change through his artwork.

The dance group that I am part of, Butterflies in Spirit, was also part of the series. We are a group that raises awareness of violence against Indigenous women and the missing and murdered Indigenous women and girls across Canada through dance. All members of the group have been impacted by violence in some way, with many who have family members of those missing or murdered. This group was started in 2012 by Lorelei Williams (Skatin and Sts'ailes Nations) in order to get the picture of her missing aunt Belinda Williams out there, as well as honor her cousin Tanya Holyk who was murdered by serial killer Robert Pickton. Butterflies in Spirit have shared all over Canada, and in 2017 went international when we were invited to present at the Women's World Peace Conference in Bogotá, Colombia. We also shared our experience of travelling to Bogotá with the students, informing and demonstrating to them our efforts to raise awareness. Thus, these modes of communication and education brought into the classroom provide an additional way to learn about Indigenous realities and truths—by learning directly from community change-makers. This provides the opportunity for criminology classrooms to become places to raise awareness and be part of a change.

This chapter began by outlining how Indigenous injustice is rooted in colonialism, explaining how the public, as well as the discipline of criminology, is largely colonized. Engaging in mainstream approaches of public criminology thus is not a useful initial intervention. Efforts must first work toward exposing, challenging, and eliminating the entrenched colonial discourse with the aim of reducing injustices that continue to face Indigenous peoples. Steps must be taken towards anti-colonial politics in everyday life, including changing the discipline of criminology to be more reflective of Indigenous truths and perspectives. In this regard, this chapter has criticized mainstream criminology for its focus on the Indigenous "problem," the lack of colonial context, and the disregard of Indigenous criminologies. It has also highlighted Indigenous change-makers and suggested to listen, learn, support, and create spaces for Indigenous community voices within criminology—including in our very own classrooms—in order to transform them into places of consciousness raising so that students become part of the change.

In conclusion, this chapter offers a reminder that it is key for criminologists to listen and learn perspectives from Indigenous persons who are putting themselves out there to be heard. As Anishinaabekwe-Métis-Nehiowé educator Janice Acoose (1995, p. 118) teaches us,

> art, music, dance, literature, and drama are much more than elusive energies emanating from outside our beings, it is vitally important that we, as Indigenous peoples, remain strongly attached to our cultures and continue to represent our own realities. Besides, who can represent our realities better than those whose ancestral roots are nourished in cultural memories that extend well beyond the Euro-Canadian experience?"

Criminologists must engage with and be authentic partners with Indigenous persons. It is imperative to assist in breaking down entrenched colonial systems and public ignorance of what these colonial systems continue to perpetrate. Only then will we be on a path to achieving real impacts in the public realm. And only then will we be able to help guide the way towards real justice in Turtle Island.

References

Acoose, J. (1995). *Iskwewak Kah' Ki Yaw Ni Wahkomakanak: Neither Indian Princesses nor Easy Squaws*. Toronto: Women's Press.

Bigelow, B., & Peterson, B. (1998). Introduction: Why rethink Columbus. In B. Bigelow & B. Peterson (Eds.), *Rethinking Columbus: The next 500 years* (pp. 10–11). Milwaukee: Rethinking Schools Ltd.

Bombay, A., Matheson, K., & Anisman, H. (2014). The intergenerational effects of Indian residential schools: implications for the concept of historical trauma. *Transcultural Psychiatry, 51*(3), 320–338.

Bonds, A., & Inwood, J. (2016). Beyond white privilege: geographies of white supremacy and settler colonialism. *Progress in Human Geography, 40*(6), 715–733.

Boots, F. A. (1989). Iroquoian use of wampum. In J. Bruchac (Ed.), *New voices from the longhouse: An anthology of contemporary Iroquois writing* (pp. 34–39). Ann Arbor, MI: Greenfield Review Press.

Borrows, J. (2002). Wampum at Niagara: The royal proclamation, Canadian legal history, and self-government. In M. Asch (Ed.), *Aboriginal treaty rights in Canada*. Vancouver: University of British Columbia Press.

Bowker, K. M. (2007). *The boarding school legacy: Ten contemporary lakota women tell their stories*, Doctoral thesis. Montana State University. Retrieved from https://scholarworks.montana.edu/xmlui/bitstream/handle/1/958/BowkerK1207.pdf?sequence=1.

Cain, M. (2000). Orientalism, cccidentalism and the sociology of crime. *British Journal of Criminology, 40*(2), 239–260.

Chansonneuve, D. (2005). *Reclaiming connections: Understanding residential school trauma among Aboriginal people: A resource manual*. Ottawa: Aboriginal Healing Foundation. Retrieved from www.ahf.ca/downloads/healing-trauma-web-eng.pdf.

Chrisjohn, R., & Young, S. (2006). *The circle game: Shadows and substance in the Indian residential school experience in Canada*. Penticton: Theytus Books.

Corntassel, J. (2012). Living in a longer now: moving beyond The State-Centric system. In Waziyatawin & M. Yellow Bird (Eds.), *For indigenous minds only: A decolonization handbook* (pp. 85–98). Santa Fe, NM: School for Advanced Research Press.

Cote, H., & Schissel, W. (2008). Damaged children and broken spirits: A residential school survivor story. In C. Brooks & B. Schissel (Eds.), *Marginality & condemnation: An introduction to critical criminology* (2nd ed., pp. 220–237). Black Point, NS: Fernwood Publishing.

Cote-Meek, S. (2014). *Colonized classrooms: Racism, trauma and resistance in post-secondary education*. Halifax & Winnipeg: Fernwood Publishing.

Currie, E. (2007). Against marginality: Arguments for a public criminology. *Theoretical Criminology, 11*(2), 175–190.

Dion, S. D. (2009). *Braiding histories: Learning from Aboriginal peoples' experiences & perspectives*. Vancouver: UBC Press.

Dunbar-Ortiz, R. (2014). *An Indigenous peoples' history of the United States*. Boston, MA: Beacon Press.

Fear-Segal, J., & Rose, S. D. (2016). Introduction. In J. Fear-Segal & S. D. Rose (Eds.), *Carlisle Indian industrial school: Indigenous histories, memories, and reclamations* (pp. 1–34). Lincoln and London: Board of Regents of the University of Nebraska.

Fournier, S., & Crey, E. (2006). "Killing the Indian in the child": Four centuries of church-run schools. In R. C. Maaka & C. Andersen (Eds.), *The indigenous experience: Global perspectives*. Toronto: Canadian Scholars' Press Inc.

Friedland, H. (2014). *IBA accessing justice and reconciliation project: Final report*. Retrieved from http://indigenousbar.ca/indigenouslaw/wp-content/uploads/2013/04/iba_ajr_final_report.pdf.

Gehl, L. (2014). *The truth that wampum tells: My debwewin on the Algonquin land claims process*. Black Point: Fernwood Publishing.

Hansen, J. G. (2012). Countering imperial justice: The implications of a cree response to crime. *Indigenous Policy Journal, 23*(1), 1–16.

Kelly, F. (2008). Confession of a born again pagan. In M. Brant Castellano, L. Archibald, & M. DeGagné (Eds.), *From truth to reconciliation: Transforming the legacy of residential schools* (pp. 11–40). Ottawa: The Aboriginal Healing Foundation.

King, J. T. (2007). The value of water and the meaning of water law for the Native Americans known as the haudenosaunee. *Cornell Journal of Law and Public Policy, 16*(3), 449–472.

Lakota People's Law Project. (2015). Native lives matter. Santa Cruz. Retrieved from http://docs.lakotalaw.org/reports/NativeLivesMatterPDF.pdf.

Loder, I., & Sparks, R. (2011). *Public criminology?* Abingdon: Routledge.

Lookingbill, B. D. (2006). *War dance at Fort Marion: Plains Indian war prisoners*. Norman: University of Oklahoma Press.

Malakieh, J. (2018). Adult and youth correctional statistics in Canada, 2016/2017. *Juristat. Canadian Centre for Justice Statistics*. 1–20. Retrieved from https://www150.statcan.gc.ca/n1/en/pub/85-002-x/2018001/article/54972-eng.pdf?st=25xb34ZP

Martin, F. A. (2014). The coverage of American Indians and Alaskan natives in criminal justice and criminology introductory textbooks. *Critical Criminology, 22*(2), 237–256.

Molin, P. F. (1988). *Training the hand, the head, and the heart": Indian education at Hampton Institute*. St. Paul, MN: Minnesota Historical Society. Retrieved from http://collections.mnhs.org/MNHistoryMagazine/articles/51/v51i03p082-098.pdf.

Monchalin, L. (2016). *The colonial problem: An Indigenous perspective on crime and injustice in Canada*. Toronto: University of Toronto Press.

Monture-Angus, P. A. (1998). Lessons in decolonization: Aboriginal overrepresentation in Canadian criminal justice. In *Visions of the Heart: Canadian Aboriginal Issues* (pp. 361–386). Scarborough: Thomson Nelson.

Navarro, J. (2014). Solarize-ing native hip-hop: Native feminist land ethics and cultural resistance. *Decolonization: Indigeneity, Education & Society, 3*(1), 101–118.

News, C. B. C. (2014, January 3). JB The first lady: Changing hip-hop one beat at a time. *CBC News*. Retrieved from www.cbc.ca/news/indigenous/jb-the-first-lady-changing-hip-hop-one-beat-at-a-time-1.2479593.

O'Connor, L., & O'Neal, M. (2010). *Dark legacy: Systemic discrimination against Canada's First Peoples*. Canada: Totem Pole Books.

Paul, D. N. (2006). *First Nations history: We were not the savages: Collision between European and Native American civilizations* (Third). Black Point, NS: Fernwood Publishing.

Peat, F. D. (1997). Blackfoot physics and European minds. *Future, 29*(6), 563–573.

Sheffield, C. L. (2011). Native American hip-hop and historical trauma. *Studies in American Indian Literatures, 23*(3), 94–110.

Sioui, G. (1992). *For An Amerindian Autohistory: An Essay on the Foundations of a Social Ethic*. Montreal: McGill-Queen's University Press.

Smith, L. T. (2012). *Decolonizing methodologies: Research and Indigenous peoples: Second edition*. London: Zed Books.

Starblanket, T. (2018). *Suffer the little children: Genocide, Indigenous Nations and the Canadian state*. Atlanta: Clarity Press, Inc.

Truth and Reconciliation Commission of Canada. (2015). *Honouring the truth, reconciling for the future: Summary of the final report of the Truth and Reconciliation Commission of Canada*. Retrieved from www.myrobust.com/websites/trcinstitution/File/Reports/Executive_Summary_English_Web.pdf.

Victor, W. (2007). Indigenous justice: Clearing space and place for Indigenous epistemologies. *Prepared for the National Centre for First Nation Governance*, December 2, 1–28. Retrieved from http://fngovernance.org/ncfng_research/wenona_victor.pdf.

Wanjek, C. (2011, October). Top 5 misconceptions about Columbus. *LiveScience*. Retrieved from www.livescience.com/16468-christopher-columbus-myths-flat-earth-discovered-americas.html.

Widdowson, F., & Howard, A. (2008). *Disrobing the Aboriginal industry: The deception behind Indigenous cultural preservation*. Kingston: McGill-Queen's University Press.

Yazzie, R. C. J. (2005). Healing as justice: The navajo response to crime. In W. D. McCaslin (Ed.), *Justice as healing Indigenous ways: Writings on community peacemaking and restorative justice from the native law centre* (pp. 121–133). Saint Paul, MN: Living Justice Press.

Zinn, H. (2012). *The indispensable Zinn: The essential writings of the "people's historian."* (T. P. McCarthy, Ed.). New York: The New Press.

23

TIME TO THINK ABOUT PATRIARCHY?

Public Criminology in an Era of Misogyny

Meda Chesney-Lind

Introduction

Progressive criminologists, particularly in the United States, face a daunting set of challenges, and the situation is even more acute for feminist criminologists. It is now clear that right-wing politics, particularly racism and sexism, were central to Donald Trump's surprising election, not the politics of inequality as some initially speculated (Schaffner, MacWilliams, & Nteta, 2017). Worse, it appears that the strategy employed in the last election—that of directly appealing to racism and sexism of White voters—may continue to dominate political discourse in the United States going forward. The calculus goes as follows: In the current political climate, Republicans are unlikely to garner much support among racial and ethnic minorities, and Trump's long, public history of sexism is both widely acknowledged and not seen by his core voters as disqualifying for the presidency. Direct appeals to racism and sexism will, it seems, become a routine feature of U.S. politics in ways unimaginable since the *de jure* defeat of segregation and the rise of the civil rights movement.

The United States is not alone in experiencing these trends. Many nations in the global North, in particular, have seen the rise of an unapologetic right-wing (often nativist) populism, which seems to have emerged in response to a set of transnational political factors, including immigration and globalization. Another key, but sometimes overlooked, aspect of these emerging rightwing movements globally has been the same direct appeal to White male dominance and an implicit endorsement of misogynistic attitudes particularly regarding women's rights and the policing of women's sexuality (Vieten, 2016; Jacobs, 2018).

For feminist criminologists, the current global political climate is particularly challenging, given the centrality of violence against women to the field's intellectual agenda. Donald Trump is an unapologetic misogynist, one who bragged about grabbing women in their genitals; he has also been accused of sexual misconduct by over a dozen women (Talking Points News, 2018). During the campaign for president, he also raised eyebrows by suggesting that women who seek abortions should be "punished," something that even the anti-abortion movement up until that point had had avoided suggesting (White, 2016). His campaign pandered shamelessly to nativism, racism (including constructing immigrants as criminals), and anti-abortion sentiments, while belittling his female opponent as "nasty," unattractive, and "corrupt," with many of his rallies characterized by chants of "lock her up" and T-shirts arguing to "Trump that Bitch" (Sanghani, 2016).

Upon taking office, Trump's presidency has been characterized by additional troubling patterns. Importantly, because of the issues surrounding his dubious election victory, Trump's allies have been targeting the very legitimacy of the U.S. criminal justice system itself (in an effort to undercut what might likely be an effort to prosecute him for obstruction of justice). On a political and policy level, however, Trump appears to have established an effective coalition with conservative establishment Republicans in Congress. In exchange for their silence surrounding his most egregious political and personal blunders and missteps, his administration has facilitated the advance of a social and economic agenda that many note often betrays his populist election rhetoric, delivering instead a narrow but troubling set of victories for traditional conservative core constituencies (including the wealthy Republican donor base and evangelical Christians) (Wagner & Eilperin, 2017)

Trump's endeavors include the continued efforts to undermine and ultimately repeal the Affordable Care Act and the recent tax cuts (that largely benefited the rich and corporations), which are clear examples of his hewing to traditional conservative issues. Perhaps the least discussed, at least until his most recent nomination of Brett Kavanaugh to the U.S. Supreme Court (New York Times, 2018), was his administration's dramatically stepped up efforts to curtail and even criminalize girl's and women's access to the full range of reproductive rights, including various forms of abortion (Rovner, 2018). Placing these abortion politics within the larger context of women's place in patriarchal society is a necessary first step in considering women's rights and women's resistance in the new century.

The issue of abortion (and abortion rights as a human right) clearly demonstrates the need for feminist criminology to engage directly with the policy and political worlds—to explicitly do what has been described as "public criminology" (Currie, 2007; Uggen & Inderbitzin, 2010). This means stepping outside of the academy (and academic journals) to do more in the realm of policy work, public education, and what some have called "newsmaking" criminology (Barak, 2007). In this chapter, an attempt is made to put abortion rights in their historical and political context. Following that, I discuss the relevance of current efforts to recriminalize abortion as part of broader policing of girls and women's bodies (and sexuality) in patriarchy. Finally, the facts of abortion (and its widespread use) are reviewed, as well as facts about abortion trends. These clearly indicate that while abortion use is down, medical abortion (not surgical abortion) is increasingly the norm, and access to affordable abortion is a vital resource for low-income women, young women, and people of color as they seek to control their life trajectories.

Reproductive Rights in the United States: A Brief History

The movement to establish a woman's right to control her own sexuality and reproduction started at the beginning of the twentieth century in the United States (Sinding, 2007). Activists like Emma Goldman, who worked as a nurse among immigrant women, saw that the absence of contraception risked women's lives because of botched efforts to induce abortion. She, and later Margaret Sanger, were struggling to establish a women's right to avoid unwanted pregnancies, focusing on individual woman and her wellbeing. During that time, the term "birth control" did not even exist and discussion of the "prevention of conception" was seen as "obscene" and a crime (Mlitt, 1980).

Goldman was arrested, put on trial, and eventually jailed in 1916 for attempting to give women information about contraception, and she took a broader view of the issue than did Sanger, who eventually focused narrowly on a more medical approach to the discussion of contraception (Berkeley Library, 2018a). Here is Emma Goldman commenting on her jailing for attempting to distribute birth control information in 1916 (Berkeley Library, 2018b):

> while I am not particularly anxious to go to jail, I should yet be glad to do so, if thereby I can add my might to the importance of birth control and the wiping off our antiquated law upon the statute.

Goldman ended up spending two weeks in a prison workhouse. The Carnegie Hall meeting that marked her release that May drew more than 3,000 people who wanted to celebrate her return—and to obtain information about birth control (Berkeley Library, 2018a).

During the second wave of feminist activism, the family planning movement gained further ground as efforts to decriminalize abortion in the 1960s and 1970s ultimately prevailed with the issuing of the landmark Supreme Court Decision, *Roe v. Wade* in 1973 (Chesney-Lind & Hadi, 2017; Doan, 2007; Planned Parenthood Federation of America, 2014). Women's rights activists' use of the phrase "Reproductive Politics" emerged in the mid- twentieth-century and signaled that the movement no longer dealt with just women's right to avoid unwanted pregnancies. Instead, it expanded the struggle over contraception to include abortion, race and sterilization, class and adoption, women and sexuality, and other related concerns (Solinger, 2005).

In the decades that followed, some contend that a "narrow" focus on the legal right to abortion meant that the more inclusive platform originally envisioned by the early reproductive rights advocates failed to develop. Knudsen (2006, p. 10) makes this argument forcefully:

> the best-known reproductive rights organizations historically focused almost exclusively on issues that were most important to white, upper- and middle-class American women rather than addressing matters that more directly affected the less privileged. Narrowly concentrating on a woman's legal right to abortion, for example, American feminists until recently have largely neglected other reproductive rights issues that greatly affect women of color and poor women, such as sterilization abuses and inadequate access to health services, not to mention access to information and contraception. While the issue of abortion clearly has a tremendous impact on all women, the greatest obstacle to procuring a safe abortion for poor women and women of color in the United States is usually a matter of access and not one of legality. The legalization of abortion may ensure that a wealthy white woman can obtain an abortion from her private physician, but legalization by itself does not ensure that a poor, Black woman in a rural area will have the financial resources or physical access to get an abortion.

These shortcomings became abundantly clear in the context of recent efforts to effectively re-criminalize abortion in the United States. These legal and political moves, in turn, provide a case study of the larger issue of the specific role of the government in the enforcement of patriarchal control over women's sexuality (and ultimately their lives).

After the 2010 off-year election—where Republicans scored major victories in many state races, taking over both governorships and legislatures (Balz, 2010)—U.S. anti-abortion activists shifted their focus to the states and in particular began to work on restricting access to abortion (rather than federal court battles about the legality of the procedure). Restrictions on abortion proliferated—some so severe that they essentially render abortion unavailable for broad swaths of the country. As a result of these sorts of changes, the Guttmacher Institute concluded, the proportion of women living in restrictive states went from 31% to 56% between 2000 and 2013, while the proportion living in supportive states fell from 40% to 31% over the same period (Nash, Gold, Rowan, Rathbun, & Vierboom, 2014). As of January 1, 2014, at least half of the states have imposed excessive and unnecessary regulations on abortion clinics, mandated counseling designed to dissuade a woman from obtaining an abortion, required a waiting period before an abortion, required parental involvement before a minor obtains an abortion, or prohibited the use of state Medicaid funds to pay for medically necessary abortions (Guttmacher Institute, 2016). These restrictions had a discernable impact as the number of U.S. abortion providers declined 4% between 2008 and 2011 (Guttmacher Institute, 2015). Since that time, the number of abortions has continued to fall. In 2014, approximately 926,200 abortions were performed, down 12% from 1.06 million in 2011 (Guttmacher Institute, 2018). The number of abortion providers also continued to decline. The number of clinics providing abortion services declined 6% between 2011 and 2014 (from 839 to 788) (Guttmacher Institute, 2018).

This state by state strategy of rending abortion unavailable was decisively blocked by a surprisingly strong decision in *Whole Women's Health et al. v Hellerstedt*. On June 27, 2016, by a vote of 5 to 3, the Supreme Court reaffirmed and strengthened constitutional protections for abortion rights, by striking down parts of a restrictive Texas law that reduced the number of abortion clinics in the state by half, leaving them only in the largest metropolitan areas. Specifically, the court found that the Texas requirements that abortion clinics had to meet the relatively high standards of "ambulatory surgical centers" and that doctors performing abortions had to have admitting privileges at local hospitals violated earlier Supreme Court requirements that the state's not place an "undue burden" on girls and women seeking abortions (Liptak, 2016).

Abortion opponents had hoped this case would provide the deeply divided Supreme Court with an opportunity to gut *Roe v. Wade* and reverse the 1992 case *Planned Parenthood v. Casey*, which held that abortion laws that created an "undue burden" on women were unconstitutional. Instead, the court both clarified and strengthened Casey while striking down the Texas requirements. One analysis concluded that the case "could invalidate anti-abortion laws in another 25 states" (Martin, 2016, para. 2). This relatively unexpected decision, hailed by one abortion right's advocate as a "game changer," essentially "leaves the right to an abortion on much stronger footing" (Martin, 2016, para. 1).

This decision, though, energized abortion opponents in the United States, and it has not prevented a number of states to continue trying to impose draconian restrictions. In point of fact, efforts to essentially re-criminalize abortion by prohibiting it at earlier and earlier stages in pregnancy continue. Most recently, early abortion bans have been passed in a number of U.S. states, explicitly outlawing abortion when performed after a certain point early in the pregnancy. The laws vary, with some forbidding abortion after six weeks of pregnancy, and some after eight weeks. Alabama's law is the most extreme: It aims to outlaw abortion at any point, except if the woman's health is at serious risk. So far in 2019, nine U.S. states have passed laws of this type, and more states are considering similar legislation (Gordon & Hurt, 2019). More globally, these burdensome regulations are not an anomaly—they are the rule when it comes to abortion access in the United States, particularly since Trump's election (Balmert, 2017).

Even before the most recent Supreme Court decision, abortion was clearly a key issue in the 2016 race for the presidency in the United States, and ultimately may have been a factor in Trump's surprising victory. As noted earlier, on the campaign trail, Trump recently said not only do you have to "ban" abortion, but also that there "has to be some sort of punishment" for women who seek abortions (Berenson, 2016, para. 1). Those comments were so controversial, even among abortion opponents, that he quickly backed away from them (White, 2016); they were also a warning of how seriously Trump's election would impact availability of the procedure. Trump also bragged on the campaign trail that he would put an abortion foe on the Supreme Court.

Since his election, Trump and his Vice President Michael Pence have been extremely visible and impassioned about their opposition to abortion. Trump became the first sitting President to address the "March for Life" (Woellert, 2018). He has also named an anti-abortion Judge to the U.S. Supreme court, Neil Gorsuch, one of his very few congressional achievements.

Gorsuch's appointment is related to another worrying trend as more religious groups are seeking to avoid having to provide their employees with access to legal contraceptives, after the U.S. Supreme Court earlier voted narrowly to grant a private, for profit corporation the right to deny their employees access to insurance to cover the cost of contraception on the basis of the religious beliefs of the owners of the company (Liptak, 2016). Gorsuch issued a key ruling earlier on this same case, arguing to dramatically expand the "religious protections" afforded owners of corporations (Totenberg, 2017). Since "the upfront cost for an IUD can be a thousand dollars", which translates, as Justice Ruth Bader Ginsburg noted in her strongly worded dissent, "to nearly a month's wages for a low-income worker", this exemption hits young and low-income women especially hard (Joffe, 2016, p. 148).

When anti-abortion protesters gathered in Washington for the 45 annual "March for Life" rally, Trump declared in a video address from the Rose Garden to the group: "In my administration, we will always defend the very first right in the Declaration of Independence, and that is the right to life" (Rovner, 2018, para. 4). More recently, Vice President Mike Pence has argued that abortion will end "in our time" (Levy, 2018). The administration most recently has attempted to prohibit organizations, like Planned Parenthood, that receive federal funds for non-abortion medical services, from even referring patients for abortion (Van Sant, 2019). That said, despite many attempts, Congress has so far failed to pass a federal ban on abortions occurring after 20 weeks, it did not cut off Planned Parenthood's federal funding, and also did not write into permanent law the Hyde Amendment, which bans most federal abortion funding but needs annual renewal (Rovner, 2018).

The abortion issue continues to color the Trump presidency. One of the most egregious examples of this is provided by Scott Lloyd, an anti-contraceptive and anti-abortion activist, who was appointed by the President to serve as head of refugee resettlement. In that capacity he has tried to block abortions for young, undocumented immigrants being held in custody in a detention center in Texas. In fact, Lloyd visited a teen while in custody, asking her if she was comfortable, if she had the food she liked, but most importantly, he wanted to counsel her against having an abortion (Peters, 2018).

How Lloyd, an appointee of President Trump, turned a small office in the Department of Health and Human Services that provides social services to refugees into a battleground over abortion rights is part of the larger story of the Trump administration's push to enact rules that favor socially conservative positions on issues like abortion, contraception and gay, lesbian and transgender rights across the board (Peters, 2018). Ultimately, the courts blocked Lloyd's efforts due to a suit filed by the American Civil Liberties Union in 2018 (Stevens, 2018), but the case speaks volumes about the Trump administration's commitment to anti-abortion politics and practices.

Naming Brett Kavanaugh to the Supreme Court, a selection now clouded by a claim of sexual assault, poses an additional threat to abortion rights. Kavanaugh was one of the judges in the Lloyd case that dissented, arguing, "a new right for unlawful immigrant minors in U.-S. government detention to obtain immediate abortion on demand" (Savage, 2018, para. 8). During the George W. Bush administration, he also argued, "I am not sure that all legal scholars refer to Roe as the settled law of the land at the Supreme Court level since Court can always overrule its precedent." He also added that some conservative justices then on the court "would do so." (Biskupic, 2018, para. 6). His record is certainly as troubling as that of Neal Gorsuch, and his confirmation jeopardizes women's access to safe and legal abortions.

Patriarchy Matters

When Donald Trump was elected President of the United States, a wide range of commentators argued the White working class, hard hit by the loss of manufacturing jobs, was not moved by

Hillary Clinton's campaign (Bump, 2017). This was a widely accepted explanation, and one with which scholars of race and gender are familiar. Once again, those concerned about sexism and racism are reminded that social class is the defining social issue of our time; this is, in fact, a longstanding tradition within sociology and most of the social sciences (Chesney-Lind & Chagnon, 2015). This time, however, there is convincing data to suggest that this is not the case. Reviewing results of a nationally representative survey data just prior to the election, Schaffner, MacWilliams, and Nteta (2017) found that voters' measures of sexism and racism correlated much more closely with support for Trump than did economic dissatisfaction, particularly among Whites without a college degree. So Clinton's loss, rather than being a fluke or the product of a bungled campaign, might in fact be a harbinger of a dangerous and toxic form of racism and misogyny. These patterns suggest that misogyny, like the racism that has long haunted U.S. elections (see Chambliss, 1999), will become an enduring feature of the U.S. political process. These political developments require a revisiting of the concept of patriarchy, with some important updates.

As discussed elsewhere (Chesney-Lind & Hadi, 2017), patriarchal systems exert control over women's sexuality, sexual expression, and reproduction (Renzetti, Curran, & Maier, 2012). As Lerner (1986, p. 212) argues in *The Creation of Patriarchy*, the commodification of women's sexual and reproductive capacity is an essential feature of women's subordination: "Women themselves became a resource, acquired by men much as the land was acquired by men." Accordingly, women have been subsumed as the sexual property of men, with expectations that they provide sexual and reproductive services. Lerner (1986, p. 215) elaborates:

> For women, class is mediated through their sexual ties to a man. It is through the man that women have access to or are denied access to the means of production and to resources. It is through their sexual behavior that they gain access to class. "Respectable women" gain access to class through father and husbands, but breaking the sexual rules can at once declass them. The gender definition of sexual "deviance" marks women as "not respectable," which in fact consigns her to the lowest class status possible.

This presents a double standard, sometimes called the whore/Madonna dichotomy, that is the cornerstone of longstanding norms governing female (but not male) behavior across multiple domains of social life. As Chesney-Lind and Hadi (2017, p. 74) explain further, "Societal discussions, then, of issues such as contraception, abortion, and sex education need to be understood as occurring within this patriarchal context." Women are often accused of being "bad," "sluts," or even criminals when they are seeking medical services that allow them to control their sexuality and reproduction. This view of them is lodged within the centuries old patriarchal view of women as male sexual property.

The understanding of patriarchy as a system of gender stratification has recently received an important theoretical update. In response to Trump's election, among other things, Enloe, argues in her recent book, *The Big Push: Exposing and Challenging the Persistence of Patriarchy* (2018), that it is past time to start thinking about patriarchy. She confesses, though, that she did not always feel this way: "I almost broke into a run to get away from the first person I heard utter the word 'patriarchy,'" thinking it "so heavy, so blunt, so ideological" (Enloe, 2018, p. ix). In subsequent decades, though, the feminist political theorist has gradually seen a particular utility in the concept. She proposes we use patriarchy as a "searchlight" whereby we see what we would otherwise miss: "the connective tissues between large and small, subtle and blatant forms of racialized sexism, gendered misogyny and masculine privilege" (pp. ix–x).

Enloe (2018, p. 166) suggests that we need to do research that showcases the questions that feminists must ask, and she cautions against timidity:

The antidote to a patriarchally complicit lack of curiosity is asking new feminist-informed questions. Lots of questions. Conducting deep and ongoing feminist investigations of the institutions apparently at the forefront of modern life is a crucial form of resistance.

Aimed at documenting how this works, Enloe argues that we need to explore both the "persistence" of patriarchy, through feminist research, while also documenting the scope and forms of "feminist resistance" (Enloe, 2018). Significantly, Trump does not loom large in her thinking about patriarchy. Enloe (p. x) argues that we should not be diverted by the "patriarchal machinations of any outsized figure," and instead focus on "more insidious dynamics that are perpetuating patriarchal ideas and relationships."

In terms of resistance, Enloe and many others were much moved by an anti-Trump set of events, starting with the largest single-day protest in U.S. history—the Women's March on January 21, 2017. Enloe (2018, p. 7) found the "personal spontaneity" of march participants infectious and the "irreverent defiance of … misogyny" embodied in the pussy hats a great "collective feminist message." What particularly intrigued her, though, was the global scope of the protest, with the amazing number of "sister marches" (all 673 of them) with an estimated attendance of 4.9 million (p. 5). Finally, and most importantly, the marches also focused, in very direct ways, on the politics of women's reproductive rights with march organizers prominently featuring the issue on their website (Women's March, 2019), saying,

> We believe in Reproductive Freedom. We do not accept any federal, state or local rollbacks, cuts or restrictions on our ability to access quality reproductive healthcare services, birth control, HIV/AIDS care and prevention, or medically accurate sexuality education. This means open access to safe, legal, affordable abortion and birth control for all people, regardless of income, location or education.

Feminist criminologists must use the tools of public criminology to join efforts to protect women's rights to abortion. Research agendas to prioritize both theorizing about reproductive rights as human rights and doing activist research on the impact of current state level efforts to render abortion unavailable are clearly needed. The academic silence about abortion must be shattered. Current narrow thinking about abortion as an issue of medical privacy truncates our ability to think and act politically. Note that the public/private divide in current legal thinking disadvantages and renders invisible injuries to girls and women and has never been a friend to women's rights (Boyd, 1997).

Recriminalizing Abortion?

It is hard to imagine a system more in need of this sort of critical feminist exploration than the series of legal and political initiatives trying to dramatically reduce women's access to reproductive rights, both in the United States and around the world. Efforts to criminalize—or, rather, recriminalize—family planning and abortion place the criminal justice system firmly in the center of patriarchal controls on girls and women's behavior, particularly since women's sexual and reproductive health is a matter of grave concern worldwide. Recent data indicated that roughly 39% of the world's population still lives in countries with highly restrictive laws governing abortion (Center for Reproductive Rights, 2014). These countries either prohibit abortion completely or allow the procedure only to save a woman's life or to preserve her health (CRR, 2014). As a result, nearly half of all abortions worldwide are unsafe (Guttmacher Institute, 2015).

The proportion of abortions that are performed under unsafe conditions is not currently known. However, complications from unsafe abortions are more common in developing regions, or where the procedure is often highly restricted (Guttmacher Institute, 2015). Estimates for 2012 indicate that 6.9 million women in these regions were treated for complications from unsafe abortions, corresponding to a rate of 6.9 women treated per 1,000 women aged 15–44. Furthermore, most recent estimates suggest that some 40% of women who experience complications from unsafe abortions never receive treatment (Guttmacher Institute, 2015). More will be said about the global issues surrounding access to abortion, and the key role played by U.-S. domestic policy in dramatically reducing reproductive rights, later in the paper.

Suffice to say here that girls' and women's "reproductive rights," particularly their access to abortion, are some of the most vigorously contested issues in contemporary American political life, arguably key to deciding presidential elections. Because discussion of these issues tends to be quite heated and ideological (often relying on deeply held cultural beliefs like religion), the larger political and social meaning of female access to abortion services can get lost in the religious rhetoric. For this reason, it is very important to put the discussion of girls' and women's access to contraception and abortion into a socio-political and criminological context, rather than simply reducing the discussion to one about the legal, moral, biological, and medical aspects of a set of "procedures." It is important to recall that access to contraception was initially framed as a political and human right rather than medical or "privacy" right, as is the case even in some of the progressive supporters of women's rights.

Abortion Trends in the United States: Facts Versus Rhetoric

An important aspect of the politics of abortion is to review the facts about abortion, both in terms of numbers of procedures and in terms of what sort of women seek these services. First, and significantly, the numbers of abortions are going down. According to the Guttmacher Institute (2016), in the United States in 2011, 1.06 million abortions were performed, down 13% from 1.21 million abortions performed in 2008.

Reasons for this decline are "not fully understood" according to a recent national study conducted by the National Academies of Sciences, Engineering, and Medicine. It may well be that increasing use of more effective forms of contraception (especially longer acting forms such as intra uterine devices and implants), as well as declines in the rates of unintended pregnancies, and possibly the increasing number of state regulations that "limit the availability of otherwise legal abortion services" (National Academies of Sciences, Engineering and Medicine, 2018, p. 5).

As reported by the National Academies of Sciences, Engineering and Medicine (2018, p. 5), since abortion became legal in the United Sates, most of them (91.6%) occur "in early pregnancy (i.e., ≤13 weeks)." Because of recent technological advances such as

> highly sensitive pregnancy tests and the availability of medication abortion, abortions are being performed at increasingly earlier gestation. According to the Centers for Disease Control and Prevention, the percentage of early abortions performed at ≤6 weeks' gestation increased by 16% from 2004 to 2013. In 2013, 38% of early abortions occurred at ≤6 weeks' gestation.
>
> *(National Academies of Sciences, Engineering and Medicine, 2018, p. 5)*

This figure is expected to rise as use of medication abortions becomes more common.

Recent history provides additional insight into these trends. As the National Academies of Sciences, Engineering, and Medicine (2018, p. 6) reports, "In 2014, the vast majority of abortions were performed in nonhospital settings: either in an abortion clinic (59 percent) or a clinic offering a variety of medical services (36 percent). Fewer than 5% of abortions were provided in hospitals." That said, the number of abortion providers is declining, with "greatest proportional decline" emerging "in states that have enacted abortion-specific regulations" (p. 6). In 2014, there were 17% fewer abortion clinics (272) in the United States than there were in 2011. Furthermore, "39% of women of reproductive age resided in a county without an abortion provider. Twenty-five states have five or fewer abortion clinics; five states have only one abortion clinic," and "an estimated 17% of women travel more than 50 miles to obtain an abortion" (p. 6).

It is important to keep in mind that "half of pregnancies among American women are unintended, and 4 in 10 of these are terminated by abortion. The vast majority of women who receive abortions are either poor or low-income, and they are quite young" (Chesney-Lind & Hadi, 2017, p. 79). In fact, 2012 figures show that "the majority of those seeking abortions were in their 20s (60%), with women in their 30s accounting for an additional 25%. The number of teens seeking abortions actually declined by 32% between 2008 and 2014, accounting for 12%." While overwhelmingly low income, nearly half living at less than the federal poverty level (Jerman, Jones, & Onda, 2016), the women who seek abortions comprise a diverse group, "with White women accounting for 39% of abortion seekers; Black women, 28%; and Hispanic women, 25%" (Chesney-Lind & Hadi, 2017, p. 79). Looking at these data slightly differently, though, over half of the girls and women who seek abortions (61%) are women of color; over half are either African American or Hispanic (National Academies of Sciences, Engineering, and Medicine, 2018). In terms of religion, 39% identify as Protestant and 28% as Catholic. In total, the Guttmacher Institute (2016) estimates that 30% of U.S. women get an abortion by the time they turn 45. These data indicate that access to affordable abortion is hardly a marginal political issue. Yet, one might not conclude that given the current silence about abortion in both feminist criminology and public criminology. Abortion is central to the rights of women, particularly women of color. That nearly a third of all women in the United States access the procedure means that efforts to recriminalize abortion are profoundly misogynistic and racist and need to be identified as such.

Abortion Access Worldwide and U.S. Policies: The Global Gag Rule

As noted earlier, women's sexual and reproductive health is a matter of grave concern worldwide. The World Health Organization estimates that 19 million unsafe abortions take place every year (Ahman & Shah, 2002). Despite the adverse impact on women's health, roughly one-third of the world's women live in countries with strict abortion legislation that do not allow women to opt for abortion under any circumstances or only in extreme cases of rape, incest, or where the woman's health is in serious danger (Mishra, 2001). Moreover, whether legal or illegal, induced abortion is usually stigmatized and frequently opposed by political and/or religious groups (Grimes et al., 2006). Today, despite all sorts of medical advances, women worldwide still do not have the power to make their own sexual and reproductive choices without government interference.

Women's right to control their sexuality and reproduction has become an international struggle, with strong opposition emerging from organized religious groups like the Catholic Church and other sexually conservative religions. Maguire (2003, p. 13), analyzing the case of contraception and abortion in the international arena, stated:

> What is not notoriously difficult to say is that religions seriously affect national and international policy on contraception and abortion. The Vatican from its unduly privileged perch in the United Nations along with the 'Catholic' nations, newly allied with conservative Muslim nations, blocked reference to contraception and family planning at the United Nations conference in Rio de Janeiro in 1992. This alliance also disrupted

proceedings at the 1994 UN conference in Cairo and impeded any reasonable discussion of abortion. As the then Prime Minister Brundtland of Norway said of the Rio conference: "States that do not have any population problem—in one particular case, even no births at all [the Vatican]—are doing their best, their utmost, to prevent the world from making sensible decisions regarding family planning.

Maguire (2003) notes that most of the world's religions originated at a time when the global population was 50 to 450 million people in comparison to six billion at the beginning of the second millennium and thus the laws and edicts articulated at that time to guide (control) human behavior are not applicable or appropriate now; in fact, they are counterproductive.

While these conservative religious forces have affected the availability of abortion globally, contrary pressures were also present, at least in the later part of the twentieth century. In fact, for decades, the developing world's reproductive health programs and policies were primarily driven by quite a different set of forces. Driven by fears of "over population," family planning programs shaped and funded by countries in the Global North pursued an aggressive agenda to control women's fertility in these economically marginalized societies (United Nations, 2014). Throughout the latter half of the twentieth century, developed countries poured substantial resources into controlling "Third World" population growth, "garnering support for their campaigns through racist imagery that depicted the Western world being overrun by people from poor countries" (Knudsen, 2006, p. 4). These programs frequently used coercion rather than a human rights-based approach in an attempt to reduce total fertility levels. However, opposition by women's health activists coupled with international organizations' push to establish reproductive rights among basic human rights helped re-direct global policies to some extent (see Chesney-Lind & Hadi, 2017 for details).

The eighties, though, marked a change in the U.S. overseas programs for family planning and reproductive health, as policymakers who were anti-abortion and increasingly anti–family planning gained political control (Barot & Cohen, 2015). Restrictive policies, most notably the Mexico City policy, also known as the global gag rule (GGR), first instituted in 1984 by President Ronald Reagan and reintroduced by President George W. Bush in 2001, prohibited foreign nongovernmental organizations (NGOs) that receive U.S. family planning assistance from using non-U.S. funding to provide abortion services, information, counseling, or referrals and from engaging in advocacy to promote abortion (Barot, 2013). While GGR was in effect between 2001 and 2009 (the Bush era), it forced many clinics to cut back on a range of critical health services that have nothing to do with abortion, such as family planning, obstetric care, and even HIV testing (EngenderHealth, 2011). Although an intent of the GGR was to reduce the global incidence of abortion, by dramatically impairing the delivery of sexual and reproductive health services, its actual impact has been to increase the number of unintended pregnancies and the abortions that inevitably follow (EngenderHealth, 2011).

According to The Center for Reproductive Rights (2003), GGR penalized NGOs in 56 countries that received family planning assistance funds from the United States. Among these were many South Asian countries. In Bangladesh, where abortion is generally prohibited, U.S.-funded NGOs that spoke publicly about abortion issues were severely affected. The GGR stifled their free speech rights, lobbying efforts to liberalize abortion laws, and censored open and honest political participation and debate (Hetterly, 2013). The GGR policy disqualified many foreign Bangladeshi NGOs from receiving USAID funding if they engaged in abortion-related activities (Hetterly, 2013). The International Planned Parenthood Federation, which refused to sign the GGR, immediately lost $12 million in USAID funding (Hetterly, 2013). Additionally, a $34 million funding that had been approved by the U.S. Congress for UNFPA previously was withheld in 2002 (Hetterly, 2013). While President Obama repealed the rule in his first week in office, for developing nations, such funding cuts over the past decades have had a lasting impact to the existing and prospective reproductive services to women who desperately need them (Nasaw, 2009).

While the GGR has been brought in and out of existence as the Presidency changed hands, the Trump presidency has massively expanded its impact. Now, the rule powers no longer apply solely to family planning assistance given by the US government, but also to funding given to NGOs focusing on disease control. Efforts to address Ebola, Zika, and other threats to world health might be compromised. Essentially, Trump's version of the gag rule will apply to roughly 9.5 billion U.S. dollars in global health funding, as opposed to roughly $575 million in family planning and reproductive health funding, according to Population Action International (PAI), a global family planning advocacy organization. Ironically, research has shown that because of the GGR, abortions in many poor countries actually increased because the health clinics that had been providing contraception were closed due to the GGR (PAI, 2018).

In essence, U.S. political efforts to restrict family planning and abortion services have created not only a major threat to global women's reproductive health and rights, they also pose a terrible threat to human health globally.

Feminist Resistance and Abortion as a Human Right

As noted at the outset of this chapter, intense reaction to Trump's election spawned the Women's March on January 21, 2017. And while march organizers expressed concern over a wide range of social policies, most of the rallies focused on Trump, largely due to statements that he had made and positions that he has taken that were regarded by many as anti-woman and misogynistic. There was also a clear emphasis on reproductive rights. The marches constituted the largest single-day protest in the history of the United States (Cauterucci, 2017), but what impressed political observers was the global scope of the protest drawing nearly five million women (Enloe, 2018).

March participants were right to be concerned. Both nationally and globally, we have seen the emergence of policies and practices that seek the control of female sexuality and, ultimately, girl's and women's bodies. Girls and women in both the United States and the developing world have seen their access to contraceptive and abortion services greatly restricted due to the conservative and patriarchal political attitudes of those in power in the United States. These androcentric views have put at risk the lives of thousands of women not only domestically but also in the developing countries. The U.S. imposition of the "global gag rule," which has recently been greatly expanded, has, for decades, denied girls and women around access to not only abortion services but a vast array of critical health services that have nothing to do with abortion, such as family planning, obstetric care, and even HIV testing. Now, it may even put global health at risk, given its recent expansion under the Trump presidency.

One key recent development on the side of reproductive rights was an important report released February 2013. Juan Mendez, UN special rapporteur on torture, "focused on the lack of access to abortion" as a form of abuse in health-care settings (much like forcing drug addicts to detox without medical support). The report noted that the denial of reproductive justice is discrimination on the basis of gender and denial of that right can cause "tremendous and lasting physical and emotional suffering" to women (Bolourian, 2013, para. 6). Mendez noted that such violations include (Bolourian, 2013, para. 7): "denial of legally available health services such as abortion and post-abortion care … violations of medical secrecy and confidentiality in health-care settings, such as denunciations of women by medical personnel when evidence of illegal abortion is found," and forcing confessions to criminalize those who have undergone abortion.

The ongoing role of the United Nations (UN) in advocating legal reforms in nations with restrictive abortion laws is impressive. Recently, for example, the UN's human rights committee has called on the Irish government to reform its restrictive abortion legislation, after ruling that it subjected a woman, Amanda Mellet, to cruel, inhuman, and degrading treatment and violated her human rights (The Guardian, 2016). A panel of UN human rights committee experts found that Ireland's prohibition and criminalization of abortion services subjected Ms. Mellet to severe physical and mental suffering after she was denied of abortion in 2011 by doctors even though the fetus had serious congenital defects. The ruling concluded that because of Ireland's restrictive abortion laws Ms. Mellet had to choose "between continuing her non-viable pregnancy or travelling to another country while carrying a dying fetus, at personal expense, and separated from the support of her family, and to return while not fully recovered" (The Guardian, 2016, para. 4). Ireland, a signatory of the International Covenant on Civil and Political Rights, was required to compensate Ms. Mellet and to prevent similar violations from occurring in the future (Ibid.).

In a world that is increasingly examining ways to reduce mortality and morbidity, it is appalling that tens of thousands of girls and woman are dying or being disabled from botched or self-induced abortions. Every one of these could be prevented through sexuality education, use of effective contraception, the provision of safe, legal induced abortion, and timely care for complications. For this reason, abortion rates and maternal mortality due to unsafe abortion are the lowest in the world in Western Europe, home to the most permissive abortion laws (Center for Reproductive Rights, 2014). Ironically, even in the United States, where restrictions on access to abortion have been proliferating, nearly a third of all women seek the procedure at some point in their lives. The liberalization of abortion laws, accompanied by expanded access to contraceptive services and sexuality education, allows governments to prevent unwanted pregnancy while ensuring that safe and legal abortion is available to any woman who chooses to terminate a pregnancy.

While in the United States and elsewhere a political backlash has developed around girls' and women's access to abortion, there are actually global counter trends, such as the recent efforts by the UN's special rapporteur on torture calling denial of abortion services, when such services are available, equivalent to "torture" and a form of gender discrimination. Given the toxic role that U.S. politics has played globally in denying women safe and legal access to the full range of reproductive rights, including abortion, it is clearly time for women's rights activists in the United States, in particular, to make access to safe and legal abortion a centerpiece of their political agenda both in their own country and globally. More generally, though, safe, legal, affordable access to this vital reproductive right needs to be prioritized and spoken about in bold, clear, and unapologetic terms in every forum that considers the human rights of the world's women and girls.

References

Ahman, E., & Shah, I. (2002). Unsafe abortion: Worldwide estimates for 2000. *Reproductive Health Matters*, *10*(19), 13–17.

Balmert, J. (2017, January 17). What a Trump presidency will mean for abortion access. *Cincinnati Inquirer*. Retrieved from www.cincinnati.com/story/news/politics/elections/2017/01/17/what-trump-presidency-will-mean-for-abortion-access/96403486/.

Balz, D. (2010, November 13). The GOP takeover in the states. *Washington Post*. Retrieved from www.washingtonpost.com/wp-dyn/content/article/2010/11/13/AR2010111302389.html.

Barak, G. (2007). Doing newsmaking criminology from within the academy. *Theoretical Criminology*, *11*(2), 191–207.

Barot, S. (2013). Abortion restrictions in U.S. foreign aid: The history and harms of the helms amendment. *Guttmacher Policy Review*, *16*(3), 9–13.

Barot, S., & Cohen, S. A. (2015). The global gag rule and fights over funding UNFPA: The issues that won't go away. Retrieved from www.guttmacher.org/gpr/2015/06/global-gag-rule-and-fights-over-funding-unfpa-issues-wont-go-away.

Berenson, T. (2016, March 30). Donald Trump backs "punishment" for women who get abortions, then backtracks. *Time*. Retrieved from https://time.com/4276862/donald-trump-abortion-ban-punishment/.

Berkeley Library. (2018a). Birth control pioneer. *The Emma Goldman Papers*. Retrieved from www.lib.berkeley.edu/goldman/MeetEmmaGoldman/birthcontrolpioneer.html.

Berkeley Library. (2018b). Letter to "The Press," February 15, 1916. *The Emma Goldman Papers*. Retrieved from www.lib.berkeley.edu/goldman/pdfs/letter14.pdf.

Biskupic, J. (2018, September 6). Roe v Wade is "precedent," Kavanaugh says, but there's more to the future of abortion. *CNN*. Retrieved from www.cnn.com/2018/09/05/politics/kavanaugh-roe-v-wade-planned-parenthood-casey/index.html.

Bolourian, L. (2013, March 25). UN report classifies lack of access to abortion as "torture". *Mic*. Retrieved from http://mic.com/articles/30925/un-report-classifies-lack-of-access-to-abortion-as-torture#.OGtTOvTCV.

Boyd, S. (1997). *Challenging the public/private Divide: Feminism, law, and public policy*. Toronto: University of Toronto Press.

Bump, P. (2017, March 29). Places that saw more job loss to robots were less likely to support Hillary Clinton. *Washington Post*. Retrieved from www.washingtonpost.com/news/politics/wp/2017/03/29/places-that-saw-more-job-loss-to-robots-were-less-likely-to-support-hillary-clinton/?utm_term=.c47ddae42ea1.

Cauterucci, C. (2017, January 12). The Women's March on Washington has released an unapologetically progressive platform. *Slate*. Retrieved from https://slate.com/human-interest/2017/01/the-womens-march-on-washington-has-released-its-platform-and-it-is-unapologetically-progressive.html.

Center for Reproductive Rights. (2003). The global gag rule's effects on NGOs in 56 countries. Retrieved from www.reproductiverights.org/document/the-global-gag-rules-effects-on-ngos-in-56-countries.

Center for Reproductive Rights. (2014). A global view of abortion rights. Retrieved from www.reproductiverights.org/sites/crr.civicactions.net/files/documents/WAM_GlobalView_2014%20EN_0.pdf.

Chambliss, W. (1999). *Power, politics, and crime*. Boulder: Westview Press.

Chesney-Lind, M., & Chagnon, N. (2015). Gender, delinquency, and youth justice: Issues for a global century. In M. Krohn & J. Lane (Eds.), *Handbook on juvenile delinquency and juvenile justice*. Hoboken, NJ: Wiley-Blackwell.

Chesney-Lind, M., & Hadi, S. T. (2017). Patriarchy, abortion, and the criminal system: Policing female bodies. *Women and Criminal Justice, 27*(1), 73–88.

Currie, E. (2007). Against marginality: Arguments for a public criminology. *Theoretical Criminology, 11*(2), 175–190.

Doan, A. E. (2007). *Opposition and intimidation: The abortion wars and strategies of political harassment*. Ann Arbor: University of Michigan Press.

EngenderHealth. (2011). Raise your voice: End the global gag rule! Retrieved from www.engenderhealth.org/media/info/globalgagrule-video.php.

Enloe, C. (2018). *The big push: Exposing and challenging the persistence of patriarchy*. Oakland: University of California Press.

Gordon, M., & Hurt, A. (2019, June 26). Early abortion bans: Which states have passed them? *NPR News*. Retrieved from https://khn.org/news/states-abortion-bans-early-pregnancy-women-health-heartbeat/.

Grimes, D. A., Benson, J., Singh, S., Romero, M., Ganatra, B., Okonofua, F. E., & Shah, I. H. (2006). Unsafe abortion: the preventable pandemic. *The Lancet, 368*(9550), 1908–1919.

The Guardian. (2016, June 9). UN calls on Ireland to reform abortion laws after landmark ruling. Retrieved from www.theguardian.com/world/2016/jun/09/ireland-abortion-laws-violated-human-rights-says-un.

Guttmacher Institute. (2015). Facts on induced abortion worldwide. Retrieved July 27, 2016, from www.guttmacher.org/pubs/fb_IAW.html#6.

Guttmacher Institute. (2016). Induced abortion in the United States. Retrieved July 27, 2016, from www.guttmacher.org/fact-sheet/induced-abortion-united-states.

Guttmacher Institute. (2018). Induced abortion in the United States. Retrieved July 22, 2019, from www.guttmacher.org/fact-sheet/induced-abortion-united-states.

Hetterly, E. G. (2013). *Reproductive rights of young married women in urban slums of Bangladesh* (unpublished master's thesis) University of Delaware, Newark, DE. Retrieved from http://dspace.udel.edu/bitstream/handle/19716/12675/Hetterly,%20Elizabeth.pdf?sequence=1&isAllowed=y.

Jacobs, T. (2018, April 4). More evidence that racism and sexism were key to Trump's victory. *Pacific Standard*. Retrieved from https://psmag.com/social-justice/more-evidence-that-racism-and-sexism-were-key-to-trump-victory.

Jerman, J., Jones, R. K., & Onda, T. (2016). Characteristics of U.S. abortion patients in 2014 and changes since 2008. Retrieved from www.guttmacher.org/report/characteristics-us-abortion-patients-2014.

Joffe, C. (2016). Putting Hobby Lobby in context: The erratic career of birth control in the United States. In L. Wade, D. Hartmann, & C. Uggen (Eds.), *Assigned: Life with gender* (pp. 145–150). New York: W.W. Norton.

Knudsen, L. M. (2006). *Reproductive rights in a global context: South Africa, Uganda, Peru, Denmark, United States, Vietnam, Jordan.* Nashville: Vanderbilt University Press.

Lerner, G. (1986). *The creation of patriarchy*. Oxford: University Press.

Levy, G. (2018, February 12). Pence sees end to abortion "in our time". *U.S. News and World Report*. Retrieved from www.usnews.com/news/national-news/articles/2018-02-27/pence-sees-end-to-abortion-in-our-time.

Liptak, A. (2016, June 28). Supreme Court strikes down Texas abortion restriction. Retrieved from www.nytimes.com/2016/06/28/us/supreme-court-texas-abortion.html.

Maguire, D. C. (Ed.). (2003). *Sacred rights: The case for contraception and abortion in the world religions*. Cary, NC: Oxford University Press.

Martin, N. (2016, June 30). Game changer: The best analysis of the Supreme Court's abortion decision. *ProPublica*. Retrieved from http://nmpoliticalreport.com/55203/game-changer-the-best-analysis-of-the-supreme-courts-abortion-decision/.

Mishra, Y. (2001). Unsafe abortions and women's health. *Economic and Political Weekly*, 36(4), 3814–3817.

Mlitt, D. W. (1980). Margaret Sanger: Birth control's successful revolutionary. *American Journal of Public Health*, 70(7), 736–742.

Nasaw, D. (2009, January 23). Obama reverses "Global gag rule" on family planning organisations. *The Guardian*. Retrieved from www.theguardian.com/world/2009/jan/23/barack-obama-foreign-abortion-aid.

Nash, E., Gold, R. B., Rowan, R., Rathbun, G., & Vierboom, Y. (2014). *Laws affecting reproductive health and rights: 2013 state policy review*. Retrieved from www.guttmacher.org/statecenter/updates/2013/statetrends42013.html.

National Academies of Sciences, Engineering, and Medicine. (2018). The safety and quality of abortion care in the United States. *National Academy of Sciences*. Retrieved from www.nationalacademies.org/hmd/Reports/2018/the-safety-and-quality-of-abortion-care-in-the-united-states.aspx.

New York Times. (2018, July 9). Trump chooses Brett Kavanaugh for the Supreme Court. Retrieved from www.nytimes.com/2018/07/09/us/politics/trump-supreme-court-nominee.html.

Peters, J. (2018, April 5). Under Trump, an office meant to help refugees enters the abortion wars. *New York Times*. Retrieved from www.nytimes.com/2018/04/05/us/politics/refugee-office-abortion-trump.html.

Planned Parenthood Federation of America. (2014). Roe V. Wade: Its history and impact. Retrieved from www.plannedparenthood.org/files/3013/9611/5870/Abortion_Roe_History.pdf.

Population Action International. (2018). Understanding Trump's global gag rule. Retrieved from http://trumpglobalgagrule.pai.org/understanding-the-policy/.

Renzetti, C. M., Curran, D. J., & Maier, S. L. (2012). *Women, men, and society*. Boston, MA: Pearson.

Rovner, J. (2018, January 22). In Trump's first year anti-abortion forces make strides. *National Public Radio*. Retrieved from www.npr.org/sections/health-shots/2018/01/22/579661047/in-trumps-first-year-anti-abortion-forces-make-strides.

Sanghani, R. (2016, June 9). The sexist Hillary Clinton merchandise that will make you cringe. *The Telegraph*. Retrieved from www.telegraph.co.uk/women/life/the-sexist-hillary-clinton-merchandise-that-will-make-you-cringe/.

Savage, C. (2018, July 10). Brett Kavanaugh on issues: Abortion, guns, climate, and more. *New York Times*. Retrieved from www.nytimes.com/2018/07/10/us/politics/brett-kavanaugh-abortion-guns-environment.html.

Schaffner, B. F., MacWilliams, M., & Nteta, T. (2017, January). *Explaining White polarization in the 2016 vote for president: The sobering role of racism and sexism*. Paper presented at the Conference on The U.S. Elections of 2016: Domestic and International Aspects, IDC Herzliya Campus. Retrieved from http://people.umass.edu/schaffne/schaffner/schaffner_et_al_IDC_conference.pdf.

Sinding, S. S. (2007). Overview and perspective. In W. C. Robinson & J. A. Ross (Eds.), *Global family planning revolution: Three decades of population policies and programs* (pp. 1–12). Herndon, VA: World Bank Publications.

Solinger, R. (2005). *Pregnancy and power: A short history of reproductive politics in America*. New York: New York University Press.

Stevens, M. (2018, March 31). Judge temporarily stops U.S. from blocking undocumented teenagers' abortions. *New York Times*. Retrieved from www.nytimes.com/2018/03/31/us/abortion-immigrant-teens.html.

Talking Points News. (2018, February 23). Porter: The Trump White House's women problem. *The Week*. Retrieved from https://theweek.com/login?issueId=406652&printArticleId=41671.

Totenburg, N. (2017, March 16). Judge Gorsuch's writings signal he would be a conservative on social issues. Retrieved from www.npr.org/2017/03/16/519501771/judge-gorsuchs-writings-signal-he-would-be-a-conservative-on-social-issues.

Uggen, C., & Inderbitzin, M. (2010). Public criminologies. *Criminology & Public Policy, 9*(4), 725–749.

United Nations. (2014). Reproductive rights are human rights. Retrieved from www.ohchr.org/Documents/Publications/NHRIHandbook.pdf.

Van Sant, S. (2019, July 21). Some Title X recipients will have more time to comply with new abortion rules. *NPR News*. Retrieved from www.npr.org/2019/07/21/743919676/trump-administration-delays-new-abortion-regulations-for-title-x-recipients.

Vieten, U. (2016). Far right populism and women: The normalisation of gendered anti-Muslim racism and gendered culturalism in the Netherlands. *Journal of Intercultural Studies, 37*(6), 621–636.

Wagner, J., & Eilperin, J. (2017, December 6). Once a populist, Trump governs like a conservative republican. *Washington Post*. Retrieved from www.washingtonpost.com/politics/once-a-populist-trump-governs-like-a-conservative-republican/2017/12/05/e73c6106-d902-11e7-b1a8-62589434a581_story.html.

White, D. (2016, May 18). Donald Trump on abortion: "I'm saying women punish themselves". *Time*. Retrieved from http://time.com/4340358/donald-trump-women-abortions-punish/.

Woellert, L. (2018, January 17). Trump's speech to March for Life marks a u-turn on abortion. *Politico*. Retrieved from www.politico.com/story/2018/01/17/trump-march-for-life-2018-343842.

Women's March. (2019). About us: Mission and principles. Retrieved from https://womensmarch.com/mission-and-principles.

24
VALUE-RESPONSIBLE DESIGN AND SEXUAL VIOLENCE INTERVENTIONS

Engaging Value-Hypotheses in Making the Criminological Imagination

Renee Shelby

There is a significant body of scholarly literature addressing limitations of the anti-gender violence movement's embrace of the criminal justice system. This research includes longstanding critiques from Black feminists on its negative impact on low-income people and persons of color (Crenshaw, 1994; Richie, 2012), and a focus on finding justice in alternative community-based accountability structures (Bumiller, 2009). In light of rape law reform's failure to effect arrest and prosecution, feminist criminologists have critiqued the conflation of "justice" with the carceral punishment of perpetrators (Daly, 2014; Larcombe, 2011; McGlynn, 2011). Rather than embrace the desire to punish, publics and counter-publics are increasingly engaging technology to support victim-centered models of justice, including through social media, digital platforms, and their relationships to body politics (Baer, 2016; Powell, 2015; Rentschler, 2017; Williams, 2015). While scholars are analyzing how technologies can be leveraged to shape and challenge rhetorical logics of violence and punishment, few analyses have focused on how the critical design process can promote victim-centered values and experiences in carceral spaces. Here, I consider the process as a possibility for public criminological engagement.

In general, *design* refers to the creation of the form and function of an object, process, or system. Value-responsible design is an approach that engages critically with how values and ideologies permeate technology, and calls for the designer to address the ethics, politics, and consequences of their design choices. For four years, I worked for a sexual violence social service agency embedded in the local juvenile justice system. During that time, we were constantly confronted with the necessity to think about how the design of local institutions entangled folks into the criminal justice system, facilitated certain kinds of experiences, and in what ways we could make relevant, local, and intersectional interventions.

Engaging questions of design is an incredibly purposeful way to both "do" and "make" public criminology. *Making* is the language we use when we produce or construct something new. In other words, making public criminology is the active practice of participation, engagement, and intervention in the carceral system. Value-responsible design is an especially useful method for making public criminology not only because it centers meaning, ethics, and experience in creating structural change, but also because it is an explicitly non-positivist way to bring "order" to "chaos." By this, I mean value-responsible design seeks to address the practical problems experienced by multiple publics without claiming there is a singular "correct" way to do so. In acknowledging and prioritizing the diversity of experiences and knowledges produced through social location or standpoints, value-responsible design acts on the critical need for plurality in responding to social problems constituted by a "matrix of domination" (Collins, 2000, p. 18).

As an intentionally creative endeavor, questions of design provide an effective way to think through the persistent gendered, classed, and racialized biases that mutually structure institutional responses to sexual and other forms of interpersonal violence, illuminate ways to engage and center marginalized voices, and create intersectionally minded interventions that embody empathetic values (Crenshaw, 1994; Daly & Chesney-Lind, 1988; Naffine, 2014). While feminists critique the positivist assumptions that scholarly epistemologies are never detached, apolitical, and objective (Nelund, 2014), value-responsible design is a knowledge-producing system that explicitly enmeshes theory and material impacts. In alignment with the feminist values of reciprocity and empathy, value-responsible design can help to catalyze purpose-driven social change, while being attentive to, rather than erasing, the power relationships that shape the experiences of violence. To extend the call by Becker (1967, p. 239), being attentive to design and values can help act on the question, "Whose side are we on?"

As public criminologists seek opportunities to craft victim-centered sexual violence interventions, being attentive to the design process is useful in navigating potential pitfalls and unintended consequences. Some scholars of technology frame unintended consequences (Tenner, 1997) as a seemingly inevitable byproduct of innovation; however, as one of my experienced design professors and colleagues proclaimed, "unintended consequences are the result of lazy design!" (Nassim JafariNaimi, personal communication, February 12, 2018). Confronting and negotiating the politics of designed "things" is an effective way to mitigate the impacts technology has on different populations. This approach stems from the feminist science and technology studies tradition that seeks not to eschew science and technology, but the White, heterosexist modes of doing science and creating technology that reify gendered and racialized power structures (Haraway, 1985; Harding, 1986; Wajcman, 2004). In doing so, value-responsible design can reveal new pathways for improved criminological knowledge creation that resists, mediates, and perhaps finds ways to step out of carceral justice.

In this chapter, I draw on Science and Technology Studies (STS) and critical design scholarship to consider: How can value-responsible design create more democratic forms of criminological knowledge creation? This is a theoretical question regarding how to engage better design practices (methods) in criminological interventions. The wording of *how can*, rather than merely *can*, value-responsible design create more democratic forms of knowledge creation is a distinctly non-essentialist approach that rejects determinist understandings of technology. As publics are already engaging with technology to support their values (Baer, 2016), attempting to abandon or side-step the increasing momentum of technological influence is an impractical approach to contemporary criminology. Scholars, advocates, and practitioners should not strive to be against technology, but against particular formations, and understand technology as a flexible social structure that mediates interaction.

Although the question of value-responsible design and criminological knowledge creation can, and should be, applied to a broad range of criminological topics, I focus on sexual violence. In the remainder of the chapter, I first synthesize theory on how designed "things" embody politics and produce cultural knowledge. Then, I describe the approach of value-responsible design and how values can serve as hypotheses to approach complex design problems, like sexual violence. Lastly, I apply these insights to analyze the values and design of two sexual violence technologies: the rape kit and the digital rape reporting app, *Project Callisto*.

These technologies are just two of many designed criminological "things" created through the criminological imaginations of victim advocates. As academics know well, all methods have limitations—even the most sophisticated of quantitative methodologies. This is also true for even the most well-intentioned designed "things." There are no magic bullets. Yet, as we collectively imagine our feminist futures, public criminologists (both with and without formal credentials) who *make* will be at the forefront of long-term criminological transformation—as this will only occur through the active *unmaking* of the current carceral system. Grosz (2000, p. 1018) writes, "the future is the domain of what endures." There are many tensions among criminologists about whether and how to do public criminology (Loader & Sparks, 2010; Piché, 2014; Ruggiero, 2012; Tonry, 2010; Turner, 2013; Uggen & Inderbitzin, 2010). Yet, most critical and feminist folx would at least agree that our future should be one unchained from the carceral present that so often fails to be inclusive, empathetic, or do much beyond proliferate harm. These logics and practices cannot be what endures.

Guiding Concepts for Addressing the Politics and Knowledge Production of Designed "Things"

Designed "things" are intimately enrolled in the logics of violence and punishment that constitute the criminological imagination (Young, 2011); however, they also provide opportunities to resist these logics. STS perspectives on the entangled relationships between humans and "things" (Callon, 1984; Latour, 1987, 1999; Haraway, 1997) are useful to think through the networked constellations of cultures, people, and objects that create criminological knowledge. Bringing STS perspectives to criminology can help expose the web of relations that stabilize crime epistemologies through technology within the carceral (Kruse, 2015; Lynch, Cole, McNally, & Jordan, 2010) and shadow-carceral state (Beckett & Murakawa, 2012). As Brown (2006, p. 236) asserts, "analyses of criminal justice can no longer rest at analyses of social interests, and motivations, but must address the technological properties of the body politic, and of the institutional landscape of control, as inseparable from their form." In other words, contemporary criminologists must be attentive to how technology is enrolled in co-producing knowledge about crime, perpetrators, and victims. For public criminologists, technology should be understood as a value-laden cultural project that shapes criminological responses. Focusing on technology can also prove useful in drawing attention to social problems that have not yet garnered widespread attention—perhaps especially among other criminologists.

Three STS insights provide a useful grounding for thinking about the relationships between designed "things," values, and the criminological knowledge they produce. The first insight is that technoscientific objects are adopted through practices of authority (Harding, 1991; Mol, 2002; Pinch & Bijker, 1984). This draws attention to how designed "things" emerge and are stabilized in networks through their relationships with other cultures, people, and objects. For thinking about the design process, it is useful to recognize that a particular technology is not adopted because it is the best solution or configuration for a specific problem; it is chosen through the relations of authority that shape and sustain its adoption. The process of designing technology is always a disorderly and controversial process that is entangled in social norms and practices of authority—even when these are seemingly invisible or naturalized (Jasanoff, 2004). Consequently, alternative designs are always possible.

The second insight is that designed "things," no matter how seemingly mundane, have politics (Winner, 1986). As the social life of "things" are often masked through appeals to rationality and efficiency, critically studying technology requires confronting the dominant belief that technology is neutral (MacKenzie & Wajcman, 1999). Despite some technologists' assertions that scientific objectivity can fight bias (Siegel, 2018), artifacts take on the cultural values of their designers (Benforado, 2015; Roberts, 2009). Consequently, biased "things" create a situation in which the "technological deck has been stacked in advance to favor certain social interests" (Winner, 1986, p. 26). This phenomenon is evident in the racial biases of contemporary digital criminological technologies, such as predictive policing that relies on big data and algorithms (Chan & Bennett Moses, 2016) and actuarial risk assessments (Hannah-Moffat, 2018; Harcourt, 2007; Goddard & Myers, 2017). Recognizing that designed "things" are political can help trace and interrogate modes of power and logics of violence in criminological networks (Lynch, Cole, McNally, & Jordan, 2010). Doing so can also destabilize the misnomer that rationality and objectivity are value-free (Harding, 1995).

The third STS insight is that technologies co-produce knowledge about a phenomenon. While in general, problems with design are most evident when the design fails to serve human needs and values, designs that we do not notice are incredibly effective in producing cultural knowledge, especially regarding race, gender, users, and authority (Oudshoorn, Rommes, & Stienstra, 2004; Kennedy, 2016). In this sense, the concept of co-production draws attention to how our knowledge about the world is reciprocally tied to the ways in which we live in it. For example, beliefs about assault shape sexual violence interventions, which then produce knowledge about assault, perpetrators, and victims. The concept of co-production moves past representationalist understandings of how "things" have politics to provide an effective framework to understand social power beyond the limiting analytical constraints of structure or agency. The concept of co-production also helps reveal the obscured values and ethical dimensions within a technology's social, material, and epistemic formations (Jasanoff, 2004) that co-construct knowledge about crime and criminological subjects.

In sum, STS provides a useful grounding for thinking about values, design, and engaging the criminological imagination. Recognizing that designed "things" are (1) adopted through practices of authority and stabilized through their relationships with people and cultures; (2) embody values and biases; and (3) co-produce knowledge, highlight the non-essentialist ways scholars, advocates, and practitioners should approach design, and the experiences technology can produce. These concepts also highlight the underlying element of responsibility that designers must accept during the design process.

The Designer's Responsibility: Rethinking the Design Process with Value-Hypotheses

The explicit translation of values into design is typically viewed as a two-step logic of identifying a value and then applying it to a design problem (Flanagan, Howe, & Nissenbaum, 2008). This logic prescribes designers should first understand values better—for example, to identify them more precisely; define them more accurately; or discover a wider range of values for the particular problem. After completing this step, the designer can then apply their more complete knowledge of relevant values to design a "thing" or intervention with great certainty. As the two-step logic attempts to break down the design process into discrete parts, its simplicity is psychologically satisfying and appealing. However, the two-step logic falsely presumes designers can adequately address values separate from action. While this is possible in scholarship, in practice, values are not removed from a situation, nor can they be resolved at a distance from the "design problem."

In their essay, "Values as Hypotheses," JafariNaimi, Nathan, and Hargraves (2015, p. 93) challenge the assumption that values can be easily enrolled in the design of an artifact, process, or system. The authors recommend an improved methodology following philosopher Dewey's (1891) conceptualization of how ethics and action are entwined through a circular question of action: "What is the situation that demands action?" and "What is the action that the situation demands?" This dialectic avoids the presumption that values can be applied to a problem as pre-established formulas that create clear and proper pathways for action. Instead, the question of action encourages designers to think of design as an entwined process of defining the problem through action, while defining action through the problem. Within this approach, values become hypotheses for best serving a particular social problem.

Take, for example, the simple design problem of needing to sit down. The shape of a chair is generally the shape of the human body in a sit position. However, the form and function of a chair's design may shift based on different value-hypotheses that serve the various situations in which one needs to sit down. Value-hypotheses—such as comfort, movement, durability, cleanliness, or efficiency—help clarify the design problem of needing to sit while simultaneously serving the demands of the situation. Whereas comfort and movement are value-hypotheses that serve the need to sit down at home, durability and cleanliness are value-hypotheses that better serve the need to sit down in public. Consequently, a recliner and bus stop bench embody different value-hypotheses to serve disparate situational needs.

However, values not only serve the situation's needs, but they also co-produce knowledge about people who sit in chairs and the desirability of the people in those spaces. Whereas a recliner may promote prolonged sitting or sleeping, a public bench may actively discourage sitting or sleeping—such as with designs that make it impossible for homeless persons to lay horizontally (Rosenberger, 2014). Testing value-hypotheses can uncover how logics of power are mobilized through particular values, while as *hypotheses*, return the designer's focus to non-determinist ways of thinking about a social problem. In other words, if one value-hypothesis fails, "test" another. For simple problems, the concept of values as hypotheses may seem an unnecessarily elaborate way to think about design. For complex problems like sexual violence, however, value-hypotheses are an invaluable approach to link theory and research with engaged community problem-solving. Like all forms of interpersonal violence, there is no essential experience of sexual violence. Not only are there many ways to perpetrate sexual violence, but the ways people internalize, cope with, and move past violence is also incredibly diverse and shaped by intersecting dimensions, such as gender, race, and social economic status, among others (Crenshaw, 1994; Richie, 1995). In short, value-hypotheses can provide a productive way to engage with how individual experiences of crime interventions are situated within a collective structural context.

Engaging Value-Hypotheses to Craft Better Criminological Responses to Sexual Violence

Value-hypotheses provide a useful approach for interrogating and clarifying the needs of sexual violence situations, as a seemingly appropriate value-hypothesis may be too broad, silence different interest groups, or provide unclear pathways to move forward. For example, the meanings of *justice* may shift based on a specific context or the actors involved in a situation, such as punishment or restoration. Even if justice seems theoretically self-evident, in practice, it may not be primarily useful to the problem at hand. Instead of justice, the values of flexibility, compassion, or community may better serve a particular sexual violence situation and produce interventions that may ultimately result in community and victim-centered justice, however that value is operationalized. Consequently, values are not procedural concepts to be readily applied to a situation, but complex strategies designers negotiate to best serve the situation at hand. We can perhaps most clearly see this application to criminology in the practices of mandatory arrest in domestic violence cases. In practice, the blind application and conflation of *justice* with *punishment*, failed to account for the contextual nuances between violent instigation and self-defense (Bible, 1998), which primarily to the detriment of women of color, resulted in the criminalization of victimization (Chesney-Lind, 2006).

The question of action is a useful method for doing public criminology as it requires designers to thoughtfully consider the end-users, institutional stakeholders, and what specific action the situation demands. Effectively working through the question of action should be a collaborative and iterative process that engages diverse stakeholders—especially end-users. It is well documented that doing so creates more useful and inclusive designs (Herring, 2009; Page, 2007); however, it is important to note that inevitable and practical constraints, such as time, money, institutional access, and culture, inject limitations into a design. Value-hypotheses can re-focus designs in light of limitations and make interventions more in service to the underlying needs of the situation.

Table 24.1 lists potential questions of action related to sexual violence. The first column provides common situations victims experience that people interested in improving criminal justice interventions could design for. The second column offers an (incomplete list) of value-hypotheses

Table 24.1 Potential Value-Hypotheses and "Questions of Action" in Sexual Violence

What's the situation that demands action?	*What's the action that the situation demands?*
Immediately after an assault	***Potential value-hypotheses (actions)***
The experience of reporting to police is shaped by the victim's race, class, and gender	adaptability; anger; autonomy; authenticity; authority; awareness; balance; compassion; equality; fairness; intersectionality; justice; knowledge; openness; power; reputation; respect; security
Victim's may be unsure about whether they want to complete a rape kit to maintain forensic evidence	autonomy; flexibility; compassion; control; curiosity; independence; respect; timeliness
The experience of receiving a rape kit is shaped by the victim's race, class, and gender	autonomy; anger; authenticity; authority; compassion; empathy; equality; fairness; intersectionality; justice; kindness; openness; power; security; respect
Victims may need on-going community and institutional support	compassion; empathy; kindness; kinship; sensitivity; solitude
Victims may not feel safe in public and private spaces following an assault	citizenship; community; happiness; independence; fairness; kinship; stability
Sexual assault prevention	***Potential value-hypotheses (actions)***
Empowering bystanders to intervene in a potential assault or uncomfortable situation	accountability; community; communication; competency; contribution; courtesy; education; knowledge; leadership
People need help getting out of uncomfortable or potentially dangerous situations without escalation	community; clarity; confidentiality; creativity; kindness; persistence; vision
Various rape myths are institutionalized or sedimented in the cultural imagination	creativity; experience; intersectionality; race and gender; transparency
Persons who feel vulnerable may want to learn self-defense	competency; control; empowerment; enjoyment
Changes to the built environment may be necessary to prioritize and promote safety	autonomy; flexibility; independence
Navigating the criminal justice system	***Potential value-hypotheses (actions)***
Actors in the criminal justice system do treat rape cases equally or do not take them seriously	authenticity; authority; balance; compassion; fairness; intersectionality; justice; knowledge; openness; power; race and gender; security; respect; trustworthiness
Prosecutors are embedded in a system that rewards them for bringing "winnable" cases	accountability; fairness; justice; influence; meaningful work; power
Gendered and racialized rape myths continue to be enacted in the criminal justice system	control; creativity; experience; race and gender; transparency; transparency
The rape kit backlog	accountability; fairness; justice; innovation; organization; process; race and gender; science; structure; sustainability

that could serve the corresponding situation. Notably, many of these value-hypotheses are not explicitly about justice or punishment but ones that center victims' experiences and promote individual and community well-being and restoration. As one could imagine, the use of different value-hypotheses could greatly re-shape the form and function of an intervention to create different experiences. In the remainder of this section, I examine two questions of action and value-hypotheses for two sexual violence interventions—forensic evidence collection and the 1970s U.S. rape kit, the Vitullo Kit, and the digital rape reporting app *Project Callisto*.

Value-Hypotheses and Unintended Consequences: The Cautionary Tale of the Rape Kit in Upholding Carceral Logics of Violence

The grassroots Citizens Committee for Victim's Assistance (CCVA) in collaboration with the Chicago Crime Lab created an early U.S. rape kit, the Vitullo Kit, in the mid-1970s (Goddard, 2003). Its purpose was to leverage science to counteract persistent rape myths and improve the medico-legal care of victims.[1] Through its long-term stabilization in the criminal justice system, the rape kit came to function as a "technoscientific witness of rape" (Quinlan, 2017, p. 7). In other words, the rape kit verifies the veracity of assault claims through the production of seemingly objective (and androcentric) scientific knowledge. The stereotype, however, that science and technology are objective and neutral practices obscures the forensic storytelling that shapes how actors in the criminal justice system produce evidence (Kruse, 2015). The discourses of science that surround the rape kit mask how evidence production is a fundamentally social process relying on conventional crime ideologies. As the Vitullo Kit was designed around the values and interests of the crime lab and its epistemologies, the kit's possibilities to radically reform, serve, and improve victims' experiences were significantly undermined (Shelby, 2018). Specifically, the CCVA did not anticipate how the rape kit could be used to maintain the status quo approach to rape investigation, and the long-term impact of the kit has been permeated with unintended consequences.

Although the rape kit is a notable feminist intervention, it is also a cautionary tale for how protocol feminism, referring to feminist strategies that re-craft and distribute technosocial practices to facilitate the care and study of the sexed body (Murphy, 2012), can perpetuate rape myths and dominant values. It also shows the limitations of the two-step logic method of design in countering logics of violence. In developing the rape kit, the CCVA conducted interviews primarily with actors in the criminal justice system and uncovered the legitimate problem of securing forensic evidence as a situation that demanded action (Goddard, 2003). Unfortunately, the CCVA assumed the positivist value of objective technoscience would overcome rape myths and transform poor evidence collection. Consequently, the value-hypotheses used to shape the design of the rape kit—for example, criminal justice control over evidence, hierarchical protocol structure, and reliance on "weak" objectivity[2]—created a medico-legal intervention that was accountable to the practical problems experienced by the crime lab, not assault survivors or how members of law enforcement perceived assault cases. One of the kit's most notable unintended consequences is that rather than function to counter gendered discourses of violence, which is what the CCVA initially identified as the "situation that demands action," the value-hypotheses of the rape kit re-constitute it as technosocial site for law enforcement to enact racialized and gendered sexual violence stereotypes (Corrigan, 2013; Mulla, 2014). That is, the rape kit has become a tool through which to double-down on, rather than challenge, rape myths that are shaped by misogyny and racism. For example, Corrigan (2013) describes the rape kit as a "trial by ordeal," whereby a "real" victim will submit to the four- to six-hour process of being swabbed, questioned, and prodded. However, there is no national law that kits must be tested; some jurisdictions will not test them if the perpetrator is known; and while we may mistakenly believe a rape kit provides probative biological evidence, the kit is especially unhelpful for the most prevalent form of sexual violence—acquaintance rape. Consequently, the kit has even failed its purposes from the perspective of the crime lab—to increase prosecutions through improved evidence collection (Du Mont & Parnis, 1999; Du Mont & White, 2007; Shelby, 2018).

Designing a medico-legal technology that was attentive to the needs of sexual violence victims required an alternative model of forensic knowledge production—one that directly empowered victims and attended to how rape myths circulated among frontline criminal justice actors. Although working with the crime lab aided the adoption and stabilization of the rape kit in the justice system, it limited the available actions that the situation—as the CCVA initially saw it—truly demanded. As hypotheses are impermanent, a re-design of rape kit protocols that engage the question of action with alternative value-hypotheses, such as autonomy, flexibility, or respect, could produce an improved system of medico-legal care—perhaps one that is even community-based or self-administered.

While self-administration may seem like an impossible forensic design, I draw attention to the history of the at-home pregnancy test. In 1967, pharmaceutical product designer Margaret Crane proposed an over-the-counter test (Kennedy, 2016). The company she worked for rejected her idea due to the prevailing belief that hysteric-prone women could not self-manage the technical procedure and consequently may attempt suicide and that it would threaten the medical authority of doctors. Crane, however, understood the values of agency and mobility would greatly serve women's need to confirm a pregnancy. Ten years later the first at-home pregnancy test became available, and today it is the primary way women learn they are pregnant. Its continued popularity is a testament to the utility of agency and mobility values to this particular problem.

The rape kit provides public criminology a lesson in the tensions and difficulties of enacting feminist interventions, in the necessity to be vigilant to the cultural economy in which interventions are embedded, and especially to the critical role of users in making meaning of designed "things." As the rape kit is currently configured, the primary users are not people who experience violence, but the hospital personnel, law enforcement, and prosecutors who interpret evidence and control the circulation of the kit throughout the criminal justice system. The rape kit means something different to these users than it does to victims. Acknowledging this tension provides an opportunity to engage new value-hypotheses in the problem of evidence posed by the rape kit. As public criminology is about confronting challenges, it is a strength, not a weakness, that value-responsible design calls for iteration. In doing so, we must use the criminological imagination to bring what Currie (2002) terms "fresh eyes" to the persistent problems that constrain responses to crime, especially in regard to users.

Designing for Victims: The Value-Hypotheses of Sexual Violence Reporting Apps in Challenging Carceral Logics of Violence

Project Callisto (projectcallisto.org) is a non-profit rape reporting technology established in 2016 that provides students a trauma-informed online platform to report campus sexual assault. Its purpose is to address, specifically within institutions, the problem of repeat offending (Lisak & Miller, 2002), the silencing of rape victims (Ahrens, 2006), the overwhelming underreporting of assault (Sable, Danis, Mauzy, & Gallagher, 2006), and the likelihood that merely reporting will result in secondary victimization (Campbell & Raja, 1999; Rich & Seffrin, 2012). Callisto allows victims to create a confidential and secure time-stamped record of an assault at a time and place that feels safe to them, while giving users the option of consulting a counselor to navigate the reporting process. Callisto also enables victims to choose how and when they want to report—either immediately or only if another person names that perpetrator. The technology was first piloted in 2015 at Pomona College and the University of San Francisco, and, as of 2017, has been adopted by 13 colleges and universities.

Callisto was developed through feedback from college students and uses the value-hypotheses of flexibility and agency to think through: "What is the action that the (reporting) situation demands?" Through its design, Callisto reconfigures the conventional power relationships between the victim, the perpetrator, fellow students, and the institution. In providing users the option to report only if another person names that perpetrator, Callisto offers control to victims where it previously did not exist and, in doing so, fundamentally transforms the overall experience of reporting to an institution. Notably, research shows that when there are multiple allegations, institutions may be more likely and quicker to respond to assault (Saul, 2017).

Callisto's design values of flexibility and agency create a reporting mechanism that allows victims to engage needed resources more easily, such as community support, multiple reporting options, and confidentiality. Consequently, Callisto provides a system of sexual violence knowledge that is more accountable to the practical problems experienced by assault victims, especially through its *multi-modal* design. *Multi-modality* generally refers to the availability of multiple means through which a person can access a social or technological resource. For thinking about sexual violence, multi-modality can facilitate public criminologies that are intersectional and attentive to the needs of diverse crime victims. Rather than a one-size-fits-all response to violence that shoehorns the needs of victims into one systemic response, multi-modality can make room to competently accommodate the varying ways crime is experienced.

While bureaucracies embrace rigid and narrow processes, technologies that take this form are fundamentally at odds with the realities of sexual violence and the needs of persons who experience assault. As there is no singular assault victim, an essentialist approach to sexual violence is bound to fail in practice and is increasingly untenable in light of growing intersectional awareness. Contemporary public criminology can—and should—embrace multi-modality as a pathway to victim-centered design. While no technology is without limitations, Callisto offers a design that more meaningfully engages with the reporting needs of campus assault victims and creates pathways to mitigate the chilling effects rape myths have on reporting. For public criminology, Callisto embodies values in a way that *unmakes* the existing carceral logics that frustrate feminist and intersectional folks, and in its place, *makes* a local and theoretically-informed intervention that can at once better serve multiple contexts and needs.

As feminism is fundamentally purpose-driven, the feminist future of public criminology must be purposeful in both leveraging knowledge on the experiences of crime to create meaningful interventions and identifying and responding to persisting carceral logics. Like the rape kit, Callisto could be co-opted into the system it seeks to change. Consequently, the feminist future of public criminology must also enthusiastically embrace iterative refinement and the active *remaking* of designed things with values that serve the ever-evolving structures and systems that shape social life. As the practice of *remaking* squarely aligns with the feminist ethics of care, repair, and restoration, it is not a futile future of meaningless labor, but a vibrant and collaborative one.

Discussion and Conclusion

As designed criminological "things" embody values and biases, and co-produce knowledge about crime, designers must think critically about the consequences of their design choices. Value-responsible design calls for the designer to address ethics and politics and engages critically with how values and ideologies permeate technology. As a method to think about the impact of interventions, the question of action enables engagement with the criminological imagination by helping us abandon the "master's tools" of positivism, determinism, and rigid hierarchy and by leveraging empirical knowledge to address the practical experiences of criminological phenomena. Rethinking how design produces knowledge about crime, victims, and perpetrators can also help us produce a just or culturally-conscious criminology that challenges taken-for-granted assumptions about crime, victims, and perpetrators. The process of intellectually working through a situation with value-hypotheses can help clarify possible courses of action and lead to diverse, non-essentialist, and intersectional responses to sexual violence that specifically intervene into the logics of violence and punishment that permeate carceral spaces.

Insights from STS help us recognize that an adopted design is not self-evident and that alternatives are accessible and possible. Like gender, race, and class, technology is a social structure that constrains interaction. However, we can augment these structures using value-hypotheses to challenge conventional crime ideologies and facilitate different ways of engaging with people who have experienced crime. Take, for example, Dr. Daniel Cooper and Dr. Ryan Lugalia-Hollon's *Million Dollar Blocks*[3] project that uses digital visualization to *remake* conversations about carceral spending. As value-hypotheses are impermanent starting points for investigation, designers should be cautious not to embrace values as permanently serving the situation. In fact, imagine what possibilities for public criminology could be opened if criminal justice interventions embraced transience and encouraged the retirement of particular values. For instance, how might we use the criminological imagination to reshape the relationships between individual "biography" and "history" through designed things? Or, as power and knowledge are connected, how might ethical "things" be used to challenge problematic criminological discourses and create more democratic forms of criminological knowledge creation? Engaging the criminological imagination in questions of design could actively encourage the cyclical revisiting of policies, processes, and technologies, and their subsequent updates based on evolving critical concerns and needs.

In sum, value-responsible design can help craft modes of criminological knowledge creation that resist, mediate, and in some cases, find ways to step out of carceral logics of violence and punishment. For practitioners, focusing on the relationships between design and values is intimately relevant to addressing victimization and harm through engaged criminological knowledge production. However, scholars should at least consider design and values, as they provide a useful site to engage their knowledge and respond to the practical problems experienced by different groups. The integration of multi-modality, in particular, may provide practical routes to community or victim-centered designs.

Amid creeping carceral expansion, attention to design can expose novel opportunities for applied and intersectional public criminologies. Within the scholarly community, there has been a lively debate about the imminent need for public criminology (Loader & Sparks, 2010; Piché, 2014; Uggen & Inderbitzin, 2010) and salient critiques of these discourses (Ruggiero, 2012; Tonry, 2010; Turner, 2013). This essay highlights how the criminological is in many ways already public. It draws attention to the responsibilities of criminology in making ethical and meaningful interventions that challenge status quo logics. If a central concern of public criminology is about creating high-quality evidence and using it to create effective and informed interventions, then engaging with design offers new pathways for improved criminological knowledge creation—as design is fundamentally an engaged and applied process. If we imagine the future as the domain of what endures, we should not forget that future is indeterminant (Grosz, 2000). The feminist future of public criminology is one we must *make*.

Notes

1 I recognize and respect individual preferences for identifying as "victim" or "survivor." In this context, I use the term "victim" to discuss rape kits and rape reporting apps, as "survivor" is most often used when someone has experienced sexual violence and also gone through a recovery process.
2 For a foundational discussion of weak versus strong objectivity, see Harding (1995).
3 The interactive visualizations are viewable at https://chicagosmilliondollarblocks.com/.

References

Ahrens, C. E. (2006). Being silenced: The impact of negative social reactions on the disclosure of rape. *American Journal of Community Psychology, 38*(3–4), 31–34.

Baer, H. (2016). Redoing feminism: Digital activism, body politics, and neoliberalism. *Feminist Media Studies, 16*(1), 17–34.

Becker, H. S. (1967). Whose side are we on?. *Social Problems, 14*(3), 239–247.

Beckett, K., & Murakawa, N. (2012). Mapping the shadow carceral state: Toward an institutionally capacious approach to punishment. *Theoretical Criminology, 16*(2), 221–244.

Benforado, A. (2015, August 12). The hidden bias of cameras. *Slate.* Retrieved from www.slate.com/articles/news_and_politics/jurisprudence/2015/08/police_body_and_dashboard_cameras_how_camera_perspective_bias_can_limit.html.

Bible, A. (1998). When battered women are charged with assault. *Double-Time, 6*(1/2), 8–10.

Brown, S. (2006). The criminology of hybrids: Rethinking crime and law in technosocial networks. *Theoretical Criminology, 10*(2), 223–244.

Bumiller, K. (2009). *In an abusive state: How neoliberalism appropriated the feminist movement against sexual violence.* Durham, NC: Duke University Press.

Callon, M. (1984). Some elements of a sociology of translation: Domestication of the scallops and the fishermen of St Brieuc Bay. *The Sociological Review, 32*(1_suppl), 196–233.

Campbell, R., & Raja, S. (1999). Secondary victimization of rape victims: Insights from mental health professionals who treat survivors of violence. *Violence and Victims, 14*(3), 261–275.

Chan, J., & Bennett Moses, L. (2016). Is big data challenging criminology?. *Theoretical Criminology, 20*(1), 21–39.

Chesney-Lind, M. (2006). Patriarchy, crime, and justice: Feminist criminology in an era of backlash. *Feminist Criminology, 1*(1), 6–26.

Collins, P. (2000). *Black feminist thought: Knowledge, consciousness, and the politics of empowerment.* New York: Routledge.

Corrigan, R. (2013). The new trial by ordeal: Rape kits, police practices, and the unintended effects of policy innovation. *Law & Social Inquiry, 38*(4), 920–949.

Crenshaw, K. (1994). Mapping the margins: Intersectionality, identity politics, and violence against women of color. In M. A. Fineman & R. Mykitiuk (Eds.), *The public nature of private violence* (pp. 93–118). New York: Routledge.

Currie, E. (2002). Preface. In K. Carrington & R. Hogg (Eds.), *Critical criminology: Issues, debates, challenges* (pp. vii–ix). Cullompton, UK: Willan Publishing.

Daly, K., & Chesney-Lind, M. (1988). Feminism and criminology. *Justice Quarterly, 5*(4), 497–538.

Daly, K. (2014). Reconceptualizing sexual victimization and justice. In I. Vanfraechem, A. Pemberton, & F. Ndahinda (Eds.), *Justice for victims: Perspectives on rights, transition, and reconciliation* (pp. 378–396). London: Routledge.

Dewey, J. (1891). Moral theory and practice. *The International Journal of Ethics, 1*(2), 186–203.

Du Mont, J., & Parnis, D. (1999). Rape laws and rape processing: The contradictory nature of corroboration. *Canadian Woman Studies, 19*(1/2), 74–78.

Du Mont, J., & White, D. (2007). The uses and impacts of medico-legal evidence in sexual assault cases: A global review. Retrieved from Geneva, Switzerland: https://apps.who.int/iris/bitstream/handle/10665/43795/9789241596046_eng.pdf.

Flanagan, M., Howe, D. C., & Nissenbaum, H. (2008). Embodying values in technology: Theory and practice. In J. van den Hoven & J. Weckert (Eds.), *Information technology and moral philosophy* (p. 322). Cambridge: Cambridge University Press.

Goddard, M. (2003, February 26). Biography/interviewer: A. Seymour. Oral History of the Crime Victim Assistance Field, The University of Akron. Retrieved from http://vroh.uakron.edu/summaries/Goddard.php.

Goddard, T., & Myers, R. R. (2017). Against evidence-based oppression: Marginalized youth and the politics of risk-based assessment and intervention. *Theoretical Criminology, 21*(2), 151–167.

Grosz, E. (2000). Histories of a feminist future. *Signs: Journal of Women in Culture and Society, 25*(4), 1017–1021.

Hannah-Moffat, K. (2018). Algorithmic risk governance: Big data analytics, race and information activism in criminal justice debates. *Theoretical Criminology.* doi:1362480618763582.

Haraway, D. J. (1985). *A manifesto for cyborgs: Science, technology, and socialist feminism in the 1980s* (pp. 173–204). San Francisco, CA: Center for Social Research and Education.

Haraway, D. J. (1997). *Modest_Witness@Second_Millennium. FemaleMan©_Meets_ OncoMouse™: Feminism and technoscience.* New York: Routledge.

Harcourt, B. E. (2007). *Against prediction profiling, policing, and punishing in an actuarial age.* Chicago, IL: University of Chicago Press.

Harding, S. G. (1986). *The science question in feminism*. Ithaca, NY: Cornell University Press.

Harding, S. (1991). *Whose science? Whose knowledge?: Thinking from women's lives*. Ithaca, NY: Cornell University Press.

Harding, S. (1995). "Strong objectivity": A response to the new objectivity question. *Synthese, 104*(3), 331–349.

Herring, C. (2009). Does diversity pay?: Race, gender, and the business case for diversity. *American Sociological Review, 74*(2), 208–224.

JafariNaimi, N., Nathan, L., & Hargraves, I. (2015). Values as hypotheses: Design, inquiry, and the service of values. *Design Issues, 31*(4), 91–104.

Jasanoff, S. (2004). *States of knowledge: The co-production of science and the social order*. New York: Routledge.

Kennedy, P. (2016, July 31). Could women be trusted with their own pregnancy tests. *New York Times*. Retrieved from www.nytimes.com/2016/07/31/opinion/sunday/could-women-be-trusted-with-their-own-pregnancy-tests.html.

Kruse, C. (2015). *The social life of forensic evidence*. Oakland, CA: University of California Press.

Larcombe, W. (2011). Falling rape conviction rates: (Some) feminist aims and measures for rape law. *Feminist Legal Studies, 19*(1), 27–45.

Latour, B. (1987). *Science in action: How to follow scientists and engineers through society*. Cambridge, MA: Harvard University Press.

Latour, B. (1999). *Pandora's hope: Essays on the reality of science studies*. Cambridge, MA: Harvard University Press.

Lisak, D., & Miller, P. (2002). Repeat rape and multiple offending among undetected rapists. *Violence and Victims, 17*(1), 73–84.

Loader, I., & Sparks, R. (2010). What is to be done with public criminology?. *Criminology & Public Policy, 9*(4), 771–781.

Lynch, M., Cole, S. A., McNally, R., & Jordan, K. (2010). *Truth machine: The contentious history of DNA fingerprinting*. Chicago, IL: University of Chicago Press.

MacKenzie, D., & Wajcman, J. (1999). *The social shaping of technology*. Buckingham: Open University Press.

McGlynn, C. (2011). Feminism, rape and the search for justice. *Oxford Journal of Legal Studies, 31*(4), 825–842.

Mol, A. (2002). *The body multiple: Ontology in medical practice*. Durham, NC: Duke University Press.

Mulla, S. (2014). *The violence of care: Rape victims, forensic nurses, and sexual assault intervention*. New York: New York University Press.

Murphy, M. (2012). *Seizing the means of reproduction: Entanglements of feminism, health, and technoscience*. Durham, NC: Duke University Press.

Naffine, N. (2014). *Feminism and criminology*. Cambridge: John Wiley & Sons.

Nelund, A. (2014). Troubling Publics: A Feminist Analysis of Public Criminology. *Radical Criminology, 4*, 67–84.

Oudshoorn, N., Rommes, E., & Stienstra, M. (2004). Configuring the user as everybody: Gender and design cultures in information and communication technologies. *Science, Technology, & Human Values, 29*(1), 30–63.

Page, S. E. (2007). *The difference: How the power of diversity creates better groups, firms, schools, and societies*. Princeton, NJ: Princeton University Press.

Piché, J. (2014). Critical reflections on "public criminology": An introduction. *Radical Criminology, 4*, 11–15.

Pinch, T. J., & Bijker, W. E. (1984). The social construction of facts and artefacts: Or how the sociology of science and the sociology of technology might benefit each other. *Social Studies of Science, 14*(3), 399–441.

Powell, A. (2015). Seeking rape justice: Formal and informal responses to sexual violence through technosocial counter-publics. *Theoretical Criminology, 19*(4), 571–588.

Quinlan, A. (2017). *The technoscientific witness of rape: Contentious histories of law, feminism, and forensic science*. Toronto: University of Toronto Press.

Rentschler, C. A. (2017). Bystander intervention, feminist hashtag activism, and the anti-carceral politics of care. *Feminist Media Studies, 17*(4), 565–584.

Rich, K., & Seffrin, P. (2012). Police interviews of sexual assault reporters: Do attitudes matter?. *Violence and Victims, 27*(2), 263–279.

Richie, B. (1995). *Compelled to crime: The gender entrapment of battered black women*. New York: Routledge.

Richie, B. (2012). *Arrested justice black women, violence, and America's prison nation*. New York: New York University Press.

Roberts, D. (2009). Race, gender, and genetic technologies: A new reproductive dystopia?. *Signs: Journal of Women in Culture and Society, 34*(4), 783–804.

Rosenberger, R. (2014, June 19). How cities use design to drive homeless people away. *The Atlantic*. Retrieved from www.theatlantic.com/business/archive/2014/06/how-cities-use-design-to-drive-homeless-people-away/373067/.

Ruggiero, V. (2012). How public is public criminology?. *Crime, Media, Culture, 8*(2), 151–160.

Sable, M. R., Danis, F., Mauzy, D. L., & Gallagher, S. K. (2006). Barriers to reporting sexual assault for women and men: Perspectives of college students. *Journal of American College Health, 55*(3), 157–162.

Saul, S. (2017, January 24). When campus rapists are repeat offenders. *New York Times*. Retrieved from www.nytimes.com/2017/01/24/us/when-campus-rapists-are-repeat-offenders.html.

Shelby, R. (2018). Whose rape kit? Stabilizing the rape kit through positivist criminology and protocol feminism. *Theoretical Criminology*. doi:10.1177/1362480618819805.

Siegel, E. (2018, February 19). How to fight bias with predictive policing. *Scientific American*. Retrieved from https://blogs.scientificamerican.com/voices/how-to-fight-bias-with-predictive-policing/.

Tenner, E. (1997). *Why things bite back: Technology and the revenge of unintended consequences*. New York: Vintage.

Tonry, M. (2010). "Public criminology" and evidence-based policy. *Criminology & Public Policy, 9*(4), 783–797.

Turner, E. (2013). Beyond "facts" and "values": Rethinking some recent debates about the public role of criminology. *British Journal of Criminology, 53*(1), 149–166.

Uggen, C., & Inderbitzin, M. (2010). Public criminologies. *Criminology & Public Policy, 9*(4), 725–749.

Wajcman, J. (2004). *Technofeminism*. Cambridge, MA: Polity Press.

Williams, S. (2015). Digital defense: Black feminists resist violence with hashtag activism. *Feminist Media Studies, 15*(2), 341–344.

Winner, L. (1986). *The whale and the reactor: The search for limits in the age of technology*. Chiacgo, IL: Chicago University Press.

Young, J. (2011). *The criminological imagination*. Cambridge: Polity Press.

25
ABOLITIONISM AS A PHILOSOPHY OF HOPE
"Inside-Outsiders" and the Reclaiming of Democracy

David Scott

Introduction

Penal abolitionism is an ethico-political approach that embraces a philosophy of liberation and human freedom and in so doing rejects legal coercion and criminal blame. Penal abolitionists are conscientious objectors to punishment and promote in its place non-punitive forms of redress for human wrongdoing, troubles, and problematic conduct. Penal abolitionists are often cast as "outsiders" when it comes to debates regarding the role and legitimacy of the penal law because they question the very existence of the penal rationale (the logic of punishment). Through their critique of the penal apparatus of the capitalist state, penal abolitionists aim to reveal the contradictions and inconsistencies within the application of the penal law, often by drawing upon evidence from people who have directly experienced its full force. By providing a platform for the often marginalized or discredited knowledge of prisoners or their families, penal abolitionists can help shine a light on the hideous realities of the prison place, thus opening it up to democratic scrutiny and public debate. But penal abolitionism is it not just about abolishing legal repression or even facilitating alternative ways of thinking about and responding to human wrongs; penal abolitionism is a *philosophy of hope* looking to promote the good society. Underscored by the principles of social justice, dignity, and a truly liberated humanity grounded in non-hierarchical, anti-oppressive, and non-exploitative human relationships, penal abolitionists aspire to build a new and thoroughly democratic society organized around human wellbeing.

The ideas of penal abolitionism should not be restricted to book shelves in university libraries or academic seminars, but rather should be infused into popular culture and be drawn upon to influence the way that people think about "crime" and punishment. In this sense, penal abolitionists should work from the "inside;" they should perform an active role in society and contribute towards everyday cultural and ideological battles for hearts and minds. Further, many prominent penal abolitionists teach in an institution key to modern day knowledge production and dissemination: the university. The penal abolitionist is an "inside-outsider" who should be committed to further enhancing democracy and building public spaces for critical reflection. They should then be both *tactically inside* and *strategically outside* the system at the same time. Following the insights of Said (1994), the penal abolitionist should deliberately *not* fully belong to a given society. It is only by sitting on the margins that they can appreciate the problems confronting the society in which they live and understand the world view of underrepresented or disadvantaged groups. This approach can help facilitate the uncovering hidden or "alternative" truths to dominant narratives, assumptions, and underlying structures of power. Being an "outsider" is also the best way to avoid co-option (Mathiesen, 2006). Yet penal abolitionists must also find the courage to both testify against oppression and engage in struggles for freedom in the here and now. They must exploit opportunities for progressive social change and attempt to implement their vision for social transformation. The penal abolitionist should explore the past and present from the point of view of the subaltern (those without a voice) and speak truth to power in the cause of freedom and social justice (Said, 1994).

As Ruggerio (2012) has argued, penal abolitionism is the only criminology he knows of that "has always adopted a public stance." Like public criminology (Loader & Sparks, 2011) more broadly, penal abolitionism aims to raise questions about common sense assumptions, generate new evidence and knowledge to debunk punitive myths, and ultimately to help reframe the debate about crime and punishment. In so doing abolitionism proposes a kind of imagination that can locate individual experiences within broader social and economic contexts and thus help transform currently neglected private troubles into public issues (Drake & Scott, 2019). Democratic engagement with the general public goes then to the very heart of abolitionist praxis, but it is an approach which differs from public criminology in one very important way: penal abolitionism aims to deconstruct the ontological and epistemological assumptions of the logic of crime and to offer alternative ways of thinking about and responding to problematic human conduct beyond the criminal process (Scott, 2018). Drawing on grass roots emancipatory politics and praxis, penal abolitionism does not conform to the criminological doxa that knowledge is generated from value free, objective, and scientific inquiry whose relevancy is shaped by government agendas and priorities. In this sense, penal abolitionism aims to foster a vision of society, political action, and human relationships which is "against criminology" (Cohen, 1988).

This chapter discusses some ways that penal abolitionists as "inside-outsiders" can challenge dominant understandings of "crime" and punishment. The chapter has three main parts. I start with a brief consideration of the current limitations of institutionalized education, knowledge production, and dissemination in the neo-liberal university (which is when an institution ostensibly designed for public education is grounded in the principles of the capitalist market place, private gain, and accumulation of profits) and the importance of considering radically alternative ways of organizing public education in the community. This is followed by an exploration of how penal abolitionists as "inside-outsiders" can help facilitate a new critical pedagogy about human conflicts, troubles, and problematic conduct as a "collective organic intellectual" (Giroux, 1988). I then discuss five interventions I adopted to illustrate how penal abolitionists can work towards reclaiming democracy through reinvigorating existing or creating alternative forms of knowledge production and public spaces for democratic dialogue. I conclude with a brief discussion of the importance of connecting abolitionist theory with public participation in democratic debates.

Beyond the Neoliberal University

The central argument of this chapter is that penal abolitionists should position themselves both inside and outside the academy at the same time. As an ideal, the university *should* work for the public good, helping to facilitate emancipatory knowledge as well as fostering and nurturing an ethico-political commitment to social justice, human rights, and democratic accountability (Giroux, 2006). While this aspiration for the University should not be abandoned, it should be located in context. One of the most enduring concerns raised against knowledge production and dissemination in the University is that it is an institution that reproduces and distributes power and cultural capital, thus performing a key part in legitimating values necessary for maintaining economically and socially unequal societies (Giroux, 1988, 2013a, 2013b; Illich, 1970). Through top down hierarchical management styles and the centralization of power, in recent times antidemocratic and authoritarian tendencies have increasingly been deployed by University management, resulting in limitations in professional autonomy and the standardization of curriculums (Walters, 2003). The demand for income and immediate results has also reduced opportunities for in-depth theoretical studies, which require several years of work.

In our time of "market-led" (Walters, 2003) criminological research, research designs and methodologies can increasingly come to reflect the interests of corporate power. As a result, research independence can be fatally undermined by the external constraints of government authorities and research funders. The basic concern is that intellectual labor and knowledge production are being used to serve corporate and technocratic priorities of neo-liberal political economies, rather than the interests of the people (Giroux, 2006; Sudbury & Okazawa-Rey, 2009). Fusing knowledge production with the logic of the capitalist marketplace (i.e., privileging the pursuit of profit and an overarching business culture) leads to a market-driven enterprise that maximizes profits through the commodification of knowledge and turns this educational institution into a space focused on service-delivery (Giroux, 2014), which then redefines students as either clients or customers.

Significantly, the neo-liberal university also fails in its basic "democratic mission" to be an institution that can inculcate civic values and ethical principles and generate concern and responsibility for tackling social problems and social divisions (Giroux, 2013a, 2013b). It is not very effective at turning students into critical citizens who can recognize the importance of participating in political culture or defending the human rights of socially marginalized groups or holding those in positions of power to account (Giroux, 2013a, 2013b). Indeed, for Henry Giroux (2014, p. 27), the neo-liberal university is part of a broader "disimagination machine" that is blocking potential for future political consciousness and public engagement. The neo-liberal university undermines critical thinking and impinges upon the mental faculties required to imagine a different kind of world grounded in social justice. It can thus become a conduit for a politics and *philosophy of despair* rather than instilling a *philosophy of hope*.

Following the insights of Illich (1970), it should be recognized that institutionalized forms of schooling, including the university, sometimes hinder learning skills for democratic participation rather than facilitate them. For Illich (1970), most learning occurs *informally*, and people often learn best in direct reciprocal dialogue and engagement with others in everyday settings than through formal timetabled educational classes. Talk of engaging in informal apprenticeships in non-traditional educational settings where the goal is skill and knowledge transfer without focus on formal educational qualifications stands in stark opposition to working in the neo-liberal university. For Illich (1970), such a scenario could be understood as a kind of "learning web" that connected people with the resources they need. The vision is for learning to be a positive, liberating, and life long experience that matches a persons' interests and motivations with the expertise and skills of those who inspire them. Underscoring this then is a commitment to capacity building and sharing knowledge and expertise outside of the university.

The vision presented by Illich (1970) is clearly appealing, yet we should not necessarily throw the baby out with the bath water. There have been times (such is as in the 1960s and 1970s) when universities have been at the forefront of developing radical and emancipatory thought and a key player in generating student protest, resistance, and dissent. This radical history also reminds us that the university is an arena for struggle rather than an inherently conservative institution. There should be attempts to transform the neo-liberal university so that it can once again be a vibrant resource in the struggles to address injustices, oppression, and exploitation. As "inside-outsiders," penal abolitionists should look to work within the academy to help reclaim the university as public spheres. Following the insights of Illich (1970), penal abolitionists should also step outside of the university and participate in a broader revitalization of public engagement in emancipatory politics, being prepared to engage in non-traditional educational settings. This suggests that penal abolitionists should transcend the boundaries between formal and informal education and between the University and the community.

Penal abolitionism therefore looks to challenge the generation of scientific knowledges in the neo-liberal university that serve the interests of the powerful and whose research agendas are shaped by governmental policy priorities. Instead, penal abolitionists aim to incorporate emancipatory politics in the education process (both formal and informal) that can challenge social and economic inequalities. Rather than just working within the existing spaces for knowledge generation and exchange which are set apart from the community (i.e., the University), as is often the case with public criminology, penal abolition presents a new challenge that demands new forms of genuinely democratic engagement that are explicitly directed at facilitating emancipatory knowledge and praxis that can aid the liberation of subjugated and oppressed groups.

Organic Collective Intellectuals

As an "inside-outsider," the penal abolitionist should aim to abolish categories, barriers, boundaries, and walls regarding educational theory and practice. This includes abolishing widely held distinctions between intellectuals and non-intellectuals. Thinking, acting, interpreting, and giving meaning to life are all intimately related and we all undertake mental labor in our ongoing everyday experiences (Mayo, 1999). For the great Italian philosopher Antonio Gramsci (1971), all people were intellectuals, but not all people in society had the role of intellectuals (i.e., academics). For Gramsci (1971), every human relationship is educative and has an influence on the kinds of political debates that develops in civil society. Education, then, is not restricted to formal educational settings, but can take place informally in the community and in ordinary human interactions and conversations. Nor for Gramsci (1971) is there an obvious distinction between the teacher and the learner. Learning can and should be a two-way process. Gramsci (1971) did, however, identify a person who offered moral leadership and facilitated informal education through direct engagement in a social movement as an "organic intellectual." Through the organization of people and dissemination of knowledge, the organic intellectual was an "insider" to a social movement who became an integral part of the local community, rather than someone from the outside simply bringing knowledge to the masses. Their overall objective of the organic intellectual is not just political engagement on a specific topic, but the transformation of an entire way of thinking about the world. Building on the insights of Gramsci (1971), Giroux (1988) talks about the importance of learning collectively and the cultivation of a collective social awareness and consciousness raising operating along "horizontal lines" (i.e., non-hierarchical relationships). For Giroux (1988), the end result of this collective learning process, where groups of people rather than individuals worked together collectively to build capacity among all of its members, is the creation of an "organic collective intellectual."

To become an organic collective intellectual means participating in and facilitating the emergence of a collective voice that can contribute towards the deepening of democracy. The penal abolitionist should work collectively, cooperatively, and in a spirit of solidarity with oppressed communities in an attempt to help find common ground for alliances and the promotion of a collective vision of a non-punitive and inclusive society (Giroux, 1988). The penal abolitionist should provide moral leadership in terms of raising ethico-political awareness and consciousness of social injustice and the harms of the penal law. This means witnessing and engaging in struggles for social justice and facilitating attempts to imagine a different kind of world through creating a coalition of progressive forces. As an insider-outsider, the abolitionist should use their privileged position (be that their educational background, networks, communication skills, knowledge, or organizational experience) to build capacity through informal ties and learning networks in the community (Illich, 1970). This sharing and building of collective power and capacity can be achieved through helping to build self-esteem, skills, and confidence of individuals or through historical recollections of past struggles and radical cultural heritage that shows another way of living and dealing with human and social troubles is possible.

This all points towards the importance of cultivating an abolitionist "critical pedagogy" beyond the (neoliberal) university setting. Friere (1970) highlights the importance of connecting politics, culture, and education together and raising the critical consciousness of individuals so they can understand their own oppression and subsequently undertake emancipatory transformative action. The liberation philosophy of Friere (1970), like that of Gramsci (1971), is intended to give hope and disrupt current understandings by looking beneath surface meanings to try and uncover the root causes of social problems. It is crucial that penal abolitionist interventions promote experiences and help transform feelings of subjugation into concrete action (Friere, 1970). This means highlighting the dialectical relationship between critical consciousness and the social action in penal abolitionist critical pedagogy (Friere, 1970). Listening, learning, and reflecting are all essential for the project of radical social transformation. For Said (1994), the aim of public engagement is to redraw the narrative—to cut against the grain, question received, and "common sense" ideas and engage in a critical encounter through dialogical transformation. This means for the penal abolitionist changing the way of seeing the world and ultimately awakening a new cultural consciousness among the masses. This can, but does not need to, take place in the university. Different sites of social practice, such as the workplace, can be transformed into sites of informal learning.

For Friere (1970), however, the community is required to be an active participant in the process of their own learning. Those engaged in critical pedagogy should actively participate in reciprocal dialogue, whereby every teacher is also a student, and look to promote critique and political engagement. Education itself was an inherently political act and its ultimate goal should be the emancipation from subjugation through the "awakening of a critical consciousness." Friere (1970) referred to this process as *conscientization* (the deepening of the coming of consciousness). Following Gramsci (1971), the "educator," whose role is almost interchangeable with that of the "learner" (Mayo, 1999), should engage in reciprocal learning—learning the unique language and culture of a given community or group of people—so to be able to convert common sense into good sense. But this is more than just critique of the prison place. It is also about trying to deepen understandings and develop the possibilities for deliberative democracy (that is informed discussion about the key issues of the day). Democracy is a constant struggle that is always unfinished. It needs to be constantly reproduced on a daily basis and this requires skills and knowledge among the people. Democracy can only survive if it is constantly reconstituted in the here and now (Giroux, 2013a, 2013b).

For the penal abolitionist, then, hierarchical forms of public engagement—that is vertical relationships between a knower (i.e., a bearer of knowledge) and a learner—can never be enough. The distinction between knower/educator and learner is false construction that individualizes knowledge production and dissemination. Public engagement for the penal abolitionist should be conceived as part of a collective and organic process that can raise the consciousness of the populace through the principles of critical pedagogy. Through working cooperatively and collectively with marginalized groups, and engaging in the process of dialogical transformation, hidden or "alternative" truths, assumptions, and underlying structures of power, can be uncovered. Placing themselves both inside and outside the formal educational system, the penal abolitionist should aspire to be an "organic collective intellectual" speaking truth to power in the cause of freedom and social justice (Said, 1994). In so doing, public engagement can be a way of helping to facilitate the reclaiming of democracy from below.

Reclaiming Democracy

To culturally embed the ideas of penal abolitionism requires the existence of appropriate public spheres through which new non-punitive meanings and understandings can be formed and popularized through a democratic and reciprocal dialogue. A meaningful understanding of democracy can only arise when it is instituted in concrete spaces that allow people to come together to discuss, think, and reflect upon social issues and their values, beliefs, and responsibility for the existence of such circumstances. These public democratic spaces, what Bauman (1999) refers to as an agora, can allow for debate and scrutiny of hegemonic ideas around "crime" and punishment and facilitate opportunities for the public to encourage decision makers to justify their actions. Democratic debate should always engage with a diverse range of dialogical encounters firmly grounded in day-to-day struggles around the meaning and interpretations of harms, troubles, and conflicts which shape contemporary society. What is also crucial is the development of a critical vernacular that is understandable to the masses; "criminological/penological illiteracy" must be eliminated by developing accessible language so that oppressions and penal injustices can be named, shamed, and eventually tackled. Effective communication is essential on the path to direct action.

Any such democratic interventions cannot be technical or merely reformist but must also aspire to a form of human living that enshrines human dignity. These new public spaces must allow for both oppositional knowledge that can challenge state-corporate and penal power and promote more utopian aspirations. In this sense, public spaces must also be both an "oppositional space" for highlighting problems and penal controversies and a "dream space" that can cultivate a radical imagination and inspiration for the transformative potential of human agency and the fulfilment of a philosophy of hope. It is essential in such a "real utopian" vision to link critical scholarship to broader forms of oppositional and idealist knowledge. Doing so allows prison abolitionists to accomplish three things: (1) facilitate concrete and pragmatic transformations; (2) expose and uncover how domination and oppression are produced and reproduced; and (3) ensure that in the long-term commitment to the penal rationale can be broken (Scott, 2013).

Below are five examples of how the abolitionist as an "inside-outsider" can help reclaim democracy regarding debates on "crime" and punishment. While the suggestions below are by no means comprehensive (indeed they draw upon examples from my own public interventions), they collectively illustrate that it is possible and desirable for penal abolitionists to make immediate and direct interventions in the public sphere.

We Should Hear Diverse Voices and Write What We Like

The place to start with reclaiming democracy is the contested space of the neo-liberal university. Abolitionists with tenure in a university are in a privileged position. They should use this to help generate momentum for the creation of organic collective intellectuals. Penal abolitionists should write not for their institution or for state sanctioned research exercises, but for the broader goals of human rights, social justice, and democratic accountability. They should write about what they consider to be the most ethically and politically important issues of the day and focus should be on movement building and local community organizing. There should be an attempt to integrate organizing into their everyday life rather than engage in organizing for "impact" or as a career vocation. The political commitment of the penal abolitionist should be to support all those, both as formal students and activists in the wider community, who are engaged in democratic struggles. The first step is to make strong connections with local abolitionist networks and directly participate in the everyday organizing of community activists. This includes organizing, publicizing (such as through leafleting and the creation of pamphlets), participating in public meetings, and direct community engagement through both informal dialogue with activists and members of the public (Scott, in press). Joining in and doing the behind the scenes work required for the building of public meetings are essential for building trust and also strong relationships with community activists.

Despite the commodification of education, there remain opportunities to *deploy* university resources to support community activism (Sudbury, 2009). Working in collaboration with local activists, the abolitionist as an inside-outsider can create spaces for critical inquiry and the sharing of wisdom through collective organizing by promoting social justice and emancipatory knowledge (Scott, 2018). To subvert the logic of the neo-liberal university it is important to avoid drawing any boundaries of exclusion and having forms of solidarity based on difference rather than sameness. This approach also requires working with a diverse group of people outside of the academy. Bringing the community into the university can add a level of commitment against penal injustice that can send a powerful message and provide inspiration for all who are prepared to listen. One example would be the International Conference for Penal Abolition (ICOPA) in London in June 15–18, 2018, which was organized by two universities (The Open University and Birkbeck University London) but which reached out to local and national abolitionist campaign groups, activist networks, and pressure groups. Here academics worked closely in a University setting with more than 40 activists to deliver an activist centered conference that was attended by more than 300 delegates. Characterized by horizontal (non-hierarchical) relationships, the aim of the organizers was to provide an opportunity of abolitionist activists to come together in solidarity and hopefully build new networks to help the U.K. abolitionist movement move forward.

As inside-outsiders in the academy, penal abolitionist should then reach out the hand of assistance to those working for liberation and freedom in the community. While it is important to recognize the limits of the university and how they currently devalue activism, the academy can also offer legitimacy to community organizing. By engaging the university as part of a pedagogy of the oppressed, new spaces can be opened up for critical pedagogy. This should entail drawing strength and inspiration from social movements to challenging elite institutions and privilege sites of expert knowledge and utilizing activism within the curriculum.

Researching and Platforming Subjugated and Marginalized Voices

The penal abolitionist should also aim to facilitate a platform for subaltern (marginalized and currently unheard) voices. As discussed above, widening participation in democratic dialogue is a key aim of the inside-outsider. Enhancing the diversity of voices heard in penal debates should also involve providing a platform for prisoners, ex-prisoners, and the families of prisoners, but it can also include doing research with prisoners. This means challenging the silencing of people in prison (Sudbury, 2009). Given the nature of the prison place, it is almost inevitable that the prisoner will be structurally prevented from participation in conversations with members of the general public and there may be no or only limited access to spaces for dialogue with debating partners within the prison place. Further, given the social backgrounds of prisoners and their broader social exclusion, many of those behind bars have found it difficult to perform the language games of normal society. Prisons are places of civil and social death and are powerful determinant of an individual's location within the knowledge economy. Engaging with prisoners establishes a new social relationship and transcends social death.

When individuals speak, they thus engage in a political process that not only starts a conversation, but which may also *ultimately lead to a* new way of conceiving the world being fostered. Hearing the voice of families, ex-prisoners, and sometimes the voice of researchers and those who have worked in the prison place can provide powerful testimony of the damage prison creates both for prisoners and the wider community. It is essential that society hears and listens to the voice of experience when it comes to prison realities. To address the potential silence, qualitative research methodologies should be used to gather testimonies of people in prison place, such as carrying out collaborative research with people in prison, so that the testimonies of prisoners are at the forefront of current debates. There are abolitionist prisoner voices, and it is important that the voice of the "abolitionist on the inside" is given due prominence in collections of abolitionist writings (Colyle & Scott, forthcoming) and also at abolitionist gatherings, such as at ICOPA annual conferences. At ICOPA in London, abolitionists activists created and published a special prisoner voice zine, facilitated ex-prisoners and prisoner families to speak at the event, and included the reading of testimonies of currently serving prisoners.

It is also crucial that this "view from below" is given a platform in any public spaces dedicated to debating "crime" and punishment, whether this be in the media or, most importantly, at public events and community meetings, the most effective way to generate connections and understandings. Readings from classic prisoner autobiographies, interviews, and collaboratively published work with activists are all important here for the wider struggle for justice.

Contesting State-Corporate Power

Since the early 1990s, the private and voluntary sectors in England and Wales have had increasing influence on the workings of the criminal process. Yet the private companies running prisons are not and cannot be held directly to account by the general public. This deficit in accountability is significant and should be addressed. *Democratic accountability* requires a public forum where the managers of corporations can be directly questioned and confronted by members of the public. In general, such opportunities are denied to citizens in relation to private companies. However, it is possible for shareholders—those with a vested interest in a private company—to challenge and question the way a private company conducts its business. This can, generally, be done through the forum of the company's annual general meeting (AGM). While "shareholder scrutiny" is in no way a satisfactory alternative to "public scrutiny," it is one means by which a privately-run corporation can be asked to account for their actions. Of course, the problem is that the AGM is a private space with access restricted to shareholders only (including activist shareholders aiming to tell truth to power) as opposed to an open and public space for all citizens. Yet possibilities remain; over the last four years, members of the *Reclaim Justice Network* have been activist shareholders at the G4S AGM (Drake & Scott, 2017).

Unsurprisingly, questions have been raised about whether the AGM could ever provide a forum for genuine accountability. Though much evidence points to how actual levels of transparency are low and not openly available to shareholders, there have been some small, but significant victories for accountability through *Reclaim Justice Network* shareholder activism at the G4S AGM. For four years, shareholder activists requested data on self-harm of prisoners published in the Annual Reports. In 2017, for the first time, G4S published details of all the prisoners who had died in their prisons in England and Wales (G4S, 2017). G4S has also continued to talk about having a policy of "zero harm" (G4S, 2017) for all of their services, although under questioning they were unable to provide specific policies in which this was being implement in their custodial services.

Following concerted protests from a range of activist groups at the G4S AGM's from 2014–2016, the company withdrew from its controversial delivery of child detention in Israel.

Ironically, while this one decision clearly indicates the real potential of the AGM to respond to the calls of shareholders, it now means that the only protest group still attending the G4S AGM is the *Reclaim Justice Network*. Though it is not without its limitations, shareholder activism can provide a means of creating a limited version of a 21st-century agora that can be part of the wider struggle to challenge the dehumanizing and sometimes deadly pursuit of profit.

Selective Engagement with the Existing Media and Creating New Forms of Media

A further form of state-corporate power shaping our understandings of democracy is the media. Despite its limitations, penal abolitionists should have a direct and concerted engagement with the media so as to question the current forms of penological illiteracy and open the debate to a more nuanced and informed debate about penal realities. The exposures of inhumane prisons in the media in the U.K. in recent years is significant politically because the message that the public are receiving about the prison estate is one of chaos, harm, and inefficiency. The public then are slowly being educated about what prison is today through such representations of a prison system in crisis. To create the appropriate public environment for downsizing the criminal process requires an informed and rationale debate about the strengths and weaknesses of punishment.

Penal abolitionists should selectively engage with both the local and national media and also independent media, such as radio, TV, newspapers, podcasts, documentaries, and internet blogs. This can also mean building and using their own media. EG Press is a good example here. Established by three academics (J. M. Moore, Emma Bell, and myself) as the publisher of the European Group for the Study of Deviance and Social Control in July 2015, this radical and independent publisher utilizes existing technologies on a voluntary basis to publish radical books by critical scholars and activists as well as the journal *Justice, Power and Resistance*. The other intervention that is of great significance is the short film/documentary. These may range from a few minutes to perhaps 60–90 minutes in length, depending on the time required. With mobile phone technologies and the ease of uploading to YouTube, the short films at least are now within the production capabilities of activists. Some medium of getting the message out is essential, but we must not become mere technicians of the state and the powerful and must be aware of pitfalls. While the media is important, it must always be secondary to the main tasks of the organic collective intellectual: building relationships and understandings within the community.

The media, then, can be utilized most effectively to publicize activism on the community and to project the event to a wider audience. Engagement with media can also help to place abolitionist arguments on the agenda and can open up abolitionist ideas to a wider audience, but interviews with the mainstream media (especially TV and radio) alone can never be enough.

Building Communities and the Production of Insurgent Knowledge

Penal abolitionists need to engage with activists inside and outside prison to create counter-carceral knowledge (Sudbury, 2009). It is important that democracy grows from the grass roots upwards, and that any organizing against the prison is thoroughly democratic in philosophy and practice. Abolitionists should build towards creating their own autonomous power bases that can foster visions of emancipation and liberation beyond the academy. This should be self-reflexive as there can be no social change without also transforming ourselves. Education of the masses should be the core goal of penal abolitionism, and for that to be achieved education about "crime" and punishment should become part of everyday life (Scott, 2018). It should not be exclusively institutionalized within specialized places of learning. Therefore, penal abolitionists envision a very different kind of educational and political participation in the community that should exist alongside the university. This starts, as discussed earlier, by helping community-based actors build political and intellectual capital. It means sharing know-how, skills, and resources with ordinary people so that we see the creation of organic collective intellectuals. But this educational approach is not just about knowledge production, but about building solidarity movements that can lead to liberation. It means engaging in organizing and activism that do not have formal ties to the Capitalist State, but rather are part of a given community.

This vision of the penal abolitionism in terms of reclaiming democracy requires the building of learning communities where people can teach each other, and where people can make resources available for such intervention. This leads us back to the ideas of Illich (1970) and his notion of the "learning web." Rather than focusing on formal qualifications and a formal teacher-learner model, the learning web is predicated on self-motivated learning and on giving individuals opportunities to links with people, places, and ideas that can help them grow at their own pace. This is a kind of apprenticeship in the community, where people learn about prisons and punishment through workshops and talking face-to-face with people who have been incarcerated. This approach would also encompass what Illich (1970) called "skill exchanges" and capacity building where abolitionists can identify their skills, the conditions under which they are willing to serve as models for others who want to learn these skills, and through "peer matching" communications networking how this can be achieved. In short, it means collectively learning together and engaging in reciprocal dialogue as organic collective intellectuals.

Liberation, Hope, and Praxis

Prisons devour the public resources necessary to restore communities devastated by racialized gendered violence and discrimination economic restructuring criminalization. The goal of the penal abolitionist is to challenge the deadly harms of incarceration and to help build the mechanisms that can be put in place to create freedom, liberation, and, most of all, human vitality and wellbeing. They cannot do this alone. There needs to be agents of change who can work together to transform communities. This work becomes increasingly necessary as the struggle from below is essential not just for democracy, but also for recapturing resources for communities in terms of promoting the paradigms of life; it is not just about dismantling the prison; it is about building communities and building hope, social justice, and a commitment to common humanity. The philosophy of hope requires collective knowledge, trust, solidarity, and listening. It cannot be driven from afar or centralized forms of control, but must grow and be locally based, drawing upon intellectual solidarities that work against broader forms of inequitable social relations. If any form of abolitionist democracy is to work, it is of crucial importance to build the cultural capital of activists.

Penal abolitionists should be prepared to take intellectual risks. The promotion of (non-penal) alternatives to prison that have demonstrated their effectiveness in addressing human conflicts troubles and illegal behaviors should be a top priority (Scott, 2013). Prisons do not create safer communities, but there are many different avenues that can be pursued to help build safer communities. This means investing in community projects and investing in the lives of people so that they have a better future. Given the widespread knowledge of the humanitarian crisis confronting prisons, it is likely that if some of the myths surrounding the idea that "prison works" were cleared away there would be public support for fiscally prudent non-punitive interventions. Any effort to reduce incarceration must begin with an investment in community welfare service, but it must also recognize the many deep wounds and traumas created from prison life, as well as the previous trauma that many of the people who are sent to prison have experienced.

Penal abolitionism is a philosophy of hope engaged in a wider struggle for social justice, freedom, and the recognition of the human dignity of all. But it is also a form of praxis, and as such abolitionists must reflect and act in the world in order to transform it in a progressive direction. It is also necessary that penal abolitionists work with people where they are at; while it may well have a utopian element, abolitionism is profoundly realistic in terms of what it can (indeed must) achieve in this historical conjuncture. One of the tasks of the abolitionist is to identify what is possible and how. Through understanding present conditions, it may become possible to highlight pathways for the democracy that is still yet to come (Said, 1994).

Reclaiming democratic spaces so that genuine dialogue and reflection can take places is a key starting point. We can only collectively move away from our current reliance on punishment and prisons once these issues have been debated and exposed for their true nature. This requires the formulation of a counter-hegemonic collective imagination and the building of alliances and relationships so that new agents of change can promote transformative political programs. The oppressed individual must perform the central role in their liberation. The penal abolitionist as inside-outsider and conduit for the formation of organic collective intellectuals can help to raise consciousness and offer some ideas that could be developed further through democratic dialogue and participation (Friere, 1970).

Penal abolitionists must continue to engage in the battle for hearts and minds in the academy and beyond its walls. Penal abolitionists should provide scholarly and nuanced accounts of the problems we face today and do the groundwork to help communities work together to find ways to address them as best we can. Critical analysis remains intellectually powerful: understanding its implications can change people's lives and influence government policies. Critical criminological writings in the past have predicted, with somewhat disturbing accuracy at times, many of the problems we face today (Hall, Critcher, Jefferson, Clark, & Roberts, 1978). Critical criminological and penal abolitionist scholarship will continue to be acknowledged and have impact in the real world and we should face the future not with trepidation, but with confidence that our arguments are strong and that collectively we can start to challenge problematic policies and practices of the corporate university. But it is also essential that as a society we put human need and inclusion before reciprocal dialogue. The very first priority is to make sure that people have the right access to the democratic process. This is part of our collective responsibility of the struggle for democracy and the creation of socially just society. Just talking about democracy, dialogue, and voice can never be enough; the material conditions must be met first for all so that people can engage in reciprocal dialogue. A firm political commitment to social justice and meeting human need is the only way to ensure that voice is heard, and that democracy is genuinely reclaimed for all (Dussel, 2013).

To achieve these ambitions aspirations, penal abolitionists must work collectively and collaboratively with the community and help to generate an organic abolitionist social movement which can operate as a genuine agent for transformative social change. Abolitionists must be both legislators (offering ideas and helping to shape organic abolitionist social movements) and interpreters (providing a way of translating the ideas of abolitionist activists into different public idioms) and use their position as "insider-outsiders" to provide a platform for prisoners, ex-prisoners and, anti-prison community activists. This requires political commitment, hard work, and above all, the recognition that abolitionism is a future orientated *philosophy of hope*.

References

Bauman, Z. (1999). *In search of politics*. Cambridge: Polity Press.
Cohen, S. (1988). *Against criminology*. Cambridge: Polity Press.
Colyle, M., & Scott, D. (Eds.). (forthcoming). *The routledge international handbook of penal abolition*. London: Routledge.
Drake, D. H., & Scott, D. (2017). Holding the corporation to account?. *Justice, Power and Resistance, 1*(2), 300–307.

Drake, D. H., & Scott, D. (2019). The criminological imagination. In J. Downes, G. Kent, G. Mooney, A. Nightingale, & D. Scott (Eds.), *Introduction to criminology* (pp. 237–257). London: Open University.
Dussel, E. (2013). *The ethics of liberation*. Durham, NC: Duke Press.
Friere, P. (1970). *The pedagogy of the dppressed*. Harmondsworth: Penguin.
G4S. (2017). *Social responsibility report*. London: Author.
Giroux, H. (1988). *Teachers as intellectuals: Towards a critical pedagogy of learning*. London: Bergen and Garvey.
Giroux, H. (2006). *The Giroux reader*. Boulder, CO: Paradigms Publishers.
Giroux, H. (2013a, February 6). The necessity of critical pedagogy in dark times. *Truthout*. Retrieved from https://truthout.org/articles/a-critical-interview-with-henry-giroux/.
Giroux, H. (2013b, October 29). Public intellectuals against the neoliberal university. *Truthout*. Retrieved from https://truthout.org/articles/public-intellectuals-against-the-neoliberal-university/.
Giroux, H. (2014). *The violence of organized forgetting: Thinking beyond America's dis-imagination machine*. San Francisco, CA: City Lights Books.
Gramsci, A. (1971). *Selections from the prison notebooks*. London: Lawrence and Wishart.
Hall, S., Critcher, C., Jefferson, T., Clark, J., & Roberts, B. (1978). *Policing the crisis*. London: Macmillan.
Illich, I. (1970). *Deschooling society*. London: Marion Boyars Publishers Ltd.
Loader, I., & Sparks, R. (2011). *Public criminology?* London: Routledge.
Mathiesen, T. (2006). *Silently silenced*. Winchester: Waterside Press.
Mayo, P. (1999). *Gramsci, Freire and adult education: Possibilities for transformative action*. London: Zed Books.
Ruggerio, V. (2012). How public is public criminology? *Crime, Media, Culture: An International Journal, 8*(2), 151–160.
Said, E. (1994). *Representations of the intellectual*. New York: Vintage Books.
Scott, D. (2013). Visualizing an abolitionist real utopia: Principles, policy and praxis. In M. Malloch & W. Munro (Eds.), *Crime, critique and utopia* (pp. 90–113). London: Palgrave.
Scott, D. (2018). *Against imprisonment*. Winchester: Waterside Press.
Scott, D. (in press). Ordinary rebels, everyone: Resisting the mega prison. In E. Hart, J. Greener, & R. Moth (Eds.), *Resisting the punitive state: Grassroots struggles across welfare, housing, education, and prisons*. London: Pluto Press.
Sudbury, J. (2009). Challenging penal dependency: Activist scholars and the anti-prison movement. In J. Sudbury & M. Okazawa-Rey (Eds.), *Activist scholarship: Antiracism, feminism, and social change* (pp. 17–36). London: Paradigms Publishers.
Sudbury, J., & Okazawa-Rey, M. (2009). Activist scholarship and the neoliberal university after 9/11. In J. Sudbury & M. Okazawa-Rey (Eds.), *Activist scholarship: Antiracism, feminism, and social change* (pp. 1–16)). London: Paradigms Publishers.
Walters, R. (2003). *Deviant knowledge*. London: Routledge.

INDEX

abolition 55, 230–231, 235, 254–255, 299–309
academic freedom 233, 256–257; and censorship 142–143, 145–146, 148–149, 155, 160, 233–234, 256–257
academic institutions: and inertia xvi, 77–78, 137–139, 143–144; institutional governance within 143–144, 149–150, 229, 261; and institutional pressure 15, 114, 137–139, 142–144, 146–147, 149, 159, 238, 256, 301, 304–305; and job security xvi, 66, 87–88, 144–147, 256, 304; publishing xvi, 4, 38, 112, 114, 123–124, 138–140, 154, 158; racism in 147, 234; *see also* racism; resistance from xvi, 52, 145–147, 149–150, 182, 229, 231–232, 234; sexism in 113–115; support from xvi, 5–6, 53, 77–78, 80, 87–92, 103, 114–115, 135–140, 143–146, 149–150, 159, 179, 182, 229, 235, 250, 254, 256
access to healthcare 120–128, 135, 216, 272–282
activism 4, 5, 13, 28, 52, 54, 78, 80, 93, 108–109, 112, 115–116, 120–122, 125–128, 133, 135, 138, 141–142, 144, 146, 149, 179, 180–182, 185–186, 199–200, 210, 239, 244–245, 251, 257, 260, 268, 277, 308; community resistance xv, 3, 13, 25, 50, 52, 54, 65–66, 77, 88, 97, 120, 125–127, 179–182, 185, 209–210, 219–224, 230–232, 241–244, 262, 264, 267, 277, 280–281, 292, 300, 304–307; scholar activism 4, 52, 64–68, 77–78, 80, 88, 93, 108–109, 112, 115–116, 120–122, 126–127, 133, 135, 137–138, 141–142, 146, 149, 179–182, 185–186, 199–200, 210, 240, 242–244, 254, 260, 268, 277, 304–305, 307; underground scholarship 121–122, 124–125, 127–128; *see also* public criminology, grounded
affordable housing 134, 168–170, 185–188, 232
apartheid 68–69, 133
Asia-Pacific 152–160, 163–175, 199, 213–224, 280; Australia 27, 107–112, 163–168, 194, 223; Bangladesh 280; China: 152–160; Fiji 165, 172; Indonesia 213–224; Melanesia 163–175; New Zealand 163, 167; Papua New Guinea 163–175, 213–224; Polynesia 164; Vanuatu 163–175; Vietnam 229

Barak, G. 34, 36, 38, 88, 272
Black Lives Matter (BLM) 62, 64
Bourdieu, P. 30, 78, 200
Braithwaite, J. 2, 4, 144, 163–165, 172, 175, 214, 219, 223, 253
Braithwaite, V. 5, 144, 214, 219
Burawoy, M. 2, 11, 22, 29–30, 36–37, 40–42, 50, 59, 70, 78–79, 141–142, 153, 159, 172, 249

capitalism 50, 60–69, 197–198, 228–229, 231, 233, 243, 301, 306–308
carceral state xv, xvi, 50, 55–56, 75–77, 79–84, 93, 121–122, 124–128, 137, 153, 194–210, 228–235, 260, 263–264, 286, 288, 290, 295, 299–300, 307–308; *see also* punitive model of crime control
civil rights movement 49, 54, 60, 75–77, 80–81, 95, 180, 205, 233, 271
climate crisis 25–26, 179, 180–188, 194; *see also* environmental crime and justice
Cohen, S. 22, 51–52, 62, 69, 148, 163, 280, 300
colonialism: colonial practices 22, 24–27, 30, 54, 62–63, 68–69, 164, 167, 214, 219, 222, 231, 235, 259–263, 265–266, 268; decolonial practices 60–63, 68–69, 166, 214, 231, 235, 253, 259, 261, 267–268; postcolonial dynamics 28–30, 165–167, 213–215, 218, 223–224, 235, 259, 261–262, 264–268
community engagement 27–28, 34–38, 40–42, 76, 108, 115, 139–142, 168, 175, 187, 222, 290; with activists 103, 115–116, 180–182, 187, 209–210, 224, 232, 234–235, 242–245, 277, 300–309; *see also* activism, scholar; community-led discussions 108, 133, 170, 173–174, 218, 232, 244–245, 267–268, 308–309; education of the public 103,

110, 134, 136, 153, 182, 250, 252, 260, 267–268, 272–273, 280, 282, 301–302, 307; with indigenous communities 260, 266–268; with marginalized communities xvi, 62, 80–81, 134–138, 140, 174, 184–186, 232; with media 15–18, 38, 41, 76, 87–89, 90–94, 107–108, 110, 112–113, 127, 155–158, 160, 181–182, 261, 307; *see also* criminology, newsmaking; with policy makers 38–39, 44–45, 75–76, 78–84, 89, 103, 107, 109–110, 148, 152, 169, 170–171, 173, 175, 182–184, 222–223, 240–241, 245, 266, 272; with racialized communities 53–54, 64–65, 209–210, 232; with students 36–37, 50, 57, 101–103, 133, 137–139, 181, 250–257, 259–260, 262, 267–268, 301; *see also* public criminology; university as a venue for
Crenshaw, K. 80, 146, 286–287, 290
crime rates 80, 96–97, 99, 111, 145–146, 152, 159, 166, 173–174, 252, 286–287, 290
criminal justice reform xv–xvi, 1, 12–13, 28, 39, 55, 75–76, 78, 82–84, 90, 93, 110–113, 128, 137, 163, 166, 174, 199, 210, 234, 254–235, 282, 286; *see also* abolition
criminological imagination 18, 28, 34, 41, 70, 288–289, 293–295, 300
The Criminological Imagination 29, 143, 159, 240, 288; *see also* Young, J.
criminology 295, 299, 302; criticisms of xv–xvi, 2–3, 5, 11, 28–30, 40, 50, 56, 78, 89, 96, 145, 148, 209–210, 231, 234–235, 239–240, 243–245, 251–252, 259–263, 268, 277, 295, 299, 302; debates in 2, 92, 193–195, 199–200, 231, 243–245; liberation criminology 59–64, 66–69; newsmaking criminology 34, 38, 88, 272; state of the field 11, 26, 78–79, 92, 102, 141, 152–156, 158–160, 163, 170, 172, 174, 197–198, 231, 238–240, 243–245, 249–257, 265–268, 271, 276, 279, 288, 302
Critical Race Theory 4, 6, 53, 156
culture 15, 18, 36, 41, 52, 173–174, 233, 261, 263–268, 289, 295
Currie, E. xiv, xvii, 3, 5, 28, 52, 78, 89, 93, 96, 152–153, 159, 249, 259, 272, 293

Du Bois, W. E. B. 30, 60, 62–67, 69, 78

early career researchers 78, 112, 137, 139, 140, 142, 147
elitism 3, 34, 41–43, 88–89, 91, 139, 141, 171–172, 241, 243–245, 249–251
environmental crime and justice xvii, 173, 179–188, 194; *see also* U.S. v. Citgo
Eurocentric sociology 60–62, 64, 68, 147, 163, 209, 261, 265

feminism: carceral feminism 56; Crunk Feminist Collective 52–53; feminist perspectives 4–5, 30, 56, 67, 96, 108–111, 113–116, 271, 276–277, 279, 287–288, 292, 294–295; feminist praxis 54, 103, 108–112, 120–121, 125–128, 272–273, 281–282, 292–293; feminist scholars 12, 52, 56, 107–108, 111, 113–116, 286; *see also* survivor-scholar; feminist theory 13, 97, 126, 287; intersectional feminism 53, 78–81
Foucault, M. 54, 79, 213

Garland, D. 68, 111, 152, 204
gender-based violence xvii, 68, 95–103, 107–116, 121–123, 127–128, 166, 173–174, 203, 268, 271, 276–277, 279, 281–282, 286–287, 290–295
genocide 60–62, 64–67, 260–264, 267, 266
global South xvi, 17, 24, 120–128, 163, 167–175, 203–210, 213–224, 280
Gramsci, A. 197, 229, 302, 303

harm reduction 121, 135–137, 184, 195–196, 201
Harney, S. 56, 143, 145, 228, 230–232; *see also The Undercommons*
Hill Collins, P. 53, 80, 287
hot climate 1, 145; *see also* Loader, I.; Sparks, R.
human rights 24, 61, 96, 98, 102, 123, 174, 204, 206–210, 214, 218–219, 222–223, 243, 277–279, 282

Inderbitzin, M. 1, 3, 34, 36, 38, 50, 59, 78–79, 102, 121, 143, 153, 204, 210, 213, 249, 272, 288, 295
intersectionality 53, 64, 68, 80, 98–100, 102–103, 111, 127, 146–147, 273, 279, 287, 290, 294–295; *see also* Crenshaw, K.

Jim Crow era 49, 60–62, 64–75, 206, 208; *see also* civil rights movement; racism

knowledge production 3, 30, 45, 96, 141–144, 200, 204, 210, 232, 235, 259, 293–294; constitutive knowledge 6, 26, 28, 35, 41–43, 45–46, 88, 97, 122, 134, 140, 249, 251, 254, 287, 295, 299–303, 308; Eurocentric and Western knowledges 2–4, 14, 25, 36, 42, 78–80, 145–146, 174, 232, 259–261, 264–265; experiential knowledge 16, 41, 287; expert knowledge 3, 13–15, 18, 27, 35, 38–40, 42, 45, 80, 89, 93, 137, 148, 155–158, 292, 302; insurgent/counter knowledge 51–56, 97, 122–123, 125–128, 143, 146, 149–150, 228–229, 253, 256, 266–268, 295, 299–300, 302, 304–305, 307–308; knowledge dissemination 12, 38, 44, 103, 125, 127, 136, 138–140, 142–143, 150, 152–160, 250, 302; plurality of 2–4, 146, 195, 252, 287–290, 294; as power 25, 41, 45, 60–61, 90, 145–156; types of knowledge 11, 35, 78

Latin America 17, 25, 125, 204–206, 210, 280; Argentina 120–122, 125–128; Brazil 120–128, 203–210; Cuba 69, 99; Dominican Republic 262; El Salvador 170; Haiti 262; Mexico 23, 28, 49, 99,

Index

205, 280; Puerto Rico 99; Uruguay 120; Venezuela 170, 256

liberation sociology/criminology 60–62, 64–68, 70

Loader, I. 1–2, 13, 29–30, 38, 42–43, 50–51, 60, 96–97, 102, 141, 145, 153, 158, 164, 167, 172, 245, 249, 250, 256, 259, 288, 295, 300

marginalization 3–4, 6, 24–26, 56, 62, 64–68, 80, 96–100, 102–104, 110–111, 135, 137, 142–144, 146–147, 149–150, 163, 166, 180, 183, 203, 205, 230–231, 233, 235, 240, 251, 253, 262, 266, 268, 280, 299, 302, 305; gender xvii, 68, 95–103, 107–116, 121–123, 127–128, 166, 173–174, 203, 268, 271, 276–277, 279, 281–282, 286–287, 290–295; LGBTQ2+ people and groups 64, 111, 147, 234; low-income communities 169, 179, 183, 187, 203–206, 210, 272, 275, 279, 286; migrant populations xvii, 22–24, 26–27, 99–101, 271, 275; racialized groups 24–26, 49, 60–70, 75, 77, 98–100, 127, 147, 150, 206–210, 229, 232, 234, 268; *see also* intersectionality; racism

Mills, C. W. 28–29, 159

misogyny 17, 271, 276–277, 279, 281, 292

moral panic 134, 148, 166, 229–230

Moten, F. 56, 143, 145, 228, 230–232; *see also* *The Undercommons*

National Association for the Advancement of Colored People (NAACP) 60, 65–66

neoliberal university 14–15, 51, 55, 114–115, 142–145, 147, 149, 179, 228–229, 232–235, 238–239, 300–303, 305, 309

non-government organizations (NGOs) 110, 136, 166–167, 217–218, 221–223, 280–281

patriarchy xvii, 3, 22, 69, 82–84, 96–101, 103, 107–116, 121–128, 166, 173–174, 203, 245, 251, 255, 268, 271–282, 286–294

Piche, J. 1, 3, 5, 50, 224, 254, 257, 288, 295

Planned Parenthood v. Casey 274

policing 165–168, 170–172, 203–209; community policing 167–168, 170–173, 205, 210; police militarization 87–89, 93–94, 166, 232, 243; police violence 60–62, 64, 76–77, 87–89, 204, 206–210, 218, 223, 231–232

politics xv–xvii, 1, 6, 11, 23, 26, 50, 75–77, 79, 83–84, 88, 91, 148, 154, 158, 184, 198, 256, 271–278, 281–282; political agendas and state xvii, 3, 51, 108, 111–112, 116, 141–143, 148–149, 154–160, 165, 184, 204, 218–219, 222–224, 229–230, 242, 261–262, 272, 274–275, 289, 300, 302

positivism 4, 59–60, 78–80, 83, 108, 114, 141, 159, 244, 249–254, 256, 287–288, 292–294

Potter, H. 52–53, 98–99

power and inequality 29, 70, 79, 82–83, 127, 147–149, 157–160, 165, 170–171, 182, 194–195, 198; confronting 3–4, 22, 30, 53–55, 90, 96, 101–102, 142, 170, 222–223, 240, 242–245, 250, 252–255, 257, 267, 293–294, 302–309; dynamics of 5–6, 56, 79, 141, 145–146, 221–224, 229–230, 232–233, 235, 287–289, 290; social control 3, 121, 123–124, 126–127, 160, 205–207, 209, 214, 218–220, 229, 241–242, 276; state power and oppression 22, 25, 37, 39, 62, 64–70, 83, 103, 148, 158, 170, 174, 203, 205–210, 213–214, 216–221, 260–261, 263–266, 279, 282; *see also* knowledge production; as power

public criminology: accessibility of 3, 13, 29, 36, 89, 136, 175, 250, 304; barriers to xv–xvi, xvii, 4–6, 11–13, 16, 27–28, 39–41, 51–52, 55, 76, 80, 102, 108, 110, 113–114, 121, 127, 137–138, 142–149, 153–155, 159–160, 163–164, 179–187, 239–245, 249–260, 266, 271, 301; critique(s) of 1–6, 25, 29, 34, 44, 92–93, 96, 122, 141, 153, 158–160, 210, 228–229, 233–235, 239–240, 244–245, 249, 251, 253–254, 257, 259–262, 266, 268, 279, 286, 288; debates in 2, 6, 14, 30, 159, 163, 201; definitions of 2–4, 21–22, 34, 36–39, 51, 78, 136, 139, 144, 164, 244–245, 249–251, 254, 260, 293; dominance of public narratives 88–89, 103, 108, 123–124, 135, 145, 148, 152, 155, 160, 181–182, 187, 198, 200, 220, 230, 239, 244, 259, 262, 266, 268, 276, 292–293, 299–300, 302, 303, 307–308; funding for xv–xvi, 15, 36, 114, 137–138, 143–146, 163, 172, 182, 305; the future of xvi, 2, 5–6, 12, 15, 18, 26, 102–104, 160, 164–165, 175, 188, 201, 224, 243–245, 266, 288, 294–295, 304; grounded 121, 127–128; impact(s) of xv, xvii, 2, 4–6, 12–13, 39, 44, 53, 55, 80–81, 84, 88, 90, 92, 96, 102–104, 109–112, 125–128, 135–137, 139–140, 153, 156–157, 160, 175, 179–187, 194, 198–200, 223–224, 239, 252–255, 259–260, 265–267, 287–288, 300, 304–307, 309; knowledge mobilization as 142–150; and labor 4, 90, 135, 138–139, 143, 145, 147, 179, 185–187, 232; legitimacy of 84, 88–89, 146, 148, 159–160, 183, 185; need for xvi–xviii, 1, 5, 25–28, 41, 43, 79, 88, 96–98, 102–103, 108–109, 112, 115, 122, 125–128, 134, 139, 149, 152, 164, 169–170, 172, 174–175, 180, 184, 186, 188, 199–200, 204, 206, 208–210, 213, 222, 239, 244–245, 250–251, 254–257, 259–268, 272, 276–279, 287–289, 293–295, 299–300, 302–303, 305–309; organic forms of 28, 41, 141, 164, 302–304, 307–309; pedagogy as 37, 249–257, 300, 303, 305; plurality of 2, 5, 40–41, 108, 110, 112, 139–141, 175, 223–234, 287; policy reform as 103, 110–112, 123, 128, 135, 171, 173–175, 180–184, 198, 204, 214, 217, 242, 250, 263, 266; in practice 2, 3, 5–6, 108–109, 139–140, 153, 155, 174–175, 179, 182–187, 210, 222–224, 229, 252–257, 259, 260, 266–268, 272, 286, 288–290, 293–295, 300, 302–307, 309; public Pacific criminology 163–165, 169–170, 172, 174–175; public support for xvii, 79, 136, 146, 148, 181–183, 221, 240; risks of doing 1, 3, 16, 42,

50–53, 66–67, 87–88, 90–93, 113–116, 125–127, 136, 138–139, 143–149, 155, 160, 179, 181, 240, 244, 256–257, 307–308; scholarly obligation to do 1, 2, 14, 18, 51–52, 64–65, 76, 78–79, 96, 126–128, 139, 140–142, 175, 179, 210, 238, 245, 252, 255–256, 295, 300, 304–305, 309; traditional forms of 1–2, 4–5, 38–39, 54–56, 109, 125, 137, 152, 235; types of public(s) 2–3, 6, 25, 37–38, 40–42, 78–79, 136, 139, 141, 174–175, 187, 221, 224, 228, 232–234, 238, 240, 243–245, 249–251, 255, 260, 266, 287, 302, 304–306; unintended consequences of 1, 16, 27, 45, 53, 55, 67, 79–80, 91–93, 97, 111, 127–128, 160, 174, 186, 196, 229; university as a venue for 133–138, 149, 164, 234–235, 267–268, 299–305

Public Criminology? 1–2, 14, 28–30, 37, 50–51, 96–97, 102, 141, 145, 153, 158, 164, 172, 245; *see also* Loader, I.; Sparks, R.

punitive model of crime control xv–xvi, 1, 2, 75, 77, 111, 116, 124, 134–135, 163, 165–166, 169, 173, 204–205, 242, 286, 288–289, 294–295, 299–300, 304; criminalization of abortion 120–128, 271–282; *see also* reproductive justice; Socorristas en Red; criminalization of immigrants 17, 22–23, 26–27, 160, 271, 275; criminalization of women 81–84, 120–122, 124–128, 272–275, 277, 279, 281–282, 290

queer studies 45; queer criminology xiv; queer scholars 3–4, 114, 145–146, 234; queer theory 13, 52

racism 60–62, 64–68, 75, 77, 127, 146, 208–209, 218, 230–234, 253, 264, 271, 276, 279–280, 289, 292; colorblind ideology 208, 231; lynching 60–62, 64–79; segregation 60–62, 64, 67, 206; white privilege 53, 56, 62, 64, 68, 111, 148–149, 231, 233, 273; white supremacy 60–62, 64, 68, 209, 262, 264, 271; *see also* academic institutions; racism in

reflexivity 80, 108, 115, 122, 179, 181, 186, 244–245, 252–254, 256, 289

reproductive justice 120–128, 271–272; *see also* Planned Parenthood v. Casey; punitive model of crime control; criminalization of abortion; *Roe v. Wade*

responsibilization 107–108, 231, 234

Rock, P. 2, 15–16, 34, 36–37, 39–42, 46, 51, 98, 102, 152–153, 159, 250–251, 257

Roe v. Wade 273–274; *see also* Planned Parenthood v. Casey; reproductive justice

slavery 49–50, 60–62, 64–65, 68–69, 194, 235, 262; *see also* racism

Socorristas en Red 120, 125–126; *see also* feminism; reproductive justice

Sparks, R. 1–2, 13, 29–30, 38, 42–43, 50–51, 60, 96–97, 102, 141, 145, 153, 158, 164, 167, 172, 245, 249, 250, 256, 259, 288, 295, 300

state violence xvii, 2, 24, 49–50, 88–89, 128, 160, 206–207, 209, 214–215, 218–224, 230, 241–242, 262–266, 281–282

survivor-scholar 108, 110, 115–116, 268

Uggen, C. 1, 3, 34, 36, 50, 59, 78–79, 102, 143, 153, 204, 210, 213, 249, 272, 288, 295

The Undercommons 56, 143, 145, 228, 230, 232

U.S. v. Citgo 182

war on drugs 2, 60, 75–76, 82–83, 89

white collar crime 37, 193–201

Young, J. 29, 141, 143, 159, 240, 288